D1571508

RESTORATION OF
Temperate Wetlands

RESTORATION OF
Temperate Wetlands

Edited by

BRYAN D. WHEELER
SUSAN C. SHAW
Department of Animal and Plant Sciences, University of Sheffield, UK

WANDA J. FOJT
English Nature, Peterborough, UK

R. ALLAN ROBERTSON
Macaulay Land Use Research Institute, Aberdeen, UK

JOHN WILEY & SONS
Chichester · New York · Brisbane · Toronto · Singapore

Other Wiley Editorial Offices

John Wiley & Sons, Inc., 605 Third Avenue,
New York, NY 10158-0012, USA

Jacaranda Wiley Ltd, G.P.O. Box 859, Brisbane,
Queensland 4001, Australia

John Wiley & Sons (Canada) Ltd, 22 Worcester Road,
Rexdale, Ontario M9W 1L1, Canada

John Wiley & Sons (SEA) Pte Ltd, 37 Jalan Pemimpin #05-04,
Block B, Union Industrial Building, Singapore 2057

Library of Congress Cataloging-in-Publication Data

Restoration of temperate wetlands / edited by Bryan D. Wheeler ... [et
    al.].
        p.   cm.
    Papers from a symposium held at the University of Sheffield,
England in Sept.   1993
    Includes bibliographical references and index.
    ISBN 0-471-95105-6
    1. Wetland ecology—Congresses.   2. Restoration ecology—
Congresses.   3. Wetland conservation—Congresses.   I. Wheeler,
Bryan D.
QH541.5.M3R47   1995
333.91'8153—dc20   94–35414
                                                            CIP

British Library Cataloguing in Publication Data

A catalogue record for this book is available from the British Library

ISBN 0-471-95105-6

Camera-ready copy supplied by the editors
Printed and bound in Great Britain by Biddles Ltd, Guildford and King's Lynn

Contents

List of Contributors

Preface

1   **Introduction: Restoration and Wetlands**   **1**
B.D. Wheeler

2   **Archaeology and Wetland Restoration**   **19**
B. Coles

3   **The Nature Conservation Importance of Fens and Bogs and the Role of Restoration**   **33**
W.J. Fojt

4   **A Focus on Fens – Controls on the Composition of Fen Vegetation in Relation to Restoration**   **49**
B.D. Wheeler & S.C. Shaw

5   **Assessing the Restoration Prospects of Degraded Fens**   **73**
A. Grootjans & R. van Diggelen

6   **Eutrophication of Fen Ecosystems: External and Internal Nutrient Sources and Restoration Strategies**   **91**
W. Koerselman & J.T.A. Verhoeven

7   **Influence of Hydrological Differentiation of Fens on their Transformation after Dehydration and on Possibilities for Restoration**   **113**
H. Okruszko

8   **Evaluation of the Present State and Mapping of the Fens in the Upper Rhinluch, Germany**   **121**
J. Zeitz

9   **Natural Revegetation during Restoration of Wetlands in the Southern Prairie Pothole Region of North America**   **129**
S.M. Galatowitsch & A.G. van der Valk

10 **Nutrient Dynamics during Restoration of Fen Meadows by Haymaking without Fertiliser Application**   **143**
J.P. Bakker & H. Olff

11 Vegetational Changes in Boreal Rich Fens Induced by Hay-making;
    Management Plan for the Sølendet Nature Reserve   167
    A. Moen

12 The Role of Seed Banks in the Revegetation of Australian Temporary
    Wetlands   183
    M.A. Brock & D.L. Britton

13 Seed Banks in Fen Areas and Their Potential Use in Restoration
    Ecology   189
    D. Maas & A. Schopp-Guth

14 Planning for the Restoration of Peat Wetlands for Birds   207
    D.E. Ward, G.J. Hirons & M.J. Self

15 The Occurence of Some Scarce East Anglian Fen Invertebrates in
    Relation to Vegetation Management   223
    A.P. Foster & D.A. Procter

16 Restoring Fen Ditches: The Case of Wicken Fen National Nature
    Reserve   241
    D.J. Painter & L.E. Friday

17 The Regeneration of Fens in Abandoned Peat Pits Below Sea Level
    in the Netherlands   251
    G. van Wirdum

18 Restoration of Acidified Rich-fen Ecosystems in the Vechtplassen
    Area: Successes and Failures   273
    B. Beltman, T. van den Broek, & S. Bloemen

19 The Ombrogenous Bog Environment   287
    M.C.F. Proctor

20 Towards an Ecohydrological Basis for Raised Mire Restoration   305
    O.M. Bragg

21 Problems in the Hydrological Management of Cut-over Raised
    Mires, with Special Reference to Thorne Moors, South Yorkshire   315
    L. Heathwaite

22 The Selection of Internal and External Water Management Options
    for Bog Restoration   331
    J.M. Schouwenaars

23 Hydrological Protection and Rewetting of Raised Bogs Influenced
    by Man   347
    R.R.F. Eggelsman

24 Effects of Damming Peat Cuttings on Glasson Moss and Wedholme
    Flow, two Lowland Raised Bogs in North-west England   349
    F.J. Mawby

25 Niche Requirements of Birds in Raised Bogs: Habitat Attributes
    in Relation to Bog Restoration   359
    B. Bölscher

26 Time to Regenerate: Long-term Perspectives of Raised Bog
    Regeneration with Special Emphasis on Palaeoecological Studies   379
    J.H.J. Joosten

27 Re-establishment of a *Sphagnum*-dominated Flora on Cut-over
    Lowland Raised Bogs   405
    R.P. Money

28 *Sphagnum* Regeneration – Toward an Optimisation of Bog
    Restoration   423
    L. Rochefort, R. Gauthier & D. Lequéré

29 Microclimate and Physical Properties of Peat: New Clues to the
    Understanding of Bog Restoration Processes   435
    Ph. Grosvernier, Y. Matthey & A. Buttler

30 Coastal Raised Mire Restoration: Mosaic of Peatland, Salt Marsh
    and Minerotrophic Wetlands for Avian Habitat Enhancement   451
    N.C. Famous, M. Spencer-Famous, J-Y. Daigle & J.J. Thibault

31 Diaspore Rain and Diaspore Bank in Raised Bogs and Implications
    for the Restoration of Peat-mined Sites   471
    P. Poschlod

32 Blanket Mires in the Upland Landscape   495
    J.H. Tallis

33 The Growth and Value of *Eriophorum angustifolium* Honck. in
    Relation to the Revegetation of Eroding Blanket Peat   509
    J.R.A. Richards, B.D. Wheeler & A.J. Willis

34 Restoration of Wet Heathland after Opencast Mining   523
    D.W. Merrilees, G.E.D. Tiley & D.C. Gwynne

35 Impacts of Conifer Plantations on Blanket Bogs and Prospects of
    Restoration   533
    A.R. Anderson, D.G. Pyatt & I.M.S. White

36 The Basis of Mire Restoration in Finland   549
    H. Heikkilä & T. Lindholm

Index   557

List of Contributors

A.R. Anderson *Forestry Authority, Northern Research Station, Roslin, Midlothian, EH25 9SY, UK*

J.P. Bakker *Laboratory of Plant Ecology, University of Groningen, P.O. Box 14, 9750 AA, Haren, The Netherlands*

B. Beltman *Department of Plant Ecology and Evolutionary Biology, Utrecht University, P.O. Box 800.84, NL-3508TB, The Netherlands*

S. Bloeman *Department of Ecology and Evolutionary Biology, Utrecht University, P.O. Box 800.84, NL-3508TB, The Netherlands*

B. Bölscher *Zoological Institute, Technical University of Braunschweig, Pockelsstrasse 10 a, D-38106, Braunschweig, Germany*

O.M. Bragg *Department of Biological Sciences, The University, Dundee DD1 4HN, UK*

D.L. Britton *Botany Department, University of New England, Armidale 2351, NSW, Australia*

M.A. Brock *Botany Department, University of New England, Armidale 2351, NSW, Australia*

A. Buttler *Laboratoire d'Ecologie Végétale et de Phytosociologie, Institut de Botanique de l'Université, Chantemerle 22, CH-2007 Neuchâtel, Switzerland*

B. Coles *Department of History and Archaeology, University of Exeter, Queen's Building, The Queen's Drive, Exeter, EX4 4QH, UK*

J-Y. Daigle *Spencer/Famous Environmental Consulting, Box 102 HCR 70, Machias, Me 04654, USA*

R.R.F. Eggelsmann *Julius-Leber-Straße 11, D-28329, Bremen, Germany*

N.C. Famous *Spencer/Famous Environmental Consulting, Box 102 HCR 70, Machias, Me 04654, USA*

W.J. Fojt *English Nature, Northminster House, Peterborough, PE1 1UA, UK*

A.P. Foster *The National Trust, 33 Sheep Street, Cirencester, Gloucestershire, GL7 1QW, UK*

L.E. Friday   *Department of Zoology, University of Cambridge, Downing Street, Cambridge, CB2 3EJ, UK*

S.M. Galatowitsch   *Departments of Horticulture and Landscape Architecture, University of Minnesota, St. Paul, MN 5510, USA*

R. Gauthier   *Département de Phytologie, Université Laval, Québec, G1K 7P4, Canada*

A. Grootjans   *Department of Plant Ecology, University of Groningen, P.O. Box 14, 9750 AA Haren, The Netherlands*

Ph. Grosvernier   *Laboratoire d'Ecologie Végétale et de Phytosociologie, Institut de Botanique de l'Université, Chantemerle 22, CH-2007 Neuchâtel, Switzerland*

D.C. Gwynne   *Environmental Sciences Department, Scottish Agricultural College, Auchincruive, Ayr, KA6 5HW, UK*

L. Heathwaite   *Department of Geography, University of Sheffield, Winter Street, Sheffield, S3 7ND, UK*

H. Heikkilä   *National Board of Waters and the Environment, Research Centre of Nature Reserve 'Friendship', Tönölä, FIN-88900, Kuhmo, Finland*

G.J. Hirons   *The Royal Society for the Protection of Birds, The Lodge, Sandy, Bedfordshire, SG19 2DL, UK*

H.J. Joosten   *Laboratory of Palaeobotany and Palynology, Heidelberglaan 2, NL-3584 CS, Utrecht, The Netherlands*

W. Koerselman   *KIWA N.V. Research & Consultancy, Groningenhaven 7, Postbus 1072, 3430 BB, Nieuwegein, The Netherlands*

D. Lequéré   *Premier Research Centre, P.O. Box 2600, Rivière-du-Loup, Québec, G5R 4C9, Canada*

T. Lindholm   *National Board of Waters and the Environment, Nature Conservation Research Unit, P.O. Box 250, FIN-00101, Helsinki, Finland*

D. Maas   *Technische Universität München, Lehrstuhl für Landschaftsökologie II, D-85350 Friesing, Germany*

Y. Matthey   *Laboratoire d'Ecologie Végétale et de Phytosociologie, Institut de Botanique de l'Université, Chantemerle 22, CH-2007 Neuchâtel, Switzerland*

F.J. Mawby   *English Nature, Wayside, Kirkbridge, Carlisle, CA5 5JR, UK*

D.W. Merrilees   *Environmental Sciences Department, Scottish Agricultural College, Auchincruive, Ayr, KA6 5HW, UK*

A. Moen   *Department of Botany, Museum of Natural History and Archaeology, University of Trondheim, N-7004 Trondheim, Norway*

R.P. Money   *Department of Animal and Plant Sciences, P.O. Box 601, University of Sheffield, Sheffield, S10 2UQ, UK*

H. Olff   *Department of Terrestrial Ecology and Nature Conservation, Agricultural University, Bornsesteeg 47, 6708 PD, Wageningen, The Netherlands*

H. Okruszko   *Institute for Land Reclamation and Grassland Farming, Falenty, 05-090 Raszyn, Warsaw, Poland*

D.J. Painter   *Department of Zoology, Downing Street, Cambridge, CB2 3EJ, UK*

P. Poschlod   *Fachbereich Biologie, Naturschutz II, Phillips Universität, D-35032, Marburg, Germany*

D.A. Procter   *Joint Nature Conservation Committee, Monkstone House, City Road, Peterborough, PE 1JY, UK*

M.C.F. Proctor   *Department of Biological Sciences, Hatherly Laboratories, Prince of Wales Road, University of Exeter, Exeter, EX4 4PS, UK*

D.G. Pyatt   *Forestry Authority, Northern Research Station, Roslin, Midlothian, EH25 9SY, UK*

J.R.A. Richards   *Department of Animal and Plant Sciences, P.O. Box 601, University of Sheffield, Sheffield, S10 2UQ, UK.*

L. Rochefort   *Département de Phytologie, Université Laval, Québec, G1K 7P4, Canada*

A. Schopp-Guth   *Technische Universität München, Lehrstuhl für Landschaftsökologie II, D-85350 Friesing, Germany*

J.M. Schouwenaars   *Department of Physical Geography, University of Groningen, Kerklaan 30, 9751 NN Haren, The Netherlands*

M.J. Self   *The Royal Society for the Protection of Birds, The Lodge, Sandy, Bedfordshire, SG19 2DL, UK*

S.C. Shaw   *Department of Animal & Plant Sciences, P.O. Box 601, University of Sheffield, Sheffield, S10 2UQ, UK*

M. Spencer-Famous   *Spencer/Famous Environmental Consulting, Box 102 HCR 70, Machias, Me 04654, USA*

J.H. Tallis   *School of Biological Sciences, University of Manchester, Williamson Building, Oxford Road, Manchester, M13 9PL, UK*

J.J. Thibault   *Spencer/Famous Environmental Consulting, Box 102 HCR 70, Machias, Me 04654, USA*

G.E.D. Tiley   *Environmental Sciences Department, Scottish Agricultural College, Auchincruive, Ayr, KA6 5HW, UK*

T. van den Broek   *Department of Plant Ecology and Evolutionary Biology, Utrecht University, P.O. Box 800.84 NL-3508 The Netherlands*

A.G. van der Valk   *Department of Botany, Iowa State University, Ames, IA 50011 USA*

R. van Diggelen   *Department of Plant Ecology, University of Groningen, P.O. Box 14, 9750 AA Haren, The Netherlands*

G. van Wirdum   *Department of Vegetation Ecology, Institute for Forestry and Nature Research, (IBN-DLO), P.O. Box 2 NL-6700 AA Wageningen, The Netherlands*

J.T.A. Verhoeven   *Department of Plant Ecology and Evolutionary Biology, Utrecht University, The Netherlands*

D.E. Ward   *Andrews Ward Associates, 62 High Street, Willingham, Cambridge, CB4 5ES, UK*

B.D. Wheeler   *Department of Animal & Plant Sciences, P.O. Box 601, University of Sheffield, Sheffield S10 2UQ, UK*

I.M.S. White   *Forestry Authority, Northern Research Station, Roslin, Midlothian, EH25 9SY, UK*

A.J. Willis   *Department of Animal and Plant Sciences, P.O. Box 601, University of Sheffield, Sheffield, S10 2UQ, UK*

J. Zeitz   *Humboldt-Universität zu Berlin, Institut für Grundlagen der Pfanzenbau-wissenschaften, Josef-Nawrocki-Straße 7, PF 1118, 12562, Berlin*

Preface

The planned restoration of wetlands is a rather recent activity, which has been stimulated by an increased awareness of the great importance of wetland ecosystems to wildlife, by a realisation that not all forms of past 'damage' to wetlands are irreversible and, in some instances, by a shrinking economic value of converted wetlands (*e.g.* owing to agricultural surplus).

Wetland restoration sits, sometimes rather uncomfortably, at the interface of a variety of disciplines and interests. It is of concern to groups with an interest in the utilisation of wetlands (farmers, foresters, peat extractors, water authorities), those who wish to safeguard their wildlife or other features (conservationists, natural historians) and those who want to study their properties and characteristics (archaeologists, biologists, ecologists, hydrologists *etc.*). Planners and politicians have the task of regulating the interaction between these activities and interest-groups.

The various wetland interest-groups do not always make comfortable bed-fellows and their differing priorities with regard to the utilisation, management, conservation or restoration of particular sites sometimes form a focus for dissent and, on occasion, litigation. Disputes are frequently fuelled by a failure to distinguish matters of fact from those of a personal choice and preference. However, they also often highlight a disconcerting scarcity of reliable scientific information of the sort needed to make informed decisions and judgements when assessing competing claims or evaluating the feasibility of alternative land-use options. In this circumstance, to help formulate a balanced, cost-effective and integrated approach to the utilisation, conservation and restoration of wetlands, scientists have a responsibility to try to acquire, synthesise and interpret relevant data in an informed and impartial way.

With such considerations in mind, in September 1993 a Symposium was held at the University of Sheffield (England) to consider and review current knowledge on the science of wetland restoration. It attracted an international audience of some 200 practitioners to hear papers presented by about 30 speakers and to read some 20 exhibited posters. This book is based around some of these papers and posters, with a small amount of supplementary material to help fill some gaps in the Symposium programme.

This book is not about wetland 'issues' but about aspects of ecological science as applied to wetland restoration. Nor is it a manual of wetland restoration, rather a broad snapshot of much current information and experience concerning this. Authors identify the problems of wetland restoration as well as the opportunities; the lack of knowledge as well as established information. In some cases they reveal how small is the fund of knowledge available and how difficult it can be to make informed decisions.

Contributions to this volume have been examined by independent referees, to whom we are particularly grateful. The editors and authors have made revisions to manuscripts in response to their recommendations. Contributors were asked to focus upon matters of science and fact rather than policy and propaganda. The editors hope that this volume will stimulate an inquiring and critical approach to the ecological principles that underpin wetland restoration. We are strongly of the view that effective wetland restoration, in both its scientific and political dimensions, demands data derived from investigation rather than assertion based on dogma.

We acknowledge gratefully the generous financial contributions made towards the running of the Symposium and publication of this book by the British Ecological Society, English Nature and the International Peat Society. We thank the Department of Animal & Plant Sciences at the University of Sheffield for providing the facilities for the Symposium and its staff and students for assisting with its organisation. We are particularly grateful for the assistance of Jane Bird, Kate Meacock, Sue Rogers, Rosie Snowden, Arthur Willis, Glyn Woods and Jayne Young, whose efforts went far beyond the call of duty.

The organisers of the Symposium were Peter Atkins, Wanda Fojt, Allan Robertson and Bryan Wheeler. In the event, serious illness prevented Peter Atkins from attending the meeting and we much regret having to report that he has since died. Although not specifically a wetland scientist, Peter made an important contribution to the advance of wetland restoration in Britain, particularly by helping to foster mutual under-standing between the competing interests of peatland exploitation and conservation and thus to provide a foundation upon which others will build. The editors would like to dedicate this book to his memory.

B.D. Wheeler
S.C. Shaw
W.J. Fojt
R.A. Robertson
January 1995

1 Introduction: Restoration and Wetlands

B. D. WHEELER

Department of Animal & Plant Sciences, P.O. Box 601, University of Sheffield, Sheffield, S10 2UQ, UK

WETLANDS AND MAN

In September 1993 a group of some 200 people with an interest in wetlands met at the University of Sheffield to share information on the science and art of wetland restoration. Most of these individuals spend a good part of their working lives in wetlands, for purposes of research, exploitation or protection, and many of them regard such ecosystems with some affection. In this last respect, they may well be unusual.

Human societies have had a long and complex interaction with wetlands. Even undrained wetlands have made a substantial contribution to some rural economies and several societies have lived in intimate association with them (Coles, 1990; and this volume). Some extensive wetlands seem to have formed through various forms of human activity (Tallis, this volume). Nonetheless, for much of the last two millennia, and especially during the last few centuries, the focus of human interest in wetlands has often been to drain them.

It is not difficult to understand the desire to drain wetlands. They can be uncomfortable places in which to work or live; they can be a source of disease, even in temperate latitudes (Dobson, 1980); and large, undrained wetlands of limited economic value may offer greater remuneration when drained and 'improved'. Aversion to wetlands is pervasive. Young schoolchildren in a city environment tend to regard wetlands with distaste (Anderson & Moss, 1993), though as their aversion increases with age it may be learnt rather than innate. But there is little reason to suppose that their attitude is unrepresentative. Even adults with an interest in wildlife most often like to visit wetlands using a boardwalk, and may prefer the surprise and visual delight generated by a mixture of mire woodland and glades to areas of greater ecological 'interest' but less visual appeal (Hammitt, 1980); for yet others, one suspects, the 'wetland experience' extends little beyond the limits of television broadcasts. Such predilections do, of course, help restrict damage to sensitive wetland surfaces

Yet the perceived inhospitability of wetlands also forms part of their appeal. They sometimes provide the closest approximation to 'wilderness' in landscapes from which this has long since disappeared. And as they are also often rich in plant and animal species, many of which are specific to wetlands (Fojt, this volume), when coupled to the vulnerability and wholesale destruction of wetland sites, there is clear justification both for wetland conservation and, where appropriate, restoration.

In England, the largest area of former wetland once occupied a region that is still known as Fenland, in a broad basin south and west of The Wash, covering much of Cambridgeshire and southern Lincolnshire. Drainage of this wetland was initiated during the Roman occupation (Hallam, 1970) and continued subsequently, with a major boost during the seventeenth century (Darby, 1956; Williams, 1990). The last big area of Fenland to be drained (1851) was a tract of fen and raised bog situated around a large shallow marl lake, Whittlesey Mere (Godwin & Clifford, 1938). The Whittlesey wetland had survived sufficiently long for nineteenth century naturalists to have noted its wildlife, and it is evident that with its drainage various bog and fen plants were lost, including the last British population of the large copper butterfly (*Lycaena dispar dispar*) (Duffey, 1970).

Awareness of the wholesale destruction of wetlands, and of the diminution in 'quality' of some extant examples (*e.g.* Fojt; Galatowitsch & van der Valk, this volume) has led naturalists and conservationists to try to protect and enhance some of the remaining examples. One of the first nature reserves in England was Woodwalton Fen, acquired by the Society for the Promotion of Nature Reserves in 1919 and made a National Nature Reserve in 1954. This site was once part of the Whittlesey Mere complex, but in the 70 years after drainage it had been subject to peat extraction and some cultivation. The subsequent redevelopment of wildlife 'interest' on this badly-damaged site provides an early example of wetland 'restoration' and illustrates both the potential and problems of the process. On the one hand, Woodwalton Fen has redeveloped a rich fenland flora; on the other, attempts to re-introduce *L. dispar* (from Dutch populations, *L. dispar bavatus*) have been largely unsuccessful, for reasons that are not fully understood. Possibilities are that, although populations of the butterfly's food plant, *Rumex hydrolapathum*[1], can be maintained, other aspects of the habitat are unsuitable; or that the site is not large enough to sustain a viable breeding population (Duffey, 1970). Woodwalton Fen epitomises the problems that may confound restoration initiatives: that the 'restored' habitat does not mimic faithfully all of the properties of the original; habitat requirements and tolerances of many species are not at all well known; and 'restored' sites are often smaller than the original wetland, isolated from comparable examples and, sometimes, divorced from the landscape processes (water supply mechanisms *etc.*) that were once critical to their former character.

Lycaena dispar still flies at Woodwalton Fen, but its populations are maintained, somewhat against the odds, by regular release of butterflies from captive breeding stock and by habitat manipulation to sustain suitable populations of *R.*

---

[1] Nomenclature for vascular plants follows Stace (1991)

hydrolapathum. To the purist, such operations may seem more like a form of zoological gardening than authentic habitat restoration and, in one sense, they are. However, pejorative overtones notwithstanding, they are but an extreme example of the fact that the maintenance of populations of many plant and animal species requires a degree of recurrent human intervention (management) even in wetlands. This is illustrated by several of the contributions to this book.

Many wetland sites have been much influenced by some form of vegetation management or habitat manipulation, usually employed in the past to increase their utility or economic value. Pools have been dug and surfaces flooded to encourage wildfowl; peat has been dug for fuel, animal bedding and (more recently) growing media for horticulture. Various crops have also been harvested: reed (*Phragmites australis*) has been cut in various fens and swamps; marsh hay and litter have been mown in very many sites (Moen, this volume); and, in Britain, 'sedge' (*Cladium mariscus*) has also been a crop of local importance. Buckwheat (*Fagopyrum esculentum*) was once widely grown on many raised bogs in north-west Europe (Joosten, this volume), and large areas of both blanket and raised bogs have been afforested (Anderson, Pyatt & White; Heikkilä & Lindholm, this volume). Many wetlands have also been used for rough, summer grazing for livestock. Some of these forms of exploitation are still practised. They have often been associated with some degree of habitat manipulation, sometimes partial drainage, and this has shaped the character of the wetlands. Indeed, the high biodiversity and natural history interest of many wetland sites is frequently a product of such manipulation, often referred to as their 'traditional' management. The 'traditional' wetlands may not have been carefully manicured ecosystems, but neither were they 'wilderness'.

The largest remaining complex of lowland fen in England, the Norfolk Broadland, is particularly rich in plant and animal species (George, 1992). These include all of the known British populations of the fenland form of the fen orchid (*Liparis loeselii*), the main populations of the swallowtail butterfly (*Papilio machaon*) and of its caterpillar's food plant (*Peucedanum palustre*). Both *L. loeselii* and *P. machaon* are exclusively associated with herbaceous vegetation types (Wheeler & Shaw; Foster & Procter, this volume) which are maintained by 'traditional' management. Without this, such vegetation readily reverts to the fen woodland which has been the main 'natural' community of these mires for much of their developmental history (*e.g.* Jennings, 1952). It would be of great interest to know in what circumstances species such as *L. loeselii* and *P. machaon* survived in Broadland before human intervention. Perhaps, before the mires were partly reclaimed and fragmented, before the rivers were embanked and diverted, and before the transition of fen with adjoining 'upland' was sharpened by drainage, natural hydrological processes and gradients helped to maintain open vegetation and shallow pools. Even so, it seems probable that some species of open fen were even less frequent in the 'natural' Broadland than they are today.

Because the character of wetlands is often critically dependent upon the nature of their water supply, they are often far more influenced by events in their surroundings ('external' factors) than are drylands. Fens may have various water sources and a wide catchment and changes in these may materially influence the quantity and quality of their water inputs (Grootjans & van Diggelen; Koerselman & Verhoeven; van Wirdum, this volume). By contrast, bogs may be less directly dependent upon the water management of their surroundings, although in some circumstances this may also affect them (Schouwenaars, this volume). In some instances the realisation of particular conservation or restoration objectives may demand control of such 'external' factors as well as 'internal' ones. Where this is not possible, it may be necessary to redefine the objectives to be compatible with the present ecohydrological *status quo*; that is, to accept that 'restoration' *sensu stricto* cannot be achieved.

THE CONCEPT OF RESTORATION

The preceding paragraphs have referred to 'restoration' without defining it. In this they have followed much general practice! However, the meaning and implications of the word 'restoration' merit consideration to help unravel the concepts that underlie restoration options and policies.

The word 'restore' has various nuances of meaning (Table 1). Common to all of them is that it implies an attempt to bring an object back into a condition which has some resemblance to a former state. The degree of match is not explicit (it may vary between a return to its 'original' state to a reproduction) but it is implicit that a restored object has some substantive similarity with a former condition (of course, it is not possible to restore any object *exactly* to its previous state).

'Restoration' can be used to accommodate various degrees of reinstatement – repair, reconstruction, reproduction and re-creation (Table 1). Thus the 'restoration' of wetlands may encompass a broad spectrum of activities, from minor reparation of damage (*e.g.* damming of ditches), through contrived re-assembly (*e.g.* deliberate reintroduction of species) to *de novo* regeneration (*e.g.* provision of appropriate starting conditions from which a new wetland can develop). At the small-scale end of this range it can be difficult to separate 'restoration' procedures from those normally thought of as routine habitat and vegetation 'management'. Perhaps the distinction should be that management practices are recurrent operations whereas restoration procedures are (hopefully) one-off or very infrequent.

Objects can be restored either to their initial ('original') state or to a 'former' condition. This distinction is important for ecosystems such as wetlands that are

Table 1. Definitions of 'restore' (paraphrased from the *Oxford English Dictionary*; Simpson & Weiner, 1989).

Restore: to give back; to make good; to set right, repair; to build up again; to re-erect or re-construct; to bring back to original state or previous condition; to reproduce or repeat in its former form; to renew; to re-establish; to bring into existence again.

---

subject to natural developmental change. In general, conservationists do not wish to restore wetland sites to their initial state, which in many cases would be wet forest or open water, but to a later seral stage (a 'former' state). Which of these is perceived to be most desirable is a matter of choice and preference. Thus, semantically, it is legitimate to restore, a damaged raised-bog *site* to woodland, open water, swamp, fen or fen carr as it is to another *Sphagnum*-rich raised bog, at least in those instances where such habitats were precursors to the bog's development. Equally, however, semantics dictate that a site cannot be 'restored' to something it never was. Thus a damaged raised bog cannt be 'restored' to wet grassland, though (semantically) it is possible to 'restore' 'wildlife' interest' to a raised-bog site by creating a habitat such as wet grassland. However, it may be more appropriate to use a quite different term from 'restoration' when the re-created habitat has no real resemblance to a previous one. The term 'rehabilitation' is sometimes used informally as a general term for the re-creation of unspecified 'wildlife interest', though it may have no greater legitimacy for this than does 'restoration' (the *Oxford English Dictionary* defines 'rehabilitation' in terms of restoration, the main difference being that it is more usually applied to people than objects). Moreover, some workers have an idiosyncratic concept of rehabilitation. 'Renaturation' is probably a more acceptable term for the restoration of unspecified 'wildlife interest', though it has little general currency in English.

The object of restoration initiatives *within* wetland sites also needs to be clearly specified. It is, semantically, quite acceptable to, say, 'restore' the water-table within a wetland to its former level without having 'restored' other aspects of the site, such as its former vegetation. This leads to a confusion that permeates restoration literature: sites are sometimes said to have been restored when just one component of their damage has been remedied. When the aim of restoration is to bring a site back into its former condition in as many respects as possible, it is desirable to recognise distinctive, but overlapping, sequential phases in the process: *viz.* re-establishment of (i) appropriate environmental conditions; (ii) characteristic biota; and (iii) features of ecosystem function and development (*cf.* Kuntze & Eggelsmann, 1981).

OBJECTIVES OF RESTORATION

The aim of restoring a damaged wetland site to a former condition often stems from a desire to re-instate characteristic, or otherwise desirable, wildlife and the objectives of restoration frequently reflect perceived conservational 'desirability'.

Conservation objectives in wetlands focus upon various features. The fundamental unit of wildlife conservation is the species, but each species may occupy a variety of different habitats and contribute to different assemblages of organisms (community-types). Moreover, wetlands also occupy, and sometimes help to form, a range of landforms and they can be categorised (with varying degrees of difficulty) into hydrotopographical types (see below). Conservationists, and others with an interest in the countryside, often consider that 'value' should be attached to examples of specific community-types and distinctive wetland-types as well as to species populations. Such an approach has significant repercussions. For example, in the UK, most of the plant species found on raised bogs are, nationally, widespread and fairly common and occur widely in other types of mire (such as poor fen or blanket bog). However, the particular *assemblage* of species which typically recurs on little-damaged raised bogs (identified by Rodwell (1991) as *Erica tetralix–Sphagnum papillosum* mire) is nowadays scarce.

Conservationists have long considered how best to assess the perceived conservation importance of different species, communities and habitats. A variety of attributes has been proposed for evaluation purposes (Ratcliffe, 1977; Usher, 1986). Only a few of these (*e.g.* area, rarity) are amenable to simple quantification. Other features can be more difficult to apply consistently and sometimes may more reflect the perceptions and preferences of individuals than an objectively-definable ecosystem property. The establishment of clear, consistent or logical guidelines for assessing conservational priorities and 'values' can become correspondingly difficult. For example, in England, the extensive blanket mires of the southern Pennines, which are sometimes near-monocultures of *Eriophorum vaginatum,* tend to be regarded as badly-damaged ecosystems in need of 'repair', whilst the great tracts of heather moor in North Yorkshire, which are near-monocultures of *Calluna vulgaris*, are prized ecosystems which form the heart of a National Park. Yet both are essentially species-poor ecosystems which have been produced by human 'damage': the difference between them presumably rests in the perceived 'visual amenity' of the two vegetation-types.

The difficulties of defining rational *conservation* objectives are sometimes more apparent than real. For example, the selection of particular management objectives within fens is often made by default by maintaining (or resuming) traditional management practices (*e.g.* Bakker & Olff; Moen, this volume), on the reasonable basis that their wildlife interest is believed to have been shaped by these. However, the question of objectives comes into much sharper focus with *restoration* initiatives for badly-damaged or disturbed ecosystems, as, depending upon the degree and nature of damage or disturbance, these may have little residual interest and a wide range of restoration possibilities.

There seem to be few guidelines to assist the selection of desirable restoration objectives and, in practice, they sometimes more reflect the preferences of individual restorers than an objectively-defensible choice. The following considerations have some relevance:

Feasibility: In some situations restoration options are largely determined by the existing environmental conditions and by the scope that exists for modifying them. For example, where peat cutting has removed all the ombrotrophic peat from a raised-bog site to expose underlying fen peat, then, initially, redevelopment of wetland will necessarily be to a minerotrophic wetland. Equally it is unlikely to be feasible to re-create low-productivity fen vegetation in a site now irrigated mainly by nutrient-rich water. In yet other situations, some restoration options may be possible, but difficult (or expensive). It is important to assess fully the feasibility and cost-effectiveness of possible objectives when planning a restoration strategy (*e.g.* Famous *et al.*; Grootjans & van Diggelen; Ward *et al.*; this volume).

Former character of the wetland: It can be argued that a rationale for restoration is provided by the character of the wetland that existed before damage, *viz.* that restoration should attempt to re-create the wetland in its 'last-known state'. On this basis, a damaged raised-bog site may be most appropriately restored to a replacement raised bog, where this is feasible. Such a dictum is less clearly applicable to formulating desirable restoration options for some fen sites, as much of the perceived conservation value of fens is often a product of some form of past 'damage' or manipulation. Indeed, some restoration initiatives in fens aim specifically to 'damage' their 'natural' state (fen woodland) by tree removal! Moreover, the application of this principle can have various curious repercussions. For example, in some parts of the Netherlands attempts are being made, mostly with some difficulty, to re-establish *Sphagnum*-dominated bog vegetation on some former, cut-over, raised-bog sites (Schouwenaars; Joosten, this volume) whilst elsewhere attempts are made to stop spontaneous, seral ombrotrophication of peat pits, by physical removal of *Sphagnum*-based vegetation, because this is seen as a threat to the valued fen communities that it replaces (Beltman *et al.*, this volume)!

Rarity: Although conservationists sometimes warn against excessive emphasis upon the importance of rarity, it is one of the more easily-defended bases of conservation strategy because species with small populations, or scarce communities, are potentially more vulnerable to loss or genetic impoverishment than are common examples. Rarity is also amenable to objective measurement. However, a practical problem of rarity, in relation to restoration, is that several rare species can provide equally desirable foci of restoration but have competing habitat and restoration requirements. For example, although raised bog is regarded as a rare 'habitat' in Britain (Fojt, this volume), restoration and conservation initiatives in former raised bogs do not always aim to re-create it: the former raised bog at Leighton Moss (Lancashire) is managed as reedbeds, for their ornithological interest. One justification of this may be that a rare reedbed bird species, such as bittern, has considerably more popular appeal than does an equally rare sphagnicolous protozoan, though this argument may not be acceptable to the conservational purist.

The application of rarity to decide restoration options can have various ramifications. In Britain, for example, it would suggest that some raised bog remnants should not be restored to raised bog but, where appropriate underlying fen peat exists, this should be exposed to regenerate species-rich herbaceous fen communities. This is because some of the very distinctive types of low-productivity fen that once preceded the development of some raised bogs are currently considerably less extensive than is raised bog.

Scarcity of opportunity: One further approach to resolving conflicting restoration options is to assess the scarcity of opportunity for achieving a particular end point. Wheeler (1992) has argued for this approach with respect to the choice of species-rich fen vegetation *versus* reedbeds in fen peat workings.

Species-rich fen vegetation is particularly associated with uncommon low-productivity habitats, irrigated by nutrient-poor water. In such conditions, restoration to reedbeds could be seen as a wasted opportunity, because these can be created readily in a wide variety of situations, including wholly artificial ones.

There is a very real need for careful consideration and identification of the criteria used to select restoration options. Without this, it will be hard to avoid decisions being made just on the basis of existing condition, historical precedent and, especially, the particular perceptions and aspirations of owners or managers.

STRATEGIES AND PROSPECTS FOR RESTORATION

The prospects for the successful restoration of damaged wetlands are, of course, inextricably determined by the restoration objectives themselves and the perceptions of 'success'. Some objectives may be realised more readily than others and it is always possible to set one's sights so low that almost any outcome can be counted as satisfactory. Equally there can be little doubt that minor damage is often more readily restored than major damage, in terms at least of the time-scale involved if not the ultimate outcome. Despite these caveats, there is plenty of evidence, both historical and experimental, that some wetland ecosystems can be effectively restored. Indeed, the present-day wildlife 'interest' of some wetland sites is, in part, a product of past damage.

To be successful, restoration initiatives need to satisfy two main conditions: to provide environmental conditions appropriate for the desired recolonist organisms; and to enable recolonisation to occur. There are two main strategies to restore habitat conditions: by *repair* and by *rebuilding*. Restoration by repair attempts to restore requisite conditions directly. It is particularly appropriate for the reparation of rather small-scale damage and, if successful, often has the advantage that a desirable outcome is realised quite quickly. Restoration by rebuilding is based on the recognition that, in some cases, appropriate conditions can be best (sometimes only) re-established indirectly, that is by taking the wetland back to an earlier developmental stage and allowing natural redevelopment. This approach is particularly suitable for sites that have been badly damaged, where this has led to irreversible change and where restoration by repair is technically difficult or prohibitively expensive. Its disadvantages are that it may demand further 'demolition' to produce a firm foundation for rebuilding, that it may take a long time for late-seral communities to redevelop and that the perceived 'interest' of the earlier seral stages may be such that these become the focus of conservation interest, and the restoration is deflected from its original objectives.

Approaches to the restoration of raised bogs that have been badly damaged by peat extraction or reclamation provide an illustration of this. In a little-damaged raised bog the uppermost peat horizon, the acrotelm, appears to play a critical rôle in hydrological self-regulation (Bragg, this volume), but it is removed by peat extraction and may be destroyed by reclamation. The 'trick' of raised bog restoration is to regenerate a fully-functional acrotelm, in particular by trying to re-establish a *Sphagnum*-dominated vegetation (*e.g.* Grosvernier *et al.*; Mawby; Money; Poschlod; Rochefort *et al.*, this volume). However, the conditions required to regenerate this are, to some extent, provided by the acrotelm itself so that in some cases, particularly in drier regions, simple attempts at repair (by blocking drainage ditches, *etc.*) may not be successful. In such situations, bog regeneration may be possible only by rebuilding. One approach which has had some success has been the construction of shallow lagoons on the bog surface in which aquatic Sphagna can regenerate (Schouwenaars, this volume), thus mimicking some properties of the acrotelm. In other cases it may ultimately be more satisfactory to remove residual 'raised' peat to the level of the groundwater table, or below, to permit natural redevelopment of bog from fen. In some parts of Britain and elsewhere (Beltman *et al.*; van Wirdum, this volume), it is not difficult to find embryonic bogs developing within fens, in some cases in sites that have been much damaged by substantial extraction of peat. The concept of giving a wetland a 'new start' in such a way falls within the *Oxford English Dictionary*'s definitions of 'restoration' (Table 1).

Perhaps the most extreme form of damage to wetland ecosystems is that found in sites which have long been drained and used for some form of agriculture. This can induce a wide spectrum of soil changes related to a reduction of water levels, application of fertilisers *etc.* (Okruszko; Zeitz, this volume). Such ecosystems may still support some residual wetland species, if only within the ditches dug to drain the wetland, but in general they can be regarded only as highly-damaged wetlands. Restoration of such sites to a more-obviously 'wetland' habitat essentially requires a reversal of the changes associated with damage. Some of these can be achieved more readily than others. It is often technically quite easy to increase the height of water tables in drained wetlands and, where sites have been enriched by fertilisation, it may be possible to reduce the fertility of the upper soil horizons, for example by appropriate vegetation management (Bakker & Olff; Koerselman & Verhoeven, this volume). Other changes, such as physical changes in soil properties, may be considered irreversible (Okruszko, this volume). Such 'irreversibility' does not, of necessity, preclude the possibility of restoration, but it may point to the need for restoration strategies based upon rebuilding rather than repair, by the creation of a different wetland habitat (such as a shallow lagoon) which may have the potential for developing some of the properties of the former wetland. The best way to restore a wetland may not always be to re-create directly the environmental conditions associated with its 'last known state'.

The development of restoration strategies is often hampered by lack of knowledge – of causes of damage; of the nature and controls upon some salient environmental variables; and of the response of organisms to these. It is often particularly important to gain an understanding of the hydrodynamics of wetlands, both to assess the effects of different types of damage and to identify potential restoration strategies (Bragg; Grootjans & van Diggelen; Heathwaite; Schouwen-aars, this volume). Various insights exist on the relationships between some wetland species and environmental conditions (*e.g.* Bölscher; Foster & Procter;

Painter & Friday; Proctor; Ward *et al.*; Wheeler & Shaw, this volume), but factual data on the environmental optima and tolerance-range of many wetland species are in short supply, and, in any case, the conditions needed to re-establish species may often be rather different from those in which they are able to persist. In consequence, restoration schemes have often proceeded on an empirical basis.

Even when firm insights do exist on species requirements, they may be difficult to implement. For example, many surfaces of the deep hill peats of the southern Pennines in England are considerably damaged by erosion. The causes of this are not fully understood (Tallis, this volume), nor are its remedies. One constraint upon revegetation is that the growth of an indigenous, potential recolonist, peat-binding species (*Eriophorum angustifolium*) is limited by the high degree of acidity of the peats, almost certainly caused by 'acid rain' (Richards, Wheeler & Willis, this volume). Its growth, and peat-stabilisation capacity, can be increased by modest application of lime, but it is far from clear whether this will prove to be an acceptable restoration procedure, not least because of possible (but not well known) detrimental effects of lime upon some other components of the ecosystem and the likely costs involved.

Restoration initiatives in wetlands may also be considerably constrained by factors external to the site. For example, it is possible – though by no means certain – that current rates of aerial nitrogen deposition may be inconducive to the re-establishment, of some *Sphagnum* species in cut-over bogs, especially perhaps some bog-building species such as *S. magellanicum*. More conclusive information on such interactions is desirable, not least because there may be little point in implementing elaborate restoration schemes if other conditions are intrinsically unsuitable for some of the target species. Similar comments apply to the rewetting of drained fen sites: the feasibility of specific restoration objectives depends not just upon the availability of water but upon its quality, so that it may be, for all practical purposes, impossible to restore the wetland to a desired condition, because of changed conditions in its surroundings. Such considerations highlight the importance of assessing feasibility in selecting restoration objectives. They also emphasise the need for a rigorous assessment of restoration opportunities to prevent rare opportunities from being squandered on a cosmopolitan objective.

Rather little is known about the capacity of many wetland species to recolonise re-created wetland habitats: indeed, even the main dispersal mechanisms are not well known for some species. The diaspores of many of the plants typical of bogs are sometimes regarded as being well suited to long-distance dispersal (Moore, 1982), though again reliable data are sparse and sometimes contradictory (Poschlod, this volume). Nor are the conditions appropriate for the effective establishment of wetland plants from diaspores generally well known.

The potential of species regeneration from diaspore banks within the upper soil horizons of damaged wetlands has received some study and seems to vary with habitat-type. For example, Poschlod (this volume) reports that the 'top spit' of raised bogs may contain a persistent diaspore bank with many typical bog species. By contrast, some types of fen may have a very restricted persistent seedbank, containing few of the more 'desirable' fen species (Maas & Schopp-Guth, this volume). This is likely to impose considerable constraints upon revegetation. Brock & Britton (this volume) also stress the importance of water regime in controlling establishment from seedbanks.

Where species have been completely lost from a former wetland site, judicious re-introduction of plant species may be required to accelerate recolonisation (*e.g.* Galatowitsch & van der Valk, this volume). Even where the species survive on-site, some transplanting, or spreading of diaspores, may materially assist natural colonisation (*e.g.* Merrilees, Tiley & Gwynne, this volume), in some cases perhaps using small vegetative fragments (Money; Poschlod; Rochefort *et al.*, this volume). Not all conservationists favour restoration policies that involve species introductions from outside the site, but this is largely a matter of choice and opinion. The 'choice' is sometimes that species re-introductions may be essential to restore isolated wetlands to their former condition. Restoration ecology is not for the faint-hearted!

TYPES OF WETLAND

Effective communication amongst wetland ecologists has long been hampered by inconsistent terminology. Numerous terms exist to refer to different types of wetland (Gore, 1983). Many lack precise definition, or are understood differently by practitioners. This is partly because groups of workers have developed their individual terminologies, because various criteria (vegetation, hydrological features, chemical characteristics, soil types, *etc.*) can form a basis for identifying wetland types and because different subdivisions are possible, even when using the same criteria. The main product of this is confusion.

Wetland terms and concepts relevant to restoration nowadays have a constituency beyond that of wetland ecologists, for example, when legislation for wetland protection and restoration is formulated. It is therefore desirable that, not only are terms, categories and concepts clearly defined, but also that they are scientifically defensible, soundly based and consistent.

The concept of wetland

The term *wetland* exemplifies terminological inconsistency and opacity. At face value it means 'land that is wet', but this raises the question: 'How wet ?' There is general agreement that 'wetland' refers to a habitat which occupies a position somewhere between dry land and deep aquatic ecosystems and differences of definition refer mainly to the exact position of its upper and lower limits (Mitsch & Gosselink, 1986). In this volume we have excluded aquatic ecosystems without emergent plants from our compass of 'wetland' on the basis that their dominant ecological processes (and requirements for restoration) are very different from those based upon semi-terrestrial waterlogged soils. The upper limit of 'wetland' can also be difficult to define, or recognise, not least because the drier parts of many wetland sites have been much modified by human activity. This is particularly pertinent for considerations of restoration as badly-damaged 'wetlands' may have lost many of their distinctive wetland features.

As used here, the concept of wetland essentially accommodates sites that have (or once had) a water table close to the ground surface for much of the year, but which may experience some periodic inundation or drying. If required, such 'wetlands' can be referred to as 'telmatic wetlands' or 'paludic wetlands', to distinguish them from open-water 'aquatic wetlands'. Their compass comes close to that of *mire*, a term which has been widely adopted as a broad unit to include many permanently waterlogged sites ('swamp, bog, fen, moor, muskeg and peatland', Gore, 1983).

Subdivision of telmatic wetlands

Wetlands may be subdivided by various criteria (Gore, 1983) and several classifications have been proposed (*e.g.* Mitsch & Gosselink, 1986; Succow, 1988; Göttlich, 1990). Many workers consider that the 'hydrotopography' of wetlands (*i.e.* their situation, 'shape' and water supply) is a particularly characteristic feature and important in their classification (Sjörs, 1950). Von Post & Granlund (1926) subdivided mires into three main types: *ombrogenous* mires were those which developed under the more-or-less exclusive influence of precipitation; *topogenous* mires were irrigated by more-or-less horizontal 'mineral soil water'; whilst *soligenous* mires were those developed on sloping sites, where laterally mobile 'mineral soil water' maintained wet conditions (Sjörs, 1950). Du Rietz (1949, 1954) emphasised that the primary division in Swedish mires was between those areas fed more-or-less exclusively by precipitation (*ombrotrophic* ('rain-fed') or *ombrogenous* ('rain-made') mires) and those in which this was supplemented by telluric water (*minerotrophic*, or 'rock-fed' mires (= topogenous + soligenous mires)). These categories are important ones. They broadly correspond with major habitat and biological differences within mires and have been widely accepted. Many wetland ecologists have come to use the word *fen* as a synonym for minerotrophic mires and *bog* to refer to ombrotrophic examples.

The concept of fen

The term *fen* has received a confused usage. For example, in Britain, *fens* have been regarded as being either (a) topographical features of the landscape (*e.g.* 'The Fens' of East Anglia); (b) wetlands encompassing a particular range of habitat conditions (Tansley, 1939); (c) wetlands encompassing a particular range of vegetation-types (Wheeler, 1980); (d) a particular, herbaceous, phase of the hydrosere interpolated between swamp and mire woodland (fen carr) (Tansley, 1939).

Anglo-Saxon use of the word '*Fenn*' had a very broad compass, as it seems then to have been a generic term for almost all types of waterlogged habitats, including those which would now be called 'bog' (Bosworth & Toller, 1882). Such breadth of usage has been perpetuated in its modern Dutch equivalent ('*veen*') and also in some vernacular use of fen in England, but English-speaking ecologists (*e.g.* Tansley, 1939) have truncated its meaning, and today it is perhaps most widely used in the ecological literature in contradistinction to 'bog', as a synonym for minerotrophic mires (Sjörs, 1950). Thus defined, it has a very broad compass, embracing a wide variety of environmental conditions and biological features. It ['fen'] is broader than the concept of peatland as it may also include sites on mineral soils. Some workers (*e.g.* Mörnsjö, 1969) consider 'true fens' to be those which are developed upon peat. Tansley (1939) distinguished wet sites on mineral soils as 'marsh'.

The minerotrophic environment is extremely variable, particularly with regard to water source, quantity and quality. Variation in base-richness has been accommodated within the concept of fen by the recognition of 'rich fen' and 'poor fen', though it is difficult to specify a clear or universal definition of these. Du Rietz (1949, 1954) recognised rich and poor fens as floristic units (*i.e.* based upon the presence or absence of plants that were thought to indicate basiphilous conditions). However, the field pH 'preferences' of many wetland plants are not always well established and may, moreover, show considerable variation between geographical regions or even amongst sites in the same region (*e.g.* Sjörs, 1950). Ultimately, the selection of the base-richness range, or the plant communities, of 'poor' or 'rich' fen may be largely arbitrary.

The range of water regimes appropriate to the concept of fen have not been well considered by ecologists. Fens are often informally regarded as wetlands that are not as wet as swamps but are wetter than, say, wet heath or wet grassland, but it is difficult to specify with much exactness the water level limits involved, or to accommodate the complications introduced by sites that are subject to strong seasonal water-level flux. Moreover, many wetland sites which support what is called 'fen vegetation' have themselves been partly drained, so that their 'natural' properties are uncertain.

The concept of bog

The term 'bog' has also not been used consistently by ecologists. For example, Tansley (1939) used it to include ombrogenous mires together with acidic minerotrophic examples ('poor fens' *sensu* Du Rietz, 1949). However, there has been a tendency for many wetland ecologists to restrict the word 'bog' to refer specifically to ombrotrophic wetlands and it is in this sense that the word is used in this volume. In this narrow sense, the concept of bog is generally more clear than that of fen, in that it essentially refers to peat-based mires that are directly and exclusively irrigated by precipitation. Such sites have a much narrower range of environmental and biological variation than minerotrophic wetlands and it is easier to specify their limits.

Whilst there is a clear conceptual distinction between bog and fen, it is less easy to specify how this can be recognised. Du Rietz (1949, 1954) suggested a floristic approach, based upon the 'fen plant limit', that is the absence of species thought to indicate groundwater influence and, despite the potential circularity, ecologists still often use floristic criteria (*e.g.* vegetation composition) to identify areas of 'bog', rather than some independent hydrological measure. However, the capacity for most 'bog' species to grow in poor fens coupled with the ability of some fen species to grow in ombrotrophic environments (in at least the more oceanic parts of their range) precludes a universal floristic separation of fen from bog. Nor can hydrochemical measures be used as universal indicators of ombrotrophy, as any simple specification of chemical thresholds is complicated by regional variation in rainwater composition (Bellamy, 1967; Proctor, 1992; Proctor, this volume). In consequence in some peatland complexes, especially oceanic mires, it can be difficult, just by using floristic or hydrochemical criteria, to determine whether a given surface is ombrotrophic or minerotrophic.

Hydrotopographical types of wetland

Perhaps the most widely-used approach to subdividing wetlands has been based upon 'hydrotopography'. This essentially refers to the 'shape' and situation of the wetland with respect to water sources. The desire to categorise wetlands by their shape, situation and water supply is beguiling, not least because it may appear to be 'simple'. However, the topography of wetlands is often not readily characterised or quantified, nor can their hydrological mechanisms always be assessed by casual inspection. Moreover, the apparent simplicity of this approach has encouraged various workers to generate hydrotopographical classifications and a plethora of rather different classifications exists. Some of these, (*e.g.* Succow & Lange, 1984; Succow, 1988) have been based upon careful synthesis and analysis of data whilst others have been more informal (*e.g.* Goode, 1972).

A limitation of many hydrotopographical classifications is that they do not

Table 2. Main topographical situations in which wetlands occur in the British Isles.

BASIN WETLANDS	Associated with discrete basins and ground hollows.
FLOOD-PLAIN WETLANDS	Associated with *current* river flood plains.
COASTAL-PLAIN WETLANDS	Associated with coastal plains, heads of estuaries, *etc.*
PLATEAU–PLAIN WETLANDS	On flat or slightly undulating ground without close association with lakes, rivers; or discrete, shallow basins; kept wet by high rainfall, impermeable substratum, high groundwater table *etc.*
VALLEYHEAD WETLANDS	Usually small, narrow wetland sites associated with the upper reaches of valleys; mainly soligenous.
HILLSLOPE WETLANDS	On sloping ground and hillsides.
LAKESIDE WETLANDS	Associated with lakes (although this 'situation' can be readily recognised, it may better subsumed within the other categories, such as basins and flood plains, rather than being given a separate identity.)

distinguish clearly between the topography of the landscape within which wetlands occur and the characteristics of the wetlands themselves. For example, in Britain, workers have distinguished 'flood-plain mires', 'basin mires', 'open water transition mires' and 'raised mires' as hydrotopographical 'types' (Ratcliffe, 1977). But raised mires, or water bodies with their associated hydroseres, often occur *within* flood plains or basins. In which category should they be placed ?

Although inevitably crude and arbitrary it is possible to identify broad 'landscape situations' in which wetlands occur (Table 2). Each of these may contain wetlands composed of one or more 'hydrotopographical elements'. In Table 3, some of the terms used by various workers for wetland types are related to their distinctive causes of surface wetness, taking as the primary division that between sites kept wet primarily by impeded drainage (retention) of water and those with relatively little restriction of water outflow but kept wet by constancy of water supply. In the minerotrophic context, these broadly correspond to the categories of topogenous and soligenous fen. In practice, specific water sources can be difficult to recognise or quantify, even in crude terms, and mixtures often occur.

Table 3. Some terms that have often been used to describe hydrotopographical components of wetland sites in relation to features of gross topography and distinctive causes of surface-wet conditions. Terms used loosely for several categories (*e.g.* valley mire) or which refer primarily to landscape features (*e.g.* basin mire) have been excluded. Note that the terms are not necessarily synonyms.

Distinctive cause of surface wetness	Topogenous sites (or parts of sites)	Sloping sites (or parts of sites)
Open water of lakes and pools	Waterfringe wetland; open water transition mire; fringing fen; limnogenous mire	
Overbank flooding from rivers and streams	Alluvial wetland; transgression mire; fluviogenous mire	
Confined groundwater (strong point-source discharge)	Spring-fed wetland; spring fen; tufa mound	Spring-fed wetland; spring fen; tufa mound
Groundwater flow (from margins or diffuse upwelling)	Percolating mire; headwater fen	Seepage fen
Run-off or local groundwater	Sump wetland; swamp(ing) mire; kettlehole mire; telmatogenous mire	Run-off fen; sloping fen; ladder fen
Precipitation	Topogenous bog; raised bog; blanket bog	Hill bog; blanket bog
Discrete zones of water flow	Soakways and water tracks	Soakways and water tracks; runnels

The hydrotopography of fens is often determined by the topography of the landscape in which they occur, but ombrogenous peat deposits sometimes shows some independence of their topographical context. Globally, bogs can occur in much the same range of landscape situations as fens, but in regions of relatively low precipitation they are restricted to topogenous situations (flat, or gentle slopes or gently undulating surfaces). Here, the ombrogenous peat is elevated above the underlying fen peat or mineral soil and sometimes forms a distinct hemi-elliptical dome independent of the surface topography. Such peatlands are often referred to as 'raised bogs'. The degree of their 'doming' appears to be a product of age, topographical situation, basal area and climate. It is often most evident in small bogs; larger examples often do not appear strongly domed, but may more form a plateau of peat with steep edges (Ratcliffe, 1964; Clymo, 1991). In Britain at least, domes of peat on ostensibly 'flat' sites sometimes conform to an underlying mineral ridge *etc*. (DAFS, 1965 and archives).

In wetter and cooler climatic regions, ombrogenous peat formation can occur on sloping ground, typically up to about 10°, but sometimes considerably steeper. This leads to the development of large tracts of ombrogenous peatland which may 'blanket' much of the landscape, conformed by its topography and restricted only by steeper slopes and other obstructions. Such peatlands are often referred to, in aggregate, as 'blanket bog', but whilst the occurrence of ombrogenous peat on hill slopes is distinctive for blanket bog, it is far from certain that the ombrogenous peatlands of the basins, flats and gentle slopes of these regions are much different – in terms of their origin, gross form and stratigraphy – from the 'raised bogs' of drier climates. Indeed, various stratigraphical sections show that some units of bog embedded within a 'blanket bog landscape' have greater similarity to 'raised bogs' elsewhere than they do to the blanket peats on adjoining slopes (*e.g.* DAFS, 1965; and archives) and it seems likely that the most distinctive hydrotopographical subdivision within ombrogenous peatlands may be that between sites in topogenous situations and those on hill slopes. This has been recognised in the categories of *hill bog* and *topogenous bog* used by the Scottish Peat Survey. On this basis, the 'blanket peatlands' of oceanic regions can be seen as a mosaic of hill bog (blanket bog), topogenous bog (raised bog) and various types of fen.

Discussion of wetland classification may seem a rather esoteric contribution to a book about wetland restoration. However, it helps to highlight the uncertainties and lack of agreement that permeate some areas of wetland ecology, as well as the frequent lack of 'hard' factual data upon which concepts (and decisions) are sometimes based. Moreover, there can be little doubt that wetland ecology (and restoration) would materially benefit from the adoption of a consistent and clear vocabulary. For whilst individual workers may be clear about their particular usage of a term, others may have a quite different understanding of it. Unless there is a particular need to do so, wetland ecologists should be encouraged to avoid the attitude of *Humpty Dumpty* – "When *I* use a word . . . it means just what I choose it to mean – neither more nor less" (Carroll, 1872), though in some situations they may have little alternative.

REFERENCES

Anderson, S. & Moss, B. (1993). How wetland habitats are perceived by children: consequences for children's education and wetland conservation. *International Journal of Science Education*, **15**, 473–485.

Bellamy, D.J. (1967). *Ecological Studies on some European Mires*. PhD thesis, University of London.

Bosworth, J. & Toller, J.N. (1882). *An Anglo-Saxon Dictionary*. Clarendon Press, Oxford.

Carroll, L. (1872). *Through the Looking Glass and What Alice Found There*. Macmillan & Co., London.

Clymo, R.S. (1991). Peat growth. In: *Quaternary Landscapes* (ed. L.C.K. Shane & E.J. Cushing), pp. 76–112. Belhaven Press, London.

Coles, B. (1990). Wetland Archaeology – a wealth of evidence. *Wetlands: a Threatened Landscape*, (ed. M. Williams), pp. 145–180. Blackwell Scientific Publications, Oxford.

Darby, H.C. (1956). *The Draining of the Fens*. Cambridge University Press, Cambridge.

Department of Agriculture and Fisheries for Scotland (DAFS) (1965). *Scottish Peat Surveys Volume 2: Western Highlands and Islands*. HMSO, Edinburgh.

Dobson, M. (1980). Marsh fever, the geography of malaria in England. *Journal of Historical Geography*, **6**, 357–389.

Duffey, E. (1970). The management of Woodwalton Fen, a multidisciplinary approach. *The Scientific Management of Plant and Animal Communities for Conservation*, (ed. E. Duffey & A.S. Watt), pp. 581–597. Blackwell Scientific Publications, Oxford.

Du Rietz, G.E. (1949). Huvudenheter och granser i Svensk Myrvegetation. *Svensk botanisk Tidskrift*, **43**, 299–309.

Du Rietz, G.E. (1954). Die Mineralbodenwasserzeigergranze als Grundlage einer natürlichen Zweigliederung der nord- und mitteleuropäischen Moore. *Vegetatio*, **5–6**, 571–585.

George, M. (1992). *The Land Use, Ecology and Conservation of Broadland*. Packard Publishing, Chichester.

Godwin, H. & Clifford, M.H. (1938). Studies of the Post-glacial history of British vegetation. I. Origin and stratigraphy of fenland deposits near Woodwalton, Hunts. *Philosophical Transactions of the Royal Society of London*, **B229**, 323–406.

Goode, D.A. (1972). Criteria for selection of peatland nature reserves in Britain. *Proceedings of the 4th International Peat Congress*, I–IV, Helsinki.

Gore, A.J.P. (ed.) (1983). *Ecosytems of the World, 4B: Mires, Swamp, Bog, Fen and Moor. Regional Studies*. Elsevier, Amsterdam.

Göttlich, Kh. (1990). *Moor- und Torfkunde*. E. Schweizerbart'sche Verlagsbuchhandlung, Stuttgart.

Hallam, S.J. (1970). Settlement around the Wash. *The Fenland in Roman Times* (ed. C.W. Phillips), pp. 22–112. Royal Geographical Research Series, London.

Hammitt, W.E. (1980). Managing bog environments for recreational experience. *Environmental Management*, **4**, 425–431.

Jennings, J.N. (1952). *The Origin of the Broads*. Royal Geographical Society, Research Series No. 2. London.

Kuntze, H. & Eggelsmann, R. (1981). Zur Schutzfähigkeit nordwestdeutscher Moore. *Telma*, **11**, 197–212.

Mitsch, W.J. & Gosselink, J.G. (1986). *Wetlands*. Van Nostrand Reinhold, New York.

Moore, P.D. (1982). How to reproduce in fens and bogs. *New Scientist*, 5 August 1982, 369–371.

Mörnsjö, T. (1969). Studies on vegetation and development of a peatland in Scania, south Sweden. *Opera botanica*, **24**, 1–187.

Proctor, M.C.F. (1992). Regional and local variation in the chemical composition of ombrogenous mire waters in Britain and Ireland. *Journal of Ecology*, **80**, 719–736.

Ratcliffe, D.A. (1964). Mires and bogs. *The Vegetation of Scotland* (ed. J.H. Burnett), pp. 426–478. Oliver & Boyd, Edinburgh.

Ratcliffe, D.A. (ed.) (1977). *A Nature Conservation Review*. Cambridge University Press, Cambridge.

Rodwell, J.S. (ed.) (1991). *British Plant Communities, Volume 2. Mires and Heaths.* Cambridge University Press, Cambridge.

Simpson, J.A. & Weiner, E.S.C. (1989). *The Oxford English Dictionary*. 2nd edn. Clarendon Press, Oxford.

Sjörs, J. (1950). On the relation between vegetation and electrolytes in North Swedish mire waters. *Oikos*, **2**, 241–258.

Stace, C. (1991). *New Flora of the British Isles*. Cambridge University Press, Cambridge.

Succow, M. (1988). *Landschaftsökologische Moorkunde*. Gebrüder Borntraeger, Berlin.

Succow, M. & Lange, E. (1984). The mire types of the German Democratic Republic. *European Mires* (ed. P. D. Moore) pp. 149–175. Academic Press, London.

Tansley, A. G. (1939). *The British Islands and their Vegetation*. Cambridge University Press, Cambridge.

Usher, M.B. (1986). *Wildlife Conservation Evaluation*. Chapman & Hall, London.

von Post, L. & Granlund, E. (1926). *Södra Sveriges tortillangar I*. Sveriges Geologiska Undersöknigar, C335, 127pp.

Wheeler, B.D. (1980). Plant communities of rich-fen systems in England and Wales. I. Introduction. Tall sedge and reed communities. *Journal of Ecology*, **68**, 365–395.

Wheeler, B.D. (1992). Integrating wildlife with commercial uses. *Reedbeds for Wildlife*. (ed. D. Ward), pp. 79–89. Royal Society for the Protection of Birds, Sandy.

Wheeler, B.D. (1993). Botanical diversity in British mires. *Biodiversity and Conservation*, **2**, 490–512.

Williams, M. (1990). Agricultural impacts in temperate wetlands. *Wetlands: a Threatened Landscape*. (ed. M. Williams), pp. 181–216. Blackwell, Oxford.

2 Archaeology and Wetland Restoration

B. J. COLES

Department of History and Archaeology, University of Exeter, Queen's Building, The Queen's Drive, Exeter, EX4 4QH, UK

SUMMARY

1. The quality of the archaeological record from wetlands is often exceptionally high, offering close integration of archaeological and palaeoenvironmental evidence.

2. The sites of Bergschenhoek (the Netherlands), Windover (United States) and the Sweet Track (Britain) illustrate the diversity of evidence available and the range of post-excavation analyses which can be applied. The influence of humans and other animals on wetland development can sometimes be traced in the peat record, as on Bourtanger Moor (the Netherlands) and in the Somerset Levels.

3. Wetland archaeology is likely to benefit from restoration programmes in the long term, but in the short term its vulnerability will need to be considered. Restoration work likely to affect buried archaeological evidence in wetlands includes earth moving operations, encouragement of certain types of vegetation and alterations in water level.

INTRODUCTION

The archaeological dimension of wetland restoration has two closely-related aspects, one of which demands consideration in restoration programmes whilst the other may contribute to the design of management procedures. The first is the high quality of the archaeological and palaeoenvironmental record, which renders even small remnants valuable for their precision and complexity; restoration work should allow for their protection or investigation. The second aspect is the significance of both the archaeological and the palaeoenvironmental record for understanding long-term trends in the evolution of wetlands. With such an understanding, encompassing the diversity of responses to influences ranging from the global to the local, restorers will be in a better position to plan individual site programmes. This paper will examine both aspects, drawing partly on the author's own experience in the Somerset Levels and partly on work elsewhere in Europe and North America, with reference where appropriate to matters raised in other contributions to this volume. All dates quoted are based on dendrochronology or on calibrated radiocarbon results; insect nomenclature is according to Kloet &

Restoration of Temperate Wetlands. Edited by B.D. Wheeler, S.C. Shaw, W.J. Fojt and R.A. Robertson
© 1995, B.J. Coles. Published in 1995 by John Wiley & Sons Ltd.

Hincks (rev. Pope) (1977); flora according to Clapham, Tutin & Warburg (1962).

QUALITY OF THE WETLAND RECORD

The significance of archaeological evidence preserved in waterlogged conditions
has been recognised for well over a century (*e.g.* Keller, 1854–79; Munro, 1890).
Rapid developments in archaeological science in recent decades have, if anything,
led to a greater increase in the information available from wetland sites than from
their dryland equivalents, and the potential now being realised is apparent from a
range of publications (*e.g.* J.M. Coles, 1984; Coles & Lawson, 1987; Purdy, 1988;
Coles & Coles, 1989; Arnold, 1990; Bocquet, 1992; B.J. Coles, 1992a; van de
Noort & Davies, 1993). In all cases, the close links between evidence for environmental conditions and that for human activities add interest to the studies, and may
greatly enhance our understanding of past diversity, as illustrated below.

Louwe Kooijmans's survey (1985, 1987) of the evidence from the Rhine-Meuse
delta includes an account of the site of Bergschenhoek. What was found could be
summed up, disparagingly, as a wadge of peat, some bits of wood, a few old bones
and broken pots. What it represented became clear as post-excavation work
proceeded. Pollen and macroscopic plant remains indicated that the peat had been
a floating mat, vegetated, just off the margins of a reed-fringed freshwater lake. It
was visited by people whose style of pottery suggested they were farmers from the
hinterland. They came for short winter visits, perhaps 11 times as there were 11
superimposed clay-lined hearths on the peat 'island', and in the winter because
many of the bones found were identified as those of wintering wildfowl, including

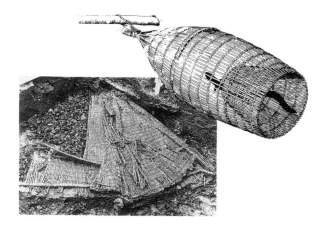

Photograph 1. A fishtrap from Bergschenhoek, *c.* 4100 BC. Woven from 1–2-year-old red
dogwood stems; the delicate structure survived for *c.* 6000 years in protective waterlogged
deposits, and it is now in the care of Leiden Museum. The reconstruction drawing shows its
original appearance and how it may have been used. *Photo: Louwe Kooijmans.*

Bewick's swan, goosander, goldeneye, widgeon and eider. Several fish traps (Photograph 1), made out of long thin stems of red dogwood, illustrate the skill of their makers. The rods used were only 1–2 years old, cut from stumps that were regularly harvested, to judge by the evidence of discarded pieces found. The fish caught with trap, nets or spears, were catfish, eel, perch, various species of carp, roach, bream and tench. Analysis of the environment and the season of the year when people came to exploit it, coupled with their likely dryland farming activities, suggests that the expeditions to Bergschenhoek were made primarily to catch waterfowl. Louwe Kooijmans suggests that the birds provided an important supplement to a lean winter diet, but may also have been valued for their feathers. Radiocarbon dating of samples from the site places the visits at around 4100 BC.

Half a world away, in an environment equally dominated by water, the prehistoric inhabitants of Florida were living off the resources of the swamps, sloughs and warm mineral springs that surrounded them (Coles & Coles, 1989; Purdy, 1992). They used the wetlands also for burial of their dead, and recent excavations at Windover have, through the combination of skeletal, artefactual, economic and environmental evidence, given one of the most complete pictures yet available of the early human settlement of North America (Doran, 1992). The Windover peat formed in a freshwater pool, and 'burial' was made by wrapping the dead in leaves and placing them in the shallow marginal waters, with stakes to anchor the corpse in at least some cases (Figure 1). Preservation conditions proved to be excellent, with fragile artefactual material such as textiles surviving, and recognisable brain tissue within some of the human skulls. Analysis of peat samples taken from the stomach area of some skeletons indicates probable food

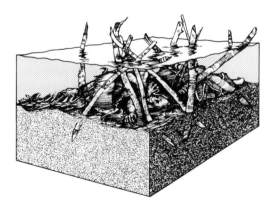

Figure 1. Diagrammatic illustration of recently-deposited human bodies in the Windover burial pool, held down on the bottom by slanting stakes. The pool was in use from about 8000 years ago, and its discovery and excavation in the 1980s has provided one of the richest sources of evidence for early Americans. *Drawn by Mike Rouillard.*

intake shortly before death, with evidence for fish and a variety of seeds and fruits (Newsom, 1988). The textiles were made from plant fibres (probably Sabal palm or saw palmetto), using several different weaves, and represent the oldest surviving textiles from the New World. Radiocarbon dating indicates a long period of use of the Windover burial pool, from about 6000 BC. Study of the human skeletons has shown that a cross-section of the population received water-burial, from young children to men and women in their late sixties or seventies. One young teenager appeared to have suffered from *spina bifida*, which must have been quite a severe handicap in the mobile, hunter–fisher–gatherer society. Yet the child was cared for well beyond the dependency period of a healthy infant.

The third example is taken from the Somerset Levels, just one short episode from the several millennia of interaction between people and wetlands which is examined in a little more detail below. Early in the history of peat formation, when much of the wetland area was dominated by *Phragmites* and the surrounding dryland was covered in primary forest, people came and felled oak and lime, ash, holly and hazel from the forest, alder, willow and poplar from the wetland fringes, and used the wood to make planks, poles and stakes with which they built a raised plank walkway across the reed swamp from a large central island to its southern margin. Their axe blades were made from igneous stone or flint, and using these and wooden wedges and mallets they felled and split trees up to 400 years old and 1 m in diameter. The trackway was used and repaired for about 11 years, after which it was rapidly lost to view in the accumulation of *Phragmites* litter and other peat-forming plant debris. Macroscopic remains of aquatic plants and beetles indicate occasional open pools, and the trackway was substantially reinforced as it crossed one of these. As they passed here, the people who used the track may have watched raft spiders on the hunt, for Girling identified the remains of *Dolomedes fimbriatus* and *Dolomedes plantarius* preserved in the peat adjacent to and contemporary with the reinforced trackway (Girling, 1984; Coles & Coles, 1986).

Dendrochronology has recently dated the trackway to 3807/6 BC (Hillam *et al.*, 1990), *i.e.* the oak trees used were felled in that winter, and the relative lack of fungal and weevil attack on the wood, coupled with evidence for plank making and track construction before the wood had seasoned, all combine to suggest that the track was made in the year of felling. Figure 2 illustrates the direct linkage of archaeological and environmental evidence which lies behind the deciphering of what is now known as the 'Sweet Track'. The essential specialist studies are published in *Somerset Levels Papers* 1–15 (1975–1989).

INTERACTION AND DEVELOPMENT IN THE LONG TERM

The direct linkage of archaeological and environmental evidence permits the analysis of long-term trends in wetland development in the light of possible human influences. These influences may have been slight by comparison with those of today, but nevertheless significant triggers or barriers to particular courses of wetland development. In this respect the activities of humans may be regarded as

THE SWEET TRACK

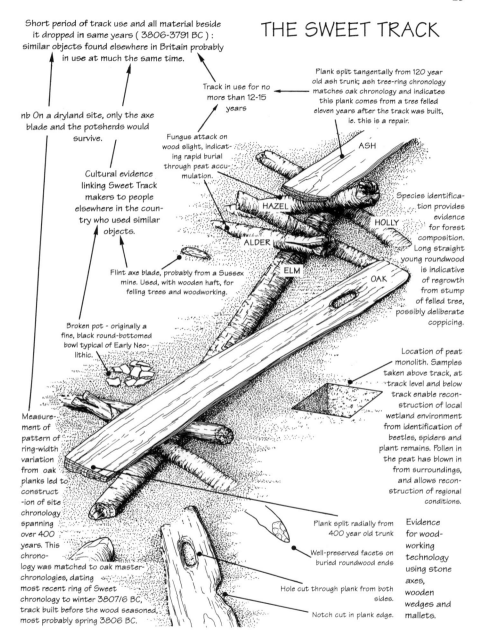

Short period of track use and all material beside it dropped in same years (3806-3791 BC) : similar objects found elsewhere in Britain probably in use at much the same time.

Track in use for no more than 12-15 years

nb On a dryland site, only the axe blade and the potsherds would survive.

Plank split tangentally from 120 year old ash trunk; ash tree-ring chronology matches oak chronology and indicates this plank comes from a tree felled eleven years after the track was built, ie. this is a repair.

Fungus attack on wood slight, indicating rapid burial through peat accumulation.

Cultural evidence linking Sweet Track makers to people elsewhere in the country who used similar objects.

ASH

HAZEL

HOLLY

ALDER

Flint axe blade, probably from a Sussex mine. Used, with wooden haft, for felling trees and woodworking.

ELM

OAK

Species identification provides evidence for forest composition. Long straight young roundwood is indicative of regrowth from stump of felled tree, possibly deliberate coppicing.

Broken pot - originally a fine, black round-bottomed bowl typical of Early Neolithic.

Location of peat monolith. Samples taken above track, at track level and below track enable reconstruction of local wetland environment from identification of beetles, spiders and plant remains. Pollen in the peat has blown in from surroundings, and allows reconstruction of regional conditions.

Measurement of pattern of ring-width variation from oak planks led to construction of site chronology spanning over 400 years. This chronology was matched to oak master-chronologies, dating most recent ring of Sweet chronology to winter 3807/6 BC, track built before the wood seasoned, most probably spring 3806 BC.

Plank split radially from 400 year old trunk

Well-preserved facets on buried roundwood ends

Hole cut through plank from both sides.

Notch cut in plank edge.

Evidence for woodworking technology using stone axes, wooden wedges and mallets.

Figure 2. Diagrammatic representation of the Sweet Track, Somerset Levels, and some of the associated evidence, to illustrate the direct conjunction of palaeoenvironmental and archaeological evidence which enhances the interpretation of both. *Drawn by Sue Rouillard.*

similar to those of certain other mammals. Studies of these influences are not yet widespread, but the work of Casparie on Bourtanger Moor in the eastern Nether- lands demonstrates the potential and may offer, from a perspective of several millennia, some suggestions for current restoration projects (Casparie, 1993).

The earliest *Sphagnum* peat of Bourtanger Moor dates to *c.* 4500 BC, and the raised bog continued to grow until about AD 1700. From *c.* 3500 BC the dry land around the bog was cleared and settled by farmers, and wind-blown soil particles from their fields along with smoke and ash from fires was deposited on the bog surface, with sand as well when agriculture intensified from *c.* 2900 BC. From *c.* 1350 BC, people dug deep into the bog for iron-ore, in the first millennium BC they attempted cultivation of the bog surface on a small scale, and *c.* 200 BC they were growing willow (*i.e.* withy beds) around the bog margin. Casparie suggests various results of this activity, including the stimulation of *Sphagnum* growth where people had built trackways, due to the weight of the track timbers and the growth of *Scheuchzeria* in the hollows of the bog surface due to localised eutrophication from the wind-borne soil and ash. But the bulk of excess nutrients, he argues were washed off the bog with the surface water discharge.

Several of the studies published in the present volume indicate that, in fens, regular mowing is necessary in order to maintain species diversity. This applies both to reed growth and to the drier fen meadows; traditionally-managed reed swamps and fen meadows are an artefact of human exploitation of wetlands. As such, their history may go back several thousand years, with evidence for the production of hay from later Neolithic and Bronze Age settlements around the margins of circum-alpine lakes, both the shallow lakes that eventually became raised bogs and the deep lakes that still exist as open water today (Higham, 1967; Greig, 1984). Reeds were cut for house-roof thatching, but probably only for the ridges, as reed-swamp development was limited at this time (Arnold, 1990). Elsewhere, brine-soaked reeds may have been dried and burnt for salt production, as was brine-soaked peat perhaps. Evidence from the East Anglian Fens suggests that salt production was well established by the later Iron Age and became an important industry in the Romano-British period (Hall & Coles, in press).

Peat was cut probably in the East Anglian Fens from the later Neolithic on- wards, and by the later first millennium BC there is evidence for its use as a fuel in the Somerset Levels also. The resulting 'peasant peat pits' (Joosten, this volume) may have provided significant refugia for bog and fen plants and invertebrates that required wetter rather than drier conditions, particularly when one considers that prehistoric peat-cutting probably only took place where conditions were relatively dry, given the lack of pumps at the time. One later prehistoric use of old peat cuts was for the deposition of bodies, normally humans but occasionally dogs and cattle (Stead, Bourke & Brothwell, 1986; Coles & Coles, 1989). The treatment of the humans suggests that most had been deliberately killed, and putting them in water-filled holes in the bog probably had considerable ritual significance.

Restoration cannot replicate the complete set of conditions which governed the development of a wetland in the past, but it may be advantageous to mimic certain key aspects once these have been identified. Taking the example of the Somerset Levels, it can be argued that minor influences such as that of mammals led to diversity within the broad trend of development governed by climate and sea-level change. In broad outline, the sequence of peat development in the Somerset Levels is similar to that observed elsewhere in lowland Britain near the coast: retreating sea, *Phragmites* domination, appearance of carr woodland, followed by the establishment and eventual dominance of raised bog species. The sequence applies to the Brue Valley rather than Sedgemoor, where little evidence for raised bog has been found as yet (Alderton, 1983). But Godwin's first studies in the Brue Valley (Godwin, 1955, 1981) indicated that raised bog was neither ubiquitous nor continuous, and subsequent work by Beckett (1978a,b), Caseldine (1986, 1988a,b), Girling (1976, 1977, 1978) and Housley (1986, 1988) has helped to define more precisely the areas that remained fen-like in character and the times when raised bog formation was checked by eutrophic floodwaters. Figure 3 indicates the distribution of the relevant evidence.

Various mammals which lived in the Somerset Levels may have influenced plant communities, and perhaps sometimes strongly enough to push development in one direction rather than another. Elk and aurochs were present in the early postglacial throughout Britain. Godwin identified elk droppings near Shapwick Station in Iron Age peats; similar droppings from Ugg Mere, Huntingdonshire, were dated to *c.* 1500 BC (Godwin, 1978). In both cases, the evidence was deposited long after most palaeozooologists reckon elk were extinct in southern Britain and it might be useful to re-examine the fossil record in view of the possible survival of the species into later prehistory. Both elk and aurochs would graze fen vegetation and browse the trees, and elk also dive after aquatic plants. Their activity might encourage species diversity, and in the Levels, areas used regularly by elk would perhaps have remained as poor-fen communities rather than developing to raised bog.

A smaller mammal, but one which possibly had a greater effect, is the beaver. Its presence in the Levels is known from beaver-chewn wood from *c.* 3000 BC and from beaver bones found at the late first millennium BC settlements (the Glastonbury and Meare Lake Villages). The impact of beaver on the prehistoric landscape in general has been discussed elsewhere (Coles & Orme, 1982, 1983; Coles, 1992b). In the Levels, their presence was probably greatest where they dammed flowing water. As the Brue carried water off limestone, dams causing it to flood would spread base-enriched waters over a wider area than they might otherwise have reached except at times of heavy rainfall. Further west, on the north edge of the Westhay island in the centre of the wetland, an episode of increased wetness in the late Neolithic, evident from beetle and plant macrofossil identifications (Girling, 1980; Caseldine, 1980), may be linked to locally-active beaver as this is where their discarded wood was found (Photograph 2). Thus beaver, like elk, may have promoted a greater diversity of wetland habitats.

Humans, the other mammal which possibly influenced the course of wetland development in the Levels, may have done so in various ways. We know they

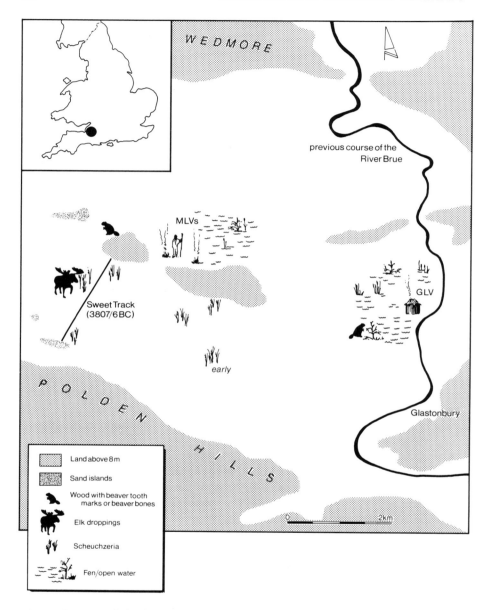

Figure 3. Map of the Somerset Levels to show location of sites and other evidence mentioned in the text, spanning the period *c.* 4000 BC to *c.* AD 50. Much of the evidence belongs only to specific short periods within that time, but in the area of the Glastonbury Lake Village (GLV) fen conditions persisted whilst raised bog developed to the south and west. The ancient course of the River Brue indicated is based on field and map evidence; it is probably close to the course taken by the river in the later prehistoric period; the present course (not shown) is an artificial one. MLV=Meare Lake Village. *Drawn by Sue Rouillard.*

Photograph 2. Wood with beaver tooth-marks, from the Baker Platform, Somerset Levels, *c.* 3000 BC. Most of the beaver-chewed wood from this site was identified as willow. *Photo: Somerset Levels Project.*

were present from the beginning of peat-formation, although perhaps not as continuously as the radiocarbon dates might at first suggest (Coles & Coles, 1992). Pollen evidence indicates widespread permanent clearance and cultivation of the dry lands from the mid-first millennium BC (Housley, 1988), and perhaps this is when we should first look for any significant human impact on the wetlands.

Godwin, Beckett and Caseldine provided evidence for the presence of *Scheuchzeria* in the upper peats of the Levels (Godwin, 1981, p.11 and plate 43; Beckett, 1978b, p.105; Coles *et al*, 1988, Fig.37). These occurrences are not directly dated, but they may confidently be assigned to the first millennium BC or later on the basis of associated evidence. Caseldine also recorded two earlier bands of *Scheuchzeria*, dating probably to the third millennium BC (Orme *et al.*, 1985, p.64–65). If Casparie's view of *Scheuchzeria*, noted above, is followed rather than Godwin's "certain indicator of extensive flooding by base-deficient water" (Godwin, 1981, p.111), then its presence could be explained by slight eutrophication following the deposition of air-borne particles from surrounding arable fields. The dating fits for all but Caseldine's early record, in so far as *Scheuchzeria* appears after the onset of widespread permanent clearance on dryland. However, there is the early record, and it should also be noted that Beckett recorded *Cladium* immediately below *Scheuchzeria* and regarded the latter as an indicator of increasing acidity following localised flooding represented by *Cladium* (Beckett, 1978b, p.105–106). It would thus be unwise to attribute the presence of *Scheuchzeria* to indirect human influence without further research.

When people settled at Glastonbury, *c.* 300 BC, they imported huge quantities of clay and wood to a "clump of cleared alder and willow fen carr surrounded by an area of shallow openwater lake with attendant stands of reedswamp, sedge fen and fen carr" (Housley, 1988, p.81). Once settled, they and their domestic animals contributed quantities of sewage to the local environment, and other nutrients in the form of food refuse including bones. The episode must have confirmed the eutrophic fen character of the locality in contrast to the contemporary raised bogs of the vicinity. For Meare, where two settlements were made at much the same time as Glastonbury, Caseldine (1986, p.96) summarises the wetland setting as follows: "In the two village areas immediately before occupation it appears that water conditions became shallower and the hydroseral succession progressed as far as a limited development of raised bog, but in the area between the two sites open water and reed swamp continued to persist". The considerable input of nutrients derived from the settlement may have put an end to raised bog development here, although generalised flooding of the area shortly afterwards would have done so whether or not the localised eutrophication had occurred.

RESTORATION AND ARCHAEOLOGY

Restoration of temperate wetlands is likely to give long-term protection to any buried archaeological evidence that still survives. But, if restoration is thorough and successful, it will no longer be possible to make new archaeological discoveries, and it will be difficult to monitor the condition of known buried material. It is a recognised paradox of wetland archaeology that the majority of discoveries are made because of operations that damage or destroy the wetland, whereas little is known of the archaeological resource preserved in intact wetlands. Palaeoenvironmental evidence may be recovered through coring, but not archaeology. It will be necessary therefore to take on trust the presence of archaeo-logical evidence, where opportunities for discovery have been limited, and for the restoration of wetlands and their subsequent management to be designed to care for presumed waterlogged wood below the surface as well as the flora and fauna on top. This should not be too difficult, given a common requirement for saturation with water of suitable quality. Along the way, however, the process of restoration may have some impact on the archaeological record.

Wetland restorers may engage in a variety of landscaping activities, ranging from sod-removal in order to reverse the acidification of fens to the simulation of hand-cut peat pits in order to promote *Sphagnum* growth. Frequently, dams and banks for retaining water are made by scraping up adjacent material, which at the same time creates an area of shallow water favourable to dragonflies or waders. Those who follow the levelling school of thought will remove any upstanding baulks and may rotavate the surface to encourage revegetation. Activities such as these may expose archaeological material, in much the same way as peat cutting or digging or clearing ditches would do, and the work should be monitored by an archaeologist just as it should be for the latter operations. If anything is discovered, it will need to be recorded, and possibly excavated. The extent of work required will depend on the nature of the find, with *in situ* structures demanding greater attention than stray objects. But it should be possible for the fieldwork to be carried out speedily, just as it would be in the context of commercial peat extraction or drainage. For exceptional finds, the restoration design could perhaps be adapted to ensure preservation *in situ* of some of the evidence, again following commercial practice where development or extraction plans have been modified to allow the continued survival *in situ* of archaeological material.

Restorers probably need to take most account of archaeology during their landscaping operations, but the impact of other operations should be briefly considered as well. Restoration of reedbeds and other fen plant communities including carr woodland may cause the roots and rhizomes of vigorous modern plants such as *Phragmites* or birch, willow and alder to penetrate archaeological levels which are now much decayed, whereas in the past the rooting took place into what were then recently deposited and little-decayed archaeological levels. It would therefore be preferable, from an archaeological point of view, if a water regime could be established which ensured that roots and rhizomes had no incentive to penetrate deeply, and further research on the rooting patterns of wetland plants would be welcome. Restoration of raised bog, which so often entails control of trees and scrub, is more likely to protect than to damage any buried archaeology in so far as removal of birch and other vegetation is concerned.

Some wetland restoration regimes call for seasonal fluctuation in water tables. This is most common where wet grassland is being restored and managed for the benefit of birds. Fluctuations within the top 15–20 cm of a restored wetland will probably have little effect on any surviving archaeological remains, for if the area was previously damaged it is unlikely that anything archaeological survives in this uppermost zone, other than inorganic remains such as flints. Greater fluctuations will cause problems, since alternation between wet and dry is probably the worst regime of all for waterlogged wood and similar materials. Archaeologists would therefore recommend that any lowering of water tables be kept to a minimum (*i.e.* within 15–20 cm of surface) and for as short a time as possible so that any buried material has a chance of remaining wet during the low phase.

Archaeological finds from wetlands may be inorganic as well as organic, witness the clay, stone, bronze and iron artefacts from the Glastonbury Lake Village. If a wetland is drained, inorganic materials are likely to survive as long as there is no ground disturbance, and in better condition than any wood. But if the ground is then rewetted, certain inorganic materials may deteriorate further, for example, iron is likely to be vulnerable (M. Corfield, personal communication) whereas flint is probably not. If a known wetland site, damaged by drainage but not destroyed by peat cutting, was likely to be rewetted during restoration, there might be an argument for selective excavation prior to rewetting, particularly if the site was dated to the second millennium BC or more recent times when metal was in use. An example of such a site would be Llyn Cerig Bach on Anglesey, where weapons, ornaments, cauldrons and diverse other metal objects had been deposited into a peat bog over the centuries, probably as votive offerings of some sort (Fox, 1946). Because the main interest of the site lay in the metal objects, had it dried out with some of the archaeological deposits otherwise undisturbed in the peat, there would be a strong archaeological case for maintaining dry conditions, or for excavation if the environmental case for rewetting was otherwise overwhelming.

At present, little is known of the precise effects of rewetting on organic archaeological and palaeoeconomic evidence which has recently dried out and it is an area requiring further investigation. Field observation suggests that rewetting is likely to halt biological decay by excluding the moles, worms and beetles that tend to invade buried wood and archaeological layers once they cease to be waterlogged. But deterioration can never be reversed, it can only be checked.

CONCLUSION

There are various other aspects of wetland restoration which require further research before their impact on archaeology can be assessed, and often their significance in terms of restoration itself has still to be investigated. A survey of wetland management practices will consider these questions further (B.J. Coles, in press). However, there is one fundamental question where archaeology can perhaps contribute to the debate – how far the restorer should interfere to create particular wetland conditions, rather than letting things follow their own course. As discussed above, the archaeological and palaeoenvironmental evidence from wetlands indicates that humans have a very long history of interference in these environments. In part, wetlands of the past, and especially the recent past, developed as they did because of human activity. In part, those of the remote past in particular developed in response to the activity of other animals and the nature of hydrological regimes, which humans have since altered. Seen in this light, human interference is but a normal part of the ecosystem and wetland restorers may wish to mimic some of the former influential activities. Seen in another light, restoration is in effect the domestication of wetlands and as such it deserves investigation for the light it could throw on initial processes of domestication in prehistory. For the present, let us rest with the shared long-term aims of archaeologists and restorers to preserve at least some small part of our wetland heritage.

ACKNOWLEDGEMENTS

My thanks to Wil Casparie for his comments and advice on the first draft of this paper. Much of the research for this paper was carried out as part of a survey of wetland management techniques funded by English Heritage.

REFERENCES

Alderton, A.M. (1983). The Sedgemoor Survey 1982: environmental results. *Somerset Levels Papers,* **9**, 9–15.

Arnold, B. (1990). *Cortaillod-Est et les villages du lac de Neuchâtel au Bronze final. Structure de l'habitat et protourbanisme.* Saint-Blaise, Editions du Ruau, Archéologie Neuchâteloise, 6.

Beckett, S.C. (1978a). The environmental setting of the Meare Heath Track. *Somerset Levels Papers,* 4, 42–46.

Beckett, S.C. (1978b). Palaeobotanical investigations at the Difford's 1 site. *Somerset Levels Papers,* 4, 101–106.

Bocquet, A. (ed.) (1992). *Archéologie et environnement des milieux aquatiques.* Editions du Comité des Travaux historiques et scientifiques, Paris.

Caseldine, A.E. (1980). Palaeoenvironmental reconstruction at the Baker Site. *Somerset Levels Papers,* 6, 29–36.

Caseldine, A.E. (1986). The environmental context of the Meare Lake Villages. *Somerset Levels Papers,* 12, 72–96.

Caseldine, A.E. (1988a). A reinterpretation of the pollen sequence from Meare. *Somerset Levels Papers,* 14, 53–56.

Caseldine, A.E. (1988b). A wetland resource: the evidence for environmental exploitation in the Somerset Levels during the prehistoric period. *The Exploitation of Wetlands* (eds P. Murphy & C. French), pp. 239–266. British Archaeological Reports British Series 186, Oxford.

Casparie, W. (1993). The Bourtanger Moor: endurance and vulnerability of a raised bog system. *Hydrobiologia,* 265, 203–215.

Clapham, A.R., Tutin, T.G. & Warburg, E.F. (1962). *Flora of the British Isles.* 2nd edn. Cambridge University Press, Cambridge.

Coles, B. (ed.) (1992a). *The Wetland Revolution in Prehistory.* The Prehistoric Society and WARP, Exeter.

Coles, B.J. (1992b). Further thoughts on the impact of beaver on temperate landscapes. *Alluvial Archaeology in Britain* (eds. S Needham & M.G. Macklin), pp. 93–99. Oxbow Monograph 27, Oxbow, Oxford.

Coles, B.J. (1994) (in press). *Wetland Management: a survey for English Heritage.* WARP Occasional Paper, No. 9.

Coles, B. & Coles, J. (1986). *Sweet Track to Glastonbury.* Thames & Hudson, London.

Coles, B. & Coles, J. (1989). *People of the Wetlands.* Thames & Hudson, London.

Coles, J.M. (1984). *The Archaeology of Wetlands.* Edinburgh University Press, Edinburgh.

Coles, J.M. & Coles, B.J. (1992). Passages of time. *Archäologische Mitteilungen aus Nordwestdeutschland,* 15, 29–44.

Coles, J.M., Coles, B.J., Morgan, R.A. & Caseldine, A.E. (1988). The Meare Heath Track 1985. *Somerset Levels Papers,* 14, 6–33.

Coles, J.M. & Lawson, A.J. (1987). *European Wetlands in Prehistory.* Clarendon Press, Oxford.

Coles, J.M. & Orme, B.J. (1982). Beaver in the Somerset Levels: some new evidence. *Somerset Levels Papers,* 8, 67–73.

Coles, J.M. & Orme, B.J. (1983). *Homo sapiens* or *Castor fiber? Antiquity,* 57, 95–102.

Doran, G. (1992). Problems and potential of wet sites in North America: the example of Windover. *The Wetland Revolution in Prehistory* (ed. B. Coles), pp.125–134. The Prehistoric Society and WARP, Exeter.

Fox, C.F. (1946). *A Find of the Early Iron Age from Llyn Cerig Bach, Anglesey.* National Museum of Wales, Cardiff.

Girling, M.A. (1976). Changes in the Meare Heath Coleoptera fauna in response to flooding. *Somerset Levels Papers,* 2, 28–33.

Girling, M.A. (1977). Fossil insect assemblages from Rowland's Track. *Somerset Levels Papers*, **3**, 51–60.

Girling, M.A. (1978). Fossil insect assemblages from Difford's I site. *Somerset Levels Papers*, **4**, 107–113.

Girling, M.A. (1980). The fossil insect assemblage from the Baker Site. *Somerset Levels Papers*, **6**, 36–42.

Girling, M.A. (1984). Investigations of a second insect assemblage from the Sweet Track. *Somerset Levels Papers*, **10**, 79–91.

Godwin, H. (1955). Studies of the post-glacial history of British vegetation. XIII. The Meare Pool region of the Somerset Levels. *Philosophical Transactions of the Royal Society*, B, **239**, 161–190.

Godwin, H. (1978). *Fenland: Its Ancient Past and Uncertain Future*. Cambridge University Press, Cambridge.

Godwin, H. (1981). *The Archives of the Peat Bogs*. Cambridge University Press, Cambridge.

Greig, J. (1984). A preliminary report on the pollen diagrams and some macrofossil results from Palafitta Fiavé. *Scavi Archeologici nella zona Palafitticola di Fiavé-Carera* (ed. R. Perini) pp.305–322. Servizio Beni Culturali della Provincia Autonoma di Trento, Trento.

Hall, D. & Coles, J. (in press). *Fenland Survey: an Essay in Landscape and Persistence*. English Heritage Monograph Series.

Higham, C.F.W. (1967). Stock rearing as a cultural factor in prehistoric Europe. *Proceedings of the Prehistoric Society*, **33**, 84–106.

Hillam, J., Groves, C.M., Brown, D.M., Baillie, M.G.L., Coles, J.M. & Coles, B.J. (1990). Dendrochronology of the English Neolithic. *Antiquity*, **64**, 210–220.

Housley, R.A. (1986). *The Environment of Glastonbury Lake Village*. PhD thesis, University of Cambridge.

Housley, R.A. (1988). The environmental context of Glastonbury Lake Village. *Somerset Levels Papers*, **14**, 63–82.

Keller, F. (1854–1879). *Die Keltischen Pfahlbauten in den Schweizerseen*. Mitteilungen der Antiquarischen Gesellschaft im Zürich, Zürich.

Kloet, G.S. & Hincks, W.D. (Revised Pope, R.D.) (1977). *A Checklist of British Insects, Coleoptera and Strepsiptera*. Royal Entomological Society, London.

Louwe Kooijmans, L.P. (1985). *Sporen in het land. De Nederlandse delta in de prehistorie*. Meulenhoff Informatief, Amsterdam.

Louwe Kooijmans, L.P. (1987). Neolithic Settlement and Subsistence in the Wetlands of the Rhine/Meuse Delta of the Netherlands. *European Wetlands in Prehistory* (eds J.M. Coles & A.J. Lawson), pp. 227–251. Clarendon Press, Oxford.

Munro, R. (1890). *The Lake Dwellings of Europe*. Cassell & Co. Ltd, London.

Newsom, L. (1988). Palaeoethnobotanical remains from the Windover site, Florida: human abdominal samples. *NewsWARP*, **4**, 5–7.

Orme, B.J., Coles, J.M., Caseldine, A.E. & Morgan, R.A. (1985). Third Millennium structures on Walton Heath. *Somerset Levels Papers*, **11**, 62–68.

Purdy, B. (1992). Florida's archaeological wet sites. *The Wetland Revolution in Prehistory* (ed. B. Coles), pp. 113–123. The Prehistoric Society and WARP, Exeter.

Purdy, B.A.(ed.) (1988). *Wet Site Archaeology*. Telford Press, New Jersey.

Stead, I.M., Bourke, J.B. & Brothwell, D. (1986). *Lindow Man: The Body in the Bog*. British Museum Publications Ltd., London.

van de Noort, R. & Davies, P. (1993). *Wetland Heritage. An Archaeological Assessment of the Humber Wetlands*. Humber Wetlands Project, University of Hull.

3 The Nature Conservation Importance of Fens and Bogs and the Role of Restoration

W. J. FOJT

English Nature, Northminster House, Peterborough, PE1 1UA, UK

SUMMARY

1. There has been much loss of fen and bog habitat in Britain dating from historical times, but this loss still continues both in terms of loss of extent and decline in 'quality' of the habitats.
2. These losses not only have implications for the conservation of the habitats themselves, but also for the conservation of wider biodiversity. Because of this restoration is now assuming an important role in the conservation of fens and bogs, although restoration projects are at very early stages.
3. The role of restoration is seen by conservation organisations as a means by which the current nature conservation interest of a fen or bog can be maintained or 'improved', and providing an opportunity to expand into areas from which the habitat has been lost.
4. The differences between management and restoration are difficult to define and there may be considerable overlap. Management will also play an important role in maintaining the 'restored' system. However, such management should not be so intensive that the restored habitat cannot be regarded as semi-natural as possible.

INTRODUCTION

When considering the role of restoration in the conservation of fens and bogs, it is often difficult to emerge from the constraints of our perception of these systems based upon their current condition and extent. In most cases we restrict our horizons to the maintenance of the existing nature conservation interest of these mires. Of course this is acceptable, and somewhat inevitable; the existing interest is the reason why these areas are valued. This may lead fortuitously to an improvement of what exists and even an opportunity to regain what has been lost. This may be illustrated by the restoration management of cut-over peatlands such as at Cors Caron (Dyfed, Wales) (formerly known as Tregaron Bog) where in order to reduce seepage loss the surrounding peat cuttings have been bunded and flooded. At the Meerstalblok (the Netherlands) the bunded cuttings in turn have

Restoration of Temperate Wetlands. Edited by B.D. Wheeler, S.C. Shaw, W.J. Fojt and R.A. Robertson
© 1995 John Wiley & Sons Ltd.

developed rafts of Sphagna. The expansion of fens and bogs into those areas from which the habitat has been completely lost is generally not feasible from the economic point of view, though this may well change.

In this paper I wish to highlight the conservation value of fens and bogs in Britain, emphasising the reasons for their value and to consider the role of restoration.

ASSESSMENT OF CONSERVATION VALUE

The assessment of the conservation value of semi-natural habitats in Britain takes into account such criteria as size, diversity, rarity, naturalness and typicalness (Ratcliffe, 1977). Of these the criteria of size, diversity and rarity are the most amenable to objective assessment. These three criteria may be applied at different scales to a fen or bog; one can consider the size of the site as a whole and the extent, diversity and rarity of the habitat types, communities and species within it.

The criterion of rarity is also recognised within European Union legislation. The (European) Council Directive on the conservation of natural habitats and of wild fauna and flora (1992) recognises the necessity of conserving certain natural habitats and species as a matter of priority; those relating to bogs and fens are listed in Table 1. The concept of restoration is in the forefront of this Directive where it is used partly to define the term 'conservation' "...a series of measures required to maintain or restore the natural habitats and populations of species of wild fauna and flora...".

Rarity as well as 'representivity' (which may be taken as equivalent to 'typicalness') are criteria used to assess fens and bogs for the status of internationally important wetlands under the Convention of Wetlands of International Importance especially as Waterfowl Habitat (Ramsar Convention).

Both of the above international designations also refer to the functioning of

Table 1. Fen and bog habitats (with CORINE code) found in Britain listed within Council Directive 92/43/EEC on the conservation of natural habitats and of wild fauna and flora.

Fens	
37.31	*Molinia* meadows on chalk and clay (*Eu-Molinion*)
54.5	Transition mires and quaking bogs
54.6	Depressions on peat substrates (*Rhynchosporion*) (also found in bogs)
53.3	* Calcareous fens with *Cladium mariscus* and *Carex davalliana*
54.12	* Petrifying springs with tufa formation (*Cratoneurion*)
54.2	Alkaline fens
Bogs	
51.1	* Active raised bogs
51.2	Degraded raised bogs (still capable of natural regeneration)
52.1 & 52.2	Blanket bog (* active only)

* Priority habitat types which are in danger of disappearance and for which the European Union has particular responsibility.

wetland ecosystems, referring to the system itself, or, in the case of the Ramsar Convention, to the role of the habitat within the river basin. Although the evaluation of the conservation value of fens and bogs in Britain does not make direct reference to functioning of systems (except that size may indirectly relate to this), it is given strong emphasis when considering the restoration of systems. Restoration must result in the development of self-sustaining semi-natural habitats (under a given management regime).

The distribution and size of British fens and bogs

Fens are widespread in Britain, though they are nowadays less frequent in well-drained lowland areas where there is intensive land-use than they once were. In general, they are small (Wheeler & Shaw, this volume) isolated systems, either by virtue of their intrinsic character (*e.g.* many spring-fed fens), or because of partial reclamation. However, some remaining flood-plain mires provide notable exceptions: the poor fens of the Insh Marshes, Scotland, cover approximately 1177 ha and the rich fens of Broadland, England, cover more than 3000 ha. Reed-beds, often a component of topogenous systems, occur throughout Britain and may be extensive in any one site, though they are less frequent and limited in extent in Scotland (except for the Tay Marshes). However, Bibby & Lunn (1982) have shown that the total area of reedbeds of 2 ha or more in England and Wales (including non-continuous patches within the same physical feature) is 2300 ha.

Rich fens are mainly associated with areas of base-rich substrata; for example, the chalk, chalky-boulder clay of southern and eastern England and the limestones of North Wales and northern England. Eastern England (East Anglia) and Anglesey have a concentration of small, spring-fed fens which are characterised by the *Schoeno-Juncetum subnodulosi* Association, a CARICION DAVALLIANAE community which is nationally rare in Britain. Towards the north and west poor fens become more frequent. Basin fens are also more frequently found and these are again small, often less than 10 ha.

The area of many lowland raised bogs retaining conservation value is now small in extent, being limited to upstanding remnants which have not been reclaimed, afforested or commercially cut for peat and old abandoned and reflooded turf cuttings which have redeveloped acid mire communities. However, surrounding many of these sites are large areas of drained peat which may have limited intrinsic conservation value but may play an important role in the hydrological functioning of remnant areas, as at Engbertsdijksvenen (the Netherlands) (Schouwenaars, this volume). Thorne Moors is Britain's largest raised bog, and the area of the Site of Special Scientific Interest covers some 1900 ha (Heathwaite, this volume). Raised bogs have a scattered distribution throughout Britain, but show a distinct clustering towards the north and west in Britain in areas such as Cumbria (England), central Wales and the Forth Valley (Scotland). In these areas they have developed within flood plains, such as Cors Caron in the Teifi valley; at the head of estuaries such as the Duddon Mosses at the head of the Duddon estuary in Cumbria; and within basins. They may also be found forming domes within blanket bog systems.

Blanket mires clothe the landscape and can therefore cover vast areas. This is well illustrated by the blanket mire of Caithness and Sutherland, known as the 'Flow Country', which covers an area of 401,375 ha (Lindsay *et al.*, 1988). Other substantial areas of blanket mire are found within the uplands of England and Wales. Such areas are not always exclusively ombrogenous.

The current extent of many fens and lowland raised bogs does not conform to their original area. Truncation has not only removed the natural transition zones with other semi-natural habitats, but has also often removed part of the site itself.

Diversity

Fens are very diverse in terms of type, situation and character (Chapter 1). There are numerous swamp and fen vegetation types in Britain: 28 swamp and tall-herb fen communities, 32 mire communities, two wet heath communities and six fen woodland communities have been identified by Rodwell (1991a, 1991b, in press). Wheeler & Shaw (this volume) indicate the species diversity of British fens. A number of their component species are not confined to fens (Wheeler, 1988) and fens are an important reservoir for these 'additional' species as other habitats are lost.

A number of different lowland raised bog types are recognised in Britain based upon their position within the landscape, for example whether located within a flood plain or basin (Nature Conservancy Council, 1989). However, unlike fens, as far as is known it seems that this has little significance upon their hydro-ecology. The raised bog itself may show ecological variation reflecting environmental differences associated with the cupola, rand and lagg, but it is now rare to find examples of raised bogs which still show this differentiation clearly. Cors Caron and Cors Fochno (formerly known as Borth Bog), Wales, are exceptions.

Four communities are largely restricted to ombrogenous mires and four other communities also occupy other habitats (Table 2). However, the microvariation of the distribution of plant and bryophyte species in both raised and blanket bogs

Table 2. Major bog plant communities identified by the National Vegetation Classification (Rodwell, 1991b), related to their alliances.

Communities largely confined to ombrotrophic bogs

M17	*Scirpus cespitosus–Eriophorum vaginatum* blanket mire. [ERICO-SPHAGNION]
M18	*Erica tetralix–Sphagnum papillosum* raised and blanket mire. [ERICO-SPHAGNION]
M19	*Calluna vulgaris–Eriophorum vaginatum* blanket mire. [ERICO-SPHAGNION]
M20	*Eriophorum vaginatum* blanket and raised bog. [ERICO-SPHAGNION]

Communities also found in other habitats as well as ombrotrophic bogs

M1	*Sphagnum auriculatum* bog pool community. [RHYNCHOSPORION ALBAE]
M2	*Sphagnum cuspidatum/recurvum* bog pool community. [RHYNCHOSPORION ALBAE]
M3	*Eriophorum angustifolium* bog pool community. [RHYNCHOSPORION ALBAE]
M15	*Scirpus cespitosus–Erica tetralix* wet heath. [ERICION TETRALICIS]

(Lindsay *et al.*, 1985) related to the microform of the bog surface above water table level is believed to be unique to bogs. The diversity of blanket mire vegetation communities and species is similar to that of raised bogs.

Bogs support fewer plant species than fens. Wheeler (1993) reported a total of 193 species found within the bog habitat as opposed to 653 for fens. This may reflect the rather uniform and 'exacting' habitat of bogs.

Rarity

Rarity is expressed in terms of mire type, vegetation type and species.

There are no available data on the extent of fen topographical types in Britain, or of most fen community-types. However, data have been collated on the distribution of the infrequent *Schoeno-Juncetum subnodulosi* community. They highlight the national importance of this community-type and its restricted distribution (Figure 1); 50 % of the total known resource in England (or 33 % of the known British resource) is found within the counties of Norfolk and Suffolk, where it is confined to calcareous valleyhead fens. The high conservation value of this community is due

Figure 1.   Distribution of the *Schoeno-Juncetum subnodulosi* community in Britain. (Sources: Wheeler, 1980; Wheeler & Shaw, 1987).

partly to its species richness and the frequent occurrence of rare fen species within it (Wheeler, 1988). It is also important because of its restricted geographical distribution. Individual stands are often less than 0.5 ha within each site.

A large number of nationally rare and scarce vascular plant and bryophyte species are associated with fen and carr (Appendix 1a, b). One of these, *Saxifraga hirculus*[1], is afforded protection within the European Union (Habitats and Species Directive). Fewer rare species are found in bog communities than in fens (Appendix 1c).

The extent of conservationally-valuable raised bog is now very limited. It has been estimated that from a total extent of some 67,000 ha of raised bog in Britain, there is now less than 4000 ha of 'natural, undamaged, primary raised bog' (Plantlife, 1992).

Because raised bogs and blanket bogs share some of their main plant communities, the overall area of certain ombrotrophic communities may be quite large. However, that of the *Erico-Sphagnetum papillosi*, the community-type most typically associated with raised bogs, is believed to be limited. In many bogs it has been lost from damaged surfaces and is now often confined to abandoned, flooded peat cuttings.

THE LOSSES OF FENS AND BOGS

The nature conservation value of fens and bogs relates to the attributes considered above; to the extent of loss of these habitats; and the threats posed to their future survival. However, whilst extent of loss is important, attention must also be given to the decline in *quality* of the habitat. A decline in quality results from damage and can sometimes be ameliorated or even reversed. It could be argued that some cases of damage, such as the cutting of raised bog to the level of fen peat, does not constitute a habitat loss but habitat change, because given the appropriate environmental conditions communities associated with raised bogs may eventually redevelop. However, the time-scale in which this could occur is comparatively long and therefore the habitat has, to all intents and purposes, disappeared.

Loss of 'quantity'

Traditionally, fens are recognised as both providing a variety of natural products such as reed, sedge, peat, bedding for animals and grazing; and as an obstacle to development, leading to their wholesale drainage. The loss of area of fens and bogs has been substantial. These losses can still occur despite legal protection. The loss of fen habitat is most dramatically illustrated by the demise of the East Anglian fens. This vast region once covered an area of some 3000 km^2 between Lincolnshire and Cambridgeshire, England (Darby, 1983). The long history of drainage, which began in Roman times, has resulted in the loss of most of the fen habitat to arable fields except for a scattering of small areas. The two largest of these are now the National Nature Reserves of Wicken Fen and Woodwalton Fen (Cambridgeshire). Their combined area does not exceed 500 ha. Woodwalton and Wicken Fens have

---

[1] Species nomenclature follows Stace (1991).

only survived through careful control of their water table by bunding and pumping. Holme Fen, Cambridgeshire, is also a relic of this vast area of fen and bog, but has not received the benefit of drainage control and consequently presents a habitat which is for the greater part more akin to birch woodland than to wetland.

This process has also occurred in south-west England with the drainage of the Somerset Levels. The Levels and Moors were a complex of fen and raised bog covering approximately 56,650 ha developed within the flood plains and low-lying ground located between the uplands and coast. Reclamation began early but, unlike the Fenland of East Anglia, this was to grazing land. Many of the resulting grazing 'levels' have escaped drastic improvement and retain substantial biological diversity.

It is not possible to extrapolate the scale of loss from these areas to the rest of the country because such big fen ecosystems were exceptional. Broadland, (Norfolk and Suffolk, England), is a large area of fen which has developed within the flood plains of the rivers Ant, Yare, Bure, Thurne and Waveney. This fen landscape has shown both regression and expansion through the years. The greatest loss of wetland was the conversion of over 16,000 ha of fen, mud flats and washlands to grazing 'levels' (Broads Authority, 1987). This loss of wetland has not been compensated by the succession of reed swamp and fen over the open water areas, the broads. In fact, whilst there has been expansion of reed in some broads, studies of 18 sample broads have shown that in 1946 some 122 ha of reed swamp existed, but by 1980 only 49 ha existed (Fuller, 1986). Such losses may be the result of coypu grazing (Boorman & Fuller, 1981). Changes in both quantity and 'quality' (see below) of the 28,300 ha estimated area of semi-natural wetland of Broadland in the 1930s have left only 8400 ha which now forms the 'best' areas of remaining semi-natural habitat (Fuller, 1986).

If we turn our attention to smaller fen systems, it is apparent that substantial losses have occurred until recently. Approximately 98% of the estimated original area of Culm grassland in Devon, England, which features JUNCO-MOLINION communities has been lost since the turn of the century (Devon Wildlife Trust and Nature Conservancy Council, 1990). Similarly, Wales has shown a startling loss of fens and bogs. Here, 711 sites were recognised as wetland at the beginning of the century, but by the 1980s only 289 were found to support wetland habitat of sufficient quality to warrant survey (Ratcliffe & Hattey, 1982).

The loss of lowland raised bogs has also been dramatic. Losses have been mainly due to agricultural reclamation, but peat extraction, urban development, afforestation and 'burning' have also contributed to loss and damage. The scale of loss is illustrated by Table 3 which shows losses in the five major areas of lowland raised bogs in Britain. These figures do not indicate the quality of the remaining habitat.

Changes have also occurred to blanket mires. There has been a 30% loss or significant damage through afforestation, hill land improvement, reclamation, burning and over grazing of upland grasslands, heaths and blanket bogs (Nature Conservancy Council, 1985). In the Flow Country of Caithness and Sutherland, Scotland, some 17% of the original area of peatland had been afforested or programmed for planting by 1987 (Lindsay et al., 1988).

Table 3. Reductions in the area of lowland raised bogs through afforestation, peat-winning, reclamation for agriculture or repeated burning between 1948 and 1978 (Nature Conservancy Council, 1985).

Area/County	Area (ha)		% loss
	1948	1978	
Lancashire	247	11	95
South Cumbria	494	156	68
Solway (Cumbria)	1124	796	32
Solway (Dumfries & Galloway)	1194	190	84
Forth Valley	1087	632	42

The loss of wetland habitat has posed a severe threat to some associated plants. More than a quarter of the 19 species which have become extinct in Britain are in this group and a further seven species are endangered (Perring & Farrell, 1983).

Loss of quality

Losses in the nature conservation 'quality' of wetlands are also widespread, as in the fens of Broadland, where nearly half of the semi-natural habitat is now covered by carr (or a herbaceous fen–carr mix) which has expanded as management has declined (Fuller, 1986). Losses of open fen to carr have also occurred in other fens where management has declined. Rowell & Harvey (1988) have shown that at Wicken Fen (Cambridgeshire), between 1936 and 1956, the proportion of scrub nearly doubled (from 59 ha to 109 ha), the area of 'sedge' (*Cladium mariscus*) declined by more than half (from 59 ha to 20 ha) and litter fen (which was managed to provide bedding for animals) declined from 14 ha to 0.5 ha.

Particularly important within parts of England has been the loss of conservation 'quality' (and even fen habitat) as a consequence of changes in hydrological regime. Many of the spring-fed valleyhead fens of the counties of Norfolk and Suffolk have been affected by drainage in the past but, though the conservation value of the fens may now be lower as a consequence, it is still substantial. However, in recent years the impact of groundwater abstraction upon fens has become increasingly apparent. This impact upon the flora and fauna of one site, Redgrave and Lopham Fen, Suffolk, has been reported by Harding (1993). He has shown a decline in the 'quality' of the flora within the former spring-fed area since 1959 (based upon a comparison of species scores; Wheeler, 1988), changes in community-types and changes in invertebrate species. Groundwater abstraction may threaten many other fens within this region, which contain nearly half of Britain's resource of the *Schoeno-Juncetum subnodulosi* (Fojt, 1994).

The decline in 'quality' of a fen or bog is difficult to define and quantify and frequently floristic change is used as a measure. This has been done by Wheeler & Shaw (1992) who have examined floristic and reported management and

Table 4. Apparent changes (%) in floristic composition and other features expressed as a percentage of the total number of examined valleyhead fen sites (*n*) in East Anglia (based upon research by Wheeler & Shaw, 1992).

	E. Norfolk (*n*=37)	W. Norfolk (*n*=40)	Suffolk (*n*=21)	Cambridgeshire (*n*=9)
Wholly/partly lost	30	47.5	19.0	55.5
Disrupted hydrology	51	62.5	71	78
Neglect	65	82.3	86	100
Change in flora	62	62.5	95	89

environmental changes in spring-fed valleyhead fens in East Anglia (Table 4), and showed that floristic change has occurred as well as the partial or total loss of sites.

THREATS TO FENS AND BOGS

Threats to the continued existence of fens may be subdivided into those occurring within the fen itself and those originating within the catchment (internal and external factors, respectively). Neglect, following a cessation in management is probably the major 'internal' threat to many fens, often leading to an overgrown vegetation dominated by bulky species at the expense of lower growing species. This is considered in some detail by Wheeler & Shaw (this volume). 'External' threats include changes in land use and water use (both surface water and groundwater) in the catchment. Water abstraction may not only pose a threat to the water input to spring-fed fens but also to those which do not appear to be spring-fed, but where permeable 'windows' in the underlying substratum are able to transmit changes in aquifer water levels to the fen.

The conservation interest of lowland raised bogs continues to be threatened by the activities which have caused much of the loss of this habitat in the past. Improved drainage within areas of former raised bog reclaimed to agriculture may still cause net water loss from the bog. A lower and fluctuating water regime encourages colonisation by trees and enhanced evapotranspiration. Peat extraction and associated drainage threaten both uncut remnants and the regeneration of abandoned and flooded peat workings (Heathwaite, this volume). An additional potential threat, the significance of which is unknown in Britain, is the vertical loss of water through the base of the bog to the aquifer (Schouwenaars, this volume), where aquifer water levels are depressed as a result of water abstraction.

THE ROLE OF RESTORATION

The limited resources available to nature conservation organisations mean that in most instances the role of any proposed restoration project must be first assessed in terms of its value to the conservation of existing nature conservation interest.

This may also be in relation to its role in preventing deterioration of the fen or bog and/or 'improving' the situation. Secondly, the role of the restoration project can be assessed in terms of the opportunity to expand the nature conservation interest back into those areas from where it has been lost. At present, this latter aspect is generally seen as a valuable by-product of safeguarding the existing interest. However, given changes in agricultural economics and developing 'green' initiatives, it is possible that future expansion may take place within targeted areas, which currently lack much existing 'interest'.

To date, the restoration of fens in Britain has been rather limited. Why this should be the case is not clear, though some sites may be considered too degraded to warrant restoration. Restoration of the early stages of the hydrosere is being attempted within the fens of Broadland. Here, turf excavation on a large scale, following earlier successes of small-scale experiments (Kennison, 1986), is creating open water habitat which will succeed to swamp and herbaceous fen, hopefully *via* a stage characterised by the development of a semi-floating raft of *Acrocladio-Caricetum diandrae* in which such species as *Liparis loeselii* may occur. In North Wales, attempts are currently in progress to restore a part of Cors Geirch which had been reclaimed for agriculture. Here, an extensive shallow lagoon has been excavated.

The restoration of lowland raised bogs damaged by peat extraction is much more widespread than fen restoration in Britain, though it is still at an early stage (Mawby, this volume). To date, restoration has focused upon controlling drainage from remnants and other areas by damming ditches and reducing evapotranspirative water loss by scrub clearance. As yet, major bunding and flooding of areas, as has occurred within Lower Saxony and Holland, has not been frequently attempted; work at Cors Caron is the only major example in Britain.

We must be mindful that any restoration attempts must aim to produce a system which is as self-sustaining as possible. We must remember that fens and bogs are semi-natural habitats, with an emphasis as much as possible upon the word natural.

REFERENCES

Bibby, C.J. & Lunn, J. (1982). Conservation of reedbeds and their avifauna in England and Wales. *Biological Conservation*, **23**, 167–186.

Boorman, L.A & Fuller, R.M. (1981). The changing status of reedswamp in the Norfolk Broads. *Journal of Applied Ecology*, **18**, 241–269.

Broads Authority (1987). *Broads Plan*. Broads Authority, Norwich.

Darby, H.C. (1983). *The Changing Fenland*. Cambridge University Press, Cambridge.

Devon Wildlife Trust & Nature Conservancy Council (1990). *Survey of Culm Grasslands in the Torridge District, Devon*. Devon Wildlife Trust, Exeter.

Fojt, W. (1994). East Anglian fens and the threat posed by groundwater abstraction. *Biological Conservation*, **69**, 163–175.

Fuller, R.M. (1986). Taking stock of changing Broadland. II Status of seminatural and man-made habitats. *Journal of Biogeography*, **13**, 327–337.

Harding, M. (1993). Redgrave and Lopham Fens, East Anglia, England: A case study of change in flora and fauna due to groundwater abstraction. *Biological Conservation*, **66**, 35–45.

Kennison, G.C. (1986). Preliminary observations on plant colonisation of experimental turf ponds in a Broadland fen. *Transactions of Norfolk and Norwich Society*, **27** (3), 193–198.

Lindsay, R., Riggall, J & Burd, F. (1985). The use of small-scale patterns in the classification of British peatlands. *Aquilo Seria Botanica*, **21**, 69–79.

Lindsay, R., Charman, D., Everingham, F., O'Reilly, R., Palmer, M., Rowell, T. & Stroud, D. (1988). *The Flow Country. The peatlands of Caithness and Sutherland.* Nature Conservancy Council, Peterborough.

Nature Conservancy Council. (1989). *Guidelines for the Selection of Biological SSSIs.* Nature Conservancy Council. Peterborough.

Nature Conservancy Council. (1985). *Nature Conservation in Great Britain. Nature Conservancy Council.* (Published in Shrewsbury), Peterborough.

Perring, F.H. & Farrell, L. (1983). *British Red Data Books 1: Vascular Plants.* 2nd edn, Society for the Promotion of Nature Conservation, Nettleham.

Plantlife (1992). *Commission of Inquiry into Peat and Peatlands. Commissioners Report, Conclusions and Recommendations.* Plantlife, London.

Ratcliffe, D.A. (1977). *A Nature Conservation Review.* 2 volumes. Cambridge University Press, Cambridge.

Ratcliffe, J. & Hattey, R. (1982). *Welsh Lowland Peatland Survey.* Research Report No. 431. Nature Conservancy Council, Bangor.

Rodwell, J (1991a). *British Plant Communities: Volume 1. Woodlands* and Scrub. Cambridge University Press, Cambridge.

Rodwell, J (1991b). *British Plant Communities: Volume 2. Mires and Heaths.* Cambridge University Press, Cambridge.

Rodwell, J (in press). *British Plant Communities: Volume 4. Aquatic communities, swamp and tall-herb fen.* Cambridge University Press, Cambridge.

Rowell, T. & Harvey H. (1988). The recent history of Wicken Fen, Cambridgeshire, England: A guide to ecological development. *Journal of Ecology*, **76**, 73–90.

Stace, C. (1991). *New Flora of the British Isles.* Cambridge University Press, Cambridge.

Stewart, A., Pearman, D.A. & Preston, C.D. (eds) (1994). *Scarce Plants in Britain.* Joint Nature Conservation Committee, Peterborough.

Wheeler, B.D. (1980). Plant communities of rich-fen systems in England and Wales. II> Communities of calcareous mires. *Journal of Ecology*, **68**, 405–420.

Wheeler, B.D. (1984). British fens – a review. *European Mires* (ed. P.D. Moore) pp. 237–281. Academic Press, London.

Wheeler, B.D. (1988). Species richness, species rarity and conservation evaluation of rich fen vegetation in lowland England and Wales. *Journal of Applied Ecology*, **25**, 331–353.

Wheeler, B.D. (1993). Botanical diversity in British mires. *Biodiversity and Conservation*, **2**, 490–512.

Wheeler, B.D. & Shaw, S.C. (1987). *Comparative Survey of Habitat Conditions and Management Characteristics of Herbaceous Rich-fen Vegetation Types.* Contract Survey 6, Nature Conservancy Council, Peterborough.

Wheeler, B.D. & Shaw, S.C. (1992). *Biological Indicators of Dehydration and Changes to the East Anglian Fens Past and Present.* English Nature Research Report No. 22. Peterborough.

Appendix 1. Rare plant and bryophyte species associated with (a) fen, (b) carr and (c) bog communities in Britain. Rare species are derived from Rodwell (1991a, b & in press). Those communities for which no rare species have been listed in the National Vegetation Classification are not contained in the table. *Status data is updated from that presented in the SSSI selection guidelines (Nature Conservancy Council, 1989). (Stewart *et al.*, 1994). **Status unknown, though regarded by Stace (1991) as scarce. (H) species noted within European Habitats and Species Directive. RDB: species noted in Red Data Book (Perring & Farrell 1983) (these are species recorded in ≤ 15 10-km squares since 1930). Schedule 8 species are listed within Schedule 8 of the Wildlife and Countryside Act 1981. [†]Nationally rare bryophytes (<15 10-km squares); [#]Nationally scarce bryophytes (16–100 10-km squares). S: *Sphagnum*; C: *Carex*.

Community	RDB[R] / Schedule 8 species[8]	Nationally scarce higher plants and ferns *	Nationally rare[†] or scarce[#] bryophytes
(a) Fen communities			
M1: *S. auriculatum* bog pool	*Scheuchzeria palustris*[R]	*Hammarbya paludosa; Rhynchospora fusca; Utricularia intermedia* **	*Sphagnum pulchrum*[#]
M2: *S. cuspidatum / S. recurvum* bog pool		*Carex magellanica*	*Sphagnum pulchrum*[#]
M4: *C. rostrata–S. recurvum* mire	*Carex chordorrhiza*[R]	*Lysimachia thyrsiflora*	
M7: *C. curta–S. russowii* mire	*Carex rariflora*[R]		*Sphagnum lindbergii*[†]
M8: *C. rostrata–S. warnstorfii* mire			*Homalothecium nitens*[#]
M9: *C. rostrata–Calliergon cuspidatum* mire	*Liparis loeselii*[R,8]	*C. appropinquata; Cicuta virosa; Dactylorhiza traunsteineri; Potamogeton coloratus; Pyrola rotundifolia; Sium latifolium; Utricularia intermedia*	*Cinclidium stygium*[#]
M10: *C. dioica–Pinguicula vulgaris* mire	*Bartsia alpina*[R]*; Kobresia simpliciuscula*[R]*; Minuartia stricta*[R,8]*; Schoenus ferrugineus* [R]	*Carex capillaris; Equisetum variegatum; Juncus alpino articulatus; Minuartia verna; Primula farinosa; Sesleria caerulea*	

Appendix 1. *continued*

Community	RDB^R / Schedule 8 species[8]	Nationally scarce higher plants and ferns *	Nationally rare[+] or scarce[#] bryophytes
M11: *C. demissa– Saxifraga azoides* mire	*C. atrofusca*[R]; *C. microglochin*[R]; *Kobresia simpliciuscula*[R]; *Schoenus ferrugineus*[R]	*C. vaginata*; *Equisetum variegatum*; *Juncus alpino articulatus*; *J biglumis*; *J castaneus*; *Salix reticulata*	*Calliergon trifarium*[#]; *Meesia uliginosa*[#]
M13: *Schoenus nigricans– Juncus subnodulosus* mire		*Dactylorhiza traunsteineri*; *Potamogeton coloratus*	
M15: *Scirpus cespitosus–Erica tetralix* wet heath			*Campylopus atrovirens var. falcatus*[+] (RDB); *Campylopus setifolius*[#]
M16: *Erica tetralix–S. compactum* wet heath	*Erica ciliaris*[R]	*Gentiana pneumonanthe*; *Lycopodiella inundata*; *Rhynchospora fusca*	
M21: *Narthecium ossifragum–S. compactum* valley mire	*Erica ciliaris*[R]	*Hammarbya paludosa*	
M22: *Juncus subnodulosus– Cirsium palustre* fen meadow		*Peucedanum palustre*	
M24: *Molinia caerulea–Cirsium dissectum* fen meadow	*Selinum carvifolia*[R,8]	*Hypericum undulatum*; *Peucedanum palustre*	*Homalothecium nitens*[#]
M25: *Molinia caerulea– Potentilla erecta* mire	*Erica vagans*[R], *Lobelia urens*[R]		

contd

Appendix 1. *continued*

Community	RDB[R] / Schedule 8 species[8]	Nationally scarce higher plants and ferns *	Nationally rare[†] or scarce[#] bryophytes
M26: *Molinia coerulea–Crepis paludosa* mire		*Primula farinosa*	
M29: *Hypericum elodes–Potamogeton polygonifolius* soakway	*Galium debile*[R]	*Pilularia globulifera*	
M31: *Anthelia julacea–S. auriculatum* spring			*Anthelia juratzkana*[#]; *Pohlia ludwigii*[#]
M32: *Philonotis fontana–Saxifraga stellaris* spring	*Koenigia islandica*[R]	*Cerastium cerastioides; Epilobium alsinifolium; Myosotis stolonifera; Phleum alpinum; Sedum villosum*	*Bryum schleicheri* var. *latifolium*[†]; *Scapania paludosa*[†]; *Bryum weigelii*[#]; *Oncophorus virens*[#]; *Pohlia ludwigii*[#]; *P. wahlenbergii* var. *glacialis*[#]; *Tritomaria polita*[#]
M38: *Cratoneuron commutatum–C. nigra* spring	*Saxifraga hirculus*[R] (H)		*Oncopherus virens*[#]
S1: *C. elata* swamp			
S4: *Phragmites australis* swamp		*Calamagrostis stricta*	
S9: *C. rostrata* swamp	*Eriocaulon aquaticum*[R]	*Cicuta virosa*	

Appendix 1. *continued*

Community	RDB ^{R} / Schedule 8 species^8	Nationally scarce higher plants and ferns *	Nationally rare† or scarce# bryophytes
S10: *Equisetum fluviatile* swamp		*Calamagrostis stricta; Lysimachia thyrsiflora*	
S11: *C. vesicaria* swamp		*Carex aquatalis*	
S12: *Typha latifolia* swamp		*Cicuta virosa*	
S13: *Typha angustifolia* swamp	*Elatine hydropiper*^{R}	*Elatine haxandra*	
S14: *Sparganium erectum* swamp		*Wolffia arrhiza*	
S21: *Scirpus maritimus* swamp	*Juncus subulatus*^{R}		
S24: *Phragmites australis–Peucedanum palustre* tall herb fen		*Carex appropinquata; Cicuta virosa; Lathyrus palustris; Peucedanum palustre; Sium latifolium; Thelypteris palustris*	
S25: *Phragmites australis–Eupatorium cannabinum* tall herb fen		*Thelypteris palustris*	
S27: *C. rostrata–Potentilla palustris* tall herb fen		*Carex appropinquata; C. aquatalis; Lysimachia thyrsiflora; Peucedanum palustre; Sium latifolium*	
(b) Carr communities			
W1: *Salix cinerea–Galium palustre*		*Lysimachia thyrsiflora*	
W2: *Salix cinerea–Betula pubescens*	*Dryopteris cristata*^{R}	*Carex elongata; Peucedanum palustre; Pyrola rotundifolia; Thelypteris palustris*	
W3: *Salix pentandra–C. rostrata*		*Carex appropinquata; Corallorhiza trifida; Lysimachia thyrsiflora*	
W4: *Betula pubescens–Molinia caerulea*	*Dryopteris cristata*^{R}		
W5: *Alnus glutinosa–C. paniculata*	*Dryopteris cristata*^{R}	*Carex appropinquata; Carex elongata; Cicuta virosa; Peucedanum palustre; Thelypteris palustris*	

contd

Appendix 1. *continued*

Community	RDB ^{R} / Schedule 8 species[8]	Nationally scarce higher plants and ferns *	Nationally rare[†] or scarce[#] bryophytes
(c) Bog communities			
M15: *Scirpus cespitosus–Erica tetralix* wet heath			*Campylopus atrovirens* var. *falcatus*[†] (RDB); *Campylopus setifolius*[#]
M17: *Scirpus cespitosus–Eriophorum vaginatum* blanket bog			*Campylopus atrovirens* var. *falcatus* [†]; *Sphagnum imbricatum*[#]; *Campylopus setifolius*[#]; *C. shawii*[#]
M18: *Erica tetralix–S. papillosum* raised and blanket bog		*Andromeda polifolia*	
M19: *Calluna vulgaris–Eriophorum vaginatum* blanket mire		*Betula nana; Vaccinium microcarpum*	*Kiaria starkei*[#]

4 A Focus on Fens – Controls on the Composition of Fen Vegetation in Relation to Restoration

B. D. WHEELER & S. C. SHAW
Department of Animal & Plant Sciences, P.O. Box 601, University of Sheffield, Sheffield, S10 2UQ, UK

SUMMARY

1. The formulation of objectives in the development of effective restoration strategies for damaged fens requires an understanding of the primary controls on the composition of fen vegetation. A brief review is given of these, based primarily upon material from Britain.
2. A synoptic survey was carried out to examine some vegetation–environment relationships within fens in Britain. Canonical Correspondence Analysis suggested that the three main axes extracted broadly correspond to variation in base-richness, soil fertility and water level. The relationships between these factors and fen vegetation composition and species richness are discussed.
3. The importance of succession and vegetation management to the character and species richness of fen vegetation is examined.
4.. The importance of past peat-cutting to the present character of fen vegetation is considered with particular respect to the use of peat excavation as a tool for the conservation and restoration of fens.

INTRODUCTION

Fens (for definition see Chapter 1) are extremely variable ecosystems, which occur in a range of waterlogged situations, fed, at least in part, by telluric water. They are (or once were) very widespread in temperate regions. In aggregate they have high biodiversities, with a large number of plant species organised into a wide range of plant communities, reflecting variations of environmental conditions, natural processes of development and degree of human influence. The formulation of objectives of restoration strategies for damaged fens requires an understanding of the basic controls on the composition of fen vegetation. This chapter provides a brief review of this, based primarily upon material from Britain.

Restoration of Temperate Wetlands. Edited by B.D. Wheeler, S.C. Shaw, W.J. Fojt and R.A. Robertson
© 1995 John Wiley & Sons Ltd.

Fens in Britain

The fen resource of the United Kingdom has yet to be quantified properly, but there are undoubtedly numerous fen sites, though many of these are small (< 5 ha). The distribution of some sites is shown in Figure 1. In aggregate they support some 46 plant community-types, containing some 653 plant species, of which about 294 can be regarded as being particularly characteristic of fens (Wheeler, 1993; Fojt, this volume). This botanical diversity is coupled with considerable entomological and ornithological richness (Foster & Procter; Ward, Hirons & Self, this volume) and these give many sites high conservation value (Ratcliffe, 1977). Various sites wait to be surveyed fully and some may remain to be discovered, particularly, perhaps, in Scotland.

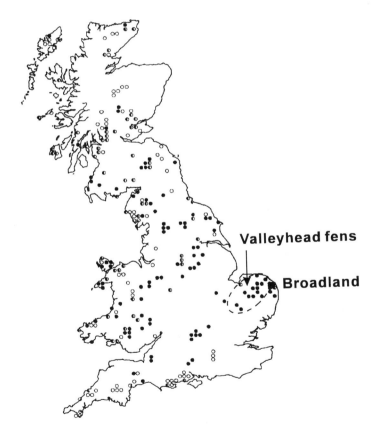

Figure 1. Map of Britain, showing location of mires examined in a 'synoptic survey' of British fens, plotted on a 10 km grid: ● rich-fen sites; ○ poor-fen sites. Half-filled circles indicate sites with both rich- and poor-fen community-types. Location of Broadland and East Anglian valleyhead fens are also shown.

Whilst some quite detailed ecological studies have been made on a small number of individual fen sites in Britain (reviewed by Wheeler, 1984), in general British fens have received but limited investigation. Recently, a broad-brush, synoptic survey has been completed to examine some environmental and management conditions associated with the main types of herbaceous fen vegetation throughout their range in Britain (Figure 1), referred to here as the 'synoptic survey' (Wheeler & Shaw, 1987; Shaw & Wheeler, 1990, 1991).

CONTROLS ON THE COMPOSITION OF FEN VEGETATION

The diversity of fen vegetation-types, and the variability of the fen habitat, permit only an outline to be drawn of the importance of some of the variables that control fen vegetation composition. Species richness can often be used as a simple, surrogate measure of the perceived conservational 'value' of fen vegetation. This is not because species-rich fen vegetation is intrinsically more 'valuable' than species-poor types, but because it is often more rare and threatened and supports a larger number of uncommon fen plant species (Wheeler, 1988). Three species-richness terms are used here: *species density* (SPD), *principal fen species score* (PFS) and *rare fen species score* (RFS) are respectively the mean number of species, fen species and rare fen species in a 4 m^2 sample (Wheeler, 1988).

Phytogeography and climate

The composition of fen vegetation varies very considerably with altitude, latitude and longitude. This is illustrated by the range of vegetation-types discussed in other contributions to this volume. In general, whilst the broad distribution of fen plants is well known for some regions, much less is known about the precise controls upon this. Ratcliffe (1977) categorised British mire plants into phytogeographical groups, though in some instances the association of species with particular regions more reflects the current distribution of suitable edaphic conditions than fundamental geographical trends (Wheeler, 1993). There is some clear evidence for responses to climatic variables that are likely to influence the distribution of some fen plants. One of the earliest, and best-studied examples is provided by *Cladium mariscus*[1]. Von Post (1925) considered *Cladium* to be a climatic indicator species and Conway (1938b) demonstrated that its growing point can be damaged by temperatures below about -2°C. However, its response to climate is influenced by other variables. For example, in colder regions the plant may be largely confined to swamps, where the deeper water confers some protection of the meristem against frost, than is the case in regions with milder winters (in Britain the plant occupies a wide range of wetness: summer water table -72 to $+28$ cm). Conway (1938a) considered growth of *Cladium* to be favoured by

---

[1] Nomeclature follows Stace (1991) for vascular plants, Smith (1978) for bryophytes and Wheeler (1984) for community-types.

warm summers and bright sunlight, though she also recognised the difficulties of extrapolating from experimental results to field distributions, by pointing to the prevalence of this species in the cool, dull, blanket-bog climates of western Ireland.

The occurrence of species at outliers from their main centres of distribution attracts special interest, especially when, in their outlying localities, the species are absent from nearby sites with apparently appropriate habitats. 'Relict status' is sometimes invoked as an explanation for such localisation. For example, Rose (1957) suggested that the occurrence of such bryophytes as *Homalothecium nitens* and *Leiocolea schultzii* in a few valleyhead fens in East Anglia (Figure 1) may reflect relict status. The handful of sites of *Schoenus ferrugineus* in Scotland may also suggest relict status, though it is equally possible that the species may be a recent colonist (Wheeler, Brookes & Smith, 1983). It is desirable not to invoke relict status as an explanation of last resort, just because none other is obvious!

Hydrochemical variables

Mire ecologists have long made measurements of water and peat chemistry, often accompanied by records of vegetation composition and there is a rich supply of field chemical data for individual plant species and vegetation-types (*e.g.* Malmer, 1962a,b; Pietsch, 1976). The development of such techniques as Canonical Correspondence Analysis (CCA) (Ter Braak, 1987) have provided powerful tools for exploring complex vegetation–environment relationships (*e.g.* Wassen *et al.*, 1990). However, many data refer to specific sites and in general the overall 'tolerances' and 'requirements' of particular species and vegetation-types with respect to particular variables are not well known. Indeed, it is clear that environmental limits which clearly circumscribe the distribution of a species or vegetation-type in one site may be inapplicable in another (Sjörs, 1950) and that the distribution of certain species can transcend major environmental boundaries (Gorham, 1950). Various experimental studies have been made on the relationship between the performance of fen plants and hydrochemical variables (*e.g.* Conway, 1938a, b; Verkamp *et al.*, 1980; Snowden & Wheeler, 1993), but they are far from comprehensive. Moreover, the difficulties of relating the results of single-species experiments to field distributions are well known.

The synoptic survey of Wheeler & Shaw examined some vegetation–environment relationships within British fens. Values of pH, conductivity and alkalinity were determined for water samples, and pH and concentrations of metal cations, N and P were measured in soil sample extracts (Wheeler, Shaw & Cook, 1991). An innovative feature of this study was the use of 'phytometer' species to provide simple, but reliable, estimates of soil fertility from a large number of sites (Wheeler *et al.*, 1991). Ranges of some variables are summarised in Table 1. Vegetation–environment relationships were examined by CCA. Several of the environmental variables are strongly correlated and the variation shown in Figures 2a and 2b can be schematically simplified into a three-dimensional model in which

Table 1. Ranges of some environmental variables measured in the substrata of British fens (Shaw & Wheeler, 1991). * $n = 4975$, except for fertility ($n = 9950$); ** values corrected for contribution made by hydrogen ion activity; *** fertility estimates were made phytometrically by growing seedlings of *Epilobium hirsutum* and *Phalaris arundinacea* on soil samples in controlled conditions; values are mg dry weight of the phytometers.

Variable	Mean*	Median*	Minimum	Maximum
Water pH	5.6	5.6	2.9	8.3
Soil pH	5.7	5.7	2.2	7.8
Water conductivity** (μS cm^{-1})	336	195	0	5354
Water alkalinity (mg l^{-1})	135.5	42.3	0	1806
Summer water depth (cm)	0.2	0.0	$^{-}$100	25
Redox potential (mV)	274	278	10	545
Soil fertility*** (mg)	10.8	7.4	0.5	42.3

the three main axes broadly correspond to variation in base-richness, soil fertility and water level (Figure 2c). These axes are substantially independent of one another.

Base-richness

The axis of base-richness inferred from the CCA ordination (Figure 2) is comprised of several variables. Positive loadings correspond to increases in water pH, conductivity and alkalinity together with soil pH and extracted concentrations of Ca and Mg. Negative loadings correspond to increased concentrations of soil-extracted Fe, Mn and Al. The overall trends identified by CCA should not, of course, be allowed to obscure some important exceptions. Thus, whilst high concentrations of soil-extracted Fe and Mn are most typically associated with base-poor conditions, high concentrations of both elements also occur in some rich-fen soils (*e.g.* Wheeler, Al-Farraj & Cook, 1985). However, high concentrations of extracted Al were invariably associated with low pH fen soils (< 5.0–5.5).

The importance of base-richness as a primary determinant of the composition of mire vegetation has long been recognised, as reflected in the gradient of bog → poor fen → rich fen (*e.g.* Du Rietz, 1949; Sjörs, 1950; Jeglum, 1971). Axis 1 of the CCA of British fen data (Figure 2) essentially represents an ordination of community-types along this gradient, from *Schoeno-Juncetum* (CARICION DAVALLIANAE) at the highest loadings to *Sphagnum cuspidatum–recurvum* bog pool communities (RHYNCHOSPORION) at the lowest. The reasons for floristic change along the base-richness gradient are not fully understood. For many vascular plant species, variation in pH *per se* is probably of rather little *direct* importance, at least within the range pH 4–7.5. Adaptation to growth in low-pH

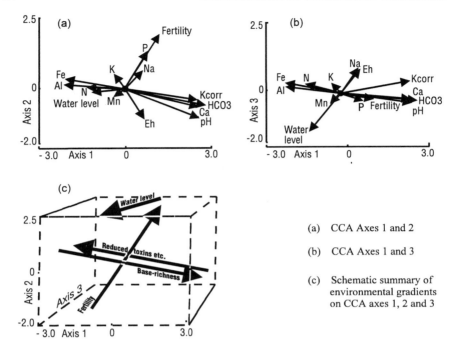

(a)   CCA Axes 1 and 2

(b)   CCA Axes 1 and 3

(c)   Schematic summary of
       environmental gradients
       on CCA axes 1, 2 and 3

Figure 2.   Canonical Correspondence Analysis ordination of floristic data and
environmental variables from British fens.

mires may partly depend upon tolerance to toxic metals such as Al, Fe and Mn
(Clymo, 1962; Sparling, 1967; Snowden & Wheeler, 1993), though not all base-
poor fens are necessarily rich in these elements. Moreover, in some base-rich fens,
both Fe and Mn may reach concentrations that are toxic to some typical fen
species.

Various calcifuge species, perhaps most notably many species of *Sphagnum,* are
typically absent from base-rich fens. Some experimental studies have confirmed
that high values of pH or calcium concentration are unfavourable to some such
species (Clymo, 1962; Jefferies & Willis, 1964), but the reasons for this are not
generally well established. In strongly oceanic climates, acidic niches often occur
even in the most base-rich fens, permitting the growth of various calcifuge species.

The base-richness relationships of various fen plant species show considerable
geographical variation, a feature which helps to blur the floristic distinction
between rich fen, poor fen (Sjörs, 1950) and even bog. Various species that are
largely confined to base-rich fens in much of their European range may occur in
more base-poor environments in oceanic regions (Aletsee, 1967; Müller, 1976;
Malmer, 1986). This gradient is clearly seen within the UK. For example, both
Cladium mariscus and *Schoenus nigricans* are confined to rich fens in eastern

England, but also occupy poor fens in western Britain and yet further west, in the far west of Ireland, also grow in blanket mire (Tansley, 1939).

As in some drier habitats, base-rich fens tend to be considerably more species-rich than base-poor examples (Table 2). In general the base-richness of fen sites is an intrinsic, natural feature and conservationists and restorers are often content to maintain its *status quo*. However, some base-rich sites may show progressive acidification, on account of artificial changes such as reduction of inputs of base-rich groundwater (Grootjans & van Diggelen, this volume) or of spontaneous successional changes (van Wirdum, this volume). In both of these situations such acidity increase is sometimes regarded as undesirable, so that remedial restoration to a more base-rich condition is undertaken (Beltman, van der Broek & Bloemen, this volume).

Deposition of 'acid rain' has been suggested as an additional cause of acidification of fens in NW Europe and for possible loss of some fen species (*e.g.* Kooijman, 1992), but in oceanic fens it can be difficult to separate such effects from their natural propensity for acidification. The impact of any such influence will depend upon the nature, quantity and quality of telluric water sources to the fens. Sites with high pH, but weakly buffered, water may be particularly vulnerable to change.

Table 2. Correlations between environmental variables and species-richness terms in British fens. Groups of variables are discussed together in the text. SPD: number of species in 4 m^2; PFS: number of fen species in 4 m^2; RFS: number of rare fen species in 4 m^2. Asterisks denote significance: *** = P<0.001; ** = P<0.01; * = P<0.05. (Shaw & Wheeler, 1991.) Data for chemical elements refer to concentrations extracted from soil samples.

	SPD	PFS	RFS		
pH	***	***	***	}	
Calcium	***	***	***	}	Positive
HCO$_3^-$	***	***	***	}	
Iron	***	***	***	}	Negative
Aluminium	***	***	***	}	
Fertility	***	***	***	}	
Phosphorus	***	***	***	}	Negative
Potassium	***	***	***	}	
Nitrogen	***	***	***	}	
Water level	**				Negative
Redox potential	*				Positive
Manganese					
Sodium					
Magnesium	*				Positive

Fertility

In the CCA ordination (Figure 2a), the gradient of fertility is most clearly expressed by phytometric response, which is paralleled by variation in extracted-P (extractant Na_2HCO_3). The fertility gradient is almost orthogonal to (*i.e.* largely independent of) the gradient of base-richness, a feature which strongly argues against any specification of the trophic status of fens in terms of pH (*e.g.* Ratcliffe, 1977). In fact, the gradient is slightly skewed towards base-rich conditions (Figure 2c), but this is because of the scarcity of very fertile soils in base-poor fens, not because of absence of low fertility soils from base-rich sites. Succow & Jeshcke (1986), amongst others, also observe some independence between pH and trophic status and, considering soil carbon:nitrogen ratios, recognise that base-rich fens can be both 'mesotrophic' and 'eutrophic' in character. They restrict the category of 'oligotrophic' to refer just to ombrotrophic sites, but as the net above-ground annual production of vegetation in some fens (*e.g.* Wheeler & Shaw, 1991) can be smaller than that of bogs (*e.g.* Forrest & Smith, 1975), it is hard to see a good justification for not recognising 'oligotrophic' fens as well. However, because the terms 'oligotrophic', 'mesotrophic' and 'eutrophic' are sometimes used as base-richness terms and have also been adopted by limnologists with specific connotations that are inapplicable to mires, it may be preferable to replace them with less ambiguous terms such as 'nutrient-rich', 'nutrient-poor', 'large productivity', 'small productivity', *etc.*

Availability of nutrients such as N, P and K is undoubtedly of key importance to plant growth and vegetation composition in fens, but general relationships are sometimes difficult to demonstrate (*e.g.* Vermeer & Berendse, 1983; Verhoeven, Koerselman & Beltman, 1988; Wheeler *et al.*, 1991). This may be because simple measurements of N and P concentrations in fen waters or peat do not adequately represent the availability of these nutrients, or because different nutrients are limiting in different situations. In the CCA ordination of British data, extracted concentrations of soil nitrogen (extractant KCl) bore no relationship to either phytometric yield or extracted P concentration. This may mean either that N is not generally as important a determinant of fertility across the fens examined as is P or that concentrations of N measured in soil extracts did not adequately represent plant-available N *in situ*. Koerselman & Verhoeven (this volume) further address the question of growth-limiting nutrients in fens.

There is strong floristic change associated with the fertility gradient identified in the CCA ordination of British fens (Figure 2). The communities occupying the lowest loadings on this axis are both CARICION DAVALLIANAE types (*Pinguiculo-Caricetum dioicae* and *Schoeno-Juncetum subnodulosi*). Some examples of the latter have extremely low above-ground 'productivity' (assessed as seasonal increment of biomass), with measured values of around 80 g m^{-2} a^{-1} (which are comparable with some values reported from the arctic tundra) (Wheeler & Shaw, 1991). At the highest loadings of the fertility gradient, the vegetation-types include the most robust and productive types (*e.g. Glyceria maxima* sociation; *Phragmites–Urtica* fen). The fertility of fen soils shows a strong negative correlation with vegetation species richness (Table 2). However, this overall trend requires some qualification because it is evident that, whilst high soil fertility is *usually* associated with low species richness, this is not a *necessary* condition. In some instances high species richness occurs in very fertile sites. One reason for this is that there may be an interaction between soil fertility and vegetation management in which some forms of vegetation management help to maintain species-rich vegetation even in fertile fen sites (Wheeler & Shaw, 1994). This is discussed further below.

'Eutrophication' of fens (*i.e.* enrichment with nutrients such as N, P and K) is widely regarded as an important cause of vegetation change (in particular, loss of species richness) within fens in NW Europe, though its influence has been more often inferred than demonstrated (*e.g.* Boller-Elmer, 1977; Verhoeven *et al.*, 1983, 1988). Restoration of enriched fens to a less fertile condition is seen as an important objective of fen restoration (Koerselman & Verhoeven, this volume). Bakker (1989) and Bakker & Olff (this volume) discuss options for reducing the fertility of wet grasslands and fen meadows and these may also apply to various other fen types.

Water level

The third axis of the CCA ordination of British fen data essentially corresponds to water level, with values of summer water table forming a gradient inverse to redox potential (Figure 2b). As the 'summer water level' data were necessarily based just upon spot measurements (a consequence of the breadth of the survey), they must be assessed with caution, as the hydroperiod of fens can be complex. Nonetheless, they show clearly that certain plant community-types occupy distinctive ranges of summer water table. The communities with highest loadings (water levels) along this axis include *Potentillo-Caricetum rostratae*, (MAGNOCARICION), *Acrocladio-Caricetum diandrae* (CARICION LASIOCARPAE); those with lowest loadings include *Phragmites–Urtica* fen, *Peucedano-Phragmitetum* and *Angelico-Phragmitetum*. The differences in mean values amongst these community-types are, nonetheless, rather small, probably because all examples are characteristic vegetation-types of fens.

The data from the synoptic survey of British fens do not show a significant relationship between summer water-table height (or redox potential) and the number of fen species and rare fen species in the vegetation. This is almost certainly because the majority of sites examined had a high, and narrow, range of summer water levels (Table 1). The negative relationship between species density and summer water table probably reflects the generally species-poor character of more swampy vegetation, caused by a failure of more waterlogging-sensitive species to grow in these particularly wet situations.

Various studies have examined the relationship between field water levels and distributions of plant species and vegetation-types (*e.g.* Spence, 1964; Balátová-Tuláčková, 1968; Grootjans & Ten Klooster, 1980). Such analyses are complicated by the difficulties of characterising the water regime of fens in a way relevant to the composition of fen vegetation (the cumulative period for which water levels exceed specific values may provide an appropriate approach; Niemann, 1973; Grootjans & Ten Klooster, 1980). It is, however, clear that, whilst it is possible to identify broad trends in water regimes associated with specific vegetation-types, there is often considerable variance and examples sometimes occur in water conditions strikingly different from those which are 'typical'. From the point of view of identifying broad environment–vegetation inter-relationships, such examples may be considered anomalous. But, providing they are stable, their ability to persist at such extremes is of considerable importance for their conservation. Of course, the conditions needed to regenerate communities may be more stringent than those under which they are able to persist.

Most examples of fen vegetation support plant species that are more-or-less confined to waterlogged habitats mixed with others that occur much more widely in drier situations (Wheeler, 1988). A wide range of 'dryland' species (*e.g. Agrostis stolonifera*) can grow in extremely wet fens. Conversely, various 'typical' fen species can grow in surprisingly dry conditions (*e.g. Schoenus nigricans* (Zwillenberg & de Wit, 1951)). Wheeler & Shaw (in press) have reviewed some information on the water level 'tolerances' and 'preferences' of fen plants.

The loss of certain species from drying-out fens is not always a direct consequence of lowering of the water table, as the effects of this may be compounded by associated environmental changes. Drying-out may be accompanied by increased rates of mineralisation in the substratum, leading to the development of a coarse and productive vegetation (Grootjans, Schipper & van der Windt, 1986), but this is not a universal phenomenon (Grootjans & van Diggelen, this volume) and, in particular, skeletal fen soils with small nutrient capital may be little affected by such processes. Changes in the degree of waterlogging may also modify other natural checks upon growth of vigorous species. For example, in laboratory experiments *Epilobium hirsutum* has been shown to grow less well on some soils when waterlogged than when they are drier, on account of greater availability of soluble iron, which retards the growth of this species (Wheeler *et al.*, 1985). Ellenberg (1954) pointed to the potential importance of competition between wetland and dryland species in regulating their field distributions.

Conservation managers frequently focus on the problems of the drying-out of fens and often give less attention to the effects of high water levels on fen ecosystems, probably because this is not a such pervasive threat. However, high water levels can also influence the growth and distribution of wetland plant species. This is obvious when excessively high water levels lead to deep inundation of peat surfaces, but a modest, continuous rise in water table may also lead to vegetation change. Even typical wetland plant species show considerable variation in their response to waterlogging, in terms of differential sensitivity to anoxia (Schat, 1984; Braendle & Crawford, 1987) or reduced toxins such as Fe^{2+} (Snowden & Wheeler, 1993) or S^- (Sellars, 1991). Sensitive species may be able to survive in waterlogged sites only because of their occupation of better-drained microtopographical niches, or by shallow-rooting into an uppermost oxic soil horizon (and perhaps also because of photosynthetic oxygenation associated with carpets of bryophytes). Even a small, but sustained, increase in water level may materially change the redox potentials of the uppermost soil horizons, unless these have some capacity for flotation. Grootjans & van Diggelen (this volume) suggest that some rare fen species may benefit from minor drainage of fens.

Such considerations may be particularly important in soligenous fens. These distinctive fens are characterised by a lateral through-flow of water. The character and importance of this has not been well studied, but in some sites it helps to maintain relatively high redox potentials even in waterlogged soils. It may thereby promote the growth of some waterlogging-sensitive species (both wetland and dryland) in soligenous sites and contribute to the high species richness that is a particular feature of many such systems. Soligenous fens are often irrigated by groundwater and abstraction of groundwater can in some instances diminish their water supply, threatening or damaging some important fen ecosystems (Harding, 1993; Fojt, 1994). One conservational response to this, sometimes, is to try to retain water on the fens by damming major outflows, but, whilst this may be effective in retaining water, it may also substantially alter the redox potential profiles of the soils.

Ultimately, despite the need to do so (van Diggelen et al., 1991), it is still difficult to predict the effects that changes in the water regime are likely to have upon the composition of fen vegetation. This reflects a lack of detailed under-standing of the way in which site wetness controls the composition of fen vegetation. The reasons for this are essentially lack of knowledge about (a) the nature of the tolerance of wetland species to wet conditions; (b) the range of water conditions particular species (and communities) can tolerate; (c) the importance of species interactions (competition etc.) in determining the field response of species to specific water conditions; (d) the importance of different phases of the hydro-period upon species survival (e.g. degree of flooding (or drying) in winter vs. summer); (e) the importance of the amplitude of water level flux vs. mean values; (f) the possibility that community-distributions are a legacy of former hydrological environments (van Diggelen et al., 1991); and (g) that other environmental conditions are primary influences upon community distribution, or modify the direct effects of water regimes. Coupled with potential inter-site variation in features that may be influenced by, but which are also partly independent of, water levels (e.g. the extent to which soils release N by mineralisation upon drying), it is not surprising that it may be difficult to predict effects of water level change except in closely circumscribed and well-studied situations. Of course, this problem is partly one of degree: it may be possible to predict that a sustained drop of water table by about 1 m would lead to an eventual loss of many fen species from the vegetation, but the consequences of a permanent change of mean summer water table height by, say, 5 cm are far less obvious.

Succession and vegetation management

The vegetation of many fen ecosystems is intrinsically unstable – that is, it is liable to change spontaneously towards a more stable, climax, state. In many temperate fens the climax state seems usually to be some form of woodland or bog, though sometimes certain types of herbaceous vegetation may also be self-maintaining for long periods. Vegetation change towards a stable state usually occurs either because of on-going, progressive successional development or because of the relaxation of some previously-arresting influence, such as vegetation management.

It is important to distinguish the spontaneous changes that occur through primary succession from those consequent upon dereliction (abandonment of past management regimes). The essential difference is that autogenic succession involves a linked change in vegetation and environment towards the climax condition, whereas changes induced by dereliction involve population flux and colonisation within an environment that is already capable of supporting the later successional species and communities. Nonetheless, the two processes can be closely interlinked.

Vegetation succession

The term 'hydrosere' is sometimes used (wrongly) as a generic term for successional processes and vegetation development in wetlands, but it is strictly applicable only to those systems which have developed by the terrestrialisation of open water. Hydroseral successions within wetlands can be complex. Autogenic (*i.e.* 'self made') successions, that is successions which are largely determined by the autochthonous accumulation of plant material, can follow a variety of pathways to the ultimate development of fen woodland or bog (*e.g.* Walker, 1970). When open waters are also strongly affected by external influences (such as allochthonous input of river silts) rather different successional processes occur, as illustrated at Esthwaite Water (Pearsall, 1918; Tansley, 1939; Pigott & Wilson, 1978).

Concepts of hydroseral succession are inapplicable to many fens, such as those which have developed by paludification (by which once relatively dry land becomes wet). In these instances, the development of the mire may be determined by a variety of processes. Many of the most extensive fens in Britain, such as those of the Norfolk Broadland, have developed primarily by paludification (Lambert & Jennings, 1951; Jennings, 1952). Nonetheless, very often the development of paludified fens cannot be completely divorced from hydroseral processes. Swamps and pools can develop within paludification fens as a result of external constraints upon their drainage (*e.g.* land–sea level change; deliberate damming) or they can be created by such activities as peat excavation. In England, a most detailed analysis of the hydrosere was reported by Lambert (1951) from the flooded basins of deep mediaeval peat workings (or 'Broads') within the paludification fens of Broadland. Also, of course, the development of both hydroseral and paludification fens can converge to a similar climax of fen carr, woodland or bog.

Table 3 Occurrence of specific management regimes in British fens (1985–90) (Shaw & Wheeler, 1991). * : $n = 1038$; ** : $n = 331$; *** : includes sites deliberately grazed and sites with open access to livestock; **** : mainly for reed (*Phragmites australis*) and 'sedge' (*Cladium mariscus*); 'marsh hay' or 'litter' only cut as part of conservation management.

	All fens*	Rich fens**
Unmanaged	39%	64%
Grazed***	51%	28%
Burnt	6%	2%
Mown****	3%	5%
Other	1%	1%

Vegetation management

It is difficult now to appreciate fully the contribution that fens once made to some rural economies. Throughout Britain, fens have provided – and some still provide – rough summer grazing for sheep and cattle (Table 3). Various crops have also been mown from fen sites. The most widespread, which has now all but disappeared, was marsh hay and litter (bedding) for livestock, produced by annual summer mowing. Other products are reed (*Phragmites australis*) and 'sedge' (*Cladium mariscus*), both used for thatching and still harvested locally. Numerous fen plants once had a variety of minor uses: rushes (*Juncus effusus*) were once widely used to make 'rush candles' and the wiry stems and leaves of *Schoenus nigricans* have provided thread for horse-collars made from *Scirpus lacustris* (Bird, 1909).

In various parts of Britain, at about the start of the nineteenth century (in some cases earlier), numerous areas of fen were designated as 'Poor's Land' or 'Fuel Allotments' as part of the Parliamentary Inclosure of parish land. Such land was designated for use by the parish poor for such purposes as the acquisition of fuel and was probably selected partly because it had limited alternative economic value. The *Charities Commissioners Report* for Hevingham parish (Norfolk) in 1838 observed that "This allotment [now an important valleyhead fen site] consists of very bad land; it is not let but given up to the poor for the purposes of cutting fuel thereon." Likewise the Tithe File of the parish suggests, for the same area, that "The western part is heathy interspersed with belts of Scotch fir and it is a poor black gravel fit for nothing." – except, presumably, the Poor! Even the most enthusiastic agricultural improvers of the day (*e.g.* Young, 1804) saw little merit in the reclamation of these unproductive sites (Burrell & Clarke, 1913) and many of these have persisted to the present day. They were undoubtedly once of much value to the parish poor – as a source of fuel, rough grazing, marsh hay, sedge and reed, the precise products and rights varying between parishes. Often the rights still exist, but twentieth-century parishioners have become increasingly reluctant to exercise them. Turf extraction was the first practice to be abandoned, except very locally. Grazing and cutting of sedge or reed continued for longer, but also dwindled. Today, few contemporary right-holders have an interest in harvesting fen products or have a couple of cows they want to graze and in consequence many of these fens have become derelict. In some sites occasional fires have helped to check scrub invasion and sometimes conservationists have resumed abandoned management regimes, often with considerable success (and effort). However, except for the small number of sites for which adequate resources are available, the areas managed are rarely as extensive as they once were; nor can continuity of management always be guaranteed.

Depending on its nature, vegetation management often has two main effects upon the composition of fen vegetation: it prevents or retards scrub invasion and the development of fen woodland and it helps to maintain the composition of low-growing herbaceous vegetation. Fen dereliction is most typically marked by a loss of low-growing species from the once-managed sward, first as monopolistic species attain dominance and then as scrub encroaches. However, neither of these processes is an axiomatic consequence of dereliction, as their occurrence or magnitude is influenced *inter alia* by the starting conditions, vegetation-type, management regime and the time-scale involved. For example, in Broadland, reedbeds, although regularly mown, show little relationship between species richness and management status (Table 4), probably because winter cropping of the dead stems has little impact on the subsequent summer biomass and light penetration into the stand (Figure 3). By contrast, sedgebeds, which are mown on a 3–5 year summer rotation, show a strong management–species richness interaction, probably because managed stands have smaller summer biomass and show much less light attenuation through the canopy than do unmanaged examples (Wheeler & Giller, 1982; Figure 3).

Table 4. Species richness and management of UK fen vegetation. Values are means (± SE) of species-richness terms: SPD: number of species in 4 m^2; PFS: number of fen species in 4 m^2; RFS: number of rare fen species in 4 m^2 (Shaw & Wheeler, 1991).

		SPD	PFS	RFS
All fens	Summer managed	23.6 ± 0.8	18.2 ± 0.5	5.3 ± 0.3
	Unmanaged	19.2 ± 0.7	15.1 ± 0.5	2.5 ± 0.4
Rich fens	Summer managed	26.7 ± 0.1	20.0 ± 0.1	5.6 ± 0.2
(pH > 5.5)	Unmanaged	19.9 ± 0.2	15.4 ± 0.3	3.0 ± 0.3
Poor fens	Summer managed	17.2 ± 0.1	13.4 ± 0.2	1.1 ± 0.1
(pH < 5.5)	Unmanaged	15.5 ± 0.1	12.2 ± 0.3	0.8 ± 0.1
Sedgebeds	Summer mown	23.3 ± 0.1	20.2 ± 0.1	9.3 ± 0.1
	Unmanaged	11.4 ± 0.1	8.3 ± 0.1	2.5 ± 0.2
Reedbeds	Winter mown	11.3 ± 0.2	9.3 ± 0.1	4.0 ± 0.1
	Unmanaged	12.8 ± 0.3	10.1 ± 0.2	4.2 ± 0.2

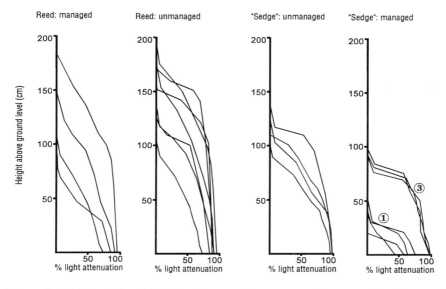

Figure 3. Light profiles (July) through vegetation canopy of unmanaged and managed stands of reed and 'sedge' in the Norfolk Broadland, as a percentage of above-canopy illumination. Managed reed was winter mown; managed sedge was summer mown on 3–5 year rotation; results relate to stands last mown 1 or 3 years previously.

It is noteworthy that, whilst some specific vegetation types, such as sedgebeds, can show a considerable difference in species-richness terms between managed and unmanaged examples, the difference is considerably less, though still significant (P < 0.05) when all types of herbaceous fen vegetation are considered together. The difference is particularly small when all examples of poor-fen vegetation are considered alone. This may reflect the intrinsically smaller number of species in low-pH fen vegetation, coupled with the generally lower fertilities of poor-fen soils (Tables 2 and 5).

There is some evidence for an interaction between vegetation management and soil fertility in relation to the species richness of fen vegetation. Comparison of examples of soligenous rich-fen stands indicated a significant (P < 0.05) negative

Table 5. Soil fertility of British fens in relation to soil pH and vegetation management (managed = summer grazed or mown). Values are mean (± S.E.) fertility estimated phytometrically (mg per plant *Phalaris arundinacea*).

Rich fens		Poor fens		All fens	
Unmanaged	Managed	Unmanaged	Managed	Unmanaged	Managed
14.8 ± 0.2	10.3 ± 0.11	9.9 ± 0.3	8.3 ± 0.2	12.9 ± 0.2	9.3 ± 0.2

relationship between species density and fertility for unmanaged stands, but no significant trend when comparing managed examples. However, the number of fen species and number of rare fen species showed a significant negative relationship with fertility in sets of both managed and unmanaged soligenous fen vegetation. (Wheeler & Shaw, 1994). One interpretation of this is that, when appropriately managed, fertile fens can be just as species rich as infertile ones, but their richness is largely a product of a greater number of common generalist species rather than fen species or, particularly, rare species. A corollary is that, in low fertility fens, species richness may be rather little influenced by management status.

Some forms of vegetation management may help to reduce soil fertility in fens through nutrient export (Bakker & Olff, this volume) though little information is available on this from British fens. The proposition is compatible with the differences recorded in Table 5, but equally the fertility and management status may both be regulated by an independent influence. For example, rich-fen sites adjoined by arable farming may be both unmanaged *and* receive increased nutrient influx compared to sites adjoined by pasture (*e.g.* Wheeler, 1983).

The importance of vegetation management in preventing scrub invasion is well known, though there are rather few studies in Britain which have carefully documented the process of replacement of herbaceous fen by fen carr (*e.g.* Godwin, Clowes & Huntley, 1975; Pigott & Wilson, 1978). In some situations scrub encroachment is slow. This is sometimes the case in dense, unmanaged tall fen vegetation (including reed and sedgebeds), where thick mattresses of litter may prevent establishment of tree seedlings, and in hydroseral sites where conditions may be too wet for substantial scrub establishment. Scrub also does not readily colonise some long-unmanaged examples of soligenous fen, pointing perhaps to some natural mechanisms for the maintenance of open conditions.

PEAT CUTTING

The effects of peat cutting upon the vegetation of fens are largely mediated through the environmental variables and vegetation processes discussed above. However, as it has had a big impact on some fen ecosystems, and is particularly germane to fen restoration, it is considered here separately.

In Britain, fen peat is dug commercially only in the Somerset Levels where some 1200 ha currently has planning consent for peat extraction. Much of this is fen ('sedge') peat dug from sites which have long been partly drained and used for agriculture. Elsewhere in Britain hand digging of fen peat has all but ceased, but was nonetheless once of great importance. Data on the occurrence, and effects, of past peat cutting in fens are still being compiled, but it seems likely that most, if not all, lowland fens have been subject to some peat removal, in some instances over much or all of the surface.

The current legacy of past peat removal depends largely upon the configuration of the workings and the drainage characteristics of the sites. Frequently excavation has generated a series of pits (sizes vary between 0.1 and > 10 ha) which have reflooded to form a hydroseral environment that has recolonised with swamp and wet fen vegetation. This process has not been universally welcomed: Vancouver (1794) comments that much of Burwell Fen (Cambridgeshire) "has been greatly injured by digging turf . . . constantly inundated . . . a most deplorable situation . . . water encourages the growth of reed and sedge . . . cut by the poor." However, today such peat pits may provide a wet fen habitat in regions from which this has otherwise largely disappeared (*e.g.* Shuckert, Poschlod & Pfadenhauer, 1992). Even within undrained fens, terrestrialising peat pits may support a distinctive vegetation and provide some of the main sites for a number of uncommon fen plants (*e.g.* Giller & Wheeler, 1986, 1988).

Recolonisation of turf ponds

The term 'turf pond' is used to refer to shallow peat pits that have reflooded and contain (or once contained) standing water. Flooded peat workings may revegetate in several ways (Figure 4). Some examples have developed a semi-floating mat of vegetation (or a loose peat infill that also has some vertical mobility). Such mats sometimes show more than 50cm vertical movement in response to water level flux and have a profound effect upon the nature and development of the recolonist vegetation, by acting as a 'hydrostat' which helps to minimise fluctuations of water level relative to the peat surface (Buell & Buell, 1941; Giller & Wheeler, 1986, 1988), thus avoiding substantial surface drying or deep inundation. Such situations are favourable for the occurrence of a number of uncommon fen plant species as well as for the establishment of some *Sphagnum* species and acidification (Giller & Wheeler, 1986, 1988; van Wirdum, this volume; Beltman *et al.*, this volume).

Semi-floating mats of vegetation may owe their buoyancy both to aerenchyma and lacunae within rhizomes and roots and, particularly, to gas bubbles (N_2 and CH_4) entrained within the raft. Raft bouyancy may show seasonal change (Hogg & Wein, 1988a,b). Rafts may form either by the centripetal invasion of open water from solid margins or by detachment and flotation of plants originally rooted in the substratum. Rather little is known about the relative importance of these two mechanisms, but the former is the only possibility where the water is too deep for emergent plants to root in the underlying peat. Reported rates of centripetal spread vary enormously (Tallis, 1973) and in some cases floating mats make little advance upon open water. Rafting by the detachment of already-rooted plants has received little detailed study, but appears to be of considerable importance, especially in situations where plants once attached to a firm peat surface are flooded (*e.g.* Björk, 1974). It appears that gas production leads to the detachment of the plants.

As turf ponds within fens are usually flooded to only a shallow depth (< 1 m), semi-floating rafts and loose-peat infills are likely to be transient: ongoing plant growth and peat accumulation leads to 'grounding' and consolidation of the rafts,

Cutting shallow flooded:
Colonisation mainly by
rooting of tall emergents

Cutting deep flooded:
Some rooting colonisation
by tall emergents plus limited
marginal rafting

Cutting wet / damp:
Rooting colonisation by
various species, including
moist grassland taxa *etc*.

Cutting initially wet / damp,
then flooded:
Some rooted plants "lift" with
rising water table to contribute
to formation of raft

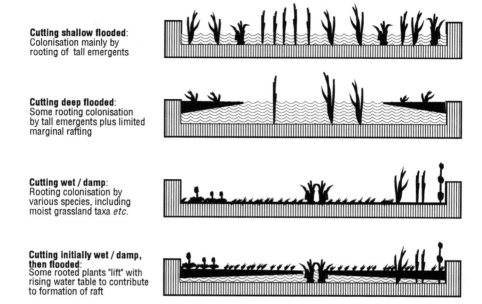

Figure 4. Recolonisation mechanisms in abandoned turbaries. For explanation, see text.

so that they may lose some of their distinctive hydrological properties and notable plant species (Giller & Wheeler, 1986).

Turf ponds occur widely. Examples from the Netherlands, and their successional processes, are described by van Wirdum (this volume) and Beltman *et al.* (this volume). In Britain, some of the most extensive and best-studied examples are located in the fens of the Norfolk Broadland (Giller & Wheeler, 1986, 1988). These were mostly excavated in the late eighteenth and early nineteenth centuries (Wells, 1989) and in some instances more than 90% of the fen surface was removed, to produce pits of varying configuration, from narrow rectangular plots to extensive (>10 ha) compartments. They support a range of vegetation-types, of hydroseral origin, and include community-types and plant species that are absent, or rare, upon the solid peat surfaces (*e.g. Dryopteris cristata, Liparis loeselii*). These species are scarce even within the turbaries, partly because they occupy a transient phase of the hydrosere. Retention and re-creation of such vegetation is likely to require rejuvenation of the hydrosere by further removal of the peat infill.

Revegetated turf ponds in Broadland show a general pattern of recolonisation that can be related to the character of the underlying substratum (Figure 5). Peat pits over estuarine clay (deposited in the 'Romano-British' marine transgressive overlap) tend to have *Phragmites australis* and *Typha angustifolia* as primary colonists, whilst in those upon continuous peat (which are higher up the river

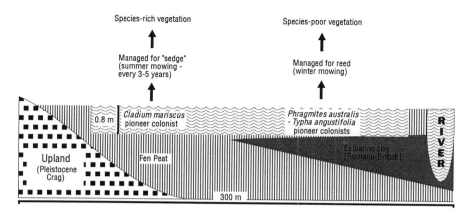

Figure 5. Schematic diagram of recolonisation of reflooded, shallow turf ponds in Broadland, Norfolk.

valleys or close to the 'upland' margins) *Cladium mariscus* is usually most important. Sometimes both seres occupy different parts of the same turf pond. The outcome of any 'restoration' by further peat digging is therefore likely to be influenced strongly by the location of the pits. The *Cladium*-sere has strong similarlities to the *Carex lasiocarpa*-sere described by van Wirdum (this volume); it contains most of the rarer plant species and is regarded as especially 'desirable'.

Attempts to restore (or create) turf ponds may be constrained by ignorance of the water regime appropriate for their desired revegetation. It is often assumed that spontaneous recolonisation of existing turf-ponds started by terrestrialisation of shallow water but, as turf-ponds were often drained whilst they were being dug, their initial revegetation may have been by plant colonisation of the peat on the wet bottoms of the cuttings followed by flotation as the pits reflooded, rather than by direct colonisation of open water. If this is correct, it may imply that the revegetation of new turf ponds could be facilitated if the fens containing them were partly drained.

Recolonisation of moist peat pits

Frequently, old peat workings in fens have not reflooded, but rather provide an uneven series of moist pits or, in some cases, a surface that has been uniformly skinned of peat. In Britain, examples of this are found in the 'valleyhead fens' of East Anglia (Figure 1). These comprise a number (>100) of mostly small (<10 ha) mires at, or close to, the headwaters of streams and rivers. They most typically occupy shallow valleys, mostly below 50 m a.s.l., with gentle, soligenous slopes irrigated by base-rich water, often derived from a chalk aquifer and supporting various fen plant communities. Stands of *Schoeno-Juncetum* (CARICION DAVALLIANAE) are characteristic and are notable as they are generally scarce in many other regions of Britain (Fojt, this volume).

Many of these sites were designated as Fuel Allotments in the Parliamentary Enclosures and at least some had been turbaries long before this (*e.g.* mediaeval turbary at Dernford Fen, Cambridgeshire). However, in many cases there is little surface indication of extensive peat removal, probably because the sites have been uniformly stripped. This makes it difficult to quantify the impact of past peat extraction, but some crude estimates can be made, at least for sites that were Fuel Allotments. At Inclosure, eligible households frequently had rights to extract up to 4000–5000 turves each year from the Fuel Allotments, with up to 8000 turves in some parishes (the size of a 'turf' varied between parishes, but dimensions of 4 x 4 x 12 inches ($\cong$ 3 litres) were frequent). On a (conservative) assumption of 20 right-holders each removing 3000 turves every year, the equivalent of 1 m depth of peat would be removed from 1 ha of fen every 50 years. As the sites are generally small, given such rates it is not surprising that even at Inclosure some had largely been stripped of their peat (*e.g.* Wendling Fuel Allotment: "Turf has been cut without restriction and is now almost exhausted" *Report of Charities Commissioners,* 1838), nor that their present peat depth is negligible.

The pre-turbary condition of these soligenous fens cannot be determined, but the suggested rate of domestic peat extraction implies either that they once had a very limited life as a fuel-peat resource, or that they had much deeper peat than they do today. It is possible that the CARICION DAVALLIANAE communities that currently occupy some of these sites may sometimes be a product of the skeletal substrata and strong springs exposed by peat removal.

These various examples of the effects of peat extraction upon lowland fens exemplify (a) the paucity of good information concerning the former character of some of the most important remaining British fen sites; (b) that many, probably most, sites have had a long and complex history of human management and manipulation and this is partly the cause of their present conservational interest; and (c) that many sites have shown remarkable powers for self-restoration after considerable damage. Such observations should not be taken as a mandate for on-going damage or *laissez-faire* with regard to vegetation management, but they do suggest that, on occasion, drastic operations may be needed to produce desired restoration results. They also provide some re-assurance that, should this prove to be necessary, such operations will by no means constitute unprecedented human intervention within a 'natural wilderness'.

REFERENCES

Aletsee, L. (1967). Begriffliche und floristiche Grundlagen zu einer pflanzen-geographischen Analyse der europäischen Regenwassermoorstandorte. *Beih. Biol. Pflanzen.*, **43**, 117–160.

Balátová-Tuláčková, E. (1968). Grundwasserganglinien und Wissengesellschaften. *Acta Scientiarum Naturalium Academiae Scientiarum Bohemoslovacae Brno*, **2**, 1–37.

Bakker, J.P. (1989). *Nature Management by Grazing and Cutting.* Geobotany 14. Kluwer Academic Publishers, Dordrecht.

Bird, R. (1909). The rural economy, sport and natural history of East Ruston Common. *Transactions of the Norfolk & Norwich Naturalists Society*, **8**, 631–666.

Björk, S. (1974). The conservation of degraded wetlands. *Proceedings of the International Conference on the Conservation of Wetlands and Waterfowl* (ed. M. Smart), pp. 349–354. International Waterfowl Research Bureau, Slimbridge.

Boller-Elmer, K.C. (1977). Stickstoff-Düngungseinflüsse von Intensiv-Grünland auf Streu- und Moorwiesen. *Veröffentilichungen des Geobotanisches Institues der ETH/Stiftung Rübel/Zürich*, **63**, 1–103.

Braendle, R. & Crawford, R.M.M. (1987). Rhizome anoxia tolerance and habitat specialization in wetland plants. *Plant Life in Aquatic and Amphibious Habitats.* (ed. R.M.M. Crawford), pp. 397–410. Blackwell Scientific Publications, Oxford.

Buell, M.F. & Buell, H.F. (1941). Surface water level fluctuation in Cedar Creek Bog, Minnesota. *Ecology*, **22**, 317–321.

Burrell, W.H. & Clarke, W.G. (1913). Topographical notes on some rarer Norfolk plants. *Transactions of the Norfolk & Norwich Naturalists Society*, **9**, 622–632.

Clymo, R.S. (1962). An experimental approach to part of the calcicole problem. *Journal of Ecology*, **50**, 707–731.

Conway, V.M. (1938a). Studies in the autecology of *Cladium mariscus* R.Br. IV. Growth rates of the leaves. *New Phytologist*, **37**, 254–278.

Conway, V.M. (1938b). Studies in the autecology of *Cladium mariscus* R.Br. V. The distribution of the species. *New Phytologist*, **37**, 312–328.

Du Rietz, G.E. (1949). Huvudenheter och granser i Svensk Myrvegetation. *Svensk Botanisk Tidskrift*, **43**, 299–309.

Ellenberg, H. (1954). Über einige Fortschritte der kausalen Vegetationskunde. *Vegetatio*, **5–6**, 199–211.

Fojt, W.J. (1994). Dehydration and the threat to East Anglian fens, England. *Biological Conservation*, **69**, 163–175.

Forrest, G. I., Smith, R.A.H. (1975). The productivity of a range of blanket bog vegetation types in the northern Pennines. *Journal of Ecology*, **63**, 173–202.

Giller, K.E. & Wheeler, B.D. (1986). Past peat cutting and present vegetation patterns in an undrained fen in the Norfolk Broadland. *Journal of Ecology*, **74**, 219–244.

Giller, K.E. & Wheeler, B.D. (1988). Acidification and succession in a flood-plain mire in the Norfolk Broadland, UK. *Journal of Ecology*, **76**, 849–866.

Godwin, H., Clowes, D.R. & Huntley, B. (1974). Studies in the ecology of Wicken Fen. V. Development of fen carr. *Journal of Ecology*, **62**, 197–214

Gorham, E. (1950). Variation in some chemical conditions along the borders of a *Carex lasiocarpa* fen community. *Oikos*, **2**, 217–240.

Grootjans, A.P., Schipper, P.C. & van der Windt, H.J. (1986). Influence of drainage on N-mineralisation and vegetation response in wet meadows. *Oecologia Plantarum*, **7**, 3–14.

Grootjans, A.P. & Ten Klooster, W.P. (1980). Changes of ground water regime in wet meadows. *Acta Botanica Neerlandica*, **29**, 541–554.

Harding, M. (1993). Redgrave and Lopham Fens, East Anglia, England: a case study of change in flora and fauna due to groundwater abstraction. *Biological Conservation*, **66**, 35–45

Hogg, E.H. & Wein, R.W. (1988a). The contribution of *Typha* components to floating mat buoyancy. *Ecology*, **69**, 1025–1031.

Hogg, E.H. & Wein, R.W. (1988b). Seasonal change in gas content and buoyancy of floating *Typha* mats. *Journal of Ecology*, **76**, 1055–1068.

Jeglum, J.K. (1971). Plant indicators of pH and water level in peatlands at Candle Lake, Saskatchewan. *Canadian Journal of Botany*, **49**, 1661–1676.

Jefferies, R.L. & Willis, A.J. (1964). Studies on the calcicole-calcifuge habit. II. The influence of calcium on the growth and establishment of four species in soil and sand culture. *Journal of Ecology*, **52**, 691–707.

Jennings, J.N. (1952). *The Origin of the Broads.* Research Series No. 2. Royal Geographical Society, London.

Kooijman, A.M. (1992). The decrease of rich fen bryophytes in the Netherlands. *Biological Conservation*, **59**, 139–143.

Lambert, J.M. (1951). Alluvial stratigraphy and vegetation succession in the region of the Bure Valley broads. III. Classification, status and distribution of communities. *Journal of Ecology*, **39**, 149–170.

Lambert, J.M. & Jennings, J.N. (1951). Alluvial stratigraphy and vegetation succession in the region of the Bure Valley broads. II. Detailed vegetational–stratigraphical relationships. *Journal of Ecology*, **39**, 120–148.

Malmer, N. (1962a). Studies on mire vegetation in the Archaean area of southwestern Götaland (South Sweden). I. Vegetation and habitat conditions on the Åkhult mire. *Opera Botanica*, **7(1)**, 1–322.

Malmer, N. (1962b). Studies on mire vegetation in the Archaean area of southwestern Götaland (South Sweden). II. Distribution and seasonal variation in elementary constituents on some mire sites. *Opera Botanica,* **7(2)**, 1–67.

Malmer, N. (1986). Vegetation gradients in relation to environmental conditions in northwestern European mires. *Canadian Journal of Botany*, **64**, 375–383.

Müller, K. (1976) Zur frage der 'Mineralbodenwasserzeiger' auf ombrogenen Moor-komplexen. *Beiträge zur Biologie der Pflanzen.*, **52**, 311–318.

Niemann, E. (1973). Grundwasser und Vegetationsgefüge. *Nova Acta Leopold*, **6**, 1–147.

Pearsall, W.H. (1918). The aquatic and marsh vegetation of Esthwaite Water. *Journal of Ecology*, **5**, 53–74.

Pietsch, W. (1976). Vegetationsentwicklung und wasserchemische Faktoren in Moor-gewässern verschiedener Naturschutzgebiete der DDR. *Archiv für Naturschutz und Landschaftforschung*, **16**, 1–43.

Pigott, C.D. & Wilson, J.F. (1978). The vegetation of North Fen at Esthwaite in 1967–9. *Proceedings of the Royal Society of London*, A, **200**, 331–351.

Ratcliffe, D.A. (1977). *A Nature Conservation Review.* Cambridge University Press, Cambridge.

Rose, F. (1957). The importance of study of disjunct distributions to progress in understanding the British flora. *Progress in the Study of the British Flora,* (ed. J.E. Lousley), pp. 61–78. Botanical Society of the British Isles, London.

Schat, H. (1984). A comparative ecophysiological study on the effects of waterlogging and submergence on dune slack plants: growth, survival and mineral nutrition in sand culture experiments. *Oecologia (Berlin)*, **62**, 279–286.

Sellars, B. (1991). *The response and tolerance of wetland plants to sulphide.* PhD thesis, University of Sheffield.

Shaw, S.C. & Wheeler, B.D. (1990). *Comparative Survey of Habitat Conditions and Management Characteristics of Herbaceous Poor-Fen Vegetation Types.* Survey Report 129, Nature Conservancy Council, Peterborough.

Shaw, S.C. & Wheeler, B.D. (1991). *A review of the habitat conditions and management characteristics of herbaceous fen vegetation types in lowland Britain.* Nature

Conservancy Council, Peterborough.

Shuckert, U., Poschlod, P. & Pfadenhauer, J. (1992). Torfstich im Niedermoor – ein Beitrag zum Arten- und Biotopschutz ? *Telma*, **22**, 253–265.

Sjörs, H. (1950). On the relation between vegetation and electrolytes in north Swedish mire waters. *Oikos*, **2**, 241–258.

Smith, A.J.E. (1978). *The Moss Flora of Britain and Ireland.* Cambridge University Press, Cambridge.

Snowden, R.E.D. & Wheeler, B.D. (1993). Iron toxicity to fen plants. *Journal of Ecology*, **81**, 35–46.

Sparling, J.H. (1967). The occurrence of *Schoenus nigricans* L. in blanket bogs. II. Experiments on the growth of *Schoenus nigricans* under controlled conditions. *Journal of Ecology*, **55**, 15–31.

Spence, D.H.N. (1964). The macrophytic vegetation of freshwater lochs, swamps and associated fens. *The Vegetation of Scotland* (ed. J.H. Burnett), pp. 306–425. Oliver & Boyd, Edinburgh.

Stace, C. (1991). *New Flora of the British Isles.* Cambridge University Press, Cambridge.

Succow, M. & Jeschke, L. (1986). *Moore in der Landschaft.* Urania Verlag, Leipzig.

Tallis, J.H. (1973). The terrestrialization of lake basins in north Cheshire, with special reference to the development of a 'schwingmoor' structure. *Journal of Ecology*, **61**, 537–567.

Tansley, A.G. (1939). *The British Islands and their Vegetation.* Cambridge University Press, Cambridge.

Ter Braak, C.J.F. (1987). The analysis of vegetation-environment relationships by canonical correspondence analysis. *Vegetatio*, **69**, 69–77.

Vancouver, C. (1794). *General View of the Agriculture of the County of Cambridge.* Board of Agriculture, London.

van Diggelen, R., Grootjans, A.P., Wierda, A., Berkunk, P. & Hoogendoorn, J. (1991). Prediction of vegetation changes under different hydrological scenarios. *Hydrological Basis of Ecologically Sound Management of Soil and Groundwater*, pp. 71–80. IAHS Publication No 202.

Verkamp, M.T., Corré, W.J., Atwell, B.J. & Kuiper, P.J.C. (1980). Growth rate and phosphate utilisation of some *Carex* species from a range of oligotrophic to eutrophic swamp habitats. *Physiologia Plantarum*, **50**, 237–240.

Verhoeven, J. T. A., van Beek, S., Dekker, M. & Storm, W. (1983). Nutrient dynamics in small mesotrophic fens surrounded by cultivated land. I. Productivity and nutrient uptake by the vegetation in relation to the flow of eutrophicated ground water. *Oecologia (Berlin)*, **60**, 25–33.

Verhoeven, J. T. A., Koerselmann, W. & Beltman, B. (1988). The vegetation of fens in relation to their hydrology and nutrient dynamics; a case study. *Handbook of Vegetation Science*. Vol 15. *Vegetation of Inland Waters* (ed J.J. Symoens), pp. 249–282. Kluwer Academic Publishers, Dordrecht.

Vermeer, J. G. & Berendse, F. (1983). The relationship between nutrient availability, shoot biomass and species richness in grassland and wetland communities. *Vegetatio*, **53**, 121–126.

Von Post, L. (1925). Gotlands-agen (*Cladium mariscus* R.Br.) i Sveriges postarktikum. *Ymer*, **45**, 295.

Walker, D. (1970). Direction and rate in some British post-glacial hydroseres. *Studies in the Vegational History of the British Isles* (eds. D. Walker & R.G. West), pp. 117–139. Cambridge University Press, London.

Wassen, M.J., Barendregt, A., Palczynski, A., de Smidt, J.T. & de Mars, H. (1990). The relationship between fen vegetation gradients, groundwater flow and flooding in an undrained valley mire at Biebrza, Poland. *Journal of Ecology*, **78**, 1106–1122.

Wells, C.E. (1989). *Historical and palaeoecological investigations of some Norfolk Broadland flood-plain mires and post-medieval turf-cutting.* PhD thesis, University of Sheffield.

Wheeler, B.D. (1983). *Turf Ponds in Broadland.* Broads Authority, Norwich.

Wheeler, B.D. (1984). British Fens. *European Mires* (ed. P.D. Moore), pp.237–281. Academic Press, London.

Wheeler, B.D. (1988). Species richness, species rarity and conservation evaluation of rich-fen vegetation in lowland England and Wales. *Journal of Applied Ecology*, **25**, 331–353.

Wheeler, B.D. (1993). Botanical diversity in British mires. *Biodiversity and Conservation*, **2**, 490–512.

Wheeler, B.D., Al-Farraj, M.M. & Cook, R.E.D. (1985). Iron toxicity to plants in base-rich wetlands: comparative effects on the distribution and growth of *Epilobium hirsutum* L. and *Juncus subnodulosus* Schrank. *New Phytologist*, **100**, 653–669.

Wheeler, B.D., Brookes, B.A. & Smith, R.A.H. (1983). An ecological study of *Schoenus ferrugineus* L. in Scotland. *Watsonia*, **14**, 249–256.

Wheeler, B.D. & Giller, K.E. (1982). Species richness of herbaceous fen vegetation in Broadland, Norfolk in relation to the quantity of above-ground plant material. *Journal of Ecology*, **70**, 179–200.

Wheeler, B.D. & Shaw, S.C. (1987). *Comparative Survey of Habitat Conditions and Management Characteristics of Herbaceous Rich-fen Vegetation Types.* Contract Survey 6, Nature Conservancy Council, Peterborough.

Wheeler, B. D. & Shaw, S. C. (1991). Above-ground crop mass and species-richness of the principal types of herbaceous rich-fen vegetation of lowland England and Wales. *Journal of Ecology*, **79**, 285–301.

Wheeler, B.D. & Shaw, S.C. (1994). Conservation of fen vegetation in sub-optimal conditions. *Conservation and Management of Fens* (eds. H. Jankowska-Huflejt & E. Golubiewska), pp. 255–265. International Peat Society and Institute for Land Reclamation and Grassland Farming, Falenty.

Wheeler, B.D. & Shaw, S.C. (in press). Plants as Hydrologists? An assessment of the value of plants as indicators of water conditions in fens. *Hydrology and Hydrochemistry of Wetlands* (eds J. Hughes & L. Heathwaite). John Wiley, Chichester.

Wheeler, B.D., Shaw, S.C. & Cook, R.E.D. (1991). Phytometric assessment of the fertility of undrained rich-fen soils. *Journal of Applied Ecology*, **29**, 466–475.

Young, A. (1804). *General View of the Agriculture of the County of Norfolk.* Board of Agriculture, London.

Zwillenberg, L.O. & De Wit, R.J. (1951). Observations sur le *Rosmarineto-Lithospermetum schoenetosum* du Bas-Languedoc. *Acta Botanica Neerlandica*, **1**, 310–323.

5 Assessing the Restoration Prospects of Degraded Fens

A. GROOTJANS & R. VAN DIGGELEN

Department of Plant Ecology, University of Groningen, P.O. Box 14, 9750 AA Haren, The Netherlands

SUMMARY

1.   In fen restoration it would be practical to distinguish between a fen, being the vegetation and its ecological requirements and a fen system, being that part of a landscape system that keeps the fen in a steady state. Restoration should be aimed at restoring the fen system, not at 'restoring' fen species.

2.   Harvesting the productivity or even sod cutting has become an integrated aspect of the fen system.

3.   The occurrence of rare fen species is practically always associated with the presence of very specific hydrological conditions. The best chances for restoration of fen systems in the immediate future lies in using the least affected ones. The restoration of fens is doomed to fail in the long run, without an ecologically sound water management based on the restoration of hydrological cycles.

INTRODUCTION

In NW European countries there is an increasing public demand to restore fens following their damage on an unprecedented scale by drainage, pollution or both. This demand is based mainly on the notion that we should try to preserve endangered species for later generations and it is generally believed that fens are suitable sites to preserve a large number of such species. Originally 'fens' meant minerotrophic, peat-forming mires that received a water supply from the mineral soil (Sjörs, 1950). Such fens are still present in, for instance, Scandinavia, and the vegetation mainly consists of specialised mosses and sedges (Dierssen, 1982). However, few people are familiar with such vegetation types – the general public and politicians are generally shown species-rich meadows or reedbeds, which have been used by farmers for centuries and represent a successional stage after the original mires have been drained. These vegetation types are not restricted to former mires and can also occur on mineral soils influenced by base-rich groundwater. Wheeler (1988), therefore, suggested that (rich) fens should be

Restoration of Temperate Wetlands. Edited by B.D. Wheeler, S.C. Shaw, W.J. Fojt and R.A. Robertson
© 1995 John Wiley & Sons Ltd.

regarded as wetland sites with a characteristic vegetation, irrigated by base-rich water (pH range 5.5–8.0) and with organic or mineral soils. So fens are sites with hydrological and ecological characteristics but are recognised by their species composition. Fens described by Wheeler include a wide range of vegetation types to which almost every endangered wetland species can be assigned. For practical reasons we would like to make a distinction between a fen, being the vegetation and its ecological requirements and the fen (landscape)system, being that part of a landscape system that keeps the fen in a steady state (see also van Wirdum, 1993). The fen system can be defined by geo-hydrological characteristics on various scales. If we regard fens as sites to be recognised by their species composition, this raises the problem of which vegetation types we accept as a fen vegetation. Of course this is an arbitrary matter. We can only indicate the range of vegetation types that are widely accepted as occurring in fens. They include plant communities belonging to the alliances CARICION DAVALLIANAE, CARICION CURTO-NIGRAE, RHYNCHOSPORION ALBAE, JUNCO-MOLINION, EU-MOLINION and some also include spring fed communities (CARDAMINO-MONTION). In a specific site, these vegetation types are practically always accompanied by other types which are not characteristic of fens, because fens are usually very heterogeneous. This implies that we can only discuss fens if the vegetation is clearly specified.

The present paper will focus on how fens are supplied with (ground)water and how this may satisfy the ecological requirements of the fen vegetation. Only fens and fen meadows with low productivity vegetation (less than 400 g m^{-2}; Klapp, 1965) will be discussed as they harbour most of the endangered wetland species.

Literature on recent attempts to restore damaged fens is very scarce (see also Klötzli, 1991). This paper therefore deals with approaches to assess possibilities for fen restoration instead of presenting an overview of successful projects. In this approach, the fen ecosystem is seen as a patient and the ecologist as a doctor who must diagnose the illness and is expected to cure the patient to a stage where the fen system is able to support species that have become endangered. It does not suffice to answer traditional ecological questions as to how ecosystems respond to hydrological changes or how species are adapted to the environment. The restoration ecologist is expected to produce viable populations of endangered species. Since a common feature of all fens is that the abiotic conditions within the ecosystem are governed by the hydrological features of the surrounding landscape, the most important question is which sites still have suitable growing conditions for endangered fen species, given the present hydrological conditions.

CHARACTERISTICS OF THE FEN SYSTEM

We know a great deal about the ecological requirements of low-productivity fen vegetation (Wassen, 1990; Koerselman & Verhoeven, 1992; Wheeler & Shaw, this volume). The fen must be saturated with base-rich water for most of the season, each fen type has a limited pH range and the availability of nutrients must be low at all times. Much less is known about the mechanisms that are responsible for this low nutrient availability. Many mechanisms have been suggested, such as reduced nitrogen mineralisation (Yerly, 1970), phosphorus fixation by calcium or by iron (III) hydroxides (Patrick & Khalid, 1974; see also Verhoeven, Kemmers & Koerselman, 1993) or loss of potassium by mowing (Egloff, 1983; Kapfer, 1987; Koerselman & Verhoeven, 1992). Which nutrient is limiting the productivity of a fen depends on the type of fen, and it may alter by mowing, atmospheric contamination, changes in water level or by changes in the groundwater composition. Fens generally become more eutrophic and lose their characteristic species through increased flooding, cessation of mowing (Koerselman & Verhoeven, 1992), or by an increase of polluted surface water input. In agricultural science it is generally believed that drainage of mires will also lead to increased productivity. This is not always correct. Russian scientists have done extensive research into this problem and found that drained fens had a lower productivity then undrained (virgin mires) ones (Platonov, 1967; see Schipper & Grootjans, 1986 for more references). Eutrophication may occur after a severe loss of soil structure (Okruszko, 1977) leading to excessive aeration of the topsoil ('muck forming'). Under such conditions base-rich groundwater can no longer reach the topsoil, resulting in a low calcium saturation, desorption of phosphorus and raised levels of P in the soil solution (Kemmers & Jansen, 1988). Drainage in unfertilised fen meadows also leads to a lower productivity (Grootjans, Schipper & van der Windt, 1986). This is in contrast to species-rich hay meadows that have previously been fertilised (Grootjans, Schipper & van der Windt, 1985).

Our knowledge of the hydrological conditions that keep fen vegetation in a steady state is modest. We know from palynological research that calciphilous fen vegetation can exist for centuries. Succow (1988), working in the large stream valleys of Eastern Germany, stresses the importance of groundwater flowing through the peat itself. This is only possible if the peat is extremely permeable and the top layer floats on the mire surface similar to the acrotelm in bogs (see Ingram, 1983; Dembek, 1992). A fen vegetation on mineral soil may also remain present in a pioneer stage for decades. In some dynamic spring mires (Pietsch, 1984), for instance, where tufa is formed, accumulation of organic matter is prevented by rapid mineralisation, followed by removal of nutrient from the fen sites by water flow. New springs can be formed when older ones are blocked by the continuous tufa accumulation, creating new opportunities for pioneer fen species. Similar fen vegetation may persist for 10–80 years under natural conditions in sand-blown dune valleys in local seepage areas (Lammerts et al., in press). Considering the increasing loads of atmospheric deposition in the central European lowlands, it is unlikely that the vast majority of fens, as we know them today, can survive without a mowing regime, even if the hydrological conditions are optimal (see also Wassen, 1990). So harvesting the productivity or even completely removing the entire organic layer is, or has become, an integrated aspect of the fen system.

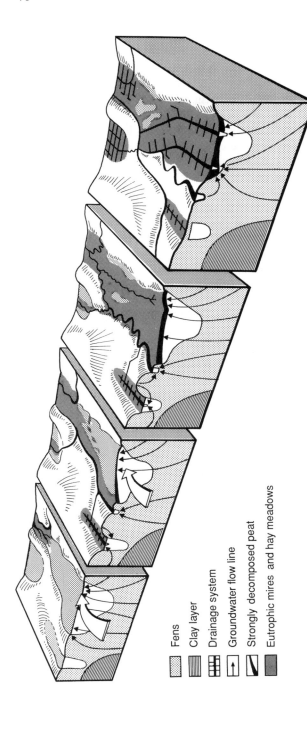

Figure 1. Hypothetical fen system development under the influences of human activities in a fen valley during many centuries. The undisturbed low productivity (mesotrophic) fens were probably permanently fed with groundwater, which did not flood the vegetation but could have moved slowly through the loosely packed top layers or through open water. This hydrological system collapsed when ditches were dug in the landscape, leading to increased flooding and silt deposition. The mire surface followed the drawdown of the groundwater level and the peat was compressed to a stage that it could no longer transport groundwater through the peat. Erosion of the fens proceeded and fens were connected by new streams. Loss of soil structure by drainage improved the nutrient availability. In this stage most fen valleys were used by farmers for hay making. The productivity remained low until the introduction of fertilisers, which promoted deep drainage of practically all fen meadows. Most streams were replaced by drainage channels and fen vegetation remained only in hydrologically isolated areas at the valley flanks or in former stream beds.

Fens

Clay layer

Drainage system

Groundwater flow line

Strongly decomposed peat

Eutrophic mires and hay meadows

FEN SYSTEM DEVELOPMENT

Fen systems supporting peat-forming fen vegetation have become rare in the central European lowlands. Due to interferences with the hydrology the larger (regional) hydrological systems supporting the former extensive fens in stream valleys have been split up into numerous smaller hydrological systems (Wassen, 1990). Practically all existing fen systems in the lowlands are man made. In the Netherlands, for instance, peat reclamation has existed for at least ten centuries (Borger, 1992). The least affected fen systems are probably the smaller stream valleys situated in the Pleistocene plateaux. But, although stream valleys may be rich in fen species, the peat-forming fen vegetation was lost long ago as the fens changed into fen meadows by drainage and after fertilisation into hay meadows. In many parts of Europe this fertilisation of stream valleys was achieved by artificial flooding, leading to silt deposition, shrinkage and subsidence of the peat and eventually to a better nutrient availability (Krause, 1959; Burny, 1986). Figure 1 shows a possible development of an hypothetical stream valley system with fens and bog in a NW European lowland area. The figure illustrates that the present nature reserves with fen species may be situated in disconnected streams, which were once dug by mediaeval man to drain more original fens, which could have expanded after their grandparents had cut the forests in the surroundings (Rybnícek & Rybníckovà, 1974) or, for instance, installed a water mill in a mire outlet (Schwaar, 1980). This example shows that, with historical changes in land use, the fen systems have also changed enormously and that fens encountered nowadays are very different from those found in the peat deposits and now occur in different parts of the landscape.

FEN DEVELOPMENT

Figure 2 illustrates the possible change in fen vegetation as the original fen systems were modified by man. This model is not based on firm evidence, but a reflection of views presented in phytosociological literature as, for instance, in Ellenberg (1978). The vegetation development in two types of fen systems is shown, both originating from more natural fen systems.

Within the mire system, lowering of the drainage base in the surroundings (for example by a drawdown in downstream lake levels) causes increased outflow of groundwater. A mire system may respond to this by shrinkage and compression of the peat. If the inflow of groundwater is not severely affected the mire remains wet. But in the course of time the character of the fen vegetation changes. New plant communities arise, some consisting mainly of calciphilous fen species but, with increased infiltration of precipitation water, acidophilous species move in or expand. The increased resistance to water flow in the peat body will lead to erosion and spring mire species can establish populations (Pfadenhauer & Kaule, 1971; Wolejko et al., in press). This erosion also triggers flooding in downstream

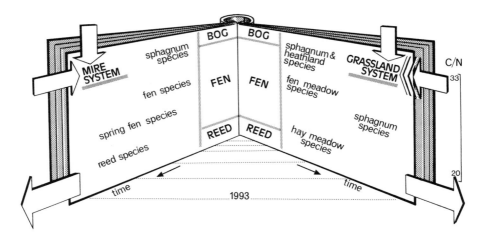

Figure 2. Model of vegetation development in a mire- and a grassland-system during the fen system development described in Figure 1. Both the mire system and the grassland system originate from natural peat-forming low-productive fens. The mire system remains wet, by a continuous inflow of groundwater, but suffers from a lowering of the drainage base in the surroundings. The grassland system is also drained internally and has a reduced input of groundwater. The model shows the spread of species from various ecosystems into the original fen vegetation. In the mire system, *Sphagnum* species may expand in the beginning, due to increased influence of precipitation water, but more often shrinkage of the mire and erosion by streams lead to eutrophic reeds or even to the spread of spring fen species. The grassland system is extremely rich in species at modest drainage intensities. Both acidophilous and calciphilous fen meadow species may expand. In a later stage, when deep drainage is applied, the calciphilous species disappear and the acidophilous species remain as long as the fen meadows are flooded.

areas. Both processes decrease the C:N ratio of the peat and also several constraints on phosphorus availability are lifted. After several decades the mesotrophic fen has become eutrophic or it has become a bog.

In the grassland systems created by farmers, first by mowing and digging shallow ditches, later by deep drainage and fertilisation, other vegetation types emerged. Many authors now regard, for instance, the species-rich small sedge communities belonging to the calciphilous alliance CARICION DAVALLIANAE as typical fens (Wheeler, 1988; Wassen, 1990; Boeye, 1992).

It seems likely that shallow drainage of rich fens stimulated the spread of calciphilous fen species such as *Epipactis palustris*[1], *Dactylorhiza incarnata*, *Liparis loeselii*, *Schoenus nigricans*, and *Parnassia palustris* (see Succow, 1970). Shallow ditches of some decimetres deep tend to diminish the influence of acid precipitation water. Slight drainage removes the precipitation water from the

---

[1] Nomenclature of plant species follows van der Meijden *et al.* (1983).

uppermost soil layers and, if sufficient seepage intensity is present, promotes the upward movement of base-rich groundwater (see also Beltman *et al.*, this volume). Even under atlantic conditions, extremely calcareous conditions may occur in the top soil due to evapotranspiration in the summer (Wind, 1986). In fact, most endangered calciphilous fen species are most abundant in fens that are no longer peat forming and are developing towards fen meadow communities, or they occur in pioneer communities on mineral soils that precede true fen communities (*e.g.* calcareous dune slacks, marine flood plains; Lammerts *et al.*, 1992). Deep drainage in a grassland system stimulates acidification of the topsoil, due to the formation of precipitation lenses – this is why *Sphagnum* species and *Eriophorum angustifolium* have spread in almost all Dutch unfertilised fen meadows (Grootjans *et al.*, 1986). The loss of soil structure will eventually lead to a low productivity grassland community with no fen species (Bakker, 1989).

FEN RESTORATION AND HYDROLOGICAL SYSTEMS

From palaeoecological research we know that low productivity fen vegetation can develop from calciphilous *Betula* forests (Schwaar, 1980), from *Phragmites* reedbeds, tall sedges and from *Cladium* sedge-beds (Succow, 1988; Jasnowka & Jasnowski, 1991). Most of these changes were related to changes in the climate, deforestation by man or changes in (lake) water levels for agricultural purposes. We know very little about the hydrological systems and the time spans involved in the transformation of eutrophic mires into more mesotrophic ones. Walker (1970) showed that even in fens little-disturbed by man, specific predictions about future fen development can only be made in terms of probability of occurrence, because numerous alternative succession pathways are possible (see also Tallis, 1983) depending on the local hydrological conditions.

What has been published under the name of fen restoration is usually a description of fen development, often without a description of the hydrological system involved. From such sources we know that it is possible to develop fen species in bogs after (deep) peat mining (van Leeuwen, 1964; Gremer & Poschlod, 1991), after peat dredging in drowned bogs (van Wirdum, 1992) or after peat cutting in stream valleys (Succow, 1971).

Several cases have been described of successful regeneration of fen species in small hydrological systems on mineral ground. Jansen & Maas (1993) described the reappearance of calciphilous fen species in small depressions in a heathland after sod cutting and hydrological measures. In these depressions the calcareous groundwater from deeper layers only reached the surface at the borders of the pond during the winter period (Figure 3). Hydrological measures to increase the water level in the surrounding areas stimulated this temporary discharge of calcareous groundwater. Additional sod cutting created new opportunities for low productivity fen species.

A similar case was presented by Stuyfzand *et al.* (1992) in a dune area on the

Wadden Sea island of Schiermonnikoog. Hydrological research showed that an observed acidification of a dune slack, which 30 years ago had abundant calci-philous fen species (Grootjans *et al.*, 1991), was caused by abstraction of groundwater by a nearby well field, by afforestation and by drainage activities in the surrounding area. The combined effects of these influences caused the water table to drop some 10–20 cm, which in turn decreased the duration of flooding by 1–2 months. The valley had one small seepage zone, which was only active in late winter and early spring, when the valley was flooded and water tables in the hinterland were high. The recent interferences with the hydrology had diminished the inflow of base-rich groundwater and increased the build-up of organic matter, leading to the disappearance of calciphilous pioneer species, such as *Schoenus nigricans*, *Epipactis palustris* and *Dactylorhiza incarnata*. Measures are now being prepared to remove part of the groundwater abstraction facilities and block the drainage channels during the winter. Sod cutting will be applied next in those parts of the dune slack that still receive base-rich groundwater. Sod cutting to restore calciphilous fen species in dune valleys is at present effective for a period of 5–15 years (Lammerts *et al.*, in press). In the beginning of this century, sand blowing and very active hydrological systems kept calciphilous dune fens in a pioneer stage at least twice that long (one record of over 80 years).

Boeye (1992) presented a case of fen development within a former heathland under the influence of up-welling, base-rich surface water from an irrigation canal. A well-developed fen vegetation with *Carex dioica*, *Eriophorum latifolium* and *Eleocharis quinqueflora* was present at discharge sites. An interesting phenomenon was that the surface water from the irrigation canal was relatively rich in nutrients, which disappeared from the groundwater during its stay in the aquifer. This was not an attempt to regenerate a fen, but just a coincidence, where a local hydrological system had been created by man which supplied nutrient-poor base-rich groundwater to the fen.

Attempts to regenerate drained fen systems with organic soils have been reported by van Diggelen *et al.* (1991) and Grootjans *et al.* (1992). The mires concerned are very complex systems in the outflows of a terminal moraine area in eastern Germany (Figure 4). Stratigraphic boring revealed that the mires started as lakes some 13,000 years ago, became kettle hole mires and then calciphilous fens (which produced layers of brown moss peat up to 2 m thick). In hydrologically isolated parts of the mires acidophilous bog vegetation developed. Attempts to drain the mires were carried out around 1870. This resulted in expansion of woodland communities along the edges and also expansion of a pine bog (*Ledo-Pinetum*) at the cost of the fen vegetation. Most of the fen now consists of fen species such as *Carex diandra*, *C. appropinquata*, *C. lasiocarpa*, fen meadow species such as *Molinia caerulea* and shrubs (*Salix repens*, *Betula* spp.). *Scorpidium scorpioides*, *Eleocharis quinqueflora* and *Liparis loeselii* are only present in hollow-like structures, created or enlarged by wild pigs. The most interesting phenomenon is that most of the central part remained almost treeless and stayed in the oligo/mesotrophic range for almost 100 years after the drainage

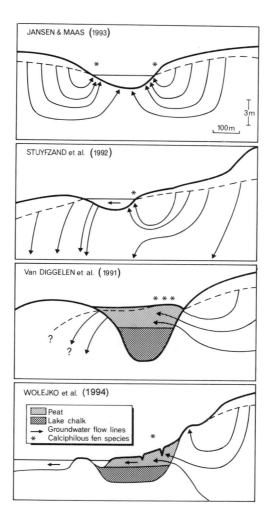

Figure 3. Pattern of flow lines in fen systems studied by various authors to assess the possibilities of restoring fen vegetation.

attempts. An explanation could be that the mire had responded by shrinkage causing a considerable lowering of its surface. This prevented desiccation and the fen vegetation remained supplied with calcium-rich groundwater. The productivity of fen also remained low, and does not appear to have changed during the last 20 years (Succow, *personal communication*) despite the sharp rise in atmospheric deposition of nitrogen (up to 40 kg N ha^{-1} yr^{-1}). This points to factors other than nitrogen limiting the productivity of the fen (see also Egloff, 1983).

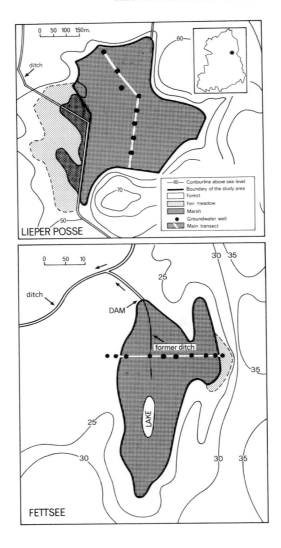

Figure 4. Location of the fen complexes 'Lieper Posse' and 'Fettsee' in eastern Germany (modified from: van Diggelen *et al.*, 1991).

Hydrological research (van Diggelen *et al.*, 1991) revealed, however, that very little discharge of groundwater remained and was restricted mainly to a shallow top layer. In deeper layers, calcium-poor water was predominant, even in the central parts of the mire. The hydrological system of the pine bog (Figure 5), providing local infiltration water, had apparently become more important than the previous subregional hydrological system providing calcareous groundwater from the moraine area. Attempts to rewet the mire by erecting a dam in the drainage ditch failed because of the extremely dry years with annual precipitation of less than 400 mm during three successive years.

A very similar mire was rewetted successfully some 5 years ago. An elevation of the water table by *c.* 30 cm led to flooding of those parts previously influenced by a drainage ditch. Undrained areas, with peat and organic lake deposits over 8 m deep, had maintained the ability to swell and rise with the water table. The acidophilous fen vegetation (*Sphagno-Betuletum*) around the small lake expanded, in contrast to the basidophilous (rich-)fen vegetation, where most of the low productivity fen species disappeared. Large tussock-forming sedges such as *Carex elata* and *C. appropinquata* responded vigorously and aquatic plants, such as *Chara* spp. and *Utricularia* spp. spread. Hydrological research (Grootjans *et al.*, 1992) showed that the fen system was still fed by calcareous groundwater, but that much of the surface water originated from precipitation (Figure 5). The pH in the top layer remained well over 6, so acidification has not yet taken place. The results of rewetting here indicate that it is essential not to flood the mire permanently, but to keep the water close to the surface to prevent release of nutrients.

These observations suggest that a slight drainage of a fen system may not affect the mesotrophic conditions of the fen vegetation during prolonged periods (up to 100 years), but that a slight, but permanent, flooding triggers a rapid response to more eutrophic conditions.

Wolejko *et al.* (in press) presented a case study in which the deterioration of a fen system provided possibilities for the development of very rare spring moss communities. The authors studied one of the largest spring mires in western Pomerania (Poland) and found that this seemingly-natural mire system used to be a treeless percolating mire (sloping fen). The spring mire appeared to have evolved a few centuries ago, possibly as a result of a water table drawdown in the outflow lake. The development of the spring mire was probably a reaction to the increased resistance to water flow in the peat body, forcing the groundwater to discharge high up at the sand borders. The eroding effect of the spring water courses increased the drainage and, although the springs also provided new habitats for many rare moss communities, a considerable eutrophication in the present spring alder wood can be noticed. This example shows that sometimes an alteration of the fen system must be accepted in order to preserve (temporarily) an even more endangered ecosystem than the one that is being lost.

We may conclude that the current knowledge of the conditions for successful fen restoration is mainly based on unplanned incidents and from carefully diagnosing the hydrological mechanisms responsible for the decline of these ecosystems. Furthermore, the occurrence of rare fen species is practically always associated with very specific hydrological conditions, which implies that fens with rare fen species can only be restored when such conditions can be provided.

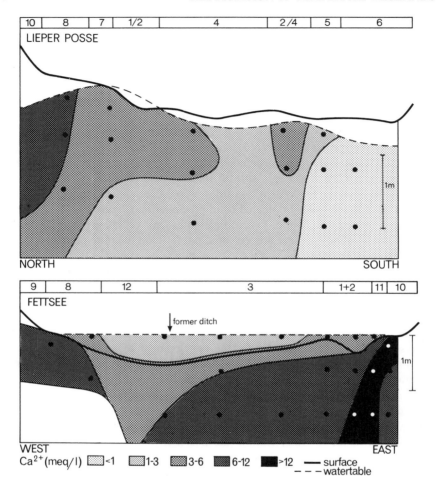

Figure 5. Distribution of calcium concentrations of groundwater to a depth of 2 m along transects through a drained fen (Lieper Posse, September 1988) and a rewetted fen (Fettsee, June 1991) in eastern Germany (modified from Grootjans *et al.*, 1992). Groundwater levels are indicated by a dashed line. 1 = *Eleocharetum quinqueflorae*; 2 = *Caricetum lasiocarpae*; 3 = *Caricetum elatae*; 4 = *Betuletum–Salicetum repentis*; 5 = *Sphagno-Betuletum pubescentis*; 6 = *Ledo-Pinetum sylvestris*; 7 = *Thelypterido-Alnetum*; 8 = *Carici elongatae-Alnetum*; 9 = *Fraxino-Alnetum glutinosae*; 10 = *Melico-Fagetum*; 11 = *Carex acutiformis* stands; 12 = *Salix* scrub.

RESTORE FENS WHERE?

The best chances for restoration of fen systems lies in using the least damaged ones: former species-rich fen meadows which have lost some endangered species but not all (see also Zeeman, 1986). Rapid success is also ensured when mowing is reapplied in hydrologically well-preserved, but abandoned fen meadows (Kapfer, 1987; Moen, 1990; Klötzli, 1991). Klötzli (1987) has shown that, even when the hydrology of the original site has been completely destroyed, an entire fen meadow vegetation could be transplanted to a hydrologically more suitable site without immediate loss of the character of the vegetation type. But restoration of low productivity fen communities in areas formerly used by modern agriculture is extremely difficult. Usually an extensive hydrological analysis of the entire area is necessary to evaluate sites suitable for future fen regeneration and even then rapid results must not be expected. Prolonged stages of eutrophic mire development are likely. Nevertheless, hydro-ecological approaches to assess future fen developments in former polder areas have been presented in the Netherlands using distribution patterns of fen species as guidelines for hydrological research (Grootjans et al., 1992; van Diggelen et al., 1994). In this approach hydrological modelling on various spatial scales has been incorporated with ecological knowledge of fen species and stratigraphic knowledge of the peat deposits present. It is more or less a diagnosis of the past and present capabilities of a landscape to support fens or fen species. Distribution patterns of fen and fen-meadow species were used to refine the scale of hydrological research and to target it to certain 'promising' sub-areas.

Many hydrological studies in the Netherlands, however, have made it clear that only small parts of former seepage areas are still suitable for fen regeneration due to huge interferences with the hydrology. Often such areas are local hydrological systems created by man.

ECOLOGICALLY SOUND WATER MANAGEMENT

In most areas the use of groundwater by agriculture, forestry and groundwater abstraction facilities is so excessive that the discharge from large hydrological systems is often not sufficient to initiate and sustain mesotrophic fen peat formation in existing nature reserves. Nowadays, possibilities arise to use relatively large agricultural areas for nature development. Those examples situated in (former) seepage areas may provide new opportunities, but only if the abstraction of groundwater is diminished. It is difficult to convince politicians that rare species should be preserved in areas now used by agriculture or for the production of drinking water. It is easier to explain that a society should not tolerate that billions of litres of clean groundwater are being pumped into the sea by applying deep drainage in low lying polder areas or evaporate into the air by the extensive use of sprinkling installations. In the Netherlands automatic devices exist to pump clean groundwater from agricultural areas to be replaced almost immediately by polluted surface water from the River Rhine. This costly practice has devastating effects on practically all wet ecosystems in these areas (van Buuren & Kerkstra, 1993).

Figure 6 shows how an ecologically sound management based on the restoration of hydrological cycles could provide new opportunities for fen regeneration.

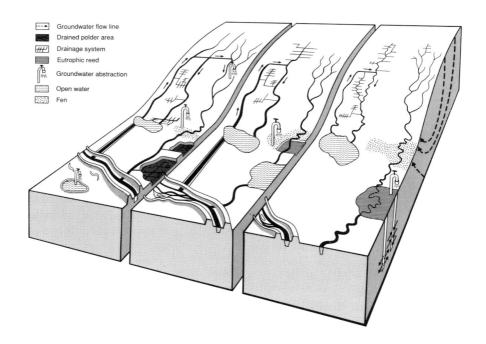

Figure 6. Future development of an imaginary landscape in the Netherlands, showing possibilities for fen restoration in seepage areas if an ecologically sound water management were to be applied, with alternative methods to produce drinking water, with reduced drainage, surface water suppletion and ecological flood control (see also text).

Deeply drained polder areas should be given new functions, for instance as reservoirs for drinking water, where eutrophic marshes are used as sinks for nutrients (Duel *et al.*, 1993). Surface water can then be used in alternative methods to produce drinking water, such as deep infiltration in aquifers (Bakker & Stuyfzand, 1993). Even eutrophic marshes may in time turn into mesotrophic ones if the discharge of base-rich groundwater is restored. Flooding hazards may be reduced by building large embankments, but also by creating flood plains. The latter also provides new opportunities for a type of fen regeneration that is suitable for wildfowl development.

We cannot satisfy the expectations of politicians to present rapid results with respect to the restoration of damaged fens. We do have, however, a responsibility to conserve and restore endangered fen species in existing nature reserves. And for this we need to monitor, diagnose and put forward suggestions for wiser use of groundwater, leaning on all the knowledge we can gather.

ACKNOWLEDGEMENTS

We are grateful to Bryan Wheeler for stimulating comments on a previous draft and to Evert Leeuwinga for preparing the figures.

REFERENCES

Bakker, J.P. (1989). *Nature Management by Grazing and Cutting.* Junk, Dordrecht.

Bakker, T.W.M. & Stuyfzand, P.J. (1993). Nature conservation and extraction of drinking water in coastal dunes; the Meyendel area. *Landscape Ecology of a Stressed Environment* (eds C.C. Vos & P. Opdam), pp. 219–243. Chapman & Hall, London.

Boeye, D. (1992). *A recent transformation from poor to rich fen caused by artificial groundwater recharge.* Thesis, University of Antwerp.

Borger, G.J. (1992). Draining – digging – dredging; the creation of a new landscape in the peat areas of the low countries. *Fens and Bogs in the Netherlands* (ed. J.T.A. Verhoeven), pp. 131–171. Kluwer, Dordrecht.

Burny, J. (1986). Het landgebruik in en rond de vallei van de Zwarte Beek te Koersel (Limburgse kempen) in het begin van de 20e eeuw. *Het Oude Land van Loon,* **41**.

Dembek, W. (1992). Soligenous peat lands in Poland and some problems with their protection and utilization. *Proceedings of the 9th International Peat Congress,* pp. 278–293.

Dierssen, K., (1982). *Die wichtigsten Pflanzengesellschaften der Moore NW Europas.* Conservatoire et Jardin botaniques, Genève.

Duel, H., During, R. & Kwakernaak, C. (1993). Artificial wetlands; a device for restoring natural wetland values. *Landscape Ecology of a Stressed Environment* (eds C.C. Vos & P. Opdam), pp. 219–243. Chapman & Hall, London.

Egloff, Th. (1983). Phosphorus as prime limiting nutrient in litter meadows (Molinion). Fertilization experiment in the lower valley of the Reuss. *Berichte des Geobotanischen Institutes der ETH Stiftung Rübel, Zürich,* **50**, 119–148.

Ellenberg, H. (1978). *Vegetation Mitteleuropas mit dem Alpen.* Ulmer, Stuttgart.

Gremer, D. und Poschlod, P. (1991). Vegetationsentwicklung im Torfstichgebiet des Haigauer Rieds (Wurzacher Ried) in Abhängigkeit von Abbauweise und Standort nach dem Abbau. *Verhandlungen der Gesellschaft für Ökologie,* **20**, 315–324.

Grootjans, A.P. Schipper, P.C., & van der Windt (1985). Influence of drainage on N-mineralisation and vegetation response in wet meadows. I: *Calthion palustris* stands. *Oecologia Plantarum,* **6**, 403–417.

Grootjans, A.P. Schipper, P.C., & van der Windt (1986). Influence of drainage on N-mineralisation and vegetation response in wet meadows. II: *Cirsio-Molinietum* stands. *Oecologia Plantarum,* **7**, 3–14.

Grootjans, A.P., van Diggelen, R., Kemmers, R.H. & Succow, M. (1991). The hydro-ecological history of a calciphilous fen; the case study of the Lieper Posse (GDR). *Phytocoenosis,* **3** (N.S.), *Supplementum Cartographiae Geobotanicae,* **2**, 263–272.

Grootjans, A.P., van Diggelen, R., Succow, M. & Tolman, M. (1992). Regeneration perspectives of groundwater fed mires; two examples from eastern Germany. *Proceedings of the 9th International Peat Congress,* pp. 377–389.

Ingram, H.A.P. (1983). Hydrology. *Ecosystems of the World 4A. Mires: Swamp, Bog, Fen and Moor* (ed. A.J.P. Gore), pp. 67–158. Elsevier, Amsterdam.

Jansen, A.J.M. & Maas, C. (1993). Ecohydrological processes in almost flat wetlands. *Proceedings of Symposium on Engineering Hydrology.* pp. 150–155. San Francisco, July 25–30, 1993.

Jasnowka, J. & Jasnowski, M. (1991). The dynamic of the peat-forming vegetation in nature reserve "Klocie Ostrowickie". *Zeszyty Naukowe, Akademia Rolnicza W Szczecinie,* **149**, 11–52.

Kapfer, A. (1987). Untersuchungen zur Renaturierung ehemaliger Streuwiesen im südwestdeutschen Alpenvorland. *Erfassung und Bewertung Anthropogener Vegetationsveränderungen.* (eds R. Schubert & W. Hilbig), pp. 178–195. Martin-Luther-Universität, Halle-Wittenberg.

Kemmers, R.H. & Jansen, P.C. (1988). Hydrochemistry of rich fen and water management. *Agricultural Water Management,* **14**, 399–412.

Klapp, E. (1965). *Grünlandvegetation und Standort.* Verlag Paul Parey, Berlin.

Klötzli, F. (1987). Disturbance in transplanted grasslands and wetlands. *Disturbance in Grasslands* (eds J. van Andel, J.P. Bakker & R.W. Snaydon), pp. 79–96. Junk, Dordrecht.

Klötzli, F. (1991). Möglichkeiten und erste Ergebnisse mitteleuropäischer Renaturierungen. *Verhandlungen der Gesellschaft für Ökologie,* **20**, 229–242.

Koerselman, W. & J.T.A. Verhoeven (1992). Nutrient dynamics in mires of various trophic status: Nutrient inputs and outputs and the internal nutrient cycle. *Fens and Bogs in the Netherlands* (ed. J.T.A. Verhoeven), pp. 397–432. Kluwer, Dordrecht.

Krause, W. (1959). Über die natürlichen Bedingungen der Grünlandberieselung in verschiedenen Landschaften Südbadens mit Ausblick auf den Wirtschaftserfolg. *Zeitschrift für Acker und Pflanzenbau,* **107**, 245–274.

Lammerts, E.J., Sival, F.P., Grootjans, A.P. & Esselink, H. (1992). Hydrological conditions and soil buffering processes controlling the occurrence of dune slack species on the Dutch Wadden Sea islands. *Coastal Dunes* (eds R.W.G. Carter, T.G. Curtis & M.J. Sheehy-Skeffington), pp. 265–272. Balkema, Rotterdam.

Lammerts, E.J., Grootjans, A.P., Stuyfzand, P.J. & Sival, F.P. (in press). Endangered dune slack plants; gastronomers in need of mineral water. *Proceedings of the 4th EUCC Congress.*

Moen, A. (1990). The plant cover of the boreal uplands of central Norway. *Gunneria,* **63**, 1–451.

Okruszko, H. (ed.) (1977). Differentiation in ecological conditions of a grassland ecosystem in the Wizna fen as influenced by reclamation. *Polish Ecological Studies,* **3/3**, 5–85.

Patrick, W.H. Jr. & Khalid, R.A. (1974). Phosphate release and sorption by soils and sediments: effect of aerobic and anaerobic conditions. *Science,* **186**, 53–55.

Pfadenhauer, J. & Kaule, G. (1971). Vegetation und Ökologie eines Waldquellenkomplexes im bayerischen Inn-Chimse-Vorland. *Berichte des Geobotanischen Institutes der ETH Stiftung Rübel, Zürich,* **39**, 74–87.

Pietsch, W. (1984). Die Standortverhältnisse im Naturschutzgebiet "Kalktuff-Niedermoor" (Vorderrhön). *Archief für Naturschutz und Landschafsforschung, Berlin,* **24**, 259–273.

Platonov, G.M. (1967). The shift of bog vegetation under the influence of drying. *Interrelation of Forest and Bog* (ed. P'Yavchenko), pp. 129–140. Amerid, New Delhi, (1976).

Rybnícek, K. & Rybnícková, E. (1974). The origin and development of waterlogged meadows in the central part of the Sumava Foothills. *Folia Geobotanica & Phytotaxonomica, Praha,* **9**, 45–70.

Schipper. P.C. & Grootjans, A.P. (1986). Bibliographie der Arbeiten über Grundwassermanipulationen in Pflanzengesellschaften. *Excerpta Botanica, B,* **24**, 217–230.

Schwaar, J. (1980). Sind die hygro- und xeroklinen Phasen der Hochmoorbildung und bestimmte Phasen der Niedermoorbildung synchrone Vorgänge gleicher Ursache? *Epharmonie* (eds O. Wilmanns & R. Tüxen) pp. 95–116. Cramer, Vaduz.

Sjörs, H. (1950). On the relation between vegetation and electrolytes in North Swedish mire waters. *Oikos*, **2**, 241–258.

Stuyfzand, P.J., Lüers, F. & Grootjans, A.P. (1992). *Hydrochemie en hydrologie van het Kapenglop, een natte duinvallei op Schiermonnikoog.* KIWA N.V. Nieuwegein, report SWE 92.038.

Succow, M. (1970). Zur Verbreitung und Soziologie der orchideen in der mecklenburgischen Talmooren. *Mitteilungen der Arbeitskreises heimischer Orchideen*, **6**, 1–26.

Succow, M. (1971). Die Talmoore des nordostdeutchen Flachlandes, ein Beitrag zur Charakterisierung des Moortyps "Niedermoor". *Archief für Naturschutz und Landschaftsforschung*, **11** (3), 133–168.

Succow, M.(1988). *Landschaftökologische Moorkunde.* Gustav Fischer Verlag, Jena.

Tallis, J.H. (1983). Changes in wetland communities. *Ecosystems of the World 4A. Mires: Swamp, Bog, Fen and Moor* (ed. A.J.P. Gore), pp. 311–347. Elsevier, Amsterdam.

van Buuren, M. & Kerkstra, K. (1993). The framework concept and the hydrological landscape structure; a new perspective in the design of multifunctional landscapes. *Landscape Ecology of a Stressed Environment* (eds C.C. Vos & P. Opdam), pp. 219–243. Chapman & Hall, London.

van der Meijden, R., Weeda, E.J., Adema, F.A.C.B. & de Joncheere, G.J. (1983). *Flora van Nederland.* 20th edition. Wolters-Noordhoff, Groningen.

van Diggelen, R., Grootjans, A.P., Kemmers, R.H., Kooijman, A.M., Succow, M., de Vries, N.P.J. & van Wirdum, G. (1991). Hydro-ecological analysis of the fen system Lieper Posse, eastern Germany. *Journal of Vegetation Science*, **2**, 465–476.

van Diggelen, R., Grootjans, A.P. & Burkunk, R. (1994). Assessing restoration perspectives of a disturbed brook valley (Gorecht-area, the Netherlands). *Restoration Ecology*, **2**, 87–96.

van Leeuwen, C.G. (1964). Restoration of modified wetlands in the Netherlands. IUCN publications. New series, **3**, (Part. I/D), 347–350.

van Wirdum, G. (1993). An ecosystem approach to base-rich freshwater wetlands, with special reference to fenland. *Hydrobiologia*, **265**, 129–153.

Verhoeven, J.T.A., Kemmers, R.M. & Koerselman, W. (1993). Nutrient enrichment of freshwater wetlands. *Landscape Ecology of a Stressed Environment* (eds C.C. Vos & P. Opdam), pp. 33–59. Chapman & Hall, London.

Walker, D. (1970). Direction and rate in some British post-glacial hydroseres. *Studies in the Vegetational Hisory of the British Isles* (eds D. Walker & R.G. West), pp. 117–139. Cambridge University Press, Cambridge.

Wassen, M.J. (1990). *Water flow as a Major Landscape Ecological Factor in Fen Development.* Thesis, University of Utrecht.

Wheeler, B.D. (1988). Species richness, species rarity and conservation of rich-fen vegetation in lowland England and Wales. *Journal of Ecology*, **25**, 331–353.

Wind, G.P. (1986). Slootpeilverlaging en grondwaterstandsdaling in veenweidegebieden. *Cultuurtechnisch Tijdschrift*, **25**, 321–330.

Wolejko, L., Aggenbach, C., van Diggelen, R. & Grootjans, A.P. (1994). Vegetation and hydrology in a spring mire complex in Western Pomerania, Poland. *Proceedings of the Koninklijke Nederlandse Akademie van Wetenschappen*, **97**, 219–245.

Yerly, L. (1970). Ecologie comparée des prairies marécageuses dans les Préalpes de la Suisse occidentale. *Veröffentlichungen des Geobotanischen Institutes der E.T.H, Stiftung*

Rübel, Zürich, **44**, 1–119.

Zeeman, W.P.C. (1986). Application in land, nature and water management; the Reitma case study. *Water Management in Relation to Nature, Forestry and Landscape Management,* TNO Committee on hydrological research, Proceedings and Information, **34**, 117–126.

6 Eutrophication of Fen Ecosystems: External and Internal Nutrient Sources and Restoration Strategies

W. KOERSELMAN
KIWA N.V. Research & Consultancy, Groningenhaven 7, Postbus 1072, 3430 BB, Nieuwegein, The Netherlands

J. T. A. VERHOEVEN
Department of Plant Ecology and Evolutionary Biology, Utrecht University, The Netherlands

SUMMARY

1.   Eutrophication of fens can be attributed to (i) increased external inputs of nutrients ('external eutrophication') and/or (ii) acceleration of nutrient cycling within the fen soil associated with a change of environmental conditions ('internal eutrophication'). The processes responsible for eutrophication are reviewed, with special attention to fens in Western Europe.

2.   In the Netherlands, recharge fens fed by polluted river water have often been eutrophicated, while fens fed by calcium-rich clean groundwater have usually maintained their mesotrophic character. In particular, N inputs have increased strongly over recent decades. Nonetheless, differences in trophic status among fens cannot always be explained from differences in nutrient mass balance, but rather from differences in soil nutrient release rates.

3.   Laboratory experiments show that the interaction of polluted river water with peat soil (*Sphagnum* and *Carex* peat) may result in the release of P from soil chemical complexes ('internal eutrophication'), probably because the high sulphate content of river water causes the release of phosphate that is adsorbed on to Fe(II)-hydroxides. When peat was incubated in clean calcium-rich groundwater, P release rates were very low.

4.   Although external eutrophication has often been held almost entirely responsible for eutrophication, internal eutrophication can be very important as well, particularly in older successional stages with huge soil organic-bound and inorganic nutrient pools.

5.   When reduction of the trophic status of fens is desired, the availability of the nutrient that limits plant growth should be addressed first, but the ultimate aim should be to establish colimitation of plant growth. In fens, plant growth is mostly limited by the availability of N or P.

6.   Management options to reduce the availability of nutrients are discussed in the context of hydrologic management strategies for the conservation of fens. Reducing P availability requires different measures from reducing N availability.

Restoration of Temperate Wetlands. Edited by B.D. Wheeler, S.C. Shaw, W. J. Fojt and R.A. Robertson
© 1995 John Wiley & Sons Ltd.

INTRODUCTION

Eutrophication is one of the most important disturbances to fens and its detrimental effects on the vegetation have been frequently reported (Klötzli, 1986; Wheeler, 1983; Verhoeven, Koerselman & Beltman, 1988). Nutrient availability in fens is determined by external nutrient inputs and by soil biogeochemical processes (*e.g.* mineralisation, chemisorption of P). Eutrophication of fens can be attributed to (i) increased external inputs of nutrients ('external eutrophication') and/or (ii) acceleration of nutrient cycling within the wetland soils associated with a change of environmental conditions ('internal eutrophication'). The latter concerns nutrients already present in the fen ecosystem, but in organic- or chemically-bound forms, and thus unavailable to the vegetation.

So far, studies have not attempted to establish the relative importance of external and internal eutrophication, and until recently processes involved with internal eutrophication have received hardly any attention (but see Curtis, 1989; Caraco, Cole & Likens, 1989, 1990; Roelofs, 1991; Koerselman, van Kerkhoven &

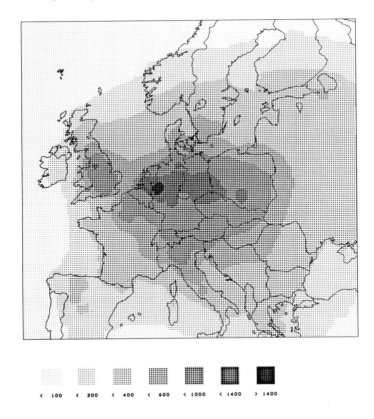

Figure 1. Deposition of NO_x in Europe, in 1988 (mol ha^{-1} a^{-1}) (Erisman & Heij,1991). Reproduced by permission of Elsevier Science Publishers BV and the author.

Verhoeven, 1993). This is unfortunate, as strategies towards conservation or restoration of nutrient-poor fen ecosystems can only be successful if the processes responsible for eutrophication are understood. In this review, which is mainly based on research in Western Europe (especially the Netherlands), the ways in which major plant nutrients (N and P) are made available to fen vegetation are examined, with particular focus on eutrophication processes. Restoration strategies aimed at reducing the trophic status of fens are then discussed.

EXTERNAL EUTROPHICATION

External nutrient sources in relation to the position of the fen in the landscape

External eutrophication of fens is due to (1) atmospheric N deposition and (2) eutrophication of groundwater, river water and surface water. Figures 1 and 2 show deposition rates of NO_x and NH_x in Europe (Erisman & Heij, 1991). There is much geographic variation, the focus of NO_x deposition being on industrial areas (Midlands UK, the Netherlands and parts of Germany and Poland). NH_x

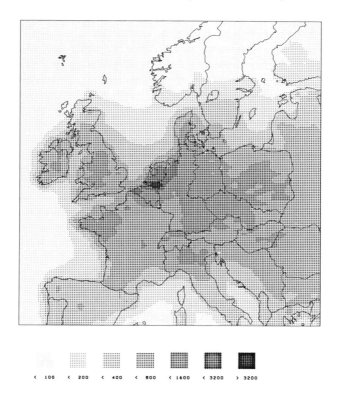

< 100   < 200   < 400   < 800   < 1600   < 3200   > 3200

Figure 2. Deposition of NH_x in Europe, in 1988 (mol ha^{-1} a^{-1}) (Erisman & Heij, 1991). Reproduced by permission of Elsevier Science Publishers BV and the author.

deposition focuses particularly on the south-eastern part of the Netherlands, mainly due to livestock wastes. Background N deposition averages 5 kg N ha^{-1} a^{-1} (Erisman, 1990). Currently, within Europe, such low N deposition rates are found only in the northern parts of Scandinavia. In most Western-European countries, total N deposition is 4–10 times background deposition values (Figures 1 & 2). Two-thirds of total N deposition occurs as dry deposition (Erisman & Heij, 1991).

Background P deposition is *c*. 0.05 kg P ha^{-1} a^{-1} (Stuyfzand, 1993). Higher deposition rates established locally may have resulted from pollution of rain gauges with bird droppings (Stuyfzand, 1993). There is no evidence that P deposition has increased over the last decades.

In addition to atmospheric water, fens may receive groundwater, surface water or river water inputs. The relative quantities of these strongly depend on the landscape ecological setting of the fen (Figure 3). Discharge fens receive groundwater inputs, which may be enriched with nutrients during its transport from areas of recharge (high topography) to areas of discharge (low topography). Riverine fens may also receive water-borne nutrient inputs during periods of flooding.

Most Dutch fen ecosystems are small 'islands' within an agricultural matrix, and exposed to lateral inflow of water from channels, ditches and other open water bodies in summer, when evapotranspiration exceeds precipitation and water is artificially supplied to maintain water levels suitable for agricultural practices. Artificial water supply, usually derived from the River Rhine, is more intense in recharge than in discharge areas, because of the greater water losses in the former during the summer. It typically contains high nutrient levels (particularly N and P) and may be an important source of nutrients (Koerselman & Verhoeven, 1992).

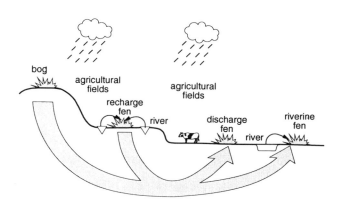

Figure 3. Schematic cross-section illustrating the position of three main mire types in the Dutch landscape. Bogs are fed entirely by precipitation, recharge fens receive an additional supply of river water inputs, and discharge fens are fed by precipitation, groundwater and (sometimes) river water. Main water flows indicated by arrows.

The nutrient mass balance of fen ecosystems

Data on the nutrient mass balance of Dutch fens are summarised in Table 1. In particular, N inputs proved to be strongly increased over background inputs. Historic N inputs for the discharge fen are estimated at $c.$ 20 kg N ha^{-1} a^{-1}, and have increased fourfold. Historic P inputs compare well to current inputs (Koerselman, 1990). Most fens in the Netherlands are mown every year, and this results in the removal of considerable quantities of N and P. For N, harvest compensates for the high N inputs, resulting in an N mass balance that is approximately in equilibrium. For P, harvesting causes a net loss from the ecosystem (Table 1).

Although individual budget components vary among the three fens studied, the eutrophic fen does not receive higher inputs than both mesotrophic fens[1]. Thus, differences in the trophic status of fens cannot be explained from differences in their contemporary nutrient mass balance. Surveys show that fens fed by clean Ca-rich groundwater (typically in discharge areas, but sometimes in recharge areas with good surface water quality) are much less affected by eutrophication than those fens that are located in recharge areas and receive polluted river water inputs (Beltman & Verhoeven, 1988; Verhoeven et al., 1988a). This raises the question whether we must instead attribute eutrophication of recharge fens to internal eutrophication processes, for example, an acceleration of the internal nutrient processing associated with the inflow of polluted river water.

INTERNAL EUTROPHICATION

Internal nutrient sources

Internal nutrient sources are more important than external sources in providing nutrients to plants and/or microbes in three fens where the cycling of nutrients was intensively investigated (Table 2). Clearly, nutrient release rates in the eutrophic fen much exceed those in the two mesotrophic fens.

Microbial mineralisation rates of N and P depend on soil-organic nutrient pools and environmental conditions (temperature, water content, pH). It is reported for a range of soil types that soil moisture contents of $c.$ 50–90% saturation are optimal for mineralisation (Miller & Johnson, 1964; Reichman, Grunes & Viets, 1966; Stanford & Epstein, 1974; Skopp, Jawson & Doran, 1990). Isotalo (1951) reported optimum soil moisture conditions of $c.$ 60% saturation for peat soil. Most studies cited here found a reduction of mineralisation rates at very high moisture saturation, owing to oxygen limitation (see also Moore & Knowles, 1989). How-

---

[1] In herbaceous vegetation, we consider 'summer biomass' the best indicator of the trophic status of fens. The floristic composition of the vegetation can also be used as an indication (cf. van Wirdum 1991). The term 'mesotrophic' is used here to refer to species-rich sites with a summer biomass typically in the range of 250–750 g m^{-2}, that are typically dominated by narrow-leaved sedges. The term 'eutrophic' is used here to refer to sites with a summer biomass in the range of 750–1500 g m^{-2}, that often have a species-poor vegetation dominated by tall sedges, reeds and/or megaforbs. Summer biomass data are for sites where the vegetation is harvested every year.

Table 1. Annual nitrogen and phosphorus budgets (kg ha^{-1} a^{-1}) of fens at Stobbenribben (recharge fen; van Wirdum, 1991), Westbroek (discharge fen; Koerselman, Bakker & Blom, 1990), and Molenpolder (recharge fen; Koerselman *et al.*, 1990a).

Site	Stobbenribben	Westbroek	Molenpolder
Trophic status	Mesotrophic	Mesotrophic	Eutrophic
NITROGEN			
Inputs			
Atmospheric deposition	45	42	44
Groundwater	0	20	0
Surface water	11	1	7
N fixation	20	13	2
Total	**76**	**76**	**53**
Outputs			
Water flow	8	21	10
Denitrification	n.d.	1	1
Harvest	57	66	38
Total	**65**	**88**	**49**
Net exchange	**+11**	**−12**	**+4**
PHOSPHORUS			
Inputs			
Atmospheric deposition	0.3	0.7	0.6
Groundwater	0.0	0.5	0.0
Surface water	0.4	0.1	0.5
Total	**0.7**	**1.3**	**1.1**
Outputs			
Water flow	1.3	0.7	1.0
Harvest	3.2	5.6	3.9
Total	**4.5**	**6.3**	**4.9**
Net exchange	**−3.8**	**−5.0**	**−3.8**

ever, a second 'peak' in ammonium-mineralisation may occur under completely waterlogged conditions (Miller & Johnson, 1964; Williams & Wheatley, 1988). Microbial mineralisation may be adversely affected by pH, when pH values are lower than 6 (*cf.* Kemmers & Jansen, 1985).

The behaviour of P is more complex than that of N, as phosphate may be adsorbed[1] to Ca, Fe and Al minerals in several ways (Patrick & Khalid, 1974; Stumm & Morgan, 1981; Nichols, 1983; Richardson & Marshall, 1986), and this chemisorption is strongly controlled by environmental conditions. Adsorption of

---

[1] Adsorption is used here in a broad sense, including physical sorption, chemical sorption and precipitation (Nichols, 1983).

Table 2. External and internal nutrient sources (kg ha^{-1} a^{-1}) of fens at Stobbenribben (recharge fen), Westbroek (discharge fen) and Molenpolder (recharge fen). Inputs for Stobbenribben: van Wirdum (1991); for Westbroek and Molenpolder sites: Koerselman *et al.* (1990a). Soil nutrient release rates for Stobbenribben: Verhoeven, Kooijman & van Wirdum (1988); for Westbroek and Molenpolder sites: Verhoeven & Arts (1987).

Site	Stobbenribben	Westbroek	Molenpolder
Trophic status	Mesotrophic	Mesotrophic	Eutrophic
Nitrogen			
Inputs	76	76	53
Soil release	115	67	315
Phosphorus			
Inputs	0.7	1.3	1.1
Soil release	5.2	3.4	43.8

phosphate on to Ca-hydroxides occurs at pH > 6.5, and onto Fe- and Al-hydroxides at lower pH (Stumm & Morgan, 1981). Moreover, phosphate is adsorbed more strongly on to Fe(III)-hydroxides than on to Fe(II)-hydroxides (Patrick & Khalid, 1974) so that phosphate availability in weakly-acid to neutral conditions is affected by the groundwater level. Adsorption is to a certain extent reversible: when environmental conditions change, desorption and dissolution processes may result in the release of part of the physically and chemically adsorbed phosphates (see Grootjans, Schipper & van der Windt, 1986).

In conclusion, a change of environmental conditions may affect both mineralisation rates and chemisorption of phosphate, thereby modifying soil nutrient status.

Effect of water chemistry on P availability in peat

As eutrophicated fens were particularly found in areas with a strong supply of polluted river water, it was postulated that polluted river water accelerates phosphate availability in fens owing to desorption and dissolution processes (Koerselman *et al.*, 1990b). This hypothesis was tested experimentally in two fens studied for their nutrient mass balance (Westbroek and Molenpolder fen in Table 1). In an experimental study, soil cores from *Sphagnum* peat from the Molenpolder fen and *Carex* peat from the Westbroek fen were exposed to three different artificial media: (1) clean moderately Ca-rich groundwater, (2) polluted river water and (3) rainwater (Table 3). The water found in fens is always a mixture of these three types, their relative quantities being determined by the hydrologic regime.

First, the soil cores were percolated to replace the original soil water by artificial media. After the percolation, the cores were incubated in the artificial media for 6 weeks at 20 °C at two water levels (1 cm above soil level, 'inundated'; and 10 cm below soil level, 'wet'). Soil chemical analyses were performed after each step in the procedure. Results of these experiments are discussed in detail by Koerselman

Table 3. Chemical composition of artificial rainwater, groundwater and river water that was used experimentally. Concentrations in mg l^{-1}, EC_{20} in μS cm^{-1}, ionic ratio (IR) $= 2[Ca]/(2[Ca] + [Cl])$ (after van Wirdum, 1991); molar concentrations.

	Rainwater	Groundwater	River water
SO_4	7	3	61
NO_3-N	0.8	0.9	4.3
Cl	4	14	113
Mg	0.2	3.5	9.6
Ca	1	26	39
Na	2	9	70
K	0.2	0.4	6.9
NH_4-N	1.5	0.4	2.2
PO_4-P	0.00	0.03	0.68
Fe	0.0	0.2	0.2
Al	0.0	0.0	0.1
HCO_3	0	78	49
pH	4.4	6.8	7.1
IR	0.2	0.9	0.4
EC	51	199	533

et al. (1993). Here, we will discuss results only for the water-soluble P fraction (P-w) and Biologically Available P (BAP)[1].

When *Sphagnum* peat was exposed to artificial groundwater, P-w values were hardly affected over the 6 weeks' time interval (Figure 4b). In contrast, rainwater and river water treatments resulted in the release of P-w over the 6 weeks' incubation interval. P-w release rates were higher in 'inundated' soil cores than in 'wet' cores. Thus, artificial river water and rainwater mobilised labile-P in *Sphagnum* peat. A similar phenomenon was absent in *Carex* peat where P-w release rates were very low in every treatment (Figure 4a). Most P in the *Carex* peat is stored in complexes that do not dissolve in water.

BAP release rates by *Sphagnum* peat were very high when the peat was exposed to river water at high water table. At lower water table, river water had much less effect (Figure 4d). In *Carex* peat, BAP values strongly increased directly after percolation with artificial river water (Figure 4c). This increase cannot be explained from the phosphate content of the percolation water, and must be attributed to rapid desorption or dissolution reactions. Other treatments did not result in high BAP release rates from *Carex* peat.

Summarising the results, it was observed that artificial river water caused the release of P from peat soil, particularly in *Sphagnum* peat that was inundated. The fact that river water did not stimulate N release (Koerselman *et al.*, 1993), and that

---

[1] P-w is a measure for the immediately available P pool whereas BAP represents the potentially available P fraction, determined after extraction with an acetic acid–ammonium lactate solution (after Egnér, Rhiem & Domingo 1960).

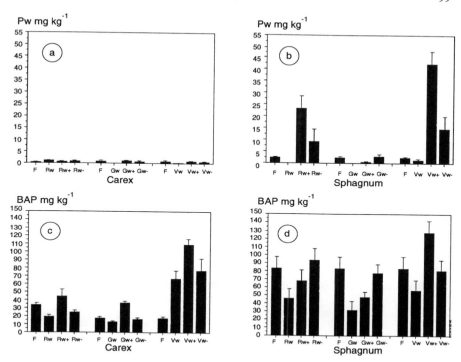

Figure 4. P concentrations (mg kg^{-1}) in fresh (F) samples of *Sphagnum* or *Carex* peat, immediately after percolation with artificial rainwater (RW), groundwater (GW) or water from the river Vecht (VW), and after 6 weeks' incubation in artificial rainwater, groundwater or river water under inundated conditions (RW+, GW+, VW+) or with water levels 10 cm below the soil surface (RW-, GW-, VW-). Values are means of 5 replicates $\pm$ s.e. After: Koerselman *et al.* (1993) (reprinted by permission of Kluwer Academic Publishers.). (a) and (b): water-soluble P (Pw); (c) and (d): Biologically Available P (BAP).

short-term effects were observed, proves that the effects are not biologically induced but must be the result of chemical reactions. The pH of the *Sphagnum* peat and the fact that effects were stronger when the peat was inundated than when the water table was 10 cm below the peat surface suggest that Fe is the most likely compound involved in P dynamics. Fe(III)-oxyhydroxide is capable of binding P more firmly than Fe(II)-oxyhydroxide (Patrick & Khalid, 1974). The relatively high redox potentials in the 'wet' *Sphagnum* peat (Eh$_7$ 208–260 mV, see Koerselman *et al.*, 1993) indicate the occurrence of Fe(III) whereas Fe will have occurred in its reduced state (Fe(II)) in the 'inundated' *Sphagnum* cores (Eh$_7$ 23–68 mV, see Koerselman *et al.*, 1993) (Stumm & Morgan, 1981). Thus, artificial river water may have caused desorption of labile Fe(II)-phosphates in inundated *Sphagnum* cores, resulting in the release of P.

Kemmers (1986a) and Wassen (1990) showed that, in samples with pH <6, ortho-P concentrations often are oversaturated with respect to iron salts, which further supports the theory postulated here.

The mechanism responsible for the P desorption by river water is as yet unknown. However, a recent correlative study of 23 aquatic systems by Caraco *et al.* (1989) revealed that the relative P release from sediments was strongly correlated with the sulphate concentration of surface waters, especially at low concentrations of sulphate (3–20 mg l⁻¹; Figure 5). These authors postulated that sulphides (from sulphate reduction) bind Fe in anoxic sediments, and that formation of iron sulphides both prevents the resupply of Fe-oxides and the formation of Fe(III)- and Fe(II)-oxide-phosphate compounds. This mechanism may be involved in our experiments as well: the synthesised river water is much higher in sulphate than the 'rainwater' and 'groundwater' media (Table 3). The possible interaction of sulphate and phosphate deserves further study.

When soil cores were incubated in synthesised, clean, moderately Ca-rich 'groundwater', phosphate release rates were always low. However, it may well be that the absence of sulphate rather than the presence of high calcium concentrations is responsible for the observed low phosphate availability in many discharge fens in the Netherlands. Earlier theories on the role of calcium in the P

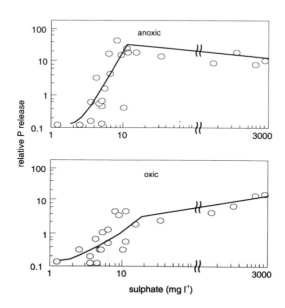

Figure 5. Relative P release under oxic (bottom) and anoxic (top) conditions against sulphate concentration of surface waters for 23 aquatic systems (Caraco *et al.*, 1989). Reprinted with permission from *Nature*, Copyright (1989) Macmillan Magazines Limited.

cycling of fens (see Kemmers, 1986b; Koerselman *et al.*, 1990b; van Wirdum, 1991) may be restricted to essentially alkaline fens with pH over 6.5, where fen water is often oversaturated with respect to 'P sinks' such as calcite, hydroxyapatite or octocalcium-phosphate (*cf.* Kemmers, 1986a; Boyer & Wheeler, 1989; Wassen, 1990).

INTERNAL AND EXTERNAL EUTROPHICATION IN RELATION TO THE SUCCESSIONAL STAGE

Internal and external eutrophication are not equally important in every successional fen stage. This is illustrated for the terrestrialisation sere in shallow open water bodies (Figure 6). Early successional stages ('semi-aquatic phase', Figure 6) are characterised by floating and submerged aquatic vegetation in small open water bodies. Nutrient cycles are open and turnover rates of water and nutrients are high (Howard-Williams, 1985). During the early stages of succession, peat and nutrients accumulate in the vegetation and within the bottom sediment. As only small amounts of organic matter have accumulated at this stage, mineralisation rates on an area basis are low. This phase of succession is characterised by the storage and immobilisation of nutrients that enter the system primarily from external sources, particularly in groundwater, surface water and precipitation.

Within several decades, fen vegetation develops to the point where the root-mats are firm enough to permit access, and harvest operations may take place ('brownmoss phase', Figure 6). Meanwhile, the accumulation of peat in the young fen induces a marked change in its hydrologic regime. As the vegetation mat expands, the peat deposit is gradually isolated from the surrounding surface water and groundwater bodies. Flow rates of water through the peat are reduced and nutrient inputs through groundwater and surface water become less important as nutrient

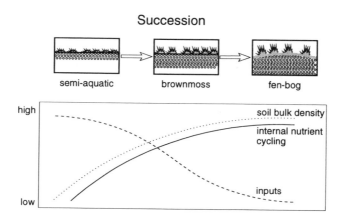

Figure 6. Successional sere depicting qualitative changes in nutrient cycling, hydrology and bulk-density during fen development.

sources for the vegetation. However, mineralisation rates in the peat increase and become sufficiently high to be of quantitative importance to the nutrient availability (Verhoeven, Maltby & Schmitz, 1990). The nutrients accumulated in early successional stages become available through mineralisation or chemisorption. The peat soil, previously a sink for nutrients, becomes a nutrient source. Most importantly, mineralisation and chemisorption are modified by the hydrologic regime (groundwater level and groundwater chemistry).

In late stages of succession, when the fen is isolated from surface water and groundwater bodies and is fed mainly by precipitation ('fen-bog phase', Figure 6) plant growth is almost entirely dependent on rates of mineralisation and chemisorption processes. Although mineralisation rates and nutrient availability are often high (Waughman, 1980; Verhoeven et al., 1990), the vegetation maintains its nutrient-poor character, probably owing to inhibition of nutrient uptake.

Inherent in the change of nutrient dynamics during fen succession is that fens of different stages differ in susceptibility to eutrophication. Early 'open' fen phases are especially susceptible to external eutrophication, whereas late 'isolated' phases may be severely affected by internal eutrophication.

RESTORATION OF NUTRIENT-POOR FEN ECOSYSTEMS

Nutrient limitation

The availability of the growth-limiting factor determines whether a plant experiences its environment as eutrophic or oligotrophic. Thus, if we aim to reduce the trophic status of fens, it is vital to reduce the availability of the limiting nutrient.

Of a total of 24 mires where the nature of nutrient limitation was investigated with reliable methods, bogs were mostly P-limited, while fens were mostly N-limited (Table 4). However, exceptions to this rule are widespread: K limitation was observed only twice, and K fertilisation has even been reported to reduce plant growth in fens (Hayati & Proctor, 1991).

Although the apparent disagreement on the nature of nutrient limitation in mires raises questions as to the influence of geographic variation and differences in soil and vegetation type, it is possibile that differences in experimentation are a key factor. For instance, Tamm (1954) studied the response of *Eriophorum vaginatum* to fertilisation (and concluded that P limited plant growth in pristine bogs), while Aerts et al. (1992) based their conclusion that primary production in pristine bogs was limited by N on growth responses by the dominant *Sphagnum* species. It may well be that growth of Sphagna and phanerogam species is limited by *different* nutrients, as the species clearly exploit different nutrient pools.

Some points of interest that emerge from the fertilisation data are:
(1)   In fens subject to prolonged annual harvesting, P limitation was reported (Egloff, 1986; Verhoeven & Schmitz, 1991). Harvest leads to high net exports of P from the ecosystem (Verhoeven et al., 1993; see also Table 1). It has further been shown that harvesting leads to a decrease of soil P pools (Vermeer, 1985).

Table 4. Growth-limiting nutrients in fens and bogs. * Limiting nutrient established under laboratory conditions, using test plant species ('phytometers').

Mire type (site)	Limiting nutrient	Reference
(a) Raised bogs		
Mörhults Mosse (south Sweden)	P	Tamm (1954)
Stordalen (north Sweden)	N	Aerts, Wallén & Malmer (1992)
Akhult (south Sweden)	P	id.
Tregaron (Wales, UK)	K	Goodman & Perkins (1968a, b)
(b) Blanket bogs		
Bovey Heath (Devon, UK)	P*	Hayati & Proctor (1991)
Crane Hill (Devon, UK)	P*	id.
Brecon Beacons (Wales, UK)	K	Goodman & Perkins (1968a, b)
(c) Poor fens		
Biebrza valley (Poland)	N	Verhoeven & Wassen (unpubl.data)
Haytor (Devon, UK)	N*	Hayati & Proctor (1991)
Lower Cherrybrook Bridge (Devon, UK)	N*	id.
Wistmen's Wood (Devon, UK)	P*	id.
Molenpolder (Vechtplassen, NL)	N	Verhoeven & Schmitz (1991)
't Hol (Vechtplassen, NL)	P	id.
(d) Rich fens		
Buitengoor (Mol, Belgium)	P	Boeye (pers. comm.)
Brackloon Lough (Crossmolina, Ireland)	P	Kooijman (1993)
Two sites at Biebrza valley (Poland)	N	Verhoeven & Wassen (unpubl.data)
Westbroek (Vechtplassen, NL)	N	Vermeer (1986a)
Gagelpolder (Vechtplassen, NL)	N	id.
Groot Zandbrink (Gelderse Vallei, NL)	N	Vermeer (1986b)
Zwartebroek (Gelderse Vallei, NL)	N	id.
Westbroek (Vechtplassen, NL)	N	Verhoeven & Schmitz (1991)
Badley Moor* (Norfolk, UK)	P	Boyer & Wheeler (1989)
Valley of Reuss (Zürich, Switzerland)	P	Egloff (1983)

(2)   In Swedish bogs it was established that in the northern part, with N deposition rates < 3 kg N ha^{-1} a^{-1}, *Sphagnum* growth was N limited, while in the southern part at deposition rates of 12–13 kg N ha^{-1} a^{-1}, *Sphagnum* production responded to P fertilisation (Aerts *et al.*, 1992). Thus, high N deposition may induce a shift from N limitation to P limitation. Similar results, however, were not observed in Dutch fens at much higher N deposition rates (Verhoeven & Schmitz, 1991). This discrepancy may be because in the absence of a root system Sphagna depend almost entirely on atmospheric inputs for their nutrition, while the prevailing phanerogams in Dutch fens can also exploit soil nutrient pools.

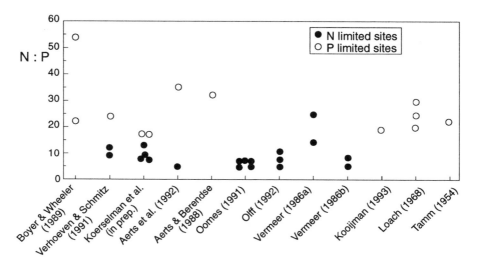

Figure 7. Vegetation N:P ratios in wet terrestrial ecosystems where the growth-limiting factor was established in fertilisation experiments.

Currently, it is being investigated whether the growth-limiting factor can be established from the plant tissue N:P ratio[1] (Koerselman, 1992). It is assumed that, under conditions of relatively low supply of P, the N:P ratio in plant tissue will be higher than under conditions of relatively high P supply (*cf.* Shaver & Mellilo, 1984; Wassen, 1990). The plant tissue N:P ratio is thus used as an indicator of the *relative* (not absolute!) amounts of plant-available N and P in the soil. This approach has long been used in aquatic ecology, where the N:P ratio of the water (known as the 'Redfield ratio') is used to establish the growth-limiting factor for algae (*e.g.* Downing & McCauley, 1992).

Figure 7 shows plant tissue N:P ratios in 31 wet terrestrial ecosystems (fens, bogs, dune slacks, wet heathlands and wet grasslands) where the growth-limiting nutrient was established in a fertilisation experiment. This figure illustrates that vegetation N:P ratios at N-limited sites are lower than at P-limited sites. The borderline between N and P limitation is at a vegetation N:P ratio of *c.* 16.

The paradox of calcareous fens: N or P limitation?

Often, calcareous fens are considered P limited, and adsorption of phosphate on to Ca-hydroxides is usually held responsible for this (Kemmers, 1986b; Boyer & Wheeler, 1989; Wassen, 1990). This assumption is often derived from statistical evidence that phosphate availability in calcareous fens is usually very low, most of the P being strongly bound in complexes usually considered unavailable to plants.

---

[1] This method cannot be applied in situations where K regulates plant growth, a condition that is usually fulfilled in mires (see Table 4).

However, fertilisation studies in calcareous fens in the Netherlands and in the Biebrza Valley (Poland) showed that plant growth responded only to N fertilisation, and not to the addition of P (Verhoeven & Schmitz, 1991; Vermeer, 1986a, b; Verhoeven & Wassen, unpublished data). The same holds for calcareous wet dune slacks (Koerselman & Meuleman, in prep.). Although P limitation has been observed in calcareous fens (Boyer & Wheeler, 1989; Kooijman, 1993) it may not be so general as sometimes stated.

The explanation of this apparent paradox may be that characteristic plant species that grow in calcareous fens ('lithotrophic species'[1] *sensu* van Wirdum, 1991) have adaptations for dissolving/adsorbing the large store of inorganic complexed phosphate accumulated in these systems. In this way these species have overcome the P limitation of their habitat and would become N limited. The possible role of phosphate solubilising by acids or enzymes excreted by plant roots is currently being investigated. Other species lacking such adaptations would experience the site as extremely P-poor. If, however, the P availability increases owing to eutrophication, the 'lithotrophic' species would lose their advantage over other species and may get outcompeted by more common species that invade the site.

An important implication of this hypothesis is that, even under conditions of N limitation, P eutrophication may adversely affect the species composition in calcareous fens.

Restoration strategies

Short-term strategies should specifically address the reduction of the availability of the nutrient that controls plant growth (Figure 8, phase 1). As the fertility of the site is reduced, characteristic low-productive plant species may find opportunities for establishment and growth as competition for light is strongly reduced (Wheeler & Shaw, 1991). During the second phase of restoration (*long-term strategies*), the reduction of the availability of limiting as well as non-limiting nutrients should be addressed (Figure 8, phase 2). The ultimate aim of restoration projects should be to reduce the availability of all major plant nutrients, as the most stable situation in terms of biomass production is reached when all major plant nutrients have low availabilities. Under conditions of single-nutrient limitation, biomass production varies with (natural) fluctuations in the availability of that particular nutrient. The system is unstable in terms of trophic status. Under conditions of colimitation, stochastic increases in the availability of one particular nutrient will not result in the increase of the trophic status of the ecosystem because other nutrients will take over control of plant growth. Stability of the trophic status may be important for sustainable development of nutrient-poor ecosystems. Also, as noted already, a

---

[1] 'Lithotrophic' refers to sites that are influenced by unpolluted calcareous (ground)water, that derives its chemical character from an intensive contact with the lithosphere. The term forms part of a system to classify water samples based on their resemblance to the three most extreme water types in the hydrological cycle (1) rainwater ('atmotrophic'), (2) clean groundwater ('lithotrophic') and (3) sea water ('thalassotrophic') (see van Wirdum, 1991). Lithotrophic fens are usually dominated by characteristic very species-rich plant communities (see van Wirdum *et al.*, 1992).

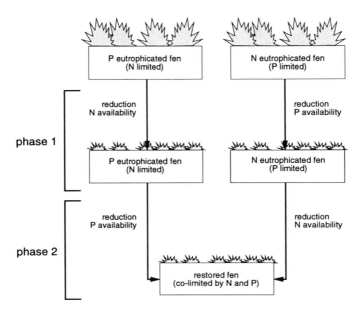

Figure 8. Development pathways in fen ecosystems following eutrophication and proposed management strategy for restoration of nutrient-poor fen ecosystems. Biomass production in fens is proportional to the height of the symbols on top of the boxes.

high level of non-limiting plant nutrients possibly adversely affects the species composition of fen vegetation.

Measures to reduce N and P availability

It is essential to reduce external nutrient inputs to the ecosystem when restoration of characteristic nutrient-poor fen vegetation is to be achieved. However, additional measures are usually required to reduce further the availability of nutrients already present (Table 5). Here it is important to differentiate between N and P, as reducing N availability requires other measures than reducing P availability.

It may be possible to reduce N availability by restoring high groundwater levels, to reduce soil N mineralisation rates and stimulate denitrification. As stated before, however, it has sometimes been observed that high N mineralisation occurs under completely waterlogged conditions. Harvest may not always be an important tool to reduce N availability, as in many Dutch fens the amount of N removed with the harvest hardly exceeds the amount deposited with precipitation (Koerselman & Verhoeven, 1992; see also Table 1). Removal of the topsoil can reduce N availability, but may have important adverse effects on the vegetation (destruction of vegetation, removal of seed bank). Van der Valk & Verhoeven (1988) showed that the seed bank of certain fen species is long lasting. Thus, the potential to restore a degraded fen may be reduced when the seed bank is removed by sod

Table 5. Management options to reduce nutrient availability. * This may increase P availability.   ** Only if standing stocks of N exceed inputs.

Measures	N	P
Reduce nutrient inputs	Yes	Yes
Restore high groundwater level	Yes	No?*
Sod removal	Yes	Yes
Mowing	No?**	Yes
Restore discharge of clean Ca/Fe-rich groundwater	No	Yes

cutting. In semi-aquatic phases, removal of the bottom mud may be essential to reduce effects of internal eutrophication.

Unlike N, deposition of P in precipitation is relatively low and harvest operations are well suited to remove P from the fen ecosystem (Koerselman & Verhoeven, 1992; see also Table 1). Ortho-P availability is strongly controlled by chemisorption on to Ca-, Al- and/or Fe-hydroxides (see above). Knowledge of biogeochemical processes that act as P stores can be used to reduce P availability, for example, by hydrological measures that stimulate discharge of Fe- and Ca-rich groundwater in fen ecosystems. Suitable measures are briefly discussed below.

In weakly acid and circum-neutral soils, restoring a high groundwater table may *decrease* N availability (owing to a reduction of mineralisation rates and an increase of denitrification) but is expected to *increase* P availability, as ortho-P is more effectively bound to Fe(III)-hydroxides than to Fe(II)-hydroxides (Patrick & Khalid, 1974). This once more shows that knowledge of the limiting nutrient is of utmost importance when restoration projects are planned.

Implications for hydrological management

Often, restoring or conserving fen ecosystems requires measures that prevent eutrophication of the groundwater in remote upstream areas, land use regulations in recharge areas and in surroundings of fen complexes, and hydrologic measures. Here, we focus on hydrologic measures only.

In the Netherlands, where hydrology is strongly regulated by man in order to favour agricultural practices, water management often involves artificial supply of water during the summer and the discharge of excess rainwater and groundwater in winter (Verhoeven *et al.*, 1988a; Koerselman, 1989). The supply of eutrophic and sulphate-rich river water to fen reserves must be strongly rejected, as this causes internal and external eutrophication.

If polluted river water is the only water source available for supplementation, one has to consider the possibility of not supplying any water at all (*e.g.* allowing groundwater levels in fens to drop during summer months). If soil pH is below 6.5, drainage may reduce P availability owing to fixation of phosphates onto Fe(III)-compounds as has been observed by Grootjans *et al.* (1986). However, the availability of N, often the limiting factor for plant growth in fens, will probably increase, because of increased microbial activity (Grootjans, Schipper & van der Windt, 1985; Hill, 1988). Moreover, a reduction of the water table may cause acidification, and also directly affects the fen vegetation, as there are strong correlations between water level and the species composition of fen vegetation. Therefore, drainage can under no circumstances be advocated in fen complexes, not even where polluted river water is the only available water source.

If lowering of groundwater tables during the summer is unacceptable, and supply of polluted river water is highly undesirable, what alternative hydrologic options are left? It is important to assess possible options from a broader perspective than that of nutrient dynamics alone. The macro-ionic composition of water is an important factor for vegetation succession, and must be taken into account. When discussing hydrologic management options, we must differentiate between rich fens, dominated by phanerogams and 'brown mosses', and *Sphagnum*-dominated poor fens.

Rich fens dominated by phanerogams and 'brown mosses'

It was discussed earlier that when clean Ca-rich groundwater discharges into fens, nutrient availability will be low. Hydrological management operations should therefore stimulate natural groundwater discharge in nature conservation areas where this has been strongly reduced over the last decades. If discharging groundwater cannot be made available directly, it can be stored in basins during winter periods (when discharge rates are high) and artificially supplied to fens via open water systems (ditches and channels). Alternatively, unpolluted groundwater now discharging into lakes could be artificially supplied into fen reserves where water shortage occurs during the summer. In assessment of the possibilities of artificial supply of water to rich fen complexes, water quality criteria should include low contents of nutrients, sulphate and toxicants. Water supply sources should in general have a quality comparable to that of clean 'lithotrophic' groundwater (Table 3, see also van Wirdum, 1991).

In the case of groundwater discharge, valuable vegetation types of the 'brown moss phase' may develop over the entire fen surface. When the inflow of clean 'lithotrophic' water in fens occurs by lateral subsurface flow, a groundwater–rainwater gradient (base-rich to base-poor, the so-called 'poikilotrophic zone' *sensu* van Wirdum, 1991) develops along the flow lines, that may support a variety of species-rich vegetation types (van Wirdum, 1991). Central parts of the fen mainly fed by precipitation will develop into a 'fen-bog phase', while the borders that are strongly influenced by subsurface inflow of 'lithotrophic' water will support a 'brown moss phase' vegetation. Thus, the mechanism by which groundwater is made available to the fen strongly affects the vegetation structure.

We advise strongly against artificial recharge of rainwater to rich fens, as this can be expected to cause severe acidification of the soil and subsequent deterioration of the base-rich fen vegetation (*cf.* Wassen, 1990; van Wirdum, 1991).

Sphagnum-*dominated poor fens*

Conservation of the excess rainwater during winter periods in open water bodies, and supply of this water to fens during the summer is the best solution for poor fens that suffer from water losses. If the poor fen character is to be conserved, 'lithotrophic' water must never be supplied by flooding, as the base-poor character of the fen would be totally destroyed. However, if clean Ca-rich groundwater were to be supplied to poor fens by subsurface inflow, a very species-rich vegetation of high nature conservation value may develop along the rainwater–groundwater gradient. The poor fen character will be maintained in the central part of the fen, while rich fen vegetation types develop at the borders.

Conclusion

Hydrologic management options vary with the type of fen ecosystem as well as with goals for nature conservation. Nature conservation aims should therefore be clearly defined. Options for the use of polluted river water as a source for additional water supply should be carefully evaluated for each project. This requires a multi-disciplinary approach, considering all aspects of water management, and its relation with fen ecology. It is very fortunate that this approach has become increasingly common in the Netherlands.

ACKNOWLEDGEMENTS

The authors thank Dr Bryan Wheeler, Prof. A.J. Willis, Ir. Jos Peters, Drs Arthur Meuleman, Drs Harrie van der Hagen and Drs André Jansen for their critical comments on the draft of this paper.

REFERENCES

Aerts, R. & Berendse, F. (1988). The effect of increased nutrient availability on vegetation dynamics in wet heathlands. *Vegetatio*, **76**, 63–69.

Aerts, R., Wallén, B. & Malmer, N. (1992). Growth-limiting nutrients in *Sphagnum*-dominated bogs subject to low and high atmospheric nitrogen supply. *Journal of Ecology*, **80**, 131–140.

Beltman, B. & Verhoeven, J.T.A. (1988). Distribution of fen plant communities in relation to the hydrochemical characteristics in the Vechtplassen area, the Netherlands. *Vegetation Structure in Relation to Carbon and Nutrient Economy* (eds J.T.A. Verhoeven, M.J.A. Werger & G.W. Heil), pp. 121–136. SPB Academic Publishing, The Hague.

Boyer, M.L.H. & Wheeler, B.D. (1989). Vegetation patterns in spring-fed calcareous fens: calcite precipitation and constraints on fertility. *Journal of Ecology*, 77, 597–609.

Caraco, N.F, Cole, J.J. & Likens, G.E. (1989). Evidence for sulphate-controlled phosphorus release from sediments of aquatic systems. *Nature*, **341**, 316–318.

Caraco, N.F., Cole, J.J. & Likens, G.E. (1990). A comparison of phosphorus immobilization in sediments of freshwater and coastal marine systems. *Biogeochemistry*, **9**, 277–290.

Curtis, P.J. (1989). Effects of hydrogen ion and sulphate on the phosphorus cycle of a

Precambrian Shield lake. *Nature*, **337**, 156–157.

Downing, J.A. & McCauley, E. (1992). The nitrogen:phosphorus relationship in lakes. *Limnology and Oceanography*, **37**, 936–945.

Egloff, T.B. (1983). Der phosphor als primair limitierender Nahrstof in Streuwiesen (Molinion); Dungungsexperiment im unteren Reusstal. *Berichte des Geobotanischen Institutes ETH Stiftung Rübel*, Zürich, **50**, 119–148.

Egloff, T.B. (1986). *Auswirkungen und Beseitigung von Dungeinflussen auf Streuwiesen.* Veröffentligungen des Geobotanischen Institutes ETH Stiftung Rübel, Zürich, **89**.

Egnér, H., Rhiem, H. & Domingo, W.R. (1960). Untersuchungen über die chemische Bodenanalyse als Grundlage für die Beurteilung des Nahrstoffzustandes der Böden. II. Chemische Extractionsmethoden zur Phosphor- und Kaliumbestimmung. *Kungliga Landbrukshögskolans annaler*, **26**, 199–215.

Erisman, J.W. (1990). *Acid deposition in the Netherlands.* National Institute of Public Health and Environmental Protection (RIVM) report nr. 723001002. Bilthoven.

Erisman, J.W. & Heij, G.J. (1991). Concentration and deposition of acidifying compounds. *Acidification Research in the Netherlands; Final report of the Dutch priority programme on acidification* (eds G.J. Heij & T. Schneider). Studies in Environmental Science **46**, pp. 51–138. Elsevier, Amsterdam.

Goodman, G.T. & Perkins, D.F. (1968a). The role of mineral nutrients in *Eriophorum* communities. III. Growth response to added inorganic elements in two *E. vaginatum* communities. *Journal of Ecology*, **56**, 667–683.

Goodman, G.T. & Perkins, D.F. (1968b). The role of mineral nutrients in *Eriophorum* communities. IV. Potassium supply as a limiting factor in an *E. vaginatum* community. *Journal of Ecology*, **56**, 685–696.

Grootjans, A.P., Schipper, P.C. & van der Windt, H.J. (1985). Influence of drainage on N mineralization and vegetation response in wet meadows. I. *Calthion palustris* stands. *Oecologia Plantarum*, **6**, 403–417.

Grootjans, A.P., Schipper, P.C. & van der Windt, H.J. (1986). Influence of drainage on N mineralization and vegetation response in wet meadows. II. *Cirsio-Molinietum* stands. *Oecologia Plantarum*, **7**, 3–14.

Hayati, A.A. & Proctor, C.F. (1991). Limiting nutrients in acid-mire vegetation: peat and plant analyses and experiments on plant responses to added nutrients. *Journal of Ecology*, **79**, 75–95.

Hill, A.R. (1988). Nitrogen transformations in a small forested headwater wetland. *Wetlands: Inertia or Momentum* (eds M.J. Bardecki & N. Patterson), Proceedings of a conference held in Toronto, Ontario, 1988, 309–313. Federation of Ontario Naturalists, Don Mills, Ontario.

Howard-Williams, C. (1985). Cycling and retention of nitrogen and phosphorus in wetlands: a theoretical and applied perspective. *Freshwater Biology*, **15**, 391–431.

Isotalo, A. (1951). Studies on the ecology and physiology of cellulose-decomposing bacteria in raised bogs. *Acta Agric Fennici*, **74**.

Kemmers, R.H. (1986a). Perspectives in modeling of processes in the root zone of spontaneous vegetation at wet and damp sites in relation to regional water management. *TNO Committee for Hydrological Research, Proceedings and Information*, **34**, 91–126.

Kemmers, R.H. (1986b). Calcium as hydrochemical characteristic for ecological states. *Ekológia (CSSR)*, **5**, 271–282.

Kemmers, R.H. & Jansen, P.C. (1985). *Stiksofmineralisatie in Onbemeste Half-natuurlijke Graslanden.* Instituut voor Cultuurtechniek en Waterhuishouding (ICW), New Series nr. 14, Wageningen.

Klötzli, F. (1986). Shifts in vegetation and site conditions due to eutrophication in wetlands. *Veröffentligungen des Geobotanischen Institutes ETH Stiftung Rübel, Zürich*, **87**, 343–361.

Koerselman, W. (1989). Groundwater and surface water hydrology of a small groundwater-fed fen. *Wetlands Ecology and Management*, **1**, 31–43.

Koerselman, W. (1990). Is er nog toekomst voor trilvenen? *De Levende Natuur*, **91**, 203–210.

Koerselman, W. (1992). The nature of nutrient limitation in Dutch dune slacks. *Coastal Dunes; Geomorphology, Ecology and Management* (eds R.W.G. Carter, T.G.F. Curtis & M.J. Sheehy-Skeffington), pp. 189–199. A.A. Balkema, Rotterdam.

Koerselman, W., Bakker, S.A. & Blom, M. (1990a). Nitrogen, phosphorus and potassium mass balances for two small fens surrounded by heavily fertilized pastures. *Journal of Ecology*, **78**, 428–442.

Koerselman, W., Claessens, D., ten Den, P. & van Winden, E. (1990b). Dynamic hydrochemical gradients in fens in relation to the vegetation. *Wetlands Ecology and Management*, **1**, 73–84.

Koerselman, W. & Verhoeven, J.T.A (1992). Nutrient dynamics in mires of various trophic status: nutrient inputs and outputs and the internal nutrient cycle. *Fens and Bogs in the Netherlands: Vegetation, History, Nutrient Dynamics and Conservation* (ed. J.T.A. Verhoeven), pp. 397–432. Kluwer Academic Publishing, Dordrecht.

Koerselman, W., van Kerkhoven, M.B. & Verhoeven, J.T.A. (1993). Release of inorganic N, P and K in peat soils; effect of temperature, water chemistry and water level. *Biogeochemistry*, **20**, 63–81.

Kooijman, A.M. (1993). Causes of the replacement of *Scorpidium scorpioides* by *Calliegonella cuspidata* in eutrophicated rich fens. I. Field studies. *Lindbergia*, **18**, 78-84.

Loach, K. (1968). Relations between soil nutrients and nutrient uptake in a Molinietum. *Journal of Ecology*, **56**, 117–127.

Miller, R.D. & Johnson, D.D. (1964). The effect of soil moisture tension on carbon dioxide evolution, nitrification, and nitrogen mineralization. *Soil Science Society of America Proceedings*, **28**, 644–647.

Moore, T.R. & Knowles, R. (1989). The influence of water table levels on methane and carbon dioxide emissions from peatland soils. *Canadian Journal of Soil Science*, **69**, 33–38.

Nichols, D.S. (1983). Capacity of natural wetlands to remove nutrients from wastewater. *Journal of the Water Pollution Control Federation*, **55**, 495–505.

Olff, H. (1992). *On the mechanisms of vegetation succession.* PhD thesis, State University of Groningen, the Netherlands.

Oomes, M.J.M. (1991). Effects of groundwater level and the removal of nutrients on the yield of non-fertilized grasslands. *Acta Oecologia*, **12**, 461–469.

Patrick, W.H. Jr. & Khalid, R.A. (1974). Phosphate release and sorption by soils and sediments: effect of aerobic and anaerobic conditions. *Science*, **186**, 53–55.

Reichman, G.A., Grunes, D.L. & Viets, F.G. Jr. (1966). Effect of soil moisture on ammonification and nitrification in two northern plain soils. *Soil Science Society of America Proceedings*, **30**, 363–366.

Richardson, C.J. & Marshall, P.E. (1986). Processes controlling movement, storage, and export of phosphorus in a fen peatland. *Ecological Monographs*, **56**, 279–302.

Roelofs, J.G.M. (1991). Inlet of alkaline river water into peaty lowlands: effects on water quality and *Stratiotes aloides* L. stands. *Aquatic Botany*, **39**, 267–293.

Shaver, G.R. & Mellilo, J.M. (1984). Nutrient budgets of marsh plants: efficiency concepts and relation to availability. *Ecology*, **65**, 1491–1510.

Skopp, J., Jawson, M.D. & Doran, J.W. (1990). Steady-state microbial activity as a function of soil water content. *Soil Science Society of America Journal*, **54**, 1619–1625.

Stanford, G. & Epstein, E. (1974). Nitrogen mineralization-water relations in soils. *Soil Science Society of America Journal*, **38**, 103–107.

Stumm, W. & Morgan, J.J. (1981). *Aquatic Chemistry*. John Wiley & Sons Inc., New York.

Stuyfzand, P.J. (1993). *Hydrochemistry and Hydrology of the Coastal Dune area of the Western Netherlands*. KIWA Nieuwegein/Free University of Amsterdam.

Tamm, C.O. (1954). Some observations on the nutrient turnover in a bog community dominated by *Eriophorum vaginatum* L. *Oikos*, **5**, 189–194.

van der Valk, A.G. & Verhoeven J.T.A. (1988). Potential role of seed banks and understory species in restoring quaking fens from floating forests. *Vegetatio*, **76**, 3–13.

van Wirdum, G. (1991). *Vegetation and Hydrology of Floating Fens*. Datawyse, Maastricht.

Verhoeven, J.T.A & Arts, H.H.M. (1987). Nutrient dynamics for small mesotrophic fens surrounded by cultivated lands. II. N and P accumulation in plant biomass in relation to the release of inorganic N and P in the peat soil. *Oecologia (Berlin)*, **72**, 557–561.

Verhoeven, J.T.A, Kemmers, R.H. & Koerselman, W. (1993). Nutrient enrichment of freshwater wetlands. *Landscape Ecology of a Stressed Environment* (eds C.C. Vos & P. Opdam), pp.33–59. Chapman & Hall, London.

Verhoeven, J.T.A, Koerselman, W. & Beltman, B. (1988). The vegetation of fens in relation to their hydrology and nutrient dynamics; a case study. *Vegetation of Inland Waters. Handbook of Vegetation Science* (ed. J.J. Symoens), vol. 15, pp. 249–282. Kluwer Academic Publishing, Dordrecht.

Verhoeven, J.T.A., Kooijman, A.M. & van Wirdum, G. (1988). Mineralization of N and P along a trophic gradient in a freshwater mire. *Biogeochemistry*, **6**, 31–43.

Verhoeven, J.T.A., Maltby, E. & Schmitz, M.B. (1990). Nitrogen and phosphorus mineralization in fens and bogs. *Journal of Ecology*, **78**, 713–726.

Verhoeven, J.T.A. & Schmitz, M.B. (1991). Control of plant growth by nitrogen and phosphorus in mesotrophic fens. *Biogeochemistry*, **12**, 135–148.

Vermeer, J.G. (1985). *Effects of nutrient availability and groundwater level on shoot biomass and species composition of mesotrophic plant communities*. PhD thesis, Utrecht University, the Netherlands.

Vermeer, J.G. (1986a). The effect of nutrients on shoot biomass and species composition of wetland and hayfield communities. *Oecologia Plantarum*, **7**, 31–41.

Vermeer, J.G. (1986b). The effect of nutrient addition and lowering the water table on the shoot biomass and species composition of a wet grassland community (*Cirsio-Molinie-tum*). *Oecologia Plantarum*, **7**, 145–155.

Wassen, M.J. (1990). *Water Flow as a Major Landscape Ecological Factor in Fen Development*. Ph.D. thesis, Utrecht University, the Netherlands.

Waughman, G.J. (1980). Chemical aspects of ecology of some South German peatlands. *Journal of Ecology*, **68**, 1025–1046.

Wheeler, B.D. (1983). Vegetation, nutrients and agricultural land use in a north Buckinghamshire valley fen. *Journal of Ecology*, **71**, 529–544.

Wheeler, B.D. & Shaw, S.C. (1991). Dereliction and eutrophication in calcareous seepage fens. *Calcareous Grasslands – Ecology and Management* (eds S.H. Hillier, D.W.H. Walton & D.A. Wells), pp.154–160. Bluntisham Books, Bluntisham, UK.

Williams, B.L. & Wheatley, R.E. (1988). Nitrogen mineralization and water-table height in oligotrophic deep peat. *Biology and Fertility of Soils*, **6**, 141–147.

7 Influence of Hydrological Differentiation of Fens on their Transformation after Dehydration and on Possibilities for Restoration

H. OKRUSZKO
Institute for Land Reclamation and Grassland Farming, Falenty, 05-090 Raszyn, Warsaw, Poland

SUMMARY

1.   A basic factor in the formation and development of peatlands is the high moisture content of the sites involved. Any change in their state of hydration can markedly affect the nature of both soils and vegetation.

2.   Two main phases in the development of peatlands are distinguished, the accumulative stage, characterised by waterlogged conditions and the accumulation of organic matter, and the decession (or recession) stage where, owing to dehydration and aeration, the decomposition of organic matter exceeds accumulation resulting in wastage and shrinkage of the soil mass.

3.   In this paper, the effect of different soil water regimes on the physical and chemical properties of fen soils and the environmental impact of such transformations are presented and discussed. The results are used to establish some principles of restoration for fens of various hydrological types.

INTRODUCTION

Changes in the water regime of a peat site have a bearing both on the nature of its plant communities and the soil conditions. Peat soil is formed as a result of the development of a peat-forming ecosystem, leading to the build-up of an organic, soil–geological formation, *i.e.* peat. This constitutes the accumulative stage in the evolution of the mire. In dehydrated conditions, which arrest the process of peat accumulation, the peat soil undergoes a transformation as a result of the onset of another soil process, known as 'moorshing'.[1] This process involves a quantitative

---

[1] Changes caused by drainage of organic soils, particularly peat soils, involving biological, chemical and physical transformations, leading to humification. Equivalent to the formation of 'earthy peat soils' (UK) and 'muck soils' (USA).

Restoration of Temperate Wetlands. Edited by B.D. Wheeler, S.C. Shaw, W.J. Fojt and R.A. Robertson
© 1995 John Wiley & Sons Ltd.

and qualitative transformation of the peat, resulting in a decrease in the amount of the organic soil on the site. This is described as the decession (or recession) stage in the evolution of a mire (Okruszko, 1985).

During the phase of decession, there may be considerable differences in the state of dehydration of the site, as reflected in the level of the groundwater table and in the degree of hydration of the soil mass in the zone above the groundwater level (the zone of aeration). Groundwater levels in a mire depend on the nature and relative amounts of its inflow and outflow, that is, on the hydrological regime of the site.

Soil moisture content in the zone above the groundwater table is closely related to the structure of the soil mass. This structure determines the capacity of the peat to store and conduct water. It is usual to consider the structure of the soil mass from the point of view of the volume of its micro-, meso- and macro pores. Optimum water conditions are found in peats having a predominant proportion of mesopores. The structure and related water conditions of fen peats depend on their degree of decomposition and botanical composition (Table 1).

The higher the degree of decomposition of the peat, the lower its potential to retain a high moisture content. In dehydrated conditions, the structure of peat soils undergoes further transformation by the process of 'moorsh' formation. The hydrological regime and structure of the peat mass determine the impact of drainage on the fen and the nature of the measures necessary for restoration. The object of this paper is to provide information on the changes in soil processes in peat based on results from many years of research conducted on fens in Poland.

DIFFERENTIATION OF FENS BASED ON THEIR WATER REGIME

Three types of water-feeding systems may be distinguished in rheophilous mires: soligenous, topogenous and fluviogenous. The first two are distinguished by the way in which groundwater flows into and out of the site; the third represents the

Table 1. Comparison of porosity in fen peats in relation to their degree of decomposition and botanical origin (Okruszko & Szuniewicz, 1974). [PUR, potential useful water retention; EUR, effective useful water retention]. Pore sizes: macropores: $30-1200 \ \mu m$; mesopores: $0.2-30 \ \mu m$ (PUR: $0.2-30 \ \mu m$; EUR: $6.0-30 \ \mu m$); micropores: $< 0.2 \ \mu m$.

Peat type	Total porosity (%)	Proportion of total pore volume (%)			
		Macropores	Mesopores		Micropores
			PUR	EUR	
Moss–sedge; fibric	92.0	25.7	53.3	30.7	13.2
Reed, tall-sedge; hemic	90.9	18.3	49.6	21.5	23.1
Alder swamp; hemic	90.1	23.4	45.5	22.2	21.2
Reed, tall-sedge; sapric	86.5	10.0	44.4	12.4	32.1
Alder swamp; sapric	88.5	24.8	35.2	14.5	28.5

supply by surface (river) water (Figure 1).

There is a correlation between the nature of the water-feeding system of fens and the nature and structure of the peat developed. Soligenous deposits primarily include moss-sedge peats with a fibric structure or tall-sedge peats with a hemic structure. The type of peat depends on the permeability of the aquifer supplying the fen. An increase in permeability is accompanied by a greater fluctuation in the groundwater level in the fen, visible as a transition from moss-sedge to tall-sedge communities and an increasing degree of decomposition of the peat mass.

Topogenous fens contain a range of peats, most frequently the hemic and sapric types. The latter typically develop from rush or alder swamp communities.

Fluviogenous fens are characterised by the greatest fluctuation in the level of groundwater in the site, which stimulates biological processes associated both with the accumulation of the biomass and with its transformation into soils. Such conditions produce strongly decomposed, amorphous (sapric) peats or muds.

The type of peat or of other organic soil formations have a major bearing on the nature and intensity of changes taking place in the soil following the dehydration of the site.

GENERAL RULES OF PEAT SOIL TRANSFORMATION AFTER DEHYDRATION

The dehydration of a mire typically induces secondary humification, an increase in the compactness of the peat mass and its disintegration into grains. Secondary humification involves the decomposition of unhumified plant fibre found in the aeration zone of peat soil. The result is a change of structure from fibrous to amorphous. The increase in the compactness of the peat is caused by the shrinkage of its amorphous mass, correlated with the moisture content of its colloids.

Shrinking of the peat mass increases in proportion to the diminishing content of plant fibre. This brings about a concentration of humus into aggregates and grains leading to the formation of a grainy, macroporous structure. The transformation of the structure of the soil mass leads to changes in its properties. With periodic drying the soil mass gradually loses its capacity to hold water (Table 2) (Okruszko & Szuniewicz, 1974).

Table 2. Porosity in basic moorsh types (Okruszko & Szuniewicz, 1974). [PUR, EUR and pore sizes: see Table 1.]

'Moorsh'-type structure	Total porosity (%)	Volume (%)			
		macropores	mesopores PUR	EUR	micropores
Peaty-fibrous	88.5	16.1	50.7	25.7	21.7
Humic-aggregate	83.0	17.2	38.2	18.6	27.6
Grainy	82.5	24.9	29.1	12.2	28.5

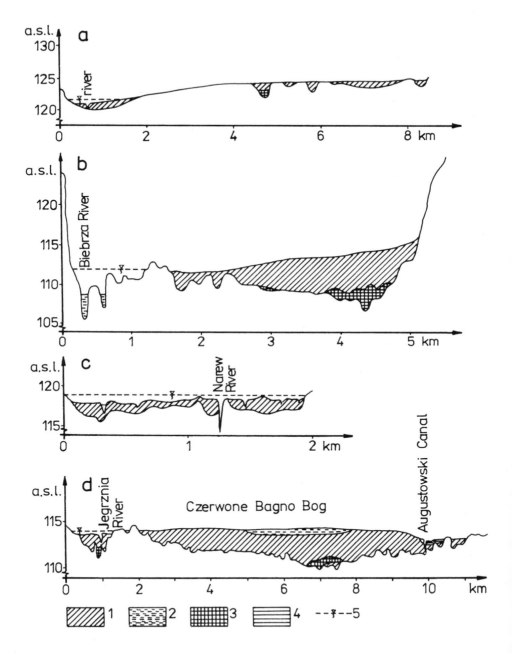

Figure 1. Types of water-feeding system of wetlands: (a) topogenous; (b) soligenous; (c) fluviogenous; (d) ombrogenous on topogenous wetland. (1) fen peat; (2) bog peat; (3) gyttja; (4) moorsh; (5) flood water maximal level. Vertical axis: m above sea level.

Bearing in mind the phenomena just described, it may be said that fibric (mesoporous) peats forming in soligenous sites retain high moisture contents even after dehydration owing to their considerable water capacity and effective capillary rise. After draining they are less prone to transformation than sapric, amorphous peats occurring in fluviogenous or topogenous sites (Table 3).

Table 3. Moisture content regimes in soils of the reclaimed fen 'Wizna' in the growing seasons during the 5-year period of investigations (Szuniewicz & Szymanowski, 1977). Reproduced by permission of Elsevier Science.

| | Type of fen-peat soil | | |
	Fibric	Hemic	Sapric
Mean groundwater level in May (cm)	49	60	57
Mean groundwater level during a drought period (cm)	79	97	90
Moisture content in the root layer of the soil (0–30 cm) at pF 2.7 (% by volume)	78.4	67.7	55.6
Moisture content at wilting point, pF 4.2 in the root layer (% by volume)	21.6	24.1	24.8
Retention capacity (volume of mesopores) in the root layer (% by volume)	53.2	43.5	30.8
Mean moisture content in the root layer, June–September (% by volume)	80.7	72.6	57.7
Mean air content in the root layer, June–September (% by volume)	8.3	14.5	28.6
The lowest moisture content in the root layer during a long drought period (% by volume)	72.7	47.6	29.6
Decrease of the moisture content in the 0–10 cm layer of the soil caused by a drop of 10 cm in the water table (% by volume)	0.6	2.9	5.7

IMPACT OF FENLAND TRANSFORMATION ON ENVIRONMENTAL CONDITIONS

Transformations of peat soils under the influence of the 'moorsh'-forming process have a vital impact on the environmental conditions, both in sites found on such soils and the situation of these sites in the landscape.

In brief, this impact may be described as follows (Okruszko, 1993):
(1) Changes in the structure of the soil mass, leading to the development of an amorphous (humified) formation replacing fibric peat or of a grainy (cloddy) formation replacing amorphous peat, affect air and water conditions in the soil. This impact is detrimental in the case of the humification of fibric peat (increased number of micropores, decreased permeability); it is, however, to some extent positive in the case of the humification of decomposed amorphous peat (increased aeration and permeability). Excessive deterioration of the soil mass

into grains makes it more vulnerable to overdrying.

(2) Differentiation of the structure of the soil profile into strata by the process of 'moorsh' formation is a negative development as it favours the occurrence of soil drought in the root layer in conditions of low precipitation.

(3) Transformation of the structure of the soil mass and of the structure of the soil profile accelerate both the infiltration of water into the soil and its lateral circulation. This facilitates retention of water from precipitation and its circulation through the water-feeding system. In consequence, the peat deposit becomes a reservoir storing available water, unlike the body of inert water found in non-dehydrated deposits.

(4) Processes associated with the humification of the dehydrated peat mass bring about an increase in the absorptive ability of the soil, resulting in the decreased availability of some cations for plants. Blocking of Fe, Al and Ca cations by humic acids decreases the capacity to fix soil phosphorus and as such improves its availability for plants.

(5) Mineralisation causes the loss of organic matter and consequently a steady decrease in the depth, and even total loss, of organic soils from the site. This is usually accompanied by the lowering of the level of groundwater by the drainage network, accompanied by subsidence due to the 'moorsh'-forming process, leading to changes in site conditions frequently affecting relatively large tracts of land.

In general, it may be said that the changes taking place in peat soils following their dehydration (the 'moorsh'-forming process) in most cases result in a deterioration of soil properties, both physical and chemical.

PRINCIPLES OF FEN RESTORATION

The first objective in fen restoration is to re-establish a high moisture content on the site by raising the groundwater level. Observations show that in the case of soligenous fens this is easily achieved. When there is a constant inflow of groundwater, its outflow can be rapidly curbed by blocking or filling-in the drainage network. The paludification is followed by the development of a new peat-forming system.

In topogenous fens, restoration is less simple. To achieve paludification, the groundwater must be raised over the entire area of which the given mire forms a part. Frequently this proves to be an impossible task. In such cases it becomes necessary to irrigate the fen locally. It should be remembered, however, that the water will percolate to areas with lower groundwater levels surrounding the fen.

To what extent, then, is it possible to restore topogenous fens by raising the water table? As a result of the subsidence and mineralisation following drainage, the flat, even surface, typical of topogenous fens becomes uneven, with a microrelief of depressions and elevations. Because the water table formed during repaludification assumes a level position, flooding of the lower-lying areas occurs (limnetic or telmatic communities), leaving exposed tracts of land dry.

Because of such conditions, restoration of typical peat-forming ecosystems which existed prior to reclamation is not feasible.

In the case of fluviogenous fens, difficulties occur during the restoration of the flooded zone. Usually, as a result of dehydration, peat deposits close to the water course undergo considerable subsidence. In order to reinstate the former fluviogenous character of these areas, the water has to be raised to a very high level; frequently this may be achieved only by the construction of large hydrotechnical installations (high embankments).

Apparently, the effect of a renaturalisation process which relies on raising the groundwater level in a formerly drained fen will vary depending on the nature of its water-feeding system.

CONCLUSIONS

The basic conclusions from the analysis of the problem of restoration of fens are as follows:

(1) Transformations of organic matter in a fen resulting from its dehydration depend on the moisture conditions prevalent in the aeration zone of the soil profile.

(2) The moisture conditions in the aeration zone of the peat depend on the depth of the groundwater table in the soil and on the structure of the peat mass.

(3) The groundwater level in the soil is directly correlated with the type of water regime of the site.

(4) The structure of the peat mass depends on its degree of decomposition and botanical composition, that is, the type of peat.

(5) The type of fen peat is related to the type of water-feeding system of the site.

(6) The type of water-feeding system of the site has a critical bearing both on the direction and extent of transformations occurring in the fen following its reclamation and on the conditions and feasibility of its restoration.

REFERENCES

Okruszko, H. (1985). Decession in the natural evolution of low peatlands. *Intecol Bulletin*, **12**, 89–94.

Okruszko, H. (1993). Transformation of fen-peat soils under the impact of draining. *Zeszyty Problemowe Postepów Nauk Rolniczych.* **406**, 4–73.

Okruszko, H. & Szuniewicz, J. (1974). Porositätsdifferenzierung und damit verbundenes Luft- und Wasserverhältnisse in den Niedermoorböden. *International Symposium zu Problemen der Wasserregulierung auf Niedermoor. Eberswalde-Berlin.* pp. 227–250. Akademie der Landwirtschsfteswissenchaften der DDR.

Szuniewicz, J. & Szymanowski, M. (1977). Physico-hydrological properties and formation of air–water conditions of distinguished sites of the Wizna fen. *Polish Ecological Studies*, **3**, 17–31.

8 Evaluation of the Present State and Mapping of the Fens in the Upper Rhinluch, Germany

J. ZEITZ

Humboldt-Universität zu Berlin, Institut für Grundlagen der Pflanzenbau-wissenschaften, Josef-Nawrocki-Straße 7, PF 1118, 12562, Berlin

SUMMARY

1.   The fen soils of the Upper Rhinluch have long been reclaimed for intensive agriculture (grassland), which has led to drying, oxidation and loss of the peat. However, the area sustains considerable wildlife interest, including a number of protected animal species, and a change in land use to prevent further degradation is desired.
2.   Data have been obtained on the topography, depth and character of the fen soils and the effects of rewetting have been modelled using the program SURFER.

INTRODUCTION

Fen soils in East Germany have been used very intensively for agriculture over the past 20 years. Over one-third of the fodder needed for animal husbandry was provided by these areas. Oriented towards economic independence and high productivity, the management of the organic soils has led to a drastic decrease of soil fertility. The main reason for the complex cause–effect mechanisms was the lowering of the ground water level to permit intensive utilisation. This effective drainage made the sites open to access and management at all times. The degradation and drying of the fens were increased by intensive grass cultivation with regular cutting three to four times each year. After initial maximum yields, minimum values have been recorded since the middle of the 1970s, due to major management problems arising from soil degradation, damage from wind erosion, dryness in the top 50cm of soil and very large diurnal temperature variations.

The Upper Rhinluch (Figure 1) has been reclaimed and used for 200 years, leading to a high proportion of degraded fen peat sites. Up to 1970, the fen soils were used extensively for agriculture, with cutting once or twice a year, minimal drainage by ditches and a high water table (20–40 cm below the surface). Subsequently, agricultural practices became more intensive, with pump drainage (water table lowered to 50 cm below the surface), use of fertilisers and cutting

Restoration of Temperate Wetlands. Edited by B.D. Wheeler, S.C. Shaw, W.J. Fojt and R.A. Robertson
© 1995 John Wiley & Sons Ltd.

Figure 1. Location of the Upper Rhinluch, Germany.

three or four times per year. If further agricultural production is planned, a change in management and farming practices is necessary to prevent further degradation of the mire. Changed economical and agropolitical circumstances demand a reconsideration of agricultural production methods. The nature conservation agencies also have an interest in this site, since it is a breeding, feeding, or rest area for many protected animal species, such as bustard, white-tailed eagle, osprey, crane, grey goose, curlew, white stork, otter and beaver. Plans and ideas for tourism, industrial development, city and rural development and water management also have to be considered. Such complex use of a landscape can be planned only by considering the sociological and economic problems.

A change in use of the fen soils is the first step to stop their further degradation. This requires a precise knowledge of the present condition of the sites in order to be able to define the current adverse features and the methods of improvement needed to reach the desired state. It is thus important to determine the properties of the sites which would affect the success of such procedures. Procedures to initiate and control such improvements were formulated with special reference to the fen area, Upper Rhinluch. In the context of peat-soil protection, and to work out methods for comparable projects, important characters of the site were mapped and evaluated and compared with records of 20 years ago.

RESEARCH AREA

The research area is located in the Upper Rhinluch, north-west of Berlin (Figures 1 and 2). It covers *c.* 12,000 ha, being part of the Thorn-Eberswalde ice-marginal meltwater channel. It is a paludification mire. The mires developed here have an average depth of 2 m, but in rills and depressions they may be up to 10 m deep. This area is located in a dry region in Germany; average annual precipitation was 501 mm from 1969 to 1989.

METHODS

Fen soils covering an area of 8820 ha were mapped and 300 profiles examined between October 1991 and December 1992 to determine the substratum and soil types. All coring points were levelled. Soil samples from representative profiles were analysed for chemical and physical properties in the laboratory. The plant associations of the research area were mapped. Based on the sample descriptions and laboratory results, maps of elevation, fen depth, substratum type, soil type and water classes were prepared at a scale of 1:10,000.

For selected areas with potential for waterlogging, different levels of rewetting were modelled with the program 'SURFER'[1]

RESULTS

Surface relief

Knowledge of the topography is important:
(a)   to assess the effectiveness of groundwater regulation through drainage or irrigation (distance from the surface soil to the groundwater level, capillary rise from the groundwater);
(b)   to choose a certain production level (heterogeneity of relief may affect production);
(c)   to assess the impact of rewetting (*e.g.* percentage of open water).

The surface topography is very heterogeneous in the fens with underlying sand. Differences in elevation of more than 1 m in an area of 100 ha are common (Figure 3), reflecting variations in the underlying valley sands (Figure 4). The surface of fens with underlying calcareous gyttja is comparatively flat.

Fen depth

The 'fen depth' includes the depth of peat and gyttja. This is important for the ecological evaluation of a fen landscape. The deeper the mire, the more important it is for the water budget of the landscape and renaturation is probably more feasible. Parts with more than 1 m depth are considered to be of ecological value. The present mire depth in the research area varies from 0.2 to 10 m; 6307 ha (71.5%) has a depth of up to 1.2 m; 1906 ha (21.6%) is up to 2 m deep and 607 ha

---

[1]   SURFER, Version 4; Golden Software Inc.; Golden Colorado, USA.

124

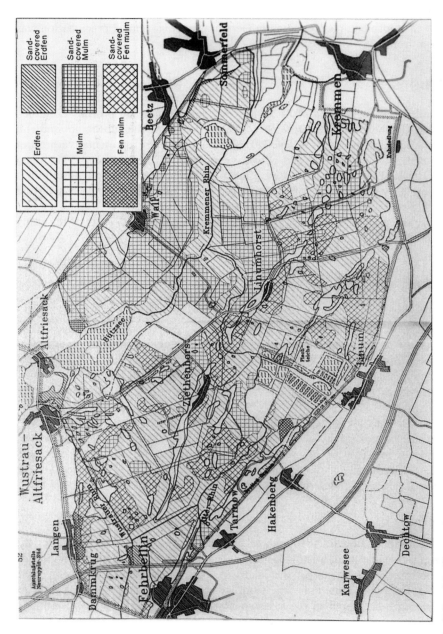

Figure 2. Soils of the Upper Rhinluch.

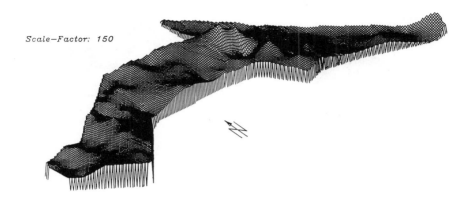

Scale—Factor: 150

Figure 3. Surface relief of a sample site (113 ha) resulting from the heterogeneous relief of the mineral subsoil and fen subsidence.

(6.9%) over 2 m deep. Hence, the mire area is mainly of shallow to medium depth. In comparison with the mire depth of 1969/70, there had been a fen loss of 783 ha by 1992. Of this loss, 280 ha was because of the establishment of deep plough cultivation. The remaining 503 ha was lost by oxidation and microbial peat decomposition. There was a shift of the mire contour lines, mainly in the range of up to 0.8 m.

Soil types

The soil types reflect the soil development, which depends on mire genesis and cultivation history. Information on soil types has been available only since the 1970's; before that the surface soil was characterised only by its apparent degree of decomposition (Vererdungszustand). This makes the mapping of 1991/92 especially valuable. Of the research area, 41.5% is characterised by the soil type 'Erdfen'; 56.5%, an area of 4984 ha, belongs to the more degraded soil types 'Fenmulm' (2229 ha or 25.3%) and 'Mulm' (2755 ha or 31.2%).

Two areas may be especially noted. The small area underlain by calcareous gyttja and cut by a meltwater gully (between Bützsee, Kremmener Lake, Beetzer Lake and Linumhorst) is characterised by the soil type 'Mulm'. Often the peat layer above the calcareous gyttja is only 0.2–0.4 m deep. In summer these peats dry out readily. In many cases, the calcareous gyttja has been brought to the surface by continued deep ploughing. The resulting rise in pH has increased peat decomposition and it seems likely that the peat cover will decompose completely in the near future. Around the melt water gully along the river Rhin the soil type 'Erdfen' (less decomposed type) is still predominant. These areas are very low-lying and have never been used for agriculture. The surface soil has always been moist owing to a shallow groundwater level, and the more decomposed soil type 'Mulm' did not develop.

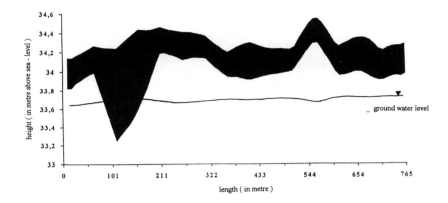

Figure 4. Cross section of the sample site (see Figure 1), showing the peat surface and the peat–mineral interface.

The second and larger part of the Upper Rhinluch has completely different soil types. Here, the mire was used from 1790 to 1890 for fuel peat production. The river system was dammed to facilitate water transport of peat and, in consequence, the present level of the river Rhin is up to 1.5 m above the surface. This leads partly to a discharge of river water on to the adjoining, lower areas of fen. Large areas here have been used for intensive agriculture since 1971. From experience in other mire areas, one could expect that much of this area would have developed the decomposed soil type 'Mulm' but this did not occur. There are still large areas with the soil type 'Erdfen' because of the influence of discharge water and the strong relief of the sandy subsurface as well as the surface relief which parallels that of the valley ground. Where the peat is shallower, the soil types 'Mulm' or 'Fenmulm' are present. The interruption of the surface by sandy islands and tongues increases the heterogeneity of the soil type mosaic. Large areas of these islands are covered by peaty soils.

Plant associations

Over 80% of the main areas in the Upper Rhinluch are covered with grassland vegetation of varying floristic composition. In comparison, the more natural remnant sites cover only 5.5%, and only 1.6% is not deep-ploughed grassland; 12.4% of the whole area cannot be related to the biotope list for fen deposits in the state of Brandenburg. These areas are mainly field and dry valley meadow communities. The latter are on the mineral soil islands of the Rhinluch or in marginal areas. The number of rare species (*e.g. Cuscuta europaea*) is very low owing to the intensive cultivation; 40% of the area is used only for pasture with 1% mown once a year and the rest two to three times a year. Because the survey was finished in September, the third cut could not be monitored; 20% of the sites are used exclusively for pasture, 55% of these intensively and 45% extensively;

16.8% of the whole area is not used at all and about half of the sites have been unused for more than 2 or 3 years. Many sites are used for pasture as well as for mowing; 11% of the area is used for extensive grazing with an additional mowing once or twice a year. Altogether, a high percentage of the sites in the Upper Rhinluch are used relatively intensively.

Soil properties

The bulk density of the peats in the research area can mainly be classified as 'dense' (Segeberg, 1960). The peats are compacted even at depth because of the drainage. The sites with the degraded soil type 'Mulm' show a decreased capacity for capillary rise of groundwater, which results in dry surface soils near wilting point (pF 4.2) in summer (Figure 5).

The Upper Rhinluch can be classed as a 'eutrophic' site by its chemical properties (Succow & Jeschke, 1986). The C:N ratio is between 10 and 15, the P and K contents are low, and the pH value is 6.0.

Rewetting

The Upper Rhinluch has an excellent hydrotechnical system of groundwater regulation, allowing both drainage and irrigation as appropriate. The Water and Soil Association and the author developed a map of the sites which are potentially suitable for rewetting. The sites are located in the reclaimed area of the embanked Rhin rivers.

The essential site properties have been evaluated. Fen soil changes and possible reasons for them have been described in detail at 14 sample sites. With the information from the survey and the software 'SURFER', a three dimensional

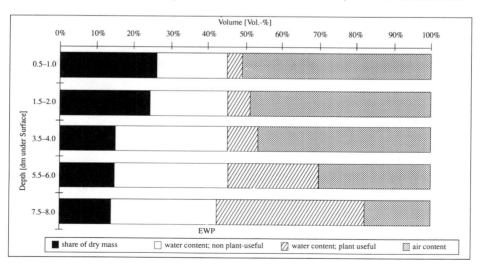

Figure 5. Soil moisture dynamics at a sample site.

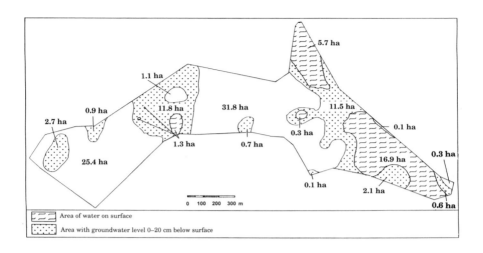

Figure 6. The predicted effects of raising the groundwater up to 30 cm above the soil surface at an example site (Figure 1), based on information from the topographical survey and the software 'SURFER'.

mire complex and the influence of rewetting was modelled. Calculation of the water storage after the groundwater was raised showed, for a sample site, that the use of the fen deposits to store water in times of water surplus (winter months) is efficient only if the sites are flooded. Figure 6 shows the predicted effects of raising the groundwater up to 30 cm above the soil surface at the sample site.

ACKNOWLEDGEMENTS

Sponsoring agency: Ministerium für Umwelt, Naturschutz und Raumordnung des Landes Brandenburg

REFERENCES

Segeberg, H. (1960). Moorsackung durch Grundwasserabsenkung und deren Vorausberechnung mit Hilfe empirischer Formeln. *Zeitschrift für Kulturtechnik und Flurbereinigung*, **1** (**3**), 144–161.

Succow, M. & Jeschke, L. (1986). *Moore in der Landschaft.* Urania Verlag, Leipzig.

9 Natural Revegetation during Restoration of Wetlands in the Southern Prairie Pothole Region of North America

S. M. GALATOWITSCH* & A. G. VAN DER VALK

Department of Botany, Iowa State University, Ames, IA 50011 USA
* Current address: Departments of Horticulture and Landscape Architecture, University of Minnesota, St. Paul, MN 55108 USA

SUMMARY

1.   Although restoration of prairie wetlands is assumed to occur within a few years of reflooding, basins reflooded for three years only had approximately half of the wetland plant species of comparable natural wetlands.
2.   Wetlands drained with ditches retained a refugium for wetland species. Consequently, when ditched basins reflooded they were rapidly recolonised by vegetatively-spreading emergent perennials.
3.   By contrast, tile-drained basins were more thoroughly drained and lacked a refugium for wetland plants during cultivation. Upon reflooding, tiled basins are initially recolonised by mudflat annuals and submersed aquatics. Recolonisation by some species, especially submersed aquatics, is probably the result of dispersal rather than recruitment from the seed bank.
4.   Regardless of drainage history (ditched vs. tile), reflooded prairie wetlands lack the perimeter zones of wet prairie and sedge meadow vegetation. Little evidence of recolonisation by these species was observed, suggesting they may need to be planted for complete restoration of prairie wetland vegetation.

INTRODUCTION

The furthest advance of the most recent continental glaciation marks the southern boundary of the prairie pothole region in North America while its western, eastern and northern boundaries are marked by the transition from prairie to forest vegetation. These Wisconsin-age glaciers left a blanket of till over this region that is dotted by numerous shallow depressions. These depressions, called prairie potholes, are not normally connected to streams because natural drainage networks have not yet developed. Prairie pothole wetlands have distinctive vegetation zones

Restoration of Temperate Wetlands. Edited by B.D. Wheeler, S.C. Shaw, W.J. Fojt and R.A. Robertson
© 1995 John Wiley & Sons Ltd.

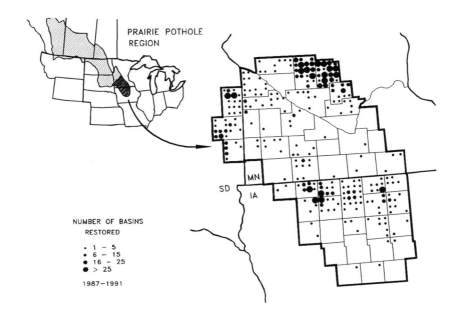

Figure 1. Wetland restorations by township completed between 1987 and 1991 in the southern prairie pothole region.

along their water depth gradients and have been classified according to the zone present in the deepest, usually also the central, part of their basins (Stewart & Kantrud, 1971). This central zone is surrounded by concentric rings of vegetation that are flooded for shorter periods. The shallowest wetlands have a sedge meadow (dominated by sedges and grasses) in the centre surrounded by wet prairie. Open water, interspersed with emergent perennials, such as *Scirpus,* and submersed aquatics, such as *Potamogeton,* occupy the centre of larger, deeper wetlands. Shallow emergents (with species such as *Sagittaria* and *Sparganium*), sedge meadow and wet prairie perennials form zones outward toward the perimeter in these wetlands. The vegetation of prairie potholes is described in detail by Kantrud, Miller & van der Valk (1989).

Wetland drainage and conversion to agricultural use have been widespread across the region, but wetland loss has been most severe in the southern portion, where agriculture is most productive and profitable. Conversion to agriculture was facilitated by an intensive network of surface drainage ditches and subsurface tile drains, starting in the late 1800s. About 90% or more of the wetlands in the southern prairie pothole region were drained, mostly 25–75 years ago (Hewes, 1951; Dahl, 1991). The effectiveness of drainage ranged from sites thoroughly drained by tile and intensively farmed every year, to sites drained with ditches and farmed only during dry years. Restoration of thousands of acres of drained prairie potholes has been attempted since the mid-1980s by a variety of private, state and federal agencies (Galatowitsch, 1993). Today, the greatest concentration of recent wetland restoration attempts in the United States is in this region (Figure 1). These projects were carried out by interrupting tile lines, plugging drainage ditches, or blocking natural drainage ways with earthen dams. The basins and surrounding hillsides are usually planted to an upland cover crop such as brome (*Bromus inermis*)[1] or switchgrass (*Panicum virgatum*) as part of the restoration. There is no attempt, however, to seed or plant native wetland plant species as it is assumed that these (and animal species) will recolonise naturally.

Early accounts of the vegetation of reflooded wetlands suggested that plant species quickly re-established and that these wetlands resembled natural wetlands within a few years (Madsen, 1988; LaGrange & Dinsmore, 1989; Sewell & Higgins, 1991). This resulted in the general impression within and outside the region that prairie potholes can be easily restored by simply re-establishing their pre-drainage hydrology (National Research Council, 1992). Unfortunately, these early accounts, particularly of the vegetation in reflooded wetlands, were based on relatively few sites and on only superficial surveys of the vegetation. No attempt was made to quantify the composition of vegetation in reflooded wetlands or to compare the vegetation of reflooded wetlands with that of natural wetlands. The latter, in our opinion, is the most definitive test of whether a wetland has been successfully restored or not (Galatowitsch & van der Valk, 1994).

The large number of recent prairie wetland restoration attempts provides an opportunity to examine the variability of revegetation and to test the assumption that natural revegetation will result in restored wetlands whose composition and structure is comparable to that of natural wetlands. Our study had two specific goals: (1) to determine if there were any patterns in the composition and structure of the vegetation among reflooded wetlands, and (2) to compare the vegetation of reflooded and natural wetlands. We analysed vegetation data from 62 semi-permanent wetlands with natural drainage re-established in 1988 to determine if there were patterns in the composition of their vegetation and if these patterns could be related to historical factors such as method of drainage or to environmental conditions within basins. In addition, the vegetation zones present in 22 of these wetlands reflooded for three years were examined. We also compared the number of species in eight guilds (*e.g.* mudflat annuals, submersed aquatics) in 10 of the 22 wetlands reflooded for three years with those in nearby extant natural wetlands and with published vegetation surveys of natural wetlands.

VEGETATION OF REFLOODED WETLANDS

Vegetation in reflooded wetlands can re-establish only if plants or propagules of wetland species are present on the site or reach the site, *i.e.* revegetation occurs because of the presence of refugial adult plant populations, remnant seed banks, dispersal of seeds and propagules to the site or a combination of these. In the case

---

[1] Nomenclature follows the Great Plains Flora Association (1986).

of prairie potholes, revegetation is believed to occur rapidly because of the presence of a vestigial seed bank (Madsen, 1988; Dornfield & Warhurst, 1988; van der Valk & Pederson, 1989). Environmental conditions at the time of reflooding can affect plant establishment (*e.g.* mean water depth, soil organic carbon content) and how and when the wetland was drained is known to affect seed bank (Weinhold & van der Valk, 1989) and vestigial vegetation composition (*e.g.*, type of drainage, date of drainage). Information on selected environmental conditions and method and date of drainage were therefore collected along with data on the species composition and structure of the vegetation for 62 wetlands.

The importance of environmental and historical factors was tested by determining to what extent they account for the vegetation patterns observed. Wetlands were sampled for three years. Because not all the basins flooded during their first year, wetlands were placed in three classes based on the number of years they were flooded. Data from all wetlands flooded for one year were combined in the same class regardless of whether the first year of flooding was in 1989, 1990 or 1991. Data from wetlands in their second and third year of flooding were placed in the flooded two years and three years classes, respectively. Vegetation of wetlands in each flooding-class was classified with a TWINSPAN analysis. A matrix of environmental and a matrix of historical dissimilarity values were also constructed for each flooding-class. An 'environmental distance' between each pair of wetlands within a flooding-class was calculated from midsummer water surface area, midsummer mean water depth and percentage of organic carbon in the top 20 cm of soil. Environmental distances were calculated from standardised values of each parameter, following Manley (1985). The duration of drainage, type of drainage (ditch or tile), and number of years since 1980, and the number of years between 1950 and 1980 that a site was used for row crop production were used to construct 'historical distances'. A matrix of historical distances was constructed for each age class based on ranks of each variable (Mantel & Valand, 1970). A matrix of stand dissimilarity (a semi-quantitative Sorenson's index based on cover class estimates) for each age class was constructed for comparisons with the environmental and historical matrices (Mueller-Dombois & Ellenberg, 1974). The concordance between stand dissimilarity value matrices and environmental and historical matrices was evaluated with Mantel tests.

Results

The TWINSPAN analysis distinguished two groups for each flooding-class (Figure 2). The basic characteristics of each group are common to all three flooding-classes, although differences between the two groups became less pronounced over time. Reflooded wetlands within Group 1 have a perimeter colonised primarily by mudflat annuals such as *Polygonum lapathifolium* and *Amaranthus rudis* and an open-water area of submersed and floating aquatics, such as *Potamogeton foliosus* and *Lemna* spp. Group 1 includes wetlands that had been effectively tile-drained, mostly in northern Iowa. In contrast, restorations in

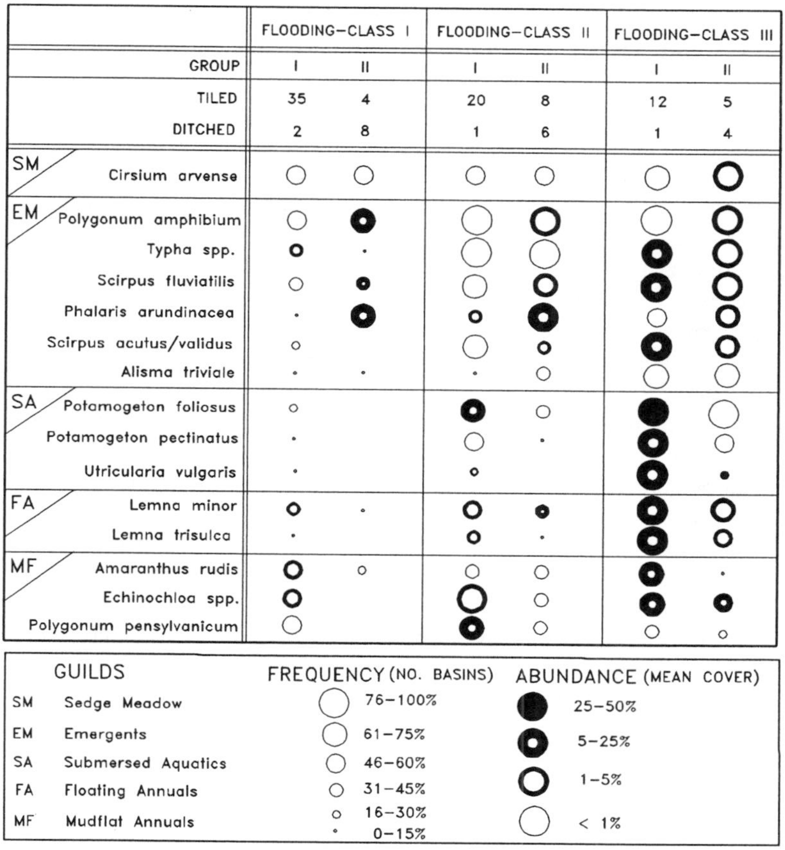

	FLOODING–CLASS I		FLOODING–CLASS II		FLOODING–CLASS III	
GROUP	I	II	I	II	I	II
TILED	35	4	20	8	12	5
DITCHED	2	8	1	6	1	4

SM
- Cirsium arvense

EM
- Polygonum amphibium
- Typha spp.
- Scirpus fluviatilis
- Phalaris arundinacea
- Scirpus acutus/validus
- Alisma triviale

SA
- Potamogeton foliosus
- Potamogeton pectinatus
- Utricularia vulgaris

FA
- Lemna minor
- Lemna trisulca

MF
- Amaranthus rudis
- Echinochloa spp.
- Polygonum pensylvanicum

GUILDS

SM	Sedge Meadow
EM	Emergents
SA	Submersed Aquatics
FA	Floating Annuals
MF	Mudflat Annuals

FREQUENCY (NO. BASINS)

- 76–100%
- 61–75%
- 46–60%
- 31–45%
- 16–30%
- 0–15%

ABUNDANCE (MEAN COVER)

- 25–50%
- 5–25%
- 1–5%
- < 1%

Figure 2. A comparison of the two vegetation groups recognised by TWINSPAN analysis of wetlands flooded for one, two and three years. Only species present in more than 67% of the basins in any year are shown. The analysis used data on all species. Flooding-classes include all basins reflooded for (I) one year or less; (II) one to two years; and (III) two to three years.

Group 2 have a periphery and shallow water zone dominated by emergent species such as *Phalaris arundinacea, Polygonum amphibium* and *Scirpus fluviatilis* with fewer mudflat annuals and submersed and floating aquatics. The wetlands of Group 2 include most of the ditched wetlands and all of the South Dakota restorations. In 10 of the Group 1 wetlands, emergent vegetation became established during the second or third year of flooding, and their vegetation became similar to that in Group 2 wetlands.

The Mantel tests and TWINSPAN analysis indicated that only historical factors were significantly correlated with vegetation composition in the first year after reflooding. Mantel tests indicated that historic factors (*i.e.* type of drainage, date of drainage) accounted for a significant portion of the variation in vegetation composition of flooding-class I basins. The index of matrix similarity between vegetation composition and historical factors declined from 3.68 in flooding-class I (P < 0.001), to 1.39 in flooding-class II (P= 0.08), and 1.00 in flooding-class III (P=0.19). How and when a wetland was drained primarily determines the composition of the initial vegetation in a reflooded pothole although these patterns are less pronounced over time.

Environmental factors showed no relationship to vegetation composition in any flooding-class. The failure of environmental factors to explain recolonisation patterns seems surprising, given what is known of the importance of soil moisture and water depth to natural regeneration in prairie marshes (*e.g.* van der Valk, 1981; Galinato & van der Valk, 1986; van der Valk & Pederson, 1989). There are two possible explanations for this lack of correspondence: (1) all the restorations were essentially identical with respect to the measured variables (water depth, size, organic carbon) or (2) suitable conditions occurred to allow a common group of species to colonise at least periodically. The first reason does not seem satisfactory since restorations included in the study had considerable variability for each environmental factor. The second possibilty appears more reasonable. Mudflats present along the perimeter were suitable for the establishment of mudflat annuals and emergent perennials and even small, shallow patches of open water were colonised by submersed and floating aquatics. It may be that species not colonising recently reflooded basins are those with specific environmental requirements, whereas these initial invaders are environmental generalists.

THE EXTENT OF RESTORATION

We used two approaches to compare the vegetation of reflooded wetlands with that of natural wetlands: (1) number of vegetation zones present and (2) number of species present in selected species guilds.

Most restoration attempts involve seasonal and semi-permanent wetlands. The former have a central zone of emergent vegetation that is flooded only in wetter years and is surrounded by sedge meadow and wet prairie zones. Semi-permanent wetlands have a central zone of submersed vegetation that is flooded in all except drought years, surrounded by emergent, sedge meadow and wet prairie zones. The presence or absence of different vegetation zones is a simple index of whether the vegetation structure in a reflooded wetland is comparable to that in a natural one. Our criterion for the presence of a vegetation zone was a total cover of 25% of the appropriate submersed, emergent, sedge meadow or wet prairie species. We examined vegetation data from 22 semi-permanent restorations that had been flooded for three years to determine which vegetation zones were present.

From the 22 basins that held water for three years, 10 were selected in northern Iowa that had been thoroughly drained by tile for at least 20 years before reflooding. A comparable natural wetland was located near each reflooded site. The vegetation of both was sampled at the same intensity (Galatowitsch, 1993). Contemporary natural wetlands have limitations as baselines for evaluating the success of vegetation re-establishment in reflooded wetlands. Natural wetlands today are islands in a sea of agricultural fields and most of the water that they receive is agricultural run-off (Neely & Baker, 1989). Consequently, the flora of these natural wetlands may have been affected by years of inputs of nutrients and pesticides and a reduction of inputs of seeds and propagules of wetland species. Several published floristic studies of wetlands in northern Iowa were conducted when these wetlands were in a more pristine condition (Pammel, 1898, 1908; Catlin & Hayden, 1927; Aikman & Thorne, 1956; Currier, 1979; Woodley, 1983). We also compared the species present in the 10 restored and 10 natural wetlands with those reported in published studies for seven wetlands in the same region.

Species were classified into eight guilds based on their life history characteristics (*sensu* van der Valk, 1981; Stewart & Kantrud, 1971) and their water-depth tolerances The eight guilds recognised were wet prairie perennials, sedge meadow perennials, shallow emergent perennials, deep emergent perennials, submersed aquatics, floating annuals, mudflat annuals and woody plants.

Results

Sixteen of the 22 wetlands reflooded for three years had an emergent zone and 13 a submersed zone. Only two wetlands had a sedge meadow zone and none had wet prairie vegetation. More permanently flooded vegetation zones are re-established quickly while less frequently flooded zones are largely absent. The mean number of species in the flora of natural wetlands was 45.8 per basin while reflooded wetlands had a mean of only 26.9 species per basin (Table 1). Forty-six (43%) of the 106 wetland species observed in the 20 reflooded and natural wetlands were only found in natural wetlands (Table 2). Not surprisingly, the most pronounced differences in floristic composition were in the wet prairie and sedge meadow zones. The 46 species found only in natural wetlands included 16 wet prairie perennials, 21 sedge meadow species, six shallow emergent species, and one each of deep emergent, submersed aquatic and mudflat annuals.

Ten species (9%) were found only in reflooded wetlands. These included *Cyperus esculentus*, an introduced perennial, an improved strain of *Panicum virgatum* that was planted to limit soil erosion and two mudflat annuals, *Xanthium strumarium* and *Amaranthus rudis*. The margins of reflooded wetlands are occupied by mudflat annuals (*e.g. Bidens cernua)* and, to a lesser extent, by emergent perennials, such as *Sparganium eurycarpum* and *Scirpus validus* rather than sedge meadow species. Emergent species found in reflooded wetlands are, however, the same as those found in natural wetlands. Emergent and floating species richness was lower in reflooded wetlands than in natural wetlands. By contrast, submersed aquatics, including *Potamogeton* spp., are more diverse in reflooded wetlands than in natural wetlands. The remaining six of 10 species

Table 1. Species richness in reflooded and natural wetlands. * Indicates significant difference between means (P<0.05, Wilcoxon Rank Sum Test).

Plant Guild	Reflooded Wetlands		Natural Wetlands		
	Mean	Range	Mean	Range	
All species	26.9	17–38	45.8	32–56	*
Wet-prairie perennials	1.1	0–2	6.0	1–12	*
Sedge meadow perennials	4.8	0–11	16.9	10–25	*
Shallow emergent perennials	5.0	2–7	12.1	8–14	*
Deep emergent perennials	2.3	1–4	2.4	1–3	
Submersed aquatics	5.8	2–9	1.2	0–3	*
Floating annuals	2.2	0–5	3.6	0–5	*
Mudflat annuals	4.6	2–9	2.8	0–8	
Woody plants	1.1	0–3	0.8	0–2	

unique to reflooded wetlands were submersed aquatics.

When compared with wetlands in previously published studies, both extant natural wetlands and reflooded wetlands had fewer species (Figure 3). Published studies indicate between 57 and 126 species per wetland, while extant natural wetlands had between 31 and 51 species. When wetlands were still surrounded by intact prairies, they had many wet prairie perennial species. In extant wetlands with no or with only a narrow prairie fringe, few of these species were present. Extant wetlands seem to have lost many species, and the most severe losses have occurred in the less frequently flooded zones. Wet prairie and sedge meadow species such as *Lilium michiganense, Cypripedium candidum, Parnassia glauca, Carex aquatilis,* and *Carex lasiocarpa* are much less common than they were reported to have been historically. Several non-indigenous species, most importantly *Phalaris arundinacea,* dominate the margins of many natural wetlands. Emergent species such as *Zizania aquatica* and *Acorus calamus* have declined while the recent invader *Typha angustifolia* and the hybrid *Typha* x *glauca* have taken over many prairie wetlands. The perimeter of extant natural wetlands are affected by 'edge effects' from adjacent agricultural lands including herbicide and fertiliser drift (Pearson & Loeschke, 1992). However, floristic shift in sedge meadow and wet prairie species probably occurred over 50 years ago, before any attempts to link agricultural use to changes in species distributions.

PATTERNS OF RECOLONISATION

There were many differences in the vegetation of restored and natural wetlands. In general, there were fewer wetland species in most guilds in reflooded than in natural wetlands. This is undoubtedly due to the fact that the oldest reflooded wetlands sampled had only been reflooded for three years. With time, reflooded and natural wetland vegetation composition will become more similar. One

Table 2. Species found only in reflooded or natural wetlands.

Reflooded wetlands only	Natural wetlands only
Wet prairie perennials	
Panicum virgatum (planted)	*Andropogon gerardii, Anemone canadense, Allium canadense, Desmodium canadense, Galium aparine, Hypoxis hirsuta, Phlox pilosa, Poa pratensis, Pycnanthemum virginianum, Rosa* spp.*, Silphium perfoliatum, Solidago canadensis, Thalictrum dasycarpum, Veronicastrum virginicum, Zigadenus elegans, Zizea aurea*
Sedge meadow perennials	
Cyperus esculentus	*Asclepias incarnata, Calamagrostis canadensis, Caltha palustris, Carex lanuginosa, C. scoparia, C. stricta, Cicuta maculata, Lathyrus palustris, Lycopus americanus, L. uniflorus, Lysimachia thyrsiflora, Lythrum alatum, Mentha arvensis, Poa palustris, Polygonum hydropiper, P. persicaria, Scutellaria galericulata, S. lateriflora, Spartina pectinatus, Stachys palustris, Urtica dioica*
Shallow emergent perennials	
None	*Acorus calamus, Carex atherodes, C. lacustris, Glyceria grandis, Iris virginica, Scolochloa festucacea*
Deep emergent perennials	
None	*Phragmites communis*
Submersed aquatics	
Ceratophyllum demersum, Myriophyllum exalbescens, Najas flexilis, Potamogeton nodosus, P. pusillus, P. zosteriformis	*Ranunculus flabellaris*
Mudflat annuals	
Amaranthus rudis, Xanthium strumarium	*Penthorum sedoides*

surprising feature is that reflooded wetlands had more species in one species guild, submersed aquatics, than natural wetlands. There were also differences in the composition of the vegetation in ditch- and tile-drained wetlands.

Why is species diversity of submersed aquatics lower in natural wetlands than in reflooded wetlands? Is there preferential dispersal of seed or other propagules of some submersed aquatic species to recently reflooded wetlands? Or are conditions for the establishment and survival of submersed aquatic species better in recently reflooded wetlands? Because both reflooded and natural wetlands in this study

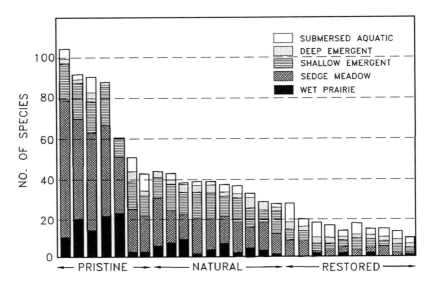

Figure 3. A comparison of species richness of five guilds of perennial species among 10 tiled, restored wetlands, 10 nearby natural wetlands, and published floras of high-quality natural wetlands (pristine).

were nearby, it seems unlikely that reflooded wetlands had or receive more propagules of submersed species than natural wetlands. However, this possibility cannot be ruled out. It seems more likely that in natural wetlands some submersed species become less common or are eliminated with time because of competition, herbivory or disease.

Why did wetlands drained with drainage ditches have more emergent species than tile-drained wetlands? We believe it is because ditch-drained wetlands often have relict or refugial populations of emergent species. Refugial populations of shallow emergent species are common along drainage ditches, and they rapidly expanded into reflooded wetlands. Even in the first year after flooding, populations of shallow emergents, such as *Polygonum amphibium, Phalaris arundinacea,* and *Scirpus fluviatilis,* were large and composed of vegetatively reproducing mature individuals. Refugial populations are much less important in thoroughly drained basins. However, refugial populations of some emergent species were also found in tiled wetlands that were not efficiently drained. Wienhold & van der Valk (1989) noted that some emergent species, such as *Scirpus fluviatilis* and *Scirpus validus,* appear to persist vegetatively in some tiled basins. Table 3 lists 47 wetland species found in wetlands before they reflooded.

The early presence of emergent species led LaGrange & Dinsmore (1989) to conclude that reflooded wetlands readily revegetate. They observed species of *Polygonum, Scirpus, Typha, Leersia,* and *Alisma,* as well as of *Ceratophyllum* and *Lemna* from reflooded marshes in Iowa. Similarly, Sewell & Higgins (1991)

Table 3. Wetland species found in dry basins the year previous to flooding or the last year of the survey (if they remained dry), usually in ditches and in wet spots within drained fields. Species are listed in descending frequency of occurrence.

Wet prairie / sedge meadow perennials

Present in more than 5% of dry basins (maximum 48%): *Cirsium arvense, Conyza canadensis, Rumex crsipus, Urtica dioica, Solidago canadensis, Verbena hastata, Poa pratensis, Carex vulpinoidea.*

Present in 5% or less of dry basins: *Scirpus atrovirens, Asclepias incarnata, Eleocharis erythropoda, Mentha arvensis, Polygonum hydropiper, Lythrum alatum, Equisetum hyemale, Juncus dudleyi, Leersia oryzoides, Heracleum lanatum, Stachys palustris, Rumex stenophylla, Eupatorium perfoliatum, Juncus torreyi.*

Shallow and deep emergent perennials

Present in more than 5% of dry basins (maximum 28%): *Polygonum amphibium, Phalaris arundinacea, Typha spp., Carex atherodes, Eleocharis macrostachya, Scirpus acutus/validus.*

Present in 5% or less of dry basins: *Scirpus fluviatilis, Sparganium eurycarpum, Alisma triviale, Sium suave.*

Submersed and floating aquatics

Present in more than 5% of dry basins: *none*

Present in 5% or less of dry basins: *Lemna·minor*

Mudflat annuals

Present in more than 5% of dry basins (maximum 90%): *Chenopodium album, Polygonum pennsylvanicum, Rorippa palustris, Amaranthus rudis, Hordeum jubatum, Polygonum lapathifolium, Echinochloa* sp. *Xanthium strumarium, Cyperus aristatus.*

Present in 5% or less of dry basins: *Cyperus strigosus, Eleocharis acicularis, Lindernia dubia, Hibiscus trionum, Gratiola neglecta.*

---

reported emergents such as *Typha* sp., *Polygonum amphibium, Phalaris arundincea, Scirpus fluviatilis* and *Alisma triviale* as well as *Lemna trisulca, Lemna minor,* and *Utricularia vulgaris* in 1–3-year old reflooded marshes in Minnesota and South Dakota. All of the species reported in these two studies were found in the reflooded wetlands that we sampled. These publications resulted in the notion that the vegetation of prairie potholes could be restored quickly and easily without human intervention.

Sewell & Higgins (1991) reported several sedge meadow species in recently reflooded wetlands in Minnesota and South Dakota, including *Carex* spp. and *Beckmannia syzigachne*. These species were found nearly exclusively in natural wetlands in our study. Although Sewell & Higgins do not report past land use or drainage method, wetland projects in partially drained pastures or ditch-drained basins, which would provide refugia for wetland species, are more common than those in tiled basins in central Minnesota and South Dakota (Galatowitsch, 1993).

The seed banks of most reflooded wetlands seemed to have contributed little to the recolonisation of reflooded wetlands other than annuals. The mean drainage duration for the restored wetlands in our study was 32 years. In Wienhold & van der Valk's study of the seed banks of drained wetlands, those drained for 30 years had less than 10% of the seed density and approximately 50% of the species in seed banks of extant wetlands. Recently-drained wetlands, especially those drained for less than 20 years, have seed banks with the greatest density and diversity (Wienhold & van der Valk, 1989). Not all wetland species may be present in the seed banks of even recently drained wetlands. For example, *Carex* spp. often have low seed production and *Carex* seeds are not long lived (van der Valk & Davis, 1979; Bremholm, 1993).

Only two tiled wetlands in our study were drained for less than twenty years. One wetland had been drained for only five years and another for only eight years prior to reflooding. Both sites were included in Group I in the TWINSPAN analysis and had a vegetative composition comparable to that of other tiled wetlands in the first year after flooding. However, by the second and third year these wetlands were clearly different from other tiled wetlands. The wetland drained for eight years had a cover of *Scirpus atrovirens* exceeding 50% across the entire wetland. The wetland drained for five years also had high coverage of *Scirpus atrovirens,* along with *Carex vulpinoidea* in shallow areas. This wetland, with 39 species, had the highest species diversity of any tiled wetland. As suggested by Weinhold & van der Valk (1989), only in recently drained wetlands will the seed bank be of any significance for restoring wetland vegetation.

Dispersal was probably responsible for the rapid colonisation of some submersed and floating aquatics in reflooded wetlands in our study because these species lack persistent seed banks and refugial populations after many years of drainage and cultivation. Only *Lemna minor* was found growing in refugial populations along ditch margins. If dispersal plays a major role in early revegetation of reflooded wetlands, basins in close proximity to natural wetlands should have more species than those far from a natural wetland. In our study, over half of the prairie wetlands of flooding-class I (51%) were within 2 km of a semi-permanent or permanent wetland; nearly another quarter (22.4%) were within 5 km of a semi-permanent or permanent wetland, and none were more than 13 km away. We were unable to find any evidence that closer proximity to a natural wetland increased species diversity in reflooded wetlands. Such a pattern has been found by Reinartz & Warne (1993) who report that distance to nearest seed source had a particularly strong effect on the number of native wetland species present in reflooded wetlands in Wisconsin. Moller & Rordam (1985) also found 10 fewer plant species in ponds within an area with an average interbasin distance of 1040 m than in another with an average distance of 435 m.

The vegetation of reflooded wetlands after three years does not resemble the vegetation in natural wetlands in most respects. Only about half of the species present in comparable natural wetlands are present in reflooded wetlands. Only two vegetation zones out of the four expected are typically present. Both the sedge meadow and wet prairie zones show little or no sign of developing in most reflooded wetlands. Since remnant seed banks will probably not be important for recolonisation of sedge meadow species, the rate and magnitude of dispersal of propagules will probably determine how quickly these species re-establish. Dispersal rates are not expected to be high, because of low seed production in *Carex* spp. and because reflooded wetlands are usually isolated, precluding water dispersal. So, the probability of reflooded wetlands acquiring sedge meadows and wet prairies in the near future seems low unless they have refugial populations that withstand drainage and cultivation (for instance along ditch lines). Unflooded areas in many basins may be overgrown by fast-growing species, such as *Phalaris arundinacea* or *Leersia oryzoides*, which would pre-empt this largely unoccupied habitat. In order to re-establish sedge meadow and wet prairie zones in reflooded wetlands, species that are found in these two zones will need to be planted.

ACKNOWLEDGMENTS

This project was funded by Ducks Unlimited, Inc., National Fish and Wildlife Foundation, North American Wildlife Foundation and the National Audubon Society. This is Paper No. 28 of the Institute for Wetland and Waterfowl Research.

REFERENCES

Aikman, J.M. &. Thorne, R.F. (1956). The Cayler Prairie: an ecologic and taxonomic study of a northwest Iowa prairie. *Proceedings of the Iowa Academy of Science, 63,* 177–200.

Bremholm, T.L. (1993). *Evaluation of techniques for establishing sedge meadows.* M.S. thesis, Iowa State University, Ames, IA. 99 pp.

Catlin, L.A. & Hayden, A. (1927). Physiographic ecology of a Wisconsin drift lake. *Proceedings of the Iowa Academy of Science, 34,* 165–190.

Currier, P.J. (1979). *Floristic composition and primary production of the post-drawdown vegetation of Eagle Lake Marsh, Hancock County, Iowa.* M.S. Thesis, Iowa State University, Ames, Iowa.

Dahl, T.E. (1991). Wetlands status and trends in the conterminous United States, mid 1970's to mid 1980's: first update of the national wetlands status report. *U.S. Fish and Wildlife Service Report.* Washington D.C. 22 pp.

Dornfield, R.& Warhurst, R. (1988). A cooperative program for restoring drained wetlands in Minnesota. *Transactions of the 53rd North American Wildlife and Natural Resources Conference, 53,* 454–462.

Galatowitsch, S.M. (1993). *Site selection, design criteria and performance assessment for wetland restorations in the Prairie Pothole Region.* PhD dissertation, Iowa State University, Ames, Iowa.

Galatowitsch, S.M. & van der Valk, A.G. (1994). *Restoring Prairie Wetlands: an Ecological Approach.* Iowa State University Press, Ames, Iowa. 246pp.

Galinato, M.I. & van der Valk, A.G. (1986). Seed germination traits of annuals and emergents recruited during drawdowns in the Delta Marsh, Manitoba, Canada. *Aquatic*

Botany, **26**, 89–102.

Great Plains Flora Association. (1986). *Flora of the Great Plains.* University Press of Kansas, Lawrence, Kansas.

Hewes, L. (1951). The northern wet prairie of the United States: nature, sources of information and extent. *Annals of the Association of American Geographers,* **41**, 307–323.

Kantrud, H. A., Millar, J. B. & van der Valk, A. G. (1989). *Northern Prairie Wetlands* (ed. A. G. van der Valk). pp. 132–187. Iowa State University Press, Ames.

LaGrange, T. G. & Dinsmore, J.J. (1989). Plant and animal community responses to restored Iowa wetlands. *Prairie Naturalist,* **21**, 39–48.

Madsen, C. R. (1988). Wetland restoration in western Minnesota. *Increasing Our Wetland Resources.* (eds J.S. Zelazney & J.S. Feierabend), pp. 92–94. National Wildlife Federation, Washington, D.C.

Manley, B.F. (1985). *The Statistics of Natural Selection.* Chapman & Hall, New York.

Mantel, N. and R.S. Valand. (1970). A technique for nonparametric multivariate analysis. *Biometrics,* **26**, 547–558.

Moller, T.R. & Rordam, C.P. (1985). Species numbers of vascular plants in relation to area, isolation and age of ponds in Denmark. *Oikos,* **45**, 8–16.

Mueller-Dombois, D. & Ellenberg, H. (1974). *Aims and Methods of Vegetation Ecology.* John Wiley & Sons, New York.

National Research Council. (1992). *Restoration of Aquatic Ecosystems.* National Academy Press, Washington D.C. 552 pages.

Neely, R. K. & Baker, J. L. (1989). Nitrogen and phosphorous dynamics and the fate of agricultural runoff. *Northern Prairie Wetlands* (ed. A.G. van der Valk), pp. 92–131. Iowa State University Press, Ames, Iowa. 400 pp.

Pammel, L.H. (1898). Old lake vegetation in Hamilton County, Iowa. *The Plant World* **2**, 42–45.

Pammel, L.H. (1908). Flora of Iowa peat bogs. *Annual Report of the Iowa Geologic Survey,* **19**, 735–778.

Pearson, J. & Loeschke, M. (1992). Floristic composition and conservation status of fens in Iowa. *Journal of the Iowa Academy of Science,* **99**, 41–52.

Reinartz, J.A. & Warne, E.L. (1993). Development of vegetation in small created wetlands in southeastern Wisconsin. *Wetlands,* **13**, 153–164.

Sewell, R.W. & Higgins, K.F. (1991). Floral and faunal colonization of restored wetlands in west-central Minnesota and northeastern South Dakota. *Proceedings of the Eighteenth Annual Conference on Wetlands Restoration and Creation,* **18**, 108–133.

Stewart, R.E. & Kantrud, H.A. (1971). Classification of natural ponds and lakes in the glaciated prairie region. U.S. Fish and Wildlife Service, *Research Publication* **92**. Washington, D.C. 57 pp.

van der Valk, A.G. (1981). Succession in wetlands: a Gleasonian approach. *Ecology,* **62**, 688–696.

van der Valk, A.G. & Davis, C.B. (1979). A reconstruction of the recent vegetation history of a prairie marsh, Eagle Lake, Iowa from its seed bank. *Aquatic Botany,* **6**, 29–51.

van der Valk, A.G. & Pederson, R.L. (1989). Seed banks and the management and restoration of natural vegetation. *Ecology of Soil Seed Banks.* (eds M.A. Leck, V.T. Parker & R.L. Simpson), pp. 329–346. Academic Press, Inc., New York.

Wienhold C.E. & van der Valk, A.G. (1989). The impact of duration of drainage on the seed banks of northern prairie wetlands. *Canadian Journal of Botany,* **67**, 1878–1884.

Woodley, G. (1983). *The vascular flora of Doolittle Prairie.* Unpublished manuscript from the Iowa State University Herbarium reprint collection, Ames, Iowa.

10 Nutrient Dynamics during Restoration of Fen Meadows by Haymaking without Fertiliser Application

J. P. BAKKER

Laboratory of Plant Ecology, University of Groningen, P.O.Box 14, 9750 AA, Haren, The Netherlands

H. OLFF

Department of Terrestrial Ecology and Nature Conservation, Agricultural University, Bornsesteeg 47, 6708 PD, Wageningen, The Netherlands

SUMMARY

1.   A fen meadow system which was not severely affected by drainage showed a good potential for restoration management, *i.e.* continued haymaking after the cessation of fertiliser application. Restoration management resulted in a decrease of above-ground standing crop, an increase of species-richness, and a replacement of species from eutrophic to mesotrophic conditions.
2.   The fertilisation history, *i.e.* the total amount of nutrients accumulated in a field, taking into account the year when restoration management started and the removal of nutrients since then, affects the rate at which the former mesotrophic plant communities can be restored. The cumulative nitrogen balance, *i.e.* the balance between total accumulation since 1945 and offtake by restoration management, is a better predictor for the dynamics of the two most important grass species than just the number of years in which restoration management was carried out.
3.   Species replacement of common mesotrophic species can be predicted better than that of rare mesotrophic species. Dispersal might be a limiting factor for rare species.
4.   During restoration management, N and K limitation may be limiting initially, whereas P limitation becomes important later.
5.   Nutrient dynamics as a mechanism of restoration succession might be seen as proceeding from an initially very low nutrient limitation (and probably light limitation under fertilised conditions) to multiple nutrient limitation with different nutrients limiting for different plant species.

INTRODUCTION

The intensification of agricultural practices in Western Europe during the last 50

Restoration of Temperate Wetlands. Edited by B.D. Wheeler, S.C. Shaw, W.J. Fojt and R.A. Robertson
© 1995 John Wiley & Sons Ltd.

years has led to the disappearance of many species-rich, low productivity plant communities of oligotrophic and mesotrophic habitats. In oligotrophic fens the C:N ratio is > 30, in eutrophic fens < 20, with mesotrophic fen meadows intermediate (Succow & Jeschke, 1986). The former large diversity of these communities was often based on a wide variety of soils, hydrological conditions and management practices. Recent agricultural practices in many former fen systems involve high rates of fertiliser application and frequent cutting. Large areas of these grasslands are now being acquired as nature reserves in the Netherlands and the authorities in charge of the management are faced with the problem of how to restore the formerly low productivity, species-rich fen plant communities.

For the restoration management to succeed, at least four conditions should be fulfilled: (i) the original hydrological conditions should still be present or should be restored; (ii) the original management practices (or absence of management) should be restored; (iii) nutrient availability should be reduced; (iv) propagules of the appropriate target species should be available (either in the seed bank or through dispersal)..

A decreased nutrient availability can be realised by stopping fertiliser application and by removing nutrients from the system through cutting, grazing or sod removal (Bakker, 1989). The history of fertiliser application to fields is important in this respect; in cases of more intensive or longer past agricultural use it might be more difficult to restore mesotrophic conditions. Furthermore, in formerly wet areas the management practices can aim at slowing down the rate of internal circulation of nutrients in the system by restoring high groundwater tables (Myers, Campbell & Melillo, 1982; Berendse *et al.*, 1994).

This paper focuses on the potential for restoration management as judged by changes in standing crop and species composition of fen vegetation after the cessation of fertiliser applications and the continuation of cutting practices. We examine how the fertilisation history of different fields has affected their restoration potential and discuss the relationship between changes in nutrient availability and plant species replacement. These results are reported for a fen system which was not severely affected by drainage.

STUDY AREA

Chronosequence

The fen meadows discussed as an example for this study on vegetation succession and nutrient dynamics are situated in the nature reserve 'Stroomdallandschap Drentsche A' along a tributary of the brook locally known as the Anlooër Diepje (53°05'N, 6°40'E). We use the word succession to indicate a unidirectional species replacement. How this succession can be judged with respect to autogenic or allogenic processes can be derived from the review on mechanisms of vegetation succession by van Andel, Bakker & Grootjans (1993). The area features no peat accumulation, so it is referred to as a mineral-based fen system. The quotient of the mathematical mean (x) and the median (M) of the duration lines of the study area x/M is about 1.05 (Bakker, 1989). This indicates a slight discharge of seepage water (Grootjans & Ten Klooster, 1980). The seepage water is calcium-poor and is associated with plant communities belonging to the alliances CARICION CURTO-NIGRAE and JUNCO-MOLINION (Grootjans, 1980).

The acquisition of fields from farmers in the nature reserve and subsequent restoration management started about 1970 and gradually continues. This enabled us to monitor vegetational dynamics in permanent plots in several fields from 1972 onwards (Bakker, 1989). In this paper, we report results from nine different fields with similar soil and hydrology, some of which had permanent plots, while others had been recently acquired (Table 1). Before 1945, all fields had about the same agricultural management (haymaking once or twice a year with little fertiliser application). Differences between fields are therefore assumed to have been established since then. This enables us to make two types of comparison: (i) a temporal comparison of permanent plots between years in a single field ('real-time' succession), and (ii) a spatial comparison in a single year between fields which were not fertilised for different time periods (reconstructed succession or chronosequence). The temporal comparison will be used to investigate changes in peak standing crop and species replacement, while the spatial comparison will be used for investigating nutrient availability and nutrient limitation.

It should, however, be noted that, for the spatial comparison, two effects (history of fertiliser application and duration of restoration management) are confounded. Fields where fertiliser application was stopped in, for example, 1966 (field F, Table 1) have therefore received a much lower total amount of nutrients than fields where fertiliser application stopped more recently (field A). This means that for a spatial comparison in a single year the duration of restoration management is negatively correlated with the total amount of nutrients which a field has received up to the present time (fertilisation history). However, observations on the

Table 1. Overview of field characteristics.

Field	Field code in Bakker (1989)	Date last fertilised	No. of permanent plots analysed	Dates annually recorded
A	–	1989	0	–
B	–	1985	0	–
C	1376	1971	7	1972–90
D	1371	1945	5	1974–90
E	463	1971	7	1974–90
F	677	1966	7	1972–90
G	854	1966	6	1972–90
H	1378	1977	2	1979–88
J	Loefvledder recent reserve	1971	0	–

permanent plots allow us to separate these two factors. All results apply to fields which were cut once a year in late July or early August during the period of restoration management. Each field involved a gradient from a drier sandy soil to a wetter, peaty soil. Only results for the wet fen meadow parts are reported here.

History of fertiliser application and nutrient offtake

Before 1950, most grasslands in fen areas in the Netherlands received low rates of fertiliser application. In areas with a peaty soil along small brooks, grazing was not a common practice, probably due to the fact that the sod is easily destroyed by trampling. Haymaking once or twice a year was the usual management here (Bakker, 1989). Advised fertiliser application rates around 1900 for Dutch sandy or peaty grasslands were 15–30 kg N ha^{-1}, 25–40 kg P ha^{-1} and 60–120 kg K ha^{-1} (Ten Rodengate Marissen, 1905). After World War II, the average rates of fertiliser application strongly increased due to introduction of artificial fertiliser and improved education of farmers. A yearly inventory of fertiliser application practices of 27 farmers by Altena (1993) showed a strong increase of N, P and K addition rates between 1948 and 1955 (Figure 1). Later data on fertiliser application were derived from personal communications with local farmers. After this, P and K application rates decreased, probably because leguminous species became less important, and the initally poor P and K status of the soil had been improved to agriculturally satisfactory levels. It should be noted that P and K addition rates returned to their former levels, while N addition rates showed a two or threefold increase. Between 1960 and 1980 the average annual rate of atmospheric deposition of N increased from 20 to 45 kg ha^{-1} (Figure 2). The

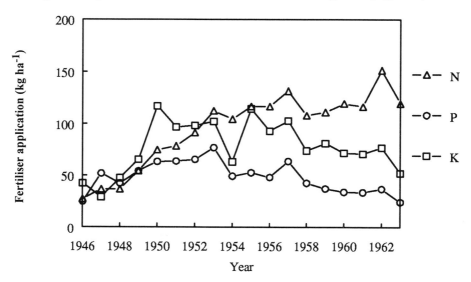

Figure 1. Average annual fertiliser application rates to permanent grassland during 1946–63 (means of 27 fields, adapted from Altena, 1993).

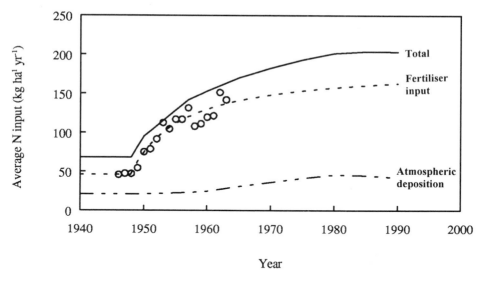

Figure 2. Reconstructed changes in annual average N input rates to permanent grassland in the Netherlands. Data on fertiliser input from Figure 1 ($y=136(t-1948)/((t-1948)+8.06)+47$, $R^2=0.84$, $p<0.001$), data on atmospheric deposition from de Boer & Thomas (1991).

(interpolated) changes in total N input to grasslands between 1940 and 1990 are also shown in Figure 2, where fertiliser application and atmospheric deposition are added. In areas with intensive dairy farming, these rates increased even more after 1970 (to 200–300 kg ha^{-1}), but this has not happened in the fen grasslands which are discussed in the current paper.

These changes in nutrient input to grasslands imply that fields where fertiliser application ceased in 1945 received much fewer nutrients up to the present than fields where fertiliser application was terminated recently. This might affect the rate at which the former mesotrophic communities can be restored. A history of several decades of fertiliser application may have produced a large pool of high quality soil organic matter, resulting in high N and P mineralisation rates. Furthermore, the soil adsorption complex might be saturated with P, and it could therefore take a long time before soil available P is depleted. In order to account for this 'fertilisation history' effect, we calculated the cumulative N input per field since 1945 for each year until 1990 (Figure 3A), using information on average N input (Figure 2) and the duration of restoration management (Table 1). Field D only received atmospheric deposition, while the other fields received more N since fertiliser application continued for longer. From these cumulative N inputs we subtracted the estimated offtake by cutting (Figure 3B) resulting in a 'cumulative N balance' (CNB, Figure 3C). The N offtake was estimated from data given by Olff, Berendse & De Visser (1994) for fields A, B, C and D. It was assumed that this represented the offtake from 2, 6, 18 and 45 years after stopping fertiliser

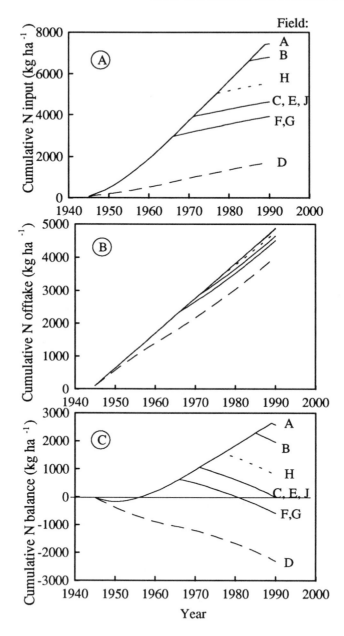

Figure 3. Estimated cumulative N input (A, sum of fertiliser application and atmospheric deposition), cumulative N offtake (B) and cumulative N balance (C, difference between input and offtake) to nine permanent grassland fields since 1947. Fertiliser input ended in different years in each field (see Table 1). Offtake rates interpolated from standing crop and tissue N concentrations in four fields not fertilised for 45, 20, 6 and 2 years, respectively.

application, where intermediate years were interpolated. It was found that field D had a negative cumulative balance (more offtake than input) over the whole period, while the balance of fields F and G became negative in 1980, and the balance for fields C, E and J became negative in 1990 (Figure 3C). The data per field in Figure 3C incorporate the nutrient input and offtake history in each field, and it will be investigated if this information can be used to understand more of the dynamics of species replacement during restoration management. It is hypothesised that fields which received more nutrients (higher cumulative balance) will take longer to reach the same species composition as a field which was under restoration management for the same time, but received fewer nutrients in the past (because fertiliser application was stopped earlier).

CHANGES DURING RESTORATION MANAGEMENT

Grassland yield

The cessation of fertiliser application in field J led to a significant decrease of peak standing cropat cutting from about 750 to 300 g m^{-2} (y=739e$^{-0.081t}$, r=0.61, P<0.01, Figure 4). An exception to this decrease was 1983, which was a very wet year and when there was a high yield (Olff & Bakker, 1991). Using the chronosequence approach, we compared 14 fields in 1990 which had then been under restoration management for different periods. In some of these fields, patches of *Juncus*

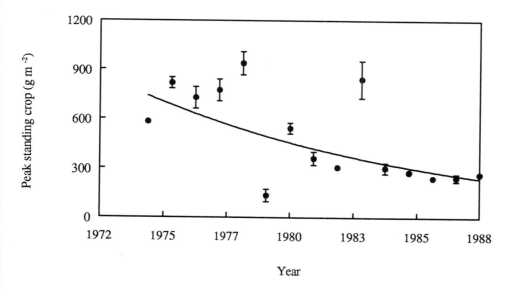

Figure 4. Changes in standing crop (mean and S.D., $n = 10$) in July of field J after fertilisers were last applied in 1971. The line gives an exponential decrease (y=739.681exp(-0.081(t+1974)), r=0.61, P<0.05).

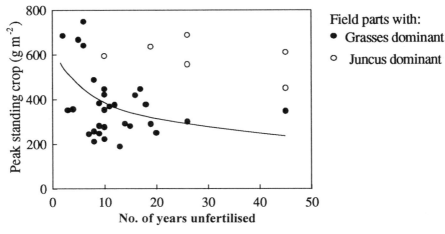

Figure 5. Peak standing crop, including litter, in 14 different fields as a function of the number of years which a field had not been fertilised. Within each field, a distinction was made between parts which were dominated by *Juncus acutiflorus* clones and parts which were dominated by grasses.

acutiflorus[1] were found, a clonal species with extensive rhizomes, which is therefore very different in growth form from the grasses dominating the rest of the field. These spots were therefore sampled separately. The peak standing crop of the grass-dominated parts was clearly lower in fields which had been longer under restoration management (Figure 5). However, peak standing crop, including litter, in the *Juncus acutiflorus* stands was always quite high compared to the rest of the field, and small differences between fields were found. This might be explained by the high storage/remobilisation of biomass and nutrients which has been observed in *Juncus acutiflorus*. Combined with long-lived leaves, this feature seems to enable this species to maintain a high biomass even at low nutrient availability (Olff *et al.*, 1994).

Species replacement in permanent plots

In order to study vegetation succession in the permanent plots, the six most abundant species were selected, according to the maximum percentage cover which a species had in any of the years, in any field. Only average percentage cover data were used (based on 2–7 plots, see Table 1). This and the frequency of occurrence (the fraction of total number of plots per field per year) were plotted against the duration of restoration management (Figure 6) and against the cumulative nitrogen balance (CNB) (Figure 7). The changes with time in cover and frequency of occurrence of individual species were described by using a set of hierarchical models for species response analysis as proposed by Huisman, Olff &

---

[1] Nomenclature of species follows van der Meiden *et al.* (1990).

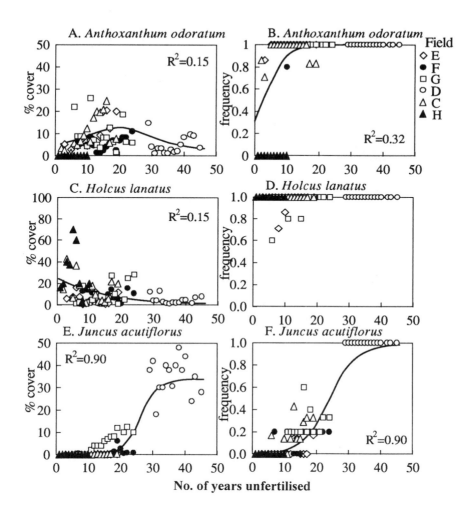

Figure 6. Percentage cover and frequency of occurrence (fraction of total no. of plots) of six most abundant plant species in the permanent plots in six annually cut fields (Table 1), as dependent on the duration of restoration management (number of years unfertilised). All presented response models were significant, as tested by an F-test based on non-linear regression (see text).

Fresco (1993) and applied by Olff, Huisman & van Tooren (1993). *Holcus lanatus* was almost always present, and decreased during the whole successional series (Figure 6). Between 10 to 20 years after the beginning of restoration management, *Anthoxanthum odoratum*, *Ranunculus repens* and *Rhinanthus angustifolius* became dominant. During this period, *Plantago lanceolata* entered the

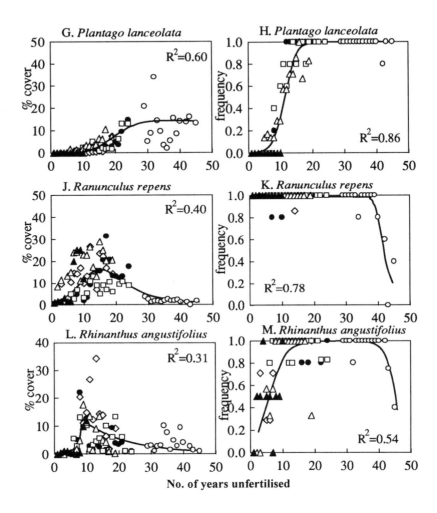

Figure 6, continued.

successional series and increased in importance (see also Olff & Bakker, 1991). *Juncus acutiflorus* was the last species to enter the successional series and became the final dominant. It should be noted that *Anthoxanthum* and *Plantago* remained absent from field H, although they were expected to become important here. This may be explained by the differences in history in fertiliser application between fields. Neither species was found when the CNB exeeded 1000 kg ha^{-1} (Figure 7). It appears that the additional six years during which field H had been fertilised compared with fields C and E has delayed the increase of both species by 5 to 10 years (Figures 6 and 7). Comparison of the R^2 of the response models between

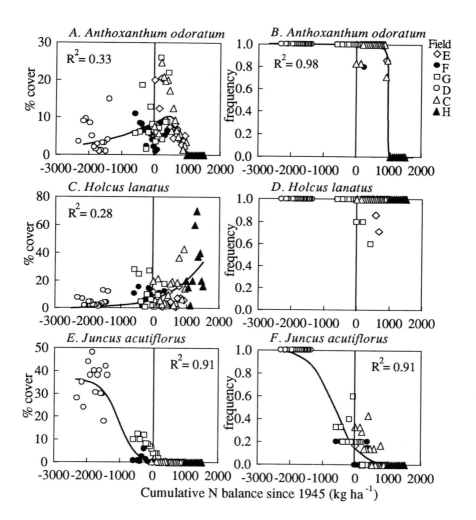

Figure 7. Percentage cover and frequency of occurrence (fraction of total no. of plots) of the six most abundant plant species in the permanent plots in six annually cut fields (Table 1), as dependent on the cumulative N balance since 1945 (see Figure 3C). Symbols as in Figure 6. All presented response models were significant, as tested by an F-test based on non-linear regression (see text).

Figures 6 and 7 revealed that the CNB was a better explanation for the variation in cover and frequency of the two most important grasses, *Anthoxanthum odoratum* and *Holcus lanatus* (explained variance increased by 13–66%). The fit of *Juncus acutiflorus* and *Plantago lanceolata* was already very good, and did not improve further. For the other species, numbers of years of restoration management or

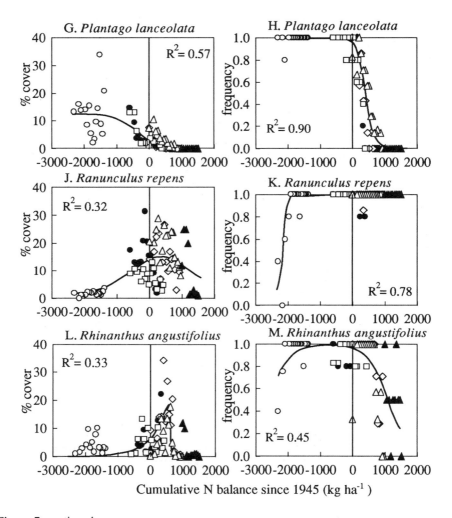

Figure 7, continued.

CNB were equally good predictors for the variance in abundance and frequency of occurrence.

The six aforementioned dominant species occur frequently in the study area along ditches and road verges and dispersal limitations are therefore not expected. This may not apply for less widespread species. Four species occurring in the permanent plots are relatively rare (they occur in less then 5% of the 5 x 5 km grid cells into which the Netherlands can be subdivided (Anonymous, 1991)). Three of these species (*Carex aquatilis, Crepis paludosa* and *Viola palustris*) occur in only one or a few plots in one field (Figure 8). *Carex aquatilis* occurs here at the

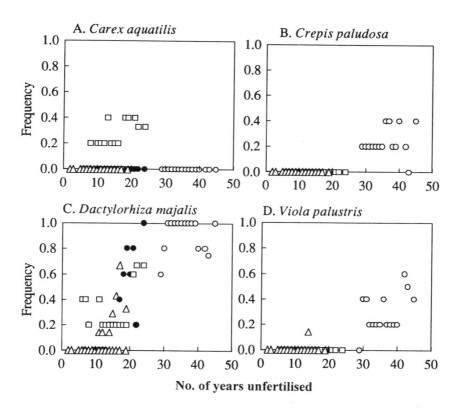

Figure 8. Percentage cover and frequency of occurrence (fraction of total no. of plots) of four rare plant species occurring in permanent plots in six annually cut fields (Table 1), as dependent on the duration of restoration management. Symbols as in Figure 6. Trends were tested by second-order polynomial regressions, which were all significant (P<0.001).

southern limit of its distribution and has poor reproductive capacity; it persists mainly by vegetative reproduction (Grootjans & van Tooren, 1984). *Crepis* and *Viola* do reproduce generatively, but seem to have failed to colonise the other fields from field D. The only rare, mesotrophic species which has readily colonised the other fields is the orchid *Dactylorhiza majalis* (Figure 8). This species produces very many small seeds, which are probably easily dispersed by wind and cutting machinery. After 20 years of restoration management it occurs in most plots. Other species occurring frequently after 20 years were *Potentilla anserina, Poa pratensis, Ranunculus acris* and *Ranunculus repens* (Olff & Bakker, 1991). Details of species replacement are given by these authors and by Bakker (1989, Tables VI.12 & 14; 1994, Table 2). It appears that the vegetational succession reveals a shift from *Poö-Lolietum* via *Lolio-Cynosuretum* towards JUNCO-MOLINION, which is a desirable objective for fen meadow restoration.

Table 2. Nitrogen (N), potassium (K), phosphorus (P) and carbon (C) concentrations in the shoot of several species in four fields ($n = 1$–5 per field) (from Olff, 1992b).

Species	Field	Concentration (g kg^{-1} dw)			
		N	K	P	C
Agrostis stolonifera	A	19.2	16.7	3.3	42.0
	B	10.9	4.8	1.8	35.6
Poa trivialis	A	21.3	22.4	3.2	40.2
	B	13.9	7.9	2.6	36.2
	C	14.4	4.8	2.4	–
Glyceria fluitans	B	14.1	6.1	2.6	40.3
Holcus lanatus	B	16.8	7.8	3.3	35.2
	C	19.0	4.4	2.8	40.4
	D	14.6	6.6	1.5	42.3
Deschampsia cespitosa	C	13.9	3.5	1.7	40.3
Anthoxanthum odoratum	C	19.2	2.9	2.2	35.8
	D	8.9	4.2	0.9	44.8
Plantago lanceolata	D	15.1	4.1	1.5	39.0
Agrostis capillaris	D	15.8	4.0	1.6	38.7
Juncus acutiflorus	D	17.1	4.9	1.9	32.6
Other dicots	B	17.8	7.6	4.3	35.6
	C	19.7	4.8	3.2	30.3
	D	20.6	3.7	1.7	35.8
Other monocots	A	19.2	16.7	3.3	41.0
	B	10.8	5.9	2.3	35.8
	C	22.2	5.0	2.6	–
	D	16.3	3.3	1.4	33.7

succession reveals a shift from *Poö-Lolietum* via *Lolio-Cynosuretum* towards JUNCO-MOLINION, which is a desirable objective for fen meadow restoration.

These results may be used to judge the potential of restoration management in different areas on similar soil when the fertilisation history is known. Such information improves predictions on the dynamics of dominant species after fertiliser application ceases. Fields fertilised over a long period took longer to reach the species composition found in those fields fertilised for a shorter time. For rare species, dispersal limitation should also be taken into account. When they are totally absent from an area, their re-establishment may be difficult (without artificial introduction).

Species-richness changes

Some further information on dispersal as a potentially limiting factor is obtained from data on the total number of species per plot and per field (Figure 9). In each plot, species can be present or absent due to local processes such as microsite colonisation, coexistence, competitive exclusion or random events. These processes are expected to be related to the history of fertiliser application. It was indeed found that the CNB accounted better for the number of species per plot than did the number of years without fertiliser application (Figure 9, 15% improvement of explained variance). The number of species per plot decreased strongly when the CNB was positive. For negative values of CNB we did not observe any clear trend. The number of species per field showed a less clear trend, and was explained somewhat better by the number of years of restoration management than by CNB (Figure 9). Field E was deviant from the other fields, since at the start of the observations this field already had more species than the other fields. The number of species increased, but at a higher absolute level. This supports the hypothesis that, whilst the number of species per plot was fully 'explained' by the CNB, this does not account adequately for the number of species per field. For this, the initial number of species was important, which

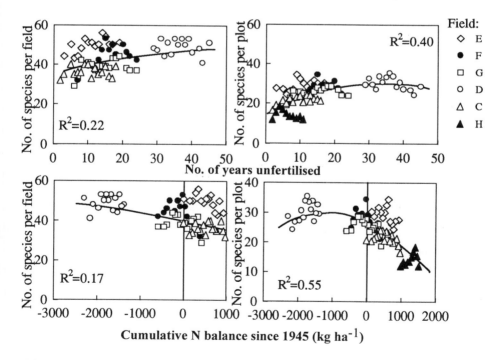

Figure 9. Number of species per field and number of species per plot in permanent plots in six annually cut fields, as dependent on the duration of restoration management and on the cumulative N balance since 1945 (see Figure 3C).

makes it likely that dispersal between fields can be an important limiting factor for the rate of increase of species richness.

NUTRIENT DYNAMICS DURING RESTORATION SUCCESSION

The decrease of total above-ground biomass during restoration management by haymaking might be caused by limitation of nutrients and changes in nutrient supply. This hypothesis was tested by growing intact sods in the glasshouse on nutrient solutions from which various nutrients were omitted. The reaction of the vegetation and individual plant species to a shift in nutrient limitation was studied by assessing the concentration of nutrients in total biomass and pool size in individual shoots. We also studied changes in tissue nutrient concentrations in individual species in the field. Changes in the availability of nitrogen were estimated by determining the rate of mineralisation *in situ* in soil.

Type of nutrient limitation

Five nutrient omission treatments were carried out by collecting undisturbed sods from each of the fields A, B, C and D in 1991 (Olff & Pegtel, 1994). The sods were placed on top of a bucket filled with demineralised water. After one month roots had grown into the buckets and the demineralised water in most buckets was replaced by various nutrient solutions. We compared the effects of demineralised water (control), a complete nutrient solution, and three nutrient solutions lacking N, P or K, respectively. By this means, the relative nutrient deficiencies were screened, assuming that the yield reduction (compared with the full nutrient solution) was a measure of how much of the nutrient lacking from the solution could be taken up from the soil of the sod (Pegtel, 1987; van der Woude, Pegtel & Bakker, 1994). The sods were clipped after 46, 86, 125 and 164 days.

The effect of omitting all nutrients simultaneously resulted in the largest cumulative (summed over all harvests) yield reduction in all fields (Figure 10). However, substantial differences were observed in the effect of the other treatments. Fields A and B were limited by both N and K, as were fields C and D. The effect of omitting K was larger in fields C and D than in earlier successional fields. Furthermore, in field C the effect of omitting P was significant, and the magnitude of this effect increased towards field D. This means that during succession the type of nutrient limitation changed from both N and K during early succession, to simultaneous N, P and K limitation in the later successional stages. In field D (where restoration management took place for the longest time) the effect of omitting either N, P or K was almost as large as omitting N, P and K simultaneously (Figure 10).

There were treatment-dependent differences between the various species groups in their contribution to the cumulative yield (Figure 10). The contribution of non-leguminous forbs was larger in the full nutrient treatment than in the other treatments, in every field. The contribution of rushes in field D was larger in the

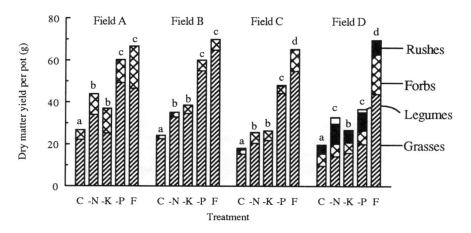

Figure 10. The effect of omitting various nutrients from a nutrient solution on the cumulative shoot dry matter yield (over four harvests) per pot ($n = 4$) of undisturbed sods, originating from four successional hayfields which were not fertilised for various periods (Field A, 2 years; Field B, 6 years; Field C, 19 years; Field D, 45 years), when grown with the roots in nutrient solutions which were either complete (F), N-deficient (–N), K-deficient (–K), P-deficient (–P) or lacking N, P and K (C). Bars with the same letter were not significantly different ($P>0.05$) within each field (Student–Newman–Keuls contrasts after one-way analysis of variance) (after Olff & Pegtel, 1994).

–N and the –P treatment. In full nutrient solution, the rushes did not increase compared with the control; the increased yield in this treatment was fully accounted for by grasses and non-leguminous forbs. Legumes increased in field D in the –N treatment compared with the control, and to a lesser extent in the –P treatment. In other fields, legumes and rushes were not important.

Tissue nutrient concentrations in the field

Tissue nutrient concentrations in the various plant species differed markedly (Table 2). Furthermore, the same species often had different concentrations in different fields. This may provide some further insight into differences in the type and extent of nutrient limitation between the chronosequence stages. The highest N and K concentrations were found in the dominant species of field A: *Agrostis stolonifera* and *Poa trivialis*. The N and K concentrations of both species decreased towards field B. It was striking that, while the N and K concentrations in field A were about equal, in field B the K concentration was two to three times lower than the N concentration. The species entering the succession in field B (*Holcus lanatus* and *Glyceria fluitans*) had higher N and K concentrations in field B than the earlier successional species *Agrostis stolonifera* and *Poa trivialis*. From field B to field C, the K concentration of *Holcus lanatus* and *Poa trivialis* decreased further, while the N concentration did not change. From field C to field D, the K concentration of *Holcus lanatus* and *Anthoxanthum odoratum* slightly increased, while the N and P concentration decreased. These results indicate that N and K limitation may be important especially in the first three stages, while P limitation only became important in field D. These conclusions concur with the results of the glasshouse experiment reported above.

Carbon concentrations showed much smaller differences between species and between fields than the concentrations of N, P and K. Therefore, carbon:nutrient ratios mainly reflected the differences in nutrient concentrations.

The discrepancy between changes in nutrient concentrations within species (due to species replacement) and differences in total values per field for N and P implies that the new species entering the succession in each field compensated for the lower pool size of N and P of species originating from earlier successional stages.

Soil changes, N mineralisation and nitrification

The results of soil analysis revealed that pH slightly decreased from field A to field D. The pool sizes of N and P in the upper 10 cm of the soil decreased in accordance with the N and P concentration from field A to field D (Table 3). The C:P ratio increased from field A to D, while the C:N ratio did not change significantly.

The net mineralisation of nitrogen was estimated by measuring the accumulation

Table 3. Overview of various soil characteristics in four fields with different fertilisation history[a] (see Table 1). Means ($n = 5$) with the same letter were not significantly different (Student–Newman–Keuls test).

	Field A	Field B	Field C	Field D
Soil moisture (g 100 g^{-1} dw)	78.9a	61.3b	74.2a	70.9a
Organic matter (g 100 g^{-1} dw)	15.4a	10.3b	12.6c	7.3d
Bulk density[b] (g cm^{-3})	1.08	0.88	0.81	0.94
pH (H_2O)	5.9a	5.9a	5.7b	5.4c
pH (KCl)	4.9a	4.8b	4.6c	4.2d
Total C concentration (g 100 g^{-1} dw)	6.65a	5.09a	6.12a	3.13b
Total N concentration (g 100 g^{-1} dw)	0.471a	0.392b	0.465a	0.266c
Total P concentration (g 100 g^{-1} dw)	0.124a	0.093b	0.055c	0.030d
C:N ratio	14.1a	13.0a	13.2a	11.8a
C:P ratio	53.6a	55.9ab	111.0c	104.8b
C pool size (g m^{-2}, 0–10 cm)	7180a	4950b	4470b	2940c
N pool size (g m^{-2}, 0–10 cm)	511a	362b	365b	246c
P pool size (g m^{-2}, 0–10 cm)	134a	84b	44c	28d

[a] From Olff *et al.* (1994).
[b] Bulk samples were used, therefore differences between fields could not be tested.

of NH_4^+ and NO_3^- at intervals of 8 weeks in *in situ* incubated undisturbed soil cores in tubes. Field D showed a significantly lower total rate of mineralisation (61 kg N ha^{-1} yr^{-1}) than the other three fields (Table 4). Total mineralisation during the growing season (mid April to mid July) was highest in fields A and B and decreased towards fields C and D. In field D almost no seasonal variation in mineralisation was found, (*i.e.* in this field an important fraction of the small mineralisation occurred in winter; Olff *et al.*, 1994). Relative nitrification rates were significantly higher in fields A and B than in fields C and D. The absolute nitrification rate was significantly highest in field B, and then decreased towards fields C and D (Table 4). Nitrification rates were highest in summer; during the winter periods only ammonification was found (Olff *et al.*, 1994).

Table 4. Pool sizes, fluxes and some proportional features of the nitrogen cycle in four fields with a different fertilisation history[a] (see Table 1). Means with the same letter are not significantly different (Student–Newman–Keuls contrasts after one-way ANOVA).

	Field A	Field B	Field C	Field D
Soil organic N (kg ha^{-1}, 0–10 cm)	5110a	3620b	3650b	2460c
Shoot N at cutting[b] (kg ha^{-1})	92	91	72	106
Root N at cutting[b] (kg ha^{-1})	85	134	228	107
Total N mineralisation (kg ha^{-1} yr^{-1})	124a	176a	140a	61b
Nitrification (kg ha^{-1} yr^{-1})	109ab	132a	76b	25c
Relative nitrification (% of total mineralisation)	88a	75a	54b	41b

[a] From Olff *et al.* (1994).

[b] These variables were calculated on the basis of several variables; therefore the true variance of these features is not known, and differences between fields could not be tested.

NUTRIENT DYNAMICS AS A MECHANISM OF RESTORATION SUCCESSION

Fen meadow vegetation management in the Netherlands can generally be characterised by three periods: period I where annual haymaking without fertiliser application took place and species-rich communities were present; period II where the agricultural exploitation was intensified by fertiliser applications and increasing offtake frequency resulting in a higher productivity and decreasing species richness; and period III where restoration management was started by the resumption of haymaking once a year without fertiliser application. Observations revealed that productivity decreased and species richness increased during restoration succession. This is, however, not likely to be a general rule, since examples are known where species richness increased while peak standing crop did not change (Olff & Bakker, 1991), or peak standing crop decreased while species richness did not increase (Oomes & Mooi, 1985).

Information on historical nutrient addition rates indicate that the relative application rates of different nutrients changed strongly (Figure 1). While until 1946 equal amounts of N, P, and K were applied, in 1963 this had changed to an application ratio of 3:2:1. This could mean that fewer macronutrients were limiting, with fewer possibilities for species to coexist (Tilman, 1982). The nitrogen mineralisation was found to be lowest late in restoration succession, while the pool sizes of N and P in the soil decreased during succession. The analysis of tissue nutrient concentration and a bioassay with intact sods revealed that N and K first became limiting for shoot production during restoration succession, while subsequently P probably also became limiting. It is concluded that restoration succession proceeds from initially little nutrient limitation (and probably light limitation under fertilised conditions) to multiple nutrient limitation. This might be an explanation of the increasing species richness in these fen communities, since different species may become limited by different nutrients. There is, however, no experimental evidence available to support this hypothesis. This might be also part of the explanation for the high species richness of these fields prior to the intensification of agricultural practices. An exception to these trends in nutrient limitation were the species changes occurring during the first six years, which seemed to be related to the decreased offtake frequency. Since the cessation of fertiliser application was attended by a decreased cutting frequency, these factors cannot be separated yet.

For a succession proceeding from nutrient limitation to light limitation, Tilman (1985) expected that allocation patterns would change, where the final dominant species would be expected to allocate more to shoots (to compete for light). When succession proceeds from light limitation to nutrient limitation as in the present fen restoration succession, the opposite pattern should be expected. However, such a relationship was not found (Olff, van Andel & Bakker, 1990; Olff, 1992a). Species from early, productive fen communities did not allocate more to shoots, but displayed their leaves high in the canopy, and had a lower specific leaf area under conditions of light limitation. A possible explanation for this might be that light competition should be treated differently from nutrient competition. The position of leaves in a canopy is probably more important than the equilibrium reduction of light at the soil surface. Furthermore, an important difference from other successional series is that most above-ground vegetation is removed annually. This makes differences in growth rate (capturing the light first) potentially more important than differences in allocation patterns.

FURTHER RESEARCH ON NUTRIENT DYNAMICS

Nutrient dynamics and vegetation succession are mutually dependent. Nutrient availability often determines which plant species become dominant, but meanwhile nutrient availability is influenced by the dominant plant species themselves (Vitousek & Walker, 1987; Berendse & Jonasson, 1992). The explanation for this lies in the fact that the process of nutrient mineralisation from living and dead plant parts is governed by soil (micro)organisms, which make the rate of mineralisation dependent on substrate quantity and quality. It was pointed out that during restoration succession, shoot nutrient concentrations within individual species generally decreased (Table 2). Attended by a rapid rate of species replacement, this implies that the species of the latter, less productive successional stages are characterised by lower nutrient concentrations. It is hypothesised that restoration succession, *i.e.* after the cessation of fertiliser application, can be characterised by a shift from early successional species with a low nutrient-use efficiency, high quantity and quality of litter, fast decomposition with high mineralisation rates and hence high nutrient availability in the soil, towards late successional species with high nutrient-use efficiency, low quantity and quality of litter, slow decomposition with low mineralisation rates and hence low nutrient availability (Berendse, 1992; van Breemen, 1993). Studies on the effect of plants and soil organisms on carbon and nutrient turnover in soil during succession are currently set up to test this hypothesis.

Since we now know the exact order of species replacement during restoration succession in the fen meadows examined, we are currently investigating if this order is explained by competitive interactions. For this, we are growing 12 species on a fertilised and unfertilised soil, both in monoculture and mixture. Several plant traits related to light interception and nutrient use are being measured.

PERSPECTIVES ON RESTORATION MANAGEMENT

From the aforementioned it might be concluded that restoration of fen meadow vegetation by cessation of fertiliser applications and haymaking is a success story. This is, however, only the case if the hydrological processes remain unchanged (Grootjans & van Diggelen, this volume). A lowering of the groundwater table in a fen vegetation with *Caltha palustris* resulted in a development of a stand dominated by *Holcus lanatus* and *Rumex acetosa* and was attended by the increase of the above-ground standing crop from 300 to 600 g dw m^{-2}. The mineralisation of the topsoil amounted to 400 kg N ha^{-1} yr^{-1} (Grootjans, Schipper & van der Windt, 1985). In other sites with a lowered groundwater table, long-term species replacement did not proceed beyond *Festuca rubra* and *Agrostis capillaris*. This might be caused by an irreversible loss of soil texture. A disturbed peat soil cannot maintain capillary rise of the groundwater and the vegetation suffers from drought. Some other limitations with respect to hydrological processes of restoration management are mentioned by Grootjans & van Diggelen (this volume) and Bakker (1994).

Other limitations for the restoration of fen vegetation have to be taken into account, even if the above-ground standing crop has decreased. It has been found that the soil seed bank in sites where restoration was envisaged did not contain many of the species characteristic of the site. Many fen vegetation species apparently do not have a long-term persistent seed bank from which regeneration can take place (Pfadenhauer & Maas, 1987; van der Valk & Verhoeven, 1988;

Bakker, 1989; Thompson, 1992; Maas, this volume). In that case, species have to come from elsewhere by dispersal. Wind dispersal does not seem to be an important factor for many species. Spontaneous dispersal along ditches is very poor (van Dorp, 1992). Dispersal by haymaking machinery seems to contribute to restoration (Bakker, 1989), and domestic herbivores are supposed to do so. But these mechanisms are bound to former agricultural practices where fields were scattered over the landscape. We conclude that restoration management has to face the possibility of deliberate introduction of plant species (Wells, Bell & Frost, 1981; Maas, 1988; Bakker, 1989; McDonald, 1993). Experiments on seed bank dynamics, seed dispersal and introduction are in progress.

REFERENCES

Altena, H. (1993). Utilization, yield and species richness of grassland between 1946 and 1963 (in Dutch). CABO-DLO Report 182, Wageningen, the Netherlands.

Anonymous (1991). *Botanical Database (in Dutch)*. Centraal Bureau voor de Statistiek, Heerlen.

Bakker, J.P. (1989). *Nature Management by Cutting and Grazing*. Kluwer, Dordrecht.

Bakker, J.P. (1994). Nature management in Dutch grasslands. *Grassland Management and Nature Conservation*. (eds R.J. Haggar & S. Peel), pp. 115–124. British Grassland Society Occasional Symposium 28.

Berendse, F. (1992). Ecosystem stability, competition and nutrient cycling. *Ecosystem Function of Biodiversity* (eds E.D. Schulze & H.A. Mooney), pp. 409–431. Springer Verlag, Heidelberg.

Berendse, F., & Jonasson, S. (1992). Nutrient use and nutrient cycling in Northern ecosystems. *Arctic Ecosystems in a Changing Climate – an Ecological Perspective*. (eds F.S. Chapin, R.L. Jefferies, J.H. Reynolds, G.R. Shaver, & J. Svoboda), pp. 337–358. Academic Press, New York,.

Berendse, F., Oomes, M.J.M., Altena, H.J. & de Visser, W. (1994). A comparative study of nitrogen flows in two similar meadows affected by different groundwater levels. *Journal of Applied Ecology*, **31**, 40–48.

de Boer, K.F. & Thomas, R. (1991). Emission and deposition scenarios for SO2, Nox and NH3. *Acidification Research in the Netherlands* (eds G.J. Hey & T. Schneider), pp. 151–168. Elsevier, Amsterdam.

Grootjans, A.P. (1980). Distribution of plant communities along rivulets in relation to hydrology and management. *Epharmonie* (eds O. Willmanns & R. Tüxen), pp. 143–170. Cramer Vaduz.

Grootjans, A.P. & ten Klooster, W.P. (1980). Changes of groundwater regimes in wet meadows. *Acta Botanica Neerlandica*, **29**, 541–554.

Grootjans, A.P., Schipper, P.C. & van der Windt, H.J. (1985). Influence of drainage on N-mineralization and vegetation response in wet meadows. I. *Calthion palustris* stands. *Oecologia Plantarum*, **6**, 403–417.

Grootjans, A.P. & van Tooren, B.F. (1984). Ecological notes on *Carex aquatilis* communities. *Vegetatio*, **57**, 79–89.

Huisman, J., Olff, H. & Fresco, L.F.M. (1993). A hierarchical set of models for species response analysis. *Journal of Vegetation Science*, **4**, 37–46.

Maas, D. (1988). Keimung und Etablierung von Streuwiesenpflanzen nach experimenteller

Ansaat. *Natur und Landschaft*, **63**, 411–418.

McDonald, A.W. (1993). The role of seed bank and sown seeds in the restoration of English flood-meadows. *Journal of Vegetation Science*, **4**, 395–400.

Myers, R.J.K., Campbell, C.A. & Melillo, J.M. (1982). Leaf-litter production and soil organic matter dynamics along a nitrogen-availability gradient in Southern Wisconsin (USA). *Canadian Journal of Forestry Research*, **13**, 12–21.

Olff, H. (1992a). Effects of light and nutrient availability on dry matter and N allocation in six successional grassland species: testing for resource ratio effects. *Oecologia*, **89**, 412–421.

Olff, H. (1992b). *On the mechanisms of vegetation succession*. PhD thesis, University of Groningen, the Netherlands.

Olff, H. & Bakker, J.P. (1991). Long term dynamics of standing crop, vegetation composition and species richness after the cessation of fertilizer application to hay-fields. *Journal of Applied Ecology*, **28**, 1040–1052.

Olff, H., Berendse, F. & de Visser, W. (1994). Changes in nitrogen mineralization, tissue nutrient concentrations and biomass compartmentation after cessation of fertilizer application to mown grassland. *Journal of Ecology*, **82**, 611–620.

Olff, H., Huisman, J. & van Tooren, B.F. (1993). Species dynamics and nutrient accumulation during early primary succession in coastal sand dunes. *Journal of Ecology*, **81**, 693–706.

Olff, H. & Pegtel, D.M. (1994). Characterisation of the type and extent of nutrient limitation in grassland vegetation using a bioassay. *Plant and Soil*, **163**, 217–224.

Olff, H., van Andel, J. & Bakker, J.P. (1990) Biomass and shoot:root allocation of five species from a grassland succession series at different combinations of light and nutrient availability. *Functional Ecology*, **4**, 193–200.

Oomes, M.J.M. & Mooi, H. (1985) The effect of management on succession and production of fermerly agricultural grassland after stopping fertilization. *Sukzession auf Grünlandbrachen* (ed. K.F. Schreiber). pp. 59–67. Münstersche Geographische Arbeiten 20.

Pegtel, D.M. (1987) Soil fertility and the composition of semi-natural grassland. *Disturbance in Grasslands* (eds J. van Andel, J.P. Bakker, & R.W. Snaydon), pp. 3–66. Junk, Dordrecht,.

Pfadenhauer, J. & Maas, D. (1987). Samenpotential in Niedermoorböden des Alpenvorlandes bei Grünlandnutzung unterschiedlicher Intensität. *Flora*, **179**, 85–97.

Succow, M. & Jeschke, L. (1986). *Moore in der Landschaft*. Urania Verlag, Leipzig.

ten Rodengate Marissen, J.Z. (1905) *Special crop science III. Grassland* (in Dutch). Wolters, Groningen.

Thompson, K. (1992). The functional ecology of seed banks. *Seeds: the Ecology of Regeneration of Plant Communities*. (ed. M. Fenner), pp. 231–258. CAB International, Wallingford.

Tilman, D. (1982). *Resource Competition and Community Structure*. Princeton University Press, Princeton.

Tilman, D. (1985) The resource-ratio hypothesis of plant succession. *American Naturalist*, **125**, 827–852.

van Andel, J., Bakker, J.P. & Grootjans, A.P. (1993). Mechanisms of vegetation sucession: a review of concepts and perspectives. *Acta Botanica Neerlandica*, **42**, 413–433.

van Breemen, N. (1993). Soils as biotic constructs favouring net primary production. *Geoderma*, **57**, 183–212.

van Dorp, D. (1992) Vestiging van plantesoorten; bereikbaarheid en geschiktheid van verschraalde graslanden. *Landschap*, **9**, 271–283.

van der Meijden, R., Weeda, E.J., Holverda, W.J. & Hovenkamp, P.H. (1990). *Flora van Nederland*. Wolters-Noordhoff, Groningen.

van der Valk, A.G. & Verhoeven, J.T.A. (1988). Potential role of seed banks and understorey vegetation in restoring quaking fens from floating forests. *Vegetatio*, **70**, 3–13.

van der Woude, B.J., Pegtel, D.M. & Bakker, J.P. (1994) Nutrient limitation after long-term nitrogen fertilizer application in cut grasslands. *Journal of Applied Ecology*, **31**, 405–412.

Vitousek, P.M. & Walker, L.R. (1987). Colonization, succession and resource availability: ecosystem level interactions. *Colonization, Succession and Stability* (eds A.J. Gray, M.J. Crawley, & P.J. Edwards) pp. 207–223. Blackwell Scientific Publications, Oxford.

Wells, T.C.E., Bell, S.A. & Frost, A. (1981). *Creating Attractive Grasslands using Native Plant Species*. Nature Conservancy Council, Shrewsbury.

11 Vegetational Changes in Boreal Rich Fens Induced by Haymaking; Management Plan for the Sølendet Nature Reserve

A. MOEN

Department of Botany, Museum of Natural History and Archaeology, University of Trondheim, N-7004 Trondheim, Norway

SUMMARY

1.   This paper describes results from a long-term project in the boreal uplands of central Norway using permanent plots to investigate the vegetational successions in abandoned hay fens.

2.   Outlying land in these uplands was used for hundreds of years for hay and pasturage for domestic stock, draining it of plant nutrients. It is little exploited nowadays and the vegetation and landscape are changing accordingly.

3.   The Sølendet Nature Reserve, established in 1974, includes about 200 ha of former grassland which was regularly mown for hay up to about 1950. Restoration of 160 ha, involving scrub clearance by axe and burning of brash, was carried out from 1976 to 1986, entailing more than 500 man-days of work. This area is now mown regularly using a two-wheeled tractor or scythe.

4.   Following a management plan, 18 ha is intensively managed, 140 ha is more extensively managed, and the rest is left to overgrow. The main aims are to preserve a typical upland haymaking area from the past, a varied type of vegetation and rare species.

5.   Experimental mowing using scythes commenced 20 years ago in some permanent plots and the vegetation has returned to a state of ecological equilibrium with scything as a prime ecological factor. After the first few years, the field-layer biomass in annually-scythed plots had decreased to about one-third of the first harvest, whereas it was about two-thirds in plots scythed every other year, *i.e.* the practice of traditional haymaking on outlying land.

6.   The main conclusions of studies of the below-ground biomass are that the mass of roots and rhizomes exceeds that of above-ground shoots, and that the ratio between the above- and below-ground biomass is lowest for the community that has remained unscythed for more than 40 years.

7.   Regular scything of the fens has led to an overall reduction of shrubs (*e.g. Betula* spp., *Salix* spp.), dwarf shrubs and the litter layer. The proportion of herbs is generally reduced, but graminoids have increased except for *Molinia caerulea*, which is drastically

Restoration of Temperate Wetlands. Edited by B.D. Wheeler, S.C. Shaw, W.J. Fojt and R.A. Robertson
© 1995 John Wiley & Sons Ltd.

reduced by intensive scything. Most orchids (*e.g. Dactylorhiza* spp., *Gymnadenia conopsea*) and other fen herbs do not tolerate intensive scything, but are favoured in lawn communities by extensive scything which reduces competition from shrubs, *Molinia caerulea, etc.* Many alpine species (*e.g. Carex atrofusca*) are favoured by scything.

INTRODUCTION

Ongoing study of the hay fens at Sølendet, at Røros in Sør-Trøndelag, central Norway, started in 1974 when the area became a nature reserve. A research programme to study the vegetation ecology of the hay fens and wooded grasslands has been combined with the more practical work of drawing up a management plan and supervising its implementation. Moen (1990) described the previous human impact on Sølendet, the methods employed for reclamation and management, the plant cover, and the results of the project from 1974 through 1988. The scything programme and long-term monitoring of the succession have continued. New projects are improving our understanding of the ecological conditions and processes behind the observed changes in vegetation caused by scything.

The terminology concerning mire ecology, the regional vegetation, plant nomenclature, *etc.* follow the Scandinavian tradition, full details being given in Moen (1990). The terms 'rich' and 'extremely rich' fen vegetation (slightly acid to alkaline, including calciphilous species) are used according to Du Rietz (1949). Vegetational 'zone' is used for (horizontal) units that extend more or less continuously over the Earth's surface, whereas vegetational 'region' is used in a wide sense including vertical differentiation; these units follow Moen (1987).

THE OUTLYING LAND AND HAY FENS OF CENTRAL NORWAY

Model to develop the agricultural ecology

An ecological model for long-term changes in the cultural landscape of temperate (nemoral) parts of Scandinavia was described by Emanuelsson (1988). He proposed four main levels, based on technological steps which had a marked effect in changing the natural environment into cultural landscapes:

1. Hunter-gatherer society
2. Slash and burn, shifting cultivation
3. Farming using infields and outlying land
4. Farming using artificial fertilisers.

Level 1 (lasting until *c.* 6000 years ago) supported about 1 person km^{-2} and level 2 (*c.* 6000–2000 years ago) about 20 people km^{-2}. Level 3 (*c.* 0–1900) supported about 50 people km^{-2} in the first part of the period, but utilisation of nutrients (*e.g.* manure) was much more efficient in the last part (especially the nineteenth century) and about 300 people km^{-2} could be supported. Using artificial fertilisers (level 4), all the land area of the temperate zone can (in theory)

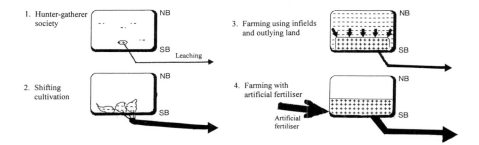

Figure 1. A model for the main levels of agriculture in central Norway (modified after Emanuelsson, 1988). - -: areas from which nutrients are taken; +++: areas which have an input of nutrients. The boxes illustrate a transect from the lowlands (SB = southern boreal) to the forest limit (NB = northern boreal).

be used as arable land and can support as many as 5000 people km^{-2}.

Figure 1 shows the model, modified to illustrate conditions typifying boreal Scandinavia with its lowland and upland areas, described in greater detail in the next sub-section.

Farming in central Norway using infields and outlying land

Only small parts of Norway are in the temperate zone; most agricultural land is in the less fertile boreal zones. Most farms in central Norway lie in the southern boreal and the lower part of the middle boreal zones, which comprise most of the lowland areas along the coast and in the valleys. The boreal uplands (*i.e.* the upper part of the middle boreal and the northern boreal regions) cover much larger areas than the lowlands. These extensive areas of outlying land were used for summer dairy farming, haymaking and grazing. The extent of infields, *i.e.* cultivated land in the lowlands around permanent settlements, was very limited in many parts of Norway and most winter fodder came from outlying land. Indeed, the supply of winter fodder primarily determined the maximum head of stock that a farmer could keep. The productivity of infields (mainly arable land) depended directly on this utilisation of the uplands. Without fodder from outlying land there was too little manure to spread on infields. In Rindal, a typical rural district area in central Norway, all the farms (about 300 in 1907) were in the lowlands, and summer dairy farms and most hay barns were situated in the uplands (Figure 2). Moen (1989) mapped the remains of 233 hay barns in Rindal, four of which were situated below 180 m a.s.l. (*i.e.* in the southern boreal region, all of them close to a river that tends to flood), one was above 650 m a.s.l. (*i.e.* in the low alpine region), and the great majority were situated 300–600 m a.s.l. (*i.e.* in the upper boreal region).

Grazing and haymaking were best and most productive where there was rich vegetation. These areas were therefore most used, as shown by the high concentration of remains of summer dairy farms and hay barns. Such farming and hay-

	Area in %	Farms (300)	Summer dairy farms (111)	Hay barn ruins (233)
Alpine regions (650-1613 m a.s.l.)	35			
Northern boreal region (450-650 m a.s.l.)	35		[black]	[black]
Middle boreal region (180-450 m a.s.l.)	25	[light]	[black]	[light]
Southern boreal region (60-180 m a.s.l.)	5	[black]		

Figure 2. Schematic representation of the occurrence of farms, summer dairy farms and hay barns in the vegetational regions in Rindal, central Norway. Total area: 595 km^2. Black shading: main occurrence; light shading: 2–10%. Number of farms and summer dairy farms after the agricultural statistics for 1907; number of hay barn ruins after Moen (1989).

making varied in intensity over time and from place to place, peaking about the mid-nineteenth century when scarcely any rich fen or wooded grassland in Norway remained unused, except in the most remote mountainous districts.

Such utilisation would obviously have been less intensive during economic depressions, for example at the time of the Black Death (*c.* 1350), but haymaking in the boreal uplands of Norway has clearly gone on for more than 1000 years (references in Moen, 1990:13). This form of land use has declined since the end of the nineteenth century, although the traditional methods were still in use in certain areas up to around 1950, and even later in some places. The agricultural statistics for 1907 show that 363 km^2 in the county of Sør-Trøndelag were used for upland haymaking, more than 2% of the entire area. (In Norway as a whole, 2681 km^2 of outlying land was used for haymaking.) The statistics for the area of outlying land mown in Sør-Trøndelag show the trend during this century quite clearly. In 1917 and 1929, 83 km^2 and 84 km^2, respectively, were scythed. In 1939, the area scythed was 40 km^2, in 1949 only 15 km^2, and in 1958, 0 km^2.

An average-sized farm in 1907 harvested 8–10 tons of hay from its upland areas, although large farms may have obtained as much as 100 tons. The upland area utilised for haymaking, expressed per inhabitant in the rural district, was as high as 1–2 ha in many places in 1907.

Farming using artificial fertilisers

The present-day farm relies on purchasing artificial fertilisers, animal feeding stuffs, implements and diesel, *etc.* from commercial sources. The resources of the outlying land are little utilised nowadays, except as grazing for a few sheep or cattle in some parts of the country and by elk and other game animals. Hence, the outlying land that was drained of nutrients for centuries now retains them, and the vegetation and landscape are changing character accordingly.

MANAGEMENT OF SØLENDET NATURE RESERVE

The Sølendet area

Sølendet Nature Reserve, set up in 1974, covered an area of 285 ha, and was extended to 306 ha in 1990. Sølendet is situated 700–800 m a.s.l. at the transition between the middle boreal and northern boreal regions. The climate is transitional between sub-oceanic and sub-continental, having a mean annual precipitation of 600 mm and a mean annual temperature of about +0.6 °C; the January and July means are –9.0 °C and +11.7 °C, respectively. The snow cover usually lasts 210–220 days.

Grey-green phyllite is the predominant bedrock, but is mostly covered by ground moraine of calcareous phyllite with a high proportion of clay particles yielding a nutrient-rich soil which readily becomes waterlogged. The nature reserve contains more than 50 marked springs (with communities of the CRATONEURION COMMUTATI alliance), mostly occurring as spring lines at about 770–780 m a.s.l., as well as a large number of more diffuse groundwater outflows. These springs carry calcareous, mineral-rich water (pH: 7.8) to the fen surface throughout the year.

Extremely rich fen vegetation covers 44% of the reserve, predominantly communities of the CARICION ATROFUSCAE alliance; additional alliances are STYGIO-CARICION LIMOSAE, CARICION LASIOCARPAE and SPHAGNO-TOMENTHYP-NION. Wooded grasslands of the LACTUCION ALPINAE alliance cover about 20%, and heathland vegetation (mainly forested) covers the rest (about 35%).

The vascular flora of Sølendet numbers 294 taxa, 25 of which are hybrids. The bryophyte flora comprises 256 species. There are many extremely rich fen species with an alpine and upper boreal distribution in Fennoscandia, for example, *Carex atrofusca*[1], *Kobresia simpliciuscula*, *Juncus castaneus* and *Pedicularis oederi*, and 25 taxa of orchids (including 12 hybrids), some being very numerous, for example, *Dactylorhiza cruenta*, *D. fuchsii*, *D. pseudocordigera*, *Gymnadenia conopsea* and *Listera ovata*. A number of species occur that are rare in Fennoscandia, for example, the orchid *Nigritella nigra*.

History and management

There are no published pollen diagrams for sites at or near Sølendet. Some palaeo-ecological evidence exists from similar areas in upper boreal central Norway (summarised in Moen, 1990: 24 ff.). It seems reasonable to conclude that a grey alder (*Alnus incana*) forest was common or dominant during the period of optimal

---

[1] Vascular plant nomenclature follows Lid (1985).

Table 1. Time spent on various management practices based on experience at the Sølendet nature reserve.

	hours ha^{-1}
Reclamation (completed):	
Clearing of dense scrub	50–100
Clearing of sparse scrub	40–50
Former working methods no longer used:	
Spreading of hay to dry	20
Drying, gathering up and transportation	30
Work which has to be done every year:	
Scything	30–40
Mowing with a 2-wheeled tractor	6
Gathering up and transport to a road	30

warmth (*c.* 8000–3500 years ago). There are now only scattered occurrences of grey alder in middle boreal parts of Sølendet, the main reason for its limited presence being the rather cold climate. Large areas of sloping fen were probably established during the climatic optimum, Hafsten & Solem (1976) having dated the establishment of a similar sloping fen to about 6000 years ago. Sølendet was almost certainly used for haymaking before the depopulation caused by the Black Death. Nevertheless, it is doubtful whether that use would have left visible signs in the area, over and above those deriving from later activities. Historical records from 1688 mention the clearance of patches at Sølendet for summer dairy farms. The area has certainly been in normal use for haymaking and summer grazing since the late-seventeenth century.

It is reasonable to assume that when utilisation of the area began, wet fens and springs were open and dominated by graminoids; the (present-day) drier fens are shrub-covered and partially forested.

Traditional haymaking at Sølendet ceased about 1950 following a gradual decline over the preceding decades. Most hay swards used to be scythed every other year, and the herbage raked, dried and taken to barns or stacks. Horse-drawn sledges were used to transport the hay down to the farms during the winter. Calculations based on data for the final decades of haymaking indicate that summer haymaking involved more than 1000 man-days annually.

A vegetational succession commenced as soon as haymaking ceased, the most obvious change being the formation of scrub and a heavy litter layer in the tall fen and swamp communities. Restoration of the former haymaking land started in 1976. Large-scale clearance (by axe) of about 56 ha of scrub-covered land was mostly completed in 1983. This reclamation took more than 400 man-days; Table 1 summarises the time spent on the various jobs. Altogether 160 ha of former haymaking land has been restored and have been mown (with a scythe or motor mower) three to seven times during 1976–93.

The management plan aims to preserve:

- a former, typical, upland haymaking area with its vegetation and flora as a feature of the farming landscape of the past;
- the varied nature of the vegetation within the reserve as it is produced by different methods of mowing and haymaking;
- rare species and species of phytogeographical interest through management specifically designed to further their growth and vitality.

The management plan makes specific provision for the following parts of the reserve:

- intensively managed areas (*i.e.* scything every 2nd or 3rd year, herbage being removed); 18 ha is scythed regularly;
- more extensively managed areas, 140 ha of formerly mown land;
- areas to be left untouched, including about 40 ha that was formerly mown.

From 1976 to 1993, 400 ha has been mown, using a two-wheeled tractor on the largest areas and scythes on smaller areas; this is an annual mean of more than 20 ha. About half of this has been raked and the herbage removed.

VEGETATIONAL CHANGES INDUCED BY SCYTHING

Permanent plots

At about 100 localities at Sølendet, analyses of the plant communities, ecological investigations, productivity and population studies, *etc.* have been carried out in visually-uniform, permanent plots of 12.5 m^2. Each locality represented a uniform area (stand) of this kind at the start of the study. Several permanent plots were established in some localities, the clearing and scything involved differing from plot to plot. The number of species and individuals in each sample plot was calculated using figures obtained by counting in three, smaller, representative sub-plots measuring 0.5 x 0.5 m.

Hay crops at Sølendet

The sward of the permanent plots was scythed about 1 August to estimate the hay yield. The dry weight was estimated at 80°C. This is an inaccurate way of estimating the total standing crop of the field layer at the peak of the growing season. Scything leaves a stubble *c.* 2–4 cm high, which, for most communities, represents 10–20% of the total standing crop of the field layer; even more in low-growing, low-production communities.

Some scythed herbage is plant litter. This varies from community to community and in relation to scything frequency (annually, biennially, *etc.*). At Sølendet, most mown communities in areas scythed every other year give about 10–20% litter.

Figure 3 shows typical changes in the dry-matter yield of a standing crop over a single decade after scything was resumed (annually or biennially) following 2–4 decades of overgrowing of former haymaking areas at Sølendet. However, the litter fraction of this tall-growing fen community is somewhat greater than the

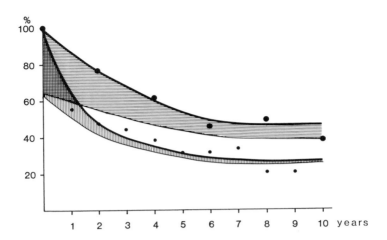

Figure 3. Schematic representation of changes in the productivity of the field layer at Sølendet induced by scything of permanent plots for 10 years, annually (lower curves) or biennially (upper curves). Standing crop shown by thick lines, litter fraction shaded, and biomass shown by thin lines. Data for the *Carex lasiocarpa–Potentilla erecta–Campylium stellatum* type of rich-fen expanse included in the CARICION ATROFUSCAE alliance (locality 1 in Moen, 1990). 100% = 3000 kg ha^{-1} of dry matter.

value usually obtained for low-growing fen communities.

The main conclusions are:

- the standing crop in biennially-scythed plots was reduced to about half that of the first harvest. The litter fraction in the first harvest was about one-third; litter subsequently made up 10–20% of the standing crop. The biomass was reduced to about two-thirds of what it was the first year;
- the standing crop in annually-scythed plots was reduced to about one-third of the first harvest, with a litter fraction of 5–10%;
- annual scything yielded about half the biomass obtained by biennial scything;
- the most economic method of utilising the plant production by scything for hay was to harvest biennially, *i.e.* as in traditional haymaking.

Biennial scything of the 53 ha of rich-fen expanse (communities dominated by *Carex lasiocarpa*, *Eriophorum latifolium*, *Scirpus cespitosus*, *Campylium stellatum*) at Sølendet gave a calculated mean dry weight yield of 1200 kg ha^{-1}. The 44 ha of drier, more low-growing, marginal communities containing *Kobresia simpliciuscula* gave a mean yield of 700 kg ha^{-1}.

Based on the yield estimates and the estimated area of different vegetational types, taken from Moen (1990), the potential hay crop at Sølendet is 107 tons, which is a realistic assessment of the maximum crop more than six decades ago. Farmers report that about 70 tons of hay was harvested from the nature reserve annually in the 1930s. A general decline in the utilisation of Sølendet for haymaking is assumed to have occurred in the decades before 1950.

Biomass of above-ground and below-ground material

Indirect sampling was used to estimate the biomass of the vascular plants above and below ground level. The method is based on counting the number of 'individuals' (*i.e.* readily-counted module, shoot, tiller) of all species in the plots and determining the mean individual weight. Aune, Kubícek & Moen (1993) describe the method and give some preliminary results from 1992. Table 2 summarises the figures obtained for one fen community during studies in 1992 and 1993. The plot scythed annually for 18 years represents an unusual, stressed situation, biennial scything being the traditional practice. It has been found that:

- the biomass decreases with increasing scything frequency;
- the mass of below-ground roots and rhizomes exceeds that of above-ground shoots;
- the ratio between the above- and below-ground biomass is lowest for the community that has remained unscythed for more than 40 years;
- *Molinia caerulea* suffers greatly from regular scything.

These conclusions agree with earlier results from the studies of hay fens (Moen, 1990). The second one verifies the conclusion of Bliss, Heal & Moore (1981) that the below-ground biomass is higher than that above-ground in wet communities. The third verifies the following published results and theories for strategies of plants (*e.g.* summarised by Fitter, 1986): scything represents a stress that forces the plants to mobilise resources to produce photosynthetic tissue to counteract the loss caused by cutting. This induces transport of nutrients (among others carbohydrates) from rhizomes and roots to shoots resulting in the below-ground biomass decreasing more than the above-ground, field-layer biomass.

Changes in species composition

The effect of scything on the plant communities at Sølendet has been studied in permanent plots using a variety of methods, *e.g.* phytosociological analysis (a 9-degree scale is used), calculating species biomass (Table 2), counting shoots (Table 3) and flowering shoots (Tables 3, 4 and 5), and measuring the heights of shoots. Additional results and comments are found in Moen (1985, 1990), Aune *et al.* (1993) and Aune *et al.* (1994). The effect of scything on the various plant populations differs from one community to another, *e.g.* biennial scything will usually reduce the number of flowering individuals of orchids in open, low-growing carpet and lawn communities, but increase their occurrence in tall-growing, scrub-invaded marginal communities. There are also considerable differences in species behaviour from one year to another (as shown in Tables 4 and 5), in part caused by differences in climate, such as the warmth-sum and precipitation in the growing season. The effect on fen species at Sølendet, based on the aforementioned analyses of the fen lawn communities (*i.e.* the *Campylium stellatum*-dominated communities) is suggested in Table 6.

Table 2. The biomass of the dominant vascular plants (g m^{-2}) in plots scythed annually, biennially and unscythed for about 40 years. Figures represent mean values for 1992 / 93, using an indirect sampling method (Aune, Kubìcek & Moen, 1993). *Molinia caerulea–Kobresia simpliciuscula–Campylium stellatum* type of rich fen margin, in the CARICION ATROFUSCAE alliance (Locality 3 in Moen, 1990). Ab=above ground; Be=below ground.

	Annually scythed			Biennially scythed			Unscythed		
	Ab	Be	A/B	Ab	Be	A/B	Ab	Be	A/B
Succisa pratensis	–	–	–	4	5	0.84	26	39	0.67
Thalictrum alpinum	7	9	0.77	11	11	0.92	4	6	0.67
Carex dioica	13	10	1.37	22	28	0.76	10	11	0.93
Carex panicea	5	5	0.86	16	19	0.83	17	34	0.50
Eriophorum angustifolium	2	4	0.59	3	7	0.46	2	3	0.61
Kobresia simpliciuscula	3	9	0.29	5	12	0.38	13	22	0.58
Molinia caerulea	4	10	0.39	5	25	0.20	23	114	0.21
Scirpus cespitosus	28	60	0.47	11	25	0.42	32	192	0.17
Total	61	105	0.58	77	138	0.56	128	425	0.30

Effect on *Carex dioica* and *Molinia caerulea*

Along with *Scirpus cespitosus*, *Carex dioica* is the most numerous (based on numbers of shoots) of all the vascular plant species forming rich-fen lawn communities at Sølendet (>1000 shoots m^{-2} are common; Table 3). It is usually sterile in areas that have remained unscythed for a long period and becomes progressively more scattered as overgrowth (recovery) by other plants takes place. Scything has favoured it in every lawn community investigated. More shoots have appeared, from successfully germinated seedlings and particularly through vegetative growth. There are also more flowering specimens (female and male, Table 4); in intensively-scythed lawns as many as 200–300 m^{-2}, whereas 0–3 is a 'normal' value in unscythed plots (Table 4). As this table shows, there are considerable differences in flowering frequency in *Carex dioica* (as in all other species studied) from one year to another (*e.g.* 240 flowering shoots m^{-2} in 1987 in the annually-scythed plot, compared with only 16 in 1988). There are also considerable differences between communities. In some years, *Carex dioica* has a large number of flowering shoots in low-growing fen communities (*i.e.* those with an open field layer), even in fens that have not been scythed for decades (72 flowering shoots in 1992 in plot 3C, 9 in 1993, *cf.* Table 3).

Molinia caerulea is a very common (often the dominant) species of unscythed fen lawns and damp grasslands at Sølendet, but was often drastically reduced following annual scything around 1 August for only about 3 years. This also applied to the numbers of flowering shoots (Table 5). The *Molinia* decline in fen-lawn communities was usually accompanied by an increase in *Carex atrofusca, C. dioica, C. flava* and other species capitalising on it.

Table 3. Number of individuals (I) and flowering shoots (F) m^{-2} in plots scythed annually (A), biennially (B) and unscythed for about 40 years (C). Mean values for estimations in 1992 and 1993. The same locality as in Table 2; 13 species with low occurrence are omitted. Full list for 1992 in Aune *et al.* (1993).

	A		B		C	
	I	F	I	F	I	F
Betula nana	2	–	36	–	10	–
Equisetum palustre	36	–	0	–	1	–
Equisetum variegatum	95	–	68	–	36	–
Euphrasia frigida	1	1	3	2	77	73
Gymnadenia conopsea	0	0	2	0	4	1
Leontodon autumnalis	1	0	29	1	35	2
Pedicularis oederi	2	0	14	0	37	1
Pinguicula vulgaris	1	0	11	2	2	0
Polygonum viviparum	48	0	62	2	41	0
Potentilla erecta	1	0	32	4	4	0
Saussurea alpina	1	0	15	0	46	0
Saxifraga aizoides	45	0	13	5	1	0
Selaginella selaginoides	5	–	104	–	76	–
Succisa pratensis	1	0	24	0	56	0
Thalictrum alpinum	449	1	764	59	592	3
Tofielda pusilla	11	0	49	0	15	0
Triglochin palustre	71	2	53	0	17	0
Carex capillaris	16	0	82	9	28	2
Carex dioica	851	75	1655	133	755	41
Carex flava	10	0	2	1	0	0
Carex panicea	62	4	198	18	162	7
Deschampsia cespitosa	0	0	10	0	13	0
Eriophorum angustifolium	31	1	30	1	17	1
Festuca ovina	5	0	33	3	10	0
Kobresia simpliciuscula	216	0	359	50	419	23
Molinia caerulea	134	0	221	0	294	7
Scirpus cespitosus	1859	–	964	–	1658	–
Total	**3954**		**4846**		**4409**	

The above-ground biomass and the numbers of fertile shoots of *Molinia*, however, increased in some formerly scrub-dominated communities of damp grasslands and fens at Sølendet after removal of the scrub followed by extensive mowing (5- to 10-year rotation) by tractor (*i.e.* leaving a high stubble). Comparable results were obtained from temperate zone wetlands. For instance, Godwin (1941) found that *Molinia* increased in two communities of tall-growing fen species scythed annually at Wicken Fen. Intensive scything favoured *Molinia* both in autumn (Godwin, 1941) and summer (Rowell, Guarino & Harvey (1985).

The explanation for this difference in behaviour may be that in low-growing,

Table 4. Number of flowering individuals of *Carex dioica* m^{-2} in 1987–89 in plots scythed annually (A), biennially (B) and unscythed for about 40 years (C). Tall-growing, rich-fen community dominated by *Carex lasiocarpa* (locality 1 as in Figure 3).

	1987		1988		1989		Mean 1987–89
	female	male	female	male	female	male	female + male
A	160	80	8	8	24	4	95
B	8	8	4	1	2	2	8
C	1	2	1	2	1	2	3

Table 5. Number of flowering individuals of *Molinia caerulea* m^{-2} in 1986–93 in plots scythed annually (A), biennially (B), unscythed for about 40 years (C) and unscythed until 1986, followed by annual scything (D). Rich fen margin community (*Molinia caerulea–Succisa pratensis–Campylium stellatum* type, locality 4 in Moen, 1990).

	1986	1987	1988	1989	1990	1991	1992	1993
A	0	0	0	0	0	0	0	0
B	0	0	1	0	0	0	0	0
C	42	?	40	24	11	10	17	9
D	36	3	3	1	1	0	0	0

intensively scythed fens, the club-shaped, food-storing, stem bases of *Molinia* are often destroyed by desiccation or decay. *Molinia* plants which are not damaged in this way by scything will, nonetheless, suffer greatly from annual and biennial scything owing to the increased drain on their stored food reserves. Food reserves may be more rapidly replenished in more southerly regions, because of the longer vegetational period. There, as in the extensively-mown, scrub-dominated areas at Sølendet, *Molinia* is favoured by removal of competing, taller-growing species.

Effect on some other fen species; general considerations

Shrub and dwarf-shrub species disappear or are drastically reduced in frequency by biennial scything, as do all tall herbs (Table 6). Orchids (*e.g. Dactylorhiza* spp. and *Gymnadenia conopsea*) and *Pedicularis oederi* do not tolerate intensive scything, but are favoured in tall-growing lawn communities by extensive scything which reduces competition from shrubs, *Molinia caerulea, etc.* Some small herbs, such as *Leontodon autumnalis*, *Pinguicula vulgaris* and *Thalictrum alpinum*, however, are favoured and form an increasing proportion of the total biomass. This is because most of their leaves lie close to the ground and are thus unharmed by scything. Even *Succisa pratensis* is favoured in some communities for the same reason, though it suffers a decline elsewhere. *Saxifraga aizoides* also becomes

Table 6. Schematic representation of the effect of regular scything on the relative above-ground biomass (as a proportion of the total biomass, −, • or +) and on flowering frequency (increased sterility or flowering frequency) of certain plant species in the lawn communities of the rich fens at Sølendet.

Shrubs and dwarf shrubs	−	st	Carex dioica	+	f
			C. flava	+	f
Bartsia alpina	−		C. lasiocarpa	•	st
Dactylorhiza cruenta	−	st	C. nigra	+	f
D. pseudocodigera	−	st	C. panicea	•	
Equisetum palustre	+		C. rostrata	•	st
E. variegatum	+		Eriophorum angustifolium	+	f
Gymnadenia conopsea	−	st	E. latifolium	+	f
Leontodon autumnalis	+	f	Juncus spp.	+	f
Pedicularis oederi	−	st	Kobresia simpliciuscula	•	st
P. palustris	+	f	Molinia caerulea	−	st
Pinguicula vulgaris	+		Scirpus cespitosus	•	
Polygonum viviparum	+				
Potentilla erecta	−	st	Campylium stellatum	+	
Saussurea alpina	−	st	Cratoneuron commutatum	+	
Saxifraga aizoides	+	f	Drepanocladus revolvens coll.	+	
Selaginella selaginoides	+		Homalothecium nitens	−	
Succisa pratensis	−	st	Plagiomnium spp.	−	
Thalictrum alpinum	+	f	Rhizomnium spp.	−	
Triglochin palustre	+	f	Sphagnum spp.	−	
Carex atrofusca	+	f	Aneura pinguis	+	
C. capillaris	+	f	Lophozia borealis	+	

more abundant in some communities scythed every other year. Scything also reduces the flowering frequency of *Carex lasiocarpa* and *C. rostrata*, which, like *Carex panicea* and *Scirpus cespitosus*, do not show a greater reduction in cover or biomass values than the total cover or biomass value for the community.

In addition to *Carex dioica*, the following graminoids become more common on scythed areas: *Carex atrofusca*, *C. capillaris*, *C. flava*, *C. hostiana*, *C. flava* x *C. hostiana*, *C. nigra*, *Eriophorum angustifolium*, *E. latifolium*, *Juncus alpino-articulatus*, *J. castaneus* and *J. triglumis*. All these taxa seem to be spreading vegetatively and from seeds. Most are weakly-competitive, alpine species. The common occurrence of alpine species (*e.g.* the three *Juncus* spp.) in the fen-lawn communities at Sølendet is regarded as a result of regular scything in the past.

Kobresia simpliciuscula is a dominant species in the dry, low-growing, fen-lawn vegetation at Sølendet. However, intensive scything reduces the frequency of its flowering, as shown by the wide variety of plant species (*e.g.* orchids) that become common in fen lawns some years after scything ceases. These species would certainly be eliminated in large areas if the course of natural succession was undisturbed, and *Molinia*, *Betula nana*, *Salix* spp. and other tall-growing shrubs, graminoids and herbs became more abundant. Future management at Sølendet will be designed to favour such weakly-competitive species in some areas.

Campylium stellatum is the bottom-layer species that profits most from scything in rich-fen lawn communities, although *Cratoneuron commutatum, Drepanocladus revolvens* coll., *Aneura pinguis* and *Lophozia borealis* are also favoured, at least in some communities. *Homalothecium nitens, Plagiomnium* spp., *Rhizomnium* spp., *Sphagnum* spp. (*e.g. S. warnstorfii*) and other acrocarpous or 'hummock-building' moss species become replaced by prostrate, pleurocarpous ones (especially *Campylium stellatum*).

In general, scything at Sølendet has so far brought about few changes in species richness in the plant communities because regular scything as a prime ecological factor has achieved equilibrium over past centuries and the time elapsing since its cessation has been too short for major changes to occur.

In some tall-growing communities, mainly in fen margins, the increase of some species (*e.g. Betula nana, B. pubescens, Salix* spp. and *Molinia caerulea*), and of litter, has already led to a decline in the number of species present. In such areas of overgrowing, which cover enormous tracts of the outlying land of Norway, the successions will result in a decrease in species richness over several decades. However, the overgrowing process is much slower in boreal uplands than in temperate wetlands (*e.g.* Wheeler & Shaw, 1991), mainly because of the lower productivity of the upland areas.

ACKNOWLEDGEMENTS

I am grateful to Trond Arnesen, Egil I. Aune, Ferdinand Kubícek and Dag-Inge Øien for pleasant collaboration during the Sølendet project and Richard Binns for correcting my English. Financial support in 1992–93 came from the Norwegian Research Council's Cultural Landscape Research Programme and the Directorate for Nature Management.

REFERENCES

Aune, E.I., Kubícek, F. & Moen, A. (1993). Studies of plant biomass in permanent plots at Sølendet Nature Reserve, Central Norway. *Universitetet i Trondheim, Vitenskaps-museet. Rapport. Botanisk Serie,* **1993 (2)**, 7–20.

Aune, E.I., Kubícek, F., Moen, A. & Øien, D.-I. (1994). Biomass studies in semi-natural ecosystems influenced by scything at the Sølendet Nature Reserve, Central Norway. *Ecology* (Bratislava), **13 (3)**, 283–297.

Bliss, L.C., Heal, O.W. & Moore, J.J. (eds.) (1981). Tundra ecosystems: a comparative analysis. *International Biological Programme,* **25**, 1–813.

Emanuelsson, U. (1988). A model describing the development of the cultural landscape. *The Cultural Landscape – Past, Present and Future.* (eds. H.H. Birks, H.J.B. Birks, P.E. Kaland & D. Moe), pp. 111–121. Cambridge University Press, Cambridge.

Du Rietz, G. E. (1949). Hovudenheter och hovudgränser i svensk myrvegetation. (Main units and main limits in Swedish mire vegetation.) *Svensk Botanisk Tidskrift*, **43**, 274–309.

Fitter, A.H. (1986). Acquisition and utilization of resources. *Plant Ecology*. (ed. M.J. Crawley), pp. 375–405. Blackwell Scientific Publications, Oxford.

Godwin, H. (1941). Studies in the ecology of Wicken Fen, IV. Crop-taking experiments. *Journal of Ecology*, **29**, 83–106.

Hafsten, U & Solem, T. (1976). Age, origin, and palaeo-ecological evidence of blanket bogs in Nord-Trøndelag, Norway. *Boreas*, **5**, 119–141.

Lid, J. (1985). *Norsk, svensk, finsk flora.* New ed. by O. Gjærevoll. Det Norske Samlaget, Oslo. 837 pp.

Moen, A. (1985). Vegetasjonsendringer i subalpine rikmyrer i Norge. (Vegetational changes in subalpine rich fen vegetation in Norway.) *Memoranda Soc. Fauna Flora Fennica*, **61**, 7–18.

Moen, A. (1987). The regional vegetation of Norway, that of Central Norway in particular. *Norsk Geografisk Tidsskrift*, **41**, 179–225, 1 map.

Moen, A. (1989). Utmarksslåtten – grunnlaget for det gamle jordbruket. *Spor – Fortidsnytt fra Midt-Norge*, **4 (1)**, 36–42.

Moen, A. (1990). The plant cover of the boreal uplands of Central Norway. I. Vegetation ecology of Sølendet nature reserve; haymaking fens and birch woodlands. *Gunneria*, **63**, 1–451, 1 map.

Rowell, T.A., Guarino, L. & Harvey, H.J. (1985). The experimental management of vegetation at Wicken Fen, Cambridgeshire. *Journal of Ecology*, **22**, 217–227.

Wheeler, B.D. & Shaw, S.C. (1991). Above-ground crop mass and species richness of the principal types of herbaceous rich-fen vegetation of lowland England and Wales. *Journal of Ecology*, **79**, 285–301.

12 The Role of Seed Banks in the Revegetation of Australian Temporary Wetlands

M. A. BROCK & D. L. BRITTON
Botany Department, University of New England, Armidale 2351, NSW., Australia

SUMMARY

1.   This paper describes current research into the seed banks of temporary wetlands in the Northern Tablelands of New South Wales, Australia.
2.   The aim of the research is to gain an understanding of the role of seed banks in revegetating temporary wetlands following periods of drought, and to use this information to manage the vegetation of Australian wetlands more predictively.
3.   Experiments which assess (a) the influence of water regime on germination from wetland seed banks, (b) the effect of season of wetting on germination and (c) the longevity of wetland seed banks and their decay and dormancy properties are described. The relevance of this research to wetland management is also considered.

INTRODUCTION

Many Australian wetlands are naturally ephemeral. Grazing and cropping of wetlands in dry years and drainage in wet years have been common practice since European occupation 150 years ago. Recent conservation awareness has emphasised the need for wetland restoration on both private and public land. Therefore there is a need to understand wetland vegetation processes and to develop effective restoration techniques (Land and Water Resources Research and Development Corporation, 1992).

The water levels of many wetlands in Australia fluctuate naturally or through manipulation. Some wetlands dry completely, remaining dry for months or even years. Seed banks play a major role in ensuring the survival of wetland vegetation through dry periods as evidenced by the rapid appearance of seedlings following wetting. Nevertheless, little information on Australian wetland seed banks is available. Studies on rice weeds (McIntyre *et al.*, 1989), monsoonal wetlands (Finlayson, Cowie & Bailey, 1990) and temporary wetlands (Casanova & Brock, 1990; Brock & Casanova, 1991) include information on seed banks, but do not

Restoration of Temperate Wetlands. Edited by B.D. Wheeler, S.C. Shaw, W. Fojt and R.A. Robertson
© 1995 John Wiley & Sons Ltd.

address their rôle in maintaining diverse plant communities, or their potential for rehabilitating degraded wetlands.

Our research focuses on temporary, high-altitude, temperate wetlands in the Northern Tablelands of New South Wales. The goals of this research are: (a) to increase our understanding of the germination response of Australian temporary wetland seed banks to timing and extent of wetting, and (b) to use such information to manage the vegetation of both undamaged and degraded wetlands in Australia more predictively. In this paper, we present the preliminary results of a number of germination trials designed to increase our knowledge of wetland seed banks.

METHODS

Six temporary wetland sites were chosen to reflect the range of water regimes: the least temporary sites dry on average once every 15 years in contrast to more temporary wetlands some of which dry several times a year, others once a year and some once every three or more years.

To test the influence of water regime on germination, sediment samples were collected in 1990 using a cylindrical coring device, and, after a drying pre-treatment, were subjected to either waterlogged or submerged water regimes. Germinating individuals were identified, counted and removed at approximately six-week intervals. Similar trials conducted in successive years, both in the glasshouse and in the field, also tested fluctuating water regime (see Table 1). Collection and experimental methods are discussed in Brock, Theodore & O'Donnell (1994).

The effect of season of wetting was tested, in both glasshouse and outdoor trials, using sediment collected from each of the six sites in early winter 1992. Sub-samples of the dry sediments were wetted in spring, summer, autumn and winter; germinating individuals were identified and counted eight weeks later.

The decay and dormancy of seed banks subject to periods of drying, and hence the regenerative potential of temporary wetlands, were examined in several ways. The longevity of seeds in dried sediments was assessed by regularly wetting sub-samples of sediments collected in 1991 and identifying and counting the individuals which germinated (Table 1a). The seed bank left after germination events (where there is no replenishment of seed by plant reproduction) was assessed by subjecting sediments to successive periods of wetting and drying. The individuals which germinated during each wetting event were identified and counted (Table 1b). The extent and nature of this residual seed bank was also examined for a sub-set of sites by counting the number of seeds germinating in one wetting event, as a proportion of viable seeds counted in sub-samples of sediment. In this way, information on the resilience of species in wetlands with unpredictable water regime can be assessed.

Table 1. Survival potential of propagules in the seed bank was determined by assessing: (a) germination from sediments which have been dry for various lengths of time; (b) residual germination from seed banks during successive wetting events.

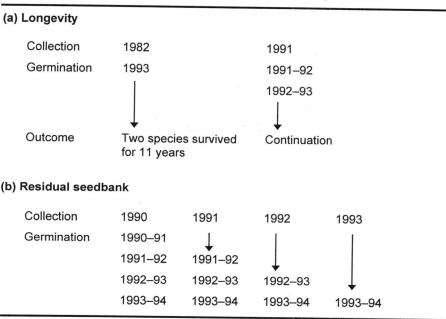

(a) Longevity

Collection	1982	1991
Germination	1993	1991–92
		1992–93
Outcome	Two species survived for 11 years	Continuation

(b) Residual seedbank

Collection	1990	1991	1992	1993
Germination	1990–91			
	1991–92	1991–92		
	1992–93	1992–93	1992–93	
	1993–94	1993–94	1993–94	1993–94

RESULTS

Of a total of 58 species germinating from sediments collected from six sites in 1990, between 21 and 38 occured in each site. Species richness was highest in a relatively undisturbed wetland, and lowest in one with a history of hydrological modification and other disturbances. Species composition varied with site; 25 % of species were site-specific and only 3.5% germinated from all six sediments (Figure 1). Different taxonomic groups were broadly represented (Figure 2). At some sites, a few species dominated germination events.

The numbers of species and individuals germinating varied with water regime (Figure 3). Some species germinated in both flooded and damp water regimes, others in only one regime. More angiosperms (monocotyledons and dicotyledons) germinated in damp conditions, although a considerable number germinated in both regimes. Charophyte germination was favoured by flooded conditions whereas bryophytes were favoured by damp conditions. Subsequent trials indicated that for many species, a fluctuating water regime stimulates a greater number of germinations.

In the seasonality trials, the greatest number of outdoor germinations occured in autumn (autumn > winter > spring >> summer) for each wetland. High

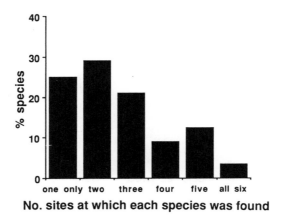

Figure 1. Site specificity: percentage of species occurring in all sites, five sites, four sites, three sites, two sites and one site only.

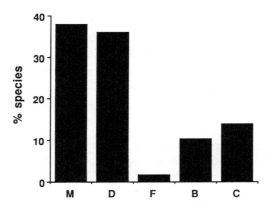

Figure 2. Taxonomic groups: Percentage of species that are monocotyledons (M), dicotyledons (D), ferns (F), bryophytes (B), and charophytes (C), (all six sites combined).

temperatures appeared to inhibit germination in summer.

Sediments collected from one study site in 1982 still to contained viable seeds, demonstrating their ability to survive an 11-year dry-storage period. Only two species (*Juncus articulatus* L. and *Myriophyllum variifolium* J. Hook) out of the 21 which are known to occur in the seed bank at this site germinated, however, suggesting that species differ greatly in their potential to survive in the seed bank. Further trials with the 1991 material should shed more light on the longevity of individual species.

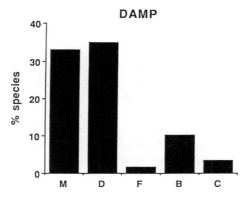

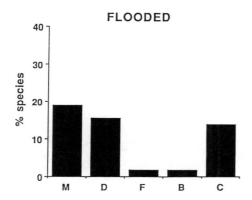

Figure 3. Percentage of the total number of species germinating in damp or flooded water regimes (presented for different taxonomic groups for all six sites combined) (see Figure 2).

The proportion of seeds germinating in one wetting event is small. Of the 11 species counted in sub-samples of sediment collected from one wetland, less than 2.5% of the viable seed of any species germinated in the first 90 days.

RELEVANCE TO WETLAND MANAGEMENT

Both the composition of the seed bank and the number and type of species germinating from it are influenced by the hydrological regime. Thus, water levels could be manipulated to favour the germination and establishment of certain species and inhibit the growth of others. Manipulation of the water regime to maximise biodiversity is clearly desirable in both wetland restoration and management.

For plants in temporary wetlands in the Northern Tablelands of NSW, the most favourable season for germination and establishment is autumn, when ambient temperatures and evapotranspiration rates are falling. Autumn may therefore be the best season for commencing rehabilitation work.

Long-lived seeds, together with the small proportion of seeds germinating in one wetting event, may indicate that we have a suite of species well-adapted to unpredictable water regimes. This resilience of the seed bank should be exploited in plans for management and rehabilitation. Species clearly differ in their potential to persist in the unreplenished seed bank, however, and so it may not be possible to rely solely on relict seed banks to revegetate wetlands which have remained dry for long periods. Transplanting seed banks and vegetative propagules may also be necessary for the revegetation of degraded temporary wetlands.

ACKNOWLEDGEMENTS

We thank Kevin Theodore, Laurie O'Donnell and Geoff Smith for both field and laboratory assistance and Rosemary Torbay for help with manuscript preparation. Dr John Weir donated samples collected in 1982. Financial support for this work was provided by Land and Water Resources Research and Development Corporation (LWRRDC) and the Australian Research Council (ARC).

REFERENCES

Brock, M.A., Theodore, K & O'Donnell, L. (1994). Seed bank methods for Australian wetlands. *Australian Journal of Marine and Freshwater Research,* **45** (4), 483–493.

Brock, M.A. & Casanova, M.T. (1991). Plant survival in temporary waters: a comparison of charophytes and angiosperms. *Verhandlungen Internationale Vereinigung fur Theoretische und Angewandte Limnologie,* **24**, 2668–2672.

Casanova, M.T. & Brock, M.A. (1990). Charophyte germination and establishment from the seed bank of an Australian temporary lake. *Aquatic Botany,* **36**, 247–254.

Finlayson, C.M., Cowie, I.D. & Bailey, B.J. (1990). Sediment seed banks in grassland on the Magela Creek Floodplain, Northern Australia. *Aquatic Botany,* **38**, 163–176.

Land and Water Resources Research and Development Corporation (1992). *Research and Development Plan 1992.* LWRRDC, Canberra. 28 pp.

McIntyre, S., Mitchell, D.S. & Ladiges, P.Y. (1989). Germination and seedling emergence in *Diplachne fusca*: a semi-aquatic weed of rice fields. *Journal of Applied Ecology,* **26**, 551–562.

13 Seed Banks in Fen Areas and Their Potential Use in Restoration Ecology

D. MAAS & A. SCHOPP-GUTH
Technische Universität München, Lehrstuhl für Landschaftsökologie II, D-85350 Freising, Germany

SUMMARY

1.   The seed banks of natural and semi-natural fen plant communities (partially used for litter harvesting, partially managed by nature conservation groups or without regular use) of intensively managed forage meadows on former fen sites, and of an arable field on a fen site were investigated and compared with respect to their usability for restoration of the former fen vegetation.

2.   The results indicate that the size of the seed bank and the species' proportions under different fen plant communities depend on the management of the sites, but that this does not influence the species composition. Intensive agricultural use changes the seed bank composition by increasing the proportion of forage plants and weeds. In the arable soil, few remnants of the former fen vegetation were found.

3.   Comparison of the seedling emergence from soil samples taken in spring and autumn of the same year, with seedling emergence from field quadrats after an observation period of three years allowed the seed bank constituents to be classified into different types according to their longevity. Generally, typical fen plant species have a transient or short-term persistent seed bank, whereas many weedy and forage plants have long-term persistent seed banks, as do fen *Carices*.

4.   The proportion of fen plants in the seed bank declined to less than 4% during *c.* 10 years after intensification of agricultural management. In arable sites on fen soils, the seed bank declined to less than 1% during the same period. This means that restoration of fen plant communities is only possible within a maximum of five years after a disturbance has removed the original plant cover.

INTRODUCTION

Although a lot of seed bank studies have been carried out in recent years, not all habitats are equally represented among the published results. This is particularly regrettable, because some of the more important objects of nature conservation, namely bogs and fens, have been largely overlooked, as a glance through the literature citations in review articles confirms (Roberts, 1981; Leck, Parker & Simpson, 1989). As many of the mire sites, in Europe at least, have been damaged

Restoration of Temperate Wetlands. Edited by B.D. Wheeler, S.C. Shaw, W.J. Fojt and R.A. Robertson
© 1995 John Wiley & Sons Ltd.

by agricultural use or industrial peat extraction, restoration of such sites regionally demands considerable investments of time and money. Besides the appropriate regulation of the hydrological conditions, restoration means the re-establishment of plant communities which were formerly present (Pfadenhauer, 1986). Initially, even in our own restoration experiments (Pfadenhauer & Maas, 1987), great hope was placed on the use of seed banks to provide restoration sites with at least some of the species belonging to the former vegetation cover. Only very limited experience on what kind of species are present in undisturbed fen soils was available (Chippindale & Milton, 1934; Champness & Morris, 1948; Mika, 1978; Vyvey, 1983). It was not clear to what extent the seed bank found beneath undisturbed fen communities would be comparable to the remnants expected to be present after several years of intensive agricultural use, except for some examples in the Netherlands (Bakker, 1983). The type of seed bank that typical fen species are able to form was not known, whereas for at least some of the species of forage meadows the type of seed bank had been investigated (Thompson & Grime, 1979). However, no comparison existed of their relative proportions in the seed bank as compared with typical fen plants.

This lack of knowledge of the seed banks of undisturbed as well as disturbed *Molinietum* and *Primulo-Schoenetum* vegetation types stimulated our studies in different areas of the pre-alpine region in southern Germany, where these communities were traditionally used for harvesting of litter until progress in agriculture stopped this demand and facilitated intensification of the sites by drainage and fertilisation. The results are presented for three series of seed bank investigations of original litter meadows with different mowing frequencies, a comparison of original meadows with improved meadows on former fen community sites and of the seed bank left after 10 years of crop farming on a fen site.

STUDY SITES AND METHODS

Study sites sampled in series 1

The sampling region lies *c*. 50 km south of München, Bavaria. All study sites are located on base-rich fen peat and their vegetation is referable to the *Schoenus ferrugineus*-community. This type of vegetation in fen areas is favoured by nature conservation policy. The different management practices for the study sites are given in Appendix 1.

Study sites sampled in series 2

These sample sites lie in the western pre-alpine region of southern Germany, *c*. 40 km east of Lake Constance. They include intact litter meadows of *Molinia*- and *Schoenus ferrugineus*-communities as well as forage meadows on former sites of this vegetation and land use type (see Appendix 2).

Study site sampled in series 3

Only one site was sampled in this investigation, lying 20 km south-west of München, Bavaria. Its former use was as a litter meadow, which had been changed into a forage meadow at an unknown date. Ten years before sampling, the forage meadow was ploughed and the area was used for cereal production. It is situated on base-rich drained fen peat. No soil treatment was applied after the last harvest before the year the soil was sampled for the seed bank investigation. At that time a ruderal vegetation mainly consisting of arable weeds had established.

On all sampled sites a rectangular sampling plot was selected and marked within an area of homogeneous vegetation. In series 1, 15 soil samples were extracted with a spade from the plot, which measured 20 x 18 m; in series 2 and 3 the plots measured 10 x 15 m and 10 soil samples were taken from each. The area of each sample was 16 x 16 cm, cut to a depth of 12 cm (series 1 and 2), or 30 cm (series 3), according to the expected depth gradient of germinable seed content (Chippindale & Milton, 1934). The samples of series 3 were subdivided into three layers of 10 cm each, which were examined separately. Sampling pattern had to follow a regular spacing, because plots for other investigations had to be avoided. In series 1, the vegetation was removed from the soil samples by application of a total herbicide (Round-up) and clipping off the dead plant material, leaving the soil undisturbed. The samples of series 2 and 3 were processed by hand to remove all vegetative parts which might resprout. The remaining soil was laid out in a layer of c. 4–5 cm in plastic trays and exposed to natural weather conditions. The samples were kept moist by watering with tap water, as necessary. Emerging seedlings of each species were counted and removed at intervals of one to two weeks. The botanical nomenclature follows Oberdorfer (1983). When no further germination was detected for at least two weeks, the samples of series 2 and 3 were stirred and turned over to expose seeds buried in the lower part of the sample to light, in order to encourage further germination.

The samples of series 1 and 2 were monitored for three growing seasons and series 3 for one growing season. Sampling in series 1 and 2 was replicated in the two following years. As only minor differences in the numbers of seedlings of individual species were found from year to year, mainly due to climatic influences on the annual seed production (Schopp-Guth, 1993), only the results of the first of the three replicate sampling years are presented here. The soil samples were taken at the beginning of the growing season in early May, except in series 1, where an additional series of soil samples was extracted in mid-September.

In series 2, plots for counting emerging seedlings were installed in six of the ten sampling sites. Ten replicate quadrats (20 x 20 cm) were laid in each sampling plot in a restricted randomised pattern, so as not to interfere with additional plots for other studies. The vegetation of these field quadrats was removed by application of a total herbicide (Round-up) and clipping the dead plant parts at soil level to avoid resprouting, shading, and competition. The edges of the field quadrats were protected by plastic sheets stuck in the soil to keep out underground rhizomes. Seedlings in the field quadrats were counted and removed in weekly periods.

RESULTS

The results of the seed bank studies are displayed as tables listing the cumulative numbers of seedlings m^{-2} for each species. These data were subjected to principal components analysis (Appendix 1), and detrended correspondence analysis (Appendix 2), respectively. Species and sites in these tables are ordered according to the results of the numerical data analysis (Wildi & Orloci, 1990).

Appendix 1 lists the results of study series 1 with soil samples from undisturbed, but differently managed *Schoenus ferrugineus*-communities. The size of the seed bank ranged between *c.* 500 and 3000 seedlings m^{-2}, depending on the management. Smaller seed banks were found in samples of sites with annual mowing. With irregular cutting the size of the seed bank increased and reached its maximum values in the samples of former fallows where cutting has been reintroduced. The mean number of species per soil sample was about 30. Nearly all species found in the seed bank were also present in the vegetation of the sites (Schopp-Guth, 1993). Many of them showed no distinct pattern with respect to their presence in soil samples of sites with different management. The highest number of species was found in the soil of site Em II, which received additional fertilisation, thus offering the possibility for growth of more nutrient-demanding species of forage meadows (*e.g. Lotus corniculatus, Trifolium* spp., *Lychnis flos-cuculi*).

The most important species in the seed bank of all sites are those which are dominant in the vegetation. The seven species with the highest numbers of emerging seedlings are listed at the top of the table. Other important species of the seed bank were found in the group of *Carex* species. Among the seven most important seed bank constituents a distinction can be found in the numbers of seedlings emerging from different sites. Both *Schoenus ferrugineus* and *Molinia caerulea* are found with a greater seed bank in the former fallow sites Ett I and Ett II and in the site Ro with a mowing frequency every three or four years. Generally, the number of emerging seedlings of *Schoenus ferrugineus* is higher in soil samples which receive no annual management. *Juncus alpino-articulatus* and *Potentilla erecta* follow approximately the same pattern, while *Primula farinosa* achieves a higher number of germinating seedlings in soil samples from sites with current and recent annual cutting regimes. A comparable distribution in the soil samples can be found for *Tofieldia calyculata*. *Linum catharticum* is similar to *Molinia caerulea* with a slight concentration of higher seedling numbers in samples from sites with medium cutting frequencies or a fallow history. In contrast to the other more important species, *Parnassia palustris* is more irregular in its occurrence with respect to the management of the sites investigated.

Out of the group of species with considerable contribution to the total seed bank of the sites, only *Potentilla erecta* has higher seedling numbers emerging in the spring samples (S). By contrast, *Molinia caerulea* and *Parnassia palustris* regularly have higher numbers of emerging seedlings in the autumn samples (A). *Juncus articulatus, Primula farinosa, Linum catharticum* and *Schoenus ferrugineus* show no clear pattern with respect to the temporal variation of their seed bank sizes. The latter is also consistent for most of the other species with smaller proportional contribution to the seed bank.

A higher number of species where occurrence in the seed bank depends on the management of the sites is found in study series 2, with a comparison including fen litter meadows and forage meadows (Appendix 2). The upper two-thirds of the table is occupied by species restricted to the seed bank of forage meadows. Not all species of this group are also present in the vegetation of these sites. Those species in the lower third of Appendix 2 contribute to the seed bank of forage meadows as well as to that of fen communities. A distinctive group of only four species dominates the seed bank of site R, the vegetation of which is dominated by tall herbaceous plants. They also contribute the largest proportion to the seed bank of this site (*Lysimachia vulgaris, Ranunculus lingua, Hypericum perforatum, Filipendula ulmaria, Galium uliginosum*). The seed bank of traditionally managed fen communities displays two further species groups with more general presence (*Molinia caerulea* group) in *Molinia caerulea*- and *Schoenus ferrugineus*-dominated plant communities, and another which is restricted to *Schoenus ferrugineus*-communities alone. These two groups reflect the dominant species. However, many of the species with ubiquitous occurrence in the seed bank (*e.g. Juncus articulatus, Carex panicea, Carex flava, Carex hostiana, Leontodon hispidus*) are restricted to the vegetation of only a part of the sites investigated.

Comparison of seedling numbers emerging from the soil samples and on the field plots distinguish species with regularly higher seedling numbers in the soil samples (*e.g. Ranunculus repens, Cerastium holosteoides, Juncus bufonius, Juncus alpino-articulatus, Juncus articulatus, Carex panicea, Carex flava, Carex hostiana*) from those with higher seedling numbers in the field plots (*e.g. Anthoxanthum odoratum*, and most of the species typical for *Molinia caerulea*- and *Schoenus ferrugineus*-communities). For a few species with smaller numbers of emerging seedlings the pattern remains obscure.

The seed bank composition of arable fields on fen peat with former typical vegetation types is shown in Table 1. Most of the germinable seeds detected are found in the upper 10 cm. The number declines to *c.* 15% in the soil layer between 20 and 30 cm. The total number of seedlings emerging from the samples is rather low compared with forage meadows on fen sites. The seed bank consists mainly of weedy species like *Chenopodium album, Stellaria media* or *Agropyron repens*, but also includes seeds of typical forage meadow species like *Poa pratensis* or *Lychnis flos-cuculi*, and ruderals of disturbed places and irregularly managed moist meadows (*e.g. Rumex obtusifolius, Plantago major, Epilobium hirsutum*). Only two species of the original fen communities are still present in the seed bank: *Carex elata* and *Carex acutiformis*. Their seed bank seems to concentrate in the lower soil strata.

Table 1. Numbers of seedlings m^{-2} in fen soil used as an arable field for c. 10 years. Numbers for species present only in the seed bank but not in the vegetation are underlined.

Soil layer / Species	0–10 cm	11–20 cm	21–30 cm
Plantago lanceolata	1		
Ranunculus acris	3		
Arrhenatherum elatius	1		
Dactylis glomerata	1		
Cirsium oleraceum	1		
Taraxacum officinale	2		
Poa compressa	1		
Epilobium angustifolium	2		
Agropyron repens	12		
Veronica arvensis	12		
Chrysanthemum leucanthemum	6	1	
Polygonum persicaria	8	2	
Polygonum convolvulus	1	2	
Carex elata	2	3	
Trifolium repens	1	5	
Eupatorium cannabinum	1	1	
Juncus alpino-articulatus	1	2	
Juncus inflexus	5	4	
Epilobium parviflorum	6	2	
Poa annua	1	1	
Cirsium arvense	6		1
Alopecurus pratensis	1		2
Hypericum tetrapterum	5		2
Epilobium hirsutum	34	3	1
Myosotis arvensis	14	1	1
Chenopodium album	44	18	4
Stellaria media	31	8	2
Ranunculus repens	92	22	22
Cerastium arvense	15	8	3
Veronica chamaedrys	28	12	3
Rumex obtusifolius	28	2	2
Poa pratensis	16	20	11
Lychnis flos-cuculi	171	35	13
Holcus lanatus	2	1	3
Festuca pratensis	2	1	1
Mentha rotundifolia	1	1	1
Juncus articulatus	14	5	5
Plantago major	1	4	2
Filipendula ulmaria		1	1

contd

Table 1. continued

Soil layer / Species	0–10 cm	11–20 cm	21–30 cm
Carex acutiformis		<u>8</u>	<u>2</u>
Polygonum aviculare		3	3
Trifolium pratense		1	1
Plantago media		<u>1</u>	
Lythrum salicaria		<u>1</u>	
Agrostis stolonifera		1	
Tussilago farfara		1	
Bellis perennis			2
Poa trivialis			1
Chenopodium rubrum			<u>2</u>
Mentha arvense			2
Lysimachia vulgaris			<u>2</u>
Sum of seedlings per soil layer	**563**	**181**	**95**
Total sum of seedlings			**839**

DISCUSSION

Three years of observation of the fen plant community samples of series 1 and 2 demonstrated the tendency of the seeds to remain in a dormant state: 61 to 74% of all seedlings found in the samples germinated within one year, 14 to 23% in the second, and 12 to 16% in the third year. This means, that up to 10% of all germinable seeds in the soil samples remain dormant for several years, and the seed banks of the species with such behaviour can be considered to be persistent (Thompson & Grime, 1979). This proportion is high compared with other meadow communities where only 6% of all detected seeds remained dormant after 18 months (Fischer, 1987). In arable soils, the proportion of germinable seeds after three years regularly drops below 3% (Brenchley & Warington, 1936). Though the soil samples in series 1 and 2 were treated differently, neither the timing of germination of single species, nor the numbers of seedlings detected in the soil beneath the comparable *Schoenus ferrugineus*-communities differed considerably. This may indicate that the seeds of many of those species which are present in the vegetation of these study sites are concentrated in the uppermost soil layers, as has been shown for other vegetation types (Schenkeveld & Verkaar, 1984). Whether this conclusion would also be consistent for the forage meadows sampled for this study remains to be investigated. An accumulation of seeds of species dominating the vegetation of the site is also found for the tall herb community sampled in series 2. A much less pronounced correlation between species composition of the vegetation and the seed bank was observed in forage meadows, where the early cutting suppresses seed production of many taller growing species. In these cases the seed bank may also be modified by sowing or weed control measures.

Numbers of germinable seeds found in soil beneath fen litter meadows mown each or every second year are lower compared with such sites with longer cutting intervals or fallow sites. The seed bank beneath *Schoenus ferrugineus*-communities was only about half the size of that beneath *Molinia caerulea*-communities. Though the comparison is based on only two *Molinia* samples, this tendency may be generalised from results of seed bank studies of other *Molinia caerulea*-communities (Chippindale & Milton, 1934; Mika, 1978) with seedling densities generally ranging higher than those found for *Schoenus ferrugineus*-communities. The arable field sampled in series 3 has seedling numbers comparable to the *Schoenus ferrugineus*-communities, which is lower than in other arable fields (Roberts & Chancellor, 1986; Albrecht & Bachthaler, 1989), but which can be interpreted as a result of the short history of crop farming and the short observation period (1 year). Studies on other sites with comparable histories indicate that the seed bank of crop fields on fen peat may be considerably higher (Burgi, unpublished), but does not differ much with respect to species composition.

Fen communities comparable to the *Schoenus ferrugineus*-vegetation of this study were analysed for seed bank composition by Vyvey (1983). He found even lower numbers of germinable seeds, which may be due to his shorter observation period of only three months. The plant communities sampled by Mika (1978) are comparable to the *Molinia caerulea*-type of series 2. The numbers of germinable seedlings m^{-2} are also comparable. The species composition of the seed bank differs somewhat, because the south Bohemian sites have a different management history and are situated on base-poor fen peat (Mika, 1978).

Differences in the numbers of germinable seeds detected in the study sites of series 1 and 2 can be attributed to the differing management regimes. *Schoenus ferrugineus*-communities which are annually mown have a lower seed output (Schopp-Guth, 1993) because the frequent mowing results in a loss of resources, thus limiting vegetative growth and seed production of many species. All species fruiting in autumn (*e.g. Molinia caerulea, Schoenus ferrugineus*) are subject to additional loss of seeds by the traditional cutting period during September and October. Here the ripe seeds of other species, which remained attached to the inflorescence (*e.g. Carex flava, Carex panicea*), are also removed. Under fallow conditions, the number of species in the vegetation and the annual seed production of many species is reduced owing to increasing effects of competitive interaction (Schopp-Guth, 1990; Maas, 1992), also resulting in reduced numbers of germinating seedlings in the soil samples. The largest total seed banks are found beneath sites with infrequent mowing events, or former fallows where cutting had been resumed some years ago.

Larger numbers of germinable seeds are found in the soil beneath *Molinia caerulea*-communities, where seed production may generally be higher, especially when efforts for more intensive agricultural use, like fertilisation, were made. The largest seed banks of all sites studied are found in the soils of forage meadows, and are generally larger, irrespective of the soil type (Chippindale & Milton, 1934;

King, 1976), than those found in soils beneath wetland plant communities.

The species found in soil samples of fen plant communities differ in their contribution to the annual seedling total. This feature is not restricted to fen plant communities (Roberts, 1986) and can also be seen in the results of the arable field sampled in series 3. The proportional contribution of each year's seedling guild permits their subdivision into three groups:

(i)   Germination of more than 95% of all germinable seeds in the first year after sampling (*e.g. Molinia caerulea, Briza media, Sesleria varia, Ranunculus nemorosus*).

(ii)   Germination of 60–95% of all germinable seeds in the first year after sampling (*e.g. Carex davalliana, Tofieldia calyculata, Parnassia palustris, Primula farinosa, Potentilla erecta, Polygala amarella, Linum catharticum*).

(iii)   Germination of less than 60% in the first year after sampling (*e.g. Carex hostiana, Carex panicea, Carex flava, Juncus alpino-articulatus, Juncus articulatus, Schoenus ferrugineus*). Nearly 20% of all the germinable seeds of these species germinated in the third year after sampling.

This classification conforms both with the results of the spring and autumn samples of series 1 and the differences in seedling numbers emerging from the soil samples and the field quadrats of series 2. Species which are found in higher numbers in the autumn samples correspond to those which also occur in higher numbers on the field quadrats and mostly germinate within one year out of the samples. The species which germinate to less than 60% out of the soil samples within one year are indeterminate with respect to spring and autumn sampling and are found in lower numbers on the field plots. This pattern can best be seen for dominant species like *Molinia caerulea, Schoenus ferrugineus,* and the *Carex* spp. For subdominants, this pattern can be obscured because of sampling errors as a result of the irregular spatial distribution of adult plants and seeds in the soil (Thompson, 1986; Henderson, Petersen & Redak, 1988). Differences in the surface structure of the substrate, which could have influenced the germination (Peart & Clifford, 1987), do not exist, at least for all samples of the original fen communities. The species found in the seed bank can be related to the seed bank types of Thompson & Grime (1979). Species belonging to seed bank types I were not detected. Also the distinction between seed bank types III and IV is somewhat arbitrary, because they only differ in the proportion of dormant seeds remaining in the soil from year to year, a property which can also be influenced by sampling errors, annual seed production, and other factors.

Since the seed bank types of Thompson & Grime (1979) are mainly based on the proportion of seeds surviving from year to year with regular annual seed input, but do not indicate how long remnants of the seed banks of type III and IV remain in the soil after the seed rain is interrupted, this classification can only give assistance for restoration with respect to seed bank type II in fen communities. Such species will soon be lost from the seed bank and no longer be available for restoration. It may therefore be more useful, with respect to restoration to adopt the seed bank types suggested by Bakker (1989) and Thompson (1992), using time

Table 2. Seed bank types (following Thompson 1992) of fen plant species.

Transient	Short-term persistent	Long-term persistent
Briza media	*Carex davalliana*	*Carex hostiana*
Sesleria varia	*Tofieldia calyculata*	*Carex panicea*
Molinia caerulea	*Parnassia palustris*	*Carex flava*
Ranunculus nemorosus	*Potentilla erecta*	*Carex acutiformis*
Leontodon hispidus	*Primula farinosa*	*Carex elata*
	Polygala amarella	*Carex fusca*
	Linum catharticum	*Carex rostrata*
	Pinguicula spp.	*Carex gracilis*
	Succisa pratensis	*Schoenus ferrugineus*
	Viola palustris	*Juncus alpino-articulatus*
		Juncus articulatus

spans of one year for transient, up to five years for short-term persistent and more than five years for long-term persistent seed bank types. A classification of important fen species according to these groups is given in Table 2. The seed bank types of many species can be explained to a good extent by their innate state of dormancy and their germination requirements (Maas, 1989).

The seed bank properties indicate that with respect to restoration the time-span since the species were lost from the vegetation plays an important role for the success of seed bank activation. In most cases where several years passed before restoration, only species with a long-term persistent seed bank will be available. Only the *Carex* spp. and a restricted number of other genera (*Schoenus ferrugineus, Juncus articulatus, Juncus alpino-articulatus*) fulfil this requirement. Species with a transient seed bank, like *Leontodon hispidus*, can only gain importance for restoration by invasion of wind-dispersed propagules. Seeds of most of the dominant and subdominant fen species have to be attributed to a short-term persistent seed bank type. However, not only the presence of these species in the seed bank, but also their proportion compared with the unwanted species of forage meadows or arable weeds influence the success of seed bank activation. As shown in Figure 1, after 10 years not more than 2 to 4% of the seed bank is composed of the remnants of the original fen community. In arable soils the proportion regularly drops even below this value. Such small proportions are suspected to be insufficient to re-establish the lost species in a stand of vegetation dominated by competitively superior species on sites which are enriched in nutrients and where the water table has been lowered by drainage.

From these results it can be concluded that good possibilities with respect to the use of seed banks for restoration of fen plant communities are only found within a short time-span of maximally five years. After this the seed banks of fen species decline so rapidly and the number and proportion of unwanted species increases to such amounts that it cannot be recommended to use the seed bank for restoration

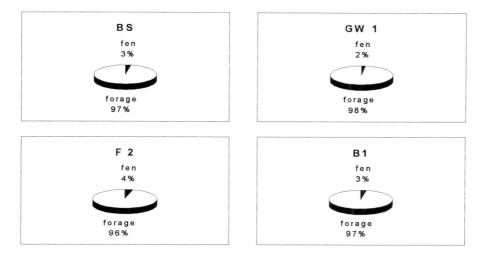

Figure 1. Proportional contribution of fen and forage plants to seed banks in four fen soils beneath forage meadows intensified *c.* 10 years ago. [For management, see Appendix 2.]

purposes any longer. In these cases a careful preparation of the sites and sufficient time spans for natural invasion or active measures of re-establishment can increase the number of species with conservational value, but may in most cases not lead to a complete reconstruction of the original plant communities.

ACKNOWLEDGEMENTS

This investigation was financially supported by grants Pf 120-4 and Pf 120-6 of the Deutsche Forschungsgemeinschaft. We gratefully acknowledge criticisms and improvements of the text by Bryan Wheeler and Ken Thompson. We also thank a considerable number of students for their support by patiently processing the soil samples, and the landowners for permission to carry away a part of their property.

REFERENCES

Albrecht, H. & Bachthaler, G. (1989). Unkrautsamengehalte und Bodeneigenschaften von Ackerflaechen in Bayern. *Weed Research*, **30**, 101–108.
Bakker, J.P. (1983). Seed bank and species diversity in moist grassland communities. *Acta Botanica Neerlandica*, **32**, 246.
Bakker, J.P. (1989). *Nature Management by Grazing and Cutting*. Kluwer, Dordrecht.
Brenchley, W.E. & Warington, K. (1936). The weed seed population of arable soil. *Journal of Ecology*, **24**, 479–501.
Champness, S.S. & Morris K. (1948). The population of buried viable seeds in relation to contrasting pasture and soil types. *Journal of Ecology*, **22**, 149–173.

Chippindale, H.G. & Milton, W.E.J. (1934). On the viable seeds present in the soil beneath pastures. *Journal of Ecology*, **22**, 508–531.

Fischer, A. (1987). Untersuchungen zur Populationsdynamik am Beginn von Sekundaersukzessionen. *Dissertationes Botanicae*, **110**, Cramer, Berlin & Stuttgart.

Henderson, C.B., Petersen, K.E. & Redak K.A. (1988). Spatial and temporal patterns in the seed bank and vegetation of a desert grassland community. *Journal of Ecology*, **76**, 717–728.

King, T.J. (1976). The viable seed contents of ant-hill and pasture soils. *New Phytologist*, **77**, 143–147.

Leck, M.A., Parker, V.T. & Simpson, R.L. (eds) (1989). *Ecology of Soil Seed Banks*. Academic Press, London.

Maas, D. (1989). Germination characteristics of some fen plant species from calcareous fens in southern Germany and their implications for the seed bank. *Holarctic Ecology*, **12**, 337–344.

Maas, D. (1992). Stress – Stoerung – Konkurrenz: Bedeutung in kalkoligotrophen Kopfbinsenriedern des Alpenvorlandes. *Verhandlungen der Gesellschaft für Oekologie*, **21**, 413–420.

Mika, V. (1978). Der Vorrat an keimfähigen Samen in südboehmischen Niedermoorboeden. *Zeitschrift fuer Acker- und Pflanzenbau*, **146**, 222–234.

Oberdorfer, E. (1983). *Pflanzensoziologische Exkursionsflora*. Ulmer, Stuttgart.

Peart, M.H. & Clifford, H.T. (1987). The influence of diaspore morphology and soil-surface properties on the distribution of grasses. *Journal of Ecology*, **75**, 569–576.

Pfadenhauer, J. (1986). Konzept zur Moorrenaturierung im süddeutschen Alpenvorland: Ziele, Verfahrensweisen, offene Fragen. *Telma*, **16**, 269–278.

Pfadenhauer, J., & Maas, D. (1987). Samenpotential in Niedermoorboeden des Alpenvorlandes bei Grünlandnutzung unterschiedlicher Intensität. *Flora*, **179**, 85–97.

Roberts, H.A. (1981). Seed banks in soil. *Advances in Applied Biology*, **6**, 1–55.

Roberts, H.A. (1986). Seed persistence in soil and seasonal emergence in plant species from different habitats. *Journal of Applied Ecology*, **23**, 639–656.

Roberts, H.A. & Chancellor, R.J. (1986). Seed banks of some arable soils in the English midlands. *Weed Research*, **26**, 251–257.

Schenkeveld, A.J. & Verkaar, H.J. (1984). The ecology of short-lived forbs in chalk grasslands: distribution of germinative seeds and significance for seedling emergence. *Journal of Biogeography*, **11**, 251–260.

Schopp-Guth, A. (1990). Wirkung unterschiedlicher Nutzungsintensität auf Populationen von Streuwiesenpflanzen. *Verhandlungen der Gesellschaft für Oekologie*, **19/2**, 356–363.

Schopp-Guth, A. (1993). Populationsbiologische Merkmale von Streuwiesenpflanzen. *Dissertationes Botanicae*, **204**, Cramer, Berlin & Stuttgart.

Thompson, K. (1986). Small-scale heterogeneity in the seed bank of an acidic grassland. *Journal of Ecology*, **74**, 733–738.

Thompson, K. (1992). The functional ecology of seed banks. *Seeds: The Ecology of Regeneration in Plant Communities* (ed. M. Fenner), pp. 231–258. CAB International, Wallingford.

Thompson, K. & Grime, J.P. (1979). Seasonal variation in the seed banks of herbaceous species in ten contrasting habitats. *Journal of Ecology*, **67**, 893–921.

Vyvey, Q. (1983). Study of the seed bank in *Schoeno-Juncetum subnodulosi* All. 1922 and in *Molinietum caerulea* All. 1922. *Acta Botanica Neerlandica*, **32**, 246–247.

Wildi, O. & Orloci, L. (1990). *Numerical Exploration of Community Patterns*. SPB Academic Publishing, The Hague.

Appendix 1. Number of germinated seedlings m^{-2} in fen soils under traditional management.† *Schoenus ferrugineus* plant communities sampled in spring (May) and autumn (September). Seedling numbers for species present only in the seed bank but not in the vegetation are underlined.

Study site / Species	Bai	Bai	Ben I	Ben I	Ben II	Ben II	Penz	Penz	Em II	Em II	Em I	Em I	Ro	Ro	Ett II	Ett II	Ett I	Ett I
	(S)	(A)	(S)	(A)	(S)	(A)	(S)	(A)	(S)	(A)	(S)	(A)	(S)	(A)	(S)	(A)	(S)	(A)
Parnassia palustris	3			5	23	49	16	18	3	16	26	227	8	39		3		5
Juncus alpino-articulatus	99	42	18	5	214	91	107	141	13	3	23	3	13	21	23	52	26	128
Potentilla erecta	21	23	31	18	292	190	195	156	115	148	406	16	3	5	13		78	21
Primula farinosa	250	193	36	23	3	5	26	193	156	247	159	263	13	5	5		5	5
Linum catharticum	44	76	104	177	143	161	258	516	99	365	159	573	771	1349	122	253	375	109
Molinia caerulea	62	70	47	62	47	42	13	21	55	44	146	104	36	206	365	661	490	690
Schoenus ferrugineus		29	182	49	419	445	203	180	83	89	174	172	370	896	1489	1286	1099	2122
Agrostis stolonifera	3	3		5	5	5	8		3	5				3	3			
Anthoxanthum odoratum	3	3												<u>5</u>		8		
Aster bellidiastrum								68	60	42								
Briza media	23					5	52	3	78	34								
Carex davalliana	3	29	5	3	49	23	31	57	49	31				5	8	3		
Carex dioica		16		3			8				16			10			8	8
Carex elata								3					8	5	23	16	13	21
Carex fusca	3				5		3	3		5					5			
Carex hostiana	44	3	16	3	8	10	52	52	44		3	3			36	5	5	10
Carex flava agg.	8		3		16	42	44	57	5		5		5	3			3	5
Carex panicea	3	13	5		49	26	10	5	3				5	5	29	18	18	44
Carex pulicaris		10				21		5	21						3			
Carex rostrata			47		47		8			13								
Cerastium holosteoides	3	<u>3</u>	3			<u>3</u>	31	21	31	78		5				<u>3</u>		3
Cirsium arvense	<u>8</u>		<u>10</u>	<u>8</u>														

contd

Appendix 1. continued

Study site / Species	Bai (S)	Bai (A)	Ben I (S)	Ben I (A)	Ben II (S)	Ben II (A)	Penz (S)	Penz (A)	Em II (S)	Em II (A)	Em I (S)	Em I (A)	Ro (S)	Ro (A)	Ett II (S)	Ett II (A)	Ett I (S)	Ett I (A)
Cirsium palustre					3	3	3		3	3				5			5	3
Deschampsia caespitosa					8													
Drosera rotundifolia													10	91				5
Eleocharis palustris			10				3	29										
Epilobium palustre			8		8	5									21		10	
Eriophorum latifolium			3	5	10			31	10	8	10	3					5	3
Eupatorium cannabinum							8	13										
Euphrasia rostkoviana										13			3					
Festuca rubra			3	3		3	8	18		57		5						
Filipendula ulmaria						8									3			
Galium boreale									39	47								
Galium palustre										3						3		8
Galium uliginosum			5		3		3			3						3		
Gentiana clusii										3	31	26						
Gentiana pneumonanthe																5		
Hypericum tetrapterum							3			3					3			
Juncus subnodulosus															13		3	146
Leontodon hispidus					3	3	3	16	44	34	26	5	5	10	13		3	3
Lotus corniculatus									8	49								
Lychnis flos-cuculi										3	3							
Lysimachia vulgaris	10								8	31					13	10	62	
Lythrum salicaria										3					44			70
Mentha aquatica	3							10							73	13	10	57
Pinguicula spp. *		5								10								

Appendix 1. continued

Study site / Species	Bai (S)	Bai (A)	Ben I (S)	Ben I (A)	Ben II (S)	Ben II (A)	Penz (S)	Penz (A)	Em II (S)	Em II (A)	Em I (S)	Em I (A)	Ro (S)	Ro (A)	Ett II (S)	Ett II (A)	Ett I (S)	Ett I (A)
Plantago lanceolata							3		13									
Poa trivialis									10	16								
Polygala amarella		3	5	18	21	55	16	65	23	3		10	3	5	3	3	5	5
Prunella grandiflora							3	10				10	3	5				
Ranunculus acris									3									
Ranunculus nemorosus			3	5		3			73	81	3		13		3		5	
Serratula tinctoria									3									
Sesleria varia			16	8	10		3	5	62	21	34	36			5		5	
Stachys officinalis				5						3				10				
Succisa pratensis						5				3								
Tofieldia calyculata	13	18	16	13			8	26		5	47	29	5	34				3
Trichophorum cespitosum	21	23	3				5	8	8	8	3		10					
Trifolium montanum										8								
Trifolium pratense										3								
Triglochin palustre				21			3											
Valeriana dioica						8											8	
Sum of all seedlings	612	560	529	437	1393	1211	1101	1729	1138	1547	1115	1479	1281	2713	2307	2344	2242	3466

* *Pinguicula vulgaris* and *Pinguicula alpina* are both present on a number of sites, but cannot be distinguished in the seedling stage.

† Management of the study sites: **Bai:** litter meadow, mown every two years, last cutting was applied the year before sampling; **Ben I:** litter meadow, mown yearly; **Ben II:** fallow of a litter meadow, last cutting more than 15 years ago; **Penz:** litter meadow, last cutting was applied two years before sampling, used as a pasture for young cattle each year for *c.* six weeks; **Em II:** litter meadow, mown every year; **Em I:** litter meadow, mown every year, fertilised with sludge at irregular intervals; **Ro:** litter meadow, mown every three or four years, last cutting was applied three years before sampling; **Ett I:** former litter meadow, left as fallow in *c.* 1970, mown again in 1985, and once yearly since then. **Ett II:** former litter meadow, left as fallow in *c.* 1970, mown again in 1986, and once yearly since then.

Appendix 2. Number of germinated seedlings m^{-2} in fen soil sampled in spring (soil) and on field plots (field) on the study sites[†] observed during two growing seasons. Seedling numbers for species present only in the seed bank but not in the vegetation are underlined.

Study site / Species	BS soil	GW1 soil	R soil	GW2 soil	F2 soil	F2 field	B1 soil	B1 field	F1 soil	F1 field	B2 soil	B2 field	D soil	D field	L soil	L field
Ranunculus repens	488	1647	74		1680	344	252	270		<u>4</u>				<u>4</u>		
Cerastium holosteoides	2165	2975	22	56	607	181	2620	2379	52	137	<u>22</u>		<u>4</u>			
Trifolium pratense	52	285	7		126	44	7	15								
Polygonum persicaria		<u>15</u>			15	15	<u>37</u>									<u>63</u>
Myosotis scorpioides	470	673	33		15	11	4	11		<u>19</u>						
Lychnis flos-cuculi	858	803	155	4	100	148	625	603						48		
Plantago lanceolata		4	222		11	1795	7	11	85	466						
Holcus lanatus	122	229	4		33	1117	26	4		15						
Poa trivialis	44	4388		4	100	204	<u>19</u>	<u>19</u>								
Ranunculus acris	30	41	26		11		15	89	4							
Galium palustre	<u>15</u>	<u>4</u>	15	<u>37</u>	<u>4</u>											
Anthoxanthum odoratum	19	226	333	26	192	2579	104	1462	22	19	30					
Cardamine pratensis	85	<u>33</u>	133	4	155	67	59	189	4	7	4		4			
Cerastium arvense		4	4		15											
Trifolium repens	30	163	<u>4</u>		19	11	15	7								
Veronica arvensis	<u>26</u>	22		7	130	19	11	48	<u>4</u>						<u>4</u>	
Poa pratensis	3023	1306	<u>7</u>	<u>7</u>	847	2079	414	337	<u>15</u>	<u>63</u>						
Poa annua	144	85			15	7	318	37		4						
Dactylis glomerata	7	7			111	181	15	33	<u>278</u>		7					
Bellis perennis	89	466	<u>4</u>	4	22	26	59	59	<u>4</u>					4		
Chrysanthemum leucanthemum	26	115			7	7	7		<u>4</u>					7		
Rumex acetosella	26	44	59	<u>4</u>	52	133	7	932	4		<u>7</u>					
Veronica chamaedrys	<u>11</u>	63			26		<u>7</u>									

Appendix 2. continued

Study site / Species	BS soil	GW1 soil	R soil	GW2 soil	F2 soil	F2 field	B1 soil	B1 field	F1 soil	F1 field	B2 soil	B2 field	D soil	D field	L soil	L field
Veronica serpyllifolia	7	126		4	22	218	15	303								4
Veronica officinalis	26	52	26		11											
Filipendula ulmaria	22	7	48		7	11										
Arrhenatherum elatius			4			15	22	22								4
Carex acutiformis	33	15	4		11	41	7									
Carex elata	144	48	78		33	266	15							4		
Juncus bufonius	67	115	59	4	33	4	525	4	4		33				4	
Juncus alpino-articulatus	19	192	30		67	30	414	4	4		118				11	22
Agrostis stolonifera	26					104	7		4			152	7			
Carex nigra	15	4	4				11						4		4	
Carex rostrata	67	37		85												
Carex gracilis	19			115	11		4									
Agrostis tenuis	4	15	30			37			4	70	11		4	15		
Sagina procumbens		315		122		33	389	44	137		4					
Galium uliginosum	63		847		15	15	30	33	52		403	22				
Ranunculus lingua			1724		7	7			19							
Lythrum salicaria	63		1254		7				4	4	11					
Hypericum perforatum	7	11	1125	37	33						4		4	4	22	48
Lotus uliginosus	22	11	544	4	773	96	181	4	11	7			107	133	11	19
Juncus articulatus	1972	3630	736	30	11	7	2002	37	4		744		56	322	70	19
Leontodon hispidus	4		41	22	22	44	26		15	48	4		200	48	11	15
Carex panicea	15	248	244	570	11	30	78		518	100	4		33	858	26	81
Carex hostiana	4	59	19	226					141	78		15	19	15	122	178
Carex flava agg.	7		22	1413	130	292	37	52	703	26	163		85	222	4	
Luzula campestris	11	89	226	181	15	15	56	11	78		281	11	33			

contd

Appendix 2. continued

Study site / Species	BS soil	GW1 soil	R soil	GW2 soil	F2 soil	F2 field	B1 soil	B1 field	F1 soil	F1 field	B2 soil	B2 field	D soil	D field	L soil	L field
Viola palustris	11	11	4	81	4	15	4		63	818	144	4	4	19	4	52
Prunella vulgaris				81		152			15	100						4
Festuca rubra				26		270		59	22	15	189	7	7			
Molinia caerulea			4	126		4			148	300	56	255	56	603	107	181
Potentilla erecta			15	215					185	788	1214	1040	100	733	56	618
Calluna vulgaris			11				19	11	7							
Succisa pratensis				226					59	377	422	41	15	7	7	
Carex davalliana			4	7					7				33		52	
Rhinanthus minor			44	4					7	7			4			
Hypericum tetrapterum			11													
Tofieldia calyculata			4										44	355	7	7
Salix repens			4	4					4					48	15	4
Polygala amarella				7						4			107	333		26
Schoenus ferrugineus													159	1014	252	48
Parnassia palustris													67	1373	26	122
Pinguicula vulgaris													30	7	63	63
Primula farinosa													281	3304	11	22
Drosera rotundifolia														218	4	
Sesleria varia														52		
Sum of seedlings:	10356	18607	8262	3733	5517	10675	8529	7086	2683	3474	3878	1547	1465	9742	892	1639

† Management of study sites: **BS:** Forage meadow on drained base-rich fen peat for 16 years. Mown 3 times a^{-1}, fertilised. **GW1:** Forage meadow on drained base-rich fen peat for > 15 years. Fertilised, mown 3 times a^{-1}. **R:** on base poor fen peat; vegetation dominated by tall herbs after 5 years fallow. Formerly an extensively-managed forage meadow with one to two cuts a^{-1} & light fertilisation. **GW2:** *Carex–Eriophorum latifolium* community on base-rich fen peat. **F2:** Forage meadow on drained base-rich fen peat for 16 years. Fertilised and cut 3 times a^{-1}. **B1:** Forage meadow on fen peat for 10 years, cut twice a^{-1}, drained, fertilised. **F1:** *Molinia* community on base-rich fen peat. For 3 years before sampling, fertilised and cut 3 times a^{-1}. **B2:** *Molinia* meadow on base-poor fen peat. **D** & **L:** *Schoenus ferrugineus* community on base-rich fen peat.

14 Planning for the Restoration of Peat Wetlands for Birds

D. E. WARD
Andrews Ward Associates, 62 High Street, Willingham, Cambridge, CB4 5ES, UK

G. J. HIRONS & M. J. SELF
The Royal Society for the Protection of Birds, The Lodge, Sandy, Bedfordshire, SG19 2DL, UK

SUMMARY

1. It is believed that restoration of peatlands for birds should create habitats which are rare or declining, to benefit species that are threatened, rather than create already widespread habitats for common birds. To gain maximum ornithological benefit, the objectives should be clearly defined before restoration is undertaken. Assessment of birds in five habitats indicates that lowland wet grassland, reedbeds and mires have the most species of conservation importance (defined as *Red Data Book* species or candidate RDB species) associated with them.

2. Preliminary site assessments should include size, geographical location and surrounding land use of the site, and the habitat requirements and distribution of the proposed target species. Subsequent feasibility studies should include hydrological survey and assessment of the impact of proposals on existing conservation interest.

3. Some of the factors affecting the restoration of lowland wet grasslands and reedbeds are discussed. Lowland wet grassland sites will need to be large (>200 ha) to support important populations of target species. Their management involves maintenance of a suitable water regime and appropriate vegetation-types. As sward composition may be affected, existing botanical interest must be safeguarded. Changes in hydrological regime may also affect existing invertebrate populations. Reedbeds require more water per unit area than wet grassland and may be more difficult to establish on peat. Moderately large reedbeds (>20 ha) are needed to attract the key reedbed specialist birds.

4. The scope of this paper is restricted to birds and, as management needs for other taxa may be different, careful consideration of the potential interest and value for a restored site must be undertaken before any work is started. All management and restoration activities must be carefully monitored and the results evaluated and made freely available to ensure that future restoration projects are as successful as possible.

Restoration of Temperate Wetlands. Edited by B.D. Wheeler, S.C. Shaw, W.J. Fojt and R.A. Robertson
© 1995 John Wiley & Sons Ltd.

INTRODUCTION

Restoration is a 'catch all term' often used to define any improving works undertaken on a piece of land where the natural interest has been destroyed or damaged. However, in nature conservation terms, restoration is taken to define attempts to re-establish complete communities with their appropriate constituents, be they botanical, invertebrate or vertebrate. It is highly debatable that this is ever possible when a site has been extensively destroyed, even if small remnants remain. More feasible is the reconstruction of a habitat type which can then be managed for the benefit of particular and predetermined species. In the case of birds, for example wildfowl, restoration will involve the provision of appropriate cover and structures for nesting, roosting and loafing, and satisfactory feeding areas with adequate food supplies. Restoration of vegetation alone may not be sufficient to meet the requirements of the dependent species and considerable care may need to be given to the development of invertebrate communities, techniques for which are still in their infancy. Under no circumstances should large-scale destruction of one form of semi-natural habitat of wildlife importance be undertaken in an attempt to change it into another. This chapter is solely concerned with the restoration of peatlands for birds, by creating or re-creating appropriate habitats where the existing conservation interest of a peatland has diminished, for example because of drainage, or has been lost, for example by peat extraction.

Restoration of peatlands for birds has intrinsic difficulties. Restoration is often required because the peat has been drained to allow other uses and consequently rewetting is necessary before any other work may be undertaken. Subsequent incorrect management has the potential to diminish a limited resource further, for example through oxidation. Some peatland habitats can only be restored, if at all, over long time-scales that may run into centuries. An example of this is the restoration of raised bogs.

Ornithological objectives

In order to gain maximum ornithological benefit the precise restoration objectives should be clearly defined before any habitat restoration is undertaken. It is appropriate, at a time when many of the characteristic peatland habitats and their dependent bird communities are diminishing, that restoration is designed to create habitats that are rare and declining, to benefit species that are threatened rather than to create habitat that is widely available for those species which have stable or increasing populations.

Peatland habitats utilised by birds

Peatlands are widely distributed throughout Britain. In theory it should be possible to assign each bird species to a specific habitat for breeding, passage or wintering and then to identify which of these habitats occur on peat soils, in order to provide an indication of which species and habitats are particularly important on peats. In practice, however, it is not always possible to do so.

Peat soils can support a very wide range of plant communities, the composition and structures of which may be present as a result of past human management. The bird communities present on a site are there because it provides suitable feeding conditions, nesting sites or shelter, and birds may depend on several different habitats at different stages in their life cycle. The absence of a bird species from a site may be due not only to lack of suitable habitat but also to geographical location (in Britain, for example, Greenland white-fronted geese, *Anser albifrons*,[1] are confined to the north and west). Equally, the presence of a bird species on a site may not be a function of soil type or vegetation composition, but merely that there happen to be flooded areas. This is true of Garganey (*Anas querquedula*), which are found in pools on lowland wet grassland sites.

Criteria have been devised to determine which bird species should receive high priority for conservation action in the UK and, by extension, for restoration activities (Batten *et al.*, 1990). These are:
1. Breeding or non-breeding in internationally significant numbers (>20% of the north-west European population);
2. Rare breeder (<300 pairs);
3. Declining breeder (>50% sustained decline since 1960);
4. Localised breeder or non breeder (>50% of the population in 10 or fewer sites).
5. Special category – showing cause for concern or with declining numbers but inadequate data to quantify the extent of the problem.

Assessment of the species and their preferred habitats for wintering, breeding or passage is given in Table 1. This allows identification of those habitats that are most useful to re-create, either because their creation ensures that a high number of Red Data Book species (Batten *et al.*, 1990) will benefit, or because the creation of a habitat benefits RDB species that are principally found on that habitat (taken as >40% of the population). Table 1 also identifies those species which have more than 40% of their populations on peat sites (RSPB unpublished data).

From Table 1 it is apparent that, although large numbers of RDB bird species are found in tall fen communities, only one is dependent on them. This is the crane (*Grus grus*), found at one site in Britain. Carr, which supports only three RDB or candidate RDB bird species, has two RDB species, Cetti's warbler (*Cettia cetti*) and sedge warbler (*Acrocephalus schoenobaenus*), which are significantly dependent on it. Swamps hold seven RDB species, of which three are significantly dependent upon them, all of which are reedbed specialists. Bogs support a large number of RDB species (13) of which only four, Greenland white-fronted goose, golden plover (*Pluvialis apricaria*), greenshank (*Tringa nebularia*) and red-necked phalarope (*Phalaropus lobatus*), are largely dependent on the bog habitat. With the exception of Greenland white-fronted goose, these are all breeding species. The greatest number of RDB species is, however, found on lowland wet

---

[1] Nomenclature follows Cramp *et al* (1977-94).

Table 1. *Red Data Book* and candidate *Red Data Book* bird species on important peat habitats. B/P/W: substantially dependent (>40% population) for breeding / passage / wintering; b/p/w: partly dependent(<40% population) for breeding / passage / wintering; *: species substantially associated with peat substrata (>40% population).

Birds	Wet grassland	Tall fen	Carr	Swamp (reedbed)	Bog
Red Data Book *species*:					
Bittern* (*Botauris stellaris*)				(BW)	
Bean goose* (*Anser fabalis*)	W				
Greenland white-fronted goose* (*Anser albifrons*)	W				W
Whooper swan* (*Cygnus cygnus*)	W				
Bewick's swan * (*Cygnus columbianus*)	W				
Wigeon (*Anas penelope*)	w				
Pintail (*Anas acuta*)	wb	b			b
Garganey (*Anas querquedula*)	b	b			
Shoveler (*Anas clypeata*)	w	w			
Pochard (*Aythya ferina*)		b			
Marsh harrier (*Circus aeruginosa*)		w		(BW)	
Red grouse (*Lagopus lagopus*)					b
Spotted crake (*Porzana porzana*)	b	b		b	
Corncrake (*Crex crex*)	b	?			
Crane* (*Grus grus*)		B			
Golden plover (*Pluvialis apricaria*)	w				B
Ruff (*Philomachus pugnax*)	b				
Black-tailed godwit* (*Limosa limosa*)	BP				
Curlew (*Numenius arquata*)	b				b
Greenshank* (*Tringa nebularia*)					B
Red-necked phalarope* (*Phalaropus lobatus*)					B
Barn owl (*Tyto alba*)	bw	b			
Cetti's warbler (*Cettia cetti*)			BW	(bw)	
Savi's warbler (*Locustella luscinioides*)				(B)	
Marsh warbler (*Acrocephalus palustris*)		b	b		
Bearded tit (*Panurus biarmicus*)				(BW)	
***Candidate* Red Data Book *species*:**					
Short eared owl (*Asio flammeus*)	b	b			
Lapwing (*Vanellus vanellus*)	b				
Snipe* (*Gallinago gallinago*)	b	b			b
Redshank (*Tringa totanus*)	b				
Yellow wagtail (*Motacilla flava*)	b				
Sedge warbler (*Acrocephalus schoenobaenus*)		b	B	(P)	

grasslands (23), where five wintering birds are largely dependent on the habitat and a further one (black-tailed godwit, *Limosa limosa*) is dependent on it for breeding. A conclusion that can be drawn from this is that better ornithological value is likely to be provided by lowland wet grassland, reedbed or bog than by the restoration of tall fen or carr, particularly as carr can be an adjunct to other habitats and thus enhance the interest. However, other factors need to be considered, such as the relative rarity of the species in question, the trend in population numbers and the likelihood of a particular restoration project attracting the desired species.

It is also appropriate to consider the potential value of restoring habitat for those species which are substantially present on peat. Of the 10 species (six breeding and six wintering) that have more than 50% of their populations on habitats on peat, factors other than substratum appear to govern their distribution in most cases. For example, Whooper swan (*Cygnus cygnus*) and Bewick's swan (*Cygnus columbianus*) occur on a limited number of sites managed as washlands and there are no data to suggest that if the substratum was different they would be disadvantaged. Indeed, the internationally important numbers of Bewick's and Whooper swans on the Ouse Washes principally feed in the surrounding arable land. Similar considerations may pertain to black-tailed godwit, now present on very few conservation-managed sites, most of which happen to be peat, and evidence from the Netherlands suggests that the highest densities are on silt sites (M. O'Brien, *personal communication*). Distribution probably overlies the apparent preference for peat substrata in the case of Greenland white-fronted goose and greenshank as they have a north and westerly distribution, occurring over substrata that are predominantly peat. The only two species which are most likely to show a preference for peat are snipe (*Gallinago gallinago*), which are found in the highest densities on peat sites (including lowland wet grassland) in Britain (Smith, 1983), and red-necked phalarope which primarily breed on the interface between open water, emergent vegetation and bog on peat (Yates, Henderson & Dymond, 1983).

The feasibility of undertaking restoration of different peatland habitats varies. Although restoration of lowland wet grassland and reedbeds has been undertaken, there are no examples of the restoration of bogs that have been useful to declining bird populations over the significant areas necessary. The one exception has been the restoration of pools within valley mires on Fetlar (Shetland Isles, Scotland) for breeding red-necked phalaropes by raising water tables, controlling grazing and controlling *Carex rostrata* (bottle sedge) (Ausden, 1992).

PLANNING RESTORATION

Once a parcel of land has been identified as being available for restoration purposes, a preliminary assessment of the site and its potential must be made (Table 2). Old maps, aerial photographs, land records and local knowledge provide a useful basis on which to determine the original habitats present on a site and the

Table 2. Factors involved in preliminary site assessment prior to restoration planning (adapted from Ward, 1992).

Site description	Legal definition	Boundaries
		Ownership
		Conservation status (*e.g.* Site of Special Scientific Interest / National Nature Reserve / Ramsar site, Special Protection Area), archaeological interest, listed buildings, Area of Oustanding Natural Beauty, National Park, Environmentally Sensitive Area,.
	Physical description	Access (roads, bridleways, footpaths other rights of way), recreation.
		Turbary, tenancies, shooting rights, fishing leases, common rights, management agreements.
	Context of the site – situation, present interest and management	Maps available, topography, water courses, waterbodies, extent of existing cover soils and hydrology (including rainfall).
		In relation to the immediate locality and wider afield.
Wildlife interest	Past and present interest	Habitats present and their components, flora (vascular and non vascular), vegetation communities, fauna (mammals, birds, herpetofauna, fish, invertebrates)
	Potential interest	As above
	Assessment	Local, regional and national importance
Past history and management		Turbary, grazing, cutting vegetation (coppicing, pollarding, mowing, reed cutting *etc.*), ditch management, shooting, fishing, habitation, flooding, drainage, extraction
Potential constraints	Physical	Soils, topography, drainage arrangements, water availability, access, pollution
(including off site factors)	Legal	As defined above.
	Financial	Capital, long term running costs.
	Manpower	
	Timescale	
	Wildlife	Pest species (vegetative or animal), large stands of undesirable habitat types
Potential works on sites	Agencies involved	Statutory and voluntary conservation agencies, planning authorities, NRA or other statutory water agencies, local representatives.
	Objectives	
	Extent	Space and time
	Product	

notable flora and fauna. Past management practices can often be identified and these will provide some ideas for future restoration objectives and subsequent management. It is important that due consideration is given to the original habitats even where these may have disappeared, for example as a result of extraction of peat, although assessment of the feasibility of these restorations must also be made. Options for restoration in the lowlands are likely to be greater than in the uplands. A cut-over raised bog may be renatured to a grassland, rich fen, an open water body with surrounding tall fen or a reedbed, all with the ultimate objective of restoration to a raised bog in several centuries. Each of these options will benefit different bird communities as already described and it may be that, on bird conservation grounds, some are deemed to be less desirable.

Restoration objectives

Assessment of objectives for restoration on bird conservation grounds must be further defined in considerable detail if success in ornithological terms is to be achieved. Detailed restoration objectives should not only cover the habitats to be restored and the desired avifauna, but also the ground form, structure, vegetation components, invertebrate fauna and hydrology. For invertebrate groups it may prove impossible to predict with certainty, either qualitatively or quantitatively, what may occur but specific food sources may be very important in allowing successful colonisation by certain birds. Experimental restoration projects, with an attendant risk of failure, should, however, not be disregarded completely as much can be learnt from carefully monitored trials.

Knowledge of the biology of each target species and its habitat requirements is essential to determine whether a restoration project will be successful. The precise needs of many species still remain to be defined and quantified. Similarly the means by which these requirements might be met are often not well understood. It is possible to predict qualitatively what species may use a particular habitat type – a wet grassland may support breeding snipe, redshank (*Tringa totanus*) and lapwing (*Vanellus vanellus*) – but it is not yet possible to predict accurately how many pairs will use it. Size and context of the site may determine restoration practicalities. For example, bittern (*Botauris stellaris*) and marsh harrier (*Circus aeruginosa*) appear to require areas of at least 20–30 ha of suitable habitat to support a breeding pair and, with the extensive hunting range required by marsh harrier, this may be as great as 100 ha. This may reflect food availability or structural factors rather than just size. In contrast, Cetti's warbler, an inhabitant of carr, survives in much smaller areas (< 1 ha). Adjacent land may also come within the home range as a loafing area, roost, or even a feeding area. However, the value of a restoration site may depend on sympathetic management of this land and its long-term security should be assessed. Changes in Government land policy may mean that land currently receiving subsidy to maintain it in a suitable condition may not always do so. Disturbance on adjacent land or unsympathetic practices in the upper catchment may reduce the usable area and thus negate any restoration efforts. This may happen where land with shooting rights abuts the restoration site.

The wider context must also be considered when setting objectives and the potential interest assessed carefully to ensure that achievable objectives are set. However, knowledge of the biology and habitat requirements of individual target species is usually sufficient to determine whether restoration efforts are likely to succeed. The availability of habitat and its bird community and current deployment of effort may militate against some options.

The success of a restoration design will depend on the hydrological characteristics of a site and its capacity to retain sufficient water of appropriate quality at the critical times of the year. An hydrological survey needs to assess quality and quantity of water inputs and outputs, the availability and quality of additional water supplies, to measure soil characteristics and topography, to assess the effects on freeboard and flood risk and to identify the need for control structures such as sluices and bunds.

Another factor to be considered in choosing management objectives is the time-scale. Some habitats, such as open water bodies, develop interesting bird communities very rapidly and can potentially develop nationally important assemblages in a few years. By contrast, the development of a raised bog, with its characteristic species assemblages, from the underlying substratum will take much longer, possibly several centuries. Many other habitats such as tall fens, reedbeds and carr will develop their bird communities over intermediate time-scales. Undoubtedly, choice of restoration objective has to take time-scale into account as it may not be considered appropriate to acquire land and spend money on its restoration with little immediate tangible benefit. Although birds are rapid colonists and common species will rapidly arrive at almost any site there is likely to be a trade off between achieving a desired community and the time-scale available.

FEASIBILITY STUDY

The initial work should take place well before any ground work to allow a considered approach and full consultation to occur. It is important to prepare a full description of the desired bird species and their requirements, which can be matched against a quantified written description for the restoration project, which takes into account a range of factors (Table 3). The feasibility study should include hydrological studies, topographical survey, soil and vegetation survey and the results of these should be fed back to the restoration objectives, taking into account other factors such as cost.

RESTORATION OF LOWLAND WET GRASSLANDS

To date, most restoration efforts have been on grassland which has undergone agricultural improvement by drainage and reseeding or conversion to arable land.

Table 3. Factors to be considered in the feasibility study.

Bird data	Bird species
	Habitat requirements
	Geographical range
	Colonising ability
Other information	Local weather conditions (rainfall and evaporation)
	Size
Topography	Gross landform (including depths of water bodies and land heights)
	Micro landform
	Spoil disposal
	Shelterbelts
Hydrology/water budget	Water availability
	Water quality and nutrient status
	Need for water control structures
	Soil water table and drainage
	Soil characteristics, type and physical properties
Vegetation and associated fauna	Seed bank
	Planting composition
	Vegetation structure
	Likely invertebrate assemblages
Other	Artificial habitat enhancement methods
	Visiting arrangements
	Other uses, *e.g.* farming and its implementation

Recent research largely on RSPB reserves, in particular the Nene Washes (Cambridgeshire) and Ouse Washes (Northamptonshire) and West Sedgemoor (Somerset), has developed understanding of the hydrology of peat-based lowland wet grasslands and the ecological requirements of the birds dependent on it (*e.g.* Green, 1986; Silsoe College, 1989; Hooker, 1991; Chown, 1992; O'Brien, 1992; Spoor & Chapman, 1992; Walker, 1992; Green & Robins, 1993). Tables 4 and 5 summarise the general ecological requirements of key breeding wader and wintering wildfowl species. This basic research has proved invaluable in identifying key constraints that may prevent success of restoration projects and opportunities which will facilitate success.

Physical constraints

Geographical location

Geographical location can influence the probability of a site attracting particular

Table 4. Habitat variables associated with high breeding wader densities on peat-based lowland wet grassland. + = positive association; − = negative association; 0 = no association (usually due to inadequate data). [Not all associations were identified as statistically significant by all authors.] Data from: Chown (1992); Green (1986; 1988); Herbert, Heery & Meredith (1990); O'Brien (1992); Vickery *et al.* (unpublished data).

	Lapwing (*Vanellus vanellus*)	Snipe (*Gallinago gallinago*)	Redshank (*Tringa totanus*)	Black-tailed Godwit (*Limosa limosa*)
Soil water				
High ditch water	+	+	+	+
Soft soil	−	+	+	+
Early-season flooding	+	0	+	0
Surface water	+	0	+	+
Vegetation/land use				
Tall vegetation	−	+	0	−
Species-rich vegetation	−	+	−	0
Tussocks	+	+	+	0
Juncus-dominated vegetation	0	+	0	0
Grazing/mowing	+	−	−	0
Large field	+	+	+	+

target species. Sites may be outside the range of a particular species or, although they may be within the range of existing populations of the target species, they may be isolated from those remaining. This may be one reason for the relatively slow increase in wader populations (especially black-tailed godwit and snipe) on West Sedgemoor following the restoration of what were considered to be suitable conditions.

Size

The minimum size of site for lowland wet grassland recreation to be worthwhile will depend on the particular objectives of the scheme. If these are to ensure that a site holds nationally important populations, then the areas required may be very large. For example, on the best sites breeding snipe attain densities of *c.* 60 pairs per 100 ha. Therefore to create a nationally important site for this species (*i.e.* holding 1% of the estimated national population) would require an area of about 500 ha.

Soil characteristics

Lowland wet grasslands on peat substrata have a number of advantages over similar sites on marine and riverine alluvium or clay provided they have adequate

Table 5. Habitat variables associated with wildfowl species on lowland wet grasslands. + = positive association; – = negative association; 0 = no association.

	Shallow water	Deep water	Short Sward	Long sward	Seeds	Arable crops	Cover
Bean goose (*Anser fabalis*)	0	+	–	+	+	0	–
Greenland white-fronted goose (*Anser albifrons*)	+	+	+	+	+	0	–
Whooper swan (*Cygnus cygnus*)	+	+	+	0	+	+	–
Bewick's swan (*Cygnus columbianus*)	+	+	+	0	+	+	–
Wigeon (*Anas penelope*)	+	0	+	–	+	+	–
Gadwall (*Anas strepera*)	+	–	0	0	+	–	0
Teal (*Anas crecca*)	+	0	0	0	+	0	+
Mallard (*Anas platyrhynchos*)	+	+	0	0	+	+	+
Pintail (*Anas acuta*)	+	+	+	0	+	0	–
Garganey (*Anas querquedula*)	+	–	–	–	+	–	+
Shoveler (*Anas clypeata*)	+	0	–	–	+	–	–
Pochard (*Aythya ferina*)	+	+	–	–	+	–	–

water supplies and can be hydrologically isolated. These facilitate the long-term management and maintenance of sites.

Field water tables may be readily manipulated on peat sites by altering ditch water levels. On West Sedgemoor the influence of ditches may extend 20 m or more into fields due to the high hydraulic conductivity of the peat (mean 1.0 m day^{-1}), and continue to affect water table heights beyond this (Silsoe College, 1989; Hooker, 1991; Walker, 1992). By contrast, ditches on clay sites only influence the water table in the 5 m or so closest to the ditch and beyond this field water tables only fluctuate in response to variations in rainfall and evapo-transpiration. Opportunities for precise management of field conditions, such as soil water tables, surface soil moisture content and soil penetrability, are therefore greater on peat and are undertaken on a range of sites including the Nene and Ouse Washes. This ability to manage water levels precisely also facilitates the integration of specific conservation management and essential seasonal farming activities, such as mowing and grazing, which require a lower water table than optimal for, say, breeding waders (Green, 1986).

The relatively high permeability of these peat soils also allows water tables to be manipulated by the use of sub-surface pipes which allow irrigation and/or drainage. Sub-surface pipes used in conjunction with low ditch levels enable rapid draw-down of the water table to allow farming activities to take place while used in conjunction with high levels allow water to be transferred in reverse to wet the soil. Experimental work on West Sedgemoor has shown by empirical measurement that pipe intervals of 30–40 m are required to maintain uniform soil water table depth and moisture status over the whole field (Hooker, 1991)

Wet peat soils are typically soft and easy for waders to probe. At West Sedgemoor, a water table depth of about 0.35 m below the surface has been shown to maintain soft, damp conditions adequately at the surface (Silsoe College, 1989; Walker, 1992). Clay substrata would need surface wetting to provide similar conditions.

Despite these advantages, rewetting of peat soils may be difficult if a site has previously dried to a considerable depth, a situation especially likely to have occurred in topogenous peat areas in the relatively dry south and east which do not have consistently high rainfall inputs to maintain soil moisture under drained conditions. Drained soils are particularly prone to shrinkage and compaction with deep cracking and also resistance to rewetting. The exact nature of the peat also influences the likelihood of drying, with fibrous sedge peats least prone (Okruszko, this volume).

Vegetation establishment and management

Management of lowland wet grassland sites for birds involves two key components: maintenance of a suitable water regime, and appropriate vegetation management regimes, usually grazing and/or mowing. Both directly influence the abundance and diversity of plants on a site as well as the structure of the sward.

Safeguarding existing botanical interest

Lowland wet grasslands and their associated ditch systems support many scarce or declining plant species, including 20% of Britain's national rarities (for example, *Polygonum mite,* Schrank) (Perring & Farrell, 1983; Evans, 1991). Therefore, management of wet grassland for birds should take account of any existing botanical interest. Particular plant species have a limited range of water tolerance, especially during the growing season, and change in water levels is likely to influence vegetation communities (Gowing, Spoor & Mountford, 1993). Where communities or species are of particular importance, for example botanically rich sites with Site of Special Scientific Interest (SSSI) status, hydrological management for birds which benefit from high water tables and some surface flooding in the breeding season (*e.g.* black-tailed godwit) may be considerably constrained. Regular flooding of peat grassland during the growing season promotes the transition from flood pasture to relatively poor rush pasture, or even tall herb fen – a situation as potentially damaging to the botanical interest as drainage. Summer flooding on the Ouse Washes, as a result of factors beyond the control of reserve management, combined with increasing nitrate concentrations in the floodwaters, has led to considerably increased stands of *Glyceria maxima* and much management effort is expended in trying to control this advance (Burgess, Evans & Thomas, 1990)

In some instances a compromise may need to be reached between the needs of birds and plants after assessing their relative importance and potential, or areas must be managed separately for birds and botanical interest (Beintema, 1982) although it should be remembered that traditional farming methods produced floristic diversity and high wader numbers. Large sites with opportunities for compartmentalisation and hydrological isolation may therefore be more suited to restoration initiatives.

Restoring vegetation on severely damaged sites

On sites severely damaged by agricultural improvement, restoration of botanical interest can only occur if there are refuge areas on the site from which recolonisation can occur, from a seed bank or by reseeding with a lowland wet grassland mix. Recolonisation of former vegetation cover from a relict seed bank in agricultural areas is poorly documented, but experience on the Nene Washes has shown that reversion to predrainage conditions can result in re-establishment of some wetland species. The number of species returning apparently declines with time after the original drainage and recently drained wetlands are probably most readily returned to their former vegetation cover. If reseeding is being contemplated this should be with wet-tolerant species. Swards containing commercial mixes of grasses including *Lolium* may be difficult to maintain on sites managed for birds, particularly where flooding occurs during the growing season. Additionally, circumstantial evidence (RSPB, unpublished data) suggests that commercial grass mixtures may grow so fast that sward conditions suitable for breeding waders will persist for too short a time to allow successful breeding.

Invertebrates

Managing lowland wet grassland for birds also requires consideration of the impact of water level changes, grazing and mowing on the biomass, density and species diversity of invertebrates, both because of their intrinsic conservation value and their importance as bird food. For example, mowing is detrimental to invertebrates dependent on the upper parts of plants, favouring only a few adaptable species (Kirby, 1992). Grazing is generally a better option for invertebrate species diversity since vegetation changes occur progressively and provide valuable structural variation within a small area. However, high stocking rates on wet ground can result in compaction and poaching, altering its suitability for both invertebrates and the birds that feed on them. Some species may benefit while others may not.

The invertebrate diversity of wet grassland is usually enhanced if there is a gradual transition from wet to drier areas, a situation also likely to increase breeding wader use. Soil invertebrate biomass can be reduced by summer waterlogging with serious implications for breeding waders, and areas flooded during the growing season at the Ouse Washes and West Sedgemoor subsequently had very low invertebrate biomasses – as low as 10% of previous levels in one extreme case at the former site (Green, 1986; Chown, 1992). A sudden and prolonged flooding of dry sites may be particularly damaging and a gradual and progressive wetting up would enable a more water-tolerant invertebrate fauna to become established.

RESTORATION OF REEDBEDS

Many of the considerations that pertain to restoration of lowland wet grasslands on peat also apply to reedbeds. To hold populations of nationally important species, reedbeds need to be large, for example, in excess of 20 ha for bittern and bearded tits (*Panurus biarmicus*). Their location is also important as, with few exceptions, most of the current populations of the RDB species are present in southern and eastern England and colonisation rates remain uncertain. The implications of the siting of a reedbed must also be considered. It is more difficult to seal a peat site adequately than a clay or silt site and isolate it from the surrounding land, and careful consideration must therefore be given to the implications, legal and otherwise, of holding water up to 0.5 m above the ground.

One of the principal differences from lowland wet grassland is the water regime. Lowland wet grasslands may be flooded in winter and drawn-down in spring, with the water table held beneath the soil throughout the summer with a maximum difference in water height of around 0.55 m. In contrast, water is held on reedbeds at depths of up to a maximum of around 0.5 m above the ground over most of the year, to a minimum of 0.5 m below ground if draw-down occurs in winter for harvesting the reed for commercial or conservation purposes. The requirement for water is consequently greater and it usually occurs in the spring when availability starts to become limiting as rainfall declines. This difference may make it inadvisable to consider restoring a peat site to reedbed unless there is a guaranteed substantial supply of water available in the spring and summer. The amount of water that has to be manipulated in the management of a reedbed on peat will have important implications for the provision of water control structures and the cost of these may make a restoration unfeasible.

Rewetting of peat reedbeds may cause short-term problems. For example, experiences at the RSPB's Marazion Marsh showed that, on rewetting, the pH dropped to 2.5 although it subsequently rose 3 months later to 6.2 (D. Flumm, *personal communication*). This has implications for the establishment of reed, particularly where pot-grown plants are used to supplement natural stock, and also for invertebrate survival over the transition period, possibly preventing colonisation by insectivorous birds for some period.

It has been suggested that establishment of reed in peat soils may also prove problematic owing to phosphorus limitation (Haslam, 1972). Although disturbance of soils may increase nutrient concentrations and improve reed growth, Ekstam, Graneli & Weisner (1992) believe that peat is generally a poor medium in which to establish reed and that it is more vulnerable to mechanical damage and to oxygen deficiency. Despite this, it must be recognised that reed has successfully colonised many peat sites.

As reedbeds can be satisfactorily created in a range of soil types, the large amounts of water required and the management implications of this, coupled with potential difficulties over establishment, must indicate that careful consideration on a site-specific basis be given to assessing whether this is the optimum restoration goal on peat.

REFERENCES

Ausden, M.H. (1992). *The importance of bogs on Fetlar for red-necked phalaropes.* Unpublished report. RSPB, Sandy.

Batten, L.A., Bibby, C.J., Clement, P. Elliott, G.D. & Porter, R.F. (1990). *Red Data Birds in Britain.* T. & A.D. Poyser, London. 349pp.

Beintema, A.J. (1982). Meadow birds in the Netherlands. *Managing Wetlands and their Birds, a Manual of Wetland and Waterfowl Management.* pp. 83–92. International Waterfowl Research Bureau, Slimbridge.

Burgess, N.D., Evans, C.E. & Thomas, G.J. (1990). Vegetation change on the Ouse Washes wetland, England, and their conservation importance. *Biological Conservation* **53**, 173–189.

Chown, D.J. (1992). *Report on West Sedgemoor breeding wader research in 1991.* Unpublished RSPB report.

Cramp, S., Simmons, K.E.L., Ferguson-Lees, I.J., Gillmor, R., Hollom, P.A.D., Hudson, R., Nicholson, E.M., Ogilvie, M.A., Olney, P.J.S., Voous, K.H. & Wattel, J. (eds). (1977–94). *Handbook of the Birds of Europe, the Middle East and North Africa.* RSPB/Oxford University Press.

Ekstam, B., Graneli, W. & Weisner, S. (1992). Establishment of reedbeds. *Reedbeds for Wildlife* (ed. D. Ward), pp. 3–19. RSPB/University of Bristol Department for Continuing Education.

Evans, C.E. (1991). The conservation importance and management of ditch flora on RSPB reserves. *RSPB Conservation Review,* **5**, 65–71.

Green, R.E. (1986). *The management of lowland wet grassland for breeding waders.* Unpublished RSPB report.

Green, R.E. (1988). Effects of environmental factors on the timing and success of the breeding of the common snipe *Gallinago gallinago* (Aves: Scolopacidae). *Journal of Applied Ecology,* **25**, 79–93.

Green, R.E. & Robins, M. (1993). The decline in the ornithological importance of the Somerset Levels and Moors, England and changes in the management of water levels. *Biological Conservation,* **66**, 95–106.

Gowing, D.J.G, Spoor, G. & Mountford, J.O. (1993). *Determining the water regime preferences of wet grassland flora.* Unpublished document, Silsoe College, Bedford.

Haslam, S.M. (1972). Biological Flora of the British Isles, *Phragmites communis* Trin. *Journal of Ecology*, **60**, 585–610.

Herbert, I.J., Heery, S. & Meredith, C.R.M. (1990). Distribution of breeding waders in relation to habitat features on the River Shannon callows at Shannonharbour, Ireland, 1987–89. *Irish Birds*, **4**, 203–215.

Hooker, J.G. (1991). *Design and evaluation of combined drainage and sub-irrigation systems on lowland peats.* M.Phil. thesis, Silsoe College, Bedford.

Kirby, P. (1992). *Habitat Management of Invertebrates.* RSPB/JNCC/NP, Sandy. 150pp.

O'Brien, M. (1992). *Breeding wader research.* Internal Progress Report. RSPB, Sandy.

Perring, F.H. & Farrell, L. (1983). *British Red Data Book I. Vascular plants.* Royal Society for Nature Conservation, Lincoln.

Silsoe College (1989) *West Sedgemoor hydrological investigation.* Unpublished report to RSPB.

Smith, K.W. (1983). The status and distribution of waders breeding on wet lowland grasslands in England and Wales. *Bird Study*, **30**, 177–192.

Spoor, G. & Chapman, J.M. (1992). *Comparison of the hydrological conditions on the Nene Washes and West Sedgemoor reserves in relation to their suitability for breeding waders.* Unpublished Report to RSPB. Silsoe College, Bedford.

Walker, L. (1992). *Evaluation of combined drainage and sub-irrigation systems on lowland peats.* M.Phil. thesis. Silsoe College, Bedford.

Ward, D. (1992). Planning for wetland restoration in the U.K. *Integrated Management and Conservation of Wetlands in Agricultural and Forested Landscapes* (ed. M. Finlayson), pp. 74–78. *Proceedings of a Workshop, Trebon, Czechoslovakia 25–31 March 1992. IWRB Special Publication 22.*

Yates, B., Henderson, K. & Dymond, N. (1983). *Red-necked phalaropes in Britain and Ireland.* Unpublished RSPB Report.

15 The Occurrence of Some Scarce East Anglian Fen Invertebrates in Relation to Vegetation Management

A. P. FOSTER

The National Trust, 33 Sheep Street, Cirencester, Gloucestershire, GL7 1QW, UK

D. A. PROCTER

Joint Nature Conservation Committee, Monkstone House, City Road, Peterborough, PE1 1JY, UK

SUMMARY

1.   Invertebrates were sampled from Skoyles Marsh, Hickling, East Anglia, using pitfall and water-trapping techniques. Results for Hemiptera, Coleoptera, Opiliones and Araneae showed higher values for species richness, diversity and evenness in a recently cut area than for nearby unmanaged fen vegetation. Species quality, however, was lower in the cut area, with some *Red Data Book* and 'Nationally Scarce' species occurring in greater proportions, or exclusively in the unmanaged vegetation. One rare species benefited from the cut.

2.   The occurrence of 10 Red Data Book or Nationally Scarce species recorded from Skoyles Marsh is also considered in the context of 72 trapping stations sampled, using the same trapping techniques, in a wide range of vegetation types undergoing a variety of management regimes at localities throughout East Anglia. This revealed that seven of the species were most often associated with unmanaged vegetation; one occurred fairly widely in both uncut and cut situations, and one had a preference for cut sites. One species was recorded only at Skoyles Marsh.

3.   When considering the reinstatement of vegetation management, perhaps following long periods of dereliction, the habitat needs of invertebrates 'specialising' in such situations should be taken into account. Unmanaged fen vegetation should always be retained within the habitat mosaic of a site.

INTRODUCTION

In Great Britain, many rare invertebrates are only known, or most frequently recorded, from the fens of East Anglia. At least 133 rare wetland species known to occur here are given Red Data Book (RDB) status in Shirt (1987) or Bratton (1991). Moreover, some RDB species that can be locally common in East Anglian

Restoration of Temperate Wetlands. Edited by B.D. Wheeler, S.C. Shaw, W. J. Fojt and R.A. Robertson
© 1995 John Wiley & Sons Ltd.

fens, for example *Photedes brevilinea* Fenn (Lepidoptera, Noctuidae)[1], are rare in a European context.

Fenland restoration may involve the reinstatement of vegetation management to areas which have undergone long-term dereliction. The aim of this may be to harvest a crop, for example *Cladium mariscus* or *Phragmites australis*, or to increase botanical diversity by reducing scrub cover, litter cover or shading by tall herbaceous vegetation. This paper, which forms part of a much wider study funded by English Nature, considers the occurrence of certain scarce fenland invertebrates in derelict, particularly *P. australis*-dominated vegetation, which botanically is often species poor. Findings from a single derelict locality which, in part, had been recently mown are presented. The occurrence of some of the rarest species is also considered in a wider context.

METHODS

Sampling techniques

Between 1988 and 1990 invertebrates were sampled from 72 sample stations at 42 East Anglian fen localities. Standardised trapping was carried out at each sample station using five pitfall traps (white plastic vending-machine cups) of 87 mm diameter placed in a line at 1 metre intervals, and two water traps (white plastic bulb bowls) of 200 mm diameter, one placed at ground level at one end of the line of pitfalls and one mounted on a 0.5 m stake at the other end. All traps contained a 30% solution of ethylene glycol to act as a preservative and were emptied and reset at 14-day intervals. Most samples were taken during the months of June/July and August/September; some sites were sampled for three consecutive summers, others for fewer seasons.

Vegetation recording involved estimating the percentage cover of each species occurring in a 4 m^2 quadrat adjacent to the invertebrate trapping station. Additional species occurring nearby were noted. Only vascular plants were recorded to the species level. A variety of environmental variables was recorded including vegetation height and litter depth.

Further details of sampling are provided in Foster & Procter (in press).

Example study site

The study site was selected as an example of derelict *Phragmites australis*-dominated fen where vegetation management was being reinstated. Although species poor botanically, this *P. australis*-dominated stand, in common with many in this study, contained examples of rare fenland invertebrates and could be

---

[1] Nomenclature follows Stace (1991) for vascular plants, Le Quesne & Payne (1981) for Hemiptera (Auchenorhyncha), Kloet & Hincks (1964) for Hemiptera (Heteroptera), Kloet & Hincks (1977) for Coleoptera, Hillyard & Sankey (1989) for Opiliones and Roberts (1987) for Araneae. Authority names are provided for groups not covered by these works.

regarded as of high zoological conservation interest in this respect. It comprised approximately 10 ha of tall *P. australis*-dominated vegetation located in Compartment 3 (Skoyles Marsh) of Hickling Broad National Nature Reserve, Norfolk (National grid reference: TG 425221). Prior to the winter of 1988/89, when approximately half of the compartment was cut, no cutting of vegetation had taken place since 1980, and it is unlikely that the vegetation litter had been removed at that time.

Vegetation in the uncut area was dominated by tall (1.5–2 m high) *P. australis*, including both standing dead and live stems. Present at very low frequency were *Calamagrostis canescens, Lycopus europaeus, Peucedanum palustre, Hydrocotyle vulgaris, Rubus* sp. and *Dryopteris* sp.. Some scrub development had taken place (*Betula* and *Salix* spp.), though not within 20 m of the trapping station. Dense *P. australis* litter covered the ground throughout, being up to 20 cm deep adjacent to the invertebrate sample station. Little change was recorded in the vegetation composition and structure between summer 1989 and summer 1990.

Prior to cutting, the managed section of the compartment was similar in vegetation structure and composition to that described above. In the summer of 1989 the cut sward was about 0.5 m tall, *C. canescens* providing up to 80% cover, and *P. australis* contributing 15%; beneath these, *Juncus effusus* formed a cover of 30%, *H. vulgaris* 10% and *Dryopteris* sp. 5%. At very low frequency were *Peucedanum palustre, Cirsium palustre, Iris pseudacorus, Carex riparia*, and *Rubus* sp. Scrub species were manually removed following the cutting of the herbaceous vegetation, and, although much of the litter was raked up and burnt, it still formed a 30–40% cover, in places up to 2 cm deep. In 1990, the vegetation structure and composition were broadly similar to that in the previous year.

Samples

Invertebrate trapping stations were operated simultaneously in both the uncut and cut areas at Skoyles Marsh. Results from the following trapping periods are considered in this paper: 8–22 June 1989, 22 June to 6 July 1989, 21 August to 4 September 1989; 5–19 June 1990, 19 June to 6 July 1990 and 15–29 August 1990.

Several invertebrate groups have been identified to the species level. This paper concentrates on the Hemiptera (bugs), Coleoptera (beetles), Opiliones (harvestmen) and Araneae (spiders). Species reviews assessing the nature conservation status, distribution and ecology for most of these invertebrates, in a Great Britain context, have recently been completed, or are approaching completion. The Hemiptera are reviewed by Kirby (1992), the Coleoptera by Hyman & Parsons (1992) and Hyman & Parsons (1994), and the Araneae by Merrett (1990). Bratton (1991) and Shirt (1987) also review the RDB species.

RESULTS

Appendix 1 lists the species of Hemiptera, Coleoptera, Opiliones and Araneae identified from Skoyles Marsh, together with numbers of individuals recorded from the uncut and cut areas in each year. The Great Britain status categories follow Ball (1992) except where subsequently revised in either Hyman & Parsons (1994) or Kirby (1992); 49 species of Hemiptera, 104 Coleoptera, 9 Opiliones and 49 Araneae were recorded. Among these are some Red Data Book and Nationally Scarce species which are either exclusive to, or most often recorded from wetland habitats. Such rarities were represented within the Hemiptera, Coleoptera and Araneae. The nine species of Opiliones recorded are fairly common and widespread in Great Britain.

Table 1 presents the numbers of species present in the uncut and cut plots at Skoyles Marsh, according to species status category. A higher total number of species was recorded from the cut area both in 1989 and 1990; this was also true for the Local and Common species. However, for the Nationally Scarce species (Na, Nb and Notable) the converse is true, with more scarce species recorded from the uncut reedmarsh. Four RDB species were present, two in both uncut and cut areas, one exclusive to the uncut and one exclusive to the cut area. The occurrence of these rare invertebrates is discussed in more detail later in this paper.

Table 2 provides species richness, diversity and evenness values together with a species quality score (SQS). Species richness is expressed simply by the numbers of species recorded, since the same trapping techniques were used simultaneously in both the uncut and cut areas. Richness, diversity and evenness values were calculated using the Hill numbers (Hill 1973) N0, N2 and E5, respectively, following Ludwig & Reynolds (1988), who recommend their use since the diversity is expressed in units of species numbers, and the evenness is largely unaffected by species richness.

Table 1. Numbers of species of Hemiptera, Coleoptera, Opiliones and Araneae recorded from uncut and cut plots at Skoyles Marsh, Hickling, according to species status category* in Great Britain.

Status in Great Britain	Uncut			Cut		
	1989	1990	1989+90	1989	1990	1989+90
RDB1	1	1	1	1	–	1
RDB2	1	1	1	–	–	–
RDBK	1	–	1	2	1	2
Na	4	4	4	1	–	1
Nb	4	2	4	3	1	3
Notable	2	4	4	1	1	1
Local	24	22	35	28	29	44
Common	49	59	78	67	70	100
Total species	86	93	128	103	102	152

* Species status category definitions are given at the end of Appendix 1.

Table 2. Species richness, diversity, evenness and species quality scores (see text) taking into account Hemiptera, Coleoptera, Opiliones and Araneae trapped during 1989 & 1990 in uncut and cut reedmarsh at Skoyles Marsh, Hickling.

	Uncut			Cut		
	1989	1990	1989+90	1989	1990	1989+90
Richness	86	93	128	103	102	152
Diversity	6.36	14.79	8.60	22.80	31.70	34.64
Evenness	0.36	0.42	0.30	0.55	0.63	0.56
Species quality score	2.70	2.22	2.21	2.05	1.49	1.81

The SQS has been calculated following Foster (1987), whereby species are assigned a score along a geometric progression according to their national status, the common species scoring 1 and the rarest 32. This cumulative score is then divided by the number of species present, resulting in a mean score per species. Eyre & Rushton (1989) have shown that this geometric scoring system leads to clear interpretation when considering site quality for nature conservation.

From our results it is evident that the species richness, diversity and evenness were higher in the cut area. Conversely, however, the SQS was lower, indicating that although there may have been an overall increase in species present there may also have been a corresponding decline in rarer species. The index of diversity will tend toward 1, and the evenness toward 0, when a single species dominates. The lower diversity and evenness values for the uncut area can be explained by the dominance in 1989 by the carabid beetle *Agonum thoreyi*, and to a lesser extent in 1990 by the abundance of the harvestman *Oligolophus tridens*. *A. thoreyi*, the most common species at the Hickling study site, was almost exclusive to the uncut trapping station. Other studies by Decleer & Segers (1989) in Belgium and Holmes *et al.* (1993) in Wales, have also shown that this predatory insect has a preference for tall-reed-dominated habitats.

Species represented by more than five individuals at Skoyles Marsh are presented in Table 3 (data for both years has been combined for each treatment). The species are ranked by their proportional presence in the uncut and cut areas, from those exclusive to the uncut to those exclusive to the cut area. Of the 10 RDB or Nationally Scarce species featured, eight were over 80% more frequent in the uncut area, and four of these were exclusive to this unmanaged area. χ^2 with Yates' correction has been used to test the probability of each species differing from a 1:1 ratio in the plots. All eight scarce species which occur with more than 80% frequency in the uncut plot differed significantly from a 1:1 ratio. Significance levels are shown in Table 3. One scarce species, *Paraliburnea clypealis*, was confined to the cut area. The occurrence of *Stilbus atomarius* does not differ significantly from the 1:1 ratio. These rare species are further analysed in Table 4. Their occurrence from a wide range of sites sampled in East Anglia is presented using derived means ($\log x + 1$) for each species per trapping

Table 3. Ranked percentage occurrence of species with more than five individuals recorded from Skoyles Marsh, Hickling. Figures for 1989 & 1990 combined in each treatment. [χ^2 using Yates' correction P <0.05*, P <0.01**, P <0.001***. Ara = Araneae, Col = Coleoptera, Hem = Hemiptera and Opi = Opiliones.]

Species	Order	Status in GB*	Uncut (%)	Cut (%)	Total no.	χ^2
Clubiona juvenis	Ara	RDB2	100	0	9	**
Hypomma fulvum	Ara	Na	100	0	8	*
Entelecara omissa	Ara	Na	100	0	9	**
Dromius longiceps	Col	Na	100	0	10	**
Olophrum fuscum	Col	Local	100	0	7	*
Stilbus oblongus	Col	Local	100	0	8	*
Nicrophorus vespilloides	Col	Common	100	0	7	*
Lophopilio palpinalis	Opi	Common	100	0	7	*
Agonum thoreyi	Col	Local	99	1	313	***
Cerapheles terminatus	Col	Na	96	4	25	***
Oligolophus tridens	Opi	Common	95	5	169	***
Quedius balticus	Col	RDB1	90	10	10	*
Agonum fuliginosum	Col	Common	89	11	61	***
Paralimnus phragmitis	Hem	Notable	88	12	17	**
Cyphon phragmiteticola	Col	Local	83	17	6	
Cantharis thoracica	Col	Local	81	19	21	**
Silis ruficollis	Col	Nb	81	19	36	***
Baryphyma trifrons	Ara	Local	80	20	15	*
Lacinius ephippiatus	Opi	Common	79	21	14	
Kaestneria pullata	Ara	Common	78	22	9	
Cyphon hilaris	Col	Local	73	27	26	*
Leistus rufescens	Col	Common	71	29	7	
Maso sundevalli	Ara	Common	69	31	13	
Paroligolophus agrestis	Opi	Common	67	33	64	**
Pirata hygrophilus	Ara	Common	61	39	226	**
Cantharis pallida	Col	Local	59	41	22	*
Cantharis figurata	Col	Local	57	43	7	
Clubiona phragmitis	Ara	Local	57	43	21	
Lepthyphantes tenuis	Ara	Common	57	43	14	
Tachyporus hypnorum	Col	Common	56	44	9	
Nemastoma bimaculatum	Opi	Common	50	50	6	
Pardosa prativaga	Ara	Common	50	50	54	
Sitona lineatus	Col	Common	45	55	11	
Cortinicara gibbosa	Col	Common	41	59	32	
Pocadicnemis juncea	Ara	Common	41	59	22	
Meligethes nigrescens	Col	Common	40	60	10	
Mycetoporus splendidus	Col	Common	36	64	11	
Quedius maurorufus	Col	Common	33	67	12	
Stilbus atomarius	Col	RDBK	33	67	9	
Oxyptila trux	Ara	Common	33	67	12	

contd

Table 3. continued

Species	Order	Status in GB*	Uncut (%)	Cut (%)	Total no.	χ^2
Oedothorax gibbosus	Ara	Common	33	67	87	**
Bathyphantes gracilis	Ara	Common	31	69	16	
Walckenaeria vigilax	Ara	Local	30	70	10	
Pachygnatha clercki	Ara	Common	29	71	14	
Antistea elegans	Ara	Local	25	75	47	**
Paederus riparius	Col	Local	25	75	8	
Clubiona subtilis	Ara	Local	25	75	8	
Pterostichus diligens	Col	Common	23	77	31	**
Pirata piraticus	Ara	Local	23	77	13	
Anthocomus rufus	Col	Local	21	79	75	***
Streptanus sordidus	Hem	Common	17	83	6	
Javesella pellucida	Hem	Common	10	90	10	*
Rilaena triangularis	Opi	Common	10	90	10	*
Streptanus aemulans	Hem	Common	9	91	35	***
Pterostichus minor	Col	Local	8	92	38	***
Lathrobium brunnipes	Col	Common	8	92	12	**
Carabus granulatus	Col	Local	5	95	64	***
Macustus grisescens	Hem	Common	2	98	43	***
Adarrus ocellaris	Hem	Common	0	100	18	***
Arthaldeus pascuellus	Hem	Common	0	100	39	***
Conosanus obsoletus	Hem	Common	0	100	21	***
Paraliburnia clypealis	Hem	RDBK	0	100	7	*
Agonum obscurum	Col	Local	0	100	32	***

* Status in Great Britain – see definitions at end of Appendix 1.

period, according to treatment. Although there is considerable overlap between the upper and lower limits (at the 95% level) for each species between many of the treatments, seven of the eight species showing a preference for the uncut plot in Table 3 had their highest derived mean values in the unmanaged sites. In most cases, the lowest derived mean is for the sites cut within a year of sampling. *Hypomma fulvum* did not follow such a trend, although the lowest numbers were for recently cut sites. *Paraliburnia clypealis*, exclusive to the cut area at Hickling, was also absent in unmanaged conditions in the wider context of this study. *Stilbus atomarius* is excluded from Table 4 since it only occurred in the Skoyles Marsh samples. It should be noted that Table 4 encompasses a wide range of vegetation types where timing of management also varies; column 4, for example, incorporates both winter- and summer-mown communities.

DISCUSSION

Our results demonstrate that, whilst invertebrate species richness, diversity and

Table 4. Mean (log x + 1) values for nine* of the ten RDB and Nationally Scarce species featured in Table 3, per trapping period, according to treatment from a range of sites sampled in East Anglia. Upper and lower limits at the 95% level given in parentheses. Column 1, derelict sites not cut for >5 years; column 2, mown 3–5 years prior to trapping; column 3, mown 1–3 years prior to trapping; column 4, mown <1 year prior to trapping.

	1	2	3	4
	(*n*=58)	(*n*=30)	(*n*=34)	(*n*=86)
Paralimnus phragmitis	0.52 (0.25–0.84)	0.22 (0.0–0.54)	0.37 (0.08–0.73)	0.18 (0.08–0.28)
Paraliburnia clypealis	0.00 (0.00–0.38)	0.15 (0.00–0.29)	0.12 (0.00–0.07)	0.04
	(*n*=49)	(*n*=22)	(*n*=30)	(*n*=69)
Dromius longiceps	0.38 (0.32–0.45)	0.00 (0.0–0.22)	0.07 (0.0–0.09)	0.02
Quedius balticus	0.16 (0.03–0.31)	0.03 (0.00–0.09)	0.04 (0.0–0.11)	0.04 (0.0–0.09)
Silis ruficollis	2.05 (1.48–2.85)	0.55 (0.06–1.26)	0.83 (0.32–1.53)	0.58 (0.30–0.92)
Cerapheles terminatus	1.74 (1.06–2.65)	0.38 (0.05–0.8)	0.20 (0.0–0.46)	0.30 (0.11–0.51)
	(*n*=58)	(*n*=30)	(*n*=34)	(*n*=86)
Clubiona juvenis	0.69 (0.40–1.07)	0.48 (0.18–0.85)	0.44 (0.17–0.78)	0.02 (0.0–0.11)
Entelecara omissa	0.69 (0.40–1.05)	0.42 (0.10–0.83)	0.24 (0.02–0.50)	0.02 (0.0–0.08)
Hypomma fulvum	1.08 (0.69–1.55)	1.09 (0.56–1.80)	1.15 (0.62–1.84)	0.62 (0.39–0.88)

* *Stilbus atomarius* excluded as it only occurred in Skoyles Marsh.

evenness may be increased by the cutting of fen vegetation, some RDB or Nationally Scarce species show a preference for unmanaged fen vegetation.

Dithlago *et al.* (1992) sampled a nearby reedbed (also at Hickling Broad National Nature Reserve), using a randomised block design of cut, burnt and unmanaged plots. Both the sampling techniques employed and the timing of samples differed from our own study; also different species groups are considered in the analysis, so the two are not directly comparable. However, at the family level, Dithlago *et al.* demonstrated that most treatment effects were between the unmanaged and both cut or burnt plots. Species richness, diversity and evenness showed no obvious relationship to treatment when considering the Diptera (two-winged flies) or overall invertebrates, though species quality was not assessed. Some row effects were also present, particularly for soil-dwelling populations; this is likely to be related to frequency and duration of flooding, a reflection of the topography of the site. In our study, no obvious differences in flooding were recorded between the uncut and cut plots.

When sampling wetland Araneae, Decleer (1990) found that, although species richness was not necessarily correlated with the act of cutting, at the species level some specialist wetland species were adversely affected. Also, Painter & Friday (this volume) have shown the value of unmanaged, *P. australis*-dominated, fen ditches within the hydroseral succession, when considering the quality of the aquatic Coleoptera fauna. In this case some of the rarest species predominated in the unmanaged ditches. These studies, together with our own, emphasise the value of species-level information when considering nature conservation management.

Three of the scarce species considered here, the bug *Paralimnus phragmitis*, the carabid beetle *Dromius longiceps* and the spider *Clubiona juvenis* appear to be associated with tall standing fen vegetation. *P. phragmitis* (given Notable status in Kirby, 1992) is associated with its food plant *P. australis* in fens and coastal marshes. In this survey it occurred in both *P. australis*-dominated situations (reedbeds) and in other vegetation types where *P. australis* was present, for example, *C. mariscus* (sedge) beds. *D. longiceps*, ranked RDB2 in Shirt (1987), had its status revised to Na by Hyman & Parsons (1992). In Great Britain it is a scarce species of fens and large coastal reedbeds. In Europe it is also rare in some countries: in Holland, Turin, Haeck & Hengeveld (1977) consider it threatened; in Belgium there is only one record (Desender, 1986); and in Scandinavia, Lindroth (1992) reports it as extremely rare in Sweden, absent from Norway, and known from only two localities in both Finland and Denmark. Larvae have been found in reed stems (Luff, in Shirt, 1987) and the current study bred examples of this species from 'cigar galls' formed on *P. australis* by *Lipara lucens* Meigen (Diptera: Chloropidae); 38 examples were captured in this study at 12 trapping stations; 11 of these stations were dominated by tall dense *P. australis* growth and one by unmanaged *C. mariscus*. Seven of the *P. australis* sites were unmanaged. Of those undergoing management, two were cut annually, one biennially and one burnt approximately a year prior to sampling, though in all cases large areas of uncut *P. australis* were present nearby. *C. juvenis*, given RDB2 (Vulnerable) ranking in Bratton (1991), is also rare in continental Europe. Decleer & Bosmans (1989) provide a distribution map and details of European records. It is known to occupy at least two widely differing habitat types, fens and sand dunes. In Great Britain it is associated with fens, principally in East Anglia where it is widespread in the Norfolk Broadland (of the 142 examples trapped in the current study, only 2 were outside Broadland). In Ireland and Germany it is recorded from sand dunes, living in grass tussocks. Within fenland, tall standing vegetation may be the principal habitat; Decleer & Bosmans (1989) have found it hibernating in broken standing stems and seed panicles of *P. australis*, though not in the litter.

Some rare species recorded at Skoyles Marsh are likely to be more dependent upon the accumulation of vegetation litter. *Quedius balticus*, is given RDB1 (Endangered) status in both Shirt (1987) and Hyman & Parsons (1994). It is confined in Great Britain to fens in East Anglia and is a predator of other invertebrates; 22 examples were trapped during the current survey. The species was wholly absent from sites mown annually, though it occurred in sites with a longer cutting rotation, or in those cut for the first time after a long period of dereliction (*e.g.* Skoyles Marsh). The spider *Entelecara omissa* is found within *Carex* tussocks or vegetation litter in fens. It is a scarce species, given Na status in Merrett (1990), and is most frequently recorded from the fens of East Anglia. In our study it occurred widely in both *P. australis*- and *C. mariscus*-dominated situations. The beetles *Cerapheles terminatus* and *Silis ruficollis*, given Na and Nb status, respectively, in Hyman & Parsons (1992), are restricted to wetland situations. The predatory larvae are probably restricted to vegetation litter in fens.

The spider *Hypomma fulvum* occurred in a wide range of vegetation types within our survey, though most were dominated by tall fen vegetation. Decleer (1990) demonstrated that in Belgium this species is adversely affected, at a highly significant level, by cutting the vegetation in either summer or winter. Merrett (1990) notes that it is recorded on *P. australis* or in the litter.

Two of the rarities occurring at Skoyles Marsh did not occur in the uncut plot in greater numbers than in the cut plot. The beetle *Stilbus atomarius* was represented by only nine examples in the whole survey, all at this site. The bug *Paraliburnia clypealis,* listed as RDBK in Kirby (1992), is a phytophagous species associated with the grass *Calamagrostis canescens*. This species benefited from the cut at Skoyles Marsh, which resulted in a marked increase in the cover of its food plant. Derived mean numbers of *P. clypealis* were also higher in regularly mown sites sampled throughout East Anglia. This species occurred at only five trapping stations, three of which were commercially harvested *C. mariscus* beds.

Cutting of fen vegetation is an essential mechanism in arresting the natural succession of open fen to fen carr and eventually woodland. Mowing of the vegetation, particularly in summer months, can also lead to an increase in botanical diversity. In addition, some invertebrates, including rare species, also benefit from this process of management, in particular a wide range of phytophagous species associated with the many food plants represented in summer-mown fens. In Great Britain the best-known example is the swallowtail butterfly *Papilio machaon britannicus* Sietz (Lepidoptera, Papilionidae), which is now confined to the fens of the Norfolk Broadland. The larvae feed almost exclusively on *Peucedanum palustre*, unlike its continental counterpart *P. machaon gorganus* Fruhstorfer, which utilises a wider range of food plants and habitats, though in inland areas of Sweden, and other parts of north-west Europe, *P. palustre* is also a principal food plant (Wicklund, 1974). Dempster *et al.* (1976) showed that the eggs are rarely laid on food plants growing low down within a dense sward; instead, tall exposed flowering-sized examples of *P. palustre* are selected for oviposition. The combination of regular cutting of the vegetation together with high water tables is important in maintaining suitable food plants for this insect. Wicklund (1974) also reports that the individual foodplants need to be sufficiently strong to take the weight of a female or she will immediately fly away before ovipositing. The significance of this is that females will lay predominantly on young turgescent leaves which are unlikely to drop from the plant.

Mown, herb-rich fens are also of value for many flower visiting invertebrates, for example, the bee *Macropis europaea* Warncke (Hymenoptera: Melittidae), given RDB3 status in Shirt (1987) and subsequently in Falk (1991), is a species which almost exclusively visits the flowers of *Lysimachia vulgaris*, a characteristic plant in many summer-mown fens of East Anglia.

However, there are a number of invertebrates associated with uncut fen vegetation. Some of these are rare in Great Britain and continental Europe and may occur in situations that are of relatively low botanical interest. From a nature conservation standpoint the needs of such species should be considered before embarking on the restoration of vegetation management, in particular on areas which have undergone long-term dereliction. At large sites where extensive areas are unmanaged, perhaps due to the limitations of manpower, such habitats may not be considered threatened. However, at small or isolated localities in particular, care should always be taken to leave some sections of the site in an unmanaged condition.

ACKNOWLEDGEMENTS

This work was funded by English Nature. We are indebted to Dr P. Kirby for identifying all the Hemiptera, to Mr. J. Cooter & Prof. J.A. Owen who checked some Coleoptera identifications, to Mrs L. Dear, Messrs H. Bowell, P. Cardy, M. Parsons and R. Morris, who sorted some of the traps, and to K. Decleer who alerted us to the continental literature. We thank Mr F. Russell, the warden of Hickling NNR, for information on past management on the reserve and for assistance with field work, and all the other wardens and landowners who allowed us to work on their land or reserves.

REFERENCES

Ball, S.G. (1992). RECORDER: *an environmental recording package for local record centres*. Version 3.1. English Nature, Peterborough.

Bratton, J.B. (ed.) (1991). *British Red Data Books: 3. Invertebrates other than Insects*. Joint Nature Conservation Committee, Peterborough.

Decleer, K. (1990). Experimental cutting of reedmarsh vegetation and its influence on the spider (Araneae) fauna in the Blankaart Nature Reserve, Belgium. *Biological Conservation*, **52**, 161–185.

Decleer, K. & Bosmans, R. (1989). Distribution and ecological aspects of four rare wetland spiders, recently reported from Belgium. *Bulletin of the British Arachnological Society*,

8, 80–88.

Decleer, K. & Segers R. (1989). The soil surface active Araneae, Opiliones, Carabidae and Staphylinidae of a wet meadow vegetation subject to dereliction and succession. *Biologisches Jahrbücher, Dodonaea*, **57**, 103–119.

Dempster, J.P., King, M.L. & Lakhani, K.H. (1976). The status of the swallowtail butterfly in Britain. *Ecological Entomology*, **1**, 71–84.

Desender, K. (1986). Distribution and ecology of carabid beetles in Belgium (Coleoptera, Carabidae). Part 4. *Studiedocumenten Koninklijk Belgisch Instituut voor Natuurwetenschappen* **34**.

Dithlago, M.K.M, James, R., Laurence, B.R. & Sutherland, W.J. (1992). The effects of conservation management of reed beds. I. Invertebrates. *Journal of Applied Ecology*, **29**, 265–276.

Eyre, M.D. & Rushton, S.P. (1989). Quantification of conservation criteria using invertebrates. *Journal of Applied Ecology*, **26**, 159–171.

Falk, S.J. (1991). A review of the scarce and threatened bees, wasps and ants of Great Britain. *Research and Survey in Nature Conservation*, **35**. Nature Conservancy Council, Peterborough.

Foster, A.P. & Procter, D.A. (in press). *A Terrestrial Invertebrate Survey of Selected East Anglian Wetlands*. English Nature, Peterborough.

Foster, G.N. (1987). The use of Coleoptera records in assessing the conservation value of wetlands. *The Use of Invertebrates in Site Assessment for Conservation* (ed. M.L.Luff), pp. 8–17. Agricultural Environment Research Group, University of Newcastle upon Tyne.

Hill, M.O. (1973). Diversity and evenness: A unifying notation and its consequences. *Journal of Ecology* **54**, 427–432.

Hillyard, P.D. & Sankey, J.H.P. (1989). *Harvestmen. Synopses of the British Fauna (New Series)*. **4.** (2nd edn). Linnaean Society of London and the Estuarine and Brackish-water Sciences Association.

Holmes, P.R., Fowles, A.P., Boyce, D.C. & Reed, D.K. (1993). The ground beetle (Coleoptera: Carabidae) fauna of Welsh peatland biotopes – species assemblages in relation to peatland habitats and management. *Biological Conservation*, **65**, 61–67.

Hyman, P.S. & Parsons, M.S. (1992). *A review of the scarce and threatened Coleoptera of Great Britain. UK Nature Conservation 3 (part 1)*. Joint Nature Conservation Committee, Peterborough.

Hyman, P.S. & Parsons, M.S. (1994). *A Review of the Scarce and Threatened Coleoptera of Great Britain*. UK Nature Conservation **12**. Joint Nature Conservation Committee, Peterborough.

Kirby, P. (1992). *A review of the scarce and threatened Hemiptera of Great Britain. UK Nature Conservation 2*. Joint Nature Conservation Committee, Peterborough.

Kloet, G.S. & Hincks, W.D. (1964). A checklist of British Insects. Second Edition (Revised). Part 1: Small Orders and Hemiptera. *Handbooks for the Identification of British Insects*. **11(1)**. Royal Entomological Society, London.

Kloet, G.S. & Hincks, W.D. (1977). A check list of British Insects. Second Edition (Completely revised by R.D.Pope). Part 3: Coleoptera and Strepsiptera. *Handbooks for the Identification of British Insects*. **11(3)**. Royal Entomological Society, London

Le Quesne, W.J. & Payne, K.R. (1981). Cicadellidae (Typhlocybinae) with a checklist of the British Auchenorhyncha Hemiptera, (Homoptera). *Handbooks for the Identification of British Insects*, **2(2c)**. Royal Entomological Society, London

Lindroth, C.H. (1992). *Ground Beetles (Carabidae) of Fennoscandia. A Zoogeographic study. Part 1: Specific Knowledge Regarding the Species.* Intercept, Andover.

Ludwig, J.A. & Reynolds, J.F. (1988). *Statistical Ecology: a Primer on Methods and Computing.* Wiley, New York.

Merrett, P. (1990). *A Review of the Nationally Notable Spiders of Great Britain.* Nature Conservancy Council, Peterborough.

Roberts, M.J. (1987). *The Spiders of Great Britain and Ireland. Vol. 2. Linyphiidae and Check List.* Harley Books, Colchester.

Stace, C. (1991). *New Flora of the British Isles.* Cambridge University Press, Cambridge.

Shirt, D.B. (ed.) (1987). *British Red Data Books: 2. Insects.* Nature Conservancy Council, Peterborough.

Turin, H., Haeck, J. & Hengeveld, R. (1977). *Atlas of the Carabid Beetles of the Netherlands.* North-Holland Publishing Company, Amsterdam

Wicklund, C. (1974). Oviposition preferences in *Papilio machaon* in relation to the host plants of the larvae. *Entomologia Experimentalis et Applicata,* **17**, 189–198.

Appendix 1. Systematic list of Hemiptera, Coleoptera, Opiliones and Araneae recorded from plots with different management regimes at Skoyles Marsh, Hickling, during 1989 & 1990.

Species	Status in GB**	Uncut 1989	Uncut 1990	Cut 1989	Cut 1990	Total no.
Hemiptera						
Ischnodemus sabuleti	Common	–	–	1	1	2
Dolichonabis limbatus	Common	–	–	–	2	2
D. lineatus	Local	–	–	–	1	1
Anthocoris nemorum	Common	3	–	–	1	4
Tytthus pygmaeus	Local	–	–	–	2	2
Pithanus maerkeli	Common	–	–	–	1	1
Adelphocoris ticinensis	Notable	–	1	–	–	1
Stenodema calcaratum	Common	–	–	–	1	1
S. trispinosum	Common	1	–	1	–	2
S. laevigatum	Common	–	–	1	–	1
Teratocoris saundersi	Common	–	–	–	1	1
Leptopterna dolabrata	Common	–	–	–	1	1
Saldula saltatoria	Common	3	1	2	–	6
Chartoscirta cincta	Common	1	–	–	–	1
Neophilaenus lineatus	Common	–	–	–	1	1
Cicadella viridis	Common	–	–	2	–	2
Aphrodes albifrons	Common	–	1	–	1	2
A. flavostriatus	Commom	1	1	–	–	2
A. bicinctus	Common	–	–	1	4	5
Adarrus ocellaris	Common	–	–	2	16	18
Jassargus distinguendus	Common	–	–	1	–	1
Arthaldeus pascuellus	Common	–	–	5	34	39
Paralimnus phragmitis	Notable	7	8	1	1	17
Conosanus obsoletus	Common	–	–	5	16	21

contd

Appendix 1 *continued*

Species	Satus in GB**	Uncut 1989	Uncut 1990	Cut 1989	Cut 1990	Total no.
Euscelis incisus	Common	–	–	1	–	1
Streptanus aemulans	Common	–	3	7	25	35
S. sordidus	Common	–	1	5	–	6
Macustus grisescens	Common	1	–	17	25	43
Elymana sulphurella	Common	–	–	–	3	3
Zyginidia scutellaris	Common	–	–	1	3	4
Chloriona smaragdula	Common	–	3	–	–	3
C. unicolor	Common	–	–	–	1	1
Delphax pulchellus	Common	–	2	–	3	5
Euides speciosa	Common	–	1	–	–	1
Delphacodes capnodes	Notable	4	–	–	–	4
Muellerianella fairmairei	Common	–	–	–	1	1
Javesella pellucida	Common	–	1	1	8	10
Paraliburnia clypealis	RDBK	–	–	5	2	7
Florodelphax leptosoma	Common	–	–	–	1	1
Coleoptera*						
Carabus granulatus	Local	–	3	59	2	64
Leistus rufescens	Common	1	4	1	1	7
Loricera pilicornis	Common	–	–	1	2	3
Dyschirius globosus	Local	–	–	3	2	5
D. luedersi	Local	–	–	4	–	4
Trechus quadristriatus	Common	–	1	–	1	2
Bembidion assimile	Common	1	–	2	1	4
Pterostichus diligens	Common	7	–	17	7	31
P. melanarius	Common	–	1	–	–	1
P. minor	Local	3	–	35	–	38
P. niger	Common	1	1	1	2	5
P. nigrita	Common	1	–	–	–	1
Agonum fuliginosum	Common	52	2	7	–	61
A. obscurum	Local	–	–	2	30	32
A. thoreyi	Local	284	28	1	–	313
Bradycellus harpalinus	Common	–	1	–	–	1
Dromius linearis	Common	–	–	2	1	3
D. longiceps	Na	5	5	–	–	10
Hydroporus melanarius	Local	–	–	1	–	1
H. memnonius	Common	–	–	1	–	1
Agabus melanocornis	Common	–	–	1	–	1
Cercyon convexiusculus	Nb	2	–	1	–	3
Megasternum obscurum	Common	–	1	4	–	5
Amphicyllis globus	Local	1	–	–	–	1
Catops morio	Common	–	2	–	–	2
C. tristis	Common	1	–	–	–	1

contd

Appendix 1 *continued*

Species	Status in GB**	Uncut 1989	Uncut 1990	Cut 1989	Cut 1990	Total no.
Nicrophorus vespillo	Common	–	3	–	–	3
N. vespilloides	Local	–	7	–	–	7
Thanatophilus rugosus	Common	–	1	–	–	1
Silpha atrata	Common	–	1	–	–	1
Cephennium gallicum	Local	–	–	1	–	1
Olophrum fuscum	Local	3	4	–	–	7
Lesteva longoelytrata	Common	–	–	1	–	1
Anotylus rugosus	Common	2	–	–	–	2
A. sculpturatus	Common	1	1	–	–	2
Stenus bimaculatus	Common	1	1	–	1	3
S. impressus	Common	1	1	1	–	3
S. juno	Common	–	–	–	3	3
S. lustrator	Local	2	1	–	–	3
S. nitens	Local	–	–	–	1	1
S. palustris	Nb	2	2	–	–	4
Euaesthetus ruficapillus	Local	–	–	–	3	3
Paederus riparius	Local	2	–	5	1	10
Lathrobium brunnipes	Common	–	1	11	–	12
L. elongatum	Local	–	–	–	1	1
L. terminatum	Common	1	–	–	–	1
Philonthus varians	Common	–	5	–	–	5
Quedius balticus	RDB1	7	2	1	–	10
Q. fuliginosus	Common	1	–	–	–	1
Q. maurorufus	Common	4	–	8	–	12
Q. nitipennis	Common	–	–	–	1	1
Mycetoporus clavicornis	Common	–	–	–	2	2
M. splendidus	Common	1	3	4	3	11
Bolitobius cingulatus	Local	–	–	1	1	2
S. testaceus	Notable	–	1	–	–	1
Tachyporus atriceps	Local	–	–	1	–	1
T. hypnorum	Common	4	1	1	3	9
T. transversalis	Local	–	–	–	1	1
Tachinus marginellus	Common	–	–	–	1	1
T. signatus	Common	–	–	1	–	1
Bryaxis bulbifer	Common	–	–	1	–	1
Rybaxis laminata	Local	–	–	–	1	1
Aphodius fossor	Common	1	–	–	–	1
Microcara testacea	Common	–	1	–	–	1
Cyphon coarctatus	Common	–	1	–	2	3
C. hilaris	Local	17	2	7	–	26
C. padi	Local	1	–	1	–	2
C. phragmiteticola	Local	4	1	1	–	6
Heterocerus marginatus	Common	–	–	1	–	1

contd

Appendix 1 *continued*

Species	Status in GB**	Uncut 1989	Uncut 1990	Cut 1989	Cut 1990	Total no.
Trixagus dermestoides	Local	–	1	–	4	5
Cantharis decipiens	Common	1	1	–	–	2
C. figurata	Local	1	3	1	2	7
C. pallida	Local	–	13	–	9	22
C. rufa	Common	.	.	.	1	1
C. thoracica	Local	.	17	1	3	21
Silis ruficollis	Nb	14	15	4	3	36
Malthodes marginatus	Common	.	.	1	.	1
Malachius bipustulatus	Common	–	–	1	1	2
Cerapheles terminatus	Na	10	14	1	–	25
Anthocomus rufus	Local	12	4	29	30	75
Kateretes rufilabris	Common	–	–	3	–	3
Meligethes aeneus	Common	–	1	–	–	1
M. erythropus	Common	1	–	–	2	3
M. nigrescens	Common	1	3	3	3	10
M. ochropus	Notable	1	1	1	–	3
M. viridescens	Common	–	–	3	–	3
Glischrochilus hortensis	Common	–	–	2	1	3
Ootypus globosus	Local	–	–	–	1	1
Stilbus atomarius	RDBK	3	–	6	–	9
S. oblongus	Local	7	1	–	–	8
S. testaceus	Common	–	1	–	–	1
Corylophus cassidoides	Local	–	–	–	1	1
Coccinella septempunctata	Common	–	–	1	1	2
Aridius bifasciatus	Ntrls	–	2	–	1	3
A. nodifer	Common	1	–	1	–	2
Enicmus histrio	Common	–	–	–	1	1
Cortinicara gibbosa	Common	10	3	9	10	32
Lagria hirta	Common	–	–	1	1	2
Galerucella tenella	Common	1	–	–	1	2
Aphthona nonstriata	Local	–	2	–	1	3
Altica lythri	Common	1	–	–	–	1
Chaetocnema hortensis	Common	–	–	–	1	1
Barypeithes pellucidus	Common	–	–	–	4	4
Sitona lineatus	Common	3	2	1	5	11

Opiliones

Nemostoma bimaculatum	Common	1	2	–	3	6
Mitostoma chrysomelas	Common	1	2	–	–	3
Mitopus morio	Common	–	–	–	1	1
Oligolophus tridens	Common	54	106	2	7	169
Paroligolophus agrestis	Common	7	36	11	10	64
Lophopilio palpinalis	Common	1	6	–	–	7

contd

Appendix 1 *continued*

Species	Status in GB**	Uncut 1989	Uncut 1990	Cut 1989	Cut 1990	Total no
Lacinius ephippiatus	Common	1	10	1	2	14
Rilaena triangularis	Common	1	–	1	8	10
Nelima gothica	Local	1	–	1	–	2
Araneae						
Clubiona reclusa	Common	.	.	2	1	3
C. stagnatilis	Common	.	.	.	3	3
C. phragmitis	Local	10	2	7	2	21
C. juvenis	RDB2	5	4	–	–	9
C. subtilis	Local	–	1	1	6	8
Zora spinimana	Common	–	2	–	–	2
Xysticus ulmi	Local	2	–	–	1	3
Oxyptila trux	Common	–	4	8	–	12
Thanatus striatus	Local	–	–	1	–	1
Pardosa pullata	Common	–	–	4	–	4
P. prativaga	Common	6	21	27	–	56
P. amentata	Common	1	–	3	–	4
P. nigriceps	Common	–	2	3	–	5
Trochosa spinipalpis	Local	–	–	2	1	3
Arctosa leopardus	Local	1	–	2	–	3
Pirata piraticus	Local	3	–	10	–	13
P. hygrophilus	Common	128	10	68	20	226
P. latitans	Local	–	–	5	–	5
Antistea elegans	Local	12	–	27	8	47
Ero cambridgei	Common	–	–	–	1	1
Robertus lividus	Common	–	–	1	–	1
Pachygnatha clercki	Common	2	2	8	2	14
Walckenaeria obtusa	Local	–	–	–	1	1
W. unicornis	Common	–	2	–	–	2
W. vigilax	Local	2	1	7	–	10
Entelecara omissa	Na	2	7	–	–	9
Dismodicus bifrons	Local	2	1	1	1	5
Hypomma bituberculatum	Common	–	2	–	–	2
H. fulvum	Na	6	2	–	–	8
Baryphyma trifrons	Local	7	5	–	3	15
Maso sundevalli	Common	–	9	–	4	13
Pocadicnemis pumila	Common	–	2	–	–	2
P. juncea	Common	1	8	11	2	22
Oedothorax gibbosus	Common	13	16	50	8	87
Silometopus elegans	Local	–	1	1	1	3
Lophomma punctatum	Local	1	–	–	–	1
Micrargus herbigradus	Common	–	–	3	–	3
Erigone atra	Common	–	–	1	–	1

contd

Appendix 1 *continued*

Species	Status in GB**	Uncut 1989	Uncut 1990	Cut 1989	Cut 1990	Total no.
Porrhomma pygmaeum	Common	1	1	–	–	2
Agyneta ramosa	Local	–	–	–	1	1
Bathyphantes approximatus	Local	3	.	.	.	3
B. gracilis	Common	4	1	6	5	16
B. parvulus	Common	.	1	2	1	4
Kaestneria pullata	Common	3	4	1	1	9
Poeciloneta globosa	Local	1	–	–	–	1
Taranucnus setosus	Local	–	1	–	–	1
Lepthyphantes tenuis	Common	2	6	–	6	14
L. zimmermanni	Common	1	–	–	–	1
Allomengea vidua	Local	–	1	–	–	1
Total species		**86**	**93**	**103**	**102**	

* The following groups of Coleoptera are not identified to the species level: Ptilidae, Staphylinidae (Aleocharinae only) and Cryptophagidae (*Atomaria* only).

** Status in Great Britain – categories follow those in Ball (1992) except where subsequently reviewed in Hyman & Parsons (1994) and Kirby (1992). The following definitions for RDB and Nationally Scarce species are taken from Hyman & Parsons (1992) and refer to the status of species in a Great Britain context.

Red Data Book 1 (RDB1), Endangered – taxa in danger of extinction and whose survival is unlikely if casual factors continue operating.

Red Data Book 2 (RDB2), Vulnerable – taxa believed likely to move into the Endangered category in the near future if the casual factors continue operating.

Red Data Book 3 (RDB3), Rare – taxa with small populations that are not at present Endangered or Vulnerable, but are at risk.

Red Data Book Category K (RDBK), insufficiently known – taxa that are suspected but not definitely known to belong to any of the above categories.

Nationally Notable (Scarce) Category A (Na) – taxa which do not fall within RDB categories but which are nonetheless uncommon in Great Britain and thought to occur in 30 or fewer 10-km squares of the National Grid.

Nationally Notable (Scarce) Category B (Nb) – taxa which do not fall within RDB categories but which are nonetheless uncommon in Great Britain and thought to occur in between 31 and 100 10-km squares of the National Grid.

Nationally Notable (Scarce), Notable – species which are estimated to occur within the range of 16–100 10-km squares. The subdividing of this category into Na and Nb has not been attempted.

Local and common are general terms; local species, which can be widely distributed, are often confined to particular habitat types, *e.g.* wetlands. Common species are regarded as common and widespread in Great Britain and often occur in a wide range of habitats and some are ubiquitous. Ntrls (Naturalised) refers to single, now widespread, non-native species given Common status in other tables.

16 Restoring Fen Ditches: The Case of Wicken Fen National Nature Reserve

D. J. PAINTER & L. E. FRIDAY*

Department of Zoology, University of Cambridge, Downing Street, Cambridge, CB2 3EJ, UK

SUMMARY

1.   The distributions and abundances of adult Odonata, Coleoptera and other groups of aquatic macroinvertebrates were studied in order to address some of the practical problems faced by the Wicken Fen Management Committee in managing the Fen's internal ditch system.

2.   Ditches near the end of their succession have characteristic faunal elements. 'Old ditch' habitats support more rare species of water beetle than recently excavated sections. Adult males of some species of odonate are more frequently seen in heavily vegetated ditches, while other species are more characteristic of open stretches.

3.   Maximum diversity of aquatic invertebrates may be maintained by excavating short stretches of ditch in rotation, ensuring that all stages of the hydrosere are represented simultaneously on the reserve.

INTRODUCTION

Wicken Fen, Cambridgeshire, is one of the last remnants of the fenland that once covered 3800 km^2 of lowland Britain (Ratcliffe, 1977) (Figure 1). In the last century, Wicken Fen was renowned for entomological and vegetational diversity, which was maintained by cropping of *Cladium mariscus* Pohl, litter (herbaceous vegetation dominated by *Molinia caerulea* Moench) and removal of peat (Godwin, 1936, 1941; Rowell, 1983).

Since 1899, areas of the Fen have been acquired and managed by the National Trust. During the first half of this century, cessation of cropping and falling water levels led to extensive invasion by fen carr and loss of floral and faunal diversity (Dempster, King & Lakhania, 1976). However, in 1961, a management plan was drawn up systematically to arrest the Fen's decline and to restore its former habitats. Foremost among the objectives of management, now as then, is the restoration and maintenance of diversity appropriate to an East Anglian fen

---

* Honorary Secretary, Wicken Fen Local Management Committee

Restoration of Temperate Wetlands. Edited by B.D. Wheeler, S.C. Shaw, W.J. Fojt and R.A. Robertson
© 1995 John Wiley & Sons Ltd.

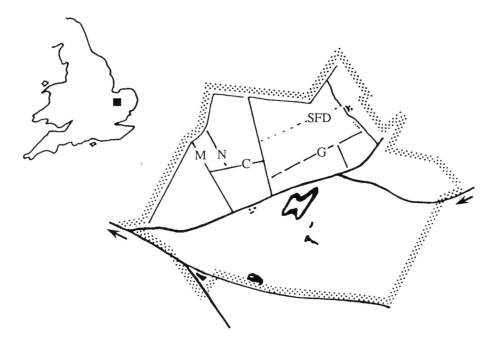

Figure 1. Map of Wicken Fen illustrating water bodies. C, Cross Dyke; G, Gardiner's Ditch; M, Malcarse Drain; N, North Dyke; SFD, Sedge Fen Drove.

system with a long history of cropping (Friday, 1994). An important element of this diversity is the flora and fauna of the internal ditches, which mostly date from the eighteenth century (Rowell, 1986) but which had largely filled with reed and detritus by 1961.

The case for and against re-excavating derelict ditches at Wicken Fen, and maintaining them by periodic excavation is summarised in Table 1. Until recently, the attitude of the Management Committee has been that the advantages outweigh the disadvantages and the policy has been to reopen as many old ditches as possible and to excavate whole ditches at intervals of 4, 8 or 12 years. In the past few years, however, this policy has been revised in view of a presumed threat to some invertebrate species with restricted populations on the Fen, which might be lost through wholesale excavation. In the most recent management plan (L.E. Friday, unpublished) only a few short stretches in each ditch are excavated each year on a strict rotation.

Is this new policy effective in attaining the objectives of the restoration project? Should some derelict ditches be left untouched and others allowed to undergo succession to near-dryness? We present here some data concerning the diversity and distribution of aquatic invertebrates on the Fen; a full analysis will form part of a PhD thesis by D.J. Painter.

Table 1. The case for and against re-excavating old ditches at Wicken Fen.

FOR

1.   Drainage or navigation obligations, which exist on some of the ditches, should be fulfilled.
2.   Open waterways are part of the historical fenland scene at Wicken.
3.   Regular clearance maintains early stages of the hydrosere and their characteristic flora and fauna.
4.   Pure stands of reed (*Phragmites*) are relatively poor in invertebrate species.
5.   Re-opening of some dry ditches may release from dormancy propagules of fenland plants that were formerly abundant but are now rare.
6.   Open ditches conduct water into the Fen in dry conditions and maintain a relatively stable high water table in their near vicinity.
7.   Ditches allow some control of visitor access and movement, and provide sources of water for fire-fighting and act as fire-breaks.
8.   Open waters are visually attractive to visitors.

AGAINST

1.   Ditches may drain the central parts of the Fen if inflow and outflow are not controlled by sluices or dams.
2.   Some (but, at Wicken Fen, not all) ditches might conduct agricultural drainage water into the Fen system.
3.   Wholesale clearance would destroy the 'old ditch' habitats, and a comprehensive excavation programme would prevent them from developing in future.
4.   Clearance of reed would destroy a proportion of nesting habitat of some bird species.
5.   Clearance of water-weed beds on a large scale may destroy entire populations of aquatic invertebrates.
6.   Ditches can make access to some parts of the Fen difficult for machinery.

METHODS

Aquatic macroinvertebrates were sampled from five ditches on Wicken Sedge Fen, varying in age since the last excavation (Table 2). Quantitative sweep samples were taken with a standard pond net (mesh diameter 0.5 mm) across the width of each ditch so as to sample both banksides and substratum. Samples were preserved in 70% alcohol and sorted and identified to species. Diptera were identified to family level.

Adult Odonata in 100-m ditch sections were counted along a transect route walked once a week during their flying season (May–September 1992). Walks started from the same point at 11.00 and finished at 14.00 h; sunny windless days were chosen whenever possible. The total number of males of different species in each section varied seasonally due to differences in species emergence times, so the results of one transect walk, on the day of maximum abundance for that species, are analysed.

Table 2. Ditches sampled at Wicken Fen (see Figure 1), with age since excavation as at 1993, physical characteristics and vegetation density.

Ditch name	Years since excavation	Width (m)	Depth (m)	Reed density (no. m^{-2})	Other macrophytes (abundance)
Sedge Fen Drove	>100	4	0.15	43	−
Gardiner's 1	13*	3	0.55	10	+++
Gardiner's 2	13*	3	0.56	49	+++
Gardiner's 3	13*	3	0.60	46	+++
Gardiner's 4	13*	3	0.78	15	+++
Gardiner's 5	13*	3	0.55	20	+++
Gardiner's 6	13*	3	0.43	48	+++
Gardiner's 7	13*	3	0.44	55	+++
Cross Dyke	13	4.1	0.70	9.2	+
Cross Dyke	2	4.1	0.93	1.4	++
Malcarse Drain	2	4	0.84	2	+
North Dyke	2	4	0.63	0	+

* Prior to excavation of six 50-m stretches in 1993.

Note: the terms Drain, Ditch and Dyke are properly attached to water bodies fulfilling subtly different functions at Wicken Fen but the terms have often been used interchangeably.

In the spring of 1993, six 50-m sections of Gardiner's Ditch were excavated. Subsequently, three habitat types within the ditch were distinguishable:

(i)   old, shallow, densely reeded;
(ii)   old, shallow, sparsely reeded;
(iii)   young, deep, clear of reed.

Twenty quantitative pond net samples were taken in one section of each habitat type in the summer and autumn 1993.

The water beetle assemblages of the old and young sections of Gardiner's Ditch were compared using a point-scoring system developed by Foster (1987) to evaluate and rank wetland sites by the rarity status of the water beetle species present. The 'wetscore' is the sum of the points scored for each species present based on a geometric progression of national abundance scores successively doubling from 1 (commonest species) to 32 (rarest). Wetscores were calculated using points assigned to East Anglian beetle species (Foster & Eyre, 1992). The 'quality score' reflects the number of rare species present at the site.

The total macroinvertebrate and adult Odonata data were ordinated using detrended correspondence analysis (DCA) (Ter Braak, 1987).

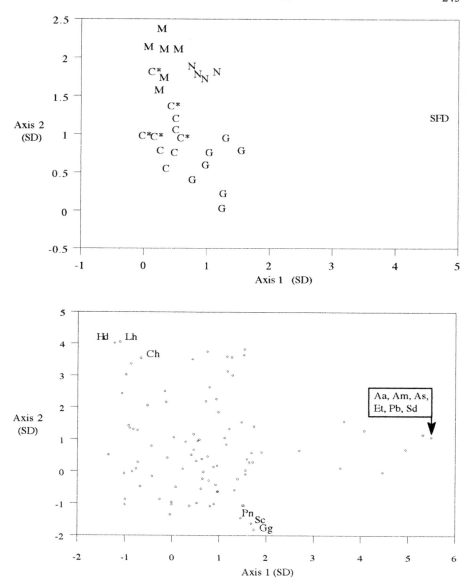

Figure 2. Detrended correspondence analysis (DCA) ordination of macroinvertebrate samples taken in autumn 1992. (a) sites; (b): species. C, Cross Dyke un-excavated; C*, Cross Dyke excavated; G, Gardiners Ditch; M, Malcarse Drain; N, North Dyke; SFD, Sedge Fen Drove. Aa, *Aedes annulipes* (Meigen); Am, *Asellus meridianus* Racovitza; As, *Agabus sturmii* (Gyllenhal); Ch, *Caenis horaria* (L.); Et, *Enochrus testaceus* (Fab.); Gg, *Graptodytes granularis* (L.); Hd, *Holocentropus dubius* (Rambur); Lh, *Laccophilus hyalinus* (Degeer); Pb, *Phacopteryx brevipennis* (Curtis); Pn, *Pyrrhosoma nymphula* (Sulzer); Sc, *Sphaerium corneum* (L.); Sd, *Suphrodytes dorsalis* (Fab.).

RESULTS

The DCA ordination plots based on macroinvertebrate samples taken from the five ditches in the autumn of 1992, reveals the distinctiveness of Sedge Fen Drove (Figure 2a). The first axis accounts for 24% of the variation and the second 9%. This is a water body at the end of hydroseral succession, which periodically dries up in the summer months and refills in autumn. It is an important breeding site for species associated with temporary conditions, such as the nationally scarce caddis *Phacopteryx brevipennis* (Wallace, 1991). Some other species that occur in large numbers and breed in the site are the *Red Data Book* (RDB) water beetle *Agabus undulatus* (Schrank) (Shirt, 1987), three species of *Dytiscus*, the mosquito *Aedes annulipes*, and the crustacean *Asellus meridianus* (Figure 2b).

The macroinvertebrate data were reanalysed after removing this outlier (Figure 3). Samples taken from within the same ditches lie together in ordination space, *i.e.* they have similar species compositions. On axis one (16% of variation), recently excavated and wide ditches with little macrophytic growth occur to the right; mature, narrow ditch sections with abundant macrophytic growth occur on the left. The un-excavated sections of Cross Dyke are clearly differentiated from the excavated sections, the former falling close to the reedy sections of Gardiner's Ditch, and the latter close to new sections of Malcarse Drain. The spread of Gardiner's samples along axis 2 (8% of variation) can be interpreted in terms of ditch succession, shallow sites with high reed density being low on the axis, and

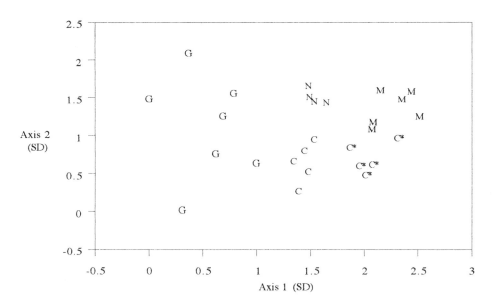

Figure 3. Detrended correspondence analysis (DCA) ordination of macroinvertebrate samples taken in autumn 1992 with the outlier Sedge Fen Drove removed. Abbreviations as in Figure 2.

Table 3. Water beetle diversity and conservation evaluation at Wicken Fen (for an explanation of 'wetscore' and 'quality score', see text).

Habitat type	Young	Old, sparse	Old, dense
Reed density (no. of stems m^{-2})	5	25	55
Total number of aquatic beetle species (a)	45	37	32
Wetscore (b)	124	114	101
Quality score (b/a)	2.8	3.1	3.2
No. of individuals of rare fen species:			
Dryops anglicanus (RDB3)	1	17	22
Hydraena palustris (RDB2)	0	15	1

deep sites with low reed density high on the axis. The RDB mollusc *Pisidium pseudosphaerium* (Schlesch) (Bratton, 1991) was found in Malcarse Drain.

The DCA of male odonate abundances (Figure 4a) reveals a strong contrast between reedy (to the left of the axis) and open water habitats (to the right). The first axis accounts for 32%, and the second 9% of variation. *Pyrrhosoma nymphula* and *Brachytron pratense* were particularly abundant in narrow ditches with high reed densities, *Erythromma najas* in wide ditches with floating *Nuphar* leaves, and *Enallagma cyathigerum*, *Aeshna grandis*, *Sympetrum striolatum*, and *Orthetrum cancellatum* were most abundant in wide ditches with a high proportion of open water (Figure 4b).

The analysis of water beetle species assemblages in the new and old ditch sections of Gardiner's Ditch (Table 3) shows that the new ditch section had the greatest number of species and highest wetscore, but the lowest quality score, while the old reedy section had the lowest number of species but the highest quality score. Wetscores in all sections exceeded 100, and can be regarded as indicating sites of high quality (Foster & Eyre, 1992). Two RDB species, *Dryops anglicanus* Edwards and *Hydraena palustris* Erichson, were present in the older sections but absent or rare in the new section.

DISCUSSION

These results illustrate the distinctive nature of different stages of the hydrosere as habitats for aquatic invertebrates. Old ditches that dry up in the summer have characteristic faunal elements and older, reedy ditches show marked contrasts with newer, more open ditches, not only in the overall composition of the macroinvertebrate fauna, but also in water beetle quality scores and the use of the habitat by adult Odonata.

Should old ditches be re-opened? If Sedge Fen Drove ditch were re-opened, it is clear that a distinctive habitat would be lost as a result. North Dyke is an example of a water body created by re-digging the course of a completely dry ditch, and its

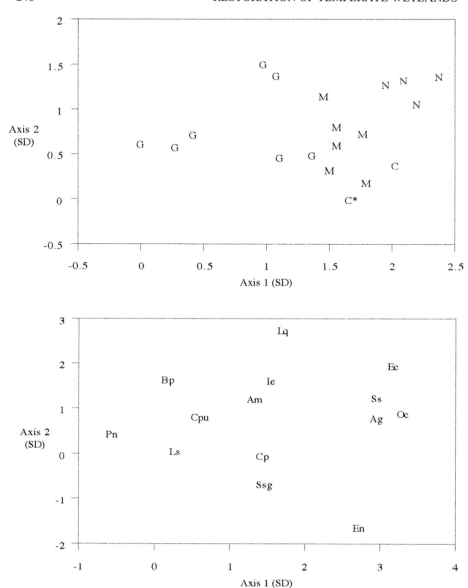

Figure 4. DCA ordination of male Odonata transect walk counts: (a) sites; (b) species. Site abbreviations as in Figure 2. Ag, *Aeshna grandis* (L.); Am, *Aeshna mixta* (Latreille); Bp, *Brachytron pratense* (Müller); Cpu, *Coenagrion puella* (L.); Cp, *Coenagrion pulchellum* (van der Linden); Ec, *Enallagma cyathigerum* (Charpentier); En, *Erythromma najas* (Charpentier); Ie, *Ischnura elegans* (van der Linden.); Ls, *Lestes sponsa* (Hansemann); Lq, *Libellula quadrimaculata* (L.); Oc, *Orthetrum cancellatum* (L.); Pn, *Pyrrhosoma nymphula*; Ssg, *Sympetrum sanguineum* (Müller); Ss, *Sympetrum striolatum* (Charpentier).

invertebrate community can be regarded as being representative of a true pioneer community of early ditch colonists, which in this isolated ditch are likely to be active dispersers. By contrast, Malcarse Drain was re-excavated in 1991 from a badly overgrown, but wet, ditch. Its present species complement will be derived from 'seed' species left *in situ* and subsequent colonists. One such 'seed' species is the rare mollusc *Pisidium pseudosphaerium*, which is described by Kerney (1991) as requiring "clear clean water in stagnant places choked with aquatic plants, often over a richly organic, even anaerobic bottom". This description fits well the previous state of the ditch, and it will be interesting to see if the population is maintained in the more open conditions prevailing at present. Cross Dyke has been excavated in alternating 50-m stretches, so the invertebrates found in the newly-excavated sections may be derived principally from migrants from the uncut 'islands'.

Once a network of ditches is established, a patchwork of diversity can be maintained by cycles of excavation. These results shed no direct light on the advisability of excavating only short sections at a time, but it seems likely that sedentary animals such as molluscs, and species represented by very localised populations, may be vunerable to local extinction as a result of wholesale excavation.

Open water habitats form an important part of many fen reserves, but are ditches to be regarded as an integral, and therefore desirable, component of a fen system? Evans (1923), writing of the flora of Wicken Fen, put his finger on the source of conflict: "lesser channels . . . have dried up completely. . .with the loss of several species. There is, however, another side to the picture. Drainage, with its new watercourses, . . . has certainly given an opportunity for. . . the intrusion of some [species] which are not sedge fen plants at all". His examples include *Hottonia palustris* L. and *Nuphar lutea* (L.), which we now accept unquestioningly as part of the Fen's flora.

Ultimately, policies regarding ditch management must be guided by the objectives of management of the whole fen system, and by consideration of the species likely to be present. If the conservation of maximum diversity of species and habitats is the aim, stretches of ditch should be maintained in each hydroseral stage. However, if the management of certain key species is perceived as more important, other strategies will be preferred. For example, a magnificent display of Odonata may be produced by excavating ditches on a short rotation, while conservation of the RDB fen beetles *Hydraena palustris* and *Dryops anglicanus* would appear to be favoured by maintaining ditches near the middle of their succession.

ACKNOWLEDGEMENTS

We thank Dr G.N. Foster and Dr M. Real for advice and comments on the manuscript.

REFERENCES

Bratton, J.H. (1991). *British Red Data Books*: 3. *Invertebrates other than insects.* Joint Nature Conservation Committee, Peterborough.

Dempster, J.P., King, M.L. & Lakhani, K.H. (1976). The status of the swallowtail butterfly in Britain. *Ecological Entomology* , **1**, 71–84.

Evans, A.H. (1923). The fens of the Great Level, their drainage, and its effect on the Flora and Fauna. *The Natural History of Wicken Fen* (eds J.S. Gardiner & A.G.Tansley), 1, 3–49, Bowes & Bowes, Cambridge.

Foster, G.N. (1987). The use of Coleoptera records in assessing the conservation value of wetlands. *The Use of Invertebrates in Site Assessment for Conservation* (ed. M.L.Luff), pp. 8–17. University of Newcastle upon Tyne.

Foster, G.N. & Eyre, M.D. (1992). *UK Nature Conservation No.1 Classification and ranking of water beetle communities.* Joint Nature Conservation Committee, Peterborough.

Friday, L.E. (1994). Wicken Fen: the management of a Nature Reserve. *A Manual of Heritage Management.* (ed. R. Harrison), pp. 135–139. Butterworth-Heinmann Ltd., Oxford.

Friday, L.E. (unpublished). *Wicken Fen Management Plan 1992–9.* Wicken Fen Local Management Committee, The National Trust.

Godwin, H. (1936). Studies in the ecology of Wicken Fen III. The establishment and development of fen scrub (carr). *Journal of Ecology*, **24**, 82–116.

Godwin, H. (1941). Studies in the ecology of Wicken Fen IV. Crop-taking experiments. *Journal of Ecology*, **29**, 83–106.

Kerney, M.P. (1991). Untitled in *British Red Data Books: 3. Invertebrates other than insects.* (ed. J.H. Bratton), pp. 82–83. Joint Nature Conservation Committee, Peterborough.

Ratcliffe, D.A. (1977). *A Nature Conservation Review, Volume 1.* Cambridge University Press, Cambridge.

Rowell, T.A. (1983). *History and management of Wicken Fen.* PhD thesis, University of Cambridge.

Rowell, T.A. (1986). The history of drainage at Wicken Fen, Cambridgeshire, England, and its relevance to conservation. *Biological Conservation,* **35**, 111–142.

Shirt, D.B. (1987). *British Red Data Books: 2. Insects.* Nature Conservancy Council, Peterborough.

Ter Braak, C.J.F. (1987). *CANOCO – a FORTRAN Program for Canonical Community Ordination by (Partial) (Detrended) (Canonical) Correspondence Analysis, Principle Components Analysis and Redundancy Analysis (Version 2.1).* Agriculture Mathematics Group, Wageningen.

Wallace, I.D. (1991). *A Review of the Trichoptera of Great Britain.* Research & survey in Nature Conservation. No 32. Nature Conservancy Council, Peterborough.

17 The Regeneration of Fens in Abandoned Peat Pits Below Sea Level in the Netherlands

G. VAN WIRDUM

Department of Vegetation Ecology, Institute for Forestry and Nature Research (IBN-DLO), P.O. Box 23, NL-6700 AA Wageningen, The Netherlands

SUMMARY

1. Restoration for nature protection involves the application of ecosystems as ecodevices. Similar ecodevices may produce different results as the environment differs. Restoration applies to the ecodevices as well as to the environment. Target states should represent a proactive optimisation of requirements with regional opportunities.

2. Critical switches in the regeneration of fen vegetation in peat pits 70–250 years old, below sea level in the Netherlands are analysed, based on previously published data and on management experience. Many sites today are of great value for nature protection, although no restoration plans have been applied.

3. Due to the depth and the steep sides of the pits, a swamp phase usually results from the formation of a floating raft, rather than from rooted, littoral vegetation.

4. Water table fluctuations relative to the vegetated surface are small in floating rafts. This promotes the development from swamp to fen, and subsequently to scrub and carr. Unless the body of mire water is brackish, open-fen vegetation on the rafts can only be maintained by harvesting.

5. When protected from drought, both harvested and non-harvested vegetation, in time, develop in to some type of poor fen. In particular, the ericaceous phase of harvested fen includes micro-sites resembling ombrogenous bog. A development of mature bog sites might occur within the next century, but there is no clear evidence so far.

6. The occlusion of ditches results in a decreasing supply of base-rich water and a rapid formation of poor fen. In surface-water-fed fens, the ditch water itself supplies bases. In groundwater-fed fens, ditches receive a lateral surface discharge, which is necessary to sustain the flow of base-rich groundwater.

7. With cyclic management regimes, problems of peat and litter disposal should be expected. Such problems can greatly reduce restoration success.

8. A hierarchical planning and realisation of restoration is suggested. The macro-level (landscape or ecological-field level) applies to the required amounts and composition of brackish or base-rich water. Opportunities for the development of various seres of succession can be assessed at this level.

9. The meso-level (ecodevice level) pertains to the gradient of base supply in the main

Restoration of Temperate Wetlands. Edited by B.D. Wheeler, S.C. Shaw, W.J. Fojt and R.A. Robertson
© 1995 John Wiley & Sons Ltd.

part of the root zone. At this level, the surface-water network can be designed so as to control atmotrophiation (ombrotrophication).

10. The micro-level (vegetation, soil and management) concerns the micro-relief and local measures, such as harvesting, scrub removal, sod cutting and pool digging. These factors control vegetation structure, succession rates, micro-site variation, and species composition in more detail. More research is needed in order to quantify the role of management in determining succession rates through the development of root systems and through the accumulation of peat.

INTRODUCTION

The natural development of fen vegetation in abandoned turbaries provides spontaneous examples of wetland 'restoration'. As regards the scope of restoration, a formal approach is followed here.

Restoration for nature protection: what it is about

Restoration defined

The drive for restoration is inspired by public concern about the impoverishment of regional floras and faunas, and by the disappearance of 'wild' landscapes. In this contribution, 'restoration for nature protection' means the re-establishment of the conditions needed to balance extinction rates and evolution, especially of higher organisms, using two main approaches: (1) to create reserves for contemporary organisms, where their populations can survive in wildlife communities, and (2) to adjust environmental conditions so that these populations can extend as far outside the reserves as we allow. Consequently, by the restoration of wetlands is meant the creation of 'functional' wetlands, rather than the restoration of particular former wetlands to some bygone state. The continuation of appropriate management is not restoration. However, some forms of management are powerful tools in the restoration of degraded wetlands.

Restoration concerns functional ecodevices for nature protection

Planning, conservation, and restoration represent deliberate human efforts to 'protect' nature from other, supposedly adverse, human influences. Certain qualities of nature are considered to be in danger through autonomous processes of human society. Nature reserves are considered to be successful when they help to protect these qualities. The reserved areas thus represent applied (sub)ecosystems: ecological devices (*ecodevices*, van Leeuwen, 1982; van Wirdum, 1982, 1986) for nature protection. By contrast with eco*systems*, eco*devices* can fail, since their application requires targets to be set for them. Accordingly, management may be needed to balance a reserve's inputs and outputs where self-regulation falls short.

Most ecodevices provide material resources and profit for human society, as in urban and agricultural land use. Such human ecodevices are distinguished from ecodevices for nature protection by using the terms *natecs* and *humecs* respectively (for definitions, see van Wirdum, 1986).

The location of a *natec* sets limits to the possible exchange of control 'currency', for example, of water, species, tourists, carbohydrates or phosphorus, with the surrounding *ecological field* (Figure 1). Too high or too low a field potential may cause a device malfunction, a defect, or excessive wear. In such situations, the device owner should consider a 'functional' restoration, rather than a 'cosmetic' restoration of insufficiently saved species assemblages. Often, the ecological field also has to be restored or adjusted, thereby minimising the need for active management and facilitating an extension of the beneficial effects over the ecological field, especially its potential flora and fauna. Running ecodevices is not a purpose in itself!

Device design should match expected field characteristics

Natec functionality can be assessed according to rather rough criteria, for example, in terms of sustained biodiversity. In the absence of any human influence the quality of nature results from unmodified ecosystems, or 'raw' *natecs*. Through the ages the most successful types of such *natecs* have varied with geological, geomorphological and human influences. Van Wirdum (1993a) emphasises that the Dutch wetlands have changed from the predominance of large areas of natural mires in prehistoric times, through the harvesting of (semi-)natural ecosystems by man, to intentional land improvement for specific human-determined functions. The dominance of human control in the latter phase has led to a wide range of alarming side-effects. Wetland restoration is one of the efforts intended to increase positive human control.

The first period distinguished in the analysis of the past is the prehistoric one. In the Netherlands the emphasis is on the Holocene, especially the subboreal and subatlantic periods, *i.e.* from about 5000 BP. Most geomorphological forces still operate today, although the hydrological ones in particular have been tamed through social demand (van de Ven, 1993). Early human influences were not too

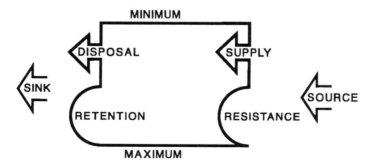

Figure 1. An ecodevice is controlled between minimum (required) and maximum (tolerated) levels by four exchange functions as regards the surrounding ecological field. After van Leeuwen (1982) and van Wirdum (1982).

different from those exerted by other large mammals. Lasting biodiversity at the country scale was controlled by the balance between the large and coherent mass of mire *versus* marine transgressions, river floods, and rising groundwater levels (see Pons, 1992).

The subsequent, historical, period in the Netherlands falls between about 1000 BP and 100–50 BP. The mass and coherence of mires was strongly diminished by flood protection, water management and land use. The human population had grown to the extent that it needed the harvest of the whole country; the landscape developed a pattern typical of human biology (Holling, 1992). However, no less diverse a flora and fauna spontaneously settled in ecosystems characterised by a large-scale and exhaustive harvesting regime.

Especially during the last century, technology enabled humans to 'squeeze' ecosystems even further, to increase their productivity artificially, and turn them into strictly-controlled *humecs* with narrowly-defined functions and with an imp-overished fauna and flora. Derelict and exhausted wastelands still serve as a refuge for nature. Under stress through overfed and leaking *humecs*, they have now been 'reclaimed' as nature reserves (Gorter, 1986). Abandoned turbaries are just one example. Human artefacts and regulations overrule biological features in the res-ulting new landscape, but in this context it may be possible to start a third, modern period. The amount of change seen today should decrease when the planned system of ecodevices for the new period is in operation, and when we successfully control our population numbers. As the potential flora and fauna have been ident-ified as a major concern, some room will be reserved for *natecs*. Hence the quest for restoration, not for the museum, but for the most appropriate nature that fits the future. Since the sequence from the prehistoric to the future template for nature is basically irreversible, restoration should refer to functional values rather than exact states. In national and international planning strategies, the best opportunities are sought for such restoration. A location thus may well end up with some target state which is new to it. Note, however, that there will be nature anyway; 'good' and 'bad' nature are defined only by the chosen goals of nature protection.

What can be learned from the abandoned turbaries?

Although abandoned turbaries cover only a limited range of mire morphology and extent, they do span a relatively wide range of hydrological-field and device-variable values, and of management. We can use the relevant data in assessing opportunities for restoration according to geographic factors, starting conditions and management with formulae of the type

$$\text{Value} = f(\text{ecological field, ecodevice}).$$

The ecological-field function concerns the local values of the driving forces for, *inter alia*, the flows of water and solutes. It includes rainfall and evapo-transpiration, and the potential flora and fauna. Hence it is a *positional* function. The device function describes the storage and transformations of 'currency' by which an ecodevice interferes with the driving forces; it is a *conditional* function.

Internal management is thus in the device function, but the social support required is in the ecological field. Value is the *operational* result, weighted by human standards derived from a comparison with fen vegetation in other environments and with palaeoecological records. This approach should result in specific local goals and in the design of optimal *natecs* and management plans to achieve these. The known variety of turbary vegetation permits some estimation of the results that can be achieved over a limited time-span, even in the absence of any purposeful planning, (the abandoned turbaries were never dug with restoration of fen vegetation in mind). The emphasis in the main part of this paper is on the device function. In the final section, attention is given to the various levels, starting with positional variation, that should be addressed in restoration planning.

Background data

Detailed floristic, vegetational and environmental data can be found in the literature cited. Species names follow van der Meijden *et al.* (1983) and Dirkse, van Melick & Touw (1988); phytosociological names follow Westhoff & den Held (1969). The discussion is based on conditions in the Netherlands where there are mild winters (mean January temperature 2°C), cool summers (mean July temperature 16°C), and a precipitation surplus (rainfall and evapotranspiration 765 and 450 mm a^{-1}, respectively, with *c.* 100 mm water deficit during April–July). The Netherlands is a low-lying country on the coast of the North Sea, with strong marine influences, which can also be traced in the water system.

THE EXAMPLE OF TURBARIES

The detailed records of den Held, Schmitz & van Wirdum (1992), and the succession schemes and ecohydrological data of van Wirdum, den Held & Schmitz (1992), together provide an extensive analysis and description of the types of vegetation in terrestrialising turbaries in the lower part of the Netherlands. These turbaries are quite different from the peat pits in bogs in the more elevated parts of the country. In the lowland turbaries, moss peat was dredged from below the regional drainage level. The original bog surface had become almost flooded owing to the post-glacial rise in sea-level and to land use. As a result, the pits filled with relatively calcareous or even brackish water, rather than base-poor bog water. This has produced base-rich, but not necessarily eutrophic, fen environments (van Wirdum, 1993a).

In the summary scheme (Figure 2) the types have been related (i) to marine influences (strong for the bulrush, less for the reed, and virtually absent for the slender-sedge sere); (ii) to mire succession from a lake phase, via swamp (semi-aquatic) and fen (rich-fen or brown-moss phase and poor-fen including sphagn-aceous and ericaceous ('fen–bog') phases) to (supposedly) a bog phase; and (iii) to harvesting (scrub and carr *vs.* open vegetation). A variety of species listed in the Dutch *Red Data Books* for vascular plants and bryophytes (Weeda, van der

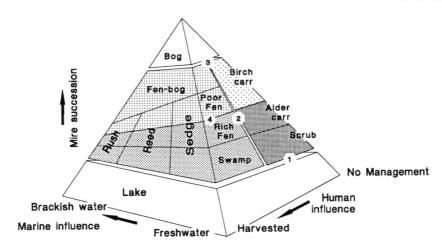

Figure 2. Ecological grouping of fen vegetation in terrestrialising turbaries, as depending on salinity (bulrush (*Scirpus lacustris* spp. *tabernaemontani*)), reed (*Phragmites australis*), and slender-sedge (*Carex lasiocarpa*) seres), harvesting (open fen *versus* scrub and carr), and succession (lake, swamp, rich fen, poor fen, fen–bog (= ericaceous phase poor fen), and bog). 1–4: breaks and transitions (lake to swamp, open fen to carr, fen–bog to bog, and rich to poor fen, respectively). After van Wirdum (1993a).

Meijden & Bakker, 1990; Siebel *et al.*, 1992) is present in the terrestrialising vegetation. Many of them (Table 1) must be considered principal rich-fen species in the Netherlands, and most of them also occur in Wheeler's (1988) list of principal rich-fen species for the UK. Although several of these species are almost entirely restricted to the terrestrialising turbaries, they are by no means common in them. The brown-moss phase of the slender-sedge sere, with similarities to CARICION DAVALLIANAE vegetation, and traditionally mown in summer, yields by far the greatest number of sites for *Red Data Book* species, but contributes less than 100 ha of the sum total of *c.* 12,000 ha of terrestrialising turbaries. However, the remaining area is no less vital to the Dutch populations of the majority of commoner principal rich-fen species.

   Three main breaks are shown in the scheme (Figure 2): transitions from (1) the lake to the swamp phase; (2) open fen to carr, and (3) fen to bog. The breaks reflect both major ecological switches and gaps in present knowledge. In addition, of particular concern within the open-fen environment is (4) the transition from rich fen to poor fen. These four points are discussed below, particularly based on the experience of managers and researchers (see Smittenberg, 1974; van Wirdum, 1979a). As experience forms the basis of day-to-day management, it is intentionally included in this treatment, with scepticism and warnings where appropriate. More formal scientific documentation is badly needed to help define ecological ground-rules more sharply. A summary such as that produced by George (1992) for the Norfolk Broadland does not exist for the Dutch fens. In this

Table 1. Sample of 'Red Data' concerning fen species in *kragge* vegetation, arranged according to phases and seres of terrestrialisation. *Red Data Book* (RDB) codes (Weeda, van der Meijden & Bakker 1990; Siebel *et al.* 1992): 1, endangered; 2, most vulnerable; 3, vulnerable; 4, rare. Seres (van Wirdum, Den Held & Schmitz 1992): B, bulrush sere; R, reed sere; S, slender-sedge sere (= quagfen sere *sensu stricto*); ( ) weak preference; – no preference. * *Kragge* fens are vital to the survival of these species in the Netherlands.

Species	RDB Code	Preferred sere
Swamp (and early brown-moss) phase:		
Calliergon giganteum	2	S–R
Eleocharis quinqueflora	2	S*
Rhizomnium pseudopunctatum	2	S–R*
Riccardia multifida	2	–
Althaea officinalis	3	R (brackish area)
Cladium mariscus	3	S–R
Cochlearia officinalis	3	R (brackish area)
Fissidens adianthoides	3	S–R
Linum catharticum	3	S–R
Pedicularis palustris	3	S*
Plagiomnium elatum	3	S–R
Sparganium minimum	3	S
Brown-moss phase:		
Bryum neodamense	1	S*
Campylium elodes	1	S*
Drepanocladus lycopodioides	1	S*
Drepanocladus sendtneri	1	S*
Eriophorum gracile	1	S*
Philonotis marchica	1	S*
Scorpidium cossoni	1	S*
Scorpidium scorpioides	1	S*
Utricularia intermedia	1	S*
Campylium stellatum	2	S*
Liparis loeselii	2	S*
Sphagnum contortum	2	S*
Dactylorhiza incarnata	3	S(–B)*
Parnassia palustris	3	S
Sagina nodosa	3	(S)
Calamagrostis stricta	4	S
Sphagnaceous phase:		
Hammarbya paludosa	1	(B–R)*
Sphagnum imbricatum	1	R* (still present?)
Sphagnum subsecundum ssp. *subsecundum*	2	S*
Sphagnum fuscum	4	S–R*
Sphagnum riparium	4	–
Sphagnum russowii	4	–

contd

Table 1. *continued*

Species	RDB Code	Preferred sere
Derived types:		
Carex pulicaris	2	–
Cirsium dissectum	2	–
Carex buxbaumii	4	–

respect a further exploration of palaeoecological and historical data sources, and their placing in an international context, such as given by Tallis (1983), would be most helpful.

(1) The transition from lake to swamp

The swamp and fen phases are not necessarily continuous with the lake phase

In most present turbaries, the open water was created 70–250 years ago. These basins, *petgaten*, have a very particular morphology (*cf.* van Wirdum, 1991, 1993a): rectangular, with steep sides, *c.* 10–50 m wide, 100–1000 m long, and 0.7–4 m deep. *Petgaten* are separated by baulks of standing peat with sandy or clayey top-spit material, 2–10 m wide. On one or more sides of a *petgat*, baulks may be missing or have gaps. In many cases, terrestrialisation only started 30–100 years ago. In one large area, this late start can be attributed to an improved water management, resulting in more stable water levels and favourable conditions for aquatic macrophytes (van Wirdum, 1991). Many accounts (*cf.* Segal, 1966) suggest a vegetation of aquatic macrophytes at the start of a continuous line of terrestrialisation, but more extensive inventories raise doubts about the general applicability of this scheme. In particular, the 'classic' development of floating plants in a dense *Stratiotes* vegetation may represent a phase of desalting coincident with increased application of fertilisers in Dutch fenlands between 1920 and 1960 (van Wirdum, 1979b, 1991). In peat deposits from the far past, a comparable hydroseral development has been found associated with rising water levels in alder carr (Gotjé, 1993). Van Wirdum *et al.* (1992) and van Wirdum (1993a) no longer regard the swamp and fen phases as necessarily continuous with the lake phase.

Raft formation

The swamp phase in the peat pits mostly starts with the formation of a floating raft (*kragge*) by such species as *Typha angustifolia*, *Phragmites australis*, *Scirpus lacustris* ssp. *tabernaemontani*, *Equisetum fluviatile*, *Thelypteris palustris*, *Cicuta virosa*, *Menyanthes trifoliata*, and *Carex* species. The *kragges* in the peat pits are *c.* 30–70 cm thick. Their development may constitute: (1) an overgrowth of the lake starting from its banks (van Donselaar-ten Bokkel Huinink, 1961; van der Toorn, 1972); (2) a settling during extreme droughts (van der Toorn, 1972); or (3) floating bottom peat or old sods returned to the *petgaten* after excavation (*cf.* Rodewald-Rudescu, 1974); or it represents (4) an outgrowth of floating plants, either incidentally arriving from elsewhere or formed in dense vegetation of *Stratiotes aloides* (van Zinderen Bakker, 1942); or (5) a regrowth of remaining, uprooted, or intentionally introduced (Haans & Hamming, 1954) rhizomes. Even when starting from rhizomes at the pit bottom, *Phragmites australis* sometimes forms a floating raft through adventitious roots and rhizomes just below the average water level. *Typha angustifolia* rafts have been reported to rise after an initial growth on the pit bottom (Havinga, 1957; in former river beds: van Donselaar-ten Bokkel Huinink, 1961). Virtually all terrestrialising peat pits thus belong to the floating fens or quagfens, the fen, as opposed to bog, type of quagmire (van Wirdum, 1991). A period of some tens of years may be needed for *kragge* formation in these unfavourably formed basins. Aquatic vegetation in the lake phase may be helpful, but it is not a *conditio sine qua non*.

The occurrence of rafts in natural mires: terrestrialisation in hostile environments

Van Donselaar (1961) and van Donselaar-ten Bokkel Huinink (1961) extensively reported on hydroseral vegetation, partly with floating rafts, in former river beds in the Netherlands. Gotjé (1993) associated prehistoric *Carex–Menyanthes* quagfens in the Noordoostpolder region of the Netherlands with phases of increased sea level rise, at a rate of *c.* 2.5 mm a^{-1}. Other palaeoecological records (*e.g.* Witte & van Geel, 1985) document the formation of a non-floating swamp phase in shallow water, and this seems to have been the most common succession in the past. Rodewald-Rudescu (1974) and Pallis (1916) discuss the formation of rafts of *Phragmites australis* up to 2 m thick, locally called *plaur*, in the Danube delta. Some are considered to be thousands of years old. Their formation is linked with the intricate geomorphology and history of the delta. Base-rich quagfen is generally associated with sheltered basins exceeding 0.5–1 m in depth, or with rapidly rising water tables. Succow & Kopp (1985) and Succow (1988) provide evidence of the association of raft formation in Germany with badly eutrophicated lakes and with acidic pools. The available data thus suggest that raft formation is a property of somewhat hostile environments for aquatic vegetation. The succession in peat pits resembles that in less anthropogenic environments, but it certainly is not representative of the main character of these.

Basin morphology, restoration and cyclic management

An initial basin width of *c.* 30 m seems most suitable for swamp and fen development. Narrower basins will terrestrialise more easily, but edge effects often remain dominant. Larger basins have more difficulty passing through the lake phase due to wave action. Gently sloping or stepped banks will accelerate the swamp start. As will be shown later, deeper basins more easily maintain a water regime favourable to fen and bog vegetation. The trade-off of their slower recolonisation has to be accepted.

Present expertise concerning the restoration of lake and swamp phases is based mainly on the removal of swamp and fen peat from already terrestrialising peat pits, rather than from new pits. Such restoration was designed as part of so-called 'cyclic' management regimes, prescribing a re-digging of peat pits after about one century (Smittenberg, 1974) and was started in the mid 1960s. The aim was to achieve a fresh formation of aquatic and swamp vegetation, hopefully developing into brown-moss-phase quagfen. Until now both the results and their documentation have been poor. While it is true that the area of late stages of succession is ever-increasing over the more transient stages of swamp and fen vegetation, there is still a large resource of lake-phase sites with almost no macrophyte vegetation. Since it is much easier to dig away a raft with open fen vegetation than it is to remove a late carr-stage *kragge* fen, insensitive application of the concept of cyclic management locally has contributed to an even further decrease of species-rich mid-successional vegetation. Moreover, in the Netherlands and some other countries, regressions from the swamp phase back to the lake phase, and a strong decline of aquatic macrophyte vegetation have been observed and attributed to various causes (van Wirdum, 1979b; de Nie, 1987; George, 1992). Problems concerning the disposal of the dredged material (see (4) below) further support the suggestion that the cyclic concept should be rethought in view of its practical applicability, side-effects and aims.

(2) The transition between open fen and carr

Floating open fen today: a (valuable) management artefact?

With the possible exception of brackish fen, fen vegetation in the Netherlands presently only remains herbaceous when regularly harvested. Most available data concerning scrub and carr formation have been summarised by Wiegers (1985, 1992). *Salix cinerea* agg. and *Alnus glutinosa* can invade wetlands even as early as the swamp phase. *Frangula alnus*, *Salix pentandra*, *Myrica gale*, *Populus tremula*, *Betula pubescens* and *Sorbus aucuparia* establish in the brown-moss and sphagnaceous fen phases. Other tree species, including *Quercus robur*, *Fraxinus excelsior* and *Pinus nigra* rarely survive the juvenile stage. The exotic *Aronia* x *prunifolia* is locally a pest, especially in desalting brackish fens in the sphagnaceous phase. Open fen undoubtedly belongs to the most species-rich types of vegetation, and it represents the main foothold for many rich-fen species (Wheeler, 1988; van Wirdum, 1991; Prins, 1993). On the other hand, scrub and carr are very important for many bird species, and mature carr may be considered a more 'balanced' type of ecosystem as regards the presence of various functional groups of organisms.

Natural factors that can keep fen vegetation open

In the past, thick layers of brown-moss-sedge peat and other sorts of herbaceous-fen peat have been formed in the absence of any strong human influences

(Stiboka, 1965). As far as we are aware, this must have been favoured by conditions no longer applicable to the Netherlands, such as (i) marine trans-gressions and (ii) a rapid post-glacial rise of sea and groundwater levels, not compensated for by water management. Direct climatic effects are thought likely to emphasise these, since tree growth currently occurs in fens in regions with much harsher winters and shorter growth periods (*cf.* Palczynski, 1984; Moen, 1990) than the Netherlands had for most of the postglacial period. Fire was probably an important factor locally in the pre-historical period in Dutch wetlands (Witte & van Geel, 1985). Gotjé (1993) reports extensive ash layers in swamp and fen deposits formed thousands of years ago. Grazing by large wild herbivores will have had local effects, as it has today. However, quagfen *kragges* only become solid enough to support large grazing mammals in the brown-moss phase. Experimental grazing of fjell cattle on derelict fen *kragges* at best slowed down scrub and carr development (Oosterveld, personal communication). Tomaszewska (1988) gives evidence that the same holds true for quite dense populations of elk in the Biebrza valley mires (Poland). However, present-day evidence relates to sites showing a combination of grazing effects and post-management relaxation (see below) rather than to unmanaged sites.

The quagfen water regime does not prevent scrub and carr formation

Gotjé (1993) provides palaeoecological evidence that scrub and carr are formed especially during geogenetic phases of a reduced rise of the groundwater table, coincident with rather large seasonal fluctuations of water level. In more stable conditions during periods with an increased groundwater-level rise, *Carex* peats were formed in his study area. In some instances carr returned to open fen or swamp due to a change in the regional drainage conditions and the question has been raised whether groundwater discharging from underlying aquifers could re-create similar conditions. Even though a strong discharge of groundwater is more common now than it was in the prehistoric period, there are no present instances where such an outflow maintains the open-fen state in peat pits. The quagfens, while floating, provide a very stable water table relative to the peat surface, which prevents the water table from drowning the surface available for tree settlement, especially on tussocks. Hence, a groundwater discharge probably maintains open fen only on solid peat deposits subject to impeded drainage, as was once the case in mires in valleys of the Pleistocene districts in the Netherlands. A higher rainfall, harsher winters, long periods of inundation in spring, and lower solute concen-trations may allow for open quagfen vegetation elsewhere (*cf.* Tallis, 1983).

Management regimes and post-management relaxation

The above considerations suggest that, if we want to preserve the open-fen environment in peat pits as a refuge for the appropriate species, we will have to consider active management at selected locations. Mowing and harvesting, either in winter or in summer, or burning will do the job (Smittenberg, 1974). Mowing in summer is often considered 'best' when considering such criteria as fen-plant species frequencies and species diversity,. In management plans, summer mowing is usually combined with other measures to accommodate birds and insects. The main difference between mowing in summer and mowing in winter is that the latter does not affect below-ground development of such species as *Phragmites australis*. More nutrients remain within the system since they have already been stored in rhizomes and fallen leaves when mowing is started. The root systems of various species of *Carex*, *Salix cinerea* agg., *Salix repens* and *Betula pubescens* apparently do not suffer from mowing in summer. The slender-sedge sere, of mesotrophic conditions, requires a summer mowing regime, *i.e.* a harvest preferably in July, but certainly before mid-September. Upon dereliction, the advanced below-ground development may cause a rapid transition to carr, for which the term *post-management relaxation* is appropriate.

Field experience indicates that post-management relaxation of swamp and early rich fen after *c.* 25 years results in a loss of most characteristic fen species. Until then it is often possible by clearing to restore species-rich open fen within 2–10 years. Of course, scrub and carr both have their own intrinsic value.

(3) The transition from fen to bog

Formation of a 'mature bog', if any, requires some 250 years

With a wetland water regime, carr, scrub and harvested open fen all develop, by natural succession, into some type of poor fen. This is due to the formation of a rainwater lens in the uppermost layers of the peat (*atmotrophiation*, van Wirdum, et al., 1992). In particular, the ericaceous phase of harvested fen in some respects comes close to wet-heath or bog vegetation. Brackish fens are known for the early establishment of such embryonic bog. Even before this phase is reached, *Sphagnum* species characteristic of bogs, such as *S. fuscum, S. imbricatum* and, more often, *S. papillosum* and *S. magellanicum*, can establish. A sphagnaceous acrotelm of 15–20 cm is formed by *S. palustre* and *S. recurvum* in 20–40 years (*cf.* van Wirdum, 1993a,b). After this rapid initial growth, peat accumulation slows down owing to slightly drier conditions at the acrotelm surface. The embryonic bog sites mature as the deeper layers of fen peat are sealed down by a sphagnaceous catotelm (*sensu* Ingram, 1983), which forms from acrotelm in about 100 years at a depth of *c.* 25 cm. Mature bog vegetation is characterised by the absence of species requiring mineral nutrients in excess of those provided by precipitation. Some of the more demanding species, helophytes as well as trees, survive in the terrestrialising *petgaten* until the fen peat layers explored by their root systems are buried below *c.* 20 cm of sphagnaceous catotelm. Adding another 100–150 years for this process (*cf.* Malmer & Holm, 1984), a sum total of *c.* 250 years is suggested for maturation of a bog embryo in a brown-moss-phase *kragge* fen (van Wirdum, 1993c). In some sites suggestive of an advanced succession, old moss peat or functionally-equivalent materials may have accelerated the process.

Witte & van Geel (1985) report the transition from CALTHION fen *via* MOLINION fen and 'wet heath' to bog vegetation in a coastal mire in about 300 years. Their detailed palaeoecological analyses suggest very slow growth, which compares well with field impressions from recent ericaceous poor-fen sites where the ericaceous phase is almost stationary! While this may contribute to the sealing properties of the catotelm, it is uncertain to what extent it automatically causes the poorer drainage conditions typical of bogs. Since most ericaceous poor-fen sites are small and freely draining into a well-maintained ditch system, there is some suspicion that bog development is arrested because of inefficient detention of rainwater.

Kragge scrub and carr apparently go through intricate cycles of atmotrophiation, eutrophication and mineralisation, but clear evidence of bog formation is missing (Wiegers, 1992). The relatively few detailed palaeoecological analyses of carr-bog sequences in peat profiles in the Netherlands (*cf.* Gotjé, 1993) are not unequivocal as regards the undisturbed and direct nature of such transitions and their applicability to floating fens. We really do not know to what extent carr is a more or less stable state, or whether it will develop into either bog or woodland.

Management for bog development

Whilst there is no clear evidence of ongoing bog formation at present, monitoring may provide important clues within one century. If the ericaceous and carr phases of poor fen prove to be almost stationary stages, a slightly improved retention of rainwater may stimulate bog growth. The 30 m width of the peat pits may now prove too small for a water regime similar to that of bogs. Where bog is the aim, a removal of baulks may be necessary in this phase.

There is no clear evidence of management facilitating bog maturation. The ericaceous phase of harvested fen is of low productivity. A gradual discontinuation of the harvesting regime, when applied, should be considered. I have seen some examples where roe deer have adequately controlled tree growth for several years in ericaceous poor-fen vegetation. Other fens became overgrown by *Betula pubescens* as a result of post-management relaxation (see above) or, in some cases, as a result of too drastic a removal of remaining trees, thereby providing bare peat spots suitable for their re-establishment.

(4) The transition from rich fen to poor fen

Different rates and causes of acidification

The transition from brown-moss (rich-fen) to sphagnaceous (poor-fen) phases has been discussed elsewhere (van Wirdum, 1991, 1993a,b; van Wirdum *et al.*, 1992; Kooijman, 1993a). Rather than the 'normal' slow atmotrophiation, a rapid transition to poor fen with a strong dominance of *Sphagnum recurvum* and *Polytrichum commune*, associated with a very species-poor vegetation (Figure 3) is often seen. The relevant sphagnaceous phases are quite different from the well-known *Carex lasiocarpa–Sphagnum* quagfen with *Sphagnum subnitens*, *S. teres*, and *S. contortum* (Segal, 1966; Westhoff & den Held, 1969; den Held *et al.*,

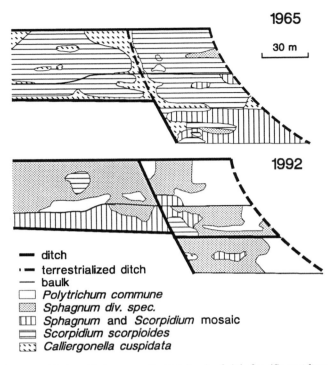

Figure 3. Atmotrophiation (*Sphagnum*, *Polytrichum*) of rich fen (*Scorpidium*, *Calliergonella*) accelerated by the terrestrialisation of ditches in a part of De Weerribben nature reserve. Terrestrialisation of ditches was in an advanced stage already in 1965, but the vegetation lagged behind; in 1992 ditches had been cleaned out and partially dug anew, but this is not yet reflected in the vegetation pattern. After van Zon-van Wagtendonk (1965) and van Wirdum (1993b).

1992), although intermediate types are common. Three causes of this rapid atmotrophiation have been suggested: (1) the exhaustion of bases, due to an increased hydrological isolation of sites, as identified by van Wirdum (1991); (2) an increased supply of nutrients due to enrichment of precipitation and surface water, followed by an expansion of *Sphagnum squarrosum* (Kooijman, 1993a, in press), which then acidifies the site; (3) an increased loss of nutrients and organic acids from plant material decomposing on the peat surface after imperfect harvests. The various causes may be linked with a changing vegetation, as with the increased abundance of *Carex elata* in a harvest-damaged moss layer first suggested by van Zon-van Wagtendonk (1965) and analysed by van Wirdum (1993b). Rather than building typical hummocks, the centrifugal growth of the shoots of *Carex elata* in mown quagfens gives way to slightly raised central pans. Rainwater and humus in the pans encourage an expansion of *Sphagnum* species, especially when coincident with a decreased supply of base-rich surface water.

The ditch system as a key to atmotrophiation control

Although the detail of the transitions discussed above are not known, there is no doubt that the supply of bases by groundwater or surface water is a primary requirement for the prolongation of the rich-fen phase. Base supply by surface water into the mire water beneath *kragges* was studied in detail by van Wirdum (1991). The relevant hydrological model can also be applied to groundwater supply (van Wirdum *et al.*, 1992). In groundwater-fed quagfens, ditches should provide for some surface drainage, so as to sustain an upward flux of base-rich groundwater. For this purpose they should be shallow enough to prevent diverting the main flow of groundwater before it reaches the *kragge*.

Whilst the existing evidence concerns the control of succession rates by ditch management, the model mentioned above and various agrohydrological formulae can also be used to determine an optimal layout of the ditch system in restoration plans. Monitoring of the water composition, for example with sounding rods (van Wirdum, 1991), can provide the information needed to fine-tune the system. Obviously, the beneficial effects of a base supply with surface water must be balanced against possible eutrophication. In the Netherlands today, groundwater is often eutrophicated as well.

Warning against possible side-effects and ineffectiveness of restoration

It is not self-evident that ditching alone is likely to be sufficient to restore strongly-acidified *kragges* back to base-rich fen, as suggested by Beltman & van den Broek (1993). Poor-fen *kragges* have to be removed, at least in part, in order to get full results from a restored ditch system, since brown-moss phase vegetation requires base-rich water.

This type of restoration initiative in existing nature reserves produces much organic material, which is often dumped, either on existing baulks or in carr, leading to potential eutrophication problems through mineralisation, and to a forced transition of fen sites into 'dry' peatland with common types of vegetation and few rich-fen species. Management authorities and dredging companies have only recently made progress towards solutions to these problems (Op't Hof, personal communication) and no records of vegetation response are available as yet. In particular, in a fairly eutrophic environment there is little chance that the early phases of terrestrialisation will really develop the vegetational properties aimed at (van Wirdum, 1983; Kooijman, 1993b). In such cases it may be much more appropriate to stimulate the development of sphagnaceous-phase vegetation to generate ericaceous poor-fen and possibly bog sites. The types of vegetation characteristic of such sites have become very rare in the Netherlands, and it has proved difficult to recreate them on cut-over bog surfaces. In many of these sites the surface peat has changed to the extent that it now provides some of the worst starting points for bog formation. In this respect, sphagnaceous phase vegetation in fens is not a 'plague' to be combated. However, where the present state is fertilised farmland, it makes sense to restore eutrophic swamp.

THE ECOLOGICAL-FIELD, ECODEVICE AND MANAGEMENT LEVELS OF RESTORATION

Three levels of scale are suggested for the planning and realisation of restoration projects. The first level (macro-level, ecological-field or landscape level) determines the properties of the ecological field with which *natecs* have to match. This level is rarely given due attention in restoration plans. Most often information about the past is tacitly considered reliable enough to assess restoration opportunities. An attempt to consider this level based on a hydrological character-isation of the ecological field is given below. The second level (meso-level or ecodevice level) particularly concerns a *natec*'s side of the same match: how much of what 'currency' (see Introduction) is exchanged with the ecological field, and which parts of a *natec* are involved. It is sufficiently illustrated by the ditch-system design mentioned above. In addition to the attention paid to management in preceding sections, the third level (micro-level or vegetation level) calls for a short discussion of micro-site patterns within the vegetation and of management control of succession rates. The higher levels provide boundary conditions for the lower ones, but it should be clear that the lower levels allow additional control over the higher ones (feedback control).

Opportunities at the ecological-field level

Mire regeneration reflects geomorphology and hydrology

Vegetation records have shown the existence of different successional seres (van Wirdum *et al.*, 1992), the main variance in the Netherlands coinciding with the saltwater–freshwater gradient (Figure 2). If the quite different succession in moorland pools and peat pits in the more elevated parts of the country is added to this, the current distribution pattern of the various seres is not very dissimilar to that of mire types earlier in the post-glacial period (Stiboka, 1965; Pons, 1992; see also van Wirdum, 1993a). This is a robust pattern suggestive of the influence of geomorphology and large-scale hydrology, which determine the water balance and water chemistry for whole mire areas. This macro-scale or landscape level apparently concerns the ecological field of the ecodevices. In spite of the overall robustness of the pattern suggested, the present situation is also strongly influenced by polders and the infiltration of polluted surface water (see also Schot & Molenaar, 1991; van Wirdum, 1980, 1991). This must be considered in the selection of suitable sites for restoration and of the environmental control measures needed. Measures may be needed to ensure the availability of the right amounts of water with appropriate chemical characteristics for the ecodevices to be restored. They include a possible restriction of land use, such as the application of fertilisers, drainage, and groundwater abstraction. The slender-sedge (*Carex lasiocarpa*) sere is particularly demanding as regards water factors.

The water cycle as a basis for planning

The connection of restoration opportunities with regional hydrology has been taken into account in planning in the Netherlands since the late 1970s according to a scheme proposed by van Wirdum (*cf.* 1980, 1991). In the hydrologic cycle, water consecutively passes through the atmosphere, the lithosphere and the ocean. Reference compositions of atmotrophic, lithotrophic and thalassotrophic water have been determined for water changed by residence in the atmosphere, lithosphere and ocean, respectively. Concise archives of water analyses suitable for the estimation of hydrological conditions at the national scale at present exist only for groundwater. Even with this limited material it is possible to determine opportunities for fen restoration according to the following rationale:

(1) In cases of an outflow of groundwater, its composition provides a good estimation of the type of water to be expected in existing or future wetlands;
(2) In cases of a substantial infiltration of water from wetlands towards the underlying body of groundwater, the latter will reflect the type of water apparently supplied from the surface-water system;
(3) When the groundwater is of the rainwater type, this is probably caused by a substantial infiltration of water in the absence of additional water sources. In the Dutch climate this indicates well-draining sites, where it will be difficult to maintain groundwater levels high enough to restore wetland conditions. However, there may still be regions with a potential for bog development (see 4);
(4) Atmotrophic water is available everywhere; where drainage is poor, measures can contribute to increase the local storage and accumulation of rainwater.

Prins (1993) compared a map of groundwater composition (Figure 4) with the present occurrence of seven main groups of fen vegetation. She found similar relations as had been found previously within individual fen sites (van Wirdum *et al.*, 1992). This means that the terrestrialising peat pits foreshadow the regional perspectives for restoration of the relevant types. A full application requires additional ecological understanding of the slender-sedge (*Carex lasiocarpa*) sere. This sere presently is almost confined to base-rich freshwater (lithotrophic situations), but van Wirdum (1991) provides evidence that it may also develop in desalting mires in the peri-marine area of the Netherlands. Other, more casual, data in support of this relation have since become available.

In the recent Nature Policy Plan for the Netherlands (Ministerie van Landbouw Natuurbeheer en Visserij, 1990) the network of existing nature reserves and projected nature reserves (derived by restoration) is based upon this scale level. This has shown a need for reliable methods to predict the likely response of plant species to restoration measures. Among the methods developed for this, the ICHORS model (Barendregt *et al.*, 1986; see also van Wirdum, 1986) should be mentioned particularly. Based on statistical relations between present species occurrences in the same region and measured water-related site factors, ICHORS estimates the probability of occurrence of species for any given set of site data supposed to apply after restoration.

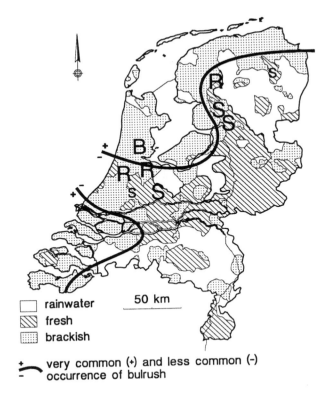

Figure 4. Dominant types of groundwater in the Netherlands, in relation to main sites of terrestrialisation (B bulrush sere, R reed sere, S slender-sedge sere). Groundwater map compiled by ir. H. Houweling (IBN, see Prins 1993), simplified. Commonness of bulrush (*Scirpus lacustris* ssp. *tabernaemontani*) roughly according to van der Meijden, Plate & Weeda (1989).

Management control of succession rates

Kragge *accrual and site heterogeneity respond to management*

On other occasions (see van Wirdum, 1991) I have drawn attention to the micro-relief in quagfen sites and its influence on ecological site heterogeneity. In particular, hummock–hollow patterns locally determine the existence of atmotrophic–lithotrophic and atmotrophic–thalassotrophic gradients expressed in the distribution of plant species. Vegetation on floating rafts is strongly influenced by the physical properties of the rafts, such as their thickness and their buoyancy. When the rafts become thicker a gradient develops between the hummocks and the hollows. Such stages are usually very rich in species of vascular plants, bryophytes and desmids due to the controlled presence of microsites with an intermediate base status. As the thickness of *kragges* increases further, they ultimately loose their capacity to follow water-level fluctuations immediately, since they are anchored to the baulks of the *petgaten*. Mineralisation then becomes more important, and a tall-herb vegetation often replaces the peat-forming mire vegetation. Alternatively, mire succession proceeds to poor-fen and embryonic bog stages as discussed previously. In both cases, site heterogeneity decreases due to the decreased presence of oligo-mesotrophic base-rich microsites (van Wirdum *et al.*, 1992; van Wirdum, 1991, 1993).

The rôle of vegetation management in the local control of raft development is very important to restoration initiatives, since the mowing of the vegetation has an obvious (but hardly studied) influence upon the thickness and buoyancy of *kragges*. When mown in winter, many helophyte species, such as *Phragmites australis*, have re-allocated above-ground nutrients to their root systems. This contributes to the accrual of below-ground biomass and peat. The relevant *kragges* usually develop faster towards the poor-fen and ericaceous phase than do summer-mown *kragges*. They also seem to suffer more from summer droughts and surface mineralisation, as mentioned above.

Experimental approach required

In the Netherlands, managers of nature reserves have a fairly good appreciation of the impact of harvesting on the succession of the vegetation (Smittenberg, 1974). However, there is a lack of understanding of the below-ground development of root systems and of peat-accumulation rates. Such understanding is of vital importance for restoration planning and to management of wetlands for long-term success. We should be aware that the expertise currently available is based on a limited set of alternatives fortuitously supplied through traditional land-use, especially peat winning and vegetation harvest. Experimental management switches and dereliction have presented puzzling examples of post-management relaxation. The accrual of *kragge* peat has been shown to interfere with the supply of water and bases at the ecodevice level, but until now no better solution has been invented than a cyclic application of old land-use methods. Rather than advertising a wide application of this unverified solution, I suggest that researchers, planners and managers should invest in the documentation of existing and new experiments and historical cases, and in the planning of new ones.

ACKNOWLEDGEMENTS

I am indebted to Drs A.H. Prins, S.C. Shaw and B.D. Wheeler and to anonymous referees for critically reading the manuscript and suggesting improvements.

REFERENCES

Barendregt, A., Wassen, M.J., De Smidt, J.T. & Lippe, E. (1986). Ingreep-effect voorspelling voor waterbeheer. *Landschap,* **3**, 41–55.

RESTORATION OF TEMPERATE WETLANDS

Beltman, B. & van den Broek, T. (1993). Verzuring van kalkrijke venen. *Landschap*, **10**, 17–33.

de Nie, W. (1987). *The decrease in aquatic vegetation in Europe and its consequences for fish populations.* EIFAC/CECPI Occasional Paper No. 19.

den Held, A.J., Schmitz, M. & van Wirdum, G. (1992). Types of terrestrializing fen vegetation in the Netherlands. *Fens and Bogs in the Netherlands; History, Nutrient Dynamics, and Conservation* (ed. J.T.A. Verhoeven), pp. 237–321. Kluwer, Dordrecht.

Dirkse, G.M., van Melick, H.M.H. & Touw, A. (1988). Checklist of Dutch bryophytes. *Lindbergia*, **14**, 167–175.

George, M. (1992). *The Land-use, Ecology and Conservation of Broadland.* Packard, Funtington.

Gorter, H.P. (1986). *Ruimte voor Natuur.* Natuurmonumenten, s'-Graveland.

Gotjé, W.(1993). *De Holocene laagveenontwikkeling in de randzone van de Nederlandse kustvlakte (Noordoostpolder).* Thesis. Vrije Universiteit, Amsterdam.

Haans, J.C.F.M. & Hamming, C. (1954). *De bodemgesteldheid van het ruilverkavelingsgebied Vollenhove.* Intern Rapport 392. Stichting voor Bodemkartering, Wageningen.

Havinga, A.J. (1957). Bijdrage tot de kennis van het rietland van Noordwest-Overijssel. *Boor en Spade*, **8**, 131–140.

Holling, C.S. (1992). Cross-scale morphology, geometry, and dynamics of ecosystems. *Ecological Monographs*, **62**, 447–502.

Ingram, H.A.P. (1983). Hydrology. *Ecosystems of the World 4A. Mires: Swamp, Bog, Fen and Moor; General Studies* (ed. A.J.P. Gore), pp. 67–158. Elsevier, Amsterdam.

Kooijman, A.M. (1993a). *Changes in the bryophyte layer of rich fens as controlled by acidification and eutrophication.* Thesis. Universiteit, Utrecht.

Kooijman, A.M. (1993b). Causes of the replacement of *Scorpidium scorpioides* by *Calliergonella cuspidata* in eutrophicated rich fens, 1, Field studies. *Lindbergia*, **18**, 78–84.

Kooijman, A.M. (in press). Species replacement in the bryophyte layer in mires: the role of water type, nutrient supply and interspecific interactions. *Journal of Ecology*.

Malmer, N. & Holm, E. (1984). Variation in the C/N quotient of peat in relation to decomposition rate and age determinations with ^{210}Pb. *Oikos*, **43**, 171–182.

Ministerie van Landbouw, Natuurbeheer en Visserij (1990). *Natuurbeleidsplan.* Staatsdrukkerij en Uitgeverij, 's-Gravenhage.

Moen, A. (1990). *The plant cover of the boreal uplands of central Norway, 1, Vegetation ecology of Sølendet Nature Reserve; haymaking fens and birch woodlands.* Gunneria, **63**, Trondheim.

Pallis, M. (1916). The structure and history of *plav*: the floating fen of the Danube. *Journal of the Linnean Society (Botany)*, **43**, 223–290.

Palczynski, A. (1984). Natural differentiation of plant communities in relation to hydrological conditions of the Biebrza valley. *Polish Ecological Studies*, **10**, 347–385.

Pons, L.J. (1992). Holocene peat formation in the lower parts of the Netherlands. *Fens and Bogs in the Netherlands; History, Nutrient Dynamics, and Conservation* (ed J.T.A. Verhoeven), pp. 7–79. Kluwer, Dordrecht.

Prins, A.H. (1993). *Laagvenen; een verkenning van mogelijkheden voor natuurontwikkeling.* NBP-onderzoeksrapport 5, DLO-Instituut voor Bos- en Natuuronderzoek, Wageningen.

Rodewald-Rudescu, L. (1974). *Das Schilfrohr.* Schweizerbart'sche, Stuttgart.

Schot, P.P, & Molenaar, A. (1991). Regional changes in groundwater flow patterns and effects on groundwater composition. *Solute Transport by Groundwater Flow to Wetland Ecosystems* (ed. P.P. Schot). Thesis, University of Utrecht.

Segal, S. (1966). Ecological studies of peat-bog vegetation in the north-western part of the province of Overijssel (the Netherlands). *Wentia*, **15**, 109–141.

Siebel, H.N., Aptroot, A., Dirkse, G.M., van Dobben, H.F., van Melick, H.M.H. & Touw, A. (1992). Rode lijst van in Nederland verdwenen en bedreigde mossen en korstmossen. *Gorteria*, **18**, 1–20.

Smittenberg, J.H. (1974). *Voorstel tot inrichting en beheer van het C.R.M.-reservaat De Weerribben*. Report, Rijksinstituut voor Natuurbeheer, Leersum.

Stiboka (1965). *De bodem van Nederland*. Stichting voor Bodemkartering, Wageningen.

Succow, M. (1988). *Landschaftsökologische Moorkunde*. Fisher, Jena.

Succow, M. & Kopp, D. (1985). Seen als Naturraumtypen. *Petermanns Geographische Mitteilungen*, **3**, 161–170, 4, map.

Tallis, J.H. (1983). Changes in wetland communities. *Ecosystems of the World 4A. Mires: Swamp, Bog, Fen and Moor; General Studies* (ed A.J.P. Gore), pp. 311–347. Elsevier, Amsterdam.

Tomaszewska, K. (1988). Plant cover of peatland in the Biebrza valley and its changes determined on the basis of aerial photographs. *Proceedings VIII International Peat Congress*, **1**, 199–207. International Peat Society, Helsinki.

van de Ven, G.P. (ed.) (1993). *Man-made Lowlands*. Matrijs, Utrecht.

van der Meijden, R., Plate, C.L. & Weeda, E.J. (1989). *Atlas van de Nederlandse flora 3, Minder zeldzame en algemene soorten*. Onderzoeksinstituut Rijksherbarium/Hortus Botanicus, Leiden.

van der Meijden, R., Weeda, E.J., Adema, F.A.C.B., & De Joncheere, G.J. (1983). *Flora van Nederland*. Wolters-Noordhoff, Groningen.

van der Toorn, J. (1972). *Variability of* Phragmites australis *(Cav.) Trin. ex Steudel in relation to the environment*. Staatsuitgeverij, 's-Gravenhage.

van Donselaar, J. (1961). On the vegetation of former river beds in the Netherlands. *Wentia*, **5**, 1–85.

van Donselaar-Ten Bokkel Huinink, W.A.E. (1961). An ecological study of the vegetation in three former river beds. *Wentia*, **5**, 112–162.

van Leeuwen, C.G. (1982). From ecosystem to ecodevice. *Perspectives in Landscape Ecology, Contributions to Research, Planning and Management of our Environment* (eds S.P. Tjallingii & A.A. de Veer), pp. 29–34. PUDOC, Wageningen.

van Wirdum, G. (1979a). Veen, venen en moerassen; Laagveenmoerassen; Hoogvenen. *Natuurbeheer in Nederland; Levensgemeenschappen* (ed Rijksinstituut voor Natuurbeheer), pp. 99–116, 117–129, 131–139. PUDOC, Wageningen.

van Wirdum, G. (1979b). Dynamic aspects of trophic gradients in a mire complex. *Proceedings and Informations*, **25**, 66–82. Committee for Hydrological Research TNO, The Hague.

van Wirdum, G. (1980). Eenvoudige beschrijving van de waterkwaliteitsverandering gedurende de hydrologische kringloop. *Rapporten en Nota's*, **5**, 118–143. Commissie voor hydrologisch onderzoek TNO, 's-Gravenhage.

van Wirdum, G. (1982). Design for a land-ecological survey of nature protection. *Perspectives in Landscape Ecology, Contributions to Research, Planning and Management of our Environment* (eds S.P. Tjallingii & A.A. de Veer), pp. 245–251. PUDOC, Wageningen.

van Wirdum, G. (1983). De mosseninventarisatie van De Weerribben. *Buxbaumiella*, **14**, 10–47.

van Wirdum, G. (1986). Water-related impacts on nature protection sites. *Proceedings and Informations*, **34**, 27–57. Committee for Hydrological Research TNO, The Hague.

van Wirdum, G. (1991). *Vegetation and Hydrology of Floating Rich-Fens.* Datawyse, Maastricht.

van Wirdum, G. (1993a). An ecosystems approach to base-rich wetlands, with special reference to fenlands. *Hydrobiologia*, **265**, 129–153.

van Wirdum, G. (1993b). Basenverzadiging in soortenrijke trilvenen. *Effectgerichte Maatregelen Tegen Verzuring en Eutrofiëring in Natuurterreinen* (eds M. Cals, M. de Graaf & J. Roelofs), pp. 97–126. Vakgroep Oecologie KUN, Nijmegen.

van Wirdum, G. (1993c). *Ecosysteemvisie hoogvenen.* Report nr. 35, Institute for Forestry and Nature Research, Wageningen.

van Wirdum, G., Den Held, A.J. & Schmitz, M. (1992). Terrestrializing vegetation in former turbaries in the Netherlands. *Fens and Bogs in the Netherlands; History, Nutrient Dynamics and Conservation* (ed. J.T.A. Verhoeven), pp. 323–360. Kluwer, Dordrecht.

van Zinderen Bakker, E.M. (1942). *Het Naardermeer.* Allert de Lange, Amsterdam.

van Zon-van Wagtendonk, A.M. (1965). *Vegetatiekartering van een gedeelte van het natuurreservaat De Weerribben te Oldemarkt.* Report, University of Amsterdam, Research Institute for Nature Management, Leersum.

Weeda, E.J., van der Meijden, R. & Bakker, P.A. (1990). Rode lijst van de in Nederland verdwenen en bedreigde planten (Pteridophyta en Spermatophyta) over de periode 1.I.1980–1.I.1990. *Gorteria*, **16**, 1–26.

Westhoff, V. & Den Held, A.J. (1969). *Plantengemeenschappen in Nederland.* Thieme, Zutphen.

Wheeler, B.D. (1988). Species richness, species rarity and conservation of rich-fen vegetation in lowland England and Wales. *Journal of Applied Ecology*, **25**, 331–353.

Wiegers, J. (1985). *Succession in Fen Woodland Ecosystems in the Dutch Haf District.* Cramer, Vaduz.

Wiegers, J. (1992). Carr vegetation: plant communities and succession of the dominant tree species. *Fens and Bogs in the Netherlands; History, Nutrient Dynamics and Conservation* (ed. J.T.A. Verhoeven), pp. 361–395. Kluwer, Dordrecht.

Witte, H.J.L. & van Geel, B. (1985). Vegetational and environmental succession and net organic production between 4500 and 800 BP reconstructed from a peat deposit in the western Dutch coastal area (Assendelver Polder). *Review of Palaeobotany and Palynology*, **45**, 239–300.

18 Restoration of Acidified Rich-fen Ecosystems in the Vechtplassen Area: Successes and Failures

B. BELTMAN, T. VAN DEN BROEK & S. BLOEMEN

Department of Plant Ecology and Evolutionary Biology, Utrecht University, P.O. Box 800.84, NL-3508TB, The Netherlands

SUMMARY

1. Acidification and eutrophication cause great changes in fen ecosystems in the Netherlands. With the aim of preventing the loss of rare species and species-rich plant communities, restoration measures are being carried out to a large extent by nature conservation agencies. For fen ecosystems little research had been carried out on the effect of measures such as sod cutting and excavation of ditches and drains.

2. This study on restoration was carried out in floating fens in which the vegetation was dominated by *Sphagnum squarrosum, S. fallax* and *Polytrichum commune* but which used to have a *Scorpidio-Caricetum diandrae* plant community with species such as *Eriophorum gracile, Scorpidium scorpioides, Carex lasiocarpa* and *C. diandra.* The main problem is a surplus of rainwater forming a water lens on top of the calcareous water. For one fen a drop in pH of the surface water from 6.2 to 4 was recorded between 1980 and 1991. In autumn 1989 a ditch was excavated along the fen and connected with the main drainage system. Experimental sites were created of which the sod was cut by removal of the top 20 cm, so different restoration measures versus control could be followed.

3. The only possibly successful restoration appeared to be a combined approach of sod cutting and drainage of surplus water. The pH increased and stabilised at *c.* 6.5, whereas with other measures, pH remained at 4; the electrical conductivity (EC) increased to 20 mS m^{-1} in the combined treatment, compared with 10 mS m^{-1} for control and sod removal only. The concentrations of calcium and bicarbonate in the surface water also showed a significant increase in the combined treatment.

4. Nitrogen concentrations in the surface water in the fen did not differ significantly between treatments. Ortho-phosphate concentrations decreased significantly after sod removal.

5. Monitoring of the vegetation development over two years after treatment showed that rich-fen species did recover in the combined treatment, although still in small percentages. Importantly, undesired species such as *Sphagnum squarrosum, S. fallax* and *Polytrichum commune* did not recover in the combined treatment, while they did in the plots where only sod removal had been carried out.

6. Failures or unattained targets after experimental restoration treatments were also

Restoration of Temperate Wetlands. Edited by B.D. Wheeler, S.C. Shaw, W. Fojt and R.A. Robertson
© 1995 John Wiley & Sons Ltd.

recorded. The only treatment which did not increase pH nor EC was removal of living *Sphagnum* plants. Excavation of large ponds, with the aim that wind and wave action would decrease the *Sphagnum* carpet, appeared not to be successful.

7.   Small-scale restoration measures might increase the acid rainwater effect due to improved shallow drainage, creating shallow puddles and trenches on top of the fen-raft.

8.   The hydrological setting of a fen in the surrounding landscape appeared to be of great importance.

INTRODUCTION

The main goal of nature conservation authorities concerning rich-fen ecosystems (*sensu* Sjörs, 1950) is the conservation of species-rich stages in the succession from open water to alder (carr) woodland (Anon., 1990). This succession is natural, but there is also a cultural dimension, due to influences of man, *e.g.* nutrient enrichment of groundwater and surface water, changes in macro-ion composition of water due to the import of water originating from the river Rhine and acid rain (which is also loaded with a rather high nutrient content). These changes in environmental conditions all lead to changes in the same direction: an increased rate of succession and a loss of species richness (*e.g. Scorpidium scorpioides*[1]). Kooijman (1993) showed that this 'rapid succession' also means that the sequence of bryophytes changed during succession. A lawn of *Sphagnum squarrosum* and *S. fallax*, develops rapidly, even in calcium-rich lowland peatlands. This carpet covers the original bryophyte community and competes strongly with the phanerogams for space, light and nutrients (Verhoeven & Schmitz, 1991). Invasion by *Polytrichum commune* in recent years seems especially to increase this 'blanket' effect. There is evidence (Bowden, 1991; Beltman & van den Broek, 1993) that the efficient use of precipitation nutrients by *P. commune* follows the acidification phase by *Sphagnum* species which occurred previously.

A change in acid conditions might also change the nutrient availability (especially PO_4^{3-}) in the water–soil environment (*e.g.* Kemmers, 1986), so acidification and eutrophication may be linked. An increase in nutrient availability for those plants, *e.g. Polytrichum*, which can explore this phosphate-enriched layer, can also contribute to the shift and/or speed of succession in many rich-fen ecosystems. The presence of macro-ions such as calcium and iron may reduce the availability of phosphate (Boyer & Wheeler, 1989).

The present succession state of the rich fens results from traditional agricultural management until the early 1950s (turf excavation, cutting of trees for fuel and hay making). When this ceased, an enormous increase of alder woodland occurred (Bakker, 1993). Restoration of the deteriorated fens was not the only option for conservationists and ideas were developed to excavate new open water bodies to give the opportunity for a wide range of succession stages: open water,

---

[1] Nomenclature of the plant species follows: Heukels & van der Meijden (1983), Jermy & Tutin (1982) and Touw & Rubers (1989).

aquatic plants, reed and sedge communities.

Because no experience was available, some experimental projects were designed, aimed at the restoration of rich-fen ecosystems, so that plant species, seed or diaspores would be maintained in the area and species would be available for re-invasion of successional stages that would be present in the (near) future. Several studies in the Netherlands have shown (Berendse et al., 1992; Kooijman, Beltman & Westhoff, 1993) that once species have become extinct in isolated fens and grasslands it is difficult for them to recolonise, even though abiotic conditions may be favourable. Until recently (1989) there was strong opposition against restoration but since the publication of the national Nature Policy Plan (Anon., 1990) restoration and nature development have become widely accepted.

The main research questions were:

- Can a base-rich environment be restored?
- Is it possible to restore a nutrient poor to moderate rich soil–water environment?
- Does the vegetation respond positively to the measures?

SITE DESCRIPTION AND EXPERIMENTAL DESIGN

The five pilot projects in fens are all situated in a lowland peat area: the Vechtplassen (Figure 1) (details in: Verhoeven, Koerselman & Beltman, 1988). In this area the peat soil is 1–2 m thick and covers a deep sandy layer, the latter being the main aquifer. The Vechtplasse area includes several polders, in which nature reserves lie scattered in between agriculturally managed meadows. A series of parallel ditches 40 m apart, discharging at the southern end into a canal, exports surplus rainwater and discharged groundwater out of the polders (Figure 1). In drought periods these ditches can be used to supply water from outside the polder to meadows, cornfields and nature reserves such as floating fens and reed-marshes. The main research has been carried out in the polder Westbroek (Figure 1). Here, discharge of calcium and bicarbonate-rich groundwater (0.5–2 mm day^{-1}) occurs into ditches and floating fens. The floating fens consist of a raft of 30 cm floating on a water layer of 0.6–1 m. The raft may be connected to uncut peat walls on one or more sides. The fens are about 40 m wide and 50–300 m long. Water budget studies and research on water chemistry (Beltman & Rouwenhorst, 1993) showed that lenses of rainwater occur in the top layer of fens with no possibilities for discharge of surplus water into ditches.

As a first restoration measure, small ditches (1 m wide, 0.8 m deep) were excavated along the research fens and connected with the polder drainage system through an adjustable culvert. The second measure was sod cutting and removal of the 15–25 cm thick *Sphagnum/Polytrichum* carpet. This measure was carried out to restore space and germination possibilities for plants and to restore the superficial run-off over the raft, which was blocked by the *Sphagnum* sponge.

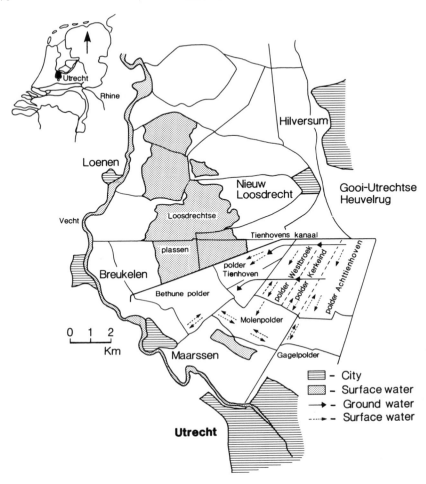

Figure 1. The Vechtplassen study area includes *e.g.* the polders Achttienhoven, Kerkeind, Molenpolder, Tienhoven and Westbroek. * Indicates restoration projects carried out in polder Westbroek. Groundwater flow direction and surface water flow through ditches are indicated. Gooi-Utrechtse Heuvelrug is an ice-pushed sandy ridge of *c.* 50 m above mean sea level; a similar difference in altitude exists between ridge and the polders in the peat area.

Thus, different combinations of experimental sites were created in the fens: control, drainage only, sod removal only and combined drainage + sod removal (Figure 2; Table 2). Each experimental site contained six 16-m^2 plots. In fen 1, two times four experimental sites were created. Adjacent to two fens (nos 2 and 3; Figure 3) new ponds (30 m wide, 100–200 m long and 1–1.5 m deep) were excavated. Here it was investigated, in small ditches *vs.* a large pond, whether wind and water currents affected the fen vegetation sufficiently to reduce the

Sphagnum carpet. Again the sod was removed locally. In fen 4 (Figure 3) the treatments were a ditch and presence or absence of sod removal. Piezometers were installed to different depths below the soil surface. Water samples from surface water and groundwater were sampled almost monthly and tested with a continuous flow analyser.

Vegetation relevées were made once a year in August, before and one and two years after the treatment. Only those from fen 1 are presented. Differences were analysed with ANOVA and tested with Tukey ($P<0.05$) (SAS, 1985).

Because water is the driving force in restoring the base-rich conditions of water and soil, this paper deals with water composition. A monitoring survey of one fen (fen 1) over several years will be compared with results from a spatial survey of several fens (fens 2, 3 and 4) at one moment. The soil aspects will be discussed in a future paper.

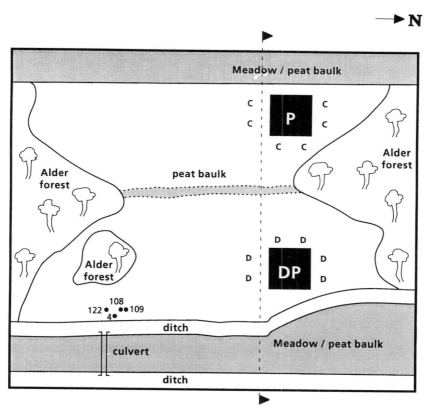

Figure 2. Floating fen in which experimental sites 1 and 2 are situated. DP: area (16 m^2) with sod removed and ditch; D: drainage only; P: only sod removed; C: control plots. Numbers indicate piezometer nests (<7 m deep). Within the plots piezometers are installed from 0.5 to 2 m deep. The hidden peat baulk inside the fen prevents exchange of water under the raft.

278

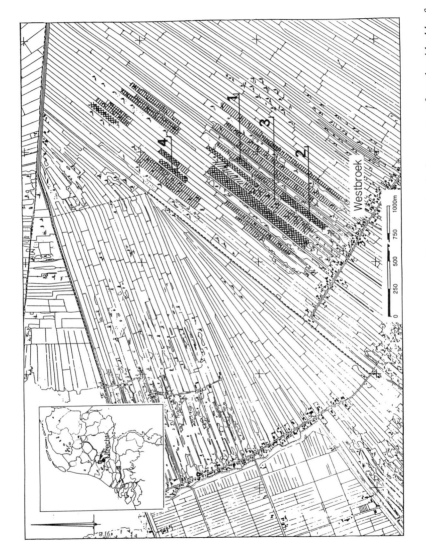

Figure 3. Detailed map of the polder Westbroek. The long parallel lines are ditches. The hatched areas are turf ponds with alder forest, the double hatched areas are ponds with floating fens. Different fens under study are indicated.

RESULTS

Surface water pH, electrical conductivity and macro-ions

Repeated measurements of water chemistry of the plots in fen 1 made clear that only at the site with combined treatment (drainage and sod removal) did the pH and electrical conductivity (EC) remain at a base-rich level (Figure 4) and were significantly higher than the values from control, drainage and the sod removal sites. After 4 months, one and two years, the pH remained fairly constant. The EC values after 4 months were lowered owing to periods of high rainfall, but increased to rather stable values after one and two years. The drained site did not show increased values; a narrow zone, 1–2 m wide along the ditches, showed higher values for EC and Ca^{2+} but beyond this no impact could be detected. Similarly, only the combined site in fen 1 showed increased values for Ca^{2+} and HCO_3^- (Table 1); the drained and sod-removed sites did not differ significantly from the control. It is clear that the groundwater below the fen differs strongly from the shallow surface water.

The survey of the experimental sites in fens 1–4 in spring 1992, one year after a restoration measure, showed (Table 2 & 3) a clear difference between the composition of surface water in the fen and that of the water in the raft (50 cm deep). An effect of sod removal was often detected. A lower pH prevailed in the shallow water layer, usually associated with low EC and low Ca^{2+}, Mg^{2+} and HCO_3^- concentrations.

The results of the second experimental site with combined treatment in research fen 1 (Table 2) are in accord with those of the first ('combined') research site (Table 1) in this fen: significantly increased values for pH, EC, but buffer ions *e.g.* Ca^{2+}, HCO_3^- are rather low. Sod removal alone is not a sufficient restoration option because the rainwater lens remains intact as is shown by the low pH, EC, Ca^{2+} and HCO_3^- values. The results from the treatments in fens 2, 3 and 4 (Table 3) are somewhat surprising. In fen 2, no significant improvements in concentrations in the surface water are measured if only 10 cm of sod (living *Sphagnum* layer) is removed. Comparing, for example, pH, EC and Ca^{2+} with groundwater analyses, it is clear that excavation of a large open water body (30 x 200 m) alone does not lead to circum-neutral, base-rich conditions in the fen soil. The same conclusion can be drawn from the analyses from fen 3, where a large pond is present but no sod removal has taken place. Excavation of ponds as a drainage measure did not affect the water composition in the shallow water layer in the fen. Floating fen 4 shows, in contrast to both experimental sites in fen 1 (Tables 1 and 2), that a low pH and low Ca^{2+}, HCO_3^- concentrations are measured in the shallow surface water of sod intact + ditch ('drainage') as well as in the sod removal + ditch ('combined') site. The experimental sites in fen 4 are situated in the topogenous area downslope of the fen, so shallow run-off from the whole fen passes through these sites and is locally even increased by sod removal.

(a)

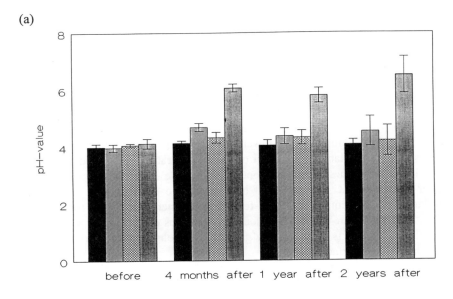

(b)

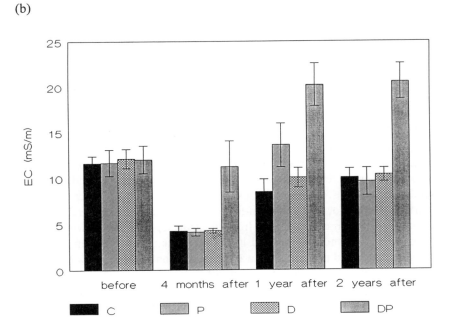

Figure 4. Mean pH (a) and electrical conductivity (EC, mS m^{-1}) (b) values for different years at the experimental sites, before and 3-times after sod-cutting. Codes: control (C), drainage (D), sod removal (P) and combined sod removal and drainage (DP); for location see Figure 2. Values for DP (sod removal + drainage) are significantly different (P<0.05).

Table 1. Mean concentrations (mg l^{-1}; ± SD, $n = 4$) of calcium, magnesium, bicarbonate and chloride in shallow groundwater and surface water in floating fen 1 with research site 1 in 1991 (see Figure 2). Drain (D), ditch excavation only; sod (P), only 20 cm sod removal; comb. (DP), combined sod removal and ditch excavation; control (C), no measures. Areas DP and D are 4 x 4 m square. Different letters indicate significant differences (P<0.05) between treatments. As there was no significant difference between D and DP or P and C, groundwater results shown are means for these pairs of treatments.

	Surface water		Groundwater		
Ion	Drain (D)	Comb. (DP)	0.5 m	1.0 m	2 m
Ca^{2+}	4.25 ± 0.95a	14.69 ± 0.97b	58.2 ± 14.1c	71.4 ± 12.6d	61.9 ± 21.0e
Mg^{2+}	0.91 ± 0.24a	1.29 ± 0.08a	3.43 ± 0.43b	5.47 ± 0.78b	7.23 ± 0.22b
HCO_3^-	6 ± 1a	32 ± 5b	206 ± 64c	311 ± 92c	262 ± 81c
Cl^-	18 ± 2.5a	22 ± 1.4a	20.8 ± 4.7a	18.8 ± 2.1a	21.0 ± 2.7a

	Surface water		Groundwater		
	Sod (P)	Control (C)	0.5 m	1 m	2 m
Ca^{2+}	4.83 ± 0.87a	2.13 ± 0.44a	35.0 ± 14.6b	45.8 ± 9.8bc	64.4 ± 18.2cd
Mg^{2+}	0.31 ± 0.05a	0.38 ± 0.08a	2.15 ± 0.81b	2.65 ± 0.56b	7.01 ± 1.05c
HCO_3^-	2 ± 1a	4 ± 1a	109 ± 61b	146 ± 41b	262 ± 67c
Cl^-	11 ± 0.8a	16 ± 2.9b	24.6 ± 3.6b	20.0 ± 1.8b	24.0 ± 2.6b

Nutrients

The nutrient status of fen water will only be discussed for fen 1. The water analyses showed high ortho-phosphate concentrations (1990: mean 0.24 mg l^{-1} SD 0.14, $n = 8$) in the uppermost profile at both sites where the sod was intact, whereas in the raft at 50 cm depth, the mean concentration was 0.06 mg l^{-1} (SD 0.02, $n = 8$) (Beltman & Rouwenhorst, 1993). In 1991, high values for ortho-P were again measured (Table 4) in the drainage and control sites, whereas in the sod-removed site as well as in the combined site significantly lower concentrations were present. The nitrogen concentrations showed no significant differences between the four sites. The concentrations measured in 1992 showed the same picture for nitrogen and phosphorus concentrations in shallow water.

Vegetation

The repeated relevées of the plots in fen 1 showed (Table 5) a persistent dominance by *Sphagnum fallax*, *S. squarrosum* and *Polytrichum commune* in the control (and drainage) site. The sod-removed site was subject to a rapid invasion by *Sphagnum* species. The combination site showed the reappearance of rich-fen

Table 2. Research fen 1; second experiment. Mean values (± SD; $n = 3$) of water composition in April 1992 of surface water (-s, 0 cm) and groundwater (-g) at 50 cm depth in fens, one year after the treatments: excavation of ditch, sod removal and combination of both. Turf ponds situated in Westbroek (see Figure 1). Ditch is $c.$ 1 m wide and 1 m deep; open water means large body of open water (30 x 50–200 m; 1 m deep) adjacent to fen. Sod removal means removal of 15–25 cm living and dead plant material. Concentrations in mg l^{-1}; EC μS cm^{-1}. Different letters indicate significant differences (P<0.05) between treatments.

	Sites without ditch		Sites with ditch	
	Control	Sod removed	Sod present	Sod removed
pH-s	4.8 ± 0.6a	4.2 ± 0.1a	3.9 ± 0.2a	5.1 ± 0.4b
pH-g	5.4 ± 0.3a	5.2 ± 0.4a	5.4 ± 0.2a	6.3 ± 0.2b
EC-s	47 ± 6.5a	45 ± 4.5a	72 ± 15a	102 ± 36a
EC-g	65 ± 20a	52 ± 11.5a	370 ± 16a	407 ± 23a
Ca-s	2.31 ± 1.93a	0.94 ± 0.43a	2.0 ± 0.90a	23.5 ± 17.5b
Ca-g	5.13 ± 2.43a	3.28 ± 1.95a	48.7 ± 22.3a	66.2 ± 20.6a
Mg-s	0.19 ± 0.19a	0.16 ± 0.14a	0.29 ± 0.23a	1.59 ± 0.95b
Mg-g	0.37 ± 0.18a	0.30 ± 0.20a	6.88 ± 2.37a	6.73 ± 3.17a
HCO$_3$-s	0 ± 0a	0 ± 0a	0 ± 0a	7 ± 7b
HCO$_3$-g	14 ± 14a	10 ± 9a	274 ± 11a	280 ± 12a

species, although the percentages were still low. The bloom of *Utricularia minor* will probably be a temporary feature.

DISCUSSION

The small-scale restoration experiments indicate that for the floating fens the import and export of water is very important. This confirms suggestions of Succow (1989), Koerselman (1989) and van Wirdum (1991). Blockage of drainage leads to rainwater lenses on top of the calcium-rich water (Beltman & Rouwenhorst, 1991, 1993). This process increases the invasion of the highly competitive *Sphagnum* species, which out-compete other characteristic rich-fen bryophytes (Kooijman, 1993). In two different experiments in fens, the combined approach of excavation of a ditch and sod removal made calcium-rich, well-buffered water conditions reappear at the surface. The importance of this is stressed by other authors such as Kemmers (1986), Boyer & Wheeler (1989) and van Wirdum (1991) (see also van Wirdum, this volume). None of the other experiments changed the pH drastically or for a long period. Similarly the (cheaper) removal of a layer of living *Sphagnum* is no option for restoration. The results from fen 4 indicate that a ditch and sod removal can also work as an extra drainage channel for superficial run-off of rainwater from areas adjacent to the sod-removed site, instead of providing the intended extra input of calcium-rich

Table 3. Mean values (mg l^{-1}; EC μS cm^{-1}; ± SD; $n = 3$) of water composition in April 1992 of surface water (-s; 0 cm) and groundwater (-g) at 50 cm depth in fens, one year after the treatment: excavation of ditch, sod removal and combination of both (see also Table 2 legend). In fen 2 only a 10 cm layer of living *Sphagnum* was removed with a pond excavated adjacent. Adjacent to fen 3, only a pond was excavated, with no other treatment. In fen 4, a ditch was excavated in combination with removal of 15–25 cm living and dead plant material. Different letters indicate significant differences (P<0.05) between treatments.

	2: Fen with open water		3: Fen with open water	4: Fen with ditch	
	Sod present	10 cm of sod removed	Sod present	Sod present	20 cm of sod removed
pH-s	4.6 ± 0.3a	4.3 ± 0.5a	5.3 ± 0.9	4.2 ± 0.2a	5.1 ± 0.5b
pH-g	6.0 ± 0.1a	6.1 ± 0.3a	5.8 ± 0.2	5.1 ± 0.4a	5.2 ± 0.4a
EC-s	87 ± 22a	63 ± 14a	96 ± 46	71 ± 11a	106 ± 6b
EC-g	186 ± 30a	184 ± 48a	159 ± 29	99 ± 36a	138 ± 60a
Ca-s	9.1 ± 8.9a	3.1 ± 1.2b	14.7 ± 11.1	2.9 ± 2.7a	10.7 ± 4.6b
Ca-g	31.5 ± 14.6a	18.8 ± 8.2a	30.3 ± 9.4	12.5 ± 11.5a	16.3 ± 10.9a
Mg-s	1.51 ± 0.93a	0.72 ± 0.06b	1.11 ± 0.63	0.61 ± 0.26a	1.95 ± 0.60b
Mg-g	3.29 ± 0.98b	1.79 ± 1.02b	2.18 ± 0.88	1.25 ± 0.72a	2.56 ± 1.71a
HCO_3-s	11 ± 20a	10 ± 7a	33 ± 37	0 ± 0a	23 ± 17b
HCO_3-g	106 ± 45a	72 ± 20a	108 ± 23	43 ± 51a	79 ± 69a

groundwater. The budget of precipitation and run-off to surface water and groundwater input in fen 4 seems to have been favoured from the start, so no improvement is reached. The eco-hydrological setting of a fen appears to be very important. The phenomenon of shallow run-off of rainwater and the effect on the plant species composition has also been mentioned by Grootjans *et al.* (1988) for dunes and wet dune-slacks, so apparently occurs in other ecosystems.

The nutrient analyses of shallow fen-water indicated that phosphate may play a key role in limiting plant growth during restoration operations. Only a combined approach of sod removal and improved drainage reduces the P concentration for a longer period. If only sod removal were to be carried out, the invading *Sphagnum* would use this extra P-nutrient source. Together with the N-fertilisation by acid rain (40 kg ha^{-1} a^{-1}, Koerselman, 1989) an increased availability of P in a water layer just underneath the *Sphagnum* carpet creates a favourable aqua-culture solution for rooting plants or those with a good internal transport system (*e.g. Polytrichum*). Exudates of *Sphagnum* species are likely to hamper phanerogam growth (Verhoeven & Schmitz, 1991).

The vegetation survey did not show a recovery of the vegetation when only one restoration measure was carried out, which confirms results from other ecosystems, for example wet grasslands (Berendse *et al.*, 1992), while in the combination plots the cover of *Sphagnum* and *Polytrichum* did not return within

Table 4. Mean nutrient concentrations (mg l^{-1}; ± SD) in shallow surface water in experimental fen 1 in 1991. $n = 40$; P, sod removed; D, drainage; C, control and DP, combined sod removal and ditch/drainage. For situation see Figure 2. Different letters indicated significant differences.

Sites	NO_3	NH_4	PO_4
Combined (DP)	0.21 ± 0.15a	0.54 ± 0.28a	0.04 ± 0.025a
Sod (P)	0.40 ± 0.22a	0.83 ± 0.28a	0.05 ± 0.025a
Drain (D)	0.13 ± 0.09a	0.49 ± 0.11a	0.37 ± 0.24b
Control (C)	0.22 ± 0.19a	0.35 ± 0.20a	0.30 ± 0.13b

Table 5. Mean percentage coverage of some bryophytes and phanerogams in the research sites DP (sod removal + drainage) and P (sod removal) and control in fen 1. Vegetation relevées (1 m^2, 5 each) made before (August 1991) and 2 years (August 1993) after sod cutting.

	Sod removal (P)		Sod removal + drainage (DP)		Control	
	1991	1993	1991	1993	1991	1993
Sphagnum squarrosum	–	16.3	24.4	–	6.8	1.6
S. fallax	44.6	36.4	46.6	–	50.0	60.0
Polytrichum commune	51.3	43.4	12.8	–	26.4	31.2
Carex diandra	–	–	–	0.3	–	–
C. lasiocarpa	0.7	0.3	2.6	3.5	0.2	3.7
C. rostrata	0.1	0.3	0.3	1.7	3.1	1.1
Pedicularis palustris	–	–	–	0.9	–	–
Juncus subnodulosus	–	–	0.2	5.8	–	–
Equisetum fluviatile	0.2	0.6	0.5	2.2	0.2	0.2
Menyanthes trifoliata	0.1	–	0.9	2.0	0.4	3.1
Utricularia minor	–	–	–	62.5	0.1	–

the 2 years. Thus, chances for a successful restoration of rich-fen plant communities still exist and the first (re)appearance of rich-fen plant species, although with low percentages, are hopeful signs.

The study suggests that a lot of (financial) effort has to be invested in the maintenance and restoration of species-rich fen ecosystems in the Netherlands. Small-scale restoration to maintain a reservoir of species within an area combined with a total rejuvenation of succession to the initial stages of terrestrialisation seems to be the most fruitful approach. In this way species are conserved in nature reserves and all possibilities for developments in or outside reserves in the wet part of the Netherlands are maintained. Isolation is an important factor to take into account in nature management (Verkaar & van Wirdum, 1991; Berendse *et al.,* 1992; Kooijman, Beltman & Westhoff, 1993). Chances of attainability are much improved when mature and young ecosystems are in close contact through water flows or are adjacent so that management itself (through mowing equipment *etc.*) functions as an export factor for diaspores (Bakker, 1989). Isolation and ecohydrological research both point to the importance of the ecological position that fens occupy in the landscape, which will affect the success or failure of restoration projects.

ACKNOWLEDGEMENTS

The authors thank the Forestry Service for enthusiastic co-operation and R. Lamoree, N. v.d. Voort, P. Senderecki and C. Witsel for supplementary fieldwork. We are indebted to J.T.A. Verhoeven, R. Aerts and A.F.M. Meuleman for their critical remarks on the typescript.

REFERENCES

Anonymous (1990). *Nature Policy Plan (Natuurbeleidsplan).* Ministry of Agriculture, Nature and Fisheries. The Hague. 272pp.

Bakker, J.P. (1989). *Nature Management by Grazing and Cutting.* Kluwer Academic Publishers, Dordrecht.

Bakker, S.A. (1993). Spatial and dynamic modelling describing the terrestrialization of fen ecosystems. *Proceedings Intecol IV International Wetland Conference,* Ohio.

Beltman, B. & Rouwenhorst, G. (1991). Ecohydrology and fen plant distribution in the Vechtplassen area, the Netherlands. *Hydrological Basis of Ecologically Sound Management of Soil and Groundwater* (eds H.P. Nachtnebel & K. Kovar), pp. 199–214. IAHS publication **202**.

Beltman, B. & Rouwenhorst, G. (1993). Impact on soil fertility by replacement of hydrologically different water types. *Hydrological, Chemical and Biological Processes of Transformation and Transport of Contaminants in Aquatic Environment.* (ed. N. Peters), pp. 187–201. IAHS-Publication **212**.

Beltman, B. & van den Broek, T. (1993). The acidification of calcareous fens: a study of curative measures. *Landschap,* **10**, 17–33.

Berendse, F., Oomes, M.J.M., Altena, H.J. & Elberse, W.Th. (1992). Experiments on the restoration of species-rich meadows in the Netherlands. *Biological Conservation,* **62**, 59–65.

Bowden, R.D. (1991). Inputs, outputs and accumulation of nitrogen in an early successional moss (*Polytrichum*) ecosystem. *Ecological Monographs,* **6**, 207–223.

Boyer, M.L.H. & Wheeler, B.D. (1989). Vegetation patterns in spring-fed calcareous fens: calcite precipitation and constraints on fertility. *Journal of Ecology,* **77**, 597–609.

Grootjans, A.P. (1985). *Changes of groundwater regime in wet meadows.* PhD thesis University of Groningen, the Netherlands.

Grootjans, A.P., Engelmoer, M., Hendriksma, P & Westhoff, V. (1988). Vegetation dynamics in a wet dune slack I: Rare species decline on the Wadden island of Schiermonnikoog in the Netherlands. *Acta Botanica Neerlandica,* **37**, 265–278.

Heukels, H. & van der Meijden, R. (1983). *Flora van Nederland*. Wolters-Noordhoff. Groningen.

Jermy, A.C. & Tutin, T.G. (1982). *Sedges of the British Isles*. Botanical Society of the British Isles. London.

Kemmers, R.H. (1986). Calcium as hydrochemical characteristic for ecological states. *Ekologia* (CSSR), **5(3)**, 271–282.

Koerselman, W. (1989). Groundwater and surface water hydrology of a small groundwater fed fen. *Wetland Ecology and Management*, **1**, 31–43.

Kooijman, A.M. (1993). *Changes in the bryophyte layer of rich fens as controlled by acidification and eutrophication*. PhD thesis, Utrecht University, the Netherlands.

Kooijman, A.M., Beltman, B. & Westhoff, V. (1993). Extinction and reintroduction of *Scorpidium scorpioides* in a rich-fen spring site in the Netherlands. *Biological Conservation*, **69**, 87–97.

SAS (1985). *SAS/STAT Guide for Personal Computers*. SAS Inst. Cary. NC-USA.

Sjörs, H. (1950). On the relation between vegetation and electrolytes in North Swedish mire waters. *Oikos*, **2**, 241–259.

Succow, M. (1989). *Landschaftsökologische Moorkunde*. G.Fisher Verlag Jena.

Touw, A. & Rubers, W.V. (1989). *De Nederlandse Bladmossen. Flora en Verspreidingsatlas van de Nederlandse Musci*. KNNV. Heiloo. The Netherlands.

van Wirdum, G. (1991). *Vegetation and hydrology of floating rich fens*. PhD Thesis Amsterdam, the Netherlands.

Verhoeven, J.T.A., Koerselman, W. & Beltman, B. (1988). The vegetation of fens in relation to their hydrology and nutrient dynamics. *Vegetation of Inland Waters* (ed. J.J. Symoens), pp. 249–282. *Handbook of Vegetation Science* **15**,. Kluwer Academic Publishers, Dordrecht.

Verhoeven, J.T.A. & Schmitz, M.B. (1991). Control of plant growth by nitrogen and phosphorus in mesotrophic fens. *Biogeochemistry*, **12**, 135–148.

Verkaar, H.J.P.A. & van Wirdum, G. (1991). (Her-)introductie: redding of face-lift van de natuur. *De Levende Natuur*, **92**:196–200.

19 The Ombrogenous Bog Environment

M. C. F. PROCTOR

Department of Biological Sciences, Hatherly Laboratories, Prince of Wales Road, University of Exeter, Exeter, EX4 4PS, UK

SUMMARY

1. Ombrogenous bogs depend on direct atmospheric inputs for water and solutes. They occur in cool temperate regions, mainly between latitudes 45° and 65°, with annual precipitation exceeding evaporation and a summer precipitation deficit < 100–150 mm.

2. *Raised bogs* occupy flat sites (*e.g.* infilled lake basins, flood plains, coastal flats), mainly within the cultural landscape; *blanket bogs,* ollowing the contours of the land, occur where summer precipitation deficit is < *c.* 25 mm, but the two types intergrade.

3. The chemical composition of surface water, especially for cations, approximates to the average composition of the local rainwater, but concentrated owing to evaporation.

4. The total of strong-acid anions (in equivalents) is always less than the total of cations. This 'anion deficit' is made up by the organic anions of the dissolved organic matter (humic substances) which account for much of the acidity in bogs.

5. Most of the cations in ombrogenous bogs are associated with the peat, which behaves as an acid cation exchanger. Divalent ions are held more strongly than univalent ions; there are *c.* 10–20 times the univalent ions and 50–100 times the divalent ions on the exchange sites as in solution in the same volume of water.

6. Substantial temporal variations in ionic concentrations reflect the interplay of precipitation and evaporation, ion exchange, and oxidation–reduction processes.

7. The peat of intact bogs is differentiated into a surface *acrotelm* of high hydraulic conductivity, within which the fluctuations of the water table and most chemical and biological activity takes place, passing downwards into the denser, more uniform, less conductive, permanently waterlogged and relatively inactive *catotelm* which forms most of the depth of the peat.

8. Bog plants typically grow slowly and do not respond vigorously to added nutrients, indicating adaptation to low nutrient supply. Nitrogen is probably generally limiting in unpolluted areas, and phosphorus in regions of high atmospheric nitrogen deposition. Vascular species in general take up ammonium- or organic nitrogen; *Sphagnum* probably gets most of its supply from atmospheric nitrate deposition.

9. The uptake and cycling of nutrients, and productivity of the dominant vascular plants, may be enhanced where drainage from the peat is concentrated into regions of rapid water flow.

10. Bogs and forests differ markedly in microclimate; radiative energy exchanges are proportionately more important in bogs, and convective exchange with the atmosphere is more important in forests. This has important consequences for geographical distribution, and in determining conditions for other organisms within the bog habitat.

Restoration of Temperate Wetlands. Edited by B.D. Wheeler, S.C. Shaw, W.J. Fojt and R.A. Robertson
© 1995 John Wiley & Sons Ltd.

INTRODUCTION

By definition, ombrogenous bogs are wholly dependent on atmospheric inputs of water and nutrients. They can occur only in regions with an annual excess of precipitation over evaporation. The accumulation of ombrogenous peat, which raises the surface above the surrounding drainage, isolating it from inputs of mineral-rich telluric water, depends on the annual production of organic matter exceeding decay. Typical ombrogenous bogs are concentrated in the cool temperate zone between latitudes 50° and 70° N in Eurasia and western North America, and about latitude 40°–55° N in eastern North America (Kats, 1958, 1959; Frenzel, 1983; Figure 1). There are more isolated occurrences at lower latitudes; thus, raised bogs are found locally around the foothills and in valleys of the Alps, and there is blanket bog on mountains in northern Japan. In the Southern Hemisphere there is much less land at suitable latitudes, but ombrogenous bogs cover substantial areas in the Magellanic region of South America (about latitude 53°–55° S; Pisano, 1983) and occur locally in the South Island of New Zealand (about latitude 45° S; Mark, Rawson & Wilson, 1979; Campbell, 1983).

Ombrogenous bogs may be divided loosely into two major types. The most widespread type are *raised bogs*, which typically develop over infilled lake-basins, or on broad river flood plains or coastal flats. They form gently domed masses of

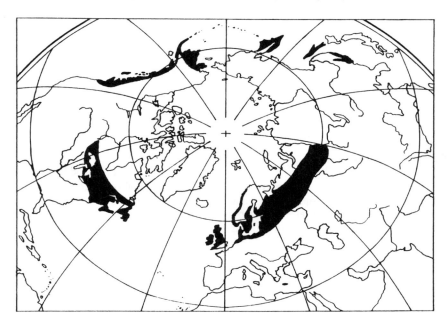

Figure 1. Main geographical area of ombrogenous bogs in the Northern Hemisphere (after Frenzel, 1983). Ombrogenous bogs occur locally in upland and mountain areas to the south and essentially ombrotrophic conditions exist within many peatlands to the north of the limits shown.

peat, typically tens or even hundreds of hectares in area, often rising 5–10 m above the nearly level water table of the surrounding country. The southern limit of raised bogs is probably determined by the maximum summer water deficit (some 100–150 mm) at which net accumulation of peat can still take place. This limit is likely to be more critical for initial establishment than for maintenance of a bog once a substantial thickness of peat has built up. Southern England is close to this limit. There were formerly large raised bogs in the Somerset Levels and around the western margins of the Cambridgeshire Fens, but there seems to be little or no tendency to ombrogenous peat development in even the most apparently suitable of the New Forest or Dorset valley bogs. Raised bog was formerly very extensive in the Shropshire–Cheshire–Lancashire plain, and south of the Humber estuary; substantial areas survive of the once larger tracts of bog around the head of Morecambe Bay and the Solway Firth, and in the Forth valley north of Glasgow. Great tracts of country were formerly occupied by raised bogs in north-west Germany and neighbouring parts of the Netherlands, as they still are in Sweden and Finland. In North America, raised bogs are locally extensive from eastern Canada and the north-eastern United States across the northern Great Lakes region to Minnesota. Generally, raised bogs lie within regions where the climax vegetation would otherwise be forest; they often form clearly discrete elements within a landscape dominated by other kinds of vegetation.

In cool moist oceanic climates ombrogenous bog can develop over any surface that is not too steep, forming extensive *blanket bogs* which follow the topography of the underlying land. In Britain and Ireland, most blanket bogs are in the uplands, or in the north and west, with summer water deficits of less than 25 mm (Green, 1964). Some areas of bog, notably the Caithness Flows, lie outside this limit, and low summer precipitation deficit undoubtedly interacts with topography in determining the geographical limits within which ombrogenous peat development can take place. In Europe, typical blanket bog is limited to Britain, Ireland and a narrow coastal strip of Norway, though some peaty plateaux in the Central European mountains might be included in this category as well. In North America, blanket bog is widespread in Newfoundland, where fogwater deposition probably provides an important part of its water supply (Price, 1992a, b), and in the Pacific north-west (Vitt *et al.*, 1990). Across the Bering Strait, blanket bogs occur in Kamchatka, and on Sakhalin and neighbouring parts of the East Asian mainland.

In fact, although 'typical' examples of 'raised bog' and 'blanket bog' can appear strikingly different, no absolute line can be drawn between them and in oceanic districts sites can be found which show all gradations between the two. Their apparent distinctness is largely an artefact of the cultural development of the landscape by man. Raised-bog-like peat domes occur on more or less flat sites within blanket bog areas, as on the Silver Flowe in Galloway and elsewhere in western Scotland. The 'ridge raised bogs' of the central plain of Ireland and elsewhere (Moore & Bellamy, 1974) spread from the basins in which they were initiated to engulf the intervening mineral ground. In the Roman or mediaeval landscape it would have been easy to see the vast bogs of Ireland, the Cheshire and Lancashire mosses and Humberside moors, the bogs of the north-west German plain and the Swedish lowlands, and the Caithness and Sutherland 'flow country', all as parts of a north-west European ombrogenous bog continuum – alternating with forest and cultivated land, and increasingly replacing them towards the Atlantic seaboard. Ecologically all ombrogenous bogs have important features in common, and many of the characteristic ombrogenous bog species occur throughout. The aim of this paper is to outline some of the main features of ombrogenous bogs as an environment for plants.

SOME RELATIONSHIPS BETWEEN RAINWATER, SURFACE-WATER AND PEAT CHEMISTRY ON OMBROGENOUS BOGS

Rainwater and surface water

At a first approximation, the average chemical composition of water from pools or established sampling pits in the bog surface is very much what would be expected from the average chemical composition of the local rainwater, but somewhat more concentrated owing to evaporation. The solutes in rainwater come from two principal sources, sea spray entrained in the atmosphere as winds blow across the oceans, and blown dust and other material of terrestrial or pollutant origin. The influences of these different sources of dissolved materials is clearly seen in a principal components analysis (PCA) of the mean rainwater composition at the 59 sites in the UK from which regular analyses were made by the Warren Spring Laboratory from 1986 to 1988 (UKRGAR, 1990). A plot of the component loadings for the concentrations of the major ions shows the three ions which come predominantly from sea spray grouped tightly together at one side of the diagram, while the ions derived mainly or entirely from terrestrial and pollutant sources form a loose cluster at the other (Figure 2). The relative importance of these two sources varies from place to place. Near the sea, marine-derived solutes are dominant, but in dry mid-continental regions the solutes in rainwater are mainly of terrestrial origin. The contribution of pollutants varies with the proximity and nature of industrial and other sources.

Table 1 compares the major-ion composition of some bog waters with rainwater from the same or a comparable site, and it is apparent that the major cations and chloride are generally present in similar proportions (Proctor, 1992). Because of the oceanic position of the British Isles, bog waters in Britain and Ireland are generally dominated by sodium and chloride, and on a molar basis magnesium almost always exceeds calcium. There are some significant differences between bog waters and rainwaters, especially among the anions (see below). Sulphate is often present in lower, and occasionally in higher, concentrations than would be expected from the rainwater input. Nitrate and ammonium are present in substantial concentrations in rainwater (UKRGAR, 1990), but are typically present in much lower concentrations, and sometimes undetectable, in ombrogenous bog

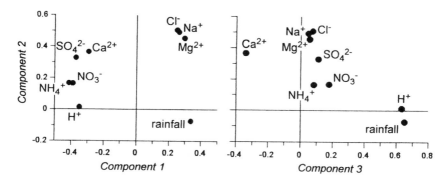

Figure 2. Principal components analysis of precipitation-weighted mean ionic concentrations in rainwater at 59 sites in the UK, from the Department of the Environment Secondary Network data for 1986–88 (UKRGAR, 1990): coefficients (loadings) of ions on Components 1–3. The marine-derived ions form a cluster on the right-hand side of the plot of Component 2 against Component 1 (left), loosely correlated with the total amount of rainfall. Pollution-derived ions are grouped on the left of the diagram, forming a loose cluster, which reflects the similar geographical distribution of their sources; their *concentrations* tend to be inversely related to rainfall, but an analysis of total deposition would show a positive relation with rainfall. Calcium, also mainly of terrestrial origin, plots close to the pollutant-derived ions here (the areas of highest deposition are associated with industrial activity and have a broadly similar distribution to the major sources of pollutant acidity), but separates from them, and is inversely correlated with H^+, in the plot of Component 2 against Component 3 (right).

surface waters. Potassium was unfortunately not included in the published Warren Spring rainwater analyses, but, from the analyses that are available, its concentration in rainwater appears to be rather variable. It is certainly variable in bog waters, probably because much of the movement of potassium takes place by movement of organisms, and the data give some support to the idea that potassium in bog surface water can be significantly depleted by plant uptake during the growing season. The ionic balance of ombrogenous bog waters generally shows a substantial deficit of inorganic strong-acid anions (Malmer, 1962a; Gorham *et al.*, 1985). This *anion deficit* is made up by organic acids derived from the organic matter of the peat. The dissolved organic matter (DOM) in the water represents in part the organic anions making up the charge balance with the cations; a further part represents undissociated organic acids (Urban, Bayley & Eisenreich, 1989; Figure 3). An additional fraction of the DOM is complexed with ferric iron and aluminium. Most of the aluminium in ombrogenous bog waters, and almost all of the iron, is bound to the DOM in this way.

Table 1. Major-ion composition of rainwaters (1986–88 means (UKRGAR, 1990)) and ombrogenous-bog surface waters from four parts of Britain, and comparisons with the proportions of major ions in seawater. Measured ionic concentrations (μequiv. l^{-1}) in **bold**; rainwater sites and data in *italic*. Carn a'Ghlinne is an unpolluted blanket-bog site in the NW Highlands of Scotland (rainfall 1861 mm a^{-1}); means of four samples collected by Dr E. Wilson, May 1992. Malham Tarn Moss, a raised bog in the Yorkshire Pennines, receives moderate acidity, SO_4^{2-}, NO_3^- and NH_4^+ (380 m a.s.l.; rainfall 1282 mm a^{-1}); means, seven sampling dates, March 1992 to March 1993. Thorne Moors, a cut-over raised bog near Doncaster, lies within the area of Britain with the highest rainwater concentrations of all the major pollutant ions (3 m a.s.l.; rainfall 568 mm a^{-1}); means for Noda 2–4 from Smart *et al.* (1989). The blanket bog above Plym Head on Dartmoor in SW England receives moderate NO_3^- and NH_4^+, but little acidity or SO_4^{2-} pollution (460 m a.s.l.; rainfall *c.*1750 mm a^{-1}); means, seven sampling dates, March 1992–March 1993. Average seawater contains (equiv. l^{-1}): 0.020 Ca^{2+}; 0.207 Mg^{2+}; 0.018 K^+; 0.851 Na^+; 0.103 SO_4^{2-}. The area of eastern England including the Jenny Hurn rainfall site and Thorne Moors has a substantial atmospheric input of non-marine Cl^-.

	H^+	Ca^{2+}	Mg^{2+}	K^+	Na^+	Cl^-	SO_4^{2-}	NO_3^-
Beinn Eighe	*12*	*8*	*34*	*–*	*150*	*178*	*29*	*5*
rel. to Cl^-	*0.07*	*0.05*	*0.19*	*–*	*0.84*	*1.00*	*0.16*	*0.028*
rel. to seawater	*–*	*1.22*	*0.92*	*–*	*0.99*	*1.00*	*1.58*	*–*
Carn a'Ghlinne	48	16	63	11	277	293	16	0.7
rel. to Cl^-	0.16	0.06	0.22	0.04	0.95	1.00	0.06	0.003
rel. to seawater	–	1.49	1.04	2.11	1.11	1.00	0.53	–
Malham Tarn	*31*	*21*	*23*	*–*	*94*	*118*	*60*	*22*
rel. to Cl^-	*0.26*	*0.18*	*0.20*	*–*	*0.80*	*1.00*	*0.51*	*0.19*
rel. to seawater	*–*	*4.81*	*0.94*	*–*	*0.94*	*1.00*	*4.93*	*–*
Malham Tarn Moss	120	28	44	9	162	181	102	2.7
rel. to Cl^-	0.66	0.16	0.24	0.05	0.90	1.00	0.56	0.015
rel. to seawater	–	4.19	1.17	2.78	1.05	1.00	5.48	–
Jenny Hurn	*92*	*56*	*26*	*–*	*72*	*135*	*120*	*46*
rel. to Cl^-	*0.68*	*0.42*	*0.19*	*–*	*0.53*	*1.00*	*0.89*	*–*
rel. to seawater	*–*	*11.22*	*0.93*	*–*	*0.63*	*1.00*	*8.63*	*–*
Thorne Moors	158	228	180	32	216	349	146	8.3
rel. to Cl^-	0.45	0.65	0.52	0.09	0.62	1.00	0.42	0.006
rel. to seawater	–	27.03	2.49	5.11	0.73	1.00	4.06	–
Yarner Wood	*17*	*13*	*29*	*–*	*124*	*150*	*44*	*18*
rel. to Cl^-	*0.11*	*0.09*	*0.19*	*–*	*0.83*	*1.00*	*0.29*	*0.12*
rel. to seawater	*–*	*2.35*	*0.93*	*–*	*0.97*	*1.00*	*2.85*	*–*
Plym Head	50	20	50	8	205	229	36	0.2
rel. to Cl^-	0.22	0.09	0.22	0.04	0.90	1.00	0.16	0.001
rel. to seawater	–	2.35	1.05	1.94	1.05	1.00	1.52	–

Temporal variations in water chemistry: water–peat relationships

The chemical composition of bog surface waters shows considerable temporal variations (Proctor, 1994). For a satisfactory understanding of these it is necessary to consider the exchangeable ions on the peat. The organic matter of which ombrogenous peats are mainly composed is a complex material derived from partial breakdown of plant constituents. It carries ionisable carboxyl and phenolic groups and behaves as a mixture of weak acids with a mean pK_a typically between 3.5 and 5.0 (Tipping, Backes & Hurley, 1988; Tipping & Hurley, 1988; Urban *et al.*, 1989), and is a major source of the acidity of ombrogenous bogs (Clymo, 1984b; Gorham *et al.*, 1985). It functions as a cation exchange medium. The quantity of cations associated with the exchange sites in a given volume of peat much exceeds those in the same volume of water. The affinity of cations for the exchange sites increases with valency. The peat:water ratio for monovalent ions is often in the range 10–20, and that for divalent ions 50–100. The partitioning of monovalent and divalent ions between water and peat varies with changing concentration in the water. Divalent ions displace monovalent ions from the exchange sites most strongly at low concentrations; at high concentrations proportionately more of the divalent ions appear in the solution. If $\log\Sigma$(divalent cations) is plotted against $\log\Sigma$(monovalent cations) round the season, the point lie close to a line with gradient 2.0, as would be predicted by Schofield's 'Ratio Law' for soils (Schofield, 1947; Schofield & Taylor, 1955). Equations governing these relationships are given by Talibudeen (1981).

There is a rather general tendency for concentrations of the major ions in bog surface waters to be higher in summer than in winter, an expected consequence of greater evaporation during the summer months (Figure 4). For reasons just outlined, the cations all tend to vary together, and the divalent cations in general show greater temporal changes of concentration than the monovalent cations. The other obvious source of variation in surface-water composition is the varying composition of the rainwater input. The interaction of varying cation inputs with the exchangeable ions stored in the peat can have consequences which are at first sight surprising. Thus, high sodium inputs in rain during stormy weather in winter lead to a peak not only of sodium, but of calcium and magnesium as well. The hydrogen ion would be expected to share in general rises of cation concentration, so pH tends to fall when (for whatever reason) cation concentrations are high, but pH is affected by other factors too.

Acrotelm and catotelm; biological and chemical activity near the bog surface

Ingram (1978, 1983), Clymo (1978, 1984a) and others have emphasised the functional differentiation of bog peats into an 'active layer' or *acrotelm* typically 25–30 cm thick and at least intermittently aerobic, overlying the *catotelm*, which is permanently waterlogged and generally occupies most of the depth of the peat. Clearly this boundary cannot be absolutely sharp; Ivanov (1981) defines it as lying at the mean minimum level of the water table in summer. The acrotelm is the

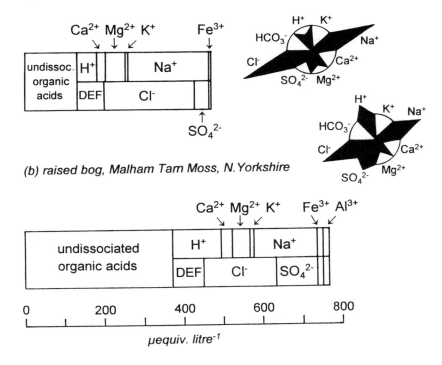

Figure 3. Major-ion composition of ombrogenous bog waters from a blanket bog and a raised bog in the UK: Maucha diagrams, and block diagrams illustrating cation–anion balance and the role of dissolved humic substances. In the Maucha diagrams, total area is proportional to total ionic concentration. The block diagrams follow the conventions of Urban, Bayley & Eisenreich (1989); the quantity of dissolved organic acids has been estimated approximately from optical absorbance at 320 nm using the regression equation for dissolved organic carbon (DOC) of Gorham *et al.* (1985) and assuming a charge density of 15 μequiv. mg^{-1} DOC (Urban *et al.*, 1989). Al^{3+} and Fe^{3+} are mostly complexed with dissolved organic matter. The diagrams are based on the same data as Table 1.

Figure 4. Temporal variation in the concentrations (μequiv. litre^{-1}) of some ions in ombrogenous bog waters at Plym Head, Dartmoor, Devon, and Malham Tarn Moss, North Yorkshire, March 1992 to September 1993. The early part of the summer was very dry at Malham Tarn in 1992 and at Plym Head in 1993; stormy westerly weather brought high Na$^+$ and Cl$^-$ inputs in the north of England in early 1993. Error bars are standard deviations, usually of six samples.

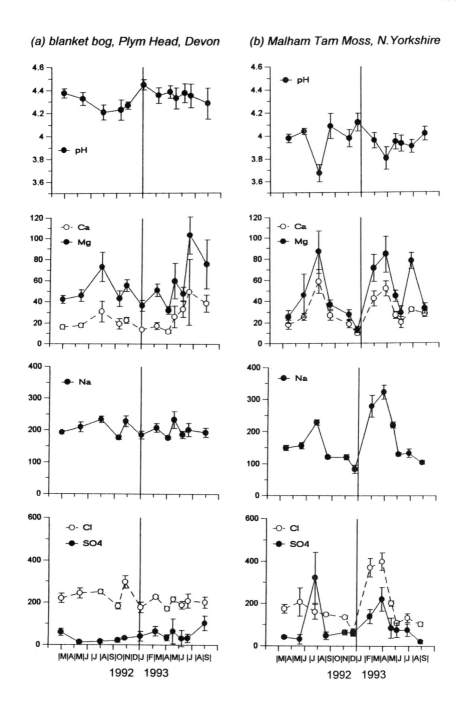

(a) blanket bog, Plym Head, Devon

(b) Malham Tarn Moss, N.Yorkshire

region within which the organic matter produced by the vegetation on the surface is progressively broken down to form peat of a greater or lesser degree of humification which is added to the surface of the catotelm as the bog grows. Decay rates of organic materials decrease down the profile to very low values once anaerobic levels are reached (Doyle & Dowding, 1990). As Ivanov emphasises, the hydraulic conductivity declines by a factor of 100–1000 (two or three orders of magnitude) between the surface and the base of the acrotelm. This has a strongly self-regulating effect on the depth of the water table (Malmer, 1962a; Ivanov, 1981). The acrotelm is thus the region within which fluctuations of the water table take place, and it is the seat of most of the chemical and biological activity in the peat.

Chemical transformations involving oxidation and reduction are prominent in the acrotelm. Much of the sulphate entering the system in rainfall is reduced to sulphides, in part incorporated into the peat organic matter, in part precipitated as FeS (Brown, 1985, 1986; Brown & Macqueen, 1985). The reduction process consumes hydrogen ions and is a major reason for the high pH values usually associated with periods of high water table (Hemond, 1980; Urban, Eisenreich & Gorham, 1987). Conversely, when the water table falls, sulphides are re-oxidised, leading to a rise in sulphate and a fall in pH; in extreme cases this can lead to autumn flushes of sulphuric acid in drainage water from bogs, which may result in severe fish kills. Bog surfaces are efficient sinks for nitrate. Mean nitrate concentrations in rainfall over ombrogenous bogs in Britain vary over a range of 1:10, from around 4 µequiv. l^{-1} in unpolluted areas of the West Highlands to around 40 µequiv. l^{-1} on the North York Moors and South Pennines. But it is rare to measure concentrations in bog surface waters above 1 µequiv. l^{-1}, except during near-freezing periods in winter, which will inhibit most biological activity Any nitrate reaching anaerobic levels in the peat would be expected to be quickly denitrified (Dickinson, 1983). Urban, Eisenreich & Bayley (1988) concluded from experiments in Minnesota and Ontario that most of the rainwater nitrate is taken up by the *Sphagnum* carpet, leaving little to reach anaerobic levels where it might undergo dissimilatory reduction to ammonium or denitrification, and their measured denitrification rates were low. Many bogs in polluted areas of Britain have, at best, an intermittent *Sphagnum* cover, so the fate of nitrate may be different here.

The solubility of several heavy metals, notably iron and manganese, is critically dependent on redox conditions. This has implications for plant nutrition, as well as for the relocation of these elements within the acrotelm (Damman, 1978, 1986). The acrotelm is the layer in which concentration by evaporation and dilution by rain are most immediately and directly felt; it is also the rooting zone for the plant cover. In general it is the acrotelm from which nutrient elements are removed by plant uptake, and to which they are returned by decomposition. Tightly-cycled nutrients will be concentrated in the plants (Chapin, van Cleve & Chapin, 1979; Jonasson & Chapin, 1985; Malmer & Wallén, 1986; Malmer, 1988, 1992) and transfers between them occur in the acrotelm; chemical analyses of water expressed from peats in the upper layers of the acrotelm reflect the complexity of the processes taking place (Malmer, 1962b, 1992; Gies & Lötschert, 1973; Clymo, 1983), but we are far from understanding them fully.

In profiles through bog hummocks in various parts of Sweden, Malmer & Holm (1984) showed that the C:N quotient tends to fall progressively with depth from values of 100 or more at the surface to values typically in the range 20–35 at the base of the acrotelm. This is essentially due to oxidation of organic carbon by micro-organisms. However, as Damman (1988) has emphasised, micro-organisms may also take up and thus immobilise inorganic nitrogen. He postulated that the final C:N quotient may be determined by limitations on microbial activity imposed by other nutrients, especially phosphorus. Certainly, acid soils including bog peats appear to be efficient sinks for rainwater ammonium inputs (Fowler, Duyzer & Baldocchi, 1991), and this is likely to be at least partly due to microbial uptake.

The acrotelm is thus a layer within which a wide diversity of processes is taking place, some of which are of great importance in, *e.g.*, plant nutrition. However, it is a thin layer, and for some purposes, as in considering the overall carbon or element balance of a bog, we can treat the acrotelm as a 'black box' and consider only its inputs (organic production, and rainwater and other materials from the atmosphere) and outputs (peat and the solutes in drainage water). The catotelm is, of course, not wholly inert, as Clymo (1984a) has shown, but processes in the catotelm are less diverse, and much slower.

THE MINERAL NUTRITION OF BOG PLANTS

Ombrogenous bogs are obviously a 'difficult' habitat for plant growth. All but a limited number of species are excluded by the prevailing high water table, low pH, and the low concentrations of many essential nutrients. The rather limited available data suggest that primary production of ombrogenous bog vegetation is commonly in the range 250–600 g m^{-2} a^{-1} (Bradbury & Grace, 1983), which is low compared with fertile temperate grasslands or forests. However, this range is far from being so low as to be unique to ombrogenous bogs.

Ombrogenous bog species often show rather little response in nutrient-addition experiments on ombrogenous peat (Figure 5). This undoubtedly in part reflects the inherently slow growth rate and efficient nutrient retention characteristic of wild species adapted to nutrient-poor habitats (Chapin, van Cleve & Chapin, 1979; Chapin, 1980; Jonasson & Chapin, 1985; Malmer & Wallén, 1986; Ohlson & Malmer, 1990). Of the essential macronutrients, calcium and magnesium are probably not a problem for the species adapted to conditions on ombrotrophic peat. Calcium is only required in rather small amounts for cell function; it is one of the paradoxes of plant nutrition that the concentrations of calcium and phosphorus in the environment and in the cell sap are approximately reversed. Potassium is required in relatively large amounts by all plants. The amount present in the vegetation cover can be an appreciable fraction of the amount present in the acrotelm peat, so potassium may be limiting on some bogs (Goodman & Perkins,

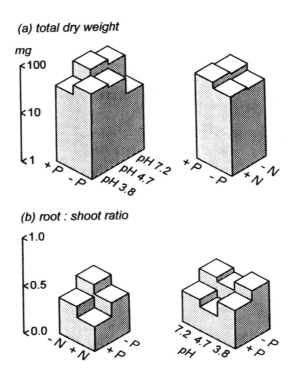

Figure 5. Growth responses from a nutrient-addition experiment with *Eriophorum angustifolium* seedlings on ombrogenous bog peat from Malham Tarn Moss, North Yorkshire, April–July 1985. Nitrogen (as NH_4NO_3) and phosphorus (as NaH_2PO_4) were added factorially at 3 initial pH levels obtained by adding 1, 3 and 10 g $CaCO_3$ per litre of sieved peat. Dry weight shows a significant but small positive response to P (P < 0.05) and is greatest at the intermediate Ca/pH (P < 0.05), with a marked interaction between these variables (P < 0.01); there is a very small and non-significant positive response to N. Root:shoot ratio is strongly and significantly depressed by both N and P (P < 0.01), but is not significantly affected by pH.

1968a, b), but is certainly not so on others (Hayati & Proctor, 1991). Iron and probably all of the micronutrients are generally available in adequate amounts. Sulphur is unlikely to be limiting in oceanic regions where there is a sulphate input from the sea-spray component in rain, or in areas with atmospheric pollution from burning of fossil fuels. Experimental studies generally indicate limitation in the field by either nitrogen or phosphorus; in some extreme cases low pH may in itself be a cause of slow growth.

Mineralisation of nitrogen on ombrogenous bogs results in release of ammonium ions. Ombrogenous bog peats do not nitrify, and in general the vascular plants growing on them show at most low levels of nitrate reductase activity. The presumption is that these plants take up nitrogen mainly as ammonium ions (Lee & Stewart, 1978), but mycorrhizal species such as *Calluna vulgaris* acquire organic nitrogen through their symbiotic fungi (Read, 1991) and, as Chapin, Moilanen & Kielland (1988) have recently shown, the non-mycorrhizal *Eriophorum vaginatum* may take up nitrogen in the field largely in the form of free amino-acids. *Sphagnum* species regularly show considerable nitrate reductase activity, especially following induction by nitrate inputs in rain, and probably obtain much or most of their nitrogen supply as nitrate (Press & Lee, 1982; Woodin, Press & Lee, 1985; Press, Woodin & Lee, 1986). Rudolph & Voigt (1986) found that *S. magellanicum* grew better and maintained a higher chlorophyll content and more normal morphology when nitrogen was supplied predominantly as nitrate than when it was supplied predominantly as ammonium.

In unpolluted areas, inputs of both nitrogen and phosphorus are small, but in such areas it is probably usually nitrogen supply that limits growth (Shaver, Chapin & Gartner, 1986; Aerts, Wallén & Malmer, 1992). In Sweden (as in Britain) the input of inorganic nitrogen from the atmosphere differs by a factor of 10 between the unpolluted north, and the much more heavily populated agricultural and industrial south. The fertiliser experiments of Aerts *et al.* showed that *Sphagnum* growth is limited by nitrogen in north Sweden, but by phosphorus in the south; a similar contrast would certainly be found in Britain and Ireland, between the unpolluted bogs of the north and west and areas such as the South Pennines with substantial rainwater and dry-deposited inputs of nitrate (from vehicle emissions and industrial sources), and of ammonium ions (largely from intensive agriculture). Even in west Wales and in south-west England nitrogen deposition is two or three times that in the least polluted areas (UKRGAR, 1990).

It has been suggested that the availability of nutrients to plants on ombrogenous peats, and the character of the vegetation, may be strongly influenced by lateral movement of water (Kulczynski, 1949; Ingram, 1967). Molecular diffusion rates in water are slow, and could be expected to limit nutrient uptake under stationary conditions (Nye & Tinker, 1977). However, over a uniform ombrotrophic bog plane, net uptake must on average be within the continuing local input from the atmosphere, and lateral water movement cannot make available more than this input. Where drainage on the bog surface is concentrated into 'water tracks', nutrients from a larger area are potentially available. Chapin *et al.* (1988) found a 2.5-fold increase in productivity in water tracks in an Alaskan tussock tundra compared with non-track areas, due almost entirely to a 10-fold greater production of the dominant *Eriophorum vaginatum*. The water tracks showed more rapid cycling of nitrogen and phosphorus; observed lateral flow-rates of about 0.6 cm h^{-1} are six and eight times as fast as diffusion rates for phosphate and ammonium, respectively. Water tracks on bogs in the British Isles often show similar features but have not been analysed experimentally. These water-track effects are different in kind from those produced by the influence of solutes derived from neighbouring mineral ground, which commonly have little influence on productivity, but profound effects on species composition.

CONCLUSION

In this paper I have concentrated particularly on water and peat chemistry as aspects of the ombrogenous bog environment because these embody some particularly obvious constraints underlying the special character of bog vegetation. I have taken for granted the wetness of bogs, but that is of course a prerequisite for the growth of the plants and as a milieu for the chemical and biological processes discussed here; hydrological characteristics of bogs are considered elsewhere in this volume (Bragg, this volume). Because of the low stature of the dominant vascular plants and the important role of *Sphagnum* carpets, microclimatic conditions for plant growth in bogs are different in important respects from those in most dry-ground communities. All the energy exchanges take place at or within a decimetre or two of the ground surface and, compared with a forest canopy, boundary-layer resistances to convective and evaporative heat transfer are rather high. For the plant cover lying within this zone the effective environment thus depends more on radiation balance and less on air temperature and windspeed than that of a forest, which is more closely coupled to the temperature of the air (Jarvis & McNaughton, 1986; Monteith & Unsworth, 1990). The microclimate within bog vegetation is less sensitive to latitude and altitude than the larger-scale climate experienced by forests. This must be a further factor in the relative uniformity of bogs and the wide distribution of many of the species within them.

REFERENCES

Aerts, R., Wallén, B. & Malmer, N. (1992). Growth-limiting nutrients in *Sphagnum*-dominated bogs subject to low and high atmospheric nitrogen supply. *Journal of Ecology*, **80**, 131–140.

Bradbury, I.K. & Grace, J. (1983). Primary production in wetlands. *Ecosystems of the World, 4A. Mires: Swamp, Bog, Fen and Moor; General Studies* (ed. A.J.P. Gore), pp. 285–310. Elsevier, Amsterdam.

Brown, K.A. (1985). Sulphur distribution and metabolism in waterlogged peat. *Soil Biology and Biochemistry*, **17**, 39–45.

Brown, K.A. (1986). Formation of organic sulphur in anaerobic peat. *Soil Biology and Biochemistry*, **18**, 131–140.

Brown, K.A. & Macqueen, J.F. (1985). Sulphate uptake from surface water by peat. *Soil Biology and Biochemistry*, **17**, 411–420.

Campbell, E.O. (1983). Mires of Australasia. *Ecosystems of the World, 4B. Mires: Swamp, Bog, Fen and Moor; Regional Studies* (ed. A.J.P. Gore), pp. 153–180. Elsevier, Amsterdam.

Chapin, F.S. (1980) The mineral nutrition of wild plants. *Annual Review of Ecology and Systematics*, **11**, 233–260.

Chapin, F.S., Fetcher, N., Kielland, K., Everett, K.R. & Linkins, A.E. (1988a). Productivity and nutrient cycling of Alaskan tundra: enhancement by flowing soil water. *Ecology*, **69**, 693–702.

Chapin, F.S., Moilanen, L. & Kielland, K. (1988b). Preferential use of organic nitrogen for growth by a non-mycorrhizal arctic sedge. *Nature*, **361**, 150–153.

Chapin, F.S., van Cleve, K. & Chapin, M.C. (1979). Soil temperature and nutrient cycling in tussock growth form of *Eriophorum vaginatum* L. *Journal of Ecology*, **67**, 169–189.

Clymo, R.S. (1978). A model of peat growth. *Production Ecology of British Moors and Montane Grasslands* (eds O.W. Heal & D.F. Perkins). *Ecological Studies* 27, pp. 187–223. Springer Verlag, Berlin.

Clymo, R.S. (1983). Peat. *Ecosystems of the World, 4A. Mires: Swamp, Bog, Fen and Moor; General Studies* (ed. A.J.P. Gore), pp.159–224. Elsevier, Amsterdam.

Clymo, R.S. (1984a). The limits to peat growth. *Philosophical Transactions of the Royal Society, London*, B **303**, 605–654.

Clymo, R.S. (1984b). *Sphagnum*-dominated peat bog: a naturally acid ecosystem. *Philosophical Transactions of the Royal Society, London*, B **305**, 487–499.

Damman, A.W.H. (1978). Distribution and movement of elements in ombrotrophic peat bogs. *Oikos*, **30**, 480–495.

Damman, A.W.H. (1986). Hydrology, development, and biogeochemistry of ombrogenous peat bogs with special reference to nutrient relocation in a western Newfoundland bog. *Canadian Journal of Botany*, **64**, 384–394.

Damman, A.W.H. (1988). Regulation of nitrogen removal and retention in *Sphagnum* bogs and other peatlands. *Oikos*, **51**, 291–305.

Dickinson, C.H. (1983). Micro-organisms in peatlands. *Ecosystems of the World, 4A. Mires: Swamp, Bog, Fen and Moor; General Studies* (ed. A.J.P. Gore), pp. 225–245. Elsevier, Amsterdam.

Doyle, T & Dowding, P. (1990). Decomposition and aspects of the physical environment in the surface layers of Mongan Bog. *Ecology and Conservation of Irish Peatlands* (ed. G. Doyle), pp. 163–171. Royal Irish Academy, Dublin.

Fowler, D., Duyzer, J.H. & Baldocchi, D.D. (1991). Inputs of trace gases, particles and cloud droplets to terrestrial surfaces. *Proceedings of the Royal Society of Edinburgh*, **97B**, 35–59.

Frenzel, B. (1983). Mires – repositories of climatic information or self-perpetuating ecosystems? *Ecosystems of the World, 4A. Mires: Swamp, Bog, Fen and Moor; General Studies* (ed. A.J.P. Gore), pp. 225–245. Elsevier, Amsterdam.

Gies, T. & Lötschert, W. (1973). Untersuchungen über den Kationhaushalt im Hochmoor. II. Jahreszeitliche Veränderungen und Einfluß der *Sphagnum*-Vegetation. *Flora, Jena*, **162**, 244–268.

Goodman, G.T. & Perkins, D.F. (1968a). The role of mineral nutrients in *Eriophorum* communities. III. Growth response to added inorganic elements in two *E. vaginatum* communities. *Journal of Ecology*, **56**, 667–683.

Goodman, G.T. & Perkins, D.F. (1968b). The role of mineral nutrients in *Eriophorum* communities. IV. Potassium supply as a limiting factor in an *E. vaginatum* community. *Journal of Ecology*, **56**, 685–696.

Gorham, E., Eisenreich, S.J., Ford, J. & Santelmann, M.V. (1985). The chemistry of bog waters. *Chemical Processes in Lakes* (ed. W. Stumm), pp. 339–363. John Wiley, New York.

Green, F.H.W. (1964). A map of annual average potential water deficit in the British Isles. *Journal of Applied Ecology*, **1**, 151–158.

Hayati, A.A. & Proctor, M.C.F. (1991). Limiting nutrients in acid-mire vegetation: peat and plant analyses and experiments on plant responses to added nutrients. *Journal of Ecology*, **79**, 75–95.

Hemond, H.F. (1980). Biogeochemistry of Thoreau's Bog, Concord, Masachusetts. *Ecological Monographs*, **50**, 507–526.

Ingram, H.A.P. (1967). Problems of hydrology and plant distribution in mires. *Journal of Ecology*, **55**, 711–724.

Ingram, H.A.P. (1978). Soil layers in mires: function and terminology. *Journal of Soil Science*, **29**, 224–227.

Ingram, H.A.P. (1983). Hydrology. *Ecosystems of the World, 4A. Mires: Swamp, Bog, Fen and Moor; General Studies* (ed. A.J.P. Gore), pp. 67–158. Elsevier, Amsterdam.

Ivanov, K.E. (1981). *Water Movement in Mirelands* (trans. A. Thompson & H.A.P. Ingram). Academic Press, London.

Jarvis, P.G. & McNaughton, K.G. (1990). Stomatal control of transpiration. *Advances in Ecological Research*, **15**, 1–49.

Jonasson, S. & Chapin, F.S. (1985). Significance of sequential leaf development for nutrient balance of the cotton sedge, *Eriophorum vaginatum. Oecologia*, **67**, 511–518.

Kats, N.Ya. (1958). O tipakh bolot i ikh razmeshchenii v kholodnoi i umerennoi zonakh severnogo polushariya. *Pochvovedeniye*, **1958(6)**, 13–20.

Kats, N.Ya. (1959). O bolotakh i torfyanikakh severnoi Ameriki. *Pochvovedeniye*, **1959 (10)**, 44–52.

Kulczynski, S. (1949). Peat bogs of Polesie. *Mémoires de l'Académie polonaise des sciences, Cracovie. Classe des sciences mathématiques et nat*urelles, B **15**, 1–356.

Lee, J.A. & Stewart. G.R. (1978). Ecological aspects of nitrogen assimilation. *Advances in Botanical Research*, **6**, 1–43.

Malmer, N. (1962a). Studies on mire vegetation in the archaean area of southwestern Götaland (South Sweden). I. Vegetation and habitat conditions on the Åkhult mire. *Opera Botanica*, **72(1)**, 1–322.

Malmer, N. (1962b). Studies on mire vegetation in the archaean area of southwestern Götaland (South Sweden). II. Distribution and season variation in elementary constituents on some mire sites. *Opera Botanica*, **72(2)**, 1–67.

Malmer, N. (1988). Patterns in the growth and the accumulation of inorganic constituents in the *Sphagnum* cover on ombrotrophic bogs in Scandinavia. *Oikos*, **53**, 105–120.

Malmer, N. (1992). IV. Geochemistry. *Peatland Ecosystems and Man: an Impact Assessment* (eds. O.M. Bragg, P.D. Hulme, H.A.P. Ingram & R.A. Robertson), pp. 165–174. Department of Biological Sciences, University of Dundee, UK and International Peat Society.

Malmer, N. & Holm, E. (1984). Variation in the C/N quotient of peat in relation to decomposition rate and age determination with ^{210}Pb. *Oikos*, **43**, 171–182.

Malmer, N. & Wallén, B. (1986). Inorganic elements above and below ground in dwarf shrubs on a subarctic peat bog. *Oikos*, **46**, 200–206.

Mark, A.F., Rawson, G. & Wilson, J.B. (1979). Vegetation pattern of a lowland raised mire in eastern Fiordland. *New Zealand Journal of Ecology*, **2**, 1–10.

Monteith, J.L. & Unsworth, M.H. (1990). *Principles of Environmental Physics*. 2nd edn. Edward Arnold, London.

Moore, P.D. & Bellamy, D.J. (1974). *Peatlands*. Elek Science, London.

Nye, P.H. & Tinker, P.B. (1977). *Solute Movement in the Soil–Root System*. University of California Press, Berkeley, California.

Ohlson, M. & Malmer, N. (1990). Total nutrient accumulation and seasonal variation in resource allocation in the bog plant *Rhynchospora alba. Oikos*, **58**, 100–108.

Pisano, E. (1983). The Magellanic tundra complex. *Ecosystems of the World, 4B. Mires: Swamp, Bog, Fen and Moor; Regional Studies* (ed. A.J.P. Gore), pp. 295–329. Elsevier, Amsterdam.

Press, M.C. & Lee, J.A. (1982). Nitrate reductase activity of *Sphagnum* species in the South

Pennines. *New Phytologist*, **92**, 487–494.

Press, M.C., Woodin, S.J. & Lee, J.A. (1986). The potential importance of an increased atmospheric nitrogen supply to the growth of ombrotrophic *Sphagnum* species. *New Phytologist*, **103**, 45–55.

Price, J.S. (1992a). Blanket bog in Newfoundland. Part 1. The occurrence and accumulation of fog-water deposits. *Journal of Hydrology*, **135**, 87–101.

Price, J.S. (1992b). Blanket bog in Newfoundland. Part 2. Hydrological processes. *Journal of Hydrology*, **135**, 103–119.

Proctor, M.C.F. (1992). Regional and local variation in the chemical composition of ombrogenous mire waters in Britain and Ireland. *Journal of Ecology*, **80**, 719–736.

Proctor, M.C.F. (1994). Seasonal and shorter-term changes in surface-water chemistry on four English ombrogenous bogs. *Journal of Ecology*, **82**, 597–610.

Read, D. J. (1991). Mycorrhizas in ecosystems. *Experientia*, **47**, 376–391.

Rudolph, H. & Voigt, J.U. (1986). Effects of NH_4^+-N and NO_3^--N on growth and metabolism of *Sphagnum magellanicum*. *Physiologia Plantarum*, **66**, 339–343.

Schofield, R.K. (1947). A ratio law governing the equilibrium of cations in the soil solution. *Proceedings of the 11th International Congress of Pure and Applied Chemistry, London*, **3**, 257–261.

Schofield, R.K. & Taylor, A.W. (1955). Measurements of the activities of bases in soils. *Journal of Soil Science*, **6**, 137–146.

Shaver, G.R., Chapin, F.S. & Gaertner, B.L. (1986). Factors limiting growth of *Eriophorum vaginatum* L. in Alaskan tussock tundra. *Journal of Ecology*, **74**, 257–278.

Smart, P.J., Wheeler, B.D. & Willis, A.J. (1989). Revegetation of peat excavations in a derelict raised bog. *New Phytologist*, **111**, 733–748.

Talibudeen, O. (1981). Cation exchange in soils. *The Chemistry of Soil Processes* (eds D.J. Greenland & M.H.B. Hayes), pp. 115–177. John Wiley, Chichester.

Tipping, E. & Hurley, M.A. (1988). A model of solid-solution interactions in acid organic soils, based on the complexation properties of humic substances. *Journal of Soil Science*, **39**, 505–519.

Tipping, E., Backes, C.A. & Hurley, M.A. (1988). The complextion of protons, alminium and calcium by aquatic humic substances: a model incorporating binding-site heterogeneity and macroionic effects. *Water Research*, **22**, 597–611.

UKRGAR (1990). *Acid Deposition in the United Kingdom 1986–1988. Third Report of the United Kingdon Review Group on Acid Rain*. Department of the Environment, London.

Urban, N.R., Bayley, S.E., & Eisenreich, S.J. (1989). Export of dissolved organic carbon and acidity from peatlands. *Water Resources Research*, **25**, 1619–1628.

Urban, N.R., Eisenreich, S.J. & Bayley, S.E. (1988). The relative importance of denitrification and nitrate assimilation in midcontinental bogs. *Limnology and Oceanography*, **33**, 1611–1617.

Urban, N.R., Eisenreich, S.J. & Gorham, E. (1987). Proton cycling in bogs: geographic variation in northeastern North America. *Effects of Atmospheric Pollution in Forests, Wetlands and Agricultural Ecosystems* (eds T.C. Hutchinson & K.M. Meema), pp. 577–598. NATO ASI Series. Vol. G16. Springer, Berlin & Heidelberg.

Vitt, D.H., Horton, D.G., Slack, N.G. & Malmer, N. (1990). *Sphagnum*-dominated peatlands of the hyperoceanic British Columbia coast: patterns in surface-water chemistry and vegetation. *Canadian Journal of Forest Research*, **20**, 696–711.

Woodin, S.J., Press, M.C. & Lee, J.A. (1985). Nitrate reductase activity in *Sphagnum fuscum* in relation to wet deposition of nitrate from the atmosphere. *New Phytologist*, **99**, 381–388.

20 Towards an Ecohydrological Basis for Raised Mire Restoration

O. M. BRAGG

Department of Biological Sciences, The University, Dundee, DD1 4HN, UK.

SUMMARY

1.   Groundwater mound theory, which explains the domed shapes of raised mires in terms of the underlying physical and biological processes, is outlined.

2.   A simple conceptual model for the raised mire system, based on ecohydrology, is described.

3.   A general account is given of possible consequences for the system of different types of human intervention, and the effectiveness of some restoration measures explored in this context.

THE GROUNDWATER MOUND THEORY FOR RAISED MIRE STABILITY

Soil physical basis

It is well established that the enigmatically domed water tables of raised mires can be explained in terms of basic soil physics. The essential characteristics of the hydrological system are that:

(i) water is supplied to the soil exclusively from above (as precipitation), and

(ii) the boundaries of the system are such that the direction of seepage is predominantly horizontal.

Under such circumstances, water will 'pile up' in the soil until the operative hydraulic gradients are sufficient to promote its dispersal by seepage at a rate which exactly equals the rate of supply. The domed body of water which results is known as a *groundwater mound*.

For a uniform, parallel-sided monolith of soil overlying a flat impermeable base and receiving a steady supply of water, an equation can be written for the shape of the groundwater mound profile at equilibrium in terms of two constant hydrological terms: water supply rate and soil permeability (Childs, 1969). Solutions of the flow equation for monoliths with other plan shapes are also available, giving a range of fairly simple quantitative models for groundwater mounds formed under such conditions (Bragg, Brown & Ingram, 1991).

Restoration of Temperate Wetlands. Edited by B.D. Wheeler, S.C. Shaw, W. Fojt and R.A. Robertson
© 1995 John Wiley & Sons Ltd.

Application to raised mires

Ingram (1982) pointed out the relevance of these principles in explaining the stability and shapes of raised mires. In a raised mire, the peat comprises a bed of soil capable of containing a groundwater mound. By contrast to mineral soils, however, this soil is formed from plant material produced at the surface; and being almost entirely organic it can persist only if decomposition is prevented, in circumboreal mires by exclusion of air by waterlogging. Thus, we may anticipate that a raised mire, left to itself, will assume the shape of a groundwater mound (Ingram, 1982). Moreover, we know sufficient about the hydraulics of the two soil layers, *acrotelm* and *catotelm* (Ingram, 1978), to indicate that raised mire morphology should be determined by the steady hydrodynamic equilibrium for the catotelm which is sustainable under all weather conditions, approached in Ingram's (1982) original quantitative test by calculation of a water balance for the driest year 'through which the mire survives without irreversible desiccation'.

By describing the steady state of the catotelm, Ingram's approach provides a realistic model for the raised mire ecosystem which is both conceptually tangible and susceptible to relatively simple quantitative analysis. However, it is important to realise that the close correspondence between the surface of the intact raised mire and the groundwater mound which sustains its catotelm is achieved through complex biological and hydrological processes within the acrotelm, whose combined effect is to confine the oscillations of the water table within a shallow layer of the soil profile (Bragg, 1982, 1989; Clymo, 1992; Ingram, 1992). Thus, the water table remains within 0.5–1 m of every part of the mire surface. The unique conditions of perennially shallow water table and isolation from mineral-enriched groundwater are appropriate to development of specialised plant communities, characterised by abundance of *Sphagnum* species. The latter are particularly sensitive to small differences in water table regime, species occurring in hollows being unable to survive even on hummock tops nearby (Ivanov, 1981; Bragg, 1982).

RESTORATION OF DEGRADED MIRE SYSTEMS

In terms of the groundwater mound model, 'degraded' mire ecosystems are those in which, often through the activities of man, the equilibrium of the steady groundwater mound has been shifted in such a way that the natural close coupling between surface and water table has been more or less seriously disrupted. Interpretation of the effects of imposed changes in these terms can be helpful in two ways. First, applied at conceptual or quantitative level, the model can furnish a basis for identification of potentially effective restoration measures. Second, with sufficient site-specific data, customised models for 'pre-disturbance' and 'post-disturbance' equilibria of the groundwater mound can be established. Changes indicated by short-term monitoring can then be assessed in relation to the quantified long-term target of a self-sustaining ecosystem based on the new groundwater mound.

Each problem in raised mire restoration is likely to be unique, in terms of both the attributes of the system before disturbance and the details of artificially imposed modifications to its hydrology. In general, however, human intervention acts on hydrodynamics at three levels: in the acrotelm, in the catotelm, and in some circumstances through regional hydrology (Schouwenaars, this volume). The discussion here will concentrate on the consequences of disturbance at the first two of these levels for the ecohydrology of the raised mire system, and attempt to illustrate how an understanding of the physical and biological foundations of the system can be helpful in interpreting existing successes and failures in restoration, and in providing pointers for rational approaches to new projects.

Acrotelm impacts: system boundaries unaltered

Impacts belonging to this category result from activities which directly affect the surface of the mire expanse; for example, digging of shallow drains, forestry and commercial peat extraction. Their effect on the equilibrium of the steady groundwater mound may be visualised in terms of modification of the water relations of the acrotelm.

Water relations of the intact acrotelm

We may think of the acrotelm as a store of water, or 'header tank', for the catotelm. The way in which it fulfils this function in intact mires is closely related to structure. Its upper surface consists largely of closely-packed *Sphagnum* capitula; moving downwards from this surface, the profile shows progression from live and newly-dead *Sphagnum* shoots retaining their macroscopic structure, through a zone where decay has reached the stage where plant structure collapses, to largely amorphous lower peat, all within a depth of 0.15–0.7 (–1) m (Bragg, 1989; Clymo, 1992). In consequence, pore structure becomes finer, and hydraulic conductivity declines sharply, as depth increases (Figure 1).

The dynamics of the acrotelm store are represented in Figure 2. When water is added (as precipitation, P) the water table rises into the coarse surface layers and lateral seepage U_{acr} occurs with increasing ease, operating an effective overflow system (Ingram & Bragg, 1984). When it stops raining, the water table falls back in to layers of finer structure, and dispersal by lateral seepage declines. By contrast, under evaporative conditions, it is vertical conduction of water through the unsaturated zone between water table and surface which controls water losses, E. As the water table recedes in consequence, coarser pores are progressively drained, and pathways for water movement become increasingly narrow and tortuous, so that the resistance of the acrotelm to the evaporative flux increases (Ingram, 1983). The roots of vascular plants may bypass this resistance, however (Bragg, 1982).

Viewed in this way, the function of the acrotelm is to integrate weather-driven

(a)   (b)

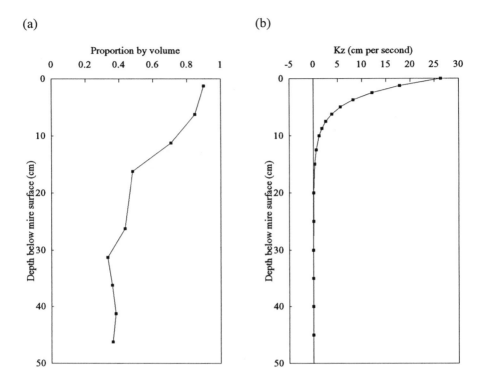

Figure 1. Some properties of the acrotelm in a *Sphagnum magellanicum* lawn: (a) variation with depth of total volume of pores of effective diameter greater than 100 μm, determined in tension table experiments; (b) variation with depth of hydraulic conductivity, K_z, measured in field flume experiments. Data from Bragg (1982).

transient fluxes of water through storage **W** to provide the steady supply U_{cat} required to maintain the catotelm. The magnitude of U_{cat} is in turn related to the height of the groundwater mound sustaining the catotelm at the critical moment when the acrotelm store is empty. It follows that alteration of the magnitude of any of the transient fluxes will alter the pattern of depletion of the store, with consequences for the hydrodynamic equilibrium of the catotelm.

Modifications imposed by disturbance

Where drains have been dug in the acrotelm, the primary hydrological effect is enhancement of lateral seepage, U_{acr}, into the drains and thence to the edge of the dome. We may surmise that introduction of exotic trees will promote evapotranspiration, E, both by increasing interception losses and by facilitating the

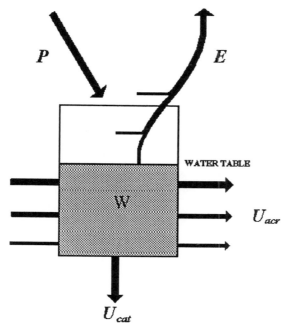

Figure 2. The water balance of a section of the acrotelm. *P*, precipitation; *E*, evapotranspiration; U_{acr}, acrotelm seepage; U_{cat}, catotelm seepage; **W**, storage. The water balance equation is: $P - E - U_{acr} - U_{cat} - W = 0$, where **W** represents change in storage.

'short-circuit route' *via* the vascular systems of introduced plants. Removal of vegetation involves loss of the whole structure of the natural acrotelm, so that the water table is relocated in the newly exposed deeper peat. Changes in aquifer yield of the upper part of the profile tending to increase the water table movement corresponding to unit change in storage (Figure 3; Ingram, 1992; Schouwenaars, 1992), and changes in albedo and evaporative resistance tending to accelerate evapotranspiration, are amongst the predictable consequences.

Usually, the initial hydrological response is manifest as an increase in the amplitude of water table fluctuation, which amounts to deepening of the acrotelm. So the system responds to enhanced opportunities for shallow seepage and evapotranspiration by increasing the capacity of the store and at the same time reducing the height of the catotelm, and thus the water supply required to maintain it (Figure 4); but this has the undesirable consequence that the water table is lowered in relation to the surface for at least part, and usually for the whole, of the year.

The restorative action dictated is to reinstate the natural water relations of the acrotelm, for example by blocking drains or removing trees. What may be surprising, unless we appreciate that the whole mire functions as a single

(a)   (b)

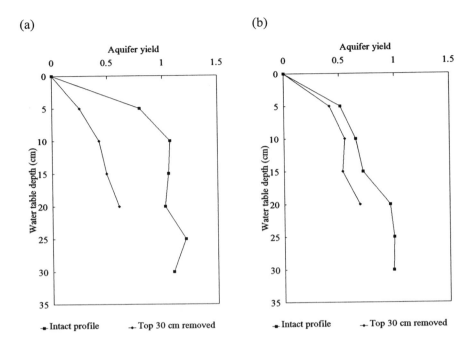

Figure 3. Variation in aquifer yield (change in storage, **W** ÷ change in water table altitude, **w**) with depth of the water table in profiles beneath (a) *Sphagnum magellanicum* and (b) *Sphagnum capillifolium*, derived from tension table determinations in which the water table was progressively lowered by 50-mm increments. In each case, the right-hand curve applies to the intact surface profile, and the left-hand curve to the profile which would remain after removal of the uppermost 0.3 m of the acrotelm. Data from Bragg (1982).

hydrological unit, is the distance over which positive results can be achieved; for example, blocking a single drain at one side of Felicia Moss is said to have led to reinstatement of *Sphagnum* communities over the whole mire expanse (R.A. Lindsay, personal communication).

Where the vegetation has been completely removed, appropriate solutions may be less obvious. However, so long as the perturbation has involved reduction only of the height of the steady groundwater mound, and not of its width, the problem remains at the mire surface. A considerable amount of attention has been paid to development of techniques for re-establishment of mire vegetation on such surfaces. Approaches which have met with success in reinstating water table conditions appropriate for growth of at least some species of *Sphagna* on level peat fields involve, in effect, artificial measures to reduce surface run-off and increase aquifer yield, for example by excavating parts of the surface (*e.g.* Beets, 1992; Money, this volume) or constructing peat dams (Eggelsmann, 1987).

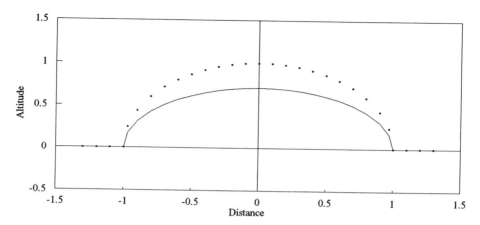

Figure 4. Projected change in groundwater mound profile for a parallel-sided mire in response to reduction of U_{cat}. Points represent the original groundwater mound profile, which is everywhere close to the mire surface; continuous curve represents the 'disturbed' equilibrium groundwater mound. Altitudes and distances expressed in 'non-dimensional' units; horizontal and vertical scales different.

Mire remnants

In the past, human influence on mires has begun at the edges – for example, in cultivating the shallower and better-drained peat at the edges of the dome, or in removing the peat here for domestic fuel use or to expose the mineral substratum for agriculture. More recently, opencast mining has imposed such patterns of disturbance over appreciably shorter time-scales (Bragg, Brown & Ingram, 1992). The remnant may have no drains or other signs of surface disturbance, but still vegetation change occurs, often advancing from the cut edges towards the centre.

Such patterns of disturbance involve reduction of the base dimension, or width, of the groundwater mound. Theory indicates that, assuming no change in (climatic) water supply or hydraulic conductivity, the height of the mound must be reduced in consequence (Bragg, 1989).

The effect for the parallel-sided model is illustrated by Figure 5. Let us suppose that the catotelm of the original, undisturbed mire corresponded to profile (a), and its base was shortened by 25%. The new equilibrium of the groundwater mound would then correspond to profile (b). Thus, the water table would retreat from the surface, leaving it 'high and dry'. A similar effect might be produced by drains which penetrate to the base of the deposit. In the purest manifestation of such disturbance, the surface of the remnant would be untouched, allowing little scope for attempting restoration by techniques such as drain-blocking or reconstitution of the acrotelm. Where both marginal cutting and surface impacts have occurred, however, surface restoration measures alone may well prove to be ineffective (Joosten, 1992).

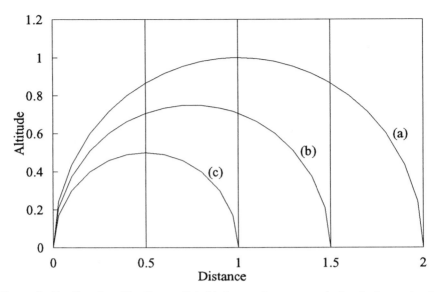

Figure 5. Family of profiles for parallel-sided groundwater mounds developing under the same climatic conditions but on bases of different widths. Altitudes and distances expressed in 'non-dimensional' units; horizontal and vertical scales different. See text for further discussion.

Attempts at restoration which have met with some success involve artificial reinstatement of the catotelm, either literally by constructing terracing against the cut faces of the remnant, or by reducing seepage losses by insertion of deep bunds of compressed peat within the new boundaries.

A more subtle approach, which may be the only practical one under some circumstances, but which seems to have been attempted only by default and rather inadequately monitored and reported, is to attempt to establish a self-sustaining mire system based on the newly imposed groundwater mound. This would require encouragement of wastage and slumping of peat so that the surface moves towards the new groundwater mound profile, whilst preventing irreversible deterioration of the system. Since hydraulic conductivity may be expected to decline as wastage proceeds (Hobbs, 1986), we may anticipate that the surface of the groundwater mound would indeed rise towards the descending mire surface as the process continues. It is worth noting that some practices which are becoming widely accepted as 'standard' restoration procedure for mires could be unhelpful if inappropriately timed in remedial management for mire remnants; for example, work in Switzerland suggests that early removal of trees, by slowing wastage and relieving overburden pressure, may actually retard progress towards a new stable system (Hobbs, 1986; Schneebeli, 1989). Thus it seems that whilst saving on major construction works, adoption of such stratagems will require considerable investment in monitoring and reactive management.

ACKNOWLEDGEMENTS

I am grateful to H.A.P. Ingram and to an anonymous referee for reading earlier drafts of this manuscript, and for their helpful comments.

REFERENCES

Beets, C.P. (1992). The relation between the area of open water in bog remnants and storage capacity with resulting guidelines for bog restoration. *Peatland Ecosystems and Man: An Impact Assessment* (eds. Bragg, O.M., Hulme, P.D., Ingram, H.A.P. & Robertson, R.A.). pp. 133–140. Department of Biological Sciences, University of Dundee.

Bragg, O.M. (1982). *The acrotelm of Dun Moss – plants, water and their relationships.* PhD thesis, University of Dundee.

Bragg, O.M. (1989). The importance of water in mire ecosystems. *Cut-over Lowland Raised Mires* (eds W. Fojt, & R. Meade). Research & Survey in Nature Conservation No. 24. Nature Conservancy Council, Peterborough.

Bragg, O.M., Brown, J.M.B. & Ingram, H.A.P. (1991). Modelling the ecohydrological consequences of peat extraction from a Scottish raised mire. *Hydrological Basis of Ecologically Sound Management of Soil and Groundwater* (Proceedings of the Vienna Symposium, August 1991). IAHS Publ. no. 202. Wallingford.

Childs, E.C. (1969). *An Introduction to the Physical Basis of Soil Water Phenomena.* John Wiley, London.

Clymo, R.S. (1992). Productivity and decomposition of peatland ecosystems. *Peatland Ecosystems and Man: An Impact Assessment* (eds O.M. Bragg, P.D. Hulme, H.A.P. Ingram, & R.A. Robertson). pp. 3–16. Department of Biological Sciences, University of Dundee.

Eggelsmann, R. (1987). Ökotechnische Aspekte der Hochmoor-Regeneration. *Telma*, **17**, 59–94.

Hobbs, N.B. (1986). Mire morphology and the properties and behaviour of some British and foreign peats. *Quarterly Journal of Engineering Geology, London*, **19**, 7–80.

Ingram, H.A.P. (1978). Soil layers in mires: function and terminology. *Journal of Soil Science*, **29**, 224–227.

Ingram, H.A.P. (1982). Size and shape in raised mire ecosystems: a geophysical model. *Nature*, **297** No. 5864, 300–303.

Ingram, H.A.P. (1983). Hydrology. *Ecosystems of the World* 4A. *Mires: Swamps, Bog, Fen and Moor* (ed. A.J.P. Gore), pp. 67–158. Elsevier, Amsterdam.

Ingram, H.A.P. (1992). Introduction to the ecohydrology of mires in the context of cultural perturbation. *Peatland Ecosystems and Man: An Impact Assessment* (eds O.M. Bragg, P.D. Hulme, H.A.P. Ingram, & R.A. Robertson), pp. 67–93. Department of Biological Sciences, University of Dundee.

Ingram, H.A.P. & Bragg, O.M. (1984). The diplotelmic mire: some hydrological consequences reviewed. *Proceedings of the 7th International Peat Congress, Dublin*, **1**, 220–234. Irish National Peat Committee / International Peat Society.

Ivanov, K.E. (1981). *Water Movement in Mirelands.* A. Thomson, & H.A.P. Ingram (translators). Academic Press, London.

Joosten, J.H.J. (1992). Bog regeneration in the Netherlands: a review. *Peatland Ecosystems and Man: An Impact Assessment* (eds O.M. Bragg, P.D. Hulme, H.A.P. Ingram, & R.A.

Robertson), pp. 367–373. Department of Biological Sciences, University of Dundee.

Schouwenaars, J.M. (1992). Hydrological characteristics of bog relicts in the Engbertsdijksvenen after peat-cutting and rewetting. *Peatland Ecosystems and Man: An Impact Assessment* (eds O.M. Bragg, P.D. Hulme, H.A.P. Ingram, & R.A. Robertson), pp. 125–132. Department of Biological Sciences, University of Dundee.

Schneebeli, M. (1989). Zusammenhänge zwischen Moorwachstum und hydraulischer Durchlässigkeit und ihre Anwendung auf den Regenerationsprozeß. *Telma*, **2**, 257–264.

21 Problems in the Hydrological Management of Cut-over Raised Mires, with Special Reference to Thorne Moors, South Yorkshire

L. HEATHWAITE

Department of Geography, University of Sheffield, Winter Street, Sheffield, S3 7ND, UK

SUMMARY

1.   The hydrological balance of Thorne Moors National Nature Reserve, a cut-over raised mire in South Yorkshire (UK), was examined.
2.   A 'ditch recharge system' was introduced as an attempt to control the mire water table close to areas of peat extraction.
3.   Seepage losses (both horizontal and vertical) appear to limit the effectiveness of this form of hydrological management. Limited information on the spatial variation in key variables, such as the saturated hydraulic conductivity, contributed to the failure of the 'ditch recharge system'.

INTRODUCTION

Field studies *vs.* models: scales of hydrological management in mires

The effective restoration and hydrological management of disturbed mires, particularly where they have been damaged by peat extraction, requires a clear understanding of the process and pattern of water movement. Unfortunately, such understanding is often limited at the scale required for management. For example, although small-scale field experiments are able to demonstrate the spatial variability in key hydrological variables such as hydraulic conductivity and the pattern of evapotranspiration from different vegetation types, they are often criticised for being too site-specific. It is also difficult to make generalisations from field or laboratory studies owing to the wide variance often demonstrated by the results. At the other extreme, hydrological models, which enable some prediction of the effect of different management strategies, are necessarily simplifications of reality. Models of water movement in raised mires may be

Restoration of Temperate Wetlands. Edited by B.D. Wheeler, S.C. Shaw, W.J. Fojt and R.A. Robertson
© 1995 John Wiley & Sons Ltd.

represented by the standard equations of groundwater flow. For example, the 'groundwater mound model' described by Ingram (1982) and Bragg (this volume), provides a steady-state analytical solution to the shape and inferred hydrological properties of intact raised mires. More complex models with time variant numerical solutions, including spatial heterogeneity and seasonal variations, are also available (Institute of Hydrology, 1992; Schouwenaars, this volume). However, such models are 'data hungry' and their output, as is the case for simplistic models, is dictated by the quality of the data input and the resolution to which the various model parameters are described. Models, therefore, depend on good empirical data and a good understanding of hydrological processes. Such understanding can only be supplied by field and laboratory experimentation, thus leading back, *via* a vicious circle, to the limitations of such smaller-scale work.

In the research described below, an examination of one of the key controls on the effective hydrological management of mires damaged by peat extraction is made. This control is water loss *via* seepage through the peat matrix. This takes place primarily in the saturated zone and may occur in both a horizontal and vertical direction in response to differences in hydraulic potential. The extent to which such seepage losses are modified in disturbed raised mires will be discussed and one attempt at reducing these losses, through hydrological management, will be described. It will be shown how a lack of detailed understanding of the spatial variation in hydraulic conductivity contributed to the failure of the management strategy described. Although the hydrological modelling of the data (Institute of Hydrology, 1992) meant that it was possible to extrapolate the patterns of water movement over a wider spatial area, the quality of the predictions was limited by the lack of detailed understanding of the variability in the key hydrological variables, even though the general patterns shown by the field results were upheld.

The water balance of undisturbed and disturbed mires

Mires develop in response to a set of unique hydrological conditions. On a small scale, the terrestrialisation or infilling of glacial relicts such as water-filled kettle holes may result in small, isolated raised mires. On a larger scale, paludification or swamping of the land surface may lead to extensive mire formation such as the raised mire of Thorne Moors in South Yorkshire which, prior to peat extraction, covered an area of at least 3400 ha and was up to 8 m deep (Limbert, Mitchell & Rhodes, 1986).

The hydrological stability of all mire types can be represented very simply by the water balance equation shown in Figure 1. For raised mires, the key input is atmospheric precipitation. Any inflow from telluric waters does not directly affect the (ombrotrophic) surface conditions of the raised mire but may be important in the minerotrophic margins. The key losses of water from raised mires are evapotranspiration and two components of discharge: (i) surface run-off and (ii) vertical and lateral seepage. Whereas lateral seepage losses occur entirely within the mire, vertical seepage *losses* may take place between the peat and the

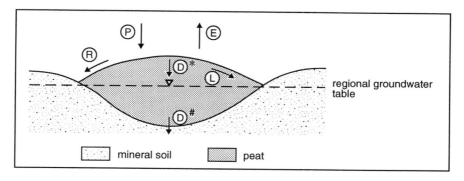

Water balance

$$P - E - R - L - D \pm S = 0$$

P = precipitation   L = lateral subsurface seepage
E = evaporation   D = downward vertical seepage
R = surface runoff   (* within peat; # between peat
S = storage   and mineral substratum)

on average Py = Dy where :
Py = P - E = precipitation surplus and Dy = R + L + D = discharge loss

Figure 1. The water balance of an undisturbed raised mire.

underlying mineral soil. This component of mire water loss is often disregarded because it is commonly assumed, for raised mires at least, that the underlying mineral substratum forms an impermeable base to the mire which then becomes the basis for the extensive waterlogging that enables the initial build-up of organic matter. Where mires have formed by paludification rather than terrestrialisation, the mineral substratum need not necessarily form an impermeable base to the peat. The significance of this boundary only becomes important when the original hydrological variables enabling mire formation are altered. Unfortunately, human intervention in the form of drainage, usually for agriculture, forestry or peat extraction, is the major source of hydrological change. Accurate estimates of seepage as a closing term in the water balance of a mire are also important. However, the high spatial variability in peat thickness, degree of decomposition and floristic composition within mire remnants make the precise evaluation of the hydraulic resistance of intact, let alone disturbed or damaged, mires difficult.

Hydrophysical properties of the acrotelm

Undisturbed mires, which posses an intact acrotelm, have a number of self-regulatory mechanisms which minimise seepage losses. In many raised mires these are related to the hydrophysical properties of the upper *Sphagnum* layer. *Sphagnum* growth is highly dependent on water movement through capillary transport. Thus evapotranspiration losses can, to a large extent, be internally regulated by the upper, living *Sphagnum* layer through their hyaline cells. This means that the intact raised mire has the ability to reduce evapotranspiration losses if the water table falls. This 'mulch' effect, which takes place as the upper *Sphagnum* layer dries out, has been shown to occur if the water table falls below 10 cm of the mire surface (Ingram, 1983). External regulation of evapotranspiration losses from intact mires also occurs because evaporation is dependent on capillary transport. Thus, only a small water table fall is needed to reduce significantly the amount of water held in the capillary bond in the acrotelm. Streefkerk & Casparie (1989) suggest that, for a little-damaged *Sphagnum*-dominated acrotelm, a 20 cm drop in the peat water table below the mire surface results in only 5% of the total water content of the mire being held in the capillary bond. This has repercussions for the hydrological management of raised mires because it implies that the water table should be at or near the mire surface in order to encourage *Sphagnum* regrowth. Such control is not always possible in cut-over mires, as will be demonstrated below.

The second key hydrological property of an intact raised mire is the capacity for shrinkage and swelling in the acrotelm in response to water table fluctuations. This property is imparted by the high permeability of the acrotelm which means that, for seepage losses from undisturbed raised mires, surface run-off is large relative to subsurface vertical and lateral seepage losses (see Figure 1). It is generally assumed that downward seepage losses in intact raised mires are of little importance because they usually amount to less than 15% of the annual mire discharge (Ivanov, 1981). This is because the resistance to vertical and horizontal water loss below the living peat surface is high, and increases with increasing decomposition. Thus, the resistance to water movement increases with peat depth and the pressure of the peat overburden (Eggelsmann, 1960; Bay, 1968). These factors taken together mean that the water balance of an intact mire is characterised by a relatively large horizontal surface run-off where low hydraulic gradients (0.1%) control the flow velocity in the acrotelm (Gafni & Brookes, 1990). It is important to recognise, however, that in disturbed mires subsurface water losses usually become more important relative to surface losses. Their significance is discussed in greater detail below.

Water losses from disturbed raised mires

Disturbed raised mires are characterised by changes in both evapotranspiration and seepage losses. Table 1 indicates the evapotranspiration losses from raised mires with differing drainage status. Evaporation losses from open water are also given for comparison. For the undisturbed mire with a distinct hummock–hollow microtopography, winter evaporation losses are greater than that from open water. This leads to a relative water surplus in the hollows and pools of the mire

Table 1. Mean evaporation from undisturbed and disturbed raised mires (after Eggelsmann, 1981).

Vegetation cover	Drainage status	Evaporation (mm a^{-1})		
		Winter	Summer	Year
Sphagnum/Calluna	Undrained	140	410	550
Calluna	Slightly drained	125	395	520
Grassland	Drained	90	410	500
Arable	Drained	75	395	470
Woodland	Drained	125	465	590
Open water	–	80	530	610

compared with the peat matrix. In effect, the mire pools serve as a water store in the winter months. In summer, in undisturbed raised mires, the evapotranspiration from the peat matrix is less than that from open water. The hollows and pools thus become points of discharge for the surrounding mire area. This important relationship between the peat matrix and the network of pools and hollows in an intact mire has been recognised by a number of researchers, and the artificial creation of areas of open water within a disturbed mire has been investigated as a means of mire restoration (Beets, 1992; Joosten, 1992). It is important to recognise, however, that topography is not necessarily the controlling factor in the hydrological stability of a mire but rather the water surplus that enables such topographical distinctions to develop in the first place. What this means is that simple simulation of the microtopography of intact mires for the restoration of *damaged* mires is not the only criteria for success – an adequate (usually excess) water supply should be the starting point.

The ability of *Sphagnum* to regulate evapotranspiration losses is also important in this context. Even in intact mires, in summer, there is often a shortage of water to the growing points of *Sphagnum* (Ingram, 1983). However, the high evapotranspiration recorded from *Sphagnum* during the growth period (max. 5–6.5 mm day^{-1}, see Table 1) is still less than that from open water (*c.* 10 mm day^{-1}).

In disturbed mires, evapotranspiration losses increase both absolutely and seasonally as a result of the reduction in the area of open water and the changing vegetation of the mire surface in response to a lowered peat water table usually initiated by drainage. This means that trees (particularly birch) and *Molinia* are able to colonise the mire surface because they are better adapted to the lowered water table (Figure 2). Woodland on drained raised mires has a high evapotranspiration loss that approaches that of open water. Furthermore, some of this evaporated water comes from the deeper peat layers via the roots of trees and scrub vegetation. This further exaggerates the falling water table, resulting in aeration of the deeper peat layers which ultimately leads to the irreversible drying and accelerated decomposition of the peat matrix.

Both surface run-off and subsurface seepage losses increase in damaged mires.

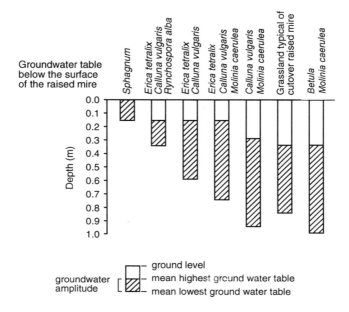

Figure 2. Water table range for different raised mire vegetation (Streefkerk & Casparie, 1989). Reproduced by permission of Staatsbosbeheer

Vertical seepage losses may increase as a result of the reduction in peat thickness either as a direct result of peat extraction (as in the case of Thorne Moors, described later) or owing to drainage and subsequent subsidence of the original mire surface. If c is the resistance (in days) of the peat layer to vertical seepage losses, it can be shown (*e.g.* Schouwenaars, Amerongen & Booltink, 1990) that this resistance is a function of the thickness of the peat layer (t) and the permeability or hydraulic conductivity of that layer (K_{sat}) where:

$$c = t/k_{sat} \ [days]$$

The relationship is non-linear because the permeability of the peat decreases with increasing depth as a result of the increasing degree of decomposition and the overburden of the upper peat layers. The rate of vertical seepage (W) can be expressed as:

$$W = \Delta h/c \ [m \ day^{-1}] \quad \text{or} \quad W = k_{sat}/t.\Delta h \ [m \ day^{-1}]$$

where Δh is the hydraulic head difference for the peat layer. The importance of vertical seepage losses has been clearly demonstrated for raised mires in the Netherlands and Germany (see, for example, Streefkerk & Casparie, 1989). The evidence for UK mires is piecemeal. It may be important for mires overlying a relatively permeable and unsaturated substratum. In the UK, where water abstraction from the underlying aquifer is important, the degree of saturation in the substratum may have altered in recent years through lowering of the regional groundwater table. In such circumstances, vertical seepage losses may be relatively more important than in the past.

Surface run-off in damaged raised mires where, for example, peat extraction has removed much of the original acrotelm, is largely controlled by the permeability or infiltration characteristics of the recently-exposed mire surface. In cut-over raised mires, this surface is likely to be part of the catotelm. The hydraulic conductivity of the remaining peat mass is also important in controlling the proportion of mire inflow discharged as surface run-off. Gafni & Brookes (1990) go so far as to suggest that the steepening of the hydraulic gradient that often occurs in disturbed (particularly cut-over) raised mires as a result of drainage operations at their periphery, is less important than the low saturated hydraulic conductivity of lower peat layers where the water table is located after drainage.

The net outcome of these changes in seepage losses from disturbed mires is shown in Table 2, which compares the seasonal distribution of surface run-off from disturbed and undisturbed raised mires. It is clear that a greater proportion of surface run-off is discharged in the first 9 months of the hydrological year from disturbed raised mires affected by peat extraction. This occurs as a result of (i) increased vertical seepage losses, (ii) enhanced lateral discharge through drains installed in the peat, (iii) higher evapotranspiration from disturbed or cultivated mires (see Table 1), (iv) decreased permeability of the exposed mires surface and (v) reduced storage capacity of the remaining peat layers. The storage coefficient (μ) of living *Sphagnum* is greater than 0.8 (Ingram, 1983); whereas that of humified peat may be as low as $\mu = 0.1$ (Streefkerk & Casparie, 1989). The storage coefficient is dependent on the porosity of the peat matrix, which decreases with increasing depth owing to the increase in the degree of decomposition and the pressure of the overlying peat (Boelter & Verry, 1977). As a consequence, there is very little 'free' water in humified (catotelm) peat, which means that the amplitude of water table movement is wider. Streefkerk & Casparie (1989) suggest that this means that renewed peat growth on catotelm peat is not spontaneous, although this will also depend on climate and the topography of the mire. Furthermore, the alteration of the seepage characteristics of the mire means that the annual distribution of the available moisture in the mire is altered. From a mire regeneration perspective, this means that cut-over mires may have too large a

Table 2. Cumulative percentage surface run-off discharged from undisturbed and disturbed raised mires for different periods of the hydrological year (after Eggelsmann, 1964; Uhden, 1967).

Drainage status	Cumulative % surface run-off leaving mire			
	Oct–Dec	Jan–Mar	Apr–Jun	Jul–Sep
Undrained	30	70	75	100
Slightly drained	30	80	90	100
Drained	30	80	95	100

moisture deficit to support mire regeneration (*i.e. Sphagnum* regrowth) during the dry summer months. This suggests that the restoration of cut-over mires to conditions which resemble their status prior to peat extraction is probably not possible because the increase in peat decomposition which occurs as the peat water table falls (through drainage and/or peat extraction) will decrease the pore volume density of the peat. This in turn will decrease the permeability and hence storage capacity of the remaining peat layers, essentially making them unsuitable for mire regeneration without modification. Thus, it is essential that ameliorative measures are undertaken to reinstate the hydrological environment necessary for regeneration to occur. Control of the water balance of the mire *must* be the starting point in any management programme. Such 'control' is invariably linked to managing seepage losses since other hydrological variables are difficult to modify, although a number of researchers have already attempted to manipulate evapotranspiration losses from disturbed mires through management of the ratio of open water to peat matrix (see Heathwaite, 1994).

Aims of the hydrological management of disturbed raised mires

The primary aim of the *hydrological* management of cut-over raised mires must be to halt the peat decomposition caused by drainage and extraction. Hydrological management to support the establishment of peat-producing vegetation may be expected to reduce rates of peat decomposition. In general, the key criteria which must be satisfied in order to meet this requirement will include:

(i)   establishment of a water surplus which will enable the saturation of the remaining peat substratum;
(ii) creation of a large water-storage capacity at the mire surface;
(iii) creation of a stable, water-saturated 'catotelm';
(iv) infiltration of the mire surface with nutrient-poor water.

The successful accomplishment of criteria (i) to (iii) relies to a large extent on a good understanding of the rate at which seepage losses occur from the disturbed mire. This means that detailed knowledge of the hydraulic conductivity of the remaining peat layers is essential if hydrological management is to be closely 'tailored' to the particular hydrological characteristics of the mire. Unfortunately, quantification of K_{sat} is not straightforward: first because it may display large spatial heterogeneity in both a horizontal and vertical direction in the peat, and second because its measurement, either in the field or the laboratory, reflects this heterogeneity thus giving rise to a wide variance around the mean value for replicated tests. Table 3 demonstrates some of the controls on the hydraulic conductivity of peat soils and the degree of variation such controls produce. The key controls are: (i) peat depth, (ii) degree of decomposition and (iii) bulk density. The latter two variables are intimately linked; as they increase, the hydraulic conductivity decreases, primarily as a result of the change in the pore size distribution in the peat. The rate at which water moves through the peat in a disturbed mire follows a complex pattern with potentially wide vertical and

Table 3. The effect of degree of decomposition and sample depth on the hydraulic conductivity of peat soils (after Boelter, 1965; Romanov, 1968).

Peat layer	Degree of decomposition	Von Post class	Sample depth (m)	Hydraulic conductivity $(m\ day^{-1})$	
				Horizontal	Vertical
Acrotelm	Living *Sphagnum*	–	–	10–109	<10
Catotelm	Fibrous	H 2–3	0.0–0.1	3.3	5.4
	Meso-fibrous	H 4–6	0.35–0.45	1.2×10^{-2}	4.4×10^{-4}
	Amorphous	H 7–10	0.50–0.60	9.6×10^{-4}	7.3×10^{-4}

horizontal variability in most mires, although for Dutch mires Streefkerk & Casparie (1989) suggest that the differences in hydraulic conductivity in the catotelm may be small and that downward seepage is generally more important than horizontal seepage. The relative importance of downward *vs.* horizontal seepage losses in UK raised mires has yet to be evaluated in detail. Site-specific field studies can encompass the variability in, for example, hydraulic conductivity to some extent. However, modelling the results, at least using the simplistic models which are often most suited to management, may not be straightforward. This is because many models, such as the groundwater mound model (Ingram, 1982), utilise a single, average value for the rate of water movement through the mire. As a result they are able only to qualify the potential outcome of hydrological management strategies, not quantify their effects. Detailed field studies therefore remain invaluable in mire restoration projects.

MIRE RESTORATION AT THORNE MOORS NATIONAL NATURE RESERVE

The objective of this study was to establish, using a field experimental approach, how the water balance of the cut-over mire (Thorne Moors, South Yorkshire) could be protected during and following peat extraction (on an industrial scale) in at least 50% of the original 1918 ha mire area. The key aim was to prevent any fall in the water table of the main mire expanse, which is contiguous with the original 73 ha National Nature Reserve (NNR).

The original raised mire, which was once up to 8 m deep (Heathwaite, 1994) has been worked, using traditional sod-cutting techniques for at least 100 years. This has left a mosaic of dry peat baulks and wet cuttings (Figure 3), within which the current conservation interest lies. More recently, peat extraction on a much larger scale and using peat-milling techniques which leave a slightly cambered peat surface devoid of vegetation, has been introduced on the Moor by the horticultural company, Fisons plc, which has planning consent to extract the peat. The research described below, examined the potential impact of peat extraction up to the original NNR boundary on the hydrological stability of the cut-over mire

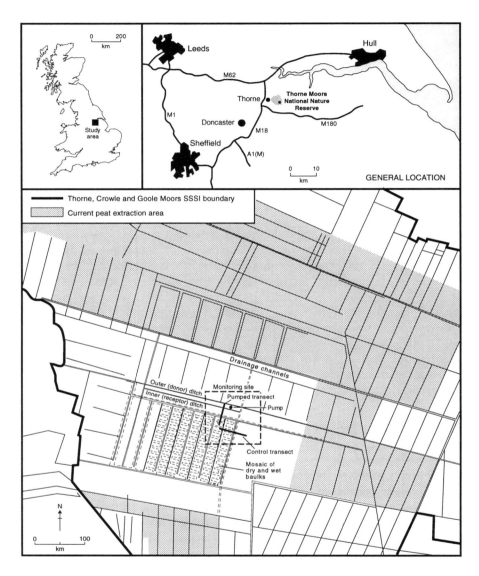

Figure 3. Location of Thorne Moors National Nature Reserve, showing the monitoring site and current peat extraction area.

remnants. At the time of the research (1990/91) the proposal was that peat extraction would leave a sharp peat face, 1–2 m deep, between the milling field and the NNR. In 1992 an agreement between Fisons and English Nature safeguarded a larger (1100 ha) area of the original cut-over mire for conservation purposes; thus peat milling up to the NNR boundary will not occur, although peat extraction will continue in other areas of the mire.

Despite the fact that the original proposal will no longer go ahead, there are still some lessons to be learnt from the failure of the particular hydrological management strategy that was developed to protect the NNR. Furthermore, water level maintenance (with which this research is concerned) is still required in Thorne Moors because the low annual rainfall (average annual rainfall: 1941–90 = 583 mm a^{-1}) emphasises the vulnerability of the mire to seepage losses because that annual recharge to the mire is very low for this mire type.

Figure 4 illustrates the method which was investigated as a means of maintaining a high water table within the NNR whilst at the same time allowing peat extraction to continue at its boundaries. As the available land area for hydrological protection was small at the time of this study, the hydrological buffer zones described in Heathwaite (1994) could not be used. The technique described here uses a minimum land area between the peat extraction zone and the protected mire remnants. The northern boundary of the NNR was used as the study site, with a control site on the eastern boundary (see Figure 3). The detailed experimental set-up is discussed in greater detail in Heathwaite (1994). The 'ditch recharge system' shown in Figure 4 was used in an attempt to control the hydraulic gradient from the NNR to the mire periphery, where peat extraction was taking place. This gradient produced considerable subsurface lateral seepage to the mire margins, as is shown by the flow-lines illustrated in Figure 5. In order to restrict the flow of water from the NNR to the mire margins, water was *pumped* from the outer drainage ditch to an inner ditch, with the objective of maintaining as high a water level as possible in the inner ditch to minimise the hydraulic gradient between it and the main peat body. The success of this strategy depended on two factors (i) the rate of *seepage* from the inner to the outer ditch, and (ii) the capacity of the outer ditch to supply water to the inner ditch. Figure 5 illustrates the pattern of

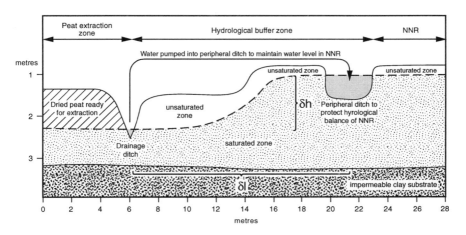

Figure 4. Schematic diagram of the 'ditch recharge system' used on the northern boundary of Thorne Moors National Nature Reserve.

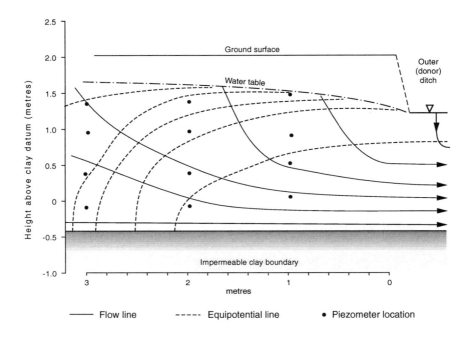

Figure 5 . Direction of water flow from the Thorne Moors National Nature Reserve to the outer ditch of the 'ditch recharge system' derived using the piezometric network shown.

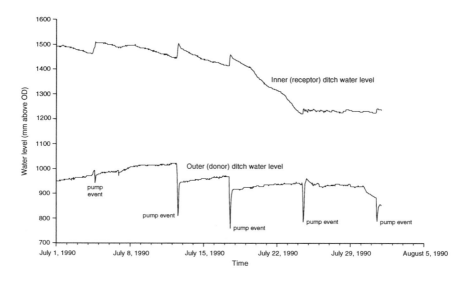

Figure 6. The effect of pumping on the water levels of the outer and inner ditches of the 'ditch recharge system'. The pump events monitored in July 1990 are shown.

water flow in the narrow buffer zone between the inner and outer ditch (see also Figure 4). It was derived from a piezometric network installed at right angles to the drainage ditch and described in more detail in Heathwaite, 1990, 1994). The flow-lines clearly demonstrate the movement of water from the NNR (at the left of the Figure) towards the outer ditch (right of the Figure). Also of importance is the evidence given by the flow-lines for water flow *beneath* the outer ditch because this suggests that flow is bypassing the drainage ditch network, which will thus reduce its effectiveness as part of the ditch recharge system. Presumably this subsurface lateral flow occurs in response to the steep hydraulic gradient between the NNR and the peripheral mire areas where peat extraction is taking place. Similar lateral subsurface flow was also recorded beneath the inner ditch (Heathwaite, 1994). The results suggest that, despite pump action, the hydraulic gradient continues to run from the NNR to the peripheral ditches. In order to 'arrest' this gradient, the capacity of the outer ditch to supply water must be greater than the rate of seepage loss from the inner to the outer ditch in response to the existing hydraulic gradient. Figure 6 shows that this was not the case, because the water level fall in the outer ditch was significantly greater than the water level rise in the inner ditch for each pump event. This was due to the limited capacity of the outer ditch to supply recharge water to the inner ditch. The net effect was an increase in the rate of seepage loss because the hydraulic gradient between the two ditches increased as their water levels were modified as a result of pumping. It is clear that pump action cannot prevent the water level fall in the inner ditch and hence fails to buffer the NNR against water level changes at the mire periphery. The net outcome of pump action is, therefore, to increase the rate of cycling of water between the two ditches rather than acting to buffer the water level in the mire remnants.

Lessons to be learnt from the ditch recharge system

Despite the general failure of the ditch recharge system in minimising seepage losses from the mire remnants, a number of valuable pointers to further research into the hydrological management of cut-over mires such as Thorne Moors can be gained. The most obvious criterion for successful management appears, at least from these results, to be a sound evaluation of the available water supply. Unfortunately, in raised mires such as Thorne, where the recharge is relatively low, the available water supply is always likely to be limited – particularly where drainage for peat extraction is accelerating the rate of seepage loss from the peatland area as a whole. This means that it is even more important that seepage losses to peripheral areas of mire remnants are minimised. Some alternative strategies to that discussed here are examined in Heathwaite (1994) and Bragg *et al.* (1992). It is important to recognise, however, that the starting point of *any* mire restoration strategy must be an accurate evaluation of the spatial variation in the hydraulic conductivity of the mire remnants, together with a careful evaluation of the vertical seepage losses to the underlying mineral subsoil – even where the subsoil is assumed to be impermeable (as is the case for Thorne Moors). This is because vertical seepage losses become relatively more important in a cut-over mire as a result of the loss of peat thickness.

It is clear that field experiments help to interpret the processes of water movement in mires and provide information from which it is possible to start to quantify the rates of water loss. Such studies also demonstrate the spatial heterogeneity and site-specific nature of the results, which tends to limit their wider applicability. Although hydrological models help to qualify the patterns of water movement in disturbed mires they give little information on the processes causing such movement. However, models often operate at a scale which is valuable to environmental management, where they form largely predictive tools. Thus the way forward appears to be a closer amalgamation of field research with simplistic hydrological models so that seepage losses can be more accurately predicted, and ultimately controlled through *effective* hydrological management.

ACKNOWLEDGEMENTS

This research was jointly funded by Fisons plc and English Nature with an additional research grant from the University of Sheffield.

REFERENCES

Bay, R. (1968). *Evapotranspiration From Two Peatland Watersheds*. North Central Forest Experimental Station, USA, 45pp.

Beets, C. P. (1992) The relation between the area of open water in bog remnants and storage capacity with resulting guidelines for bog restoration. *Peatland Ecosystems and Man: An Impact Assessment* (eds O.M. Bragg, P.D. Hulme, H.A.P. Ingram & R.A. Robertson), pp.133–140. Department of Biological Sciences, University of Dundee.

Boelter, D.H. (1965). Hydraulic conductivity of peats. *Soil Science*, **100**, 227–231.

Boelter, D.H. & Verry, E.S. (1977). *Peatland and Water in the Northern Lake States*. Forest Service, US Department of Agriculture, Minnesota, 30pp.

Eggelsmann, R. (1960). Über den unterirdischen Abfluss aus Mooren. *Wasserwirtschaft*, **50**, 149–154.

Eggelsmann, R. (1981). *Ökohydrologische Aspekte von Anthropogen Beeinflussten und Unbeeinflussten Mooren Norddeutschlands*. Bodentechnologisches Institut, Bremen.

Eggelsmann, R. (1964). Die Verdunstung der Hochmoore und deren hydrographischer Einfluß. *Deutsche Gewässerkundliche Mitt.*, **8**, 138–147.

Gafni, A. & Brookes, K.N. (1990). Hydraulic characteristics of four peatlands in Minnesota. *Canadian Journal of Soil Sciences*, **70(2)**, 239–254.

Heathwaite, A.L. (1990). *The hydrology of Thorne Moors NNR*. Unpublished Report to Fisons and English Nature, 50pp.

Heathwaite, A.L. (1994) Hydrological management of a cut-over peatland. *Hydrological Processes*, **8**, 245–262.

Ingram, H.A.P. (1982) Size and shape in raised mire ecosystems: a geophysical model. *Nature*, **297**, 300–303.

Ingram, H.A.P. (1983) Hydrology. *Mires: Swamp, Bog, Fen and Moor* Volume 4A, (ed. A.J.P. Gore) pp. 67–157. Elsevier, Amsterdam.

Institute of Hydrology (1992). *The hydrology of Thorne Moors*. Unpublished Report to Fisons plc.

Ivanov, K.E. (1981). *Water Movement in Mirelands*. Academic Press, London, 276pp.

Joosten, J.H.J. (1992) Bog regeneration in the Netherlands. A Review. *Peatland Ecosystems and Man: An Impact Assessment* (eds O.M. Bragg, P.D. Hulme, H.A.P. Ingram & R.A. Robertson), pp. 367–373. Department of Biological Sciences, University of Dundee.

Limbert, M., Mitchell, R. D. & Rhodes, R. J. (1986). *Thorne Moors Birds and Man*, Doncaster and District Ornithological Society, Doncaster, 95pp.

Romanov, V. V. (1968). *Evaporation from Bogs in the European Territory of the USSR*. Israel Programme for Scientific Translations, Jerusalem, 183pp.

Schouwenaars, J. M., van Amerongen, F., & Booltink, M. (1990) Hydraulic resistance of peat layers and downward seepage in bog relicts. *International Peat Journal*, **4**, 65–76.

Streefkerk, J. G. & Casparie, W. A. (1989). *The Hydrology of Bog Ecosystems: Guidelines for Management*, Dutch National Forestry Service, 120pp.

Uhden, O. (1967). *Niederschlag- und Abflussbeobachtungen auf unberuhrten, volentwasserten und kultivierten Teilen eines Nordwestdeutschen Hochmoores der Esterweger Dose am Kustenkanal bei Papenburg*. Paul Pary, Hamburg, 20pp.

22 The Selection of Internal and External Water Management Options for Bog Restoration

J. M. SCHOUWENAARS

Department of Physical Geography, University of Groningen, Kerklaan 30, 9751 NN Haren, The Netherlands

SUMMARY

1.   In most bog remnants and cut-over bogs the water table drops too far for the re-establishment of a *Sphagnum*-dominated vegetation. This is caused by both internal processes (drainage, peat removal, changed plant–soil relations) and external processes (increased downward and lateral water losses). Each of these processes needs specific water management measures to limit adverse effects on the potential for bog restoration.

2.   At some sites it may be sufficient to improve the hydrological conditions within the bog area (internal water management option). At others it may be necessary to create hydrological 'buffer zones' around the reserve (external water management option).

3.   This paper aims to identify the most important considerations when selecting water management options. The following measures are discussed: (a) blocking dams, (b) construction of bunds, (c) enlargement of area occupied by open water and (d) creation of hydrological buffer zones.

4.   Hydrological research may be crucial for a correct assessment of perspectives for rewetting. Criteria for the selection of research methods are given. A survey of hydraulic properties of the peat layers is essential. In hydrologically 'isolated' bog remnants/cut-over bogs, research should focus on the selection of sites with good prospects for rewetting by internal measures. In areas with higher lateral and downward water losses, however, different water management options have to be analysed and evaluated before their implementation, using hydrological models. Some examples are presented.

5.   Problems related to the ecological interpretation of hydrological studies are described; special attention is given to the impact of spatial variability. Some specific hydrological research items of wetland restoration are discussed. Here, special attention is given to feedback mechanisms between renewed peat-growth and changing hydrophysical properties of the upper peat layer.

Restoration of Temperate Wetlands. Edited by B.D. Wheeler, S.C. Shaw, W.J. Fojt and R.A. Robertson
© 1995 John Wiley & Sons Ltd.

AN INTRODUCTION TO HYDROLOGICAL PROBLEMS IN BOG REMNANTS AND CUT-OVER BOGS AND WATER MANAGEMENT OPTIONS

One of the main concerns in projects aiming at the restoration of bogs is the creation of suitable hydrological conditions for the re-establishment of a bog vegetation. In undisturbed bogs the water table depth in summer is not lower than 30–40 cm (Romanov, 1968; Ivanov, 1981; Ingram, 1992).

However, in most bog remnants (parts of a former bog which are left after other parts have been destroyed or badly damaged) and in cut-over bogs (parts which have been completely altered by peat extraction) the actual water table drops below this level. This may have been caused by several reasons:

1.   Superficial drainage (trenches, smaller open drains) has lowered the phreatic level, both in winter and in summer.

2.   Peat cuttings or drainage in surrounding areas have resulted in an increase of lateral and downward water losses through the peat.

3.   Drainage, mostly accompanied by subsequent peat cutting, has changed the hydrophysical properties of the exposed peat layers. Water storage coefficients (or 'water yield', defined as the quantity of water (measured as equivalent depth) added or removed when the water table rises or falls through a unit distance) of the exposed peat layer are lower than in an original bog. As a consequence water table fluctuations have increased.

4.   When the original *Sphagnum* vegetation has been replaced by a vegetation dominated by shrubs and grasses, the root systems of the latter facilitate water extraction from deeper peat layers. This means that in dry periods the water table may drop somewhat further than at sites covered with *Sphagnum*.

During the preparation of a bog restoration project one has to analyse which of these processes are of importance to the site under consideration. Each of them needs specific water management measures to limit adverse effects on the potential for bog restoration. At some sites it may be impossible to create the hydrological conditions required for a successful re-establishment of bog vegetation. Where it is assessed that the required conditions can be created by water management, appropriate measures have to be selected.

At some sites it may be sufficient to improve the hydrological conditions within the bog area (internal water management option). At others it may be necessary to create hydrological 'buffer zones' around the reserve (external water management option). It is obvious that the latter involves more land and costs and puts more constraints on plan preparation.

At certain sites, the need for involvement of hydrological expertise may be limited. This certainly holds for bog remnants and cut-over bogs consisting of thick peat layers with very low hydraulic conductivity. Here, the high hydraulic resistance of the peat layers will strongly limit the exchange of water with adjacent areas.

In others, however, hydrological research may be crucial for a correct

Table 1. An overview of hydrological problems and water management options in bog restoration projects

	Water management options
a. WATER BALANCE – OUTPUT TERMS	
1. Drainage (open drains)	Internal (dams)
2. Downward seepage	External (buffer zones)
3. Lateral water losses	Internal, external
4. Evapotranspiration	Internal (indirectly)
b. TOP LAYER CONDITIONS	
5. Water storage capacity	Internal (inundation)
6. Topography	Internal (digging)
c. WATER QUALITY	
7. Atmospheric deposition	

assessment of prospects for rewetting. Hydrological research may include both field and model studies. This contribution aims to identify the most important considerations, including research aspects, when selecting water management measures for bog restoration.

An overview of water management options is given in Table 1. Here, the following technical activities are distinguished:

a. Blocking drains

Most bog remnants have been drained superficially to some degree and blocking these drains seems a rewetting practice of charming simplicity. Indeed, many successful attempts have been recorded, varying from the insertion of plastic sheets at regular distances to complete refilling of drains with peat.

Whether these measures are sufficient depends *inter alia* on the hydraulic conductivity of the underlying strata. If a clay deposit lies at the base of the peat, downward seepage will be very limited. If a sandy aquifer underlies the peat, downward water losses mainly depend on the thickness of the peat layers at the bottom of these drains. For cut-over bogs in Lower Saxony, Blankenburg & Kuntze (1987) recommend a minimum thickness of 0.5 m for strongly humified peat (humification degree (von Post) >7). For less humified peat a minimum thickness of 1 m is recommended (Schouwenaars, 1993b).

However, at sites where hydrophysical properties (in particular, water storage, see above) of the exposed peat layer are strongly different from those in undisturbed bogs, blocking of drains will often be insufficient. Here, in dry summer periods, the low water storage capacity, in combination with increased evaporative losses from secondary vegetation (shrubs and grasses) when compared with the original bog vegetation dominated by *Sphagnum* mosses, will frequently result in too low water tables (den Hartog *et al.*, 1994; Schouwenaars, 1993a).

b. Construction of bunds

An increase of water storage capacity near the surface must be regarded as one of the most important management options. A large quantity of water stored in and above the upper peat layers guarantees a limited drop of the water table in a period when evaporation exceeds precipitation (summer).

In most bog remnants and cut-over bogs the upper peat layers differ strongly from those of undisturbed bogs (Romanov, 1968; Schouwenaars & Vink, 1992; Schouwenaars, 1993a). The actual shortage in water storage capacity of the upper peat layers has to be compensated artificially. The construction of bunds facilitates a shallow inundation at a given site, thus creating extra water storage near the surface. Inundation in winter and spring will inhibit growth of grasses and shrubs at these sites. Experience in the Netherlands has shown that a minimum winter-inundation of about 20 cm is needed to ensure this. A smaller inundation would frequently lead to a sharp drop of the water table below the peat surface in relatively dry summers, allowing species like *Molinia caerulea* to stay dominant at these sites. For a colonisation with *Sphagnum* species the water table should not fall much below the peat surface in summer.

c. Enlargement of area occupied by open water

The construction of bunds facilitates a partial inundation at a given site, thus creating extra water storage capacity. This can also be achieved without or in addition to bunding, by the creation of small water-holding pools or trenches. In summer, during dry periods, the water level in these pools or trenches normally is higher than the (ground)water table in the peat ridges in between. As a consequence there is a constant flow of water from the trenches into the peat ridge (infiltration), resulting in relatively high water tables in these ridges. This phenomenon is illustrated in Figure 1.

Of course, the 'buffering' effect upon water table fluctuations in the peat ridge as illustrated in Figure 1 depends on rates of water infiltration. The latter depends on permeability of the peat and distance between peat ridges. Also, the area occupied by trenches in relation to the area occupied by ridges will determine the fluctuation pattern of both the water level in trenches and the water table in the ridges. For various site conditions, differing in the relative area occupied by open water, simulations with hydrological models clearly demonstrate the importance of this factor for stabilising water table fluctuations (Schouwenaars, 1988b). This aspect will be treated in more detail later (Figure 2).

Frequently, structures of trenches and ridges are present in bog remnants, in particular when sod cutting has taken place. If present, a regular pattern of trenches, small drains and little pools at limited distances (5 to 10 m) should not be destroyed by levelling. Rather, one should take advantage of these water storage facilities and even consider their enlargement by some digging activities (Beets, 1992).

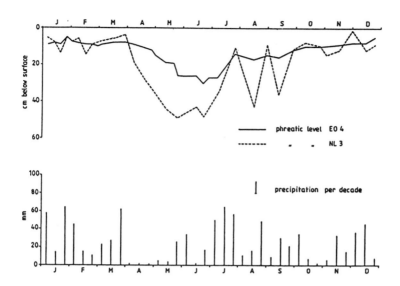

Figure 1. Groundwater fluctuations at two sites in the Engbertsdijksvenen with equal rates of downward seepage. Precipitation per 10 days (1988). The phreatic tube at site EO 4 is situated in the centre of a peat ridge, 4-m wide, which is surrounded by trenches, permanently filled with water in 1988. The phreatic tube at site NL 3 is situated 35 m from the nearest drain. Total precipitation in 1988: 895 mm; downward seepage in 1988: 80 mm.

d. Creation of hydrological buffer zones

Here, a hydrological buffer zone is defined as a zone surrounding the bog, where the water table is kept relatively high. As a result water pressure in the layers underlying the peat will also be relatively high.

At the margins of bog remnants where horizontal (lateral) water flow may occur through the peat layers towards adjacent (mostly cut-over) areas, the functioning of buffer zones is based upon the creation of a limited hydraulic gradient between the bog remnant and adjacent land. In small peat-remnants (some ha) left uncut or with minor peat extraction, with surface levels some metres above the immediate surroundings, buffer zones on shallow peat may need inundation to be effective. However, in these cases, one preferably should consider the 'sealing' of the margins of these small remnants effectively, using a low-permeability bund.

In the central parts of bog remnants and cut-over bogs, horizontal water flow through the peat layers is often negligible. When sandy aquifers underlie the peat and water flows horizontally through these aquifers towards adjacent land, a buffer zone with a high water table will lead to a relatively high water pressure in the layers underlying the peat. This leads to a reduced hydraulic head drop over the peat layers, thus limiting downward water losses. Hence, this option is important in situations where considerable water losses occur through downward seepage.

RESEARCH METHODS: FROM RAPID ASSESSMENT TO MODELLING WATER MANAGEMENT SCENARIOS

Field surveys

Well-humified peat (humification degree H > 7 (von Post scale)) has a very low hydraulic conductivity (*e.g.* Baden & Eggelsmann, 1963; Boelter, 1969). In cut-over bogs, where more than 1 m of this peat-type has been left behind, one will find a peat relict that is very isolated, hydrologically. Hence, a survey of the hydraulic properties of the peat layers is essential, *e.g.* by field- and laboratory measurements of hydraulic conductivity. A rapid assessment of humification degree at different depths by experienced people may allow a rough estimation of the hydraulic properties. Hydrological research should focus on the selection of sites within these relicts with good prospects for rewetting by internal measures (blocking ditches, creation of bunds, changing microtopography). When preparing a water management plan for such an area, one needs a well-defined scheme for removal and discharge of excess water. This includes a scheme for superficial water discharge.

Important aspects to be examined in field surveys are vegetation, type of peat, thickness of peat layers, permeability, drainage system, groundwater fluctuations and (deep) groundwater head.

Hydrological modelling

It is often difficult to make an intuitive assessment of the effectiveness of different water management options. For instance, if one expects high downward water losses, an artificial increase of water storage near the surface may be too limited, even after bunding. On the other hand, investment in hydrological buffer zones around a bog reserve may be useless if the required water storage conditions within the bog are not fulfilled. Therefore, in many cases, the different options have to be analysed and evaluated before the management practices are implemented, using hydrological models. These models allow the prediction of water balances and water table fluctuations. In general, given the high spatial variability in peatlands, modelling entails many assumptions and simplifications. Nonetheless, with these models, the sensitivity of, for example, water table fluctuations for certain water management activities can be examined, giving a better insight into the relevant mechanisms and management options.

An example of a simple one-dimensional, non-steady model

Even a one-dimensional model, describing vertical water flow, including a simple analytical description of horizontal water exchange (quasi-two-dimensional approach), can be useful for preparatory studies. The model SWAMP (Soil Water Modelling in Peat, Schouwenaars (1988a)) was developed as a tool for the evaluation of different water management options in bog relicts. In this model, site-specific information, especially about the hydro-physical properties of the peat layers and downward water losses, have to be incorporated.

Given the scarcity of reliable field data, the model was based upon a simple calculation procedure, but guarantees a good approximation of the different terms of the water balance and their variation in time (*i.e.* non-steady). In the SWAMP model, these are determined by using meteorological data (precipitation, potential evaporation), vegetation characteristics (potential transpiration, root zone depth) and hydrological properties of the peat layers and underlying mineral deposits.

For a given site, the model estimates the water balance terms, the depth of the phreatic level and water content in the unsaturated zone. To find analytical solutions for the physically-based flow equations, a number of simplifying assumptions are used. The most important are:

- the different soil layers are homogeneous;
- within each time step (decades; 10 or 11 days) water flow in the soil is regarded as steady (*i.e.* not varying in time);
- maximum capillary flux is a function of the groundwater depth;
- water uptake by plants from the root zone is a linear function of available soil moisture.

In Figure 2 some results of the model SWAMP are presented. These results describe the predicted changes in water table fluctuations in the Engbertsdijks-venen (the Netherlands), as a consequence of two different water management options. One option is to reduce downward water losses (seepage), the other is to improve the storage capacity near the surface by increasing the proportion of open water. In Figure 2 it is clearly demonstrated that a high water storage capacity of the exposed peat layer (Figure 2b) results in a higher water table, when compared to a low water storage capacity (Figure 2a). Once a high water storage capacity is present, further enlargement of the proportion of open water may be contra-effective as the increased evaporation may result in lower water levels.

The results in Figure 2 also show that the preference for each option varies and depends mainly on the actual (*i.e.* initial) amount of downward water losses. For the climatic conditions in the Engbertsdijksvenen (annual precipitation 675 mm) one can conclude that at sites with low water storage capacity, buffer zones to reduce downward seepage are only attractive when simultaneously water storage capacity is increased considerably. The latter involves enlargement of the proportion of open water at these sites.

An example of a simple two-dimensional steady state model

The 'groundwater mound theory' (Ingram, 1982; Bragg, this volume) tries to give a physically-based explanation of the shape of bogs by relating the shape to net precipitation input and hydraulic conductivity of the peat. Essentially, the analytical model which was developed to describe these relations is based upon the same assumptions as are made for drainage problems and hydrological buffer zones around bog reserves (van der Molen, 1981). Bakker (1992) presents a similar approach for the description of the shape of raised bogs.

(a)

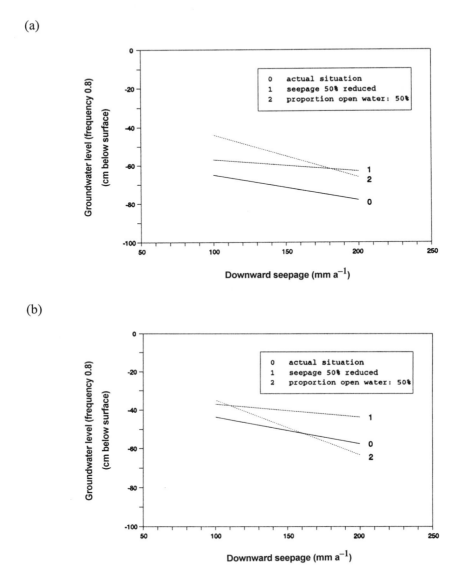

Figure 2. Expected changes in water table fluctuations in the Engbertsdijksvenen for different water management options as simulated with the SWAMP model, (a) at a site with a soil water storage coefficient $\mu = 0.15$; (b) at a site with a soil water storage coefficient $\mu = 0.30$. Option 1 is a reduction of downward water losses by 50%; Option 2 is the enlargement of the water storage capacity near the surface by enlarging the proportion of open water to 50%. The horizontal axis gives the actual downward seepage; the vertical axis gives the groundwater level which is exceeded during 80% of the growing season (1 April to 15 October), averaged for a simulation period of 30 years.

All of these approaches assume steady state flow conditions. This means that fluxes and hydraulic gradients are taken as constant (not varying in time). When applied to drainage problems, the flux is taken to be equal to precipitation surplus in periods with high rainfall (e.g. 10 mm day^{-1}). When applied to buffer zones the approach is suited for conditions during spring when average precipitation surplus is approximately 0.5 to 1 mm day^{-1}.

With this steady state approach it is not possible to simulate summer conditions in a buffer zone, simply because in summer there is no precipitation surplus. Van der Molen (1981) presents a non-steady approach for periods where precipitation equals evaporation. For a satisfactory description of summer conditions and an assessment of critical (low) water tables a non-steady approach is needed, which includes evapotranspiration losses and capillary rise in the unsaturated zone.

The shortcomings of a steady state approach are also limiting when analysing water table behaviour in bogs. In contrast to the conditions of a persistent hydraulic equilibrium with outward seepage as the critical process, as assumed in the 'groundwater-mound' model (Bragg (this volume)), upward capillary fluxes in summer are much more relevant in explaining the lowering of the water table in this period. Another serious problem when applying this model is the determination of the quantity of outward seepage through the peat body. In the 'groundwater-mound' theory this flux is taken to be equal to the average annual precipitation surplus. However, as explained above such flux actually never exists, as in winter excess water is removed superficially or through gullies and in summer upward capillary rise is the dominant flow process. Indeed, analysis of the very low hydraulic conductivity of the lower peat layers (catotelm) in combination with the very limited hydraulic gradients in bogs, indicates that the outward seepage through the lower peat layers is far less than the annual precipitation surplus.

An example of a detailed (quasi-) three-dimensional non-stationary model

During the preparation of a plan for a National Park in the Groote Peel area in the Netherlands, the SIMGRO model was applied in hydrological studies (van Walsum, 1992; van Walsum & Joosten, 1994). To support regional decision making, both internal and external water management measures were investigated. Both the internal and external measures involve changes of the hydrological system that are not constant in time. Obviously, shallow drains are only active in periods with high rainfall and in dry periods the soil moisture deficits in agricultural lands are counteracted often by means of sprinkling. Since these impacts vary temporally, they can only be modelled adequately using a non-steady model.

In the SIMGRO model, groundwater flow is modelled using a so-called quasi-three-dimensional geohydrologic schematisation, that is a schematisation into a two-dimensional horizontal flow through aquifers and a one-dimensional vertical flow through aquitards (horizontally oriented layers of lower permeability, separating aquifers). Vertical water movement in the unsaturated zone is simulated

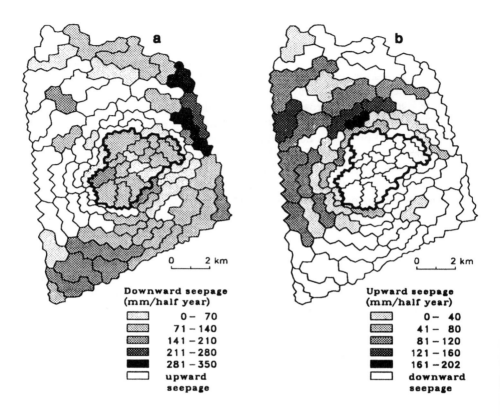

Figure 3. Subregional values of the downward seepage (a) and the upward seepage (b) in the Groote Peel area, as computed with the SIMGRO model for the summer of the year 1971 (van Walsum, 1992). Reproduced by permission of Van Walsum (1992).

one-dimensionally for groups of nodes of the two-dimensional (horizontal) groundwater model. For the description of water flow, the finite-element method is used. This is a numerical approach, where equations are solved by iteration procedures, in contrast to analytical solutions used in the models mentioned earlier.

When the model was first applied in cut-over bogs, great difficulties were experienced (van Walsum, 1992). Developed for 'rather homogeneous' agricultural lands, the high spatial variability of water levels and of hydraulic peat-properties in cut-over bogs, and especially, the crucial role of surface water, prevented a straightforward application of this model. This is probably the case with most similar hydrological models. However, after several adaptations it proved to be a suitable model for regional studies, involving cut-over bogs.

To illustrate the possibilities of these hydrological models in regional studies, an example of the output is presented in Figure 3.

Selection of research methods

In many bog remnants and cut-over bogs a better understanding of the site-specific hydrological conditions is needed to prepare plans for rewetting activities (a 'problem-oriented' approach). When there are conflicts between different interests (*e.g.* nature conservation, peat extraction, agriculture) and possible solutions have important financial consequences, great efforts are needed in plan preparation and accompanying research. Here, the use of detailed hydrological models is required. In cases where erroneous decisions have little impact in terms of values and costs, a rough approach based upon the intuitive judgement of 'experts' may be sufficient.

For process-oriented research (research aimed at a better understanding of general hydrological processes involved in bog development) both simple and detailed models can be used, depending on the specific questions involved. Here, much attention should be paid to the collection of relevant field data and some management experiments should also be included.

Table 2 presents criteria for the selection of research methods for different types of hydrological studies.

INTERPRETATION OF HYDROLOGICAL INFORMATION

In both simple and detailed hydrological models, parameter values are needed to describe the different hydrological characteristics of the sites represented by

Table 2. An overview of research methods based upon input requirements and their suitability for problem- and process-oriented studies

(relative) Input	Type of study	Problem-oriented engineering		Process-oriented research
		Internal measures	External measures	
Low	Field survey	⊤		
	Simple model	│		⊤
Medium	Field experiment	⊥	⊤	│
	Laboratory experiment		│	│
High	Detailed models		⊥	⊥

(model-) nodes. Normally, there is a large difference between the spatial scale used in hydrological models and the actual field scale relevant to understanding plant–soil–water relations. Microtopographic differences may lead to a high spatial diversity, associated with differences in plant composition.

Given the need for at least some averaging procedures in the description of a certain site (node) in simulation models, results of these models mostly present 'averaged' values for variables like water table depth and downward seepage. Probably, further progress in computer technology will allow much more detailed modelling at a very fine scale in the future. However, the collection of reliable field data appropriate to such a fine scale is very expensive and is unlikely to be possible. This implies that some procedures have to be developed for the interpretation of the 'averaged' hydrological information in a way which is relevant from an ecological viewpoint.

An important method is presented as 'range modelling' (*e.g.* van Wirdum, 1991) where the assignation of values to a variable describing field conditions takes place after the definition of a probability function for its values. Different approaches can be followed, like stochastic programming with, for example Monte Carlo procedures.

An example of the methodological problems discussed here is illustrated in Figure 4, where a comparison is made between the frequency distribution of groundwater levels at a certain moment at a hypothetical site, and the groundwater level predicted for that site with a model using average values for peat characteristics of the site. In this example, modelling neglects the spatial diversity within the site. For instance, the model suggests an actual situation where the total area has the same groundwater level of 40 cm below the surface. The model predictions for 'potential site conditions' (*e.g.* after water management measures) suggest no potential for bog regeneration, whereas in reality the potential bog area will increase from 30% to more than 40%.

In the example illustrated in Figure 4, the modelling will result in an underestimation of the potential for bog restoration. However, at other sites it may result in its overestimation. This may imply that modelling with a very fine scale results in a fairly accurate description of the spatial diversity. However, lack of reliable field data often prevents fine-scale modelling.

Van Walsum & Joosten (1993) present a method to bridge the gap between hydrological information and ecological interpretation. They assume that for permanent bog growth to be possible, the long-term average of downward seepage should not exceed a 'critical' value. This approach is illustrated in Figure 5. The curves in this figure describe the frequency distribution of the rate of downward seepage in the Groote Peel, as predicted with the SIMGRO model. Each curve represents a different situation, indicated by figures (see legend). The fraction of the area where the critical downward seepage is not exceeded is called the 'potential bog area'. For different scenarios of water management, the areal changes in 'potential bog area' were analysed and this information was used for

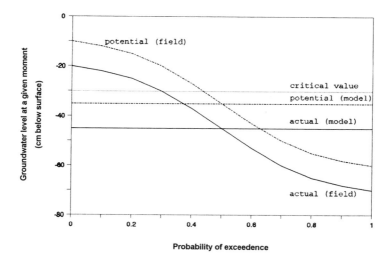

Figure 4. An illustration of possible errors in the estimation of the 'potential bog area' when using spatially averaged values in hydrological modelling. The horizontal axis gives the probability that the corresponding groundwater level, indicated by the curve, is exceeded, for example, in the actual field situation about 30% of the area has a groundwater level above −30 cm (critical value) and in 100% of the area it is above −70 cm. The area with potential groundwater levels above the 'critical value' is regarded as suitable for bog restoration.

final decision making. Although the amount of seepage regarded as 'critical' is open to question, this attempt gives a good example of the difficulties involved.

REWETTING: SOME FUNDAMENTAL RESEARCH NEEDS

In general, there is good knowledge of the hydrological aspects of drainage and agricultural land improvement. This knowledge is of some use in questions related to rewetting. Here, the main hydrological problem is to find out how rewetting processes can be stimulated by water management measures. This question can be partly answered using existing hydrological engineering approaches (see selection of research methods). However, there are many urgent new questions related to wetland restoration and new research programmes have to be started.

In the past drainage activities were mostly followed immediately by soil improvement and other agricultural activities, and plant–soil–water relations were changed rapidly. By contrast, planned activities for rewetting will be executed over a considerable period (10–30 years). At some sites, removal of the plant cover, for instance trees, or large-scale inundation may lead to relatively 'abrupt' changes in vegetation. However, the changes in vegetation will generally be spontaneous and slow and changes in plant–soil–water–atmosphere relations will

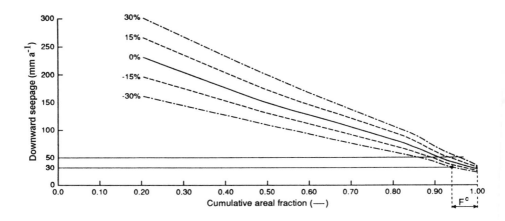

Figure 5. An example of relating the 'potential bog area' to critical values for downward seepage (van Walsum, 1992). For a given fraction of the area (comparable with the probability of exceedence in Figure 3) the downward seepage is equal to or greater than the value indicated by the curve. The figures indicated for each curve (*e.g.* +15%) indicate the relative change in average downward seepage, compared with the actual situation (0%). These changes result from water management measures and are predicted with a hydrological model. The fraction of the area (F^c) where downward seepage does not exceed a hypothetic rate, regarded as critical (*e.g.* 30 or 50 mm a^{-1}) is assumed to be suited for bog restoration. Reproduced by permission of Van Walsum (1992).

occur gradually. Hence, the temporal aspects of rewetting processes are of utmost importance.

Schouwenaars (1990) showed that the disappearance of a living *Sphagnum* layer in bogs and replacement by the grass *Molinia caerulea* (after drainage) has increased evapotranspiration during dry periods. The re-establishment of a *Sphagnum* cover will reduce evaporative water losses during dry periods. Also the water storage capacity at a site with a living *Sphagnum* cover is larger than at a site covered with *Molinia*.

These are examples of how succession in vegetation and related changes in plant cover influence local hydrology (evapotranspiration, water storage capacity, resistance to surface flow, *etc.*). Probably, water budgets will change gradually and also groundwater recharge may show a gradual increase or decrease. Also ground- and surface water flow towards ditches may change gradually and may cause changes in the temporal discharge pattern of streams around the rewetted sites.

The restoration of a *Sphagnum* vegetation in bog remnants and cut-over bogs will induce 'intrinsic mechanisms' which contribute to the recovery of wetter conditions in dry periods. These 'intrinsic self-regulating' processes need to be taken into account when simulating rewetting processes with hydrological models. This requires a new approach in modelling, which can generate a satisfactory description of relevant feedback mechanisms.

Summarised, the following fundamental questions seem to be relevant for further studies on hydrological processes relevant to bog restoration and their modelling.

- How can hydrophysical properties of the upper peat layers and micro-topography be described adequately to assess water storage capacity near the surface, including its spatial variability?
- How should temporal variability of the factors mentioned above be described to permit its inclusion in models simulating rewetting processes over several decades or centuries?
- Which modelling concepts should be used to describe the feedback mechanisms between peat growth and changing hydrophysical properties of the upper layer?
- What type of risk analysis is needed to determine and study the 'critical' ranges of relevant hydrological variables (*e.g.* water table behaviour, capillary rise)?

REFERENCES

Baden, W. & Eggelsmann, R. (1963). Zur Durchlässigkeit der Moorböden. *Zeitschrift für Kulturtechnik und Flurbereinigung*, **4**, 226–254.

Bakker, T.W.M. (1992). The shape of bogs from a hydrological point of view. *International Peat Journal*, **4**, 47–54.

Beets, C.P. (1992). The relation between the area of open water in bog remnants and storage capacity with resulting guidelines for bog restoration. *Peatland Ecosystems and Man: An Impact Assessment* (eds O.M. Bragg, P.D. Hulme, H.A.P. Ingram, & R.A. Robertson), pp. 133–140. International Peat Society/Department of Biological Sciences, University of Dundee, Dundee.

Blankenburg, J. & Kuntze, H. (1987). Moorkundlich-hydrologische Voraussetzungen der Wiedervernassung von Hochmooren. *Telma*, **17**, 51–58.

Boelter, D.H. (1969). Physical properties of peat as related to degree of decomposition. *Soil Science Society of America, Proceedings*, **83**, 606–609.

den Hartog, G., Neumann, H.H., King, K.M. & Chipanshi, A.C. (1994). Energy budget measurements using eddy correlation and Bowen ratio techniques at the Kinosheo Lake tower site during the Northern Wetlands Study. *Journal of Geophysical Research*, **99**, 1539–1549.

Ingram, H.A.P. (1982). Size and shape in raised mire ecosystems; a geophysical model. *Nature*, **297**, 300–303.

Ingram, H.A.P. (1992). Introduction to the ecohydrology of mires in the context of cultural perturbation. *Peatland Ecosystems and Man: An Impact Assessment* (eds O.M. Bragg, P.D. Hulme, H.A.P. Ingram, & R.A. Robertson), pp. 67–93. International Peat Society/ Department of Biological Sciences, University of Dundee, Dundee.

Ivanov, K.E. (1981). *Water Movement in Mirelands*. Academic Press, London, 276pp.

Romanov, V.V. (1968). *Hydrophysics of Bogs*. Ed. Monson Bindery Ltd, Jerusalem.

Schouwenaars, J.M. (1988a). The impact of water management upon groundwater fluctuations in a disturbed bog relict. *Agricultural Water Management* **14**, 439–449.

Schouwenaars, J.M. (1988b). Hydrological research in disturbed bogs and its role in decisions on water management in the Netherlands. *Proceedings of the International Symposium on the Hydrology of Wetlands in Temperate and Cold Regions.* Publications of the Academy of Finland 4/1988, **Vol.1**, 170–177.

Schouwenaars, J.M. (1990). A study on the evapotranspiration of *Molinia caerulea* and *Sphagnum papillosum*, using small weighable lysimeters. In: Schouwenaars, J.M. (1990). *Problem oriented research on plant–soil–water relations.* PhD. thesis, Agricultural University Wageningen, the Netherlands.

Schouwenaars, J.M. (1993a). Hydrological differences between bogs and bog relicts and consequences for bog restoration. *Hydrobiologia*, **265**, 217–224.

Schouwenaars, J.M. (1993b). Möglichkeiten für die Wiedervernässung von Hochmooren in Abhängigkeit von der Torfmächtigkeit. *Telma, 23*, 117–123.

Schouwenaars, J.M. & Vink, J.P.M. (1992). Hydrophysical properties of peat relicts in a former bog and perspectives for *Sphagnum* regrowth. *International Peat Journal*, **4**, 15–28.

van der Molen, W.H. (1981). Über die Breite hydrologischer Schutzzonen um Naturschutzgebiete in Mooren. *Telma*, **11**, 213–220.

van Walsum, P.E.V. (1992). Water management in the Groote Peel bog reserve and surrounding agricultural area; simulation and optimization. *Report* **49**, DLO Winand Staring Centre, Wageningen.

van Walsum, P.E.V. & Joosten, J.H.J. (1994). Quantification of local ecological effects in regional hydrologic modelling of bog reserves and surrounding agricultural lands. *Agricultural Water Management*, **25**, 45–55.

van Wirdum, G. (1991). Interface theory and the base state of fen mires. Proceedings Symposium: *Hydrological and ecological sound management of soil and groundwater, Vienna. IAHS Publication*, **202**, 173–186.

23 Hydrological Protection and Rewetting of Raised Bogs Influenced by Man

R. R. F. EGGELSMANN

Julius-Leber-Straße 11, D-28329, Bremen, Germany[1]

ABSTRACT

After a period of mire utilisation lasting nearly two centuries, more than 90% of the peatland area in Germany is now used for agriculture, forestry or peat extraction. Protection of the remaining peatlands therefore now stands in the forefront of public interest and policy.

The German Federal State of Lower Saxony is rich in mires (more than 10%). In 1981, a state mire protection programme decided that all the peat-winning areas of raised bogs and those bogs which are not used by agriculture or forestry – a total of nearly 30,000 ha – should be taken for protection, for rewetting and renaturation.

At the present time there are no actively-growing raised bogs in north-western Germany. The surface morphology of the original raised bogs has therefore been investigated from the topographic maps of the turn of the century. In addition, the work of the botanist C.A. Weber (1902) concerning the relationships between surface morphology, recent vegetation and peat growth (accumulation) of the original raised bogs in Germany has been studied.

Two comprehensive experimental areas were set up in cut-over raised bogs by the Soil Technological Institute (Bremen): since 1976 at Lichtenmoor (district Nienburg), after 'white' peat winning and since 1983 at Leegmoor (near Papenburg, district Emsland) after 'black' peat winning.

Preliminary data on water balances have been used to establish some ecohydrological principles. The ecotechnical measures described for mire restoration are based on the results of many years' field experiments, and on many surveys and discussions with colleagues in Germany and other countries. Further, experiences gained in agricultural engineering for flood irrigation have also been useful, especially for investigating rewetting processes.

---

[1] Former Professor of the Bodentechnologisches Institut, Bremen. Unfortunately, illness prevented Professor Eggelsmann giving his full presentation at the Symposium.

Restoration of Temperate Wetlands. Edited by B.D. Wheeler, S.C. Shaw, W. J. Fojt and R.A. Robertson
© 1995 John Wiley & Sons Ltd.

Mire rewetting for renaturation and regeneration is a very long-term problem. The implications and results of experiments can therefore only be regarded as preliminary indications. At present, no-one knows whether raised bog regeneration on large, flat surfaces is really possible, even in the long term, because rainfall is now acidic and contains many nutrients and damaging substances (for example, heavy metals, herbicides, fungicides). However, if peat accumulation has been initiated, after centuries or a millennium, mire research workers will be able to study the ecological situation of our time from these peat layers.

SELECTED BIBLIOGRAPHY

Baden, W. & Eggelsmann, R. (1968). The hydrological budget of high bogs in the Atlantic Regions. *Proceedings of the 3rd International Peat Congress, Quebec, Canada*, 206–211.

Blankenburg, J. & Eggelsmann, R. (1990). Regenerationsversuch auf hochmoorartigem Leegmoor im Lichtenmoor – hydrologische Ergebnisse (1976/88). (Regeneration field experiment of raised bog after peat cutting in Lichtenmoor – results of peat soil conditions and hydrology (1976/88). *Zeitschrift fur Kulturtechnik und Landentwicklung*, **31,** 117–124.

Eggelsmann, R. (1975). The water balance of lowland areas in north-western regions of the FRG. *The Hydrology of Marsh Ridden Areas.* Proceedings of the Minsk symposium, 355–368. The Unesco Press, International Association of Hydrological Sciences.

Eggelsmann, R. (1980). Hydrological aspects of peatland utilization and conservation in northwestern Germany. *Proceedings of the 6th International Peat Congress, Duluth, Minnesota*, 28–30.

Eggelsmann, R. (1984). Annual groundwater course in peatlands with different using (vegetation). *Proceedings of the 7th International Peat Congress, Dublin, Ireland*, Vol.1, 137–147.

Eggelsmann, R. (1988). Rewetting for protection and renaturation / regeneration of peatland after or without peat winning. *Proceedings of the 8th International Peat Congress, Leningrad*, Vol **3**, 251–260.

Eggelsmann, R. & Blankenburg, J. (1993). Mire and water – Leegmoor Project. The results of 5 years field experiments. *Naturschutz und Landschaftspflege in Niedersachsen,* **29.** 32pp.

Kuntze, H. & Eggelsmann, R. (1981). Zur Schutzfähigkeit nordwestdeutscher Moore. *Telma,* **11,** 197–212.

Nick, K-J. (ed.) (1993). Beiträge zur Wiedervernässung abgebauter Schwarztorfflächen. *Naturschutz und Landschaftspflege in Niedersachsen,* **29**, 1–127.

Weber, C.A. (1902). *Über die Vegetation und Entstehung des Hochmoores von Augstumal im Memmeldelta.* Paul Parey, Berlin.

24 Effects of Damming Peat Cuttings on Glasson Moss and Wedholme Flow, two Lowland Raised Bogs in North-west England

F. J. MAWBY

English Nature, Wayside, Kirkbride, Carlisle, CA5 5JR, UK

SUMMARY

1.   This paper presents the results from six years of vegetation monitoring after damming ditches on Glasson Moss and three years of water level monitoring before and after ditch damming on both Glasson Moss and Wedholme Flow. The aims of management are: (a) to maintain the characteristic raised bog vegetation on areas that have not been cut for peat; and (b) to restore conditions suitable for the regeneration of *Sphagnum* bog on cut-over areas.

2.   Vegetation data indicate that restoring *Sphagnum* to a damaged bog surface is a slow process except in those areas where flooding or high water tables are maintained. In constantly flooded conditions, *Sphagnum cuspidatum* colonises and grows rapidly.

3.   Water table monitoring shows that on little-disturbed *Sphagnum*-dominated bog the range of water table fluctuation is < 200 mm and surface flooding is rare. In cut-over bog before damming, the water table fluctuated between 100 mm below the surface in wet periods and 800 mm in dry periods. Surface flooding never occurred.

4.   The dipwell monitoring showed that water tables continue to fluctuate after damming. The fluctuation varies considerably relative to bog topography. Where water is easily contained and flooding sustained, the fluctuation is less than in sloping areas where water continues to drain through the peat.

5.   The rise and fall of the bog is measured with 'peat anchors'. These show that the surface of the uncut bog fluctuates by 30–35 mm compared with 50–60 mm in cut-over bog. They also show that the surface of the re-soaked cut-over bog is rising slightly relative to the original peat depth.

INTRODUCTION

Glasson Moss and Wedholme Flow are situated in the county of Cumbria in North West England on the lowlands by the Solway Firth (Figure 1) and are two of several important raised bogs in the area. They are both Grade 1 Nature

Restoration of Temperate Wetlands. Edited by B.D. Wheeler, S.C. Shaw, W.J. Fojt and R.A. Robertson
© 1995 John Wiley & Sons Ltd.

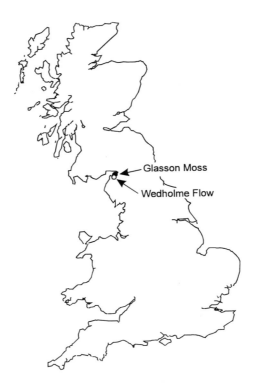

Figure 1. Location of Wedholme Flow and Glasson Moss (Cumbria, north-west England).

Conservation Review sites (Ratcliffe, 1977) and National Nature Reserves (NNR's). Until the middle of this century they were both cut for domestic fuel around the perimeter. Much of the remaining shallow peat has been converted to agricultural land. In the mid 1800s most owners marked their boundaries by cutting drains across the mosses. The first commercial cutting occurred in the early 1900s but ceased in the late 1920s. Cutting resumed in 1948 on both sites but was abandoned on Glasson Moss in 1954. Wedholme Flow has been cut continuously since 1948. English Nature acquired 168 ha of this area in 1990 in order to protect uncut areas from further damage and to rehabilitate the cuttings. The main habitats and areas distinguished on the two bogs are summarised in Table 1.

A programme of damming drains and peat cuttings around Glasson Moss and Wedholme Flow NNRs was undertaken between 1986 and 1993 in order to control water loss and stimulate regeneration of *Sphagnum*. This large-scale work, covering some 150 ha of cuttings on Wedholme Flow and 60 ha on Glasson Moss, has been largely experimental. On Glasson Moss between 1986 and 1989 over 1000 dams, covering 16 ha of cuttings, were constructed with either peat plugs incorporating a polyethylene-sheet waterproof membrane or with tin sheets. They

Table 1. Main habitats and areas distinguished on Wedholme Flow and Glasson Moss, Cumbria.

	Wedholme Flow (ha)	Glasson Moss (ha)
Uncut bog with original surface	125	38
Abandoned cuttings or damaged bog	310	152
Area currently being cut by peat milling	160	nil
Fringe habitats	185	34
Area of Site of Special Scientific Interest	780	224
Area owned orleased as National Nature Reserve	270	107

were constructed by volunteer labour and lightweight machinery. Since 1989 the remaining areas of cuttings on both sites have been dammed with substantial peat plugs by contractors using larger machines.

The aim of monitoring is to detect the effectiveness of damming by recording changes in the vegetation and water table levels of the bog. It was important to ensure that monitoring was practical. Dipwells were installed two years in advance of the damming work on Wedholme Flow, to provide a baseline from which to measure the changes.

Further details of the work are described by Mawby (1993).

VEGETATION MONITORING ON GLASSON MOSS

Methods

Permanent quadrats were established on two areas of cuttings soon after damming. Three quadrats, each 1m², were established in 1986: (i) on a baulk between two cuttings, dominated by *Calluna vulgaris* (L.) Hull; (ii) in a *Calluna*-dominated area on the fringe of the cuttings; and (iii) in an area between the cuttings and the little-damaged bog with remnants of the original surface. A transect was established in 1987 comprising 10 0.5 m² quadrats, each *c.* 10 m apart. These occupy a slope of *c.* 1 in 40, the first five on bog with original surface which retains some characteristic species, the second five on *Calluna*-dominated bog crossed by cuttings.

The occurrence of all higher plants and mosses was noted and cover was recorded using a six-point-cover scale (1, one or a few plants; 2, 2–20%; 3, 21–40%; 4, 41–60%; 5, 61–80%; 6 = 81–100% cover). Recording intervals have been annual until 1990 and biennial thereafter, during the period July to August.

Results

Changes in the mean cover of selected species in each quadrat for 1987 and 1992 are shown in Figure 2. The response of *C. vulgaris* (an indicator of relatively low

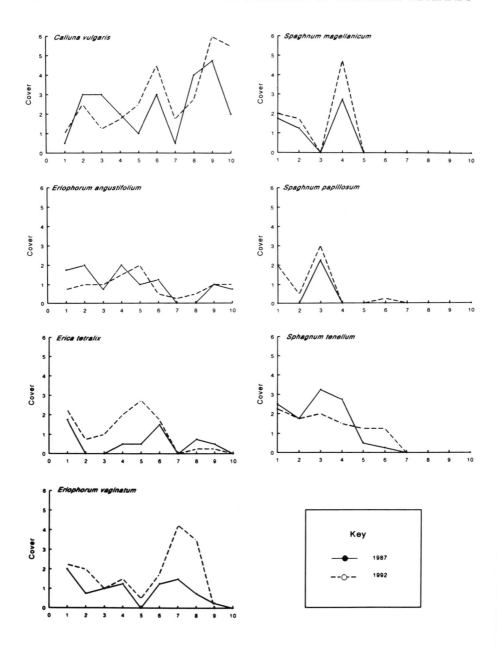

Figure 2. Occurrence of seven plant species in 10 quadrats located on a 90-m transect on Glasson Moss, crossing the interface between a cut-over area (dammed in 1987) (quadrats 1–5) and the uncut bog (quadrats 6–10), recorded in 1987 and 1992. Cover was recorded using a six-point-cover scale (see text).

or fluctuating water tables) has been variable. Whilst there has been a decline in cover of *Calluna* in part of the transect (quadrats 2, 3, 4 & 8) it has remained static or increased in the remainder and still has high cover values within the cuttings. There was a die back between 1987 and 1989 which reduced overall cover, but cover has since recovered to some degree. By contrast, *Erica tetralix* L., taken here as an indicator of rising water table levels, has shown a general increase in cover in the cut-over bog. The most significant increase in cover is shown by *Eriophorum vaginatum* L., particularly in the *Calluna*-dominated quadrats (5–9). This species seems to be a good indicator of a rising water table in these circumstances.

There has been a decline in the cover of *Eriophorum angustifolium* Honck. in quadrats 1, 2 & 4, where the Sphagna have increased. Most significantly, *E. angustifolium* has increased in the *Calluna*-dominated quadrats (5, 9 & 10) and has established in 7 & 8, probably indicating increasing wetness. However, regardless of its preference for waterlogged areas, this species has the ability to colonise dry, *Calluna*-dominated peat, as the 1987 recording shows. There has been a notable increase in *Sphagnum papillosum* Linb., including colonisation of three additional quadrats. *Sphagnum magellanicum* Brid. has also notably increased but only where it was already established. There has been a general decrease of *Sphagnum tenellum* where the other two species have increased. Nevertheless, it has increased in quadrats 5 & 6 where there is no competition from *S. magellanicum* and *S. papillosum*.

Compared with the dramatic growth of *Sphagnum cuspidatum* in flooded cuttings, all of these *Sphagnum* species are very slow to colonise. General observations are that *Sphagnum papillosum* is the first *Sphagnum* species to recolonise bare peat where water tables have been raised sufficiently, with *Sphagnum tenellum* showing a limited response.

HYDROLOGICAL MONITORING

Introduction

Dipwells were installed in March 1990 to measure water table fluctuations on Glasson Moss and Wedholme Flow. They were located in areas of uncut bog and in various locations on cut-over bog on both sites prior to damming. Three dipwells on Glasson Moss were in previously-dammed cuttings.

Methods

Dipwell transects

Three transects of dipwells have been installed on Wedholme Flow. Transect 1 (505 m), comprises 19 dipwells on undisturbed *Sphagnum*-dominated bog and 18 dipwells on an area cut until 1990. A main drain divides the two areas. Transect 2 (60 m), comprising 11 dipwells, is perpendicular to a drain dividing the current

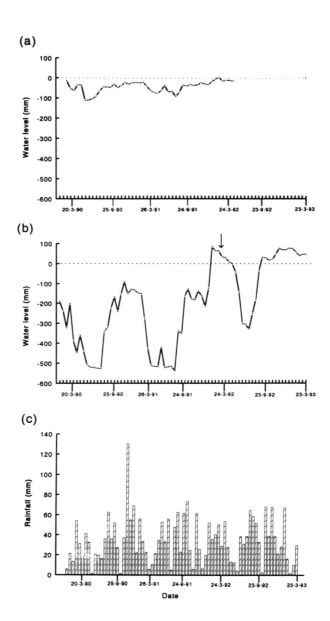

Figure 3. The water table movement in (a) undisturbed, *Sphagnum*-dominated bog on Glasson Moss and (b) cut-over bog on Wedholme Flow in relation to (c) rainfall, March 1990 to March 1993. The dotted line indicates ground level. The area on Wedholme Flow was dammed in February 1992 (↓). Annual rainfall totals: 20.3.90–26.3.91: 870 mm; 26.3.91–24.3.92: 819 mm; 25.3.92–23.3.93: 900 mm.

area of milling fields and an area that was cut between 1976 and 1985, and dammed in 1993. Transect 3 (120 m) is in another part of these abandoned cuttings. It comprises 22 dipwells, 11 either side of a drain between the cut-over area and the badly damaged but uncut bog still supporting Sphagna.

On Glasson Moss there are 10 dipwells: three on the 'best' area of uncut *Sphagnum* bog; two on a similar area but affected by adjacent abandoned cuttings; two in cuttings dammed prior to installation; and three in areas dammed in 1992.

'Peat anchors' have been installed beside each dipwell on Glasson Moss and there are twelve distributed along the transects on Wedholme Flow. These are 60 cm square metal plates set 15 cm below the surface against a datum post sunk into the mineral soil. The plate rises and falls with the expansion of the bog surface and this is measured from a datum mark on the anchor post. The peat anchors and dipwells have been surveyed to Ordnance Datum.

Rainfall data are provided by a rain gauge installed on the edge of Wedholme Flow. The rainfall, anchors and dipwells have been recorded at two-week intervals since April 1990. The water level in each dipwell is measured accurately from the top of the well using an electrical device and adjusted to give the water level relative to the ground level (to the nearest 5 mm).

Results

The results of three years of monitoring can only be analysed briefly at this stage. A representative sample of wells and anchors has been chosen to highlight some specific points.

Rainfall is a critical factor and shows a close match with the bog water table (Figure 3). In undisturbed, *Sphagnum*-dominated bog on both sites the wells show a very stable water table (Figure 3a). There is an annual fluctuation of <150 mm on Glasson Moss and <200 mm on Wedholme Flow. The greater fluctuation on Wedholme Flow is probably caused by the adjacent cuttings. Now that these are dammed, a lower fluctuation is anticipated. This limited range of movement within undisturbed *Sphagnum*-dominated bog is also shown by the peat anchors (Figure 4).

Where there has been any form of cutting, all dipwells and peat anchors show a widely fluctuating water table (Figures 3 & 4) which, although higher, still fluctuates since damming. It appears that the cut-over peat is very free draining in at least the top 500 mm, both in the recently cut-over peat on Wedholme Flow and in cuttings on Glasson Moss that have been abandoned for 40 years. The water table rarely comes within 100 mm of the surface and surface flooding is very rare. The water table fluctuates widely and freely in response to rain and dry weather. During the summer the water in most wells shows a fall to at least 500 mm and in several a drop to 700 mm or more. This clearly illustrates the problem that has to be overcome in the restoration process.

(a)

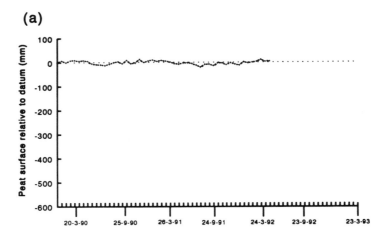

(b)

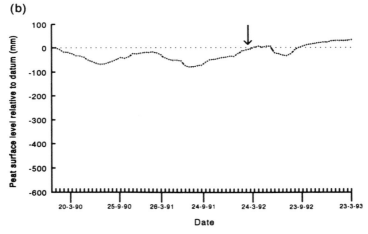

Figure 4. The vertical movement of the ground surface shown by 'peat anchors' in (a) little-damaged *Sphagnum*-dominated bog on Glasson Moss, compared with (b) cut-over bog on Wedholme Flow (dammed in February 1992 (↓)). The dotted line indicates the fixed installation datum.

DISCUSSION

The dipwells have monitored water levels for one year following the damming operations and show a very varied response. The water level continues to drop quickly during dry spells in the summer, even on areas where the bog surface is level or shallow basins have formed and surface flooding is maintained over much of the year (Figure 3). There has only been a small rise in the mean maximum and minimum water level where the bog surface slopes, and sustaining high water tables remains a problem. These maximum and minimum levels are an important aspect of restoring bog vegetation and require more detailed analysis. Summer water tables seem to be particularly critical to the regeneration of Sphagna. In any situation on dammed cuttings, the regeneration of Sphagna and other forms of bog vegetation is very slow if the water table is not maintained consistently high throughout the year. Monitoring of peat anchor levels has shown that damming leads to a rapid expansion of the peat as it reabsorbs the water, indicating that water is being retained.

Dipwell data and vegetation data illustrate the problem of sustaining consistently high water tables necessary for the restoration of the acrotelm, particularly during the summer. Where flooding of cuttings and shallow basins is sustained, *Calluna vulgaris* is rapidly killed and replaced by a vigorous growth of *Sphagnum cuspidatum* and *Eriophorum angustifolium*. But, where the water table continues to fluctuate, vegetation response is variable. If high water levels are maintained *Calluna* shows stunting and die-back. There is a relatively quick response to even a small increase in water tables by *E. vaginatum*, *E. angustifolium*, *Erica tetralix* and *Rhynchospora alba*. The response of the Sphagna also varies, depending on the stability of the water table. The most responsive species are *S. papillosum* and *S. tenellum*; both *S. magellanicum* and *S. capillifolium* are very slow to respond. *Drosera rotundifolia* and *Andromeda polifolia* also respond slowly.

These interim results show a slow but steady change in the vegetation as a result of the damming. The quadrats cover a very small area but nonetheless reflect the overall change. They do not show the more dynamic response of *Sphagnum cuspidatum* in flooded cuttings. In some of the areas dammed in 1986 the hummock-forming Sphagna, particularly *S. papillosum*, are developing over the *S. cuspidatum* mat.

ACKNOWLEDGEMENTS

I am grateful to Glyn Woods for preparing the figures and to the editors for constructive comments and help in preparation of the text.

REFERENCES

Mawby, F.J. (1993). The restoration of two lowland raised bogs in Cumbria: Glasson Moss and Wedholme Flow National Nature Reserves. Dip.CM Dissertation, Birkbeck College, University of London.

Ratcliffe, D.A. (1977). *A Nature Conservation Review*. 2 volumes. Cambridge University Press, Cambridge.

25 Niche Requirements of Birds in Raised Bogs: Habitat Attributes in Relation to Bog Restoration

B. BÖLSCHER

Zoological Institute, Technical University of Braunschweig, Pockelsstrasse 10 a, D-38106 Braunschweig, Germany

SUMMARY

1. In the western Palearctic, breeding bird assemblages of natural open raised bogs and of restored raised bog remnants are similar in guild structure and species composition. They originate from a group of about 45 species, most of which are ground nesters.

2. Habitat features of abandoned peat cuttings and drained 'still-stand complexes' which had been restored by rewetting and removal of trees differed from those of natural raised bogs, particularly in having a taller and denser vegetation, a smaller range of moisture gradient and a more uniform vegetation physiognomy. Rewetted bogs did not have an undulating surface relief of hummocks and hollows.

3. Most of the bird species were less adaptable in responding to variations in peat physical properties than to variations in vegetation structure.

4. Between locations, whinchat (*Saxicola rubetra*) and yellow wagtail (*Motacilla flava*) exhibited a clear niche shift, matching changes in vertical vegetation structures. These species evidently selected the best-suited vegetation structure within available habitat properties.

5. Golden plover (*Pluvialis apricaria*) was confined to the shortest and most sparse vegetation. Habitat properties provided by conventional restoration practices are considered suboptimal for this species. These deficiencies may be related to an undulating surface relief as well as to physical properties of the soil.

INTRODUCTION

Restoration of raised bogs in terms of bird conservation may focus upon various objectives. One ideal goal would be the re-establishment of habitats for highly specialised bird species that exclusively inhabit raised bogs in their total area of distribution. In the western Palearctic, no single bird species is exclusively confined to raised bogs. Yet, in a well-defined geographical area (*e.g.* southern Scandinavia, central European Plains) subsequent to the onset of peat accumulation in postglacial times, a small number of bird species seem to have

Restoration of Temperate Wetlands. Edited by B.D. Wheeler, S.C. Shaw, W.J. Fojt and R.A. Robertson

developed strong affinities with the particular habitat conditions on raised bogs. As trees and shrub thickets are scarce, most of these birds are ground nesters. Avian communities of typical open raised bogs in the western Palearctic are poor in species (Peus, 1928), but such bogs have abundant individuals of one or two dominant passerines. Species richness depends on area, habitat patchiness and structure, and the proportion of open water (Boström & Nilsson, 1983, *cf.* Usher & Thompson, 1993). Thus, when defining the major goal of bog restoration in ornithological terms, it may simply be suggested as 're-establishment of a bird assemblage as similar as possible to that of a natural raised bog'. This objective fits the hypothesis that rewetting is an essential restoration practice to provide bog remnants appropriate for bog-typical birds, but additional restoration practices may be of similar importance. Tracing bird–habitat relations on natural raised bogs and restored bogs, the present study focused on three major questions to examine this hypothesis:

1. How similar are breeding bird assemblages of natural raised bogs to those of habitat types established following rewetting of raised bog remnants and peat-cuttings?
2. How do different rewetting practices affect bird species richness and abundance?
3. Is habitat use by particular species on rewetted bogs similar to that on undamaged natural raised bogs?

The ideal circumstance for such an investigation would be provided by having rewetted bogs and undamaged raised bogs adjacent to one another or, at least, within the same region. However, such a situation is often difficult to find. For example, in north-western Germany, although much bog rewetting has taken place, little undamaged bog remains. In southern Sweden there are both 'natural' bogs and bogs subject to peat extraction, but little rewetting of damaged sites. Therefore a comparison was made of the bird assemblages on damaged, partly rewetted German bogs with those of 'undamaged' raised bogs in southern Sweden. The bird assemblage of these is believed to be similar to that which occupied the north German bogs before they were damaged.

STUDY AREAS

Field work was undertaken in 1985 and from 1989 to 1991 on five raised bog complexes in southern Sweden and three raised bog remnants in the central European Plains (Figure 1). The Swedish bogs (Vakö Myr, Arshult Myr, Store Mosse, Anderstorp Store Mosse, Komosse) are virtually undisturbed and thus still in a 'natural' state. Altitudes of four locations range between 140 m and 170 m. The most northern bog has an altitude of about 330–340 m. In southern Sweden mean annual temperatures range from 5°C to 7.5°C, and the mean temperature in July is about 16°C. Mean annual precipitation in the most western bog comes close to 1000 mm, while in the other four areas it ranges from 600 mm to 750 mm (see Malmer, 1988). All of these bogs have a lagg. Some of them consist of two or

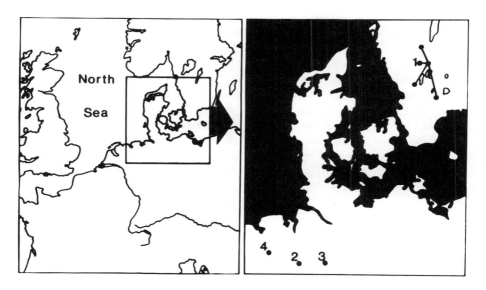

Figure 1. Location of study sites in the western Palearctic subregion. 1 = undisturbed natural raised bogs in southern Sweden, 2 = Südliches Wietingsmoor: rewetted bog remnants including former industrial peat excavation fields, 3 = Bissendorfer Moor: rewetted bog remnants containing former domestic peat cuttings, 4 = Tinner Dose: small nearly undamaged parts of a large bog complex.

more truly ombrotrophic sections which have a marginal slope and a flat plateau and are separated by strips of poor fen. Trees, mostly pine (*Pinus sylvestris*)[1], but also birch (*Betula pubescens*) and sometimes spruce (*Picea abies*), are frequent on the marginal slopes. On the plateaux, tree cover ranges from 0.3 to 2.0%. Small trees and *Betula nana* cover up to 3%. The surface of the plateaux and slopes has numerous hummocks and hollows, while lawns and soft mossy mats are confined to the plateaux. The commonest moss species on the hummocks is *Sphagnum fuscum,* while *Sphagnum magellanicum* is dominant on soft mats and *Sphagnum cuspidatum* in the hollows. Of the vascular plants, *Calluna vulgaris, Empetrum nigrum* and *Rubus chamaemorus* are dominant on large high hummock strings, and *Eriophorum vaginatum, Andromeda polifolia* and *Vaccinium microcarpum* on shallow hummocks. In the two most southern bogs, *Erica tetralix* and *Myrica gale* occur in addition to these species. Wet lawns support much *Trichophorum cespitosum,* while in the hollows *Rhynchospora alba, Scheuchzeria palustris, Carex limosa* or *Eriophorum angustifolium* predominate. On one bog there are numerous oval-shaped ponds on the plateau, which have a hollow-type vegetation. In some locations, the vegetation of the hollows had vanished and had been

---

[1] Nomenclature follows Ehrendorfer (1973) for vascular plants and Frahm & Frey (1983) for bryophytes

replaced by mudflats. Hollows and lawns retain standing water until early summer. Within the truly ombrotrophic parts of these five bogs, seven sample sites were selected, each 9–18 ha in size, and investigated in either 1989, 1990 or 1991. The Swedish sites are here collectively referred to as 'site 1'.

The three sites in the central European Plains are situated along a climatic gradient from atlantic to subcontinental conditions, distances to the North Sea being 50–150 km. Along this west–east axis mean annual precipitation ranges from 660 mm to 750 mm, mean annual temperatures are about 8.5°C, and mean temperatures in July are about 17.0°C. In the past, these bogs have been affected by drainage and domestic or industrial peat exploitation. Today, as a result of rewetting practices and conservation management, they are in different successional stages of regeneration and land use. Where hummocks are present the vegetation consists of *Sphagnum magellanicum*, *Sphagnum papillosum*, *Vaccinium oxycoccos*, *Andromeda polifolia* and *Erica tetralix*. Locally, *Calluna vulgaris* adds to these species. Lawns are dominated by *Eriophorum vaginatum* and *Erica tetralix*, supplemented in wetter places by *Sphagnum recurvum* and *Eriophorum angustifolium*. Frequently, dry peat is covered with purple moorgrass (*Molinia caerulea*).

'Site 2' is a section of the large bog complex 'Südliches Wietingsmoor' (*c*. 1200 ha), situated at an altitude of 36–40 m. The entire bog has been extensively drained until the late 1970s, and more than two-thirds has been altered by domestic and commercial peat cutting. Peat exploitation has gradually ceased during the last 15 years, and rewetting of large parts has proceeded as part of a conservation project. These habitats retain up to 30% cover of standing water until early summer. The vegetation of the wettest sections consists of pure stands of *Eriophorum angustifolium* and *Eriophorum vaginatum*. On higher elevated peat, *Calluna vulgaris* and *Erica tetralix* are dominant. A drained 'still-stand complex' of about 250 ha has been unaffected by peat cutting. Its water table in late spring is 30–50 cm below the surface. Locally, small patches covered with *Leucobryum glaucum* are found. To keep the surface free from birches and purple moorgrass various management practices are applied, in particular sheep-grazing and sometimes controlled fires. In 1985, a sample of about 131 ha at 'site 2', where there were no trees, was investigated.

'Site 3' is the open central part of 'Bissendorfer Moor', a bog at an altitude of 50–54 m. This bog is about 600 ha in size, and it has been affected by draining and domestic peat cutting in the past. In the late 1970s, ditch-blocking and scrub clearance were established as current management practices. Since then, rewetting of large areas has been in progress. The water table in late spring is 10–30 cm below the surface. Where the bog is undamaged there is a 'still-stand complex', with hummocks and lawns, but no hollows. This basic pattern is diversified by numerous artificial ponds resulting from rewetting of abandoned domestic peat cuts in different successional stages of vegetation development. Several ponds retain standing water with *Sphagnum cuspidatum*, others are dominated by *Eriophorum angustifolium* and *Eriophorum vaginatum*, a few by *Rhynchospora alba* or mud surfaces and some by *Erica tetralix*. Adjacent ponds are separated by banks of drained peat covered with *Molinia caerulea*. Old pines and birches are scattered in the open central part of the bog with numerous small trees and *Vaccinium uliginosum* covering up to 5%. In the open centre of 'site 3' a sample about 137 ha in size was investigated in 1985.

'Site 4' is a small section of the large bog complex 'Tinner Dose'. The entire mire is about 3000 ha in size. Major areas have been altered by drainage in the past. At present large sections are used as a test area by the German armed forces, which results in frequent outbreaks of fire during summer. In some small areas which are largely unaffected by fire, the vegetation is a treeless mosaic of shallow hummocks, hollows and lawns, normally with standing water in patches until late spring. Hollows are dominated by *Sphagnum cuspidatum, Rhynchospora alba* and *Eriophorum angustifolium*. In 1985, a sample of about 22 ha at this site was investigated.

METHODS

In order to conduct an investigation on bird–habitat relations, the sites were subdivided into sample squares of equal size. Aerial photographs (1:5000) of the bogs were covered with a grid net of plots 125 m x 125 m. A total of 247 plots was investigated. In every plot, breeding birds[1] and various habitat variables were recorded. Bird territories were mapped on separate copies of 1:5000 aerial photographs at least three times between mid April and mid June. Navigation on the sparsely featured bog surfaces was achieved by using a compass and by comparing certain landscape features (*e.g.* trees, ponds, rows of *Molinia*, edges of *Calluna*) with subjects on aerial photographs. Generally, the mapping method followed Svensson (1978). Thus, census techniques were similar to those applied by Brown & Stillman (1993).

In each 125 m x 125 m plot, between seven and ten sample squares of 4 m² were chosen in accordance with the proportion of different vegetation types. Various habitat variables were recorded in each square, and means were calculated for the entire plot. Cover values of bare peat, moss carpets, moss hummocks, grass/sedge tussocks and dwarf shrubs were estimated within each square. Soil penetrability was measured in the centre and edges of each square using a penetrometer (Myers, Williams & Pitelka, 1980). Several components of vegetation structure were measured at these five points within each sample square: vegetational profiles were surveyed as proposed by Cody (1968); vegetation densities at different heights (10, 20 and 30 cm) were recorded by counting contacts along a thin rod (*cf.* Rotenberry & Wiens, 1980); the height of the highest grass, forb or dwarf shrub within each square was measured as maximum vegetation height. A moisture index was calculated by applying Ellenberg's moisture indices (Ellenberg, 1974) for the predominant plant species. Floristic diversity was

---

[1] Nomenclature of bird species follows Walters (1980).

calculated using the Shannon–Weaver formula. Horizontal layer diversity was assessed by estimating the proportion of vegetation with heights of < 1 cm (moss), 1–10 cm, 10–25 cm, 25–50 cm and 50–100 cm and then applying the Shannon–Weaver formula on these data. The distances to the next pond and to the next tree were measured from the centre of each 125 m x 125 m plot. Data were processed by principal components analysis (PCA) to derive a simplified model of total habitat niche space *sensu* Hutchinson (Rotenberry & Wiens, 1980).

RESULTS AND DISCUSSION

Bird assemblages

Breeding bird assemblages on open raised bogs in the western Palearctic evidently originate from a group of approximately 45 species (Table 1). On a regional scale, 24–32 species are typical inhabitants of open raised bogs; on a local scale the range is 10–20 species. These bird assemblages may be divided into 10 major foraging 'guilds'. Most of the birds feed on invertebrates, not being monophagous or oligophagous with respect to particular food organisms, but instead specialising in one or two food-presenting strata. In bog habitats these strata are, in particular, water surface, surface of peat and mosses, surface of herbs and dwarf shrubs, tree layer and air space.

The ground-dwelling invertebrate collectors may be subdivided into two guilds according to body size. Pipits and wagtails form one of these. Meadow pipit (*Anthus pratensis*) is the commonest bird species on raised bogs all over the western Palearctic. Plovers, such as golden plover (*Pluvialis apricaria*) and lapwing (*Vanellus vanellus*) form the other guild. The third guild contains omnivorous ground-dwellers, *e.g.* skylark (*Alauda arvensis)* and reed bunting (*Emberiza schoeniclus*). Waders comprise another guild, though there may be some reasons to split it into true probers, jabbers and mudflat mowers. Such fine distinctions may relate to different foraging techniques, as well as to different affinities to water (see Burton, 1974). Widely distributed species typical of western Palearctic raised bogs are curlew (*Numenius arquata*), snipe (*Gallinago gallinago*) and wood sandpiper (*Tringa glareola)*. Further guilds are formed by perch-using aerial invertebrate hunters of sparrow-size to thrush-size, such as whinchat (*Saxicola rubetra*) and great grey shrike (*Lanius excubitor*), and by larger specialised herbivores, *i.e.* grouse species. When ponds with open water are available, dabbling or diving waterfowl and gulls will add to these species. At the higher levels of the food webs, some ground- or tree-nesting vertebrate predators may complete the bird assemblages. Locally, these primary constituents may be supplemented by members of additional guilds.

Table 1. Species composition of bird assemblages on open raised bogs in different regions of the western Palearctic. Species occasionally using single trees on bogs for nesting, but not feeding on bogs, were not taken into account. Species frequencies: > 25% +++, 5–25% ++, 1–5% +, < 1% *. Regions and references: 1, Finland (Järvinen & Sammalisto 1976, Väisänen & Järvinen 1977); 2, Central Sweden (Boström & Nilsson, 1983; Nilsson, 1986); 3, Southern Sweden (Nilsson, 1977; Boström & Nilsson, 1983; Götmark, Ahlund & Eriksson, 1986); 4, Estonia (Kumari, 1972; Irdt & Vilbaste, 1974); 5, Germany (Peus 1928, Bölscher 1988).

	Region				
	1	2	3	4	5
Red-throated diver (*Gavia stellata*)	–	+	*	*	–
Black-throated diver (*Gavia arctica*)	–	–	–	*	–
Slavonian grebe (*Podiceps auritus*)	–	–	–	*	–
Whooper Swan (*Cygnus cygnus*)	–	*	*	–	–
Mallard (*Anas platyrhynchos*)	+	*	*	*	+
Teal (*Anas crecca*)	*	*	+	+	+
Goldeneye (*Bucephala clangula*)	–	*	*	–	–
Tufted duck (*Aythya fuligula*)	–	*	–	*	–
Montagu´s harrier (*Circus pygargus*)	–	–	–	–	*
Merlin (*Falco columbarius*)	–	–	–	*	–
Hobby (*Falco subbuteo*)	*	–	–	*	
Peregrine (*Falco peregrinus*)	+	–	–	(*)	–
Red grouse (*Lagopus lagopus*)	+	–	–	*	–
Black grouse (*Tetrao tetrix*)	–	+	+	+	*
Crane (*Grus grus*)	+	+	+	*	–
Golden plover (*Pluvialis apricaria*)	+	++	++	++	+
Lapwing (*Vanellus vanellus*)	+	++	+	++	++
Ruff (*Philomachus pugnax*)	–	*	–	*	*
Snipe (*Gallinago gallinago*)	–	++	+	–	*
Black-tailed godwit (*Limosa limosa*)	–	*	–	–	+
Whimbrel (*Numenius phaeopus*)	+	*	*	+	–
Curlew (*Numenius arquata*)	++	++	+	+	++
Redshank (*Tringa totanus*)	*	–	*	*	+
Greenshank (*Tringa nebularia*)	–	–	–	*	–
Green sandpiper (*Tringa ochropus*)	–	+	+	–	*
Wood sandpiper (*Tringa glareola*)	+	++	+	++	*
Black-headed gull (*Larus ridibundus*)	+	*	–	–	*
Common gull (*Larus canus*)	+	+	+	+	+
Herring gull (*Larus argentatus*)	+	–	–	+	–
Cuckoo (*Cuculus canorus*)	–	*	+	*	+
Short-eared owl (*Asio flammeus*)	*	–	–	*	*
Skylark (*Alauda arvensis*)		+	++	+	+++
Meadow pipit (*Anthus pratensis*)	+++	+++	+++	++	+++
Tree pipit (*Anthus trivialis*)	++	–	*	++	+
Yellow wagtail (*Motacilla flava*)	++	+	+	+	+

contd

Table 1 *continued*

| | Region | | | | |
	1	2	3	4	5
Pied wagtail (*Motacilla alba*)	–	*	*	*	*
Whinchat (*Saxicola rubetra*)	+	++	++	+	+
Stonechat (*Saxicola torquata*)	–	–	–	–	+
Grasshopper warbler (*Locustella naevia*)	–	–	–	–	+
Great grey shrike (*Lanius excubitor*)	*	*	–	*	*
Red-backed shrike (*Lanius collurio*)	–	–	*	–	*
Linnet (*Carduelis cannabina*)	–	–	*	–	++
Yellowhammer (*Emberiza citrinella*)	+	–	–	–	–
Rustic bunting (*Emberiza rustica*)	–	*	–	–	–
Reed bunting (*Emberiza schoeniclus*)	+	+	*	*	++

Species densities in different rewetting stages

Estimates of densities of six bird species in three crudely-defined stages of bog rewetting in northern Germany and undamaged raised bogs in southern Sweden are shown in Table 2. Abundance of golden plover on undamaged raised bogs was much greater than on other types, although (due to the small number of samples) the difference was not significant ($\chi^2 < 3.4$, P=0.065). Maximum density was five pairs in 10 ha. All the other five species had abundances higher in at least one of the habitat types established by rewetting than on undamaged raised bogs. For lapwing, curlew and whinchat, this difference was not significant ($\chi^2 < 2.5$, P=0.11), but in meadow pipit and yellow wagtail it proved significant ($\chi^2 > 5.0$, P=0.025). At its maximum, meadow pipit exhibited a density of 30 pairs in 10 ha on former domestic peat cuttings.

Habitat characters

PCA was performed to analyse the multidimensional habitat niche space covering stages of bog rewetting as well as ombrotrophic parts of undamaged natural bogs. Four independent principal components of multidimensional habitat space were distinguished (Table 3). Habitat axis I is defined by vertical vegetation structure, ranging from sparse and low to dense and high dwarf-shrub–sedge layers. Axis II covers habitat properties related to soil moisture and presence of open water, ranging from wet to moderately dry habitats. Axis III relates to physiognomic properties of vegetation in the horizontal dimension pattern, in particular determined by the proportions of dwarf shrubs and moss hummocks on one side, and of tussock-grass on the other side. It also includes information on the surface relief. Axis IV relates to horizontal heterogeneity. Since its contribution to total habitat niche space was negligible, further application of PCA results focused on axes I, II and III.

The two-dimensional ordination of bog habitat types on biplots of axes I and II

Table 2.   Densities of bird species estimated for different restoration stages of ombrogenous bog habitats (pairs in 10 ha^{-1}). Columns: I, undisturbed natural raised bogs; II, rewetted formerly drained 'still-stand complex' (sites 2, 3); III, rewetted abandoned commercial peat-cuttings; IV, rewetted abandoned domestic peat-cuttings.

Species	Restoration stage			
	I	II	III	IV
Golden plover	1.5	0.47	0.42	0
Lapwing	0.66	0.16	0.29	1.88
Curlew	0.75	1.02	1.43	0.47
Meadow pipit	6.3	8.9	7.9	10.9
Yellow wagtail	0.28	0.16	0	2.66
Whinchat	1.13	0.7	0	1.56
area investigated (ha)	106	128	70	64

and axes I and III indicates some of the attributes that distinguish undisturbed natural bogs from various rewetting stages (Figure 2). Undisturbed natural raised bogs have a particularly sparse and low vegetation structure, but they include wet hummock–hollow complexes rich in open water as well as drier parts with eroding peat surfaces. In rewetted, once-drained bogs, vegetation is higher and denser due to partial mineralisation of peat. Similar structures may be found in minerotrophic parts of undisturbed raised bog complexes, *e.g.* laggs and pools. On the third habitat axis, vegetation physiognomy of undisturbed natural bogs is dominated by plant assemblages containing dwarf-shrubs and mosses rather than by tussock-grass. This results in a conspicuously-undulating surface relief of hummocks, hollows, lawns and carpets. At site 3, apart from hollows proper, a similar vegetation physiognomy was found in the rewetted 'still-stand complex' and in peat cuttings, but vegetation structure was much taller and denser. Site 2 was dominated by tussock-forming species (*Eriophorum vaginatum, Molinia caerulea*).

Patterns of habitat use

When habitat centroids of seven bird species were ordinated on a biplot as described above (Figure 3), these mean habitat properties proved less variable with respect to the moisture factor than to vegetation factors I and III. Some species showed distinct responses to the moisture factor that were invariably adressed to either the dryer or the wetter section, with a remarkably low variance between sites. Whinchat was associated with the drier section, while yellow wagtail and snipe showed a preference for the wetter section. On natural raised bogs, snipe is a resident of the marginal fen-like laggs and of minerotrophic pools. Since at site 1 only truly ombrotrophic parts were investigated, snipe was not found in these. But this species, as well as black-tailed godwit and redshank, was a

Table 3. Structure matrix of Principal Components Analysis for 247 sample plots on natural raised bogs and restored bog remnants. Factor loadings are only given in numerals, if P = 0.001 (r>0.210), else ** P = 0.01 (r>0.166), * P = 0.05 (r >0.127), (–) negative linear correlation. Factor loadings > 0.67 are shown in bold type.

Variables	Factor			
	I	II	III	IV
Eigenvalue	6.16	3.16	2.83	1.71
Axis length	2.48	1.78	1.68	1.31
Cumulative % variance	34.2	51.8	67.5	77.0
Vertical vegetation density in 1–10 cm height	**0.941**	ns	ns	ns
Total vegetation profile area in 0–100 cm height	**0.925**	ns	ns	0.260
Maximum height of dwarf shrub/grass/sedge	**0.884**	(–) *	0.221	ns
Horizontal cover of layers below 11 cm height	**–0.838**	ns	ns	0.382
Horizontal vegetation density in 10 cm height	**0.761**	*	0.264	ns
Cover % of bare peat	–0 .653	0.252	0.482	**
Mean stalk diameter (h=10 cm)	0.617	0.311	0.315	**
Probing depth (penetrometer)	0.229	**–0.771**	**	ns
Distance to next pond or flark	ns	**0.748**	ns	ns
Moisture index of vegetation	–0.487	**0.714**	ns	(–)**
Cover % of moss carpets	–0.433	**– 0.677**	–0.215	ns
Distance to next tree	ns	0.315	**0.825**	(–)**
Cover % of moss hummocks	–0.290	ns	**–0.711**	*
Cover % of common cotton-grass/sedges	0.251	– 0.504	**0.698**	ns
Cover % of dwarf shrubs	0.346	0.470	–0.642	ns
Horizontal layer diversity	ns	0.246	ns	**0.895**
Cover % of layer 50–100 cm	0.516	(–)*	ns	0.665
Floristic diversity	–0.401	(–)*	–0.535	0.640

member of the bird communities of rewetted bog remnants. Several bird habitats, in particular those of meadow pipit and curlew, were ordinated as somewhat intermediate, indicating a broad response to the moisture gradient. These species are likely to be capable of occupying most of the habitats available along the full gradient.

Species ordination along the vertical vegetation gradient showed a shifted pattern of niche requirements, when comparing sites 1, 2 and 3. This pattern paralleled overall differences in vertical vegetation structure between these locations. Golden plover at site 2 was found in a sector which just overlapped that of site 1, with respect to vegetation height and density. Site 3, where vegetation was much taller and denser, lacked this species. Analysis of bird centroid ordinations along gradient III showed that whinchat were confined to the two sites rich in dwarf shrubs and hummocks. In drier parts, these features may be closely associated with a sparse tree and shrub layer which is necessary for perching. Yellow wagtail, which also needs perches at least for display, occupies

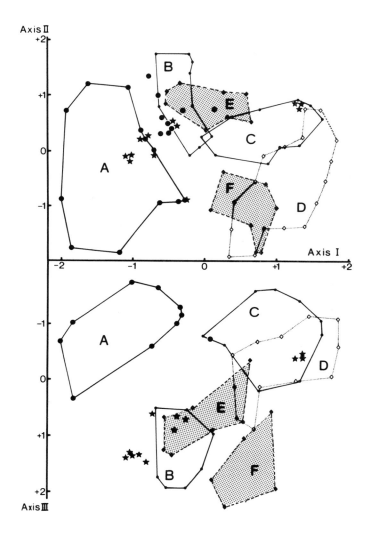

Figure 2. PCA-ordination of bog habitat types. Horizontal axis I: vegetation gradient concerning vertical structure and architecture. Upper vertical axis II: moisture gradient. Lower vertical axis III: vegetation gradient concerning horizontal physiognomy. Outer boundaries of bog habitat types were delimited by connecting peripheral factor scores of respective sample plots: A (●) undisturbed natural bogs at site 1; B (•) rewetted 'still-stand complex' at site 2; C (•) restored 'still-stand complex' at site 3; D (◊) rewetted domestic peat-cuttings at site 3; E (◆) former industrial peat-cuttings at site 2 restored by surface grading and smooth rewetting; F (◆) former industrial peat-cuttings at site 2 restored by surface grading and strong rewetting. ★: single samples from site 4.

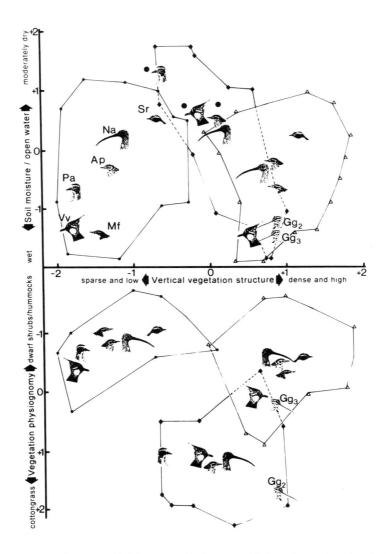

Figure 3. PCA-ordination of habitat centroids for seven bird species at sites 1 to 3. Axis I, II and III as in Figure 2. Species abbreviations: Ap meadow pipit (*Anthus pratensis*), Gg snipe (*Gallinago gallinago*); Mf yellow wagtail (*Motacilla flava*); Na curlew (*Numenius arquata*); Pa golden plover (*Pluvialis apricaria*); Sr whinchat (*Saxicola rubetra*); Vv lapwing (*Vanellus vanellus*). Outer site boundaries: (•), site 1, (◆), site 2; (Δ), site 3.

habitats with a rolling surface. Snipe seemed to avoid habitats with low proportions of tussock-forming species. The impact of vegetation physiognomy on the remaining four species seemed uncertain.

For a further analysis of the evident pattern of niche shift between the sites mentioned above, habitat gradients I, II and III were subdivided into five gradient intervals. Relative abundance of golden plover, meadow pipit and whinchat was estimated separately for the three major study sites according to their frequency distributions along these gradients. Meadow pipit used the three gradients uniformly over their site-specific extension, thus emphasising their opportunistic mode of habitat use in raised bogs. Figure 4 displays patterns of habitat use for golden plover and whinchat. Golden plover clearly preferred the shortest and most sparse vegetation at a site occupied for breeding. At site 2 this vegetation structure was established by management practices (sheep-grazing, controlled fires), but it seemed suboptimal there in being much higher and denser than in most of the golden plover habitats on natural bogs. Along the moisture gradient, the wettest habitats were avoided, but in the driest section of this gradient, there was a marked difference between natural bogs and rewetted bog remnants with former industrial peat cuttings: in the latter, only the driest sections offered the short and sparse vegetation appropriate for this species. Vegetation physiognomy, apparently, is of minor impact on golden plover's habitat choice, although pure stands of dwarf shrubs seem to have a negative effect. Whinchat preferred higher proportions of dwarf shrubs and was absent from wetter habitats, especially on natural bogs. The use of the vertical vegetation gradient showed a similar pattern of ostensibly shifted habitat preference: depending upon the habitat properties available within a certain location, whinchat preferred the highest and densest vegetation. One of the variables not included in PCA procedure, cover of perch-offering trees and shrubs, was higher in whinchat habitats than in unoccupied areas. This bird species did not just prefer a distinct vegetation structure, but evidently selected the best-suited vegetation structure within available habitat properties. A similar pattern was observed in yellow wagtail.

Surface relief

Since golden plover was the only species with densities clearly higher on natural than on rewetted bogs, a univariate analysis of habitat properties was confined to that species (Table 4). Apart from expected differences in vertical vegetation structure, a conspicuous effect of the surface relief on habitat choice became apparent. On natural raised bogs, breeding habitats of golden plovers had higher hummocks, larger moss-carpets and fewer dwarf shrubs than unoccupied adjacent patches. Similar differences were observed comparing plover habitats on natural bogs and rewetted bog remnants. On the latter, the open ground above the surface was provided by bare peat rather than by mosses. Furthermore, the levels of particular habitat properties, *e.g.* hummock height and soil penetrability, in localities not inhabited by golden plover on natural raised bogs were higher than the levels in true golden plover habitats on rewetted bog remnants. These differences in habitat properties suggest that rewetting of damaged bogs, even in combination with management practices like sheep-grazing and controlled fires,

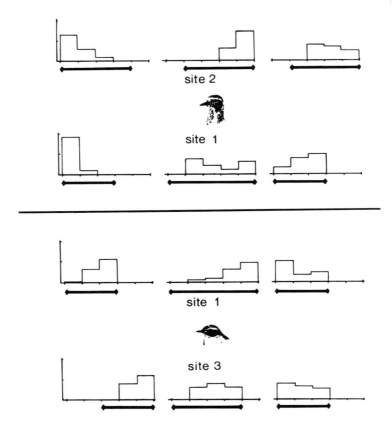

Figure 4. Habitat use of golden plover (upper part) and whinchat (lower part) according to their relative abundances along habitat gradients, as shown in the three columns of corresponding histograms. Each of the three gradients was subdivided into five intervals that covered equal proportions of that vector. Left – vertical vegetation gradient, centre – moisture gradient, right – horizontal physiognomy gradient. Underlying thick double-arrows mark the proportion of overall gradients I, II and III, which coincides with the respective site.

may provide habitats that are at best suboptimal for golden plover, since the patchy arrangement of hummocks and hollows is not restored.

It is useful to consider the 'macrohabitat' requirements of golden plover. In southern Scandinavia, this species is by far the commonest wader on undamaged raised bogs (Boström & Nilsson, 1983). The obvious preference of golden plover for drier parts of north-west German raised bog remnants may be an artefact, since the wetter parts lack the short and sparse vegetation the bird requires. Peus (1928) reported on numerous pairs resident on the then undamaged, huge raised bogs in north-western Germany adjacent to the Dutch border. These now-vanished natural

Table 4. Particular features of golden plover habitats on restored bog remnants in north-west Germany (group I) and natural raised bogs (group II) in southern Sweden compared with patches unoccupied by this species on natural raised bogs in southern Sweden (group III). * indicates significant difference between columns I & II, [#] between columns II & III (U-test; P<0.05). Data are given in terms of mean ± s.d.

Groups	I	II	III
Number of samples	9	16	45
Cover % of 0–1 cm vegetation layer	31.0±17.0*	57.5±12.6[#]	14.6±16.6
Cover % of 0–10 cm vegetation layer	52.3±19.2*	71.4±7.5[#]	57.5±13.6
Cover % of bare peat	26.8±16.0*	15.4±10.3[#]	9.4±10.4
Cover % of moss carpets	0.2±0.7*	27.4±18.9[#]	16.7±13.7
Cover % of moss hummocks	4.4±3.4*	14.4±4.2	14.1±7.5
Hummock height (cm)	15.0±3.3*	33.8±12.7[#]	24.6±7.9
Cover % of dwarf shrubs	20.4±12.0	17.9±7.6[#]	27.2±11.5
Cover % of tussock grass	27.2±18.0	14.4±4.2	18.5±7.6
Maximum height of dwarf shrubs and grass/sedge complex (cm)	36.0±12.0*	18.1±3.8[#]	20.8±4.4
Number of vegetation contacts in 20 cm height	11.0±3.8*	6.0±2.7[#]	8.7±3.9
Relative vegetation profile area in 10–25 cm height (%)[†]	8.0±3.1*	1.8±0.9[#]	3.5±2.1

[†] Calculated using the formula: 100 x (mean stalk diameter (mm)) x (no. perpendicular vegetation contacts in 10–25 cm height) / 150 mm.

habitats of that species were probably similar to those on undamaged raised bogs in southern Sweden (see Jonas, 1935). On blanket bogs in northern England golden plovers were found to be associated with mountain plateaux, avoided disturbance and gamekeeping, and preferred certain vegetation types with *Empetrum nigrum*, where cover of bracken (*Pteridium aquilinum*) as well as pasture was low (Haworth & Thompson, 1990). Findings in the eastern highlands of Scotland were similar: golden plovers were associated with high altitude and low cover of grass and bracken, and preferred habitats with a high cover of flush and flush/heath mosaic (Brown & Stillman, 1993). In the mountainous area of Hardangervidda (Norway), Byrkjedal (1989) observed a strong affinity of golden plover with vegetation types dominated by lichen heath. These results match the findings on golden plover macrohabitats on natural raised bogs in several aspects: low disturbance, heath-type vegetation, mosaic of vegetation and bare ground, presence of *Empetrum nigrum*; but evidently high altitude is not required.

Morphological and physiological niche dimensions

The three major habitat factors – vegetation profile, moisture and vegetation physiognomy – are considered to be related to various physiological, behavioural and morphological features of a particular bird species. These are genetically determined species-specific attributes as well as properties obtained by learning (see Hilden, 1965; Cody, 1985). Vegetation profile is associated with cover and microclimate, and serves as an obstacle against movement and view. Soil moisture is likely to affect two major biological functions: feeding and breeding. With respect to feeding, there are relationships with food type, food abundance and food availability. The latter in particular refers to probing waders with specialised bills, where soil penetrability works as threshold to feeding success (Burton, 1974). With respect to reproductive success, we have to recognise that the microclimatic properties of a bird's habitat must match species-specific properties of eggshells as well as juvenile thermoregulation. Thickness and porosity of avian egg shells determine their water vapour conductance and thermal resistance. Both properties are related to microclimate in the nesting habitat. Water vapour tension in a ground nest depends on the ambient atmosphere close to the nest surface and it should match the species-specific egg water vapour pressure so that total diffusive water loss during incubation can be limited (Rahn & Paganelli, 1990). In addition, ground nesters must be adapted to cold such that newly hatched chicks can survive. This kind of physiological adaptation has been observed in several species of ducks, waders and gulls (see Steen, Toien & Fiske, 1991). These genetically-determined properties may set further constraints on the capability of a species to select a breeding site.

The biological effect of vegetation physiognomy on birds is somewhat more complex, as it has relations to food type and food abundance, to camouflage, and to microclimate. It may also include proximate factors concerning habitat selection, *i.e.* direct behavioural stimuli (Hilden, 1965). A detailed study on these niche dimensions within bird communities on raised bogs still remains to be performed.

CONCLUSIONS

It could be argued that the differences observed between the 'natural' and rewetted raised bog sites studied could stem from geographic differences rather than from rewetting effects. The Swedish sites are situated about 400–500 km to the north of the German sites. This may have implications both for qualitative and quantitative differences. The first question to answer is: how similar are undamaged bogs in southern Sweden and slightly damaged bog remnants in northwestern Germany with respect to vegetation structure, vegetation physiognomy, soil moisture and resident bird species? From the literature (Jonas, 1935, Peus, 1928) it can be inferred that bird assemblages, vegetation structure, moisture and vegetation physiognomy on 'intact' bogs in north-western Germany during the first decades of this century were similar to those now found on 'intact' bogs in south-western Sweden (though bogs in north-western Germany were probably purely treeless, while Swedish bogs have a scattered tree layer). Furthermore, the present vegetational and physical properties of the north-west German site 4 coincide with those of several intact raised bogs in south-western Sweden (Figure 2).

The second major question is whether densities of particular bird species in equivalent habitats in southern Sweden and north-western Germany may be different, following a geographic gradient. The answer to this question can only be indirect and is based on fragmentary data. Along a geographic gradient covering about 500 km distance within Sweden, densities of golden plover and curlew on raised bogs in the south and in the north were not significantly different; those of meadow pipit and whinchat decreased, whilst those of lapwing and yellow wagtail increased northwards (Boström & Nilsson, 1983). On the other hand, densities of meadow pipit are higher on palsa bogs in the tundra than on raised bogs in southern Sweden, densities of yellow wagtail on meadows or pastures in eastern central Europe are higher than in northern Europe, while densities of whinchat on meadows in eastern central Europe are similar to densities on meadows in southern Finland (Glutz von Blotzheim & Bauer, 1985, 1988). All we can conclude from these data is that there is no clear trend in decreasing or increasing densities along a south–north gradient in Europe for the six species shown in Table 2.

The results presented here may be useful in tracing major habitat requirements of birds on raised bogs in the western Palearctic, although their scientific basis is still narrow. There is need for further research on natural raised bogs, particularly in Ireland (see Madden, 1987) and Russia. It appears that the habitats available to breeding birds on rewetted bog remnants, as well as in rewetted peat cuttings, generally differ from those offered by undisturbed natural bogs, in particular in having a taller and denser vegetation, a smaller range of the moisture gradient and a more uniform vegetation physiognomy (*e.g.* species-poor stands of cotton-grass). It has to be emphasised that, apart from botanical aspects, the establishment of a large patchiness in soil moisture conditions will be favourable in terms of bird conservation on rewetted bogs. However, for several bird species rewetting is not the sole condition to provide suitable habitats. Removal of trees on a drained bog surface may attract meadow pipits. Whinchat requires elevated perches for display and insect catching. Therefore, scattered shrubs, dead stems and single trees have to be conserved to support this species. Curlew is not confined to rewetted locations. But, since this species apparently avoids forest edges, the area freed from trees and shrubs may need to be at least 40 ha to attract at least one pair, 100 ha to attract perhaps five pairs. Stable populations of about 30 pairs can only be established in large areas poor in trees. To achieve this without supplementing tree-removal by rewetting will be highly expensive. Rewetting of abandoned domestic peat cuttings will have long-term effects. During different successional stages, these habitats will meet the requirements of teal (*Anas crecca*), snipe, lapwing, yellow wagtail and some rarer species.

When abandoned industrial peat cuttings are rewetted by conventional restoration practices, for example, levelling the peat surface and damming up the water table, this will initially result in the establishment of plant communities rich in cotton-grass species (*Eriophorum* spp.). At site 2, this successional stage has lasted for more than 14 years, and changes in the vegetation are hardly evident. The resulting habitats match the habitat requirements of meadow pipit, curlew and, provided rewetting is intense, probing waders such as snipe. Yet, it will require more expensive and skillfully planned restoration methods to sustain bird assemblages as similar as possible to those of natural raised bogs. For these types of 'peat deserts', *i.e.* abandoned industrial peat cuttings, it would be interesting to discuss two alternative proposals. In the first case it might be desirable to try to discover what is preventing a 'uniform' stand of cotton grass from developing greater structural heterogeneity by 'natural' developmental processes. The second, more ambitious, alternative would be to restore the undulating surface relief by forming a network of hollows and building shallow hummocks as well as higher hummock strings using poorly-humified peat. Suitable fragments of the mosses and vascular plants should be implanted instead of depending upon seed banks. This approach to bog restoration would be a fundamentally new method which has only been tried on a small scale until now. It is likely to be expensive to implement on a large scale, and there are suspicions that the hummocks and ridges will be invaded by birch, thereby presenting a considerable management problem. But, it may help to accelerate the major goal of bog restoration in ornithological terms. It would be a desirable object for science to study its impact on golden plover and other species.

ACKNOWLEDGEMENTS

I am indebted to S.C. Shaw, B.D. Wheeler and an anonymous referee for helpful comments on the text. G. O'Donovan kindly provided information on bird data from bogs in Ireland. J. Brockmann assisted in part of the fieldwork. Thanks to D. Hilfert, A. Martens, G. Rüppell, F. Suhling and A. Wendler for useful discussions on an earlier draft.

REFERENCES

Bölscher, B. (1988). *Untersuchungen zur Dispersion und Habitatwahl der Vogelarten nordwestdeutscher Hochmoor- und Grünlandbiotope: Versuch einer Biotopbewertung.* Ph.D. thesis, Technical University of Braunschweig. Braunschweig, Germany.
Boström, U. & Nilsson, S.G. (1983). Latitudinal gradients and local variations in species richness and structure of bird communities on raised peat-bogs in Sweden. *Ornis Scandinavica*, **14**, 213–226.
Brown, A.F. & Stillman, R.A. (1993). Bird – habitat associations in the eastern highlands of Scotland. *Journal of Applied Ecology*, **30**, 31–42.
Burton, P.J.K. (1974). Feeding and the feeding apparatus in waders, a study of anatomy and adaptations in the Charadrii. *British Museum (Natural History) Publications*, **719**, 1–150.
Byrkjedahl, I. (1989). Habitat use and resource overlap by breeding golden plovers and dotterels (*Pluvialis apricaria, Charadrius morinellus*). *Journal für Ornithologie*, **130**, 197–206.
Cody, M.L. (1968). On the methods of resource division in grassland bird communities.

American Naturalist, **102**, 107–147.

Cody, M.L. (1985). *Habitat Selection in Birds.* Academic Press, Orlando, USA.

Ehrendorfer, F. (1973). *Liste der Gefäßpflanzen Mitteleuropas.* (2nd ed.). Gustav Fischer Verlag, Stuttgart.

Ellenberg, H. (1974). Zeigerwerte der Gefäßpflanzen Mitteleuropas. *Scripta Geobotanica (Göttingen)*, **9**, 1–97.

Frahm, J.P. & Frey, W. (1983). *Moosflora.* Verlag Eugen Ulmer, Stuttgart.

Glutz von Blotzheim, U.N. & Bauer, K.M. (1985). *Handbuch der Vögel Mitteleuropas.* Vol. 10/II. Aula-Verlag, Wiesbaden.

Glutz von Blotzheim, U.N. & Bauer, K.M. (1988). *Handbuch der Vögel Mitteleuropas.* Vol. . 11/I. Aula-Verlag, Wiesbaden.

Götmark, F., Ahlund, M. & Eriksson, M.O.G. (1986). Are indices reliable for assessing conservation value of natural areas? An avian case study? *Biological Conservation*, **38**, 55–73.

Haworth, P.F. & Thompson, D.B.A. (1990). Factors associated with the breeding distribution of upland birds in the southern Pennines. *Journal of Applied Ecology*, **27**, 562–577.

Hilden, O. (1965). Habitat selection in birds. *Annales Zoologici Fennici*, **2**, 53–75.

Irdt, A. & Vilbaste, H. (1974). *Bird fauna of the Nigula peat-bog. Estonian wetlands and their life.* Estonian contribution to the International Biological Programme 7. (Ed. by Academy of Sciences of the Estonian S.S.R., Estonian Committee for IBP). pp. 214–229. Valgus, Tallinn.

Järvinen, O. & Sammalisto, L. (1976). Regional trends in the avifauna of Finish peatland bogs. *Annales Zoologici Fennici*, **13**, 31–43.

Jonas, F. (1935). Die Vegetation der Hochmoore am Nordhümmling (Vol. 1). *Feddes Repertorium (Beihefte)*, **78 (1)**.

Kumari, E. (1972). Changes in the bird fauna of Estonian peat bogs during the last decades. *Aquilo seria Zoologica*, **13**, 45–47.

Madden, B. (1987). The birds of Mongan Bog, Co. Offaly. *Irish Birds*, **3**, 441–448.

Malmer, N. (1988). Patterns in the growth and the accumulation of inorganic constituents in the Sphagnum cover on ombrotrophic bogs in Scandinavia. *Oikos*, **53**, 105–120.

Myers, J.P., Williams, S.L. & Pitelka, F.A. (1980). An experimental analysis of prey availibility for sanderlings (Aves: Scolopacidae) feeding on sandy crustaceans. *Canadian Journal of Zoology*, **58**, 1564–1574.

Nilsson, S.G. (1977). Häckfagelfaunan pa högmossar i sydvästra Smaland. *Fauna och Flora*, **72**, 227–233.

Nilsson, S.G. (1986). Are bird communities in small biotope patches random samples from communities in large patches? *Biological Conservation*, **38**, 179–204.

Peus, F. (1928). Beitrag zur Kenntnis der Tierwelt nordwestdeutscher Hochmoore. *Zeitschrift für Morphologie und Ökologie der Tiere*, **12**, 533–683.

Rahn, H. & Paganelli, C.V. (1990). Gas fluxes in avian eggs: Driving forces and the pathway for exchange. *Comparative Biochemistry and Physiology*, **95A**, 1–15.

Rotenberry, J.T. & Wiens, J.A. (1980). Habitat structure, patchiness, and avian communities in North American steppe vegetation: A multivariate analysis. *Ecology*, **61**, 1228–1250.

Steen, J. B., Toien, O. & Fiske, P. (1991). Metabolic adaptations to hypothermia in snipe hatchings (*Gallinago media*). *Journal of Comparative Physiology*, **161**, 155–158.

Svensson, S. (1978). Förenklad revirkarteringsmethod för inventering av faglar pa myrar och mossar. *Var Fagelvärld*, **37**, 9–18.

Usher, M.B. & Thompson, D.B.A. (1993). Variation in the upland heathlands of Great Britain: Conservation importance. *Biological Conservation*, **66**, 69–81.

Väisänen, R.A. & Järvinen, O. (1977). Structure and fluctuation of the breeding bird fauna of a north Finnish peatland area. *Ornis Fennica*, **54**, 143–153.

Walters, M. (1980). *The Complete Birds of the World*. David & Charles, Newton Abbot.

26 Time to Regenerate: Long-term Perspectives of Raised Bog Regeneration with Special Emphasis on Palaeoecological Studies

J. H. J. JOOSTEN
Laboratory of Palaeobotany and Palynology, Heidelberglaan 2, NL-3584 CS, Utrecht, The Netherlands.

SUMMARY

1.   Of the techniques available to study long-term phenomena, only palaeoecological research may provide reliable long-term data on regeneration of bog landscapes and bog vegetation types and renewed peat accumulation after natural and anthropogenic disturbance.

2.   In cases of minor natural and anthropogenic disturbance (including desiccation, fire, superficial drainage and buckwheat cultivation), self-regulation mechanisms may provide for spontaneous regeneration of bog vegetation and the bog landscape.

3.   No evidence is available of successful re-establishment of bog vegetation in large-scale cut-over bogs, except in very wet climates. Possibly this is only a matter of time, because re-establishment of bog vegetation may take several decennia up to centuries. Other restrictions, including the absence of sophisticated hydrological conditions required for the re-establishment of *Sphagnum* 'key-species', can, however, not be excluded. This failure of re-establishment of bog vegetation leads to the conclusion that restoration of bogs as self-regulating landscapes after severe anthropogenic damage is impossible within human time perspective.

4.   The developments in fine-scaled peat pits resulting from peat extraction point to good perspectives for regeneration of bog vegetation and their peat deposits. The requirements for such successful regeneration starting from open water, however, are as yet poorly understood. Long-term vegetation development in these pits, as revealed by palaeoecological research, may be attributed to climatic conditions and to human interference in local and regional hydrology. Regeneration of these complexes to a raised bog may be hampered by excessive downward seepage as a result of decreased hydraulic resistance, and the eventual loss of open water storage capacity.

5.   Long-term accumulation rates of regeneration peat produced by floating bog mats amount to 100–500 g dry weight $m^{-2} a^{-1}$. These high accumulation rates may enable the development of sustainable peat 'production' techniques in which peat accumulation in cut-over bogs is enhanced for future peat extraction.

Restoration of Temperate Wetlands. Edited by B.D. Wheeler, S.C. Shaw, W.J. Fojt and R.A. Robertson
© 1995 John Wiley & Sons Ltd.

INTRODUCTION

Raised bogs[1] are landscapes[2] with the capacity to shape the improbable paradox 'high and wet'. In the temperate part of the northern hemisphere, only a few species have the right combination of properties to create and maintain a raised bog. These species, including *Sphagnum papillosum*, *S. magellanicum*, *S. imbricatum*, *S. fuscum*, *S. rubellum*, are called 'key-species', as their dominance is a *conditio sine qua non* for bog formation. In the course of thousands of years, these and associated species develop complex self-regulation mechanisms enabling a bog landscape to maintain its basic characteristics (Joosten, 1993).

Natural mire ecosystems are often characterised by slow processes and rare events (*e.g.* Glebov, 1979; Tolonen, 1979; Tallis, 1983; Rybnícek, 1984; Zobel, 1988; Vitt & Kuhry, 1992). Slow and subtle developments may also be expected in the case of bog regeneration[3], because of the extreme nature of the wet ombrotrophic environment and resulting low growth rates of bog plants (Lötschert, 1969). Therefore, bog regeneration has to be approached by long-term ecological studies (Franklin, 1989).

This paper presents a review of long-term studies in bog regeneration with special emphasis on the contribution of palaeoecology. Nomenclature of bryophytes and vascular plants follows Landwehr & Barkman (1966) and van der Meijden *et al.* (1983), respectively.

LONG-TERM STUDIES IN BOG ECOLOGY

Various scientific techniques are available to study long-term phenomena, including direct long-term studies (observational and manipulatory), substitution of space-for-time studies, modelling, and retrospective studies based on cultural or natural records (Caraco & Lovett, 1989).

Direct observations

Continuous direct long-term observations are extremely rare in bog ecology, because of the limited life span of the researchers and the short duration of most research projects (Tallis, 1983; Weatherhead, 1986). Notable exceptions are hydrological records from the former Soviet Union, where water-balance data are available for long periods, *e.g.* for Lammin Suo since 1894 (Romanov, 1968a, b), and ornithological data (*e.g.* Irdt & Vilbaste, 1974; Joosten & Bakker, 1987).

---

[1] A raised bog is here defined as 'a landscape, dominated by ombrotrophic, peat-producing communities, which, in a given climate and as a result of the hydraulic properties of peat and vegetation, is elevated above the regional groundwater level' (Joosten, 1992a).

[2] In this paper the word landscape is used in the sense of the German 'Landschaft' to mean the integrated character of a distinctive part of the earth's surface, operating as a functional and structural unit (cf. the concept of mire massif, geotope and mesotope in Ivanov, 1981).

[3] Bog regeneration is defined here as the process of renewed development towards a bog after natural or cultural disturbance of a bog (Joosten, 1992a).

Vegetational data are available only for much shorter periods. Studies of four permanent plots in a virgin pre-alpine bog (five annual records covering the period 1957–76) show fine-scale changes in both vegetation composition and pattern (Schmeidl, 1977). An Estonian bog pool complex was studied by Mets (1982) over the period 1959–76 using photographs. Observed changes in pattern were ascribed to changes in water level and autogenic processes. Saposnikov, Juscenkova & Minaeva (1991) describe long-term vegetation changes as result of bog transgression in Russia. Tüxen (1986) presents a series of coarse vegetation maps of the 'miniature bog' Horneburg 3 in Lower Saxony (1958, 1970, 1974, 1979, 1981) showing vegetational changes as a consequence of hydrological changes. Barkman (1992) notes, that between 1960 and 1990 "suprisingly little change" has taken place in the vegetation and flora of intact bog remnants and heath pools under protection in the Netherlands. Observations on a former bog buckwheat field show that in 20 years without human activities little had changed, not even after a (superficial) fire (Barkman, 1992).

Direct observations (12 annual records covering the period 1973–92) in 80 peasant peat pits in the Liesselse Peel (the Netherlands) indicate that newly established ombrotrophic, peat-producing vegetation may hardly change in time, although rapid developments do occur sporadically (Joosten, unpublished data).

Other direct long-term studies in vegetational changes of virgin and degenerated bogs are often restricted to an occasional repetition of earlier observations (Backéus, 1972; Fetcher *et al.*, 1984; Chapman & Rose, 1986; Jortay & Schumacker, 1989; Tüxen, 1990; Boc, 1991; Meade, 1992; Boc & Smagin, 1993). Such a time-fragmentary approach may hamper the discovery of relations between observed changes in patterns and related processes.

Space-for-time substitution

Space-for-time substitution (STS) infers temporal trends from the study of different-aged sites, assuming that spatial and temporal variation are equivalent (Pickett, 1989). This technique has often been applied in mire ecology, as in Tansley's (1939) classic hydrosere from open water to bog. Palaeoecological studies, however, show much more complicated succession pathways than this conceptual model (Walker, 1970; Rybnicek, 1973, 1984; Aaviksoo, Masing & Zobel, 1984).

The theory of cyclic 'regeneration' in raised bogs was initially proposed by Aiton (1811), Sernander (1909) and von Post & Sernander (1910), who based their views (also) on stratigraphical/palaeoecological observations. The concept was later elaborated and established in STS by Osvald (1923, 1925, 1949, 1970), studying the distribution of contemporary plant communities and relief patterns in bogs. The impressive concept of 'cyclic bog regeneration' remained the dominant model of bog growth and development for a long time (Jensen, 1973), until it was largely subverted by palaeoecological research (Walker, 1961; Walker & Walker, 1961; Casparie, 1969, 1972; Klinger, 1976; Barber, 1981; Svensson, 1988).

Space-for-time substitution has been employed in describing revegetation and regeneration 'developments' in cut-over bogs, *inter alia* by Crome (cited in Wiegman, 1837), Tüxen (1928), White (1929), Podbielkowski (1960), Neuhäusl (1975) and Dietze (1981). Wiegman (1837) already pointed at Crome's faulty application of STS in comparing completely different types of ecosystem.

Modelling

Mathematical modelling has been useful in helping to understand slow processes in mire ecosystems and to forecast future changes (Wildi, 1978; Jones & Gore, 1978; Clymo, 1978, 1984, 1992; Ivanov, 1981; Miller *et al.*, 1984, Swanson & Grigal, 1988; Aaviksoo, 1988; Alexandrov, 1988; Schneebeli, 1991; Bragg *et al.*, 1991). Every model, however, needs calibration and validation with independently obtained data (Shugart, 1989), necessitating other types of long-term studies.

Dynamics of a higher order than present in the calibration and validation series cannot be simulated adequately by extrapolation (During & Joosten, 1992).

Retrospective studies

Retrospective studies require the presence of adequate cultural or natural source material. Van der Molen (1988) describes the history of Woodfield Bog (Ireland) since the eighteenth century, based on documentary and verbal evidence. Smart *et al.* (1986), Joosten & Bakker (1987), Ringler (1989) and Precker (1992, 1993) studied long-term vegetation developments in large-scale peat-extraction sites, based on old maps and photos, historical data and anecdotal evidence. Since the end of peat extraction hardly any peat-producing vegetation with key-species had re-established in these sites. Oral inquiry of peat-digging farmers indicates that the re-establishment of typical bog vegetation with *Sphagnum magellanicum* and *S. papillosum* in fine-scaled pits in Germany takes 35 to 60 years (Tüxen, 1993). This figure corresponds with historical observations of Findorff and de Luc (in Rennie, 1807), who stated that pits "dug in Duvel's moor were in a few years filled up with aquatic plants: That, in thirty years these were converted into a firm, spongy substance. That the solid surface of this, at the end of the period, nourishes heath and other ligneous plants that grow on the adjacent moor". De Luc continued with detailed observations on vegetation development in such peat pits: "That the surface of these pits is covered with all kinds of ligneous and aquatic plants, that delight in such a soil; that these alternately overtop one another; that the ligneous plants make the greatest progress in a dry summer, so that the surface seems to be entirely covered with them: That the reverse is the case in a rainy summer: That the aquatic plants overtop the ligneous and choke them, insomuch, that the whole surface seems to be entirely covered with a matting of aquatics, which, by decaying, form a soil for the ensuing season: That, if it continue rainy for a succession of years, these aquatic plants continue to prevail till a dry season ensue."

Such historical records on bog development covering a long period are very rare and are often unreliable. The Earl of Cromerty (1711), for example, claims to have actually witnessed "a standing wood of fir trees" changing into "peat moss, from which the inhabitants dug peat" between 1651 and 1699.

A bog itself, however, to paraphrase the French historian Marc Bloch, "is a witness, and like most witnesses it rarely speaks until one begins to question it". Bogs, as accumulating landscapes, preserve (part of) their history and the history of their surroundings in the successively superimposed layers of peat. Retrospective studies based on these natural records have been widely applied in bog ecology since the first systematic stratigraphical observations and palaeoecological interpretations of Dau (1829) and Steenstrup (1842). Many techniques are presently available to extract detailed information on long-term developments from these natural archives (Overbeck, 1975; Birks & Birks, 1980; Godwin, 1981; Berglund, 1986). These techniques are also helpful to reconstruct and clarify revegetation and regeneration developments in anthropogenically damaged bogs.

PALAEOECOLOGICAL STUDIES IN BOG REGENERATION

Regeneration after natural disturbance

The concept of bog regeneration was initially defined by von Post & Sernander (1910, *p.*18) as "the origin of new, local centres of bog growth, raised by local congestion (as a result of differential peat accumulation) and destruction, leading to a re-establishment of favourable humid conditions for rapid peat accumulation at those sites, that were already colonised by weakly peat-accumulating plant formations (heather–lichen mire)." (translated by J.H.J Joosten). With regard to the bog micro-forms, the term 'regeneration' was used in a semantically correct way. Confusingly, however, the content of the term was soon extended to include the process of normal peat accumulation and bog growth as a progressive develop-ment (*cf.* review by Barber, 1981).

A type of regeneration in the original sense of von Post & Sernander (1910) was described by Tolonen (1971, 1980) and Tolonen, Huttunen & Jungner (1985), who observed a short-term 'cyclic' alternation of slightly humified *Sphagnum*-peat and strongly humified layers of peat dominated by hepatics, dwarf-shrubs and lichens in bogs in Europe and North America. Less frequent and more radical changes over larger areas are illustrated by the presence of 'recurrence surfaces' and related phenomena in bog profiles (Granlund, 1932; Overbeck, 1975; Dickinson, 1975; Frenzel, 1983). Recurrence surfaces, including the 'Grenzhorizont' of Weber (1900), can be interpreted as periods of dryness, leading to interrupted *Sphagnum* growth, expansion of Ericaceae and *Eriophorum vaginatum* and increased peat decomposition, followed by a renewed accumulation of slightly humified peat. These temporary dry phases apparently did not last long enough to enable the establishment of trees on the bogs.

Palaeoecological studies also provide evidence of bog regeneration after major natural disturbances. Casparie (1972), Casparie & Streefkerk (1992) and Dupont (1986) describe regeneration after bog bursting, subsequent drainage and intensive erosion in the Bourtangerveen around 2500 BP (=^{14}C-years before present). Regeneration after bog fires was described by Menke (1963) and Tolonen *et al.* (1985). Van Geel & Dallmeijer (1986) found evidence of a severe bog fire and a subsequent establishment of extensive *Molinia caerulea*-dominated vegetation around 4000 BP. Bog vegetation re-invaded the area after the *Molinia*-vegetation had persisted for a century.

Regeneration after anthropogenic disturbance

Regeneration after fire and grazing

A detailed palaeoecological description of bog regeneration after major anthropogenic disturbance is presented by Witte & van Geel (1985). Bog growth at the Assendelver Polder (the Netherlands) was disturbed by local human habitation during the Roman Iron Age (*c.* 1800 BP). The original bog vegetation became dominated by *Molinia caerulea* until *c.* 1450 BP because of local fires and grazing by domestic animals. Subsequently a very wet *Sphagnum cuspidatum*-vegetation established itself, followed by an *Eriophorum vaginatum*-dominated vegetation until *c.* 1200 BP. Peat growth at the site ceased when the area was reclaimed during mediaeval times.

Regeneration after buckwheat fire cultivation

Buckwheat fire cultivation was practised over extensive areas in Germany and the Netherlands during the eighteenth and nineteenth centuries. This comprised superficial drainage of the bog and burning of the upper peat layers, followed by cultivation of buckwheat (*Fagopyrum esculentum*) in the ash–charcoal–peat mixture (Venema, 1855; Göttlich, 1990). Averdieck & Schneider (1977) claim the formation of a layer of slightly-humified *Sphagnum*-peat, 60 cm thick, over a former buckwheat fire horizon in the Großes Moor near Barnstorf (Lower Saxony, Germany). Local pollen values (*sensu* Janssen, 1973) of *Fagopyrum* were found in the same bog beneath a 30 cm layer of *Sphagna cymbifolia* and *S. acutifolia* peat by Schneider & Steckhan (1963). A similar phenomenon has been observed at the Brunssum I-site (the Netherlands; Janssen, 1960), where a *Sphagnum papillosum*-dominated vegetation changed into a sedge mire after buckwheat fire cultivation.

Regeneration after peat cutting

The first 'palaeoecological' observations on regeneration of bog vegetation and associated peat formation after peat-winning date from Jürgen Christian Findorff (1720–92) (in: Brüne, Lilienthal & Overbeck, 1937): "In such pits, Nature has been able to work from all sides, and it is therefore not astonishing, that they . . . have been filled up with moss in such a way, that it is hardly possible to notice the distinctive marks of such pits on the surface. Only, this increment is nothing more than a pure white moss, and keeps, in contrast to the neighbouring peat, always the distinctive mark of a light colour, of a loose, spongy substance, still being far from putrefaction and from the real peat" (translated by J.H.J. Joosten).

Peat, regenerated after peat digging, has been analysed frequently in archaeology, mainly for dating purposes (Schütrumpf, 1951, 1958; Jankuhn, 1958; Clason, 1963). Many objects, including human remains, have deliberately been deposited or buried in peat pits that were afterwards overgrown with newly formed peat (Glob, 1965; Coles & Coles, 1989; van der Sanden, 1990; Coles, this volume). Many of these studies, however, are concerned with small pits cut in a larger undamaged bog.

In some regions, peat cutting for fuel has taken place since early times (Dieck, 1983). These activities have also been discerned in 'miniature bogs' ('heathland pools', e.g. van der Voo, 1962; Schwaar, 1983; Schwaar & Brandt, 1984; Tüxen, 1986; van den Munckhof, 1988; Barkman, 1992; van Dam & Buskens, 1993), but not to their full extent, because the cut-over 'miniature bogs' have regenerated to the 'virgin' appearance of today. At present these sites, which according to their floristics, water chemistry and geomorphological situation mostly have to be considered as 'poor fens', are often covered with beautiful examples of peat accumulating vegetation types of the OXYCOCCO-SPHAGNETEA and SCHEUCH-ZERIETEA. Their regeneration, however, is obvious from the presence of a considerable hiatus in the peat stratigraphy (cf. Tüxen, 1986) and the (sometimes hardly visible) regular vegetation patterns resulting from peat cuttings (cf. Tüxen, Stamer & Onken-Gruß, 1977; Tüxen, 1983).

Chesters (1931) mentions "fresh layers of very recent origin, containing remains of Eriophorum and Erica tetralix" in "some of the oldest trenches used for peat cutting". Pfadenhauer (1989) decribes peat pits (600 x 60 m) in the Kulbinger Filz (Southern Germany), that were dug and partly filled with topspit material between 1918 and 1924. In 60 years, a layer of regeneration peat 40 cm thick was formed, consisting of little-humified and loose Sphagnum remains, covered by a vegetation of transitional mire (with Sphagnum recurvum and Carex rostrata) and local patches of bog vegetation, including Sphagnum rubellum and S. magellanicum. Stratigraphical profiles from revegetated commercial peat cuttings on Thorne Waste (S. Yorkshire, UK) indicate that since the expiration of peat excavation in 1920 no bog vegetation with key-species has re-established. Recent deposits consist of a layer of ericaceous material 5–15 cm thick, with remains of Juncus effusus, or Sphagnum fimbriatum, S. recurvum, S. cuspidatum and Drepanocladus (Smart, Wheeler & Willis, 1989).

Only rarely have Sphagnum papillosum and S. rubellum established in the older, extensive peat cuttings of Thorne Waste (B.D. Wheeler in litt. 1994).

Regeneration in fine-scaled peat pit complexes

Regeneration after peat cutting has been studied most thoroughly in fine-scaled peat pit complexes. Eshuis (1946) was the first to analyse the pollen and macrofossil content of recent *Sphagnum* peat in peasant peat pits in the Peel (the Netherlands) dating from the late 1800s. The peat consisted of *Sphagna cuspidata* with remains of *Calluna vulgaris, Oxycoccus palustris, Juncus* sp. and Cyperaceae.

A more detailed palaeoecological study of regenerative succession after peat cutting was performed by Averdieck & Schneider (1977). They discovered old peat pits completely filled with a layer of slightly humified *Sphagnum*-peat, almost 1 m thick, in a strongly-humified peat section of the Silleruper Moor (Schleswig-Holstein). The lowest regeneration peat can be dated palynologically to *c.* AD 1350 (*cf.* Dörfler 1989), indicating late-mediaeval peat extraction. The pollen types and macroremains that were probably part of the local peat-accumulating vegetation are presented in Figure 1. Regeneration in the pit (zone A) started with a vegetation of *Sphagna cuspidata* (probably *Sphagnum cuspidatum* or *S. recurvum*) and Cyperaceae (possibly *Eriophorum angustifolium* or *Rhynchospora alba*). The high degree of decomposition in the lower part of that zone represents a mixture of old and new peat. Zone B is characterised by the presence of *Sphagnum magella-nicum, Empetrum nigrum* and pollen of the *Vaccinium/Erica* type. The latter pollen type includes bog species like *Oxycoccus palustris, Andromeda polifolia*

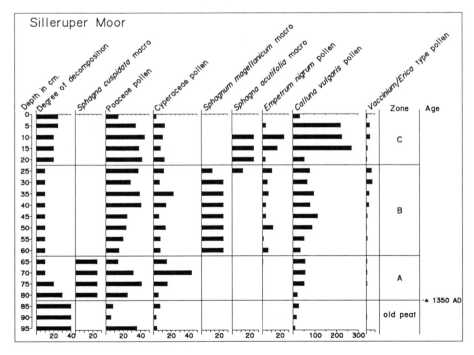

Figure 1. Pollen and macrofossil diagram of the Silleruper Moor regeneration peat section, Schleswig-Holstein, Germany (selected curves only). Pollen values are expressed as percentages of the upland tree pollen sum, macrofossils as volume percentages. After Averdieck & Schneider (1977).

and *Erica tetralix*. *Calluna vulgaris* was probably not part of the peat-accumulating vegetation, according to the values that point to regional pollen deposition (*sensu* Jensen, 1973) in that area during this period (Dörfler, 1989). The uppermost zone (zone C) shows a dominance of *Sphagna acutifolia* (probably *Sphagnum rubellum*, Overbeck, 1975), *Empetrum nigrum* and local pollen values of *Calluna vulgaris*.

Detailed stratigraphical records of recent regeneration peat in nine peasant peat pits in Lower Saxony are presented by Bertram (1988). In three pits, succession had proceeded to a vegetation consisting of *Sphagnum papillosum, Oxycoccus palustris, Eriophorum angustifolium, Erica tetralix* and *Aulacomnium palustre* via shorter or longer phases with *Sphagna cuspidata* (*S. cuspidatum* or *S. recurvum*), *Eriophorum vaginatum, E. angustifolium, Oxycoccus* and *Erica*. Present-day vegetation-types dominated by *Sphagnum magellanicum* (two pits) apparently followed in succession from a similar *Sphagna cuspidata*-dominated vegetation. In four pits, vegetation has remained in the *Sphagna cuspidata*-phase, resulting in a present vegetation dominated by *Sphagnum recurvum* with *Eriophorum angustifolium* and *Molinia caerulea*. Underlying regeneration peat is characterised by the remains of these species and *Eriophorum vaginatum*. In two of the latter pits, peat had been extracted totally, uncovering the mineral subsoil.

One of the major problems associated with palaeoecological studies of recent regeneration peat is the dating of the deposits. ^{14}C-dating is not (yet) suitable because of the relatively large error in the measurements and because large amounts of 'old' carbon have been released into the atmosphere as a result of the burning of fossil fuels since the Industrial Revolution (Birks & Birks, 1980). Also ^{210}Pb-dating is not quite reliable because of the high hydraulic conductivity of the newly formed peat deposits resulting in postdepositional re-allocation and other methodological problems (Oldfield pers. comm. 1992; Lütt, 1992).

^{210}Pb-dates of initial regeneration peat in Schleswig-Holstein are presented by Lütt (1992). Figure 2 shows the overall stratigraphy of these pits, the age of the oldest regeneration peat deposits (with an inherent error of 10–40%), the depth of the profile and the depth of the remaining original peat layer. Most of the profiles show a succession of an initial *Sphagna cuspidata*-vegetation with *Eriophorum angustifolium* to a vegetation dominated by *Sphagnum magellanicum* (L1–G3) or *S. papillosum* (F1). In one pit, succession did not proceed beyond the *Sphagna cuspidata/Eriophorum angustifolium*-phase (C2).

Joosten (1985a, b) has established a detailed chronology of regeneration peat deposits in the Peel area (the Netherlands) based on a comparison of historical data and pollen records from the nineteenth and twentieth century. Study of a site in the Mariapeel (Joosten, 1985a) included pollen analysis, determination of pollen concentrations, identification of other palynomorphs (fungi, rhizopods, animals) and macrofossil analysis (Figure 3).

The lowest zone (zone 1) consists mainly of species indicating a wet to humid environment (*Rhynchospora alba, Sphagnum cuspidatum, S. papillosum, S. recurvum*). *Pohlia nutans* (including var. *sphagnetorum*), *Drepanocladus fluitans* and

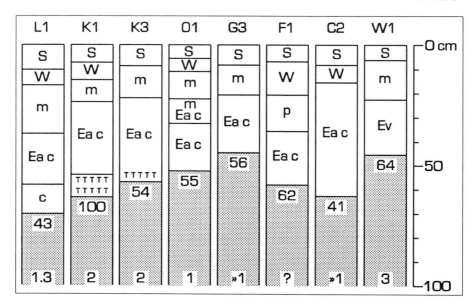

Figure 2. Stratigraphy of regeneration peat sections in Schleswig-Holstein, Germany. S = living vegetation, W = root layer, m = *Sphagnum magellanicum* peat, p = *S. papillosum* peat, c = *Sphagna cuspidata* peat, Ea = *Eriophorum angustifolium*, Ev = *E. vaginatum*, t = topspit material. Stippled = old peat. Numbers at the top of the stippled zone indicate ^{210}Pb-ages of the lowermost regeneration peat layers. Numbers at the base of each column indicate depth of the remaining old peat deposits (in m). Topspit is the vegetated and root-penetrated toplayer of a (superficially drained) mire, that is removed prior to peat extraction. After Lütt (1992).

several microfossil types point at strongly fluctuating water levels (Joosten, 1985a). Remains of *Molinia caerulea, Erica tetralix, Calluna vulgaris* and *Oxycoccus palustris* appear and disappear simultaneously with those of *Betula*. The birches near the pit probably disappeared as a consequence of buckwheat fire culture on nearby tracks. Removal of the birches may have resulted in a higher and more stable water level, favouring the more light-demanding *Sphagnum papillosum*. The abrupt change suggests a complete 'drowning' of the floating bog-mat. This event took place around 1855. The material in zone 2 consists almost entirely of remains of *Sphagnum papillosum*. The growth form, robust with feathery branches, suggests that *Sphagnum papillosum* has been growing under very wet conditions (Beijerinck, 1934); the microfossils in this zone also point to a very wet environment (Joosten, 1985a). The transition to zone 3 can be dated to 1920. The small charcoal- and *Molinia*-peaks near that transition reflect the effect of the extremely dry years of 1920 and 1921 when enormous bog fires swept the Peel area. The transition to zone 4 could be dated at 1938. In 1939 the nearby Defence Canal was dug and parts of the adjacent bog were reclaimed to agricultural land, as illustrated by the presence of sand in the lowest spectrum of zone 4. This may

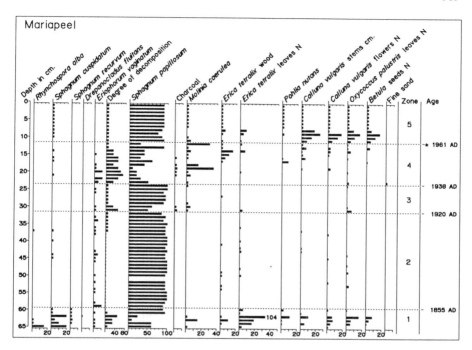

Figure 3. Macrofossil diagram of the Mariapeel-MPN regeneration peat section, the Netherlands (selected curves only). Macrofossils (including degree of decomposition – unrecognisable organic material, sand, charcoal) are expressed as volume percentages, as numbers (N) or as cumulative length (cm) per 2.5 cm^3. After Joosten (1985a).

have resulted in a lowering and destabilisation of the water level in the nearby pit. As a consequence *Molinia caerulea* could expand during and after the dry years in the 1940s and the extremely dry year 1959. The transition of zones 4 and 5 must be fixed shortly after 1960. The nature reserve Mariapeel was founded in 1963, leading to a stabilisation of the water level in the Defence Canal (which became part of the reserve), favouring the development of bog vegetation in the nearby pit. Zone 5 is characterised by an increase in macroscopic remains of *Betula*, indicating nearby presence of birches. Like zone 1, there is a conspicuous simultaneous and parallel occurrence of remains of *Calluna vulgaris*, *Oxycoccus palustris* and *Betula*.

In many other cases, however, regeneration of a vegetation dominated by 'key' *Sphagnum* species did not occur. Analyses of a site in the Ospelse Peel (Joosten, 1985b) and a site in the Liesselse Peel (Joosten, 1985a) show that succession in these pits did not proceed beyond the *Sphagna cuspidata*-stage during 150 years. Also, at a site in the Heidse Peel, a pit studied in detail remained in that stage since the beginning of renewed peat accumulation around 1900 (J.H.J. Joosten, unpublished results).

Insight into the failure of bog regeneration is of special interest for nature conservation. Peat accumulation at a Heidse Peel site (Joosten, 1985b) stopped shortly after the Second World War, in reaction to ongoing reclamations in the surroundings. A similar situation occurred in a Liesselse Peel-pit (Joosten, 1985a), as a result of nearby peat extraction in the 1960s (Joosten, 1982).

A very distinct development was found in a peat pit in the Ospelse Peel (Jansen, 1993; J.H.J. Joosten, unpublished results). Regeneration started with a phase with *Rhynchospora alba*, followed by *Sphagna cuspidata*. After some years *Sphagnum magellanicum* became established, soon accompanied by *S. papillosum*. After 1950 a sharp increase in the degree of decomposition was evident, together with the disappearance of both *S. magellanicum* and *S. papillosum* and an expansion of *Calluna vulgaris*, *Molinia caerulea* and *Erica tetralix*. *Betula* expanded slightly later. This change must be interpreted as a result of major desiccation of the site. The event is synchronous with a rise of the water level in the immediate surroundings of the pit after the establishment of the Groote Peel nature reserve in 1951 (Vermeer & Joosten, 1992), and with the reclamation and drainage of large areas of adjacent mire in the framework of land consolidation works. The sand in the peat from this level probably results from contemporary afforestations of cover sand hills close to the site (Joosten & Bakker, 1987).

Accumulation rates of regeneration peat in peasant peat pits in Germany and the Netherlands based on dated profiles are presented in Table 1.

DISCUSSION

Long-term studies

Most of the techniques available to study long-term phenomena do not provide adequate long-term information on bog regeneration. Mathematical modelling cannot be applied without independently-obtained long-term data. Retrospective studies are hampered by the absence or unreliability of cultural source material. As far as direct observational studies are concerned, the scanty availability of long-term data is reinforced by interest in bog regeneration being only recently resumed. Experiments in bog restoration[1] are often particularly hampered by the limited time-span available for evaluation, leading to strongly time-dependent results and therefore misleading conclusions (Tilman, 1989, *cf.* Rydin, 1993). Enthusiastic reports on 'apparently' successful restoration projects are frequently only based on an initial rapid (and impressive!) expansion of fruiting *Eriophorum* species. Such 'beginners optimism' will often be qualified and differentiated by longer-term developments (Joosten, 1992b).

Space-for-time substitution must always be applied with caution in describing 'developments'. For rather simple communities, such as pioneer communities of cut-over bogs, the technique may provide useful results, because little time has

---

[1] Bog restoration is here defined as the complex of human activities aiming at stimulation of bog regeneration (Joosten, 1992a).

Table 1. Accumulation rates of regeneration peat in small peat pits in Germany and the Netherlands.

Type of peat	Accumulation rate (g dry weight.$m^{-2} a^{-1}$)	Source
Sphagnum papillosum–Molinia– Ericaceae-peat	490	(Joosten 1985a)
S. papillosum-peat	240	(Joosten 1985a)
S. papillosum- + Eriophorum angustifolium–Cuspidata-peat	170	(Lütt 1992)
S. magellanicum- + E. angustifolium– Cuspidata-peat	100–390	(Lütt 1992)
S. magellanicum- + E. vaginatum-peat	400	(Lütt 1992)
S. magellanicum–S. papillosum-peat	350	(Jansen 1993)
E. angustifolium–Cuspidata-peat	470	(Lütt 1992)
E. angustifolium–Cuspidata-peat	180	(Joosten unpub.)
S. recurvum–Molinia–Erica-peat	230	(Joosten unpub.)

been available to build up complex relation systems. The usefulness of STS may, however, rapidly decrease with increasing age ('history') of the system (Joosten & Bakker, 1987).

Only palaeoecological research may provide reliable long-term data on regeneration of bogs, bog vegetation types and renewed peat accumulation after natural and anthropogenic disturbance. It has to be stressed, however, that the positive picture of bog regeneration as presented by palaeoecology may be distorted by the limitations of the research method. Regeneration can only be studied palaeoecologically when regeneration actually has taken place, *i.e.* where regenerated peat is available. Disturbances without consequent regeneration are indiscernible, because the remaining part of the bog will rapidly oxidise and eventually vanish completely (Joosten, 1993). Many bogs in the Netherlands have disappeared as a result of cultural influences and natural events leaving virtually no trace (Borger, 1975; Leenders, 1989; Pons, 1992).

Bog regeneration and restoration

The ultimate aim of bog restoration must be the regeneration of a raised bog as a self-regulating landscape (Joosten, 1993). (Re-)development of such a landscape, however, is a process of (many) centuries, especially after severe destruction. Therefore, Joosten (1992a) has suggested that bog regeneration and restoration may be considered to be 'succesful', when populations of those species that are able to rebuild a raised bog in the particular climatic conditions ('key-species') have become permanently established. In the temperate part of the northern hemisphere these species are *Sphagnum papillosum, S. magellanicum, S. imbricatum, S. fuscum* and *S. rubellum* (Joosten, 1993). Although this approach is useful, in practice it has to be remembered that a bog landscape has far more specific environmental requirements (especially climatic and hydrological) than the bog key-species, as is shown by the different distributions of raised bogs, bog vegetation types and bog key-species (Joosten & Bakker, 1987).

In case of minor disturbance, self-regulation mechanisms may provide for spontaneous regeneration of the bog landscape (Joosten, 1993). Many direct observations support the palaeoecological data on spontaneous regeneration of bog vegetation after surficial damage, especially after buckwheat fire cultivation (*cf.* Joosten, 1993). The peat record also shows that bog regeneration may take place after extensive disturbance. The abundance of remains of *Eriophorum vaginatum* in the recurrence surfaces is reminiscent of the dominance of this species in many cut-over and recently rewetted bog sites. Similarly, the renewed bog growth above the retardation layer, indicated by peat consisting of *Sphagna cuspidata*, resembles initial peat accumulation by *Sphagnum cuspidatum* in indundated peat pits. The *S. cuspidata* type of peat is called 'Vorlaufstorf' ('precursor peat', Overbeck, 1975), because it is often found in the stratigraphy below the recent slightly humified *Sphagna cymbifolia*- and *Sphagna acutifolia*-peat. Probably these regeneration phenomena were, to some extent, dependent on self-regulation processes that were still operating in the bog, even in the absence of bog vegetation and part of the acrotelm.

Until now, evidence has not been available of successful re-establishment of more than minor plots of bog key-species in large-scale commercially cut-over bogs. The only exceptions are bogs in very wet climates, *e.g.* in mountainous areas (Poschlod, 1990; see Poschlod, this volume). Re-establishment is possibly only a matter of time, because cut-over bogs were, until recently, left in a drained state for future reclamation to agricultural land or forest. The reviewed palaeoecological studies show that re-establishment of bog vegetation may take several decennia up to centuries, even under seemingly favourable hydrological conditions. The absence of bog vegetation in older large-scale cut-over areas, in contrast to fine-scaled complexes, however, indicates that other restrictions to the re-establishment of *Sphagnum* key-species cannot be excluded (*cf.* Poschlod, 1990).

In the case of severe bog disturbance, including the removal of the upper peat layers and destruction of acrotelm conditions, permanent wet conditions necessary for the re-establishment of bog vegetation can only be realised by open water storage (Beets, 1992). Open water, however, is not a suitable substratum for bog vegetation, because *Sphagnum* key-species appear to be sensitive to very wet conditions and inundation, both directly and via competitive interactions (*cf.* Rydin, 1993). Therefore the open water has to be 'covered' by a firmer substrate, *e.g.* scattered tussocks or floating mats, to enable *Sphagnum* colonisation (Joosten, 1992a; Money, this volume). Direct observations during 20 years (J.H.J. Joosten unpublished results) show that deep (>0.5 m), dystrophic bog water is normally recolonised with difficulty by plant species, including *Sphagna*. In open water, peat degradation will often exceed peat accumulation, as is known from direct observational and palaeoecological studies in virgin bogs (Boatman, 1977; Boatman & Tomlinson, 1977; Loopmann, 1988; Foster *et al.*, 1988).

The developments in fine-scaled peat pit complexes, including 'miniature bogs', point at good prospects for regeneration of bog vegetation and their peat deposits under favourable conditions. The requirements for such successful regeneration starting from open water, however, are still poorly understood. Vegetation succession in these pits, as revealed by palaeoecological studies, has a striking similarity to the vertical zonation of *Sphagnum* mosses and phanerogams along hollow–hummock gradients in virgin bogs and the associated decreasing preference for wet conditions (Beijerinck, 1934; Müller, 1965; Vitt, Crum & Snider, 1975; Overbeck, 1975; Ivanov, 1981; Clymo & Hayward, 1982; Dierssen, 1982; Andrus, Wagner & Titus, 1983; Wallén, Falkenberg-Grerup & Malmer, 1988; van der Molen, Schalkoort & Smit, 1992). According to Bertram (1988), a development towards bog vegetation in such pits can only be expected in case of early colonisation of OXYCOCCO-SPHAGNETEA-species like *Oxycoccus*, *Erica* and *Aulacomnium*, starting from a vegetation dominated by *Eriophorum angustifolium* and *Sphagnum recurvum*. Colonisation by *Molinia caerulea* would prevent a further development towards bog vegetation. Joosten (1985a, 1986), however, found a repeated re-establishment of vegetation dominated by *Sphagnum papillosum* after short phases of local expansion of *Molinia caerulea*, consequent upon the dry years 1921, 1947/49 and 1959.

The extent of regenerated bog vegetation in such complexes may be impressive, especially in 'miniature bogs'. To my knowledge, however, none of these complexes has yet regenerated to a raised bog, possibly owing to lack of time. Another problem obstructing this development might be the increased downward seepage from the bog remnant, which may be caused by decreased hydraulic resistance as a result of peat extraction. In a developing natural bog, the increase in resistance seems to be proportional to the increasing differences in hydraulic head between the bog and its surroundings, leading to a downward seepage that hardly changes in time during thousands of years of bog development (*cf.* Eggelsmann, 1960, 1981). Removal of part of that resistance by peat extraction, without a similar decrease in head differences, as has often been the case in fine-scaled pit complexes, may lead to increased downward seepage. This will result in larger water level fluctuations than in a natural bog. Initially the fluctuations can easily be followed by floating bog mats, and water levels will remain relatively stable for the newly established bog vegetation. In the long run, however, the water space below the bog mat will be filled up by accumulating peat. This rapidly waterlogged regeneration peat is much less humified and has less hydraulic resistance than the original peat and will therefore maintain a disproportionally large seepage. The accumulated peat, however, will hamper vertical mat movement in response to water level fluctuations. This may ultimately lead to desiccation of the bog vegetation (Schouwenaars, 1982), especially in drier climates.

Increased downward seepage may also result from lowering the hydraulic heads in the mineral subsoil. In areas where the subsoil has good water-transmitting properties, such increase may be the effect of hydrological changes up to several kilometres from the remnant (Poelman & Joosten, 1992; van Walsum, 1990,

1992). The resulting negative effect on sustainable bog development has been studied by van Walsum & Joosten (1994) for the Groote Peel National Park (the Netherlands). Palaeoecological research and hydrological modelling illustrate that desiccation in that area may take place as a consequence of lowering of the regional groundwater head, even if phreatic water levels inside the nature reserve are raised simultaneously (Jansen, 1993; Projectgroep de Groote Peel, 1990; van Walsum, 1992; J.H.J. Joosten, unpublished results), indicating the importance of limited downward seepage (see also Schouwenaars, this volume).

Peat accumulation

Accumulation rates of regeneration peat, produced by floating bog mats in Germany and the Netherlands in the nineteenth and twentieth centuries, amount to 100–500 g dry weight $m^{-2} a^{-1}$ (being 1000–5000 kg $ha^{-1} a^{-1}$) (cf. Poschlod, 1990). These rates are (very) high compared with long-term peat-accumulation rates in virgin mires as observed by Tolonen (1979), Reader & Stewart (1972), Jones & Gore (1978), Middeldorp (1982), Kratz & DeWitt (1986) and Ovenden (1990). The figures, however, are of the same order of magnitude as annual primary production rates of *Sphagnum* species (reviewed in Lindholm & Vasander, 1990 and Rochefort, Vitt & Bayley, 1990) and bog vegetation (Smith & Forrest, 1978; Reader, 1978; Reinikainen, Vasander & Lindholm, 1984; Francez, 1988; Vasander, 1990). Apparently the net primary production is largely accumulated as peat. This can be attributed to favourable conditions for peat formation in the floating bog mats: rather dry conditions for the vegetation, enabling a large productivity (Ivanov, 1981), and rapid inundation as the newly formed peat drowns under the weight of subsequent peat accumulation, leading to slightly humified, coarse and fibrous peat.

These high accumulation rates may enable the development of sustainable peat 'production' techniques in which peat accumulation in cut-over bogs is enhanced for future peat extraction, especially for horticultural purposes (cf. Elling & Knighton, 1984).

CONCLUSIONS

Palaeoecological and direct observational studies show that re-establishment of bog vegetation (including key-species) is a common feature in raised bogs after superficial damage including fire and superficial drainage, and after peat extraction in fine-scaled peat pit complexes.

No evidence is available of successful regeneration in largely cut-over bogs, except in very wet climates. This observation may be biased by the young age of most restoration projects. Other restrictions, including the absence of sophisticated hydrological conditions required for the re-establishment of *Sphagnum* key-species, can, however, not be excluded.

Long-term studies in bog regeneration indicate that restoration of bogs as self-regulating landscapes after severe anthropogenic damage (including peat extraction) is impossible within human time perspective, because the necessary massive re-establishment of bog key-species and renewed accumulation of peat require (many) centuries. Bog regeneration may furthermore be hampered by hydrological changes both inside and outside the bog remnant.

Accumulation rates of bog peat accumulated by floating bog mat vegetation in fine-scaled peat pit complexes are very high. This may enable the development of sustainable peat 'production' techniques in which peat accumulation is enhanced for future peat extraction.

ACKNOWLEDGEMENTS

The assistance of Peter Hoen in preparing the figures is gratefully acknowledged. The work was supported by the Foundation for Social Environmental Research (SRO), which is subsidised by the Netherlands Organization for Scientific Research (NWO).

REFERENCES

Aaviksoo, K. (1988). Natural and anthropogenous changes in a mire and its neighbourhood. *Dynamics and Ecology of Wetlands and Lakes in Estonia* (ed. M. Zobel), pp. 90–105. Academy of Sciences of the Estonian SSR, Tallinn.

Aaviksoo, K., Masing, V. & Zobel, M. (1984). Autogenic succession of mires: a markovian approach. *Estonia. Nature, Man, Economy* (ed. J.-M. Punning), pp. 56–67. Academy of Sciences of the Estonian SSR, Tallinn.

Aiton, W. (1811). *A treatise on the Origin, Qualities, and Cultivation of Moss-Earth, with Directions for Converting it into Manure.* Wilson and Paul, Air.

Alexandrov, G.A. (1988). A spatially distributed model of raised bog relief. *Wetland Modelling* (ed. W.J. Mitsch, M. Straskraba & S.E. Jørgensen), pp. 41–53. Elsevier, Amsterdam.

Andrus, R.E., Wagner, D.J. & Titus, J.E. (1983). Vertical zonation of *Sphagnum* mosses along hummock–hollow gradients. *Canadian Journal of Botany*, 61, 3128–3139.

Averdieck, F.-R. & Schneider, S. (1977). Anthropogen beeinflußte Moorprofile. *Telma*, 7, 15–26.

Backéus, I. (1972). Bog vegetation re-mapped after sixty years. Studies on Skagerhult-smosen, central Sweden. *Oikos*, 23, 384–393.

Barber, K.E. (1981). *Peat Stratigraphy and Climatic Change. A Palaeoecological Test of the Theory of Cyclic Peat Regeneration.* Balkema, Rotterdam.

Barkman, J.J. (1992). Plant communities and synecology of bogs and heath pools in the Netherlands. *Fens and Bogs in the Netherlands: Vegetation, History, Nutrient Dynamics and Conservation* (ed. J.T.A. Verhoeven), pp. 173–235. Kluwer, Dordrecht.

Beets, C.P. (1992). The relation between the area of open water in bog remnants and storage capacity with resulting guidelines for bog restoration. *Peatland Ecosystems and Man: An Impact Assessment* (eds O.M. Bragg, P.D. Hulme, H.A.P. Ingram & R.A. Robertson), pp. 133–140. International Peat Society/Department of Biological Sciences, University of Dundee, Dundee.

Beijerinck, W. (1934). *Sphagnum en Sphagnetum*. W. Versluys, Amsterdam.

Berglund, B.E. (ed.) (1986). *Handbook of Holocene Palaeoecology and Palaeohydrology*. John Wiley, Chichester.

Bertram, R. (1988). Pflanzengesellschaften der Torfstiche nordniedersächsischer Moore und die Abhängigkeit dieser Vegetationseinheiten von der Wasserqualität. *Dissertationes Botanicae*, **126**, 1–192. Cramer, Berlin.

Birks, H.J.B. & Birks, H.H. (1980). *Quaternary Palaeoecology*. Edward Arnold, London.

Boatman, D.J. (1977). Observations on the growth of *Sphagnum cuspidatum* in a bog pool in the Silver Flowe National Nature Reserve. *Journal of Ecology*, **65**, 119–126.

Boatman, D.J. & Tomlinson, R.W. (1977). The Silver Flowe. II. Features of the vegetation and stratigraphy of Brishie Bog and their bearing on pool formation. *Journal of Ecology*, **65**, 531–546.

Boc, M.S. (1991). Monitoring rastitel'nosti na ochranjaemych bolotnych territorija: zadaci, metodika, rezul'taty. *Bolota ochranjaemych territorija: problemy ochrany i monitoringa. Tezisy dokladov XI Bsesjoeznogo polebogo seminara-ekskursii po bolotovedenijoe* (ed. M.S. Boc), pp. 53–56. Bsesojuznoe Botaniceskoe Obscectvo Central'no-lesnoj Biosfernyj Gosudarstvennyj Zapovednik, Leningrad.

Boc, M.S. & V.A. Smagin (1993). *Flora i rastitel'nost' bolot severo-zapada Rossii i principy ich ochrany*. Gydrometeoizdat, Sankt-Petersburg.

Borger, G.J. (1975). *De Veenhoop. Een historisch-geografisch onderzoek naar het verdwijnen van het veendek in een deel van West-Friesland*. Buijten en Schipperheijn, Amsterdam.

Bragg, O.M., Brown, J.M.B. & Ingram, H.A.P. (1991). Modelling the ecohydrological consequences of peat extraction from a Scottish raised mire. *Hydrological Basis of Ecologically Sound Management of Soil and Groundwater* (Proceedings of the Vienna Symposium, August 1991), pp. 13–22. IASH Publication no. 202, Wallingford.

Brüne, F., Lilienthal, K. & Overbeck, F. (1937). *Beiträge und Fragmente zu einem Moorkatechismus von Jürgen Christian Findorff weyl Moorkommissar der herzogl. bremischen Moore und Anmerkungen*. Gerhard Stalling, Oldenburg.

Caraco, N.M. & Lovett, G.M. (1989). How can the various approaches to studying long-term ecological phenomena be integrated to maximize understanding? *Long-term Studies in Ecology. Approaches and Alternatives* (ed. G.E. Likens), pp. 186–188. Springer, New York.

Casparie, W.A. (1969). Bult- und Schlenkenbildung in Hochmoortorf. *Vegetatio*, **19**, 146–180.

Casparie, W.A. (1972). Bog development in Southeastern Drenthe (the Netherlands). *Vegetatio*, **25**, 1–271.

Casparie, W.A. & Streefkerk, J.G. (1992). Climatological, stratigraphical and palaeo-ecological aspects of mire development. *Fens and Bogs in the Netherlands: Vegetation, History, Nutrient Dynamics and Conservation* (ed J.T.A. Verhoeven), pp. 81–129. Kluwer, Dordrecht.

Chapman, S.B. & Rose, R.J. (1986). *An assessment of changes in the vegetation at Coom Rigg Moss National Nature Reserve within the period 1958 – 1986*. Institute of Terrestrial Ecology Report, Project 1092, Wareham.

Chesters, C.G.C. (1931). On the peat deposits of Moine Mhor. *Journal of Ecology*, **19**, 46–59.

Clason, A.T. (1963). Het Bolleveen bij Taarloo. Sporen van voorhistorische turfwinning in Drenthe. *Nieuwe Drentse Volksalmanak*, **81**, 231–240.

Clymo, R.S. (1978). A model of peat bog growth. *Production Ecology of British Moors and Montane Grasslands* (eds O.W. Heal & D.F. Perkins), pp. 187–223. Springer, Berlin.

Clymo, R.S. (1984). The limits to peat bog growth. *Philosophical Transactions Royal Society London,* **B 303,** 605–654.

Clymo, R.S. (1992). Productivity and decomposition of peatland ecosystems. *Peatland Ecosystems and Man: An Impact Assessment* (eds O.M. Bragg, P.D. Hulme, H.A.P. Ingram & R.A. Robertson), pp. 3–16. International Peat Society/Department of Biological Sciences, University of Dundee, Dundee.

Clymo, R.S. & Hayward, P.M. (1982). The ecology of *Sphagnum. Bryophyte Ecology* (ed. A.J.E. Smith), pp. 229–289. Chapman & Hall, London.

Coles, B. & Coles, J. (1989). *People of the Wetlands. Bogs, Bodies and Lake-dwellers.* Thames & Hudson, London.

Cromerty, G. (1711). An account of the mosses in Scotland. *Philosophical Transactions,* 27, 296–301.

Dau, J.H.C. (1829). *Die Torfmoore Seelands.* Gyldendahl und Hinrichs, Kopenhagen und Leipzig.

Dickinson, W. (1975). Recurrence surfaces in Rusland Moss, Cumbria (formerly North Lancashire). *Journal of Ecology,* 63, 913–935.

Dieck, A. (1983). Jungsteinzeitliche bis mittelalterliche Brenntorfgewinning – Materialen und Deutungsversuche. *Telma,* 13, 99–126.

Dierssen, K. (1982). *Die wichtigsten Pflanzengesellschaften der Moore NW-Europas.* Conservatoire et Jardin botaniques, Genève.

Dietze, G. (1981). Beobachtungen zur Neubildung von Hochmoor-Pflanzengemeinschaften im Altwarmbüchener Moor (Landkreis Hannover). *Telma,* 11, 189–195.

Dörfler, W. (1989). Pollenanalytische Untersuchungen zur Vegetations- und Siedlungsge-schichte im Süden des Landkreises Cuxhaven, Niedersachsen. *Probleme der Küstenfor-schung im südlichen Nordseegebiet,* 17, 1–75.

Dupont, L.M. (1986). Temperature and rainfall variation in the Holocene based on comparative palaeoecology and isotope geology of a hummock and a hollow (Bourt-angerveen, the Netherlands). *Review of Palaeobotany and Palynology,* 48, 71–159.

During, R. & Joosten, J.H.J. (1992). Referentiebeelden en duurzaamheid. Tijd voor beleid. *Landschap,* 9, 285–295.

Eggelsmann, R. (1960). Über den unterirdischen Abfluß aus Mooren. *Die Wasser-wirtschaft,* 50, 149–154.

Eggelsmann, R. (1981). *Ökohydrologische Aspekte von anthropogen beeinflußten und unbeeinflußten Mooren Norddeutschlands.* Dissertation Universität Oldenburg, Oldenburg.

Elling, A.E. & Knighton, M.D. (1984). *Sphagnum* recovery after harvest in a Minnesota bog. *Journal of Soil and Water Conservation,* 39, 209–211.

Eshuis, H.J. (1946). *Palynologisch en stratigrafisch onderzoek van de Peelvenen.* Thesis, Utrecht.

Fetcher, N., Beatty, T.F., Mullinax, B. & Winkler, D.S. (1984). Changes in arctic tussock tundra thirteen years after fire. *Ecology,* 65, 1332–1333.

Foster, D.R., Wright Jr., H.E., Thelaus, M. & King, G.A. (1988). Bog development and landform dynamics in central Sweden and south-eastern Labrador, Canada. *Journal of Ecology,* 76, 1164–1185.

Francez, A.-J. (1988). Production primaire et decomposition dans une tourbière à Sphaignes des Monts du Forez (Puy-de-Dôme, France). *Third International Wetlands Conference Rennes 1988,* 113–114.

Franklin, J.F. (1989). Importance and justification of long-term studies in ecology. *Long-term Studies in Ecology. Approaches and Alternatives* (ed. G.E. Likens), pp. 3–19. Springer, New York.

Frenzel, B. (1983). Mires – repositories of climatic information or self-perpetuating ecosystems. *Ecosystems of the World. Mires: Swamp, Bog, Fen and Moor. 4A General Studies* (ed. A.J.P. Gore), pp. 35–65. Elsevier, Amsterdam.

Glebov, F.Z. (1979). Classification of space-time changes of forest and mire in the taiga zone of West Siberia. *Proceedings of the International Symposium on Classification of Peat and Peatlands, Hyytiälä, Finland*, pp. 249–259. International Peat Society, Helsinki.

Glob, P.V. (1965). *Mosefolket – Jernalderens Mennesker bevaret i 2000 Ar*. Gyldendal, Kφbenhavn.

Godwin, H. (1981). *The Archives of the Peat Bogs*. Cambridge University Press, Cambridge.

Göttlich, Kh. (1990). Moorkultivierung für Land- und Forstwirtschaft. *Moor- und Torfkunde* (ed. Kh. Göttlich), pp. 385–410. Schweizerbart, Stuttgart.

Granlund, E. (1932). De Svenska högmossarnas geologi. *Sveriges Geologiska Undersökning C*, **373**, 1–193.

Irdt, A. & Vilbaste, H. (1974). Bird fauna of the Nigula peat-bog. *Estonian Wetlands and their Life* (ed. E. Kumari), pp. 204–213. Valgus, Tallinn.

Ivanov, K.E. (1981). *Water Movement in Mirelands*. Academic Press, London.

Jankuhn, H. (1958). Zur Deutung der Moorleichenfunde van Windeby. *Praehistorische Zeitschrift*, **36**, 184–219.

Jansen, R. (1993). *Vergelijking palaeoecologische gegevens uit een boerenkuil in de Groote Peel met historische gegevens uit de regio*. MSc thesis, Laboratorium voor Palaeobotanie en Palynologie, Utrecht.

Janssen, C.R. (1960). On the late-glacial and post-glacial vegetation of South Limburg (Netherlands). *Wentia*, **4**, 1–112.

Janssen, C.R. (1973). Local and regional pollen deposition. *Quaternary Plant Ecology* (ed. H.J.B. Birks & R.G. West), pp. 31–42. Blackwell, Oxford.

Jensen, U. (1973). Über Bulte und Schlenke in Mooren. *Sukzessionsforschung* (ed. R. Tüxen), pp. 71–88. Rinteln.

Jones, H.E. & Gore, A.J.P. (1978). A simulation of production and decay in blanket bog. *Production Ecology of British Moors and Montane Grasslands* (eds O.W. Heal & D.F. Perkins), pp. 160–186. Springer, Berlin.

Joosten, H. (1982). *Een oriënterend paleo-oecologisch onderzoek aan regeneratieveen in boerenkuilen in de Peel*. Rapport 20-8212-15. Staatsbosbeheer, Tilburg.

Joosten, J.H.J. (1985a). A 130 year micro- and macrofossil record from regeneration peat in former peasant peat pits in the Peel, the Netherlands: a palaeoecological study with agricultural and climatological implications. *Palaeogeography, Palaeoclimatology, Palaeoecology*, **49**, 277–312.

Joosten, J.H.J. (1985b). De betekenis van de boerenkuilen in de Peel. *Natuurhistorisch Maandblad*, **74**, 19–26 and 45–50.

Joosten, H. (1986). Moore und historische Archive: Ein Vergleich von Daten aus natürlichen und kulturellen Gedächtnissen. *Telma*, **16**, 159–168.

Joosten, J.H.J. (1992a). Bog regeneration in the Netherlands: a review. *Peatland Ecosystems and Man: An Impact Assessment*. (eds O.M. Bragg, P.D. Hulme, H.A.P. Ingram & R.A. Robertson), pp. 367–373. International Peat Society/Department of Biological Sciences, University of Dundee, Dundee.

Joosten, H. (1992b). Eigner, J. & Schmatzler, E. (1991): Handbuch des Hochmoorschutzes – Bedeutung, Pflege, Entwicklung. Rezension. *Telma*, **22**, 351–352.

Joosten, H. (1993). Denken wie ein Hochmoor: Hydrologische Selbstregulation von Hochmooren und deren Bedeutung für Wiedervernässung und Restauration. *Telma*, **23**, 95–115.

Joosten, J.H.J. & Bakker, T.W.M. (1987). *De Groote Peel in verleden, heden en toekomst.* Rapport 88–4. Staatsbosbeheer, Utrecht.

Jortay, A. & Schumacker, R. (1989). Zustand, Erhaltung und Regeneration der Hochmoore im Hohen Venn (Belgien). *Telma Beiheft*, **2**, 279–293.

Klinger, P.U. (1976). *Feinstratigraphische Untersuchungen an Hochmooren.* Thesis, Kiel.

Kratz, T.K. & DeWitt, C.B. (1986). Internal factors controlling peatland-lake ecosystem development. *Ecology*, **67**, 100–107.

Landwehr, J. & Barkman, J.J. (1966). *Atlas van de Nederlandse bladmossen.* Koninklijke Nederlandse Natuurhistorische Vereniging, Amsterdam.

Leenders, K.A.H.W. (1989). *Verdwenen venen. Een onderzoek naar de ligging en exploitatie van thans verdwenen venen in het gebied tussen Antwerpen, Turnhout, Geertruidenberg en Willemstad 1250 – 1750.* Gemeentekrediet, Brussel.

Lindholm, T. & Vasander, H. (1990). Production of eight species of *Sphagnum* at Suurisuo mire, southern Finland. *Annales Botanici Fennici*, **27**, 145–157.

Loopmann, A. (1988). Influence of mire water, oxygen and temperature conditions upon vegetation and the development of bog complexes. *Dynamics and Ecology of Wetlands and Lakes of Estonia* (ed. M. Zobel), pp. 40–57. Tartu State University, Tartu.

Lötschert, W. (1969). *Pflanzen an Grenzstandorten.* Gustav Fischer, Stuttgart.

Lütt, S. (1992). Produktionsbiologische Untersuchungen zur Sukzession der Torfstichvegetation in Schleswig-Holstein. *Mitteilungen der Arbeitsgemeinschaft Geobotanik in Schleswig-Holstein und Hamburg*, **43**, 1–249.

Meade, R. (1992). Some early changes following the rewetting of a vegetated cutover peatland surface at Danes Moss, Cheshire, UK, and their relevance to conservation management. *Biological Conservation*, **61**, 31–40.

Menke, B. (1963). Beiträge zur Geschichte der Erica-Heiden Nordwestdeutschlands. *Flora*, **153**, 521–548.

Mets, L. (1982). Changes in a bog pool complex during an observation period of 17 years. *Peatland Ecosystems* (ed. V. Masing), pp. 128–134. Valgus, Tallinn.

Miller, P.C., Miller, P.M., Blake-Jacobson, M., Chapin III, F.S., Everett, K.R., Hilbert, D.W., Kummerow, J., Linkins, A.E., Marion, G.M., Oechel, W.C., Roberts, S.W. & Stuart, L. (1984). Plant-soil processes in *Eriophorum vaginatum* tussock tundra in Alaska: a systems modeling approach. *Ecological Monographs*, **54**, 361–405.

Middeldorp, A.A. (1982). Pollen concentration as a basis for indirect dating and quantifying net organic and fungal production in a peat bog ecosystem. *Review of Palaeobotany and Palynology*, **37**, 227–282.

Müller, K. (1965). Zur Flora und Vegetation der Hochmoore des nordwestdeutschen Flachlandes. *Schriften des Naturwissenschaftlichen Vereins für Schleswig Holstein*, **36**, 30–77.

Neuhäusl, R. (1975). Hochmoore am Teich Velké Dárko. *Vegetace CSSR*, **A9**, 1–267.

Osvald, H. (1923). Die Vegetation des Hochmoores Komosse. *Svenska Växtsociologiska Sällskapets Handlingar*, **1**, 1–436.

Osvald, H. (1925). Zur Vegetation der ozeanischen Hochmooren in Norwegen. *Svenska Växtsociologiska Sällskapets Handlingar*, **7**, 1–106.

Osvald, H. (1949). Notes on the vegetation of British and Irish mosses. *Acta Phytogeographica Suecica*, **26**, 1–62.

Osvald, H. (1970). Vegetation and stratigraphy of peatlands in North America. *Nova Acta Regiae Soc. Scient. Upsaliensis Ser. V:C*, **1**, 1–96.

Ovenden, L. (1990). Peat accumulation in northern wetlands. *Quaternary Research*, **33**, 377–386.

Overbeck, F. (1975). *Botanisch-geologische Moorkunde*. Wachholtz, Neumünster.

Pfadenhauer, J. (1989). Renaturierung von Torfabbauflächen in Hochmooren des Alpenvorlandes. *Telma Beiheft*, **2**, 313–330.

Pickett, S.T.A. (1989). Space-for-time substitution as an alternative to long-term studies. *Long-term Studies in Ecology. Approaches and Alternatives* (ed. G.E. Likens), pp. 110–135. Springer, New York.

Podbielkowski, Z. (1960). Zarastanie dolów potorfowych (The development of vegetation in peat pits). *Monographiae Botanicae*, **10**, 1–144.

Poelman, A. & Joosten, J.H.J. (1992). On the identification of hydrological interaction zones for bog reserves. *Peatland Ecosystems and Man: An Impact Assessment* (eds O.M. Bragg, P.D. Hulme, H.A.P. Ingram & R.A. Robertson), pp. 414–418. International Peat Society / Dept. of Biological Sciences, University of Dundee, Dundee.

Pons, L.J. (1992). Holocene peat formation in the lower parts of the Netherlands. *Fens and Bogs in the Netherlands: Vegetation, History, Nutrient Dynamics and Conservation* (ed. J.T.A. Verhoeven), pp. 7–79. Kluwer, Dordrecht.

Poschlod, P. (1990). Vegetationsentwicklung in abgetorften Hochmooren des bayerischen Alpenvorlandes unter besonderer Berücksichtigung standortskundlicher und populationsbiologischer Faktoren. *Dissertationes Botanicae*, **152**, 1–331.

Precker, A. (1992). Das Große Göldenitzer Moor bei Rostock-Nutzungs- und Vegetationswandel der letzten 200 Jahre. Teil I: Die vorindustrielle Phase extensiver Nutzung (1788 – 1950). *Telma*, **22**, 299–315.

Precker, A. (1993). Das Große Göldenitzer Moor und das Teufelsmoor bei Horst. Ein Beitrag zur Entstehungs- und Nutzungsgeschichte Mecklenburger Regenmoore und zu ihrer gegenwärtigen ökologischen Situation. *Berichte Geologisch-Paläontologisches Institut und Museum Christian-Albrecht-Universität Kiel*, **61**, 1–127.

Projectgroep de Groote Peel (1990). *Technische maatregelen ter verbetering van de waterhuishouding in de Groote Peel en hun effecten*. Ministerie van Landbouw, Natuurbeheer en Visserij.

Reader, R.J. (1978). Primary production in northern bog marshes. *Freshwater Wetlands. Ecological Processes and Management Potential* (ed. R.E. Good, D.F. Whigham & R.L. Simpson), pp. 53–62. Academic Press, New York.

Reader, R.J. & Stewart, J.M. (1972). The relationship between net primary production and accumulation for a peatland in southeastern Manitoba. *Ecology*, **53**, 1024–1037.

Reinikainen, A., Vasander. H. & Lindholm, T. (1984). Plant biomass and primary production of southern boreal mire-ecosystems in Finland. *Proceedings 7th International Peat Congress Dublin*, **4**, 1–20.

Rennie, R. (1807). *Essays on the Natural History and Origin of Peat Moss*. Archibald Constable, Edinburgh.

Ringler, A. (1989). Zur Naturschutzbedeutung aufgelassener Torfabbauflächen im Alpenvorland: Beobachtungen zur Flächenrelevanz, Vegetationsentwicklung und floristischen Bedeutung. *Telma Beiheft*, **2**, 331–363.

Rochefort, L., Vitt, D.H. & Bayley, S.E. (1990). Growth, production and decomposition dynamics of *Sphagnum* under natural and experimentally acidified conditions. *Ecology*, **71**, 1986–2000.

Romanov, V.V. (1968a). *Hydrophysics of Bogs*. Israel Program for Scientific Translations, Jerusalem.

Romanov, V.V. (1968b). *Evaporation from Bogs in the European Territory of the USSR*. Israel Program for Scientific Translations, Jerusalem.

Rybnícek, K. (1973). A comparison of the present and past mire communities of Central Europe. *Quaternary Plant Ecology* (ed. H.J.B. Birks & R.G. West), pp. 237–261. Blackwell, Oxford.

Rybnícek, K. (1984). The vegetation and development of Central European mires. *European Mires* (ed. P.D. Moore), pp. 177–201. Academic Press, London.

Rydin, H. (1993). Mechanisms of interactions among *Sphagnum* species along water-level gradients. *Advances in Bryology*, **5**, 153–185.

Saposnikov, E.S., Juscenkova, L.N. & Minaeva. T. Ju. (1991). Izmenenija v soobscestve el'nika pusicevo-osokovo-sfagnovogo v rezultate progressirujuscevo zabolacivanija. *Bolota ochranjaemych territorija: problemy ochrany i monitoringa. Tezisy dokladov XI Bsesjoeznogo polebogo seminara-ekskursii po bolotovedenijoe* (ed. M.S. Boc), pp. 73–77. Bsesojuznoe Botaniceskoe Obscectvo Central'no-lesnoj Biosfernyj Gosudarstvennyj Zapovednik, Leningrad.

Schmeidl, H. (1977). Veränderung der Vegetation auf Dauerflächen eines präalpinen Hochmoores (Vorläufige Mitteilung). *Telma*, **7**, 65–76.

Schneebeli, M. (1991). *Hydrologie und Dynamik der Hochmoorentwicklung*. Dissertation ETH, Zürich.

Schneider, S. & Steckhan, H.-U. (1963). Das Große Moor bei Barnstorf (Kreis Grafschaft Diepholz). *Beihefte zum Geologischen Jahrbuch*, **55**, 139–192.

Schouwenaars, J. (1982). Maßnahmen im Wasserhaushalt der niederländischen Hoch-moorereste – Zur Kenntnis der Anforderungen für eine Hochmoorregeneration. *Telma*, **12**, 219–234.

Schütrumpf, R. (1951). Die pollenanalytische Untersuchung eisenzeitlicher Funde aus dem Rüder Moor, Kreis Schleswig. *Offa*, **9**, 53–56.

Schütrumpf, R. (1958). Die pollenanalytische Untersuchung der neuen Moorleichen aus dem Kreis Eckerförde. *Praehistorische Zeitschrift*, **36**, 156–166.

Schwaar, J. (1983). Spät- und postglaziale Vegetationsstrukturen im oberen Wümmetal bei Tostedt (Landkreis Harburg). *Jahrbuch Naturwissenschaftliche Verein Fstm. Lüneburg*, **36**, 139–166.

Schwaar, J. & Brandt, K.H. (1984). Pflanzenfunde aus einer vorgeschichtlichen Siedlung in Bremen-Rekum. *Abhandlungen Naturwissenschaftlichen Verein Bremen*, **39**, 171–194.

Sernander, R. (1909). De scanodaniska torfmossarnas stratigrafi. *Geologiska Föreningens Förhandlingar*, **31**, 423–448.

Shugart, H.H. (1989). The role of ecological models in long-term ecological studies. *Long-term Studies in Ecology. Approaches and Alternatives* (ed. G.E. Likens), pp. 90–109. Springer, New York.

Smart, P.J., Wheeler, B.D. & Willis, A.J. (1986). Plants and peat cuttings: historical ecology of a much exploited peatland – Thorne Waste, Yorkshire, UK. *New Phytologist*, **104**, 731–748.

Smart, P.J., Wheeler, B.D. & Willis, A.J. (1989). Revegetation of peat excavations in a derelict raised bog. *New Phytologist*, **111**, 733–748.

Smith, R.A.H. & Forrest, G.I. (1978). Field estimates of primary production. *Production*

402   RESTORATION OF TEMPERATE WETLANDS

Ecology of British Moors and Montane Grasslands (eds O.W. Heal & D.F. Perkins), pp. 17–37. Springer, Berlin.

Steenstrup, J.J.S. (1842). Geognostisk-geologisk undersögelse af skovmoserne Vidnesdam- og Lillemose i det nordlige Sjelland. *Vid. Sel. naturvid. og mathem. Afh.*, **9**, 17–120.

Svensson, G. (1988). Fossil plant communities and regeneration patterns on a raised bog in south Sweden. *Journal of Ecology*, **76**, 41–59.

Swanson, D.K. & Grigal, D.F. (1988). A simulation model of mire patterning. *Oikos*, **53**, 309–314.

Tallis, J.H. (1983). Changes in wetland communities. *Ecosystems of the World. Mires: Swamp, Bog, Fen and Moor. 4A General Studies* (ed. A.J.P. Gore), pp. 311–347. Elsevier, Amsterdam.

Tansley, A.G. (1939). *The British Isles and their Vegetation*. Cambridge University Press, Cambridge.

Tilman, D. (1989). Ecological experimentation: strengths and conceptual problems. *Long-term Studies in Ecology. Approaches and Alternatives.* (ed. G.E. Likens), pp. 136–157. Springer, New York.

Tolonen, K. (1971). On the regeneration of Northeuropean bogs. I. Klaukkalan Isosuo in S. Finland. *Acta Agralia Fennica*, **123**, 143–166.

Tolonen, K. (1979). Peat as a renewable resource: long-term accumulation rates in Northeuropean mires. *Proceedings of the International Symposium on Classification of Peat and Peatlands, Hyytiälä, Finland*, pp. 282–296. International Peat Society, Helsinki.

Tolonen, K. (1980). On the regeneration of Northeuropean bogs. II. Stratigraphic records from Germany, Denmark and S. Sweden. *Proceedings of the 6th International Peat Congress, Duluth*, pp. 119–125, Duluth.

Tolonen, K., Huttunen, P. & Jungner, H. (1985). Regeneration of two coastal bogs in eastern North America. Stratigraphy, radiocarbon dates and rhizopod analysis from sea cliffs. *Annales Academiae Scientiarum Fennicae A III*, **139**, 1–51.

Tüxen, J. (1983). Die Schutzwürdigkeit der niedersächsischen Kleinsthochmoore im Hinblick auf ihre Vegetation. *Tüxenia Mitteilungen der Floristisch-soziologischen Arbeitsgemeinschaft N.S.*, **3**, 423–435.

Tüxen, J. (1986). *Führer zur Exkursion der DGMT, Sektion I und V am 6. und 7. September 1986*. DGMT, Schneverdingen.

Tüxen, J. (1990). Zur Vegetationsentwicklung der niedersächsischen Flachland-Hochmoore in den letzten 25 Jahren – Vergleichsuntersuchungen in einigen der bedeutendsten Moorschutz-Gebiete. *Kurzfassungen der DGMT-Tagung 'Moore auf lange Sicht: ihre Vergangenheit - ihre Zukunft'* (eds G. Große-Brauckmann & H. Joosten), 2 pp., Meijel.

Tüxen, J. (1993). Lütt, S. (1992): Produktionsbiologische Untersuchungen zur Sukzession der Torfstichvegetation in Schleswig-Holstein.– Mit. Arbeitsgem. Geobot. Schlesw.-Holstein u. Hamburg *43*, 1–249, 48 Abb., 62 Tab.; Kiel. Rezension. *Telma*, **23**, 354–355.

Tüxen, J., Stamer, R. & Onken-Grüß, A. (1977). Beobachtungen über den Wasserhaushalt von Kleinstmooren. *Mitteilungen der Floristisch-soziologischen Arbeitsgemeinschaft N.F.*, **19/20**, 283–296.

Tüxen, R. (1928). Das Altwarmbüchener Moor. *Mitteilungen der Provinzialstelle für Naturdenkmalpflege Hannover*, **1**, 56–85.

van Dam, H. & Buskens, R. (1993). Ecology and management of moorland pools: balancing acidification and eutrophication. *Hydrobiologia*, **265**, 225–263.

van den Munckhof, P. (1988). *Het beheer van zwak gebufferde wateren in Nederland van ± 1850 tot heden*. Rapport 245. Laboratorium voor Aquatische Oecologie, Nijmegen.

van der Meijden, R., Weeda, E.J., Adema, F.A.C.B. & De Joncheere, G.J. (1983). *Heukels/van der Meijden Flora van Nederland*. Wolters-Noordhoff, Groningen.

van der Molen, P.C. (1988). Palaeoecological reconstruction of the regional and local vegetation history of Woodfield Bog, Co. Offaly. *Proceedings Royal Irish Academy*, **88B**, 69–97.

van der Molen, P.C., Schalkoort, M. & Smit, R. (1992). Hummock–hollow complexes on Clara Bog, Co. Offaly, Ireland. *Hummock–hollow complexes on Irish raised bogs. A palaeo/actuo ecological approach of environmental and climatic change* (ed. P.C. van der Molen), pp. 117–173. PhD thesis, Amsterdam.

van der Sanden, W.A.B. (1990). Veenlijken, offers in het veen? *Mens en moeras. Veenlijken in Nederland van de bronstijd tot en met de Romeinse tijd.* (ed. W.A.B. van der Sanden), pp. 204–229. Drents Museum, Assen.

van der Voo, E.E. (1962). Geomorfologie en plantengroei van dobben bij Ureterp (Fr.). *De Levende Natuur*, **65**, 12–19.

van Geel, B. & Dallmeijer, A.A. (1986). Eine Molinia-Torflage als Effekt eines Moorbrandes aus dem Frühen Subboreal im Hochmoor Engbertsdijksveen (Niederlande). *Abhandlungen des Landesmuseums für Naturkunde*, **48**, 471–479.

van Walsum, P.E.V. (1990). *Waterbeheer rondom de Groote Peel. Verkenning en evaluatie van scenario's*. Rapport 106. Staring Centrum, Wageningen.

van Walsum, P.E.V. (1992). *Water management in the Groote Peel bog reserve and surrounding agricultural area*. Report 49. The Winand Staring Centre for Integrated Land, Soil and Water research, Wageningen.

van Walsum, P.E.V. & Joosten, J.H.J. (1994). Quantification of local ecological effects in regional hydrologic modelling of bog reserves and surrounding agricultural lands. *Agricultural Water Management*, **25**, 45–55.

Vasander, H. (1990). Plant biomass, its productivity and diversity on virgin and drained southern boreal mires. *Publications of the Department of Botany, University of Helsinki*, **18**, 1–16.

Venema, G.A. (1855). *De Hooge Veenen en het Veenbranden*. Kruseman, Haarlem.

Vermeer, J.G. & Joosten, J.H.J. (1992). Conservation and management of bog and fen reserves in the Netherlands. *Fens and Bogs in the Netherlands: Vegetation, History, Nutrient Dynamics and Conservation* (ed. J.T.A. Verhoeven), pp. 433–478. Kluwer, Dordrecht.

Vitt, D.H., Crum, H. & Snider, J.A. (1975). The vertical zonation of Sphagnum species in hummock-hollow complexes in northern Michigan. *Michigan Botanist*, **14**, 190–200.

Vitt, D.H. & Kuhry, P. (1992). Changes in moss-dominated wetland ecosystems. *Bryophytes and Lichens in a Changing Environment* (eds J.W. Bates & A.M. Farmer), pp. 178–210. Clarendon Press, Oxford.

Von Post, L. & Sernander, R. (1910). *Pflanzen-physiognomische Studien auf Torfmooren in Närke*. XI International Geological Congress, Excursion Guide No. 14 (A7), Stockholm.

Walker, D. (1961). Peat stratigraphy and bog regeneration. *Proceedings of the Linnean Society of London*, **172**, 29–33.

Walker, D. (1970). Direction and rate in some British postglacial hydroseres. *Studies in the Vegetational History of the British Isles* (ed. D. Walker & R.G. West) pp. 117–139. Cambridge University Press, Cambridge.

Walker D. & Walker, P.M. (1961). Stratigraphic evidence of regeneration in some Irish bogs. *Journal of Ecology*, **49**, 169–185.

Wallén, B., Falkenberg-Grerup, U. & Malmer, N., 1988. Biomass, productivity and relative rate of photosynthesis of *Sphagnum* at different water levels on a South Swedish peat bog. *Holarctic Ecology*, **11**, 70–76.

Weatherhead, P.J. (1986). How unusual are unusual events? *American Naturalist*, **128**, 150–154.

Weber, C.A. (1900). Ueber die Moore mit besonderer Berücksichtigung der zwischen Unterweser und Unterelbe liegenden. *Jahresbericht der Männer von Morgenstern*, **3**, 3–23.

White, J.M. (1929). Re-colonisation after peat cutting. *Royal Irish Academy Proceedings*, **39 Section B**, 453–476.

Wiegman, A.F. (1837). *Ueber die Entstehung, Bildung und das Wesen des Torfes*. Vieweg, Braunschweig.

Wildi, O. (1978). Simulating the development of peat bogs. *Vegetatio*, **37**, 1–18.

Witte, H.J.L. & van Geel, B. (1985). Vegetational and environmental succession and net organic production between 4500 and 800 BP reconstructed from a peat deposit in the western dutch coastal area (Assendelver Polder). *Review of Palaeobotany and Palynology*, **45**, 239–300.

Zobel, M. (1988). Autogenic succession in boreal mires – a review. *Folia Geobotanica et Phytotaxonomica*, **23**, 417–445.

27 Re-establishment of a *Sphagnum*-dominated Flora on Cut-over Lowland Raised Bogs

R. P. MONEY

Department of Animal and Plant Sciences, P.O. Box 601, University of Sheffield, Sheffield, S10 2UQ, UK

SUMMARY

1.   Revegetation trends in abandoned peat workings suggest that *Sphagnum*-dominated vegetation does not readily return to cut-over raised bogs without human intervention.

2.   Water table instability, which may characterise milled peat fields, severely inhibits *Sphagnum* regeneration. However, raised bog communities can develop hydroserally to form floating rafts, which may provide a mechanism for restoring these cut-over areas.

3.   Experiments have been carried out to investigate the potential for facilitating *Sphagnum* recolonisation on abandoned peat fields. Applying *Sphagnum* inoculum encouraged recolonisation and raft establishment within flooded pits. Regeneration from fragments was more prolific than from whole plants.

4.   Shallow water conditions were optimal for raft establishment. Development of rafts may further benefit from physical assistance using materials such as brushwood to give support.

5.   *Sphagnum* growth in the field was enhanced by mineral enrichment with phosphorus. Laboratory experiments suggested that the low pH values recorded on cut-over peat fields (< pH 3) may inhibit *Sphagnum* growth. However, raising the pH in the trial pits did not improve growth, although this may have been masked by the effects of calcium toxicity.

INTRODUCTION

Raised bogs were once much more widespread in the UK than they are today. Historically, the greatest losses have occurred through reclamation for agriculture and forestry (Ratcliffe, 1977; Lindsay, 1993) but in present times commercial peat extraction is generally regarded as the greatest threat to residual areas. It is unlikely that any UK raised bogs have remained completely unmodified but even raised bog that is little disturbed now covers a small percentage of its original area. With raised bog habitat so diminished there would be obvious advantages in being able to restore sites made derelict by peat extraction.

Restoration of Temperate Wetlands. Edited by B.D. Wheeler, S.C. Shaw, W.J. Fojt and R.A. Robertson
© 1995 John Wiley & Sons Ltd.

Currently in the UK, peat production is primarily for horticulture, producing an estimated 1.76 million m^3 of horticultural grade peat annually, 75% of which is used as a growing medium (Bather & Miller, 1991). The most modern and widespread method of extraction is surface milling, which accounts for 65% of production. Milling involves iterative removal of thin layers of peat over extensive areas to leave a landscape of relatively flat peat fields, intensively drained and devoid of vegetation, with perhaps 50 cm depth of basal peat remaining.

The surface of a little-damaged bog is characterised by a spongy, actively growing layer (c. 50 cm thick) of plants, principally *Sphagnum* mosses, referred to as the acrotelm (Ingram & Bragg, 1984; see also Bragg, this volume). More specifically, the *Andromeda polifolia* sub-community of the *Erica tetralix–Sphagnum papillosum* community, (M18a in the National Vegetation Classification; Rodwell, 1991) is believed to be the vegetation type most characteristic of little-damaged UK raised bogs. A desirable goal for restoration would therefore be to return such a vegetation layer to the surface of milled peat fields where at all possible.

Results presented here are derived from current research investigating the potential for facilitating *Sphagnum* colonisation of abandoned peat fields. Full details of this research are presented by Money (1994). Patterns of spontaneous recolonisation are discussed and consideration is given to the habitat conditions of cut-over areas with implications for *Sphagnum* regrowth. Preliminary results are also presented for regeneration trials in which *Sphagnum* was reintroduced to the field.

SPONTANEOUS RECOLONISATION OF CUT-OVER BOG

In 1992 an extensive vegetation survey of abandoned peat workings was undertaken throughout the UK and Ireland. These ranged from small domestic cuttings through to abandoned commercial operations. Vegetation was recorded in 4-m^2 quadrats, using the Domin scale and the data were classified using Two Way Indicator Species Analysis (TWINSPAN) (Hill, 1979). What follows is a simplified account; details are presented elsewhere (Money, 1994).

Spontaneous re-establishment of *Sphagnum* vegetation in cut-over bogs in the UK has generally been poor. The most widespread plant communities resembled dry heathland dominated by *Calluna vulgaris*[1], *Molinia caerulea*, *Betula* spp and *Pteridium aquilinum*. Where *Sphagnum* regeneration was observed, it generally formed part of a wet heath community alongside the above species, plus abundant *Eriophorum vaginatum, E. angustifolium, Juncus effusus, Erica tetralix* and *Polytrichum* spp. Such plant assemblages do not resemble an undisturbed raised bog flora. Furthermore, the typical raised bog Sphagna were generally replaced by species such as *S. fimbriatum* and *S. recurvum*. However, one species, *S. cuspidatum*, readily recolonised flooded ditches and cuttings.

---

[1] Nomenclature follows Stace (1991) for vascular plants and Smith (1978) for bryophytes.

Before the recent introduction of milling, most commercial peat workings were block cut, whereby peat was removed in strips to leave a topography of parallel cuttings separated by upstanding baulks. Where drainage remains effective, cuttings and baulks may both become colonised by dry heath. However, cuttings lying close to the water table and acting as a focus for run-off can provide a wet niche for the regrowth of some bog species.

Excellent bog plant communities, analogous to the *Andromeda polifolia* sub-community of the *Erica tetralix–Sphagnum papillosum* community (M18a), had recolonised some locations, occurring as floating rafts in small flooded peat pits and ditches. A list of component species is given in Table 1. It is probable that successful recolonisation in these situations was due to two factors. First, a source of propagules persisted in the vicinity and second, floating rafts stay in contact with a fluctuating water table, thus providing perennially wet conditions. *Sphagnum* plants in a raft are therefore not as vulnerable to drought as are their counterparts growing on solid peat and the growth of heath species is constrained.

Table 1. Floating raft vegetation in revegetated peat pits.

Dominant *Sphagnum* species, (forming a thick 'spongy' layer):	*S. papillosum, S. magellanicum, S. cuspidatum.*
Principal vascular plant species	*Erica tetralix, Rhynchospora alba, Narthecium ossifragum, Eriophorum angustifolium.*
Additional associated bryophytes	*Sphagnum palustre, S. auriculatum, S. subsecundum, S. recurvum, S. capillifolium, S. subnitens, S. pulchrum, S. tenellum, Mylia* spp.
Additional associated vascular species	*Drosera rotundifolia, D. intermedia, D. anglica, Andromeda polifolia, Calluna vulgaris, Eriophorum vaginatum, Vaccinium oxycoccos, Molinia caerulea, Eleocharis multicaulis, Myrica gale, Potamogeton polygonifolius, Hypericum elodes, Menyanthes trifoliata, Rhynchospora fusca*

HYDROLOGICAL CHARACTERISTICS OF A MILLED PEAT FIELD

At Thorne Moors, South Yorkshire (for location, see Heathwaite, this volume, Figure 3), water table depth was recorded for an abandoned milled peat field with an average of 1m depth of peat remaining and ditches which had been blocked. Measurements were made from a series of piezometer tubes, every two months. The water table was highly unstable, lying at the surface during the winter months and falling during the summer (Figure 1). In an intact bog, the high water-storage capacity of the acrotelm layer gives it a regulatory function which contains water table fluctuations and maintains surface-wet conditions (Bragg, 1989). A milled peat field has no acrotelm layer and the water storage capacity of residual peats is not high enough to perform the same function. The problem is exacerbated by

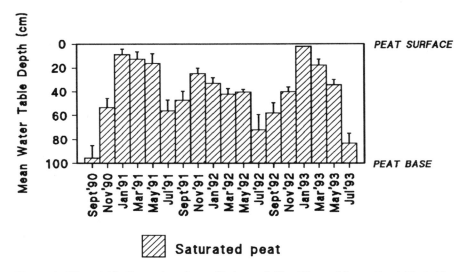

Figure 1. Water table fluctuations in a milled peat field at Thorne Moors, South Yorkshire. Each bar represents the mean value from a series of piezometer tubes. Error bars = 95 % confidence limits.

evapotranspirative loss where peat fields become colonised by *Molinia* and *Betula* (Schouwenaars, 1990). Furthermore, restoration projects may face particular problems in comparatively low rainfall locations. For example, Thorne Moors receives *c.* 550–600 mm a^{-1} compared with over 1000 mm a^{-1} received by sites further north and west.

Water table fluctuation may be reduced by creating open water areas across a peat field, thus increasing surface storage (Beets, 1992; Schouwenaars, 1992). This would require reconfiguration of the bog surface to produce, for example, a mosaic of pools. In these conditions, revegetation would be at least partly hydroseral – evidence discussed above suggests that floating raft development can result in revegetation by very desirable bog plant communities.

HYDROCHEMICAL CONDITIONS IN A CUT-OVER BOG

Water samples were regularly taken from pits dug in a milled peat field on Thorne Moors. Conductivity and pH were recorded and the samples further analysed to determine the concentration of several major ions (analytical techniques are detailed in Money, 1994). Pits were sampled every two months from June 1990 to June 1993. However, only pH and conductivity were recorded beyond June 1991.

Figure 2 shows the range of values recorded against concentrations measured by other workers for undisturbed sites. Concentrations were higher for all ions except phosphorus, which remained negligible. Concentrations of NH_4^+, SO_4^{2-} and Ca^{2+} were most increased. Water chemical conditions in the milled peat field thus resembled poor fen rather than ombrotrophic bog. However, unlike poor fen, pH in the milled peat field was generally lower than undisturbed bog, with values on average below pH 3.5 (Figure 2).

Enrichment may be due to contamination from the underlying substratum, but this is unlikely as similar water quality was recorded from another cut-over area on Thorne Moors with several metres of peat remaining (Money, 1994). Alternatively, aeration and biochemical oxidation of the peat due to drainage and water table instability may have led to a release of nutrients though the importance of this process is poorly understood. Drying of peat has been observed to increase total amounts of soluble N (Braekke, 1981; Piispanen and Lähdesmäki, 1983) and concentrations of SO_4^{2-} (Gorham, 1956). In the latter case, oxidation of sulphide to sulphate produces a drop in pH. This may explain the high SO_4^{2-} concentrations and low pH values recorded at Thorne Moors. Atmospheric pollution may also have contributed to the high NH_4^+ and SO_4^{2-} concentrations recorded, but these inputs were not measured.

Various irrigation and immersion experiments have shown *Sphagnum* species to be differentially sensitive to S pollution but generally at concentrations above current ambient values (Ferguson, Lee & Bell, 1978; Ferguson & Lee, 1980). However irrigation with 14.4 mg l^{-1} SO_4^{2-} (in the range found at Thorne Moors) has been shown to reduce the growth of some species (Ferguson & Lee, 1983). Furthermore, several workers have reported that addition of NH_4^+ even at low concentration, constrains the growth of *Sphagnum* in culture and field experiments (Clymo, 1987; Press, Woodin & Lee, 1986; Rudolph & Voight, 1986). However, by contrast, experimental N enrichment may stimulate *Sphagnum* growth or at least have no adverse effect (Aerts, Wallen & Malmer, 1992).

LABORATORY EXPERIMENTS

Effect of calcium concentration on *Sphagnum* growth

Growth experiments using up to 20 mg l^{-1} Ca^{2+} were conducted on *S. cuspidatum, S. recurvum* and *S. magellanicum*. Plants were grown in pots in a greenhouse for 60 days in a 0.1(s) nutrient solution (Boatman & Lark; 1971) at pH 4; $CaCl_2$ was used to adjust calcium concentration in the solution. Growth was measured using the capitulum correction method (Clymo, 1970) and recorded as relative growth rate (RGR), where RGR = (nL final plant dry weight − nL original plant dry weight) / time. Results are shown in Figure 3. Data were analysed using ANOVA. A significant reduction in growth (P = 0.0001) was observed only in *S. magellanicum* at 20 mg l^{-1} Ca^{2+}.

Effect of pH on *Sphagnum* growth

Experiments of similar design to the above were conducted to investigate the effect of pH on *S. cuspidatum, S. recurvum* and *S. magellanicum*. The standard nutrient solution (see above) had a pH of 4.7. Treatments were acidified using 5%

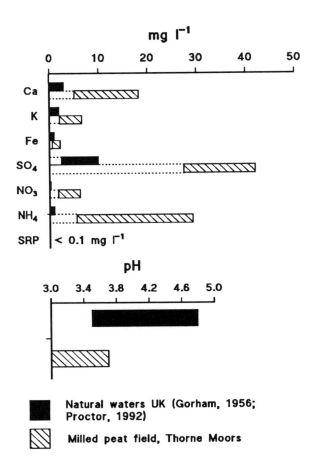

Figure 2. Hydrochemical characteristics of undisturbed *vs.* cut-over bog. Bars represent the range of values recorded; SRP = soluble reactive phosphorus.

HCl. Details of these experiments are given elsewhere (Money, 1994). Results are shown in Figure 4. There was a significant trend towards reduced growth below pH 4 in *S. cuspidatum* (P = 0.0001) and *S. recurvum* (P = 0.0001) Below pH 3.5, *S. magellanicum* showed a trend towards reduced growth but this was not significant (P = 0.1886). The implications of the above experiments are considered in the Discussion.

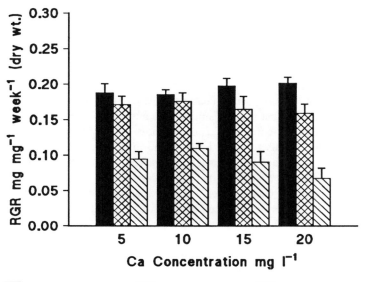

Figure 3. Effect of calcium concentration on the growth of *Sphagnum* in submerged culture. Error bars represent 95% confidence limits. RGR = relative growth rate.

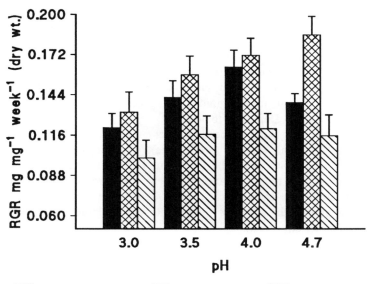

Figure 4. Effect of pH concentration on the growth of *Sphagnum* in submerged culture. Error bars represent 95% confidence limits. RGR = relative growth rate.

FIELD REINTRODUCTION EXPERIMENTS

Materials and methods

1. Water table fluctuation and Sphagnum *growth*

The aim of this experiment was to examine the effect of water table fluctuation on the regeneration of *Sphagnum* introduced to the field. Flooded pits, 4 m^2 in area and 1 m deep with an adjacent shelf of similar area and 10 cm deep, were specially dug in an abandoned block-cut area of Thorne Moors to carry out these field trials (Figure 5i). Individual plants (*c.* 5 cm long) of the following species were placed prostrate on the peat surface of the shelf: *S. magellanicum, S. papillosum, S. capillifolium, S. palustre, S. fimbriatum, S. recurvum, S. auriculatum* and *S. cuspidatum*. Fifty plants of each species were used, each species covering an area of 0.5 m^2. Similarly, plants were placed on a raft composed of netlon mesh and bamboo canes floating in the adjacent flooded pit. This experiment was set up in May 1991. Results presented document growth after 30 months. Growth was measured using a 4m^2 quadrat divided into 400 squares of 100 cm^2. Area covered and capitulum density were recorded.

2. Water regime and regeneration from whole plants

This rudimentary experiment was designed to investigate the ability of different Sphagna to regenerate from whole plants placed upon cut-over surfaces and determine the water regime most conducive to successful growth. Trenches were specially dug, approximately 16 m long and 2 m wide with sloping bottoms (Figure 5ii). This provided a range of water regimes so that a trench could be crudely divided into sections as follows:

Peat slope	Remains dry for long periods
Peat–water interface	Thin band along either side of the water's edge, comprising moist peat to very shallow water
Shallow water	Depths up to 50 cm
Deep water	Depths exceeding 50 cm, up to *c.* 100 cm

Whole plants of eight species (see above) were scattered by hand at approximately even density along the length of the trenches. Different species were placed in separate trenches. Approximately 150 litres of loosely packed *Sphagnum* was applied to each trench. Control trenches received no *Sphagnum*. Inoculum was applied in the winter of 1990/91. Results are largely descriptive and represent growth after three years.

3. Sphagnum *fragment regeneration*

This experiment investigated the propensity for *Sphagnum* to regenerate from fragments. Plants of *S. cuspidatum* and *S. recurvum* were shredded in a household blender and the resultant slurry was diluted to form a thin 'soup' in which capitula remains and fragments of stem up to 0.5 cm long remained visible. The 'soup' was

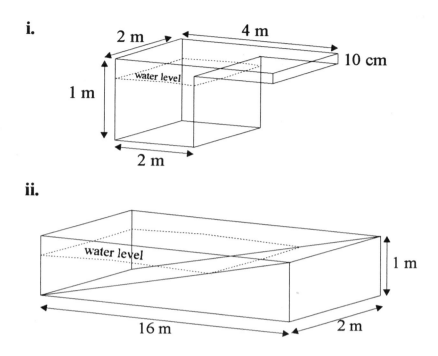

Figure 5. Design of experimental trenches used in field re-introduction trials.

then dispensed along the length of trenches as outlined above. Each trench was inoculated with approximately 5 kg spun wet weight of a single species (about half the quantity used in experiment 2). Brushwood was placed in the flooded part of some trenches to investigate whether physical support would assist growth. Inoculum was applied in March 1991. Results represent observations made in December 1993.

4. Nutrient and lime additions

The aim of this experiment was to investigate the growth response of *Sphagnum* to additions of phosphorus and increase in pH. Plants of *S. cuspidatum* and *S. recurvum* cut to 5 cm long were submerged to 30 cm depth in specially dug pits (refer to experiment 1). After 10 days, water quality in the pits was altered according to the following treatments:

Control	No treatment
Lime added	Addition of 80 g laboratory-grade $CaCO_3$; (The aim of adding lime was to reduce acidity to *c.* pH 4)
P added	Addition of 30 g laboratory-grade NaH_2PO_4
Lime and P added	Both treatments, quantities as above.

Table 2. *Sphagnum* growth after three years on an artificial raft (experiment 1). Capitulum starting density = 1 in 100 cm^2 over 0.5m^2.

	Area covered (m^2)	No. of capitula in 100 cm^2
Sphagnum cuspidatum	1.9	25–30
Sphagnum recurvum	0.4	25
Sphagnum auriculatum	0.9	35–40

Plants were harvested after 20 weeks and growth was measured using the capitulum correction method (Clymo, 1970). Results were analysed using ANOVA.

Results

1. Water table fluctuation and Sphagnum growth

For several months of the year the water levels fell by up to 38 cm below the surface of the peat shelf causing it to dry out. However, plants on the raft surface remained perennially wet. *Sphagnum* growth is summarised in Table 2. On the peat shelf, *S. magellanicum*, *S. papillosum*, *S. capillifolium*, *S. palustre*, *S. fimbriatum*, *S. recurvum* and *S. auriculatum* all completely failed to regenerate. However, *S. cuspidatum* grew to a density of 20 capitula per 100 cm^2 over 0.25 m^2. This growth mostly occurred during the final 12 months of the experiment, which was unusually wet. It was also notable that plants had become significantly displaced from their original place of inoculation, due probably to rain splash.

On the floating raft, *S. magellanicum*, *S. papillosum*, *S. capillifolium*, *S. palustre* and *S. fimbriatum* also failed to regenerate. However, *S. cuspidatum*, *S. recurvum* and *S. auriculatum* grew prolifically. Capitulum density was increased by an order of magnitude and the raft area became almost completely smothered by growth.

2. Water regime and regeneration from whole plants

Trenches to which *Sphagnum* was not added showed no signs of spontaneous recolonisation. Results for other trenches are summarised below:

Peat slope: In the first two years of the experiment, plants of all species became desiccated and failed to regenerate. In the third year, conditions were unusually wet and the peat slope was generally inundated by water a few centimetres deep. During this period a continuous cover of *S. cuspidatum*, *S. recurvum* and *S. auriculatum* developed. Very sparse regeneration was also observed for *S. papillosum* and *S. palustre*.

Peat–water interface: Successful regeneration was observed fairly immediately for *S. cuspidatum*, *S. recurvum* and *S. auriculatum*, which produced 100% cover at capitulum densities in the order of 80, 100 and 50 per 100 cm^2, respectively. *S. fimbriatum* formed clumps of very spindly plants in the inundated part of the interface, covering up to 50% of the peat surface. Plants of other species appeared to have become coated in peaty sediment and lost into the soft peat surface.

Shallow water: Successful regeneration was observed only for *S. cuspidatum*, *S. recurvum* and *S. auriculatum*. Each species developed a floating raft at capitulum densities in the order of 45, 65 and 40 per 100 cm^2 respectively. Regeneration in shallow water was slower than at the peat–water interface. In particular, at depths of 30–50cm, rafts took *c.* 18 months to become established.

Deep water: Regeneration of all species largely failed. The original inoculum could be recovered from the trench bottom, but was discoloured brown and showed no signs of growth. Small floating clumps of *S. cuspidatum*, *S. recurvum* and *S. auriculatum* did occur, but only where plants had become anchored to the trench periphery.

3. Sphagnum *fragment regeneration*

The peat slope in these trenches remained dry throughout the three years. Regeneration of *Sphagnum* fragments in this zone largely failed except for limited growth from inoculum in cracks in the peat. Along the remaining length of the trenches, regeneration of *S. cuspidatum* and *S. recurvum* was far more successful than in experiment 2 (despite no obvious differences in water quality). Continuous floating rafts developed across deeper water to cover a considerable length of the trenches. Growth of *S. cuspidatum* was notably more prolific than that of *S. recurvum*.

In the first year, trenches containing brushwood were characterised by prolific algal growth (notably the filamentous alga *Oedegonium* spp.) which appeared to inhibit *Sphagnum* regeneration. However, this effect was temporary and did not limit *Sphagnum* growth in the long term. Brushwood did not remain afloat in deep water therefore the desired effect was not achieved. However, a subsurface layer of brushwood did appear to facilitate growth of *S. cuspidatum* into deeper water compared with growth achieved when brushwood was absent.

4. *Nutrient and lime additions*

Figure 6 shows the change in water quality in response to these treatments. Phosphorus concentration was successfully increased throughout the duration of the experiment (Figure 6i). Acidity reduced to pH 4 proved difficult to maintain and six lime applications were required to keep pH elevated (Figure 6ii). This increased calcium concentrations to undesirably-high levels (Figure 6iii).

Figure 7 shows the effect of treatment on *Sphagnum* growth. Elevated phosphorus concentration significantly increased the growth of both *S. cuspidatum* and *S. recurvum* ($P = 0.0001$). Addition of lime alone decreased growth of both species though this was only statistically significant for *S. recurvum*. Addition of both lime and phosphorus produced a growth response in *S. cuspidatum* similar to that of just phosphorus but in *S. recurvum* the presence of lime appeared to negate a positive growth response to phosphorus. These growth responses were mirrored by the concentration of P in the plant tissue (Money, 1994).

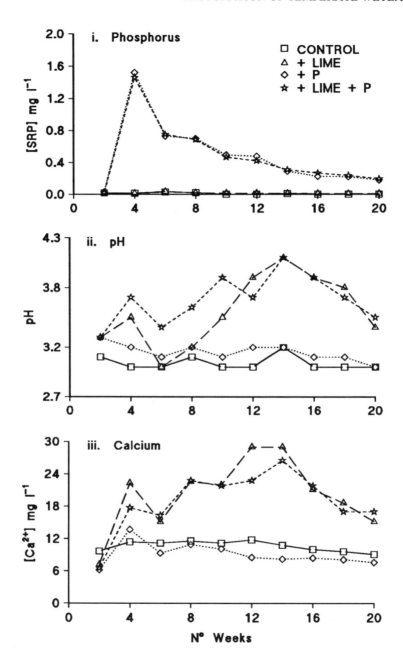

Figure 6. Field responses of water quality to mineral addition in experiment 4. SRP = soluble reactive phosphorus.

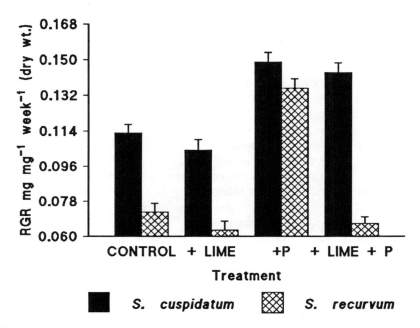

Figure 7. Growth response of submerged *Sphagnum* to mineral additions in the field (experiment 4). RGR: relative growth rate after 20 weeks. Error bars represent 95% confidence limits.

DISCUSSION

Examination of revegetation trends in cut-over raised bogs suggests that communities typical of undisturbed raised bogs do not always readily return to abandoned peat workings, and many disturbed bog relics remain too dry for regrowth of a *Sphagnum*-dominated vegetation. This is due in part to residual drainage networks but, furthermore, water storage capacity of the bog surface is reduced by removal of the acrotelm layer so that the surface of peat fields may remain prone to drought even after drains have been blocked. This was recorded at Thorne Moors and has been reported by other workers elsewhere in NW Europe (Eggelsmann, 1982; Schouwenaars, 1988, 1992; Streefkerk & Casparie, 1989; Beets, 1992; Schouwenaars & Vink, 1992).

Results from field experiment 1 suggest that water table fluctuation can severely inhibit *Sphagnum* regeneration. Notably, *S. cuspidatum* was able to tolerate periodic desiccation and grow during wet periods. However, the severity of drought experienced in this experiment was modest compared with milled areas on other parts of the peatland. Several species also failed to regenerate on the perennially wet artificial raft. This may have been due to smothering by the prolific growth of *S. cuspidatum*, *S. recurvum* and *S. auriculatum*.

The creation of bodies of open water will increase the surface storage capacity of peat fields and limit water table fluctuation (Beets, 1992; Schouwenaars, 1992). This is not incompatible with revegetation by raised bog communities, as evidence suggests these may develop as floating rafts ensuring permanent saturation of the *Sphagnum* layer and exclusion of undesirable species such as *Molinia* and *Betula* (Money, 1994, in press). It is considered by some workers that this strategy may be the only way to return raised bog vegetation to many areas (Schouwenaars & Vink, 1992; Schouwenaars, 1992).

Results from field experiment 2 suggest that applying *Sphagnum* as whole plants will encourage *Sphagnum* recolonisation. However, the surface of peat cuttings is an unstable environment and such inoculum is prone to desiccation, drowning and smothering by peat. Consequently, successful regeneration may only be achieved initially by species with an aquatic habit growing in a shallow water environment. The success of pool species may be due to their comparatively high productivity (Clymo & Reddaway, 1971; Pedersen, 1975; Pakarinen, 1978; Andrus, 1986) enabling them to progress rapidly from the vulnerable stage of recently applied inoculum. In natural colonisation of flooded peat pits, a pioneering raft of aquatic *Sphagnum* usually precedes colonisation by lawn and hummock-forming species. Restoration must therefore consider encouraging development of aquatic *Sphagnum* rafts to provide a template for other species.

The observed regenerative success from fragments, particularly of *S. cuspidatum* (experiment 3), suggests a means for using inoculum more economically. 'Hydroseeding' fragments would also be a more practical way of inoculating large areas. The propensity for *Sphagnum* to regenerate from fragments has been identified for numerous species (Baker & Macklon, 1987; Poschlod & Pfadenhauer, 1989; Rochefort, Gauthier & Lequéré, this volume). The more vigorous regeneration observed here compared with relatively intact material used in experiment 2 may be a product of stimulation of lateral buds. This phenomenon may be similar to that seen in vascular plants, hormonally controlled by the apex (Jones, 1978; Clymo & Hayward, 1982; Clymo, 1987).

Results from field experiment 3 provide limited evidence that raft development may benefit from physical assistance. Effects of brushwood may become more apparent in the future as *Sphagnum* growth continues. Further monitoring of experimental trenches is required. Restoration measures might therefore include optimising pool area and depth, using artificial or natural materials to break up the water surface and reduce disturbance by wave action, and use of raft-building vascular plants such as *Menyanthes trifoliata* and *Juncus bulbosus*.

Water chemical conditions are likely to influence growth of aquatic Sphagna and the water quality of cut-over areas may differ significantly from undisturbed bog. The relatively enriched conditions at Thorne Moors may explain the growth of poor-fen species such as *Juncus effusus* and *Sphagnum recurvum*. However, these conditions may not directly constrain growth of raised bog species (Money, 1994). In the laboratory, calcium concentrations of 20 mg l^{-1} were found to reduce growth of *Sphagnum magellanicum*. However, in the field such high calcium concentrations were rare and episodic. On average, Ca concentrations were around 10 mg l^{-1} and were therefore unlikely to influence *Sphagnum* growth (Money, 1994). The importance of the high NH_4^+ and SO_4^{2-} values recorded are difficult to assess as ambiguity in the literature particularly surrounds the effect of N (see above). However, plants of all species used in the above experiments stored in the field at Thorne Moors have continued to grow, suggesting that conditions at least are not lethal.

Bogs are naturally acid systems, so it is unusual to propose, from the evidence of these laboratory experiments, that pH values as low as 3 frequently recorded at Thorne Moors may inhibit *Sphagnum* growth. However, being a logarithmic scale proton concentration is an order of magnitude greater at pH 3 than at pH 4. Despite this, experiment 4 suggests that elevating field pH does not improve growth. However, any benefit of reducing H^+ concentration was probably masked by the effect of calcium toxicity, as inordinate amounts of lime were required to sustain a pH response in the pit water. An alternative method for reducing acidity would consequently need to be considered, though the whole concept may simply be unrealistic.

Further field evidence from experiment 4 suggests that growth of *Sphagnum* rafts is encouraged by modest addition of phosphorus to pool water. This supports suggestions made by other workers that *Sphagnum* growth in the field is limited by negligible availability of P (Boatman, 1977; Baker & Boatman, 1990, 1992). *Sphagnum* may be well adapted to growing in a low nutrient regime but this does not necessarily represent optimum conditions for growth. The extent to which growth can be encouraged before unhelpful invasion by undesirable species, notably algae, becomes problematic would benefit from further research.

This study represents early steps in understanding how a *Sphagnum*-dominated flora may be restored to milled peat fields. Encouraging results suggest that measures can be taken to encourage and enhance *Sphagnum* regrowth. However, it needs to be recognised that suggestions made here represent results of small-scale growth trials and future consideration must be given to scaling-up the process. Urgent consideration must also be given to the establishment of lawn and hummock-forming Sphagna on rafts of aquatic Sphagna. We know this can occur on a small scale but the extent to which it can be encouraged on a larger scale requires further research. There is also a fundamental need to investigate the potential for 'farming' *Sphagnum* in order to provide adequate quantities of inoculum for restoration projects.

ACKNOWLEDGEMENTS

This project was funded by Fisons plc (Horticulture division). Thanks also go to the late Peter Atkins for his enthusiasm and commitment to the project.

REFERENCES

Aerts, R, Wallén, B. & Malmer N. (1992). Growth limiting nutrients in *Sphagnum*-dominated bogs subject to low and high atmospheric nitrogen supply. *Journal of Ecology*, **80**, 131–140.

Andrus, R.E. (1986). Some aspects of *Sphagnum* ecology. *Canadian Journal of Botany*, **64**, 416–426.

Baker, R.G.E & Boatman, D. J. (1990). Some effects of nitrogen, phosphorus, potassium and carbon dioxide concentration on the morphology and vegetative reproduction of *Sphagnum cuspidatum* Ehrh. *New Phytologist*, **116(4)**, 605–612.

Baker, R.G.E. & Boatman, D.J. (1992). The effect of nitrogen, phosphorus and carbon dioxide on cell development in branch leaves of *Sphagnum*. *Journal of Bryology*, **17**, 35–46.

Baker, R.G.E. & Macklon, A.E.S. (1987). *A study of factors affecting the growth and morphology of* Sphagnum. Unpublished report for Highlands & Islands Development Board.

Bather, D.M. & Miller, F.A. (1991). *Peatland Utilisation in the British Isles*. Centre for Agricultural Strategy, Paper 21, University of Reading, Reading.

Beets, C.P. (1992). The relation between the area of open water in bog remnants and storage capacity with resulting guidelines for bog restoration. *Peatland Ecosystems and . Man: An Impact Assessment.* (eds O.M. Bragg, P.D. Hulme, H.A.P. Ingram, R.A. Robertson). pp. 133–140. International Peat Society/Department of Biological Sciences, University of Dundee, Dundee.

Boatman, D. J. (1977). Observations on the growth of *Sphagnum cuspidatum* in a bog pool in the Silver Flowe National Nature Reserve. *Journal of Ecology*, **65**, 119–126

Boatman, D.J. & Lark, P.M. (1971). Inorganic nutrition of the protonemata of *Sphagnum papillosum* Lindb., *S. magellanicum* Brid. and *S. cuspidatum* Ehrh. *New Phytologist*, **70**, 1053–1059.

Braekke, F. H. (1981). Hydrochemistry of low-pH soils of South Norway. 2. Seasonal variation in some peatland sites. *Meddelelser Norsk Institutt for Skogforskning*, **36**, 1–22.

Bragg, O. (1989). The importance of water in mire ecosystems. *Cut-over Lowland Raised Mires* (eds W.J. Fojt, & R. Meade), pp. 61–82. *Research and Survey in Nature Conservation No 24*. Nature Conservancy Council, Peterborough,.

Clymo, R.S. (1970). The growth of *Sphagnum*: methods of measurement. *Journal of Ecology*, **58**, 13–49.

Clymo, R.S. (1973). The growth of *Sphagnum*: some effects of environment. *Journal of Ecology*, **61**, 849–869.

Clymo, R.S. (1987). Interactions of *Sphagnum* with water and air. *Effects of Acidic Deposition and Air Pollutants on Forests, Wetlands and Agricultural Ecosystems* (ed. T.C. Hutchinson & K.M. Meema), pp. 513–529. Springer-Verlag, Berlin.

Clymo, R. S. & Hayward, P. M. (1982). The ecology of *Sphagnum. Bryophyte Ecology* (ed. A.J.E. Smith), pp. 229–291, Chapman & Hall, London.

Clymo, R.S. & Reddaway, E.J.F. (1971). Productivity of *Sphagnum* (bog moss) and peat accumulation. *Hidrobiologia*, **12**, 181–192.

Eggelsmann, R. (1982). Moglichkeiten und Zielzetzungen fur eine Regeneration von Hochmooren-hydrologische betrachtet. *Inf. Natursch. Landschaftspf.*, **3**. 167–177.

Ferguson, P. & Lee, J.A. (1980). Some effects of bisulphite and sulphate on the growth of *Sphagnum* in the field. *Environmental Pollution* **21**, 59–71.

Ferguson, P. & Lee, J.A. (1983). The growth of *Sphagnum* species in the southern Pennines. *Journal of Bryology*, **12**, 579–589.

Ferguson, P., Lee, J.A. & Bell, J.N.B. (1978). Effects of sulphur pollutants on the growth of *Sphagnum* species. *Environmental Pollution*, **16**, 151–162.

Gorham E (1956). The ionic composition of some bog and fen waters in the English Lake District. *Journal of Ecology* **44**, 142–152.

Hill, M.O. (1979). *TWINSPAN – A FORTRAN programme for arranging multivariate data in a two-way table by classification of the individuals and attributes.* Cornell University, Ithaca, New York.

Ingram, H.A.P. & Bragg, O.M. (1984). The diplotelmic mire: some hydrological consequences reviewed. *Proceedings of the 7th International Peat Congress, Dublin, June, 1984*, **1**, pp. 220–234. Irish National Peat Committee, for the International Peat Society.

Jones, D.G. (1978). Aspects of growth and development in *Sphagnum cuspidatum*. *Bulletin of the British Bryological Society*, **31**, 8–10.

Lindsay, R.L. (1993). Peatland conservation – from cinders to Cinderella. *Biodiversity and Conservation*, **2**, 528–540.

Money, R.P. (1994). *Restoration of lowland raised bog damaged by peat extraction – with particular reference to* Sphagnum *regeneration.* PhD thesis. University of Sheffield.

Money, R.P. (in press). Restoration of cut-over peatlands: the rôle of hydrology in determining vegetation quality. *Hydrology and Hydrochemistry of Wetlands* (eds. J. Hughes & A.L. Heathwaite). John Wiley, Chichester.

Pakarinen, P. (1978). Production and nutrient ecology of three *Sphagnum* species in southern Finnish raised bogs. *Annales Botanici Fennici*, **15**, 15–26.

Pedersen, A. (1975). Growth measurements of five *Sphagnum* species in south Norway. *Norwegian Journal of Botany*, **22**, 277–284.

Piispanen, R. & Lähdesmäki, P. (1983). Biochemical and geobotanical implications of nitrogen mobilisation caused by peatland drainage. *Soil Biology and Biochemistry*, **15**, 381–383.

Poschlod, P., & Pfadenhauer, J. (1989). Regeneration vegetativer Sprossteilchen von Torfmoosen – Eine vergleichende Studie an neun *Sphagnum*-Arten. *Telma*, **19**, 77–88.

Proctor, M.C.F. (1992). Regional and local variation in the chemical composition of ombrogenous mire waters in Britain and Ireland. *Journal of Ecology*, **80**, 719–736.

Press, M.C., Woodin, S.J. & Lee, J.A. (1986). The potential importance of an increased atmospheric nitrogen supply to the growth of ombrotrophic *Sphagnum* spp. *New Phytologist*, **103**, 45–55.

Ratcliffe, D.A. (1977). *A Nature Conservation Review*. Cambridge University Press.

Rodwell, J.S. (ed.) (1991). *British Plant Communities Vol. 2. Mires and Heaths*. Cambridge University Press, Cambridge.

Rudolf, H. & Voight, J.U. (1986). Effects of NH_{4+}-N and NO_3-N on growth and metabolism of *Sphagnum magellanicum*. *Physiologia Plantarum*, **66**, 339–343.

Schouwenaars, J.M. (1988). The impact of water management upon groundwater fluctuations in a disturbed bog relict. *Agricultural Water Management*, **14**, 439 – 449.

Schouwenaars, J.M. (1990). A study on the evapotranspiration of *Molinia caerulea* and *Sphagnum papillosum*, using small weighable lysimeters. In: Schouwenaars, J.M. (1990). *Problem oriented research on plant–soil–water relations.* PhD thesis, Agricultural University, Wageningen.

Schouwenaars, J.M. (1992). Hydrological characteristics of bog relicts in the Engberts-dijksvenen after peat-cutting and rewetting. *Peatland Ecosystems and Man: An Impact Assessment.* (eds O.M. Bragg, P.D. Hulme, H.A.P. Ingram, R.A. Robertson). pp. 125–

132. International Peat Society/Department of Biological Sciences, University of Dundee, Dundee.

Schouwenaars, J.M. & Vink, J.P.M. (1992). Hydrophysical properties of peat relicts in a former bog and perspectives for *Sphagnum* regrowth. *International Peat Journal*, **4**, 15–28.

Smith, A.J.E. (1978). *The Moss Flora of Britain and Ireland.* Cambridge University Press, Cambridge.

Stace, C. (1991). *New Flora of the British Isles*. University Press, Cambridge.

Streefkerk, J.G. & Casparie, W.A. (1989). *The Hydrology of Bog Ecosystems – Guidelines for Management.* Staatsbosbeheer, Utrecht.

28 *Sphagnum* Regeneration – Toward an Optimisation of Bog Restoration

L. ROCHEFORT, R. GAUTHIER

Département de Phytologie, Université Laval, Québec, G1K 7P4, Canada

D. LEQUÉRÉ

Premier Research Centre, P.O. Box 2600, Rivière-du-Loup, Québec, G5R 4C9, Canada

SUMMARY

1.   Four common *Sphagnum* species (*S. magellanicum, S. nemoreum, S. angustifolium* and *S. papillosum*) found in Québec (eastern Canada) showed a very good ability to regenerate vegetatively from fragments. In extreme cases, even a stem section of only 1–2 mm long can regenerate.
2.   A high water level close to the peat surface and mineral amendments (slow-release 12–12–12 NPK fertiliser and bone meal) enhanced *Sphagnum* establishment.
3.   The addition of a shade cover did not prove to be an important factor in the spreading of the *Sphagnum* mosses.

INTRODUCTION

With 170 million ha, Canada has more peatlands than any other country (Gorham, 1991). However, most of Canada's peatlands are fens or northern bogs affected by permafrost and are not usable for horticultural peat harvest. Hence, the southern ombrotrophic peatlands are under greater pressure of exploitation as only these bogs contain peat suitable for horticultural peat harvesting. At present the peat harvesting industry in Canada has reached a point in its development where certain bogs that have been harvested for the past decades are now largely depleted of their horticultural grade peat. When the harvesting operation ceases, the bog is abandoned, and, unfortunately, does not usually return to a natural cycle of bog formation. This situation is evident in New Brunswick, Québec, Manitoba, and Alberta, where such sites need to be restored to functional peatlands. However, there is little information available on North American peatland restoration. A long term goal is to implement a policy of no net loss of functions and values of wetlands in Canada (Lynch-Stewart, 1992).

Since the late 1960s, peat has been harvested by vacuum in Canada (Keys,

Restoration of Temperate Wetlands. Edited by B.D. Wheeler, S.C. Shaw, W.J. Fojt and R.A. Robertson
© 1995 John Wiley & Sons Ltd.

1992). Compared with the previously-used block-cutting method, the vacuum method leaves a flat, bare peat surface devoid of any *Sphagnum* diaspores. The recolonisation process of such peatlands is very slow compared with recolonisation of sites harvested with block-cutting methods (personal observations of 30 abandoned peatlands in eastern Canada). To facilitate the restoration of these bare, uniform substrata, different experiments were undertaken to investigate the regenerating ability of some common *Sphagnum* species found in North America. Our goal was to determine: (i) which part of *Sphagnum* can regenerate and how small a *Sphagnum* diaspore can be; (ii) the effect of the substratum humidity on the regeneration of *Sphagnum*; (iii) if the addition of minerals enhances the regeneration of *Sphagnum* mosses; and (iv) if the sole introduction of sparse *Sphagnum* diaspores in the field would initiate the recolonisation process. All these experiments were aimed at one goal: to minimise the amount of natural vegetation needed for peatland restoration. It would not be wise to destroy an equivalent surface of a natural peatland in order to restore an abandoned peat field. Thus, if we can reduce the size and density of diaspores needed to re-establish vegetation on a bare peat surface, the better it will be for the environment.

MATERIAL AND METHODS

1. *Sphagnum* vegetative diaspore experiment

Two sets of experiments were performed. One set dealt with three *Sphagnum* species, namely *S. magellanicum* Brid., *S. rubellum* Wils. and *S. angustifolium* (C. Jens. ex Russ.) C. Jens. The living plants were collected in September 1992 at the Ste-Marguerite peatland (Mistassini, Qc.). Sectioning of living parts only was performed in sterile conditions using a laminar air-flow cabinet. The living plant organs were sterilised for 30 seconds with sodium hypochlorite 1.5% solution. Cultivation was done at 22 °C in closed cabinet, on sterile 7% agar in Petri dishes with (Rudolph & Voigt, 1986) medium added with 0.1% sucrose solution. Acidity was adjusted to pH 5.8. Light intensity was similar to daylight but continuous.

The second set of experiments dealt only with *Sphagnum papillosum* Lindb. The plants were collected in May 1993 at St-Etienne-de-Lauzon peatland (Lévis County, Qc.). Living plant parts were isolated under non-sterile conditions. Cultivation occurred at room temperature in non-sterile Petri dishes on Whatman No. 1 filter paper wetted with 3 ml of (Rudolph & Voigt, 1986) solution. Acidity was adjusted to pH 4.5 using HCl 1N. Enough bi-distillated water was added when the plants began to dry, to keep the filter paper wet. Cultures were kept at room temperature and were exposed to daylight, which averaged 2000 to 3000 lux.

2. Water levels experiment

This experiment was carried out in a glasshouse on vacuum-harvested peat in small containers (25 x 30 x 10 cm, split into two compartments). The living *Sphagnum* plant material was collected at the Ste-Marguerite peatland (Mistassini,

Qc) in autumn 1992. Four species were investigated: *Sphagnum magellanicum* (section *Palustria*), *S. angustifolium* (section *Cuspidata*), and *S. fuscum* (Schimp.) Klinggr. and *S. nemoreum* Scop. (both of section *Acutifolia*). The Sphagna were dissected into four parts to test their powers of regeneration: capitulum only; 1 cm of stem below the capitulum; capitulum + stem (= 2.5 cm fragment), and branches only. A fixed number of pieces was evenly distributed on the peat surface: approximately 150 small spreading branches and 25 pieces for all the other fragments. The temperature was maintained around 20 °C with a 16 h photoperiod. The plants were left to grow for 3 months (December to March). Two different water levels, 8 cm and 1–2 cm below the peat surface, were maintained by differentially spraying with distilled water every two days. Water level was controlled with the aid of a small perforated PVC pipe inserted in every container. After 3 months of growth, the Sphagna cover of the bare surface was estimated and the number of capitula were counted. To be counted, a new capitulum needed to have at least 4–5 branches arranged in a rosette-like fashion. Two-way ANOVAs were computed for each species studied after verifying assumptions for normality and homogeneity of variances.

3. Mineral additions experiment

This experiment was designed to test the possibility of recolonisation by *Sphagnum nemoreum* on a peat substratum from a peatland abandoned in 1974 and which had not yet revegetated naturally. Nutrients were added to see if this would initiate colonisation. Six 60 litre containers (36.5 x 50 x 31 cm) were filled with a block of peat cut from the abandoned peatland. Three fertiliser treatments were applied: (i) control; (ii) addition of a slow release fertiliser (12–12–12 NPK – Grace Sierra), 10 g per container, limed with calcium carbonate and magnesium carbonate (9.25 g of each per container) in order to get a pH of 4.5; (iii) addition of bone meal (2–11–0 NPK; total P_2O_5: 15%, organic matter: 15%; So-Green Corp., Ont.), 8.55 g per container, and limed as above. The fertilisers and lime were incorporated only into the first 3 cm of the peat. Two methods of introducing the *Sphagnum* moss were tested. On one half of the surface, two cavities 3 cm deep were dug and a lump of *Sphagnum* at natural density was inserted into each one. This method was designed to simulate how *Sphagnum* would colonise a bare peat surface if bands of vegetation were left as source of diaspores during exploitation or if, for example, introducing 1 m^3 peatland vegetation plugs were introduced in the field for restoration. On the second half, pieces of mosses (0.5 to 1 cm long) were sprinkled on the surface. This method was designed to simulate the spreading of surface shredded peatland vegetation for large-scale bog restoration. The blocks were watered from the top with demineralised water and the water level was maintained at 10 cm below the surface. The containers were kept in a greenhouse, under natural light, at a temperature of 18–20 °C. The latter experiment lasted from November 1992 to May 1993. Observations of the development of the mosses were noted every two weeks, or each month towards the end of the experiment. Diameter increment of the lumps of *Sphagnum* were measured once a month.

4. Field reintroduction experiment

With this experiment we tested the ability of *S. magellanicum* and *Polytrichum strictum* Brid. to regenerate from fragments on a peatland abandoned for one year. The introduction plots were compared with similar plots where no treatment was applied to the bare peat surface (control) or where 250 ml of granular horticultural lime had been sprinkled on 1 m². The study was conducted at the Ste-Marguerite peatland (Mistassini, Qc) during the field seasons 1992 and 1993. Ste-Marguerite peatland is an ombrotrophic bog under the influence of a humid continental climate. Mean July and January temperature are 17.2 °C and −16.8 °C, respectively. Temperatures are below freezing point for at least five months of the year and the frost-free season is around 103 days (from 31 May to 12 September). Mean annual precipitation is 82 cm, of which 75% falls in the form of rain. Snow melts between March and April. During the growing season, the water level of the exploited and abandoned peatland was generally 5 cm lower than the level naturally occurring in the undisturbed part of the peatland (Figure 1).

Twenty-seven blocks of 4 x 1 m² quadrats were established on three abandoned harvesting bays on which the drainage ditches had been dammed in early spring 1992. *S. magellanicum* and *P. strictum* fragments (0.5–2 cm long) were shredded using a domestic blender. Approximately 750 ml of moss material was spread on each quadrat plot. The plant material was introduced during the beginning of July 1992. The number of individual capitula was recorded on 6 September 1992 and 8 October 1993.

Data were analysed by ANOVA in a randomised complete block design. The data for each year were analysed separately. In 1992, the numbers of capitula m^{-2}

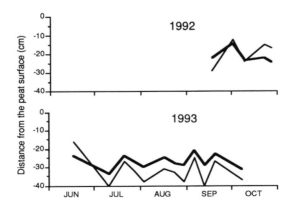

Figure 1. Fluctuation of the water table in the natural (thick line) and abandoned (thin line) part of the experimental peatland during 1992 and 1993.

for each of the four treatments were compared, based on data collected from the 27 blocks. In 1993, only 18 blocks were available to compare the effect of treatments in their second year; the other nine blocks were covered with a 40% shading cloth (and the lime and *Polytrichum* treatments received extra addition of *Sphagnum* fragments in spring 1993). Data were transformed ($\sqrt{(x+0.5)}$) prior to analysis, to reduce heterogeneity of variances. The analyses of variances were done using the GLM procedure of SAS (SAS, 1988). When the ANOVA showed a significant treatment effect at the 0.05 level, the means of treatments were compared using a Tukey test. For the *Sphagnum* treatments in 1993, we compared the number of capitula between the nine plots that were covered with a shading cloth with the 18 that were left uncovered using a T-test. Again the data were square-root transformed prior to analysis.

RESULTS

1. *Sphagnum* vegetative diaspore experiment

Preliminary results (Table 1) show that despite a severe contamination of cultures, most *Sphagnum* organs, whether entire or in parts, possess the ability to regenerate when cultivated under sterile conditions with nutrients provided. Best results were obtained with *S. rubellum* apical buds and with *S. angustifolium* entire spreading branches. In general, both of these species show a better ability to regenerate than *S. magellanicum* despite a lower contamination rate with this species.

Table 1. Preliminary results of experiments with living *Sphagnum* vegetative parts in sterile culture on agar with Rudolph & Voight (1986) medium.

Plant part	*S. magellanicum*	*S. rubellum*	*S. angustifolium*
Apical bud with leaf and branch primordia	0/6* 0/6 0/6 1/1	4/5 4/4 4/5 4/4	
Thin section of stem just below capitulum	0/9 0/9 1/9		
Stem section between capitulum and first branch fascicle	1/6 0/6		
Spreading branch with leaves	0/3 0/3 0/4	0/6 1/5 1/5	3/6 4/6 1/6
Spreading branch without leaves	0/6	1/6 0/6 0/6	0/6 0/6 0/6
Spreading branch leaf	0/9 0/12 0/8 1/9	0/12 0/11 1/9	0/12 0/12 0/10
Pendent branch with leaves	0/6 0/6 0/6		
Pendent branch without leaves	0/9 0/8 0/8 0/9		
Stem section between branch fascicles	0/6 0/6 0/6		

* Results are presented for each Petri dish as a replicate of each experiment within each species as n_1/n_2 = number of plant parts regenerating/total number of plant parts in the Petri dish. Variations with n_2 and number of replicates for each species are due to removal of plant parts contaminated with micro-organisms.

Table 2. Production of regeneration sites by some living *Sphagnum papillosum* detached organs as a function of time in non-sterile culture on filter papers wetted with Rudolph & Voight (1986) medium.

Date of observation		June			July	
	6	16	22	28	7	26
Plant parts	No. in culture	No. of regeneration sites				
Capitulum branch						
a) long	43	53	77	77	77	77
b) medium size	31	13	18	26	27	32
c) short	43	0	1	3	5	7
Apical bud	3	0	0	0	0	0
Stem section between capitulum and first branch fascicle	3	0	0	0	0	0
Stem section with a fascicle of branches	20	21	23	34	38	40
Stem section between branch fascicle	28	0	0	3	8	16

The best results were obtained with sections of stem with attached fascicle of branches, as was expected from observations by Clymo & Duckett (1986). Here the number of regenerating sites doubled the number of stem sections put into culture. Good results were also obtained with fully elongated branches from the capitulum. The medium-sized and short branches from the capitulum continued their growth to full length before any regeneration site appeared. Regeneration on stem sections between branch fascicles was delayed, but these parts proved to possess good regeneration capacity. Total absence of regeneration from apical buds could be due to low nutrient availability compared with the results obtained with *S. rubellum* in sterile culture with high concentrations of nutrients.

The second experiment clearly shows that there is better regeneration (Table 2) in non-sterile culture than in sterile culture. Contamination by micro-organisms was also extremely small, probably due to the fact that the sterilisation process is too harsh for the moss tissues or that the non-sterile culture had no sugar. In addition, regeneration began within 10 or 20 days, a much shorter period than in the sterile culture of the first experiment. In the latter, one month and sometimes two months passed before the first sign of regeneration.

2. Water levels experiment

Sphagnum fuscum

Sphagnum fuscum regenerated best from fragments containing a capitulum still attached to the stem. After 3 months, the capitula almost tripled the initial number

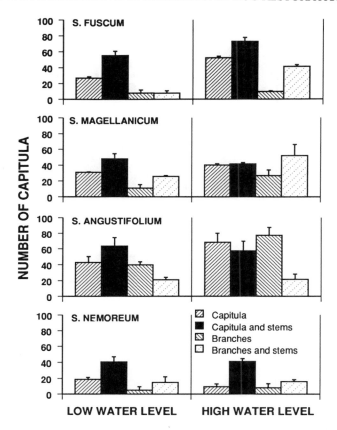

Figure 2. Regeneration of vegetative parts of four *Sphagnum* species: the number of capitula present after a 3-month incubation time in relation to two water levels (1–2 cm and 8 cm below the peat surface). The initial number of fragments was 150 for the small branches and 25 for the three other types.

(from 25 to 75; $F_{3,16} = 67.8$; $P < 0.0001$; Figure 2). Overall, the higher water level slightly increased the success of *S. fuscum* regeneration (minimum $F_{1,16} = 13.8$; $P = 0.0019$) in terms of innovations produced and coverage. Even though several new capitula were produced within the 3 months of growth, this species spread very little (barely one-fifth of the peat surface; Figure 3).

Sphagnum magellanicum

For this species, most parts regenerated well with the exception of branches alone (minimum $F_{3,16} = 6.3$; $P = 0.005$; Figures 2 & 3). After 3 months, *S. magellanicum* was beginning to form little cushions. A good coverage of the bare peat surface (Figure 3) was achieved more by the capitula which tended to increase in size rather than the number of newly formed regenerants (compare with graphs for

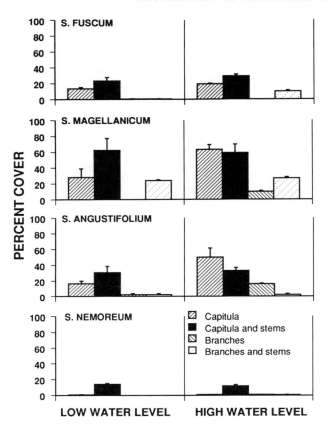

Figure 3. Regeneration of vegetative parts of four *Sphagnum* species: the *Sphagnum* cover of the bare peat surface after a 3-month incubation time in relation to two water levels (1–2 cm and 8 cm below the peat surface). The initial number of fragments was 150 for the small branches and 25 for the three other types. .

S. fuscum and *S. angustifolium*). *S. magellanicum* produced more innovations under a higher water level regime ($F_{1,16} = 6.7$; $P = 0.02$).

Sphagnum angustifolium

The types of fragment differed significantly in terms of success of regeneration (minimum $F_{3,16} = 5.2$; $P = 0.03$). In terms of production of innovations, only *S. angustifolium* showed a good ability to regenerate from fragments composed of branches alone (Figure 2). Regeneration from branches did not spread as much on the peat surface (Figure 3) as when a capitulum was introduced but it was more successful than when the branches were still attached to a stem (Figures 2 & 3; for comparison 1 cm of stem of *S. angustifolium* had *c*. 8 branches x 25 = 200 branches). In general, the maintenance of a water level closer to the peat surface

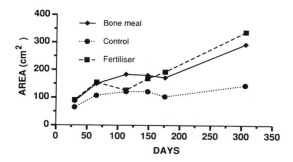

Figure 4. Growth of *Sphagnum nemoreum* on peat treated with slow-release fertiliser (12–12–12), bone meal (2–11–0) or no fertiliser.

favoured a better growth for all parts (minimum $F_{1,16} = 5.2$; $P = 0.037$) for both plant parameters measured.

Sphagnum nemoreum

With this species, only the diaspores composed of a capitulum attached to a stem succeeded in increasing its number of regenerants (from 25 to 40; $F_{3,16} = 20.3$; $P = 0.0001$; Figure 2). This species was neither vigorous nor influenced by the water level. Overall, it regenerated very poorly on the bare peat substratum (Figure 3).

3. Mineral additions experiment

Both fertiliser treatments enhanced the growth and the expansion of *S. nemoreum* compared with the control, where the peat substratum was as it occurs naturally in the bog (Figure 4). Nevertheless, differences between these two treatments were noted. Within a month, algae had developed on all the peat surfaces which had been treated with the slow release 12–12–12 fertiliser whereas, on peat where bone meal was applied, very few algae were observed and only on small areas. The algae, in some cases, covered the *Sphagnum* mosses and smothered them, reducing their total growth. However, given time, the development of the *Sphagnum* did not seem to be influenced by the algal growth, since its development in the fertilised treatment caught up with the bone meal treatment.

4. Field reintroduction experiment

In 1992, differences in the number of capitula m^{-2} were significant between treatments (($F_{3,78} = 59.1$; $P = 0.0001$. The *Sphagnum* treatment differed from all other treatments, while the three other treatments were not significantly different from each other at the 0.05 level. In 1993, the results were similar ($F_{3,51} = 9.8$; $P =$

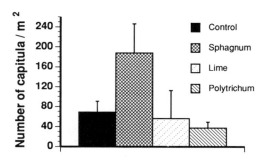

Figure 5. The effect of the addition of external *Sphagnum magellanicum* diaspores, lime and companion species (*Polytricum strictum*) on *Sphagnum* regeneration on an abandoned harvested peatland.

0.0001 for differences between treatments; Figure 5). In other terms, these results indicate that the addition of *Sphagnum* diaspores to a bare peat surface enhance the chance of *Sphagnum* recolonisation, as, even after two summers and one winter in the field, a number of the introduced diaspores were still alive. Covering the plots in the second summer did not result in a higher density of *Sphagnum* capitula in the quadrats (P = 0.216).

DISCUSSION

To restore the vegetation of boreal bogs after peat extraction, we need to know how to reintroduce *Sphagnum* species into an abandoned peaty field and to minimise the disturbance of natural bog vegetation from where diaspores will be taken. As a partial answer, we have investigated which parts of different *Sphagnum* species can regenerate and how small a fragment can regenerate.

The growth of *Sphagnum* parts on agar plates (exp. 1) indicates that all four of the North American *Sphagnum* species tested had a high power of vegetative regeneration, as was also found by Poschlod & Pfadenhauer (1989). These authors did not succeed in getting new innovations from *Sphagnum* leaves. However, as previously found by Oehlmann (1898), we observed that very small parts of *Sphagnum* such as a single branch leaf or a cross-section of a stem were able to produce a new shoot. Now that we know that almost any vegetative parts of *Sphagnum* can regenerate into new individuals, we need to obtain more information on the growing conditions which can promote this regeneration on a larger scale.

The growth of *Sphagnum* parts on bare peat substratum (exp. 2) confirms that at least three species of *Sphagnum* can readily reproduce vegetatively and established themselves on peat. The level of regeneration achieved by the *Sphagnum* fragments tested during a 3-month period was very similar to the maximum numbers of new innovations observed by Wilcox & Andrus (1987) during a 112-day incubation (from 8 to 70 for similar species). A water level close to the surface of the peat substratum favoured the regeneration of all the species and types of fragment (except for *S. nemoreum*, which did very poorly). For *S. magellanicum*, our results are not directly consistent with the findings of Wallén *et al.* (1988), where a better rate of carbon fixation was obtained when the water level was maintained 10 cm below the surface compared with 2 cm. Based on observation of cores at natural density, we should have expected more biomass production of *S. magellanicum* at our low water level.

The growing conditions of the last two experiments were closer to the conditions in which natural *Sphagnum* regeneration will have to take place. With the results obtained from these experiments, we can conclude that an external source of diaspores will significantly enhance *Sphagnum* establishment and mineral additions will help it to spread more rapidly. The effect of a cover did not influence *Sphagnum* colonisation of already established capitula. However, more work is needed to assess if it could improve the conditions at the onset of fragment establishment.

ACKNOWLEDGEMENTS

We want to thank Martine Cormier and Cécile Gauthier of Laval University, and France Cayer and Jacinthe Arsenault of Tourbières Premier, for their useful assistance with this research. This research was funded by Johnson & Johnson, Centre Québécois de la Valorisation de la Biomasse (CQVB) and Tourbières Premier Ltée. We thank Suzanne Campeau for her resourceful assistance in statistics and graphics, as well as with the follow up of some of these experiments.

REFERENCES

Clymo, R.S. & Duckett, J.G. (1986). Regeneration of *Sphagnum*. *New Phytologist*, **102**, 589–614.

Gorham, E. (1991). Northern peatlands: role in the carbon cycle and probable responses to climatic warming. *Ecological Applications*, **1**, 182–195.

Keys, D. (1992). *Canadian Peat Harvesting and the Environment*. North American Wetlands Conservation Council (Canada). Issues paper no 1992–3.

Lynch-Stewart, P. (1992). *Aucune perte nette – Mise en oeuvre d'objectifs "aucune perte nette" pour la conservation des terres humides au Canada*. North American Wetlands Conservation Council (Canada). Issues paper no 1992–2.

Oehlmann, V. (1898). *Vegetative Fortpflanzung der Sphagnuceen nebst ihrem Verhalten gegen Kalk*. Diss. Univ. Freiburg, 71 S.; Freiburg (Schweiz).

Poschlod, P. & Pfadenhauer, J. (1989). Regeneration of vegetative parts of peat mosses – A comparative study of nine *Sphagnum* species. *Telma*, **19**, 77–88.

Rudolph, H. & Voigt, J.U. (1986). Effects of NH_4^+-N and NO_3^--N on growth and metabolism of *Sphagnum magellanicum*. *Physiologia Plantarum*, **66**, 339–343.

SAS Institute Inc. (1988). *SAS/STAT User's Guide, Release 6.03*. Edition Cary, NC. 1028 pp.

Wallén, B., Falkengren-Grerup, U. & Malmer, N. (1998). Biomass, productivity and relative rate of photosynthesis of *Sphagnum* at different water levels on a South Swedish peat bog. *Holarctic Ecology*, **11**, 70–76.

Wilcox, D.A. & Andrus, R.E. (1987). The role of *Sphagnum fimbriatum* in secondary succession in a road salt impacted bog. *Canadian Journal of Botany*, **65**, 2270–2275.

29 Microclimate and Physical Properties of Peat: New Clues to the Understanding of Bog Restoration Processes

PH. GROSVERNIER, Y. MATTHEY & A. BUTTLER
Laboratoire d'Ecologie Végétale et de Phytosociologie, Institut de Botanique de l'Université, Chantemerle 22, CH-2007 Neuchâtel, Switzerland

SUMMARY

1.   Current knowledge of initial ecological conditions which allow *Sphagnum* mosses to recolonise a disturbed peatland mainly concerns the hydrosere system, as a dynamic of terrestrialisation, but few studies, if any, have described such recolonisation by paludification.

2.   Two paludification successional series encountered in the Swiss Jura Mountains are described, which lead towards the formation of a continuous *Sphagnum* carpet, with, as pioneer species (a) *Eriophorum vaginatum* and (b) *Polytrichum alpestre*. They suggest that both peat physical properties and microclimate play an important role in triggering the growth of *Sphagnum* on dry and apparently hostile bare peat surfaces.

3.   Two greenhouse experiments were undertaken in order to answer the questions: (a) which *Sphagnum* species is best adapted for recolonising dry bare peat surfaces? (b) what is the relative importance of a high water level? (c) how can peat properties help to reinitiate *Sphagnum* growth? (d) how far can a particular microclimate compensate for a low water table?

4.   Beyond its apparent sensitivity to ecological factors, *S. fallax* seems to be a very effective species in recolonising dry bare peat, particularly because of its fast growth rate and carpet-forming capacity, and its greater resistance to total desiccation in terms of recovery ability, even when growing as isolated plants.

5.   When *S. fallax* is grown on bare peat as isolated plants spread over the field (simulating establishment from diaspores), water table depth, microclimate and peat type each contributes equally to the growth variation. Pore size distribution in the upper haplotelmic peat profile, as a result of an increased mineralisation rate, appeared most relevant in influencing the water regime. On the other hand, commensalism with some pioneer species can provide an effective alternative to the lack of a suitable permanent water table by creating a favourable microclimate.

Restoration of Temperate Wetlands. Edited by B.D. Wheeler, S.C. Shaw, W.J. Fojt and R.A. Robertson
© 1995 John Wiley & Sons Ltd.

INTRODUCTION

Several workers have studied the initial ecological conditions which allow *Sphagnum* mosses to recolonise a disturbed peatland. The regeneration processes of bog vegetation in a hydrosere system, as a dynamic of terrestrialisation, have been studied in the Jura Mountains (Royer *et al.*, 1978) and elsewhere in Europe (Bertram, 1988; Jortay & Schumacker, 1989; Lütt, 1992). But few studies, if any, have described such recolonisation by paludification.

In Switzerland, wetlands have been strictly protected by law since 1987. Among them, peat bogs, *i.e.* raised and sloping mires (Succow & Lange, 1984) [also called ombrogenous and ombrosoligenous (transitional) mires (Steiner, 1985) and grouped under the general concepts of raised and mountain mires by Goodwillie (1980)], have diminished by 80–90%, essentially during the last two centuries (Grünig, Vetterli & Wildi, 1986). They are now subject to management programs to conserve whatever is left and to restore what can be restored. The conservation of well-preserved bog areas can be more or less easily achieved by preventing drainage and nutrient supply from the surroundings, but we know very little about how to restore the diplotelmic structure (Ingram, 1978) which characterises bog ecosystems. Further, raising the water table to an effective level for restoration purposes is often totally out of the question, especially in those cases where the remaining bog forms an elevated island, delimited by steep cutting walls and surrounded by intensive agricultural land.

In this paper we examine how *Sphagnum* mosses can reinitiate growth on bare peat in situations other than the 'classical' hydrosere system.

From field observations to greenhouse experiments: the testing of hypotheses

Regeneration outside the hydrosere system is not at all exceptional in the Jura mountains. In this region the bogs are developing at altitudes between 900 and 1100 m. The general climate in these sites is given by Matthey (1971): mean annual rainfall of 1446 mm (about 36% during the period June to September, with a maximum of 11 consecutive days without rainfall); mean annual temperature of 4.7 °C (with monthly mean temperatures between 9.7 and 13.3 °C for the same period, negative temperatures being possible at any time in summer); relative humidity of nearly 100% every night, leading to the formation of fog.

Situations where *Sphagnum* mosses have reappeared after peat extraction are numerous, and these plants can be observed growing in dried out situations, but rarely on a bare peat surface. They are more likely to appear among other, usually vascular, plants which had been the actual pioneers. Among the various vegetation communities recolonising bare peat surfaces, two of them are recurrent and show an evolution towards the formation of a continuous *Sphagnum* carpet.

Succession with *Polytrichum alpestre*

Very often, bare peat surfaces, more or less deeply drained with ditches of 30 to

>100 cm depth, are slowly recolonised by a *Polytrichum alpestre* lawn. This species shows itself rather resistant to desiccation and has already proved to be an excellent pioneer in other situations (Collins, 1976; Geiger, 1980; Wicky, 1988).

Our observations suggest a succession pattern as shown in Figure 1b. The detailed study of entire regenerating soil profiles of different successional stages as well as of the related microclimate conditions presented in Matthey (1993) allow us to propose the following hypothesis. During the first years after peat mining, the superficial drainage increases the mineralisation rate in the top 10–20 cm of peat. This ultimately results in the compaction of the surface peat layer (Eggelsmann, 1962; Hobbs, 1986) (Figure 2b). Even if not totally impermeable, this layer helps to keep the rainwater at the surface by hampering downward losses due to a reduced permeability (Eggelsmann & Mäkelä, 1964; Buttler, Dinel & Lévesque, in press). In turn, it also helps *Sphagnum* plants to overcome drought periods. Combined with the *Polytrichum alpestre* carpet, which prevents the formation of a hardened crust of peat and creates a canopy structure with a favourable microclimate environment, the establishment conditions for *Sphagnum* are likely to be improved.

These observations strongly emphasise the possible importance of peat physical properties in allowing *Sphagnum* plants to grow in dry and apparently hostile spots and are in accordance with results based on hydrological models (Schneebeli, 1991).

Succession with *Eriophorum vaginatum*

Most often, in the initial stages of regeneration successions, *Sphagnum* mosses reappear under the cover of vascular plants. Dwarf shrubs are very often involved, such as *Vaccinium uliginosum*, *Calluna vulgaris* or *Betula nana*, but most frequently the standing dead leaves of *Eriophorum vaginatum* tussocks, a species well known for its great ability to recolonise bare peat surfaces (Wein & MacLean, 1973; Gartner, Chapin & Shaver, 1986).

The entire succession is described in Figure 1a. In this example, the water mound was temporary, built up only after rainfall events, and the whole peat layer left behind after peat extraction was only about 70 cm thick. This suggests that ecological factors other than water level had also been effective in allowing the return of the *Sphagnum* plants. In accordance with Overbeck & Happach's (1957) statements, our hypothesis, based upon field measurements (Matthey, 1993), is that particular microclimate conditions could be the key factor in triggering the growth of *Sphagnum* plants under the cover of dead *Eriophorum vaginatum* leaves (Figure 2a).

Questions arising

Which *Sphagnum* species is best adapted for recolonising dry bare peat surfaces? What is the relative importance of a high water level? How can peat properties help to reinitiate *Sphagnum* growth? How far can a particular microclimate

(a)

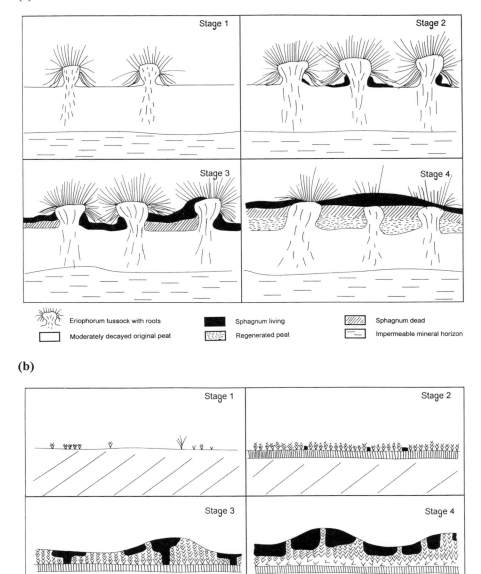

(b)

Figure 1. Schematic illustration of the vegetation succession pattern in (a) *Eriophorum vaginatum* and (b) *Polytrichum alpestre* series.

compensate for a low water table?

To answer these questions, in terms of testing the different hypotheses and quantifying the relative importance of species, water level, peat physical and chemical properties and microclimate at the surface of the soil, two greenhouse experiments were undertaken.

METHODS

Five peat soils were chosen as representative of an increasing disturbance by the process of peat extraction: (i) undisturbed bog with living *Sphagnum*, (ii) dry heathland on clear-cut and drained peat, (iii) surface and (iv) deeper layers of bare peat formerly used for harvesting horticultural peat; and (v) agriculture land peat.

In the first experiment whole cylindrical cushions of three species of *Sphagnum* (*S. fallax, S. magellanicum* and *S. fuscum*), collected in the field as living 5-cm-thick carpets, were used as a matrix. They were placed on top of the different peat cores, 45 cm in length and 13.3 cm in diameter, kept in PVC pots. Ten plants per pot, cut to exactly 5 cm length and marked with a polyester thread, were then implanted into the carpets for growth measurements.

For the second experiment, only one species was used (*S. fallax*) but three microclimate conditions were simulated: (i) perforated plastic sheet cover, (ii) shading mesh; and (iii) control without protection. Twelve isolated plants of 2 cm length were pricked directly on to the bare peat.

In both experiments, the water level was set at −1 cm (high water level) and at −40 cm (low water level). The *Sphagnum* plants were watered every 11 days from above with 300 ml of rainwater per pot to stay close to natural conditions.

The 90 PVC pots, including three replicates, were randomised. The climatic environment was kept close to natural conditions during the experiments, which lasted from June to September.

Comparisons between different treatments were made by measuring the growth in length and change in weight (dry weight at 60 °C) of *Sphagnum* plants by use of the 'capitulum correction method' (Clymo, 1970). Change in weight is given as uncorrected or corrected mass increment, as well as relative mass increment, proportional to the weight of an original stem section of 1 cm (Clymo, 1973).

Surface peat layers (0–5 cm) and deep peat layers (40–45 cm) of the five soils were characterised for all the cores at the end of the second experiment. The following analyses were conducted: pH (in KCl and in water); pyrophosphate index; total C, H and N; total Ca, Mg, K, Na, Fe, Mn and P; cation exchange capacity; bulk density and water holding capacity; total porosity, proportions of pores >200 μm, between 200 μm and 20 μm, and <20 μm. Analytical procedures followed standard methods (McKeague, 1976).

The results of these analyses were used as environmental factors to account for the influence of peat properties on *Sphagnum* growth, in relation to water level and microclimate. In the first experiment, the effect of the peat on growth was assessed

(a)

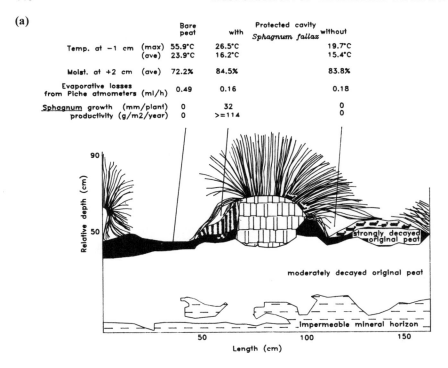

		Bare peat	with	Protected cavity *Sphagnum fallax*	without
Temp. at −1 cm	(max)	55.9°C	26.5°C		19.7°C
	(ave)	23.9°C	16.2°C		15.4°C
Moist. at +2 cm	(ave)	72.2%	84.5%		83.8%
Evaporative losses from Piche atmometers (ml/h)		0.49	0.16		0.18
Sphagnum growth (mm/plant)		0	32		0
productivity (g/m2/year)		0	>=114		0

(b)

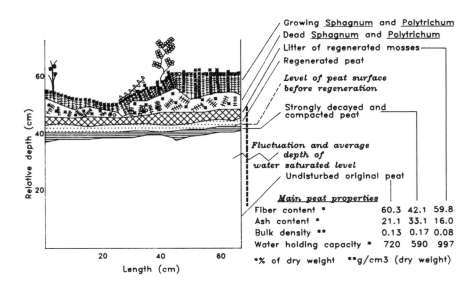

Figure 2. Field observations and measurements in (a) *Eriophorum vaginatum* and (b) *Polytrichum alpestre* successional series.

only with the five soil-types, as described above.

Analyses of variance of growth in length and of change in dry weight were conducted on each experiment using the General Linear Model procedure of the SAS program (SAS Institute Inc., 1988). Means comparisons between treatments were made using the LSMEANS procedure, and normality of the data sets was checked by the UNIVARIATE procedure of the SAS program. Data were log-transformed.

Interpretation and quantification of the different treatment effects on the growth of *Sphagnum* assessed as a result of combined growth in length and change in weight were made with multivariate analyses. Principal Components Analysis (PCA) and Redundancy Analysis (RDA) were computed using the CANOCO program (ter Braak, 1992). Statistical tests were made using the Mantel test procedure of CANOCO, and partialling out of the explanatory variables and their respective variance, according to Borcard, Legendre & Drapeau (1992)

Species names are given in accordance with Tutin *et al.* (1964–80) for vascular plants, Isoviita (1967) for Sphagna and Smith (1980) for other mosses.

RESULTS

First experiment : the species' ecology

The different factors considered for analysis of variance were: (i) species, (ii)

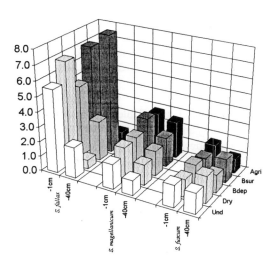

Figure 3. Change in dry weight over 130 days in the factorial combination experiment with three *Sphagnum* species, two water table levels and five peat soils. Results are given in weight per weight of unit length of stem (mg*(mg*cm of stem^{-1})$^{-1}$). See Tables 1 & 2.

Table 1. Results of change in dry weight over 130 days in the factorial combination experiment with three *Sphagnum* species, two water table levels and five peat soils. Results are given in weight per weight of unit length of stem $(\text{mg}*(\text{mg}*\text{cm of stem}^{-1})^{-1})$. For each species and water level, significant differences at P<0.01 level between peat soils are indicated with different letters. See also Figure 3.

		Water table level						
		−40 cm				−1 cm		
Species								
Peat soil	Abbr.	*mean*		*± std. error*	*n*	*mean*		*± std. error*	*n*
S. fallax									
Undisturbed	Und	**2.1**	C	0.4	*17*	**5.6**	A	0.6	*15*
Dry heath	Dry	**0.6**	A	0.2	*16*	**6.9**	A	0.8	*20*
Bare peat depth	Bdep	**2.7**	ABC	1.0	*15*	**4.8**	A	0.7	*10*
Bare peat surface	Bsur	**8.0**	D	1.2	*10*	**7.0**	A	1.7	*14*
Agriculture	Agri	**0.8**	AB	0.3	*18*	**6.2**	A	1.0	*12*
S. magellanicum									
Undisturbed	Und	**1.0**	A	1.1	*25*	**1.7**	A	1.4	*23*
Dry heath	Dry	**1.4**	AB	1.8	*15*	**2.2**	A	1.7	*26*
Bare peat depth	Bdep	**1.7**	AB	1.3	*27*	**2.3**	A	1.7	*26*
Bare peat surface	Bsur	**2.0**	AB	1.7	*28*	**3.0**	A	1.8	*26*
Agriculture	Agri	**2.5**	B	1.8	*24*	**2.8**	A	2.6	*26*
S. fuscum									
Undisturbed	Und	**1.4**	A	0.2	*22*	**1.5**	A	0.2	*20*
Dry heath	Dry	**1.8**	A	0.2	*19*	**1.2**	A	0.2	*22*
Bare peat depth	Bdep	**1.2**	A	0.1	*24*	**1.5**	A	0.2	*18*
Bare peat surface	Bsur	**1.6**	A	0.2	*24*	**1.3**	A	0.1	*26*
Agriculture	Agri	**1.0**	A	0.2	*17*	**1.6**	A	0.2	*16*

water table depth and (iii) soil type. Only the results concerning the change in weight are presented in Figure 3 and Tables 1 & 2, those of growth in length showing on the whole the same pattern. Growth results are consistent with literature (Lindholm & Vasander, 1990).

The main effects of treatments on weight change are in relation to species, water table and the interaction between species and water table, as shown with the corresponding F-values (Table 2).

The different peat soils only affected *Sphagnum* growth to a smaller extent. This effect was obvious only for *S. fallax* when the water table was maintained at a low level (Table 1).

Species sensitivity to ecological factors such as water table depth and peat soils was quantified using the principal components analysis (Figure 4). All variables were strongly correlated with axis 1, which accounts for 86.2% of the total variance and ordinates the samples on a gradient of increasing growth, both in length and in weight on axis 1.

Table 2. Variance analysis of change in dry weight in the factorial combination experiment with three *Sphagnum* species, two water table levels and five peat soils. See also Table 1.

Summary of ANOVA

Source	DF	Sum of squares	Mean square	F Value	**Pr > F**
Model	29	282.82	9.7523	16.59	**0.0001**
Error	571	335.56	0.5877		
Corrected total	600	618.38			

	R-Square	C. V.	Root MSE		Mean
	0.4574	27.4	0.7666		2.79

Source	DF	**F Value**	Pr > F
SPECIES	2	**21.02**	0.0001
WATER TABLE DEPTH	1	**96.83**	0.0001
SOIL	4	**7.13**	0.0001
SPECIES * WATER TABLE DEPTH	2	**62.93**	0.0001
SPECIES * SOIL	8	**8.36**	0.0001
WATER TABLE DEPTH * SOIL	4	**3.64**	0.0062
SPECIES * WATER TABLE DEPTH * SOIL	8	**9.87**	0.0001

Redundancy Analysis combined with the use of covariables for the partialling out procedure was used to quantify the respective influence of the so-called 'environmental variables' such as species, water table depth and peat-type. Species account for about 48% of the growth variation (total of 'explained' growth variation is 64.5%), resulting in the separation of three distinct groups of samples on the PCA diagram, each group corresponding to one species. The interaction with water table depth is almost negligible (1.2%). The effect of water level alone, which only accounts for about 10% of the growth variation, is due mainly to *S. fallax*, whose samples with a low water table show a dispersion as far right as those of *S. fuscum*. Finally, the different peat soils had a low influence on the growth of the *Sphagnum* mosses (less than 6%), without detectable interactions with either species or water table depth.

Second experiment: conditions for the regrowth of *S. fallax*

Growth response of *S. fallax* was examined by analysis of variance and showed highly significant relations with the environmental variables such as microclimate, water table depth and soil-type.

The first step of the multivariate analysis was to select, from the 32 peat physical and chemical properties (including ratios between properties), those which were

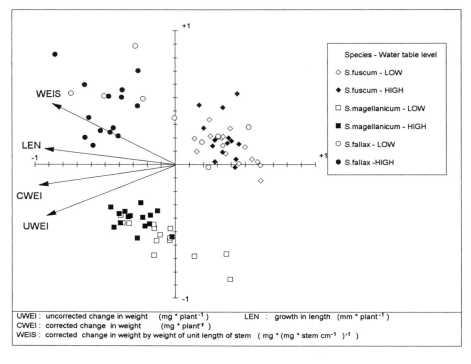

UWEI :   uncorrected change in weight   (mg * plant⁻¹)   LEN :   growth in length (mm * plant⁻¹)
CWEI :   corrected change in weight   (mg * plant⁷)
WEIS :   corrected change in weight by weight of unit length of stem (mg * (mg * stem cm⁻¹)⁻¹)

Summary of PCA

Axes	1	2	3	4
Eigenvalues	0.862	0.098	0.038	0.002
Cumulative percentage variance of species data	86.2	96.0	99.8	100.0

Figure 4. Scatter diagram of the principal component analysis of the growth measurements in the factorial combination experiment with three *Sphagnum* species, two water table levels and five peat soils. Axes 1 and 2 are represented.

best fitting in the growth model (Redundancy Analysis) of *Sphagnum fallax* and that were statistically significant ('forward selection' procedure of the CANOCO program (ter Braak, 1992). Together with the qualitative variables concerning water table depth and microclimate, three quantitative variables were selected. Their order of importance was as follows: percentage of mesopores smaller than 20 μm (positively correlated with high N, P and K concentrations, high bulk densities and pyrophosphate indices, and negatively correlated with high C:N ratios, percentage of macropores larger than 200 μm and water-holding capacity), total Na and total C of the surface layer of the peat cores.

Applying the partialling out procedure in the second step of the redundancy analysis indicated that the variance of the remaining 'explanatory' variables had approximately similar contributions: 26% for water table depth, 22% for the microclimate and 25% for the three selected soil properties (total of explained growth variation is 62.4%). However, water table depth and peat properties shared an important interaction of almost 10%, whereas microclimate proved to be independent of the other factors.

Thus, peat properties may influence the water supply of the plants, either by the

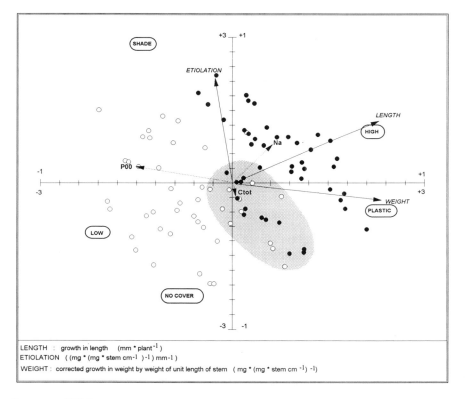

LENGTH : growth in length (mm * plant^{-1})
ETIOLATION ((mg * (mg * stem cm-1)-1) mm-1)
WEIGHT : corrected growth in weight by weight of unit length of stem (mg * (mg * stem cm^{-1}) -l)

Summary of RDA

Axes	1	2	3
Eigenvalues	0.463	0.156	0.004
Species–environment correlations	0.828	0.783	0.282
Cumulative percentage variance, species data	46.3	61.9	62.3
Cumulative percentage variance, species–environment relation	74.3	99.2	100.0

Total variance: 1.000;   Sum of all unconstrained eigenvalues: 1.000
                           Sum of all canonical eigenvalues: 0.624

Figure 5. Scatter diagram of the Redundancy Analysis (RDA) of the experiment on *Sphagnum fallax* growth in factorial combination with three microclimates, two water table levels and five peat soils assessed with their three main discriminating properties. Axes 1 and 2 are represented.

retaining capacity of atmospheric rain inputs or, to some extent, by capillarity rises, depending on the groundwater level. On the RDA scatter diagram (Figure 5), *Sphagnum* growth appeared to be negatively correlated with a high percentage of fine mesopores at the peat surface. From the redundancy analysis with all the explanatory variables, it can be further concluded that the growth of *Sphagnum* is positively correlated with the occurrence of large pores at the surface or even to variables expressing peat profiles with a decreasing pore size from the surface (with a high water-holding capacity) towards depth.

The apparent influence of microclimate is of particular interest. Whilst shading mainly emphasises etiolation and reduces change in weight (see also Clymo, 1973; Hayward & Clymo, 1983; Rydin, 1984), covering the plants with a plastic sheet, either with a high or a low water table, favoured growth, presumably as a result of a constant high ambient humidity. In the perspective of bog restoration, the most important result is the overlapping range of growth of samples combining a high water table with absence of cover and those with a low water table but a plastic sheet covering (Figure 5).

DISCUSSION

Each species has an individual response to ecological factors and to stress situations such as drought. This has clearly been demonstrated before by several authors describing ecological niches for different *Sphagnum* species (Vitt & Slack, 1984; Rydin, 1986).

One might expect *S. fuscum* to be the best-adapted species for dry bare peat conditions. Due to its dense cushion structure (Clymo & Hayward, 1982; Rydin & McDonald, 1985; Wallén, Falkengren-Grerup & Malmer, 1988), this species can be to some extent independent of both water table depth and peat soil properties. Moreover, it is very resistant to extreme conditions such as severe drought (Silvola & Aaltonen, 1984; Lindholm, 1990). However, in revegetating peat fields where drainage still is effective, the most frequent species is *S. fallax*. Our field observations and experimental results suggest that hostile ecological conditions exert a severe selection on the re-establishing species. Beyond its apparent sensitivity to ecological factors, *S. fallax* indeed seems to be a very effective species in bog restoration processes, particularly because of its fast growth rate and carpet-forming capacity (Overbeck & Happach, 1957; Francez, 1992; Lütt, 1992), and its greater resistance to total desiccation, in terms of recovery ability (Wagner & Titus, 1984), even when growing as isolated plants.

The importance of soil properties and microclimate is emphasised in the second experiment, where the mosses were grown as isolated plants spread over the field, (simulating establishment from diaspores), in contrast to the uniform cover of *Sphagnum* carpets in undamaged bogs.

In such cases, the water table, although it is a fundamental factor, like the general climate, is not an exclusive necessity for re-initiating *Sphagnum* growth.

Commensalism with species like *Eriophorum vaginatum* or dwarf shrubs can provide an effective alternative to the lack of a suitable permanent water table by providing a favourable microclimate. Comparable phenomena have already been observed with vascular plants (Carlsson & Callaghan, 1991) where *Calluna vulgaris* shrubs sheltered *Carex nigra* stands against wind. On the other hand, a vigorous growth of *Calluna* can suppress the establishment of *Sphagnum*, essentially by reducing light influx, but mainly in the mature phase of the *Calluna* cycle, which extends over about 30 years (Barclay-Estrup, 1971). In the other stages (pioneer, young, and even degenerating) bryophytes can grow and they may even find more favourable microclimate conditions. Several authors have measured reduced evapotranspiration rates, in dry summer periods, in *Calluna–Sphagnum* communities (Matthey, 1971) or drained heathlands (Eggelsmann, 1964) compared, respectively, with pure *Sphagnum* lawns and grassland. Ingram (1983) also mentions the important role of the 'markedly clumped pattern' of dwarf shrubs 'in which mutual shelter and shading create a distinctive local microclimate', and quotes Firbas (1931) who observed similar effects with tussock-formers such as *Eriophorum vaginatum* or *Trichophorum cespitosus*.

Our own field measurements (Matthey, 1993), based upon evaporative losses from Piche atmometers (Figure 2a) placed among *Eriophorum vaginatum* tussocks, are totally consistent with the observations discussed above and with Piche atmometer results from Neuhäusl (1975) who obtained similar rates while comparing a *Calluna–Sphagnum* to a *Sphagnetum magellanici* community.

Although peat properties have a limited influence on well established *Sphagnum* populations, they are much more determinant in the initial stages of recolonisation. There seems to be an optimal set of both physical and chemical properties of the surface peat layer. In our experiment, the peat originating from the surface of the bare haplotelmic peat soil presented such optimal properties. The pore size distribution in the profile, which is correlated to the degree of decomposition of the peat and influences the water regime, appeared as most relevant, in accordance with Okruszko (1993).

CONCLUSION

One common objection towards restoration schemes is that, because of their self-healing capacity, the damaged bog ecosystems finally manage to restore themselves, provided the time span is long enough (Schneebeli, 1991). In actual fact, in the Swiss Jura mountains, examples of such homeostasis processes are numerous, and the primary hypotheses that we tested in the present work are based upon observations of these spontaneous processes. On the other hand, considering that up to 90% of all the raised bogs of Switzerland have definitively disappeared because of human activities, the few remaining surfaces deserve some 'help'. Yet bog management should not to lead to some kind of manufactured ecosystem. There is a need for careful studies to assess the potential for recovery of each particular site and then, based upon experimental knowledge, encouragement of the development of those conditions relevant to the reinstatement of a *Sphagnum*-based community.

This is particularly true for severely disturbed sites where the hydrology has been considerably modified by drainage and the acrotelm totally destroyed by peat extraction. In such situations one can no longer talk about bog regeneration. One only can deal with the restoration, through re-creating secondary successions in the sense of Falinski (1991), of peatland ecosystems as close as possible to natural, *i.e.* self-regulating, ecological conditions. This also means that peat extraction cannot reasonably be considered as an ecologically sustainable economic activity in a human life-scale perspective.

ACKNOWLEDGEMENTS

The authors are grateful to L. Paganuzzi and A. Jeanneret for technical help, to E. Boss for translation supervision and to the Swiss National Research Fund for financial support. We also are indebted to B. Wheeler for constructive comments on the manuscript.

REFERENCES

Barclay-Estrup, P. (1971). The description and interpretation of cyclical processes in a heath community. III. Microclimate in relation to the *Calluna* cycle. *Journal of Ecology,* **59**, 143–166.

Bertram, R. (1988). Pflanzengesellschaften der Torfstiche nordniedersächsischer Moore und die Abhängigkeit dieser Vegetationseinheiten von der Wasserqualität. *Dissertationes Botanicae,* Band **126**, J.Cramer Verlag, Berlin – Stuttgart.

Borcard, D., Legendre, P. & Drapeau P. (1992). Partialling out the spatial component of ecological variation. *Ecology,* **73**,1045–1055.

Buttler, A.J., Dinel, H. & Lévesque, P.E.M. (in press). Implications of physical, chemical and botanical characteristics of peat on carbon gas fluxes. *Soil Science.*

Carlsson, B.A. & Callaghan, T.V. (1991). Positive plant interactions in tundra vegetation and the importance of shelter. *Journal of Ecology,* **79**, 73–983.

Clymo, R.S. (1970). The growth of *Sphagnum*: Methods of measurement. *Journal of Ecology,* **58**, 13–49.

Clymo, R.S. (1973). The growth of *Sphagnum*: some effects of environment. *Journal of Ecology,* **61**, 849–869.

Clymo, R.S. & Hayward, P.M. (1982). The ecology of *Sphagnum. Bryophyte Ecology* (ed. A.J.E. Smith), pp.229–289. Chapman & Hall, London.

Collins, N.J. (1976). Growth and population dynamics of the moss *Polytrichum alpestre* in the maritime Antarctic. Strategies of growth and population dynamics of tundra plants 2. *Oikos,* **27**, 389–401.

Eggelsmann, R. (1962). Durchlässigkeit und Grundwasserströmung am Beispiel der Moore am Steinhuder Meer und eines Moormarschpolders im Bremer Blockland. *Berichte aus der Landesanstalt für Bodennutzungsschutz,* **3**, 125–132. Bochum, Germany.

Eggelsmann, R. (1964). Die Verdunstung der Hochmoore und deren hydrographischer Einfluss. *Deutsche Gewässerkundliche Mitteilungen*, **8**, 138–147.

Eggelsmann, R. & Mäkelä, T. (1964). Einfluss von Entwässerung und landwirtschaftlicher Nutzung auf die Durchlässigkeit des Moorbodens. *Maataloustieteellinen Aikakauskirja*, **36**, 77–84. Helsinki.

Falinski, J.B. (1991). La dynamique du paysage interprétée par la dynamique de la végétation. *Colloques Phytosociologiques, XVII, Phytosociologie et Paysage, Versailles 1988* (ed. J.M. Gehu), pp.425–444. J. Cramer Verlag, Berlin–Stuttgart.

Francez, A.J. 1992 The growth and primary production of *Sphagnum* in a peat-bog of the Monts du Forez (Puy-de-Dôme, France). *Vie et Milieu*, **42**, 21–34. In French, with English summary.

Firbas, F. (1931). Untersuchungen über den Wasserhaushalt der Hochmoorpflanzen. *Pringsheims Jahrbuch für Wissenchaftliche Botanik*, **74**, 459–696.

Gartner, B.L., Chapin, F.S. III & Shaver, G.R. (1986). Reproduction of *Eriophorum vaginatum* by seed in Alaskan tussock tundra. *Journal of Ecology*, **74**, 1–18.

Geiger, W. (1980). Phytosociologie des landes de dégradation dans la tourbière du Cachot (Jura neuchâtelois, Suisse). *Documents Phytosociologiques, N.S., Lille*, **V**, 5–10.

Goodwillie, R. (1980). European Peatlands. *Nature and Environment Series, No. 19*, 75pp. Council of Europe, Strasbourg.

Grünig, A., Vetterli, L. & Wildi, O. (1986). The raised and transition bogs of Switzerland – findings from a national inventory. *Swiss Federal Institute of Forestry Research*, **286**, 58pp. Birmensdorf. In French and German, with English summary.

Hayward, P.M. & Clymo, R.S. (1983). The growth of *Sphagnum*: experiments on, and simulation of, some effects of light flux and water-table depth. *Journal of Ecology*, **71**, 845–863.

Hobbs, N.B. (1986). Mire morphology and the properties and behaviour of some British and foreign peats. *Quarterly Journal of Engineering Geology*, **19**, 7–80.

Ingram, H.A.P. (1978). Soil layers in mires: function and terminology. *Journal of Soil Sciences*, **29**, 224–227.

Ingram, H.A.P. (1983). Hydrology. *Mires: Swamp, Bog, Fen and Moor, 4A. General Studies* (ed. A.J.P. Gore), pp. 67–158. Elsevier, Amsterdam.

Isoviita, P. (1967). Studies on *Sphagnum* L. I. Nomenclatural revision of the European taxa. *Annales Botanici Fennici*, **3**, 199–264.

Jortay, A. & Schumacker, R. (1989). Zustand, Erhaltung und Regeneration der Hochmoore im Hohen Venn (Belgien). *Telma*, Beiheft **2**, 279–293. Hannover.

Lindholm, T. (1990). Growth dynamics of the peat moss *Sphagnum fuscum* on hummocks on a raised bog in southern Finland. *Annales Botanici Fennici*, **27**, 67–78.

Lindholm, T. & Vasander, H. (1990). Production of eight species of *Sphagnum* at Suurisuo mire, southern Finland. *Annales Botanici Fennici*, **27**, 145–157.

Lütt S. (1992). Produktionsbiologische Untersuchungen zur Sukzession der Torfstich-vegetation in Schleswig-Holstein. *Mitteilungen der Arbeits-gemeinschaft Geobotanik in Schleswig-Holstein und Hamburg* (ed K. Dierssen), Heft **43**, 250pp. Kiel.

McKeague, J.A. (ed) (1976). *Manual of Soil Sampling and Methods of Analysis*. Canadian Society of Soil Science, Ottawa, Canada.

Matthey W. (1971). Ecologie des insectes aquatiques d'une tourbière du Haut-Jura. *Revue Suisse de Zoologie*, **78**, 367–536.

Matthey, Y. (1993). Typologie de la régénération spontanée des hauts-marais jurassiens non boisés et approche écologique de trois séries végétales caractéristiques de la dynamique secondaire. *Thesis, Laboratoire d'Ecologie végétale*, Université de

Neuchâtel, Switzerland.

Neuhäusl, R. (1975). Hochmoore am Teich Velkè Dàrko. *Vegetace* CSSR, A9, Academia, Prague, 267pp.

Okruszko, H. (1993). Transformation of fen-peat soils under the impact of draining. *Zeszyty Problemowe Postepow Nauk Rolniczych* (eds H. Okruszko, J. Glinski, E. Sikora*), z.* 406, 3–73. Dzial Wydawniczo-Polygraficzny KUL, Lublin.

Overbeck, F. & Happach, H. (1957). Über das Wachstum und den Wasserhaushalt einiger Hochmoorsphagnen. *Flora (Jena)*, **144**, 335–402.

Royer, J. M., Vadam, J.C., Gillet & Aumonier, M.F. (1978). Etude phytosociologique des tourbières acides et alcalines du Haut-Doubs. Réflexions sur leur régénération et leur genèse. *Centre Universitaire d'Etudes Régionales*, **2**, 109–185. Laboratoire de Taxonomie expérimentale et de Phytosociologie, Université de Franche-Comté, Besançon, France.

Rydin, H. (1984). Some factors affecting temperature in *Sphagnum* vegetation. An experimental analysis. *Cryptogamie: Bryologie et Lychénologie*, **5**, 4, 361–372.

Rydin, H. (1986). Competition and niche separation in *Sphagnum*. *Canadian Journal of Botany*, **64**, 1817–1824.

Rydin, H. & McDonald, A.J.S. (1985). Photosynthesis in *Sphagnum* at different water contents. *Journal of Bryology*, **13**, 579–584.

SAS Institute Inc. (1988). *SAS/STAT – User's Guide, Release 6.03 Edition.*

Schneebeli, M. (1991). *Hydrologie und Dynamik der Hochmoorentwicklung.* Dissertation ETH Nr 9366, Eidgenössische Technische Hochschule, Zürich.

Silvola, J. & Aaltonen, H. (1984). Water content and photosynthesis in the peat mosses *Sphagnum fuscum* and *S. angustifolium*. *Annales Botanici Fennici*, **21**, 1–6.

Smith, A.J.E. (1980). *The Moss Flora of Britain and Ireland.* Cambridge University Press, Cambridge.

Steiner, G.M. (1985). The hydrological mire types of Austria and their vegetation. *Aquilo Seria Botanicae*, **21**, 53–60.

Succow, M. & Lange, E (1984). The mire types of the German Democratic Republic. *European Mires* (ed P.D. Moore), pp. 149–175. Academic Press, London.

ter Braak, C.J.F. (1988–1992). *CANOCO – a FORTRAN program for Canonical Community Ordination (version 2.1).* Microcomputer Power, Ithaca, New York.

Tutin, T.G. *et al.* (1964–1980). *Flora Europaea.* Cambridge University Press, Cambridge.

Vitt, D.H. & Slack, N.G. (1984). Niche diversification of *Sphagnum* relative to environmental factors in northern Minnesota peatlands. *Canadian Journal of Botany*, **62**, 1409–1430.

Wagner, D.J. & Titus, J.E. (1984). Comparative desiccation tolerance of two *Sphagnum* mosses. *Oecologia (Berlin)*, **62**, 182–187.

Wallén, B., Falkengren-Grerup, U. & Malmer, N. (1988). Biomass, productivity and relative rate of photosynthesis of *Sphagnum* at different water levels on a South Swedish peat bog. *Holarctic Ecology*, **11**, 70–76.

Wein, R.W. & MacLean, D.A. (1973). Cotton grass (*Eriophorum vaginatum*) germination requirements and colonizing potential in the Arctic. *Canadian Journal of Botany*, **51**, 2509–2513.

Wicky, J.D. (1988). *Die Torfmoore von Rechthalten und St.Ursen / Kanton Freiburg. Stratigraphische, ökologische und vegetationskundliche Untersuchungen im Schwandmoos, Entenmoos und Rotmoos.* Thesis, Philosophisch-naturwissenschaftliche Fakultät, 207pp. Universität Freiburg, Switzerland.

30 Coastal Raised Mire Restoration: Mosaic of Peatland, Salt Marsh and Minerotrophic Wetlands for Avian Habitat Enhancement

N. C. FAMOUS, M. SPENCER-FAMOUS, J-Y. DAIGLE & J. J. THIBAULT

Spencer/Famous Environmental Consulting, Box 102 HCR 70, Machias, ME 04654, USA

SUMMARY

1. A restoration plan was prepared for a peat-harvested maritime bog in NE New Brunswick, Canada. Elements of the plan included sequential restoration, rewetting, rapid revegetation/bog surface stabilisation, wildlife habitat enhancement, monitoring, low maintenance, and reasonable costs.

2. The plan called for the re-establishment of plant community-types characteristic of peatlands and slightly minerotrophic wetlands in topographically higher freshwater sections and the establishment of salt marsh community zonation in seawater-inundated areas.

3. Surface topography, water chemistry and vegetation communities were investigated. Salt marsh establishment on mined bog was documented on nearby sites. The restoration scheme was designed to enhance migratory and breeding wader, waterfowl, and landbird populations.

INTRODUCTION

In an effort to develop restoration guidelines for the New Brunswick peat industry, the New Brunswick Department of Natural Resources and Energy through the Canada–New Brunswick Cooperation Agreement on Mineral Development, commissioned the Peat Research and Development Center in Shippagan, New Brunswick, to prepare a restoration plan for Pokesudie Bog, located in north-eastern New Brunswick, Canada (Figure 1).

Pokesudie Bog is a 100 ha ombrotrophic maritime bog in production since the 1960s. The extractable peat is underlain by a variably thick layer of humified black peat (von Post >4) that rests on silty sands and glacial tills over sandstone bedrock. The surface of the black peat layer is fairly regular and is expected to

Restoration of Temperate Wetlands. Edited by B.D. Wheeler, S.C. Shaw, W.J. Fojt and R.A. Robertson
© 1995 John Wiley & Sons Ltd.

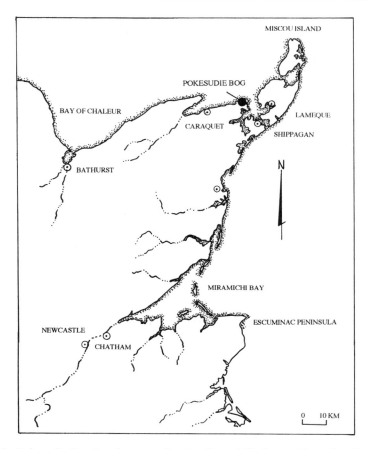

Figure 1. Pokesudie Bog location map showing Bay of Chaleur to Escuminac Peninsula, Gulf of St Lawrence, New Brunswick, Canada. Note the bog's extreme maritime location.

leave gently sloping surfaces for restoration. Sections of depleted production fields will eventually be inundated by the sea, which is currently eroding two sides of the bog and has flooded sections of six production fields. Sea level in this region is rising at a rate of 20 cm per 100 years (Rampton *et al.*, 1984). Because of erosion and eventual inundation by seawater, this plan incorporates both salt marsh and peatland restoration. Naturally established salt marsh on two nearby mined bogs served as a working example for salt marsh establishment at Pokesudie Bog.

The climate in NE New Brunswick is classified as mid-latitude continental. Mean annual precipitation is about 1108 mm of which 351 mm occurs as snowfall. Mean monthly temperatures range from –9.7 °C (January) to 18 °C (July).

Pokesudie Bog's coastal position, low-lying topography, and proximity to important waterbird habitats offers a unique opportunity to restore the bog for wildlife, far exceeding its original pre-development habitat value. Habitats adjacent to the NW side of Pokesudie Bog are very diverse and rich in birdlife, including a mixture of bog, fen, freshwater emergent marsh, brackish marsh, salt marsh, sand and cobble beach, freshwater seepages, unvegetated flat, eelgrass bed, and sand dune.

Pokesudie Bog will be restored as a combination of fresh, brackish, and saltwater ecosystems. Especially significant will be an increase in shallow water bodies and seasonally flooded wetlands. Because of the pristine shoreline and isolation, the N and NW sides of Pokesudie Island, combined with a well-implemented restoration plan, make this a natural area of province-wide significance for breeding and migratory bird populations. The major groups of birds benefiting from this restoration plan include nesting and migrating landbirds, waders, waterfowl, and raptors.

Goals of the Pokesudie Bog restoration plan include:

- restoration to functioning wetland systems;
- restoration of *Sphagnum* mosses;
- enhancement of wildlife values ;
- integration of bog development with restoration;
- development of low-cost, maintenance-free restoration methods;
- establishment of habitats that complement the regional landscape ecology.

This paper condenses the Pokesudie Bog restoration plan, the first large-scale restoration plan developed for a boreal North American bog (Famous *et al.*, 1993a). The plan provides methods for modifying existing operations and identifies information gaps in peatland restoration science and methodology. The restoration plan should be treated as a guide and therefore be flexible, with evaluations at five-year intervals to adjust for changes in production fields, plant community establishment patterns, and to utilise new peatland restoration methods. An important but speculative component of any bog restoration plan is *TIME*. Restoration of low-nutrient bog surfaces takes time, even under favourable water-table levels and with low-level nutrient enhancement.

BACKGROUND

Active peatland restoration is new to Canada and the USA. No country-wide standards have been established for either jurisdiction, nor is there agreement among academia, government, and industry on desired endpoints, *e.g.* weak fen conditions on nutrient-enhanced oligotrophic peat versus inherently species-poor habitats on ombrotrophic peat.

The definition of bog restoration we have adopted follows that of the Canadian Sphagnum Peat Moss Association (CSPMA): abandoned bog surfaces will be restored to functioning wetlands. Restoration by the CSPMA's definition does not require initial establishment of *Sphagnum* mosses. From a long-term ecological perspective, our goal is to restore freshwater portions of the bog to functioning wetlands and to create conditions favourable for plant succession to proceed toward community endpoints dominated by ericaceous shrubs and *Sphagnum* mosses. The plan is designed to speed up the recolonisation process, which may take decades without habitat manipulation.

Our predictions of plant community-types and plant community succession are based on fully documented patterns and processes occurring naturally throughout eastern and central North America (Green, 1983; Jonsson-Ninniss & Middleton, 1991; Famous *et al.*, 1991, 1993b). Natural succession begins with colonisation by wind dispersed sedges and bryophytes, forming a herbaceous or meadow-dominated (unmown) seral stage. Ericaceous shrubs, black crowberry (*Empetrum nigrum*)[1], and birches (*Betula* spp., on drier sites) follow. Moss, shrub and sedge-dominated communities develop and persist on wetter sites; tree- and tall shrub-dominated communities eventually dominate drier sites (Nilsson *et al.*, 1990).

When hydrological conditions are favourable, *Sphagnum* mosses are later colonisers, generally after about 10 years (Spencer-Famous *et al.*, 1993). *Sphagnum* growth is accelerated by the addition of thin layers of sand and gravel (*e.g.* blown from gravel access roads), thin layers of mineral substratum thrown on to the bog's surface by ditching, or from run-off draining sand and gravel (Spencer-Famous *et al.*, 1993). Vascular plant colonisation is also rapidly enhanced by this process, as is species diversity and percentage cover, usually without inhibiting colonisation of *Sphagnum* mosses (Nilsson *et al.*, 1990). Over the long term, there is an increase in cover of oligotrophic species such as *Rhododendron canadense, Juncus peleocarpus, J. effusus, Viburnum cassinoides, Scirpus cyperinus*, and *Myrica gale*. Seed production in *Eriophorum vaginatum* (*E. vaginatum* L. var. *spissum* (Fern.) B. Boivin.) more than doubles under these conditions (N.C. Famous, unpublished data).

METHODS

The preparation of the restoration plan encompassed extensive field surveys including depth coring, peat characterisation, surface elevation measurements, water chemistry analysis, vegetation sampling in naturally reclaiming bogs and adjacent salt marshes, wildlife habitat assessment, and regional landscape ecology assessment. These data were used to predict final peat surface topography and elevations and to circumscribe restoration plant community-types.

Information essential for preparing the Pokesudie Bog restoration plan is summarised in Table 1 (Famous *et al.* 1993a). The final surface topography map, sequential restoration maps, and final plant community map are presented. The remaining maps and data are presented elsewhere (Famous *et al.*, 1993a).

The coring and surveying procedures are found in Famous *et al.*, 1993a. The New Brunswick Department of Natural Resources and Energy conducted the 1976 and 1992 surveying and the 1976 coring. The Peat Research and Development Center in Shippagan, New Brunswick, conducted the 1992 coring.

Final peat surface topography was determined by first estimating the extent of

---

[1] Nomenclature for vascular plant names follows Gleason & Cronquist (1991).

Table 1. Information needed to prepare restoration plan for Pokesudie Bog.

• Surface and bottom topography maps	• Surface elevations of plant communities
• Harvestable peat thickness map	in natural and established salt marshes
• Final surface topography map	• Final plant community cover type map
• Final drainage plan	• Autecology of recolonist plant species
• Residual peat/substratum water	• Habitat requirements for selected faunal
chemistry	species
• Sequential restoration maps	• Regional landscape ecology assessment

mining. Next, abandoned areas, sections not expected to be mined or partially mined, sedimentation ponds, access roads, and staging areas were identified and their surface elevations determined or estimated. The final peat surface elevations for the remaining production areas were determined by subtracting extractable peat thickness from surface elevation, leaving a minimum of 0.6 m of peat. Contours were then drawn from the adjusted point elevation estimates.

The water chemistry variables determined in the field included specific conductivity, temperature, pH, and salinity. The variables analysed in the laboratory included Ca, NO_3, Mg, NH_4, K, total P, Na, Cl, pH, and SO_4.

Both quantitative and qualitative sampling of vegetation communities were conducted. Quantitative sampling followed the relevé sampling procedure. Percentage cover was estimated for each of four vegetation strata (moss, low shrub, high shrub and tree) using the Braun-Blanquet scale for each species within a 5 x 5 m relevé.

Pokesudie Bog was divided into four sampling areas: salt marsh, brackish marsh, disturbed bog, and undisturbed bog. Relevés were placed subjectively within the habitat types or along transects. Qualitative descriptions of the vegetation were taken throughout disturbed areas of the bog and in surrounding habitats. The vegetation on abandoned peatland inundated by seawater was sampled using relevé plots at Shippagan Bog and Pokemouche Bog.

The target plant community-types for the restoration plan were based on studies of naturally re-established communities on abandoned peat mines throughout eastern and central Canada and adjacent United States (Nilsson *et al.*, 1990; Famous *et al.*, 1991; 1993b; Famous & Spencer, 1993a,b). The target types included freshwater, brackish and saltwater types.

Criteria and factors used to select plant community-types for the restoration plan included: (1) predominance of wetland vegetation, (2) high potential for rapid establishment necessary for erosion control, (3) widespread, proven establishment on naturally restoring peatlands, (4) practicability, (5) low cost to the producer, (6) moderate to high wildlife values, and (7) role in the regional landscape ecology. Consideration was given to the ease with which the plan can be implemented, low maintenance, and potential to work in concert with the production plan.

Because it is essential to start restoration as soon as sections are abandoned, restoration sequence maps were prepared at 5-year intervals starting with 1993 (existing conditions). Maps for years 5 and 15, and final plant community-type are presented. Contoured at 0.5 m intervals, the maps were based on the thickness of extractable (*Sphagnum*) peat. A mining rate of 7.5 cm a^{-1} was used to determine the restoration sequence. Only *Sphagnum* peat with a von Post value of 4 or less was expected to be mined.

RESULTS

Final peat surface topography

The key element to the restoration plan is the final peat surface topography map, based primarily on the extent of extractable peat, thickness of the black peat layer, and location of currently abandoned production fields (Figure 2). This map is essential for determining plant community zonation and the distribution of plant community-types, on-bog watersheds, topographic slopes/gradients, drainage patterns, and the locations of on-bog sedimentation ponds. The post-mining

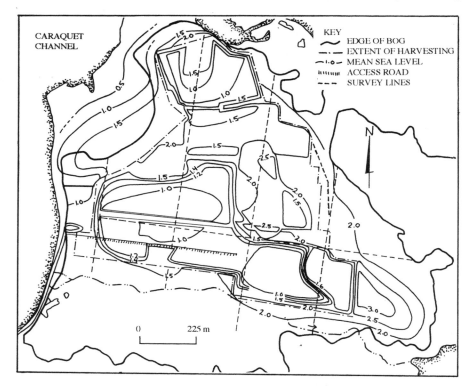

Figure 2. Pokesudie Bog final surface topography. Seawater inundation is predicted to reach the 1.4 m (mean sea level) contour during autumn and new-moon high tides and storm surges. Intertidal and brackish plant community zonation is expected to parallel contours between 1.0 m and 1.5 m (mean sea level).

surface treatments were based on elevation and topographic position such as side of slope or base of a depression. The final bog elevations determined where seawater inundation would occur and approximate zonation of saltwater-inundated plant communities. These areas were predicted using elevations taken in an adjacent salt marsh and from long-term tidal measurements at nearby tide gauges.

Sloping sections of bog (3–4% slope) will require nutrient enhancement to promote rapid revegetation for stabilisation and erosion prevention. Without modest nutrient enhancement from sand, gravel, or mineral substratum, raw low-nutrient peat may take decades to revegetate (Anderson & Kurmis, 1981; Green, 1983; Famous et al., 1991). Sections with relatively flat topography or with shallow depressions are the most likely areas to be successfully restored to typical ombrogenous communities using applications of recycled living bog surface (labelled 'top-spit' on Figures 4 and 5) (see also Poschlod, this volume).

Restoration plan plant community-types

Salt and brackish plant community-types

Salt-water community-types, presented in Table 2a, are based on salinity level and depth of tidal inundation. The ecological requirements for individual plant species are presented in Famous et al. (1993a). Intertidal communities included high-marsh (HM on Figure 5), upper marsh (UM) and brackish marsh (BM). The 'high' and 'upper' modifiers refer to the plant community's position within the intertidal zone (Thomas 1983). The high-marsh zone is located between mean tide and mean high tide (average high-tide level through a lunar cycle). Upper marsh is located between mean high tide and mean high high tide (average of the monthly highest tides during each full and new moon). Above the upper marsh is a marsh border zone (narrow, not shown on figures) and brackish marsh. The key distinction between upper marsh and brackish marsh is that the former is regularly flooded by water with a higher salinity while the latter is irregularly flooded and the salinity is generally low (e.g. 5 ppt). A low-marsh zone (too small to be shown on Figures 4 and 5) which is dominated by Spartina alternifolia and flooded by near full-strength seawater will be present within excavated sections and old ditches.

The dominant species within the high-marsh area should be salt hay or salt-meadow grass (Spartina patens), rushes (Juncus balticus and J. gerardi), and salt marsh bulrush (Scirpus maritimus). The elevation range of this zone is between 0.5 and 0.9 m mean sea level (msl). Areas between 0.8 and 1.0 m (msl) will have the same species but with a higher cover of bulrushes (Scirpus spp.), alkali grass (Puccinellia spp.), spike rushes (Eleocharis spp.), freshwater cord-grass (Spartina pectinata), and bentgrass (Calamagrostis canadensis).

Freshwater final plant community-types

Freshwater plant community-types are based on community structure, nutrient regime, and water-table depth. Community-types are summarised in Tables 2b and

Table 2. Plant communities to to be established at Pokesudie Bog (see Figures 3–5).

(a) Intertidal plant community types

Seawater	OW	Channel margins, shallow pools, shallow widened ditches; gradient from highly saline near main canals to brackish in interior; *Ruppia maritima* in pools and slow-flowing ditches; *Spartina alterniflora* lining emergent portions of highly saline areas; *Scirpus* spp. lining brackish interior areas
High marsh (intertidal)	HM	Salt marsh dominated by *Spartina patens* and *Juncus balticus*; some sections with lawns of *Plantago juncoides*, *Suaeda americana*, and *Limonium nashii*
Upper marsh (intertidal)	UM	Mean high high tide line; salt marsh dominated by *Juncus balticus*, *Scirpus maritimus*, *Puccinellia* spp., *Spartina patens*, *Triglochin maritima*
Brackish marsh	BM	Irregularly flooded dominated by *Scirpus maritimus*, *S. acutus*, *Puccinellia* spp., *Spartina pectinata*, *Calamagrostis canadensis* and *Juncus* spp.
Pannes		Bare peat areas either dry or containing highly saline water; vegetated with annuals such as *Salicornia europaea* and *Suaeda americana*; *Ranunculus cymbalaria* may be associated with brackish pannes/pools
Peat Flats		Sparsely vegetated (5–15% cover) with *Triglochin maritima*, *Puccinellia* spp., *Spartina alterniflora*, *Limonium nashii*, *Atriplex patula*, *Suaeda americana*
Upper Marsh Border		Located above the mean high high tide line; flooded by storm surges and wave action; found on dikes and irregularly flooded peat; *Myrica gale* present vegetated with *Solidago sempervirens*, *Elymus arenarius*, *Scirpus* spp., *Juncus* spp., *Ammophila breviligulata*, *Spartina pectinata*, *Aster novi-belgii*

(b) Freshwater plant community types to be established on ombrotrophic bog surfaces

Open water	OW	Ponds, blocked ditches; may dry up some years; emergent sedges present in shallow areas; floating aquatics; bordered by LM and MM communities
Mud bottom	MB	Flat, wet peat; sparsely vegetated; liverwort (and algal mats) present
Low nutrient meadow	LM	Recycled bog surface (top-spit); little/no sand; high water table; sedge/*Sphagnum* dominated (shrub cover <25%); *Eriophorum vaginatum* ssp. *spissum*, *E. angustifolium*, *Juncus peleocarpus*, *Rhynchospora alba*
Ericaceous meadow	EM	Little/no sand; high water table; dominated by sedges, bog shrubs and *Sphagnum* mosses (shrub cover >25%), *Chamaedaphne calyculata* and other ericaceous shrubs, sedges similar to LM

Table 2 (b) continued

Shrub heath	SH	Shrub dominated undisturbed bog; *Sphagnum* present in poorly drained areas; tree cover <25%; all ericaceous shrubs, *Aronia melanocarpa*, occasional *Nemopanthus mucronata* and *Sorbus americana*
Wooded shrub heath	WH	Similar to SH but with 25–50% tree cover; better drained and adjacent to ditches and production areas; *Picea mariana, Larix laricina, Betula* spp.
Forested bog	FB	In undisturbed and disturbed areas; little/no sand treatment; better drained; close to ditches and on dry slopes; tree cover >50%; *Picea mariana* and *Larix laricina*; ericaceous shrubs and occasional *Nemopanthus mucronata*

(c) Freshwater plant community types to be established on weakly minerotrophic surfaces

Open water	OW	Ponds, blocked ditches; may dry up some years; emergent sedges, *Glyceria* spp., and *Juncus* spp. present in shallow areas; floating aquatics; bordered by LM and MM communities
Minerotrophic meadow	MM	Thin veneer of sand; high water table; sedge/grass-dominated; bog and non-bog shrubs present (shrub cover <25%); dominant species include *Scirpus cyperinus*, sedges (*Carex* spp.), *Juncus effusus, Scirpus* spp.
Shrub meadow	SM	Similar to MM; water table somewhat high; mixture of graminoids (25–75% cover) & shrubs (25–75% cover); *Rhododendron canadense, Kalmia angustifolia, Myrica gale, Salix* spp., *Aronia melanocarpa, Betula* spp.
Shrub thicket	ST	Similar to MM; water table lower; tall-shrub-dominated; better-drained sloping areas; shrub cover >75%; *Salix* spp., *Aronia* spp., *Rhododendroncanadense, Ledum groenlandicum, Spiraea latifolia, Nemopanthus mucronata*
Wooded thicket	WT	Similar to ST with 25–50% tree cover; trees deciduous (*Betula* spp.) and coniferous (*Picea mariana*)
Forested Fen	FF	Higher sand/peat/mineral mixture; >50% tree cover; shrubs similar to ST; trees similar to WT

2c and described in more detail in Nilsson *et al.* (1990). The freshwater plant community types fall into two groups: low-nutrient (Table 2b) and higher-nutrient (Table 2c). Low-nutrient, oligotrophic types included sedge/ericaceous shrub meadow (SM, 25–75% cover by typical bog shrubs), shrub heath (SH), wooded shrub heath (WH), and forested bog (FB). Higher-nutrient types include minerotrophic meadow (MM, comprised of sedges and grasses), shrub meadow (SM, comprised of more robust shrubs), shrub thicket (ST), wooded shrub thicket (WT), and forested fen (FF). The term meadow is used to describe natural plant communities dominated by herbaceous species, differing from the European use which describes mowed or grazed herbaceous communities.

Meadows typically have the highest water tables, which restrict shrub growth and inhibit tree growth. Included within the sedge/ericaceous shrub meadow community-type are low-nutrient communities such as moss lawn and sedge lawn, which are dominated by *Sphagnum* mosses and sedges, respectively. The dominant sedges will include cotton grasses, wool grass (*Scirpus cyperinus*), white beak-rush, and *Carex canescens*. Both community-types will be located in areas with very high water tables. Intermediate-level water tables favour shrubs but restrict tree growth while lower water tables favour trees.

Sequential restoration and community succession maps

Peatland restoration will begin as soon as portions of the bog are no longer in production. Areas in restoration are shown on a series of production area maps presented at three intervals starting from 1993. The working restoration plan presents five 5-year intervals (Famous *et al.*, 1993a). In general, usable peat deposits in the western section of the bog will be depleted first. The SW portion of the bog which was flooded by seawater has already been abandoned. The thickest layers of usable peat are located in the SE section, which will be depleted in about 25 years of continuous extraction at 7.5 cm per year.

Figures 3–5 present a series of maps showing the projected progressive changes in plant community-types over time starting with the first plant communities to recolonise after abandonment (Figure 3) and ending with final plant community-types on Figure 5. Table 3 summarises production field changes to be completed at the 5- and 15-year intervals illustrated in Figures 3 and 4. The final plant community-types or endpoints shown in Figure 5 are those likely to remain relatively unchanged in physical structure (*e.g.* shrub dominated or tree dominated) for extended periods of time (*e.g.* 50 years) if environmental conditions remain constant.

Pokesudie Bog restoration procedures

The restoration plan includes a combination of production field changes, surface topography modifications, sand and top-spit applications, water management techniques, and if needed, seeding with higher plants. These are designed to facilitate wetland/peatland restoration and waterbird habitat enhancement.

Table 3. Production field changes and restoration work to be completed during years 5 (Figure 3) and 15 (Figure 4). TS = 'top-spit'; MM = minerotrophic meadow (see Table 2).

Additional protection for 5 years		
Production field changes	1	Excavate new sedimentation ponds (autumn)
	2	Excavate new perimeter ditches (autumn)
Restoration work	1	Widen ditches in intertidal areas (autumn)
	2	Re-profile field / fill ditches in TS areas (autumn)
	3	Build dike to prevent seawater inundation (autumn)
	4	Spread sand in areas labelled MM (winter)
	5	Spread chopped bog surface in TS areas (spring)
	6	Spread seed and mosses, if needed (spring)
	7	Flood with seawater (spring)
Additional protection for 15 years		
Production field changes	1	Re-route perimeter ditch (autumn)
Restoration work	1	Widen ditches in intertidal areas (autumn)
	2	Cut canals to sea (spring)
	3	Excavate intertidal connector ditches (spring)
	4	Level fields / fill ditches in TS area (autumn)
	5	Build new dike (autumn) / open old dike (spring)
	6	Spread sand in areas labelled MM (winter)
	7	Spread chopped bog surface in TS areas (spring)
	8	Spread seed and mosses, if needed (spring)

The production field changes shown in Figures 3 and 4 are presented for 5- and 15-year intervals (starting in 1993). Actual locations and the timing of alterations will be performed or modified as needed. They will depend on mining rates, which may vary due to weather conditions and equipment improvements. The on-bog locations of these features are estimates but approximate likely sites.

Sedimentation ponds are strongly recommended by the New Brunswick Department of Natural Resources to protect adjacent water bodies from excess siltation from suspended peat and mineral sediments. Initially, sedimentation ponds will be located in abandoned sections to intercept perimeter ditches carrying run-off from the bog. After sections of production fields are abandoned, new sedimentation ponds will be placed at strategic locations to help retain run-off on the bog and allow down-slope production field ditches to be filled to facilitate rewetting of abandoned areas. Abandoned sedimentation ponds provide habitat for waterfowl, other waterbirds, invertebrates, frogs, and salamanders and create wet areas for *Sphagnum* to recolonise.

New or relocated perimeter ditches will be excavated to divert run-off to the new on-bog sedimentation ponds. Production field ditches located down-slope from new perimeter ditches can be blocked because they are no longer functioning.

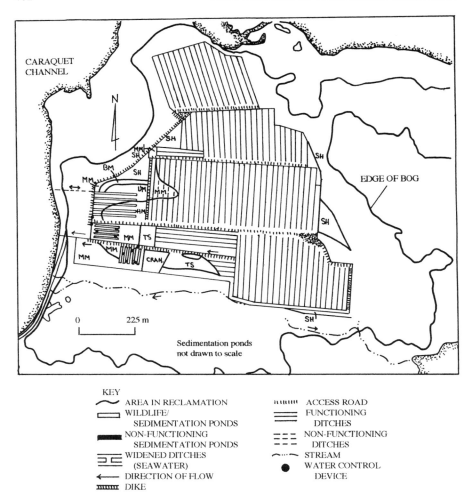

Figure 3. Predicted vegetation types and surface configuration at Pokesudie Bog after 5 years of continuous peat mining with parallel restoration management. Letters indicate vegetation types (see Table 2); TS = 'top-spit'. All depleted production fields south of the access road will be restored as ombrotrophic and weak fen community-types.

Abandoned production fields will be levelled or re-profiled (removing the crown from the centre of the field) to rewet the entire field. Best done in the autumn when the bog is driest, this procedure can be combined with ditch filling. An irregular microtopography, important to *Sphagnum* moss establishment (Wilcox & Andrus, 1987; Eggelsmann, 1988), will be created on the abandoned bog's surface prior to the application of 'top-spit' recycled from newly opened-up bogs. The microtopography prevents the removal of 'top-spit' by wind and offers support for

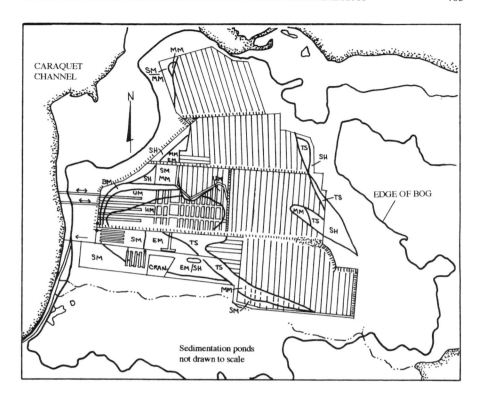

Figure 4. Predicted vegetation types and surface configurations at Pokesudie Bog after 15 years of continuous peat mining with parallel restoration management. Letters indicate vegetation types (see Table 2). Note that MM and TS plant community-types on Figure 3 are now SM and EM, respectively. Seawater-inundated sections are north of access road (see Figure 5).

early mound development. 'Top-spit' is readily available in peat mining regions of eastern Canada.

An alternative to blocking ditches is to widen ditches with a screw auger, creating a broad, low habitat with a higher water table to facilitate sedge meadow development and *Sphagnum* moss regeneration.

In sections expected to be inundated by seawater, ditches will be widened with a screw auger to create broad, low channels to enhance saltwater flow to interior areas. The microtopography will be comprised of alternating low, wet depressions (upper low-marsh and lower high-marsh communities) with raised, better-drained strips of high marsh (salt hay and Baltic rush).

Ditches will be either filled or blocked with ditch spoil to help retain run-off on the bog. Ditch filling should occur down-slope from on-bog sedimentation ponds and on completely abandoned production fields. Ditches will remain open in

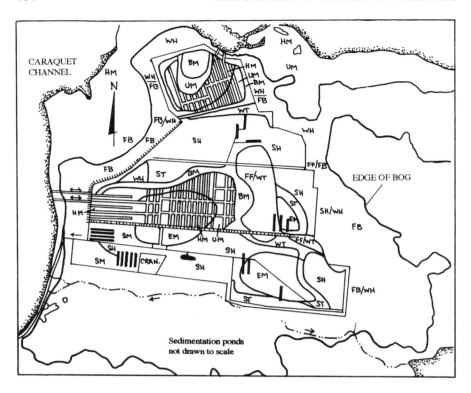

Figure 5. Predicted final plant communities and surface configuration at Pokesudie Bog following 25 years of continuous peat mining with parallel restoration management. Letters indicate vegetation types (see Table 2). Note that weak-fen treatments started with an MM seral stage (see Figures 3 & 4) followed by SM, ST, WT, and FF. Ombrotrophic community-types started with recycled chopped bog surface (TS) followed by EM, ST, WT and FB stages. Water table depths determine final plant community-type under both nutrient regimes.

sections to be restored as salt marsh.

Dikes are planned to protect adjacent production fields from seawater intrusion. Tops of the dikes need to be at an elevation of 2 m (msl). Generally, they will be about 1 m in height. Dikes will be constructed out of peat and should be breached when flooding is required.

Channels connecting abandoned production fields to the sea will be cut. Two pairs of seawater canals should be placed north of the bagging plant and at the NE corner of the production fields (see Figures 4 & 5). Protective measures should be used at the canal outlets to prevent further erosion by the sea.

Water control devices (ditch weirs) will be used to block and re-route perimeter ditches and to allow water level control of the sedimentation ponds during production and post-production phases. Post-production water control is needed for water drawdowns to enhance waterbird production.

A thin application of sand/gravel will be scattered over frozen bog to provide modest amounts of nutrients to help accelerate revegetation rates. The amount of sand/gravel needed is small, similar to that spread on highways during snowstorms. This estimate is based on the faster and more complete revegetation occurring naturally on bogs after small quantities of mineral ditch spoil were thrown onto adjacent bog surfaces. This pattern has been documented on mined bogs throughout eastern Canada and eastern Maine (Famous *et al.*, 1991). Areas designated for sand/gravel treatment include all salt marsh and brackish marsh areas and areas labelled minerotrophic meadow (MM) on Figures 3–5.

Sphagnum regeneration has even been enhanced by sand where water levels were high (Spencer-Famous *et al.*, 1993). Money (this volume) reports a similar response in *Sphagnum* growth with the addition of low levels of nutrients. Nutrient conditions are more similar to weak fen conditions. Field experiments are in progress at another site in New Brunswick (M. Spencer-Famous, unpublished).

Fresh recycled bog surface ('top-spit') will be placed on areas labelled as TS on sequential restoration figures (Figures 3–4). Areas receiving recycled bog surface will have their production fields re-profiled and drainage ditches filled. The plant community-types to be established following top-spit application include ericaceous meadow (EM), moss lawn (*Sphagnum*-moss-dominated areas with very high water tables too small to be shown on figures), and shrub heath (SH). Experiments with fresh recycled bog surface applications are in progress in New Brunswick (Rochefort *et al.*, this volume; M. Spencer-Famous, personal communication).

One or two years may be needed in some sections to rewet the bog fully before 'top-spit' can be applied. Experiments are needed to evaluate this unknown time interval, which may be site specific.

Recognising the regenerative capacity of *Sphagnum* from vegetative innovations (Sobotka, 1976; Lane, 1977; Elling & Knighton, 1984; Clymo & Duckett, 1986; Wilcox & Andrus, 1987; Rochefort & Gauthier, 1993; Money, this volume), in areas where chopped bog surface may be in short supply, an alternative method entails mixing homogenised *Sphagnum*, with homogenised *Polytrichum strictum* and seeds of *Carex canescens, Eriophorum vaginatum* ssp. *spissum, Juncus peleocarpus*, and *Rhynchospora alba*. Ombrogenous and weak-fen Sphagna such as *S. capillifolium, S. magellanicum, S. fuscum* and *S. flavocomens* are recommended. The non-*Sphagnum* species are designed to provide support for vertical *Sphagnum* growth. This process occurs naturally in undisturbed (Crum, 1983) and disturbed bogs in North America (Wilcox & Andrus, 1987; Spencer-Famous *et al.*, 1993) and Europe (Eggelsmann, 1988; Meade, 1992).

A mix suitable for higher-nutrient conditions, including minerotrophic Sphagna (*e.g. S. magellanicum, S. recurvum* and *S. fimbriatum*) should be applied to areas labelled MM on Figures 3–4. Refinements to these mixes, application rates and application schedules should be evaluated in field tests. Field experiments are needed to determine viability, timing and appropriate seed concentrations.

Transplantation or seeding of salt marsh perennials and annuals may be needed.

Bird population enhancement

The restoration plan is designed to restore and enhance pre-existing values for nesting and migratory landbirds and waterfowl. Invertebrate, amphibian, and small and large mammal populations will be restored through this plan. Habitat enhancement predictions are based on on-site qualitative surveys and quantitative surveys in nearby bogs in New Brunswick and the USA (Nilsson *et al.*, 1990).

Intertidal salt marsh and brackish marsh bird species

Increased habitat will be provided for common terns (*Sterna hirundo*)[1] nesting in a beach/dune area north of the bog. Migratory shorebirds will utilise new flats and marshes. Habitat for nesting waterfowl, currently common in adjacent brackish marshes, and migratory waterfowl, abundant in both the brackish and salt marshes, will be increased. Foraging habitat for merlins (*Falco columbarius*), an uncommon falcon, will likewise increase.

Bird populations in the brackish and salt marsh section will include nesting songbirds (*e.g.* sharp-tailed sparrow (*Ammodramus caudacutus*), song sparrow (*Melospiza meloides*), and red-winged blackbird (*Agelaius phoeniceus*)), nesting waders (*e.g.* spotted sandpiper (*Actitis macularia*) and common snipe (*Gallinago gallinago*)), nesting waterfowl (nesting on adjacent better drained land), feeding herons, migratory waterfowl, and migratory waders (especially greater yellowlegs (*Tringa melanoleuca*), lesser yellowlegs (*Tringa flavipes*), least sandpiper (*Calidris minutilla*), and semipalmated sandpiper (*Calidris pusilla*)).

The salt and brackish marshes surrounding Pokesudie Bog are used by a diverse group of waders and waterfowl. The salt, sand, and peat flats immediately north of the bog, heavily used by migratory shorebirds, terns and gulls, are expected to transgress over mined bog surfaces. Sand with it's associated invertebrate populations should be transported naturally into this small embayment. Migratory shorebirds that will benefit from the creation of intertidal habitats include white-rumped sandpiper (*Calidris fuscicollis*), semipalmated sandpiper, least sandpiper, semipalmated plover (*Charadrius semipalmatus*), black-bellied plover (*Pluvialis squatarola*), whimbrel (*Numenius phaeopus*), and Hudsonian godwit (*Limosa haemastica*), all common in adjacent habitats.

Placement of minerotrophic freshwater and brackish ponds adjacent to existing salt and brackish marshes will provide excellent habitats for nesting waterfowl which will use the ponds for feeding, loafing, courtship, and brood rearing.

Nesting landbirds and freshwater waterbirds

The creation of interspersed emergent marsh, shrub meadow, shrub thicket, and

---

[1] Common and scientific bird names follow the American Ornithologists' Union (1983).

forested habitat will increase bird species diversity and result in higher nesting densities (Nilsson *et al.*, 1990). Most typical bog species will recolonise (*e.g.* palm warbler (*Dendroica palmarum*), Lincoln's sparrow (*Melospiza lincolnii*), savannah sparrow (*Passerculus sandwichensis*), alder flycatcher (*Empidonax alnorum*), and common yellowthroat (*Geothlypis trichas*)) as well as non-bog, edge and forest nesting species (*e.g.*, magnolia warbler (*Dendroica magnolia*), white-throated sparrow (*Zonotrichia albicollis*), yellow-rumped warbler (*Dendroica coronata*), Wilson's warbler (*Wilsonia pusilla*) and gray catbird (*Dumetella carolinensis*)).

Species diversity and nesting densities will increase because of the large increase in volume of foliage (leaves serve as feeding substrates for most bird species which are insect-eating leaf gleaners), number of vegetation layers (*e.g.* ground, low shrub, tall shrub, and tree canopy), and number of habitat types. Diverse, restored habitat types collectively result in more 'niches' or places for birds to feed and breed (Nilsson *et al.*, 1990).

Waterfowl populations are expected to increase because of the higher productivity of ponds excavated into mineral substratum. The addition of mineral-rich water results in a greater diversity and biomass of plants both in the ponds and in adjacent minerotrophic areas. The bottom of most sedimentation ponds will be excavated into mineral substrate and will be more productive than the natural low-nutrient ponds found on the top of the peat deposits. These natural ponds provide limited food for waterbirds, serving primarily as resting and stopover areas for migrants. Black ducks (*Anas rubripes*), wood ducks (*Aix sponsa*), and green-winged teal (*Anas crecca*) utilise these ponds during the nesting season.

The addition of fresh and brackish ponds along the coast will provide both brood-rearing and migratory-waterbird habitat. Experimental studies evaluating brackish ponds at Pokesudie Bog are recommended to determine optimum salt water/freshwater mixtures.

RECOMMENDATIONS

Selection of post-mining treatments depends on the restoration objectives: ecological (*e.g.* specific plant community endpoints, *Sphagnum* moss re-establishment, salt and brackish marsh creation, high species diversity); wildlife (*e.g.* waterfowl/waterbirds, furbearers, amphibians and reptiles, high species diversity); or economic (*e.g.* low-cost cranberry production; sustainable harvest of living *Sphagnum*; agricultural). The Pokesudie Bog restoration plan combines ecological and wildlife objectives, and contains the following basic elements: (1) sequential restoration, (2) rewetting, (3) rapid revegetation/bog surface stabilisation, (4) wildlife habitat enhancement, (5) monitoring, (6) low maintenance, and (7) reasonable costs. Summarised in Table 4, the principles and methods are simple and cost-effective, and can be combined with routine maintenance.

Peatland restoration in North America is a new, multidisciplinary science with many information gaps. A combination of experimental studies on abandoned production fields, case history studies of naturally restoring/restored peatlands, and hydrologic modelling of the intertidal zone is needed to develop and fine-tune the methods presented in this restoration plan. Because methods have not received rigorous field testing, it is essential that the plan be flexible, carefully monitored, and updated periodically (*e.g.* at 5-year intervals) to adjust for changes in production fields, plant establishment rates, and new restoration methods.

Critical information gaps include quantitative estimates of optimum application rates and water-table depths for sand/gravel, recycled bog surface, and seed mixtures, estimates of revegetation rates for seawater-inundated peat, estimates of re-establishment rates for aquatic plants in both weakly and highly minerotrophic ponds, and autecological studies of selected restoration species. Case studies of naturally restoring peatlands are needed to monitor long-term changes in nutrient and pH levels of peat subjected to sand and lime applications, and to monitor revegetation rates, especially on bog surfaces receiving sand/gravel, seawater exposure, and nutrient amendments. Hydrologic modelling is needed to estimate canal size and optimum width and slope of widened ditches for flooding proposed salt and brackish marsh areas with seawater.

Table 4. Bog restoration principles and methods

• Sequential restoration: begin restoration as soon as large sections are abandoned	• Create irregular surface microtopography
	• Revegetate rapidly
• Integrate development with restoration	• Recycle bog surfaces ('top-spit')
• Retain run-off from production fields in abandoned sections	• Foster companion plantings with *Sphagnum*
• Block drainage and reprofile fields	• Simulate communities found on naturally restored peatlands
• Widen selected ditches/create ponds	
• Create oligotrophic conditions/spread thin layer of sand	• Secure buffer strips/undisturbed habitat islands as refugia.

REFERENCES

American Ornithologists' Union, (1983). Check-list of North American Birds. 6th edn. American Ornithologists' Union, Washington DC. 877 pp.

Anderson, M.L. & V. Kurmis (1981). *Revegetation of mined peatlands: I. Environmental properties of a mined area*. Report to Minnesota Department of Natural Resources, 47 pp.

Clymo, R.S. & Duckett, J.G. (1986). Regeneration of *Sphagnum*. *New Phytologist*, **102**, 589–614.

Crum, H. (1983). *Mosses of the Great Lakes Region*. University of Michigan Press.

Eggelsmann, R. (1988). Rewetting of raised bogs. *Die Geowissenschaften*, **11**, 317–322.

Elling, A.E. & Knighton, M.D. (1984). *Sphagnum* moss recovery after harvest in a Minnesota bog. *Journal of Soil and Water Conservation*, **39**, 209–211.

Famous, N.C. & Spencer-Famous, M. (1993a). *Peatland Restoration in Canadian Peatlands: Present status and future initiatives*. Unpublished report.

Famous, N.C. & Spencer-Famous, M.R. (1993b). *Recolonization processes in cutover bogs in North America.* Unpublished report.

Famous, N.C., Spencer, M. & Daigle, J-Y. (1993a). *Restoration Plan for Pokesudie Bog (Bog 600).* Technical report for the New Brunswick Department of Natural Resources and Energy, Geological Survey, Bathurst, New Brunswick.

Famous, N.C., Spencer, M.R. Anderson, D. & Davis, R.B. (1993b). *Restoration Patterns in Harvested North American Peatlands.* Unpublished manuscript.

Famous, N.C., Spencer, M. & Nilsson, H.D. (1991). Revegetation patterns on harvested peatlands in central and eastern North America. *Peat and Peatlands: The Resource and its Utilisation* (eds. D.N. Grubich & T.J. Malterer) pp. 48–66. Proceedings of the 1991 International Peat Symposium, Duluth, Minnesota.

Gleason, H.A. & Cronquist, A.C. (1991*). Manual of Vascular Plants of Northeastern United States and Adjacent Canada.* 2nd ed. New York Botanical Gardens, Bronx, NY, 910 p.

Green, P.E. (1983). *Natural revegetation of mined peatlands in northern Minnesota.* MS Thesis, University of Minnesota.

Jonsson-Ninniss, S. & Middleton, J. (1991). Effect of peat extraction on the vegetation in Wainfleet Bog, Ontario. *Canadian Field Naturalist,* **105**, 505–511.

Lane, D.M. (1977). Extent of vegetative reproduction in eleven species of *Sphagnum* from northern Michigan. *Michigan Botanist,* **16**, 83–89.

Meade, R. (1992). Some early changes following the rewetting of a vegetated cutover peatland at Danes Moss, Cheshire, U.K. and their relevance to conservation management. *Biological Conservation,* **61**, 31–40.

Nilsson, H.D., Famous, N.C. & Spencer, M. (1990). Harvested Peatland Reclamation, Mining impacts, case histories, and reclamation options. Unpublished manuscript. Box 102 HCR 70, Machias, Maine 04654. 317 pp.

Rampton, V.N., Gauthier, R.C. Thibault, J. & Seaman, A.A. (1984). Quaternary Geology of New Brunswick. Geological Survey of Canada. Memoir 416. 77 pp.

Rochefort, L. & Gauthier, R. (1993). The regeneration ability of four *Sphagnum* species found in Québec, Canada. Unpublished manuscript.

Spencer-Famous, M.R., Famous N.C. & Anderson, D.S. (1993). *Natural regeneration patterns of bryophytes on abandoned vacuum harvested peatlands.* Unpublished report.

Sobotka, D. (1976). Regeneration and vegetative propagation of *Sphagnum palustre* as a factor of population stability. *Acta Societatis Botanicorum Poloniae,* **45**, 365–377.

Thomas, M.L.H. (1983). Marine and coastal systems of the Quoddy Region of New Brunswick. *Canadian Special Publication of Fisheries and Aquatic Science,* **64**, 306 p.

Wilcox, D.A. & Andrus, R.E. (1887). The role of *Sphagnum fimbriatum* in secondary succession in a road salt impacted bog. *Canadian Journal of Botany,* **65**, 2270–2275.

31 Diaspore Rain and Diaspore Bank in Raised Bogs and Implications for the Restoration of Peat-mined Sites

P. POSCHLOD

Fachbereich Biologie, Naturschutz II, Philipps Universität, D-35032, Marburg, Germany

SUMMARY

1.　Diaspore rain and diaspore banks were studied in natural stands and peat-mined sites in raised bogs of the Bavarian foothills of the Alps.

2.　Not all species are adapted to long-distance dispersal by the wind. *Sphagnum* mosses can disperse by vegetative parts such as leaves and branches. Diaspores of ruderal wetland species like *Juncus effusus* and *Typha latifolia* were found in peat sites mined by milling.

3.　There are not many spermatophytes in the diaspore bank of natural stands or in the 'top spit' (surface layer) of peat pits. Of the typical raised-bog species, only *Calluna vulgaris* and *Rhynchospora alba* have a very persistent diaspore bank. However, almost all of the bryophyte species of raised bogs were found in the diaspore bank; in particular, spores and vegetative parts of *Sphagnum* mosses form a persistent diaspore bank.

4.　The results show that restoration of milled peat sites in raised bogs needs intervention. The 'top spit' could be used to initiate succession on such sites by spreading it on the bare surface, and it is thus proposed that, in sites where peat is extracted by milling, the 'top spit' should be stored. However, the diaspore bank of *Sphagnum* mosses seems to be persistent only in the case of wet storage. Therefore excavation methods like the 'Baggerverfahren' should be used, where these conditions are produced after peat mining.

INTRODUCTION

Today in raised bogs the major peat industries win peat by the milling method. With this method areas remain under harvesting for decades. The disturbance of the ecosystem is very severe, because after the end of peat harvesting bare peat areas remain, completely devoid of vegetation (Poschlod, 1992). Until recently, concepts of restoration have only been based upon the planting of typical, clonal plant species to form a vegetation cover with the aim of retarding processes of erosion and mineralisation and facilitating succession (Maas & Poschlod, 1991; Schuckert & Poschlod, 1991, 1993). However, such restoration methods can only be exceptional as they are too expensive for the huge areas which are exploited

Restoration of Temperate Wetlands. Edited by B.D. Wheeler, S.C. Shaw, W.J. Fojt and R.A. Robertson
© 1995 John Wiley & Sons Ltd.

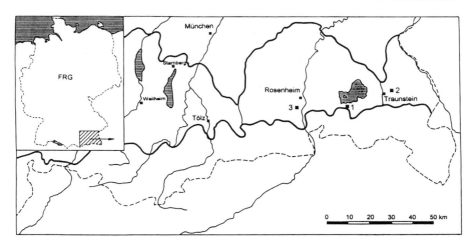

Figure 1. Study sites in the Bavarian foothills of the Alps (southern Germany).

today. It is therefore necessary to know whether the species of raised bogs can disperse their diaspores over long distances from more or less intact surrounding areas to initiate succession towards the former peat-forming raised bog-community. Would it be useful to store the 'top spit' or surface layer (vegetation horizon, after Poschlod, 1990), which is removed before peat mining, and subsequently to spread it on the bare peat surface of the milled areas, as traditionally done in combination with the hand peat-cutting method? Does this 'top spit' contain a diaspore bank of the typical peat-forming plant species which could initiate succession towards the former raised-bog community? On the peat sites mined by milling there is usually no diaspore bank of spermatophytes or bryophytes (Salonen, 1987). Therefore the diaspore rain was studied in natural stands and peat-mined sites. The diaspore bank was investigated in natural stands and in peat pits in an area where the 'top spit' was stored for years with the aim of spreading it after the end of peat mining by the milling method.

DESCRIPTION OF THE SITES

The study of diaspore rain was carried out in a large raised-bog complex, the Kendlmühlfilz south of the Chiemsee (Figure 1). The investigated sites were three natural stands in the centre of the complex, three areas peat-mined by cutting and four areas mined by milling in the north of the raised bog complex (Table 1, see Pfadenhauer, Siuda & Krinner, 1990). The natural stands were the central, peat-forming raised bog community (1), a transitional bog with *Scheuchzeria palustris*[1]

---

[1] The nomenclature of species follows Ehrendorfer (1973) for spermatophytes and Smith (1978, 1990) for bryophytes. In two cases, species could not be determined exactly. In the diaspore bank

(2) and a dwarf pine scrub (3). The stands in the peat-cut areas were a dry *Calluna* heath (4, 5) and a dry bog forest with *Betula pubescens* agg., *Frangula alnus* and *Molinia caerulea* (6). On the peat sites mined by milling (7–10) there was no vegetation at all. The milled peat fields had a length of about 1.5 km and a width of 20–30 m. Diaspore traps were placed in the middle of the strips, so that the nearest vegetation was some plant individuals (*e.g. Juncus effusus, Typha latifolia*) 10–15 m away at the edge of the ditches.

The diaspore bank of natural stands was studied in the raised bog Wieninger Filz, situated in the south-eastern part of the Bavarian foothills of the Alps near Traunstein (Figure 1). It is a typically asymmetrical raised bog with a margin of dwarf pine, developed from a former lake. The raised bog was influenced by peat cutting in the first half of this century. The studied sites were situated on the unmined surface along a transect with a different water table (Figure 3).

The investigations of the potential value of the deposited 'top spit' to regeneration took place in the Kollerfilz in the Rosenheimer basin near Rosenheim (Figure 1). The 'top spit' was set aside by an excavator in large, former (before the beginning of milling) peat cuttings (peat pits) between the sites mined by milling. This deposition of the 'top spit' happened between 1973 and 1981 in peat pit 1, in 1966 in peat pit 4, and in 1975 in peat pit 5. The water level in all peat pits was about 20–30cm below the peat surface.

The annual precipitation of the investigated region, the foothills of the Alps, is between 1100 and 1700 mm (Schmeidl *et al.,* 1970; Poschlod, 1990): Kendl-mühlfilz, 1344 mm a^{-1}; Wieninger Filz, 1541 mm a^{-1}; Kollerfilz, 1125 mm a^{-1}. The annual distribution in the Kendlmühlfilz for the period 1959–68) was as follows: Jan, 67 mm; Feb, 60 mm; Mar, 86 mm; Apr, 105 mm; May, 196 mm; Jun, 183 mm; Jul, 163 mm; Aug, 158 mm; Sep, 86 mm; Oct, 78 mm; Nov, 69 mm; Dec, 95 mm (Schmeidl *et al.,* 1970). The distribution is similar at the other sites (Poschlod, 1990).

METHODS

The diaspore rain was studied by collecting the diaspores with sticky traps, following Werner (1975). The traps consisted of a frame of 1 m^2, which was covered with plastic foil (Figure 2). The lime (Soveurode of Sovilo, Reims), which was kept sticky over the whole investigation period, was sprayed on the plastic foil in the field[2]. Trapping of diaspores started at the beginning of July (8 July 1987), when the first diaspores (*Eriophorum vaginatum*) were ripe, and ended in October 1987 (8 October 1987) so that the dispersal time of all species typical for

---

sometimes *Cephalozia loitlesbergeri* and *C. macrostachya* could not always be differentiated, because they did not form any perianths. *Leucobryum glaucum* and *L. juniperoideum* could not be distinguished because of intermediate characteristics.
[2] After the experiment the analysis of the traps showed that over 80% of the particles caught by the method used were insects. The author therefore now uses 'dry diaspore traps', which subsequent studies have shown to be satisfactory (e.g. Poschlod & Jordan, 1992).

Table 1. Vegetation and diaspore rain in the natural stands and peat-cut areas in the Kendlmühlfilz. Sites: 1, raised bog; 2, transitional bog with *Scheuchzeria palustris*; 3, dwarf pine scrub; 4 & 5, dry *Calluna* heath; 6, dry bog forest with *Betula pubescens*. Vegetation cover estimated in 9 m² relevée around the trap by Braun-Blanquet method (8 July 1987). I: species in actual vegetation and diaspore rain; II: species only in the actual vegetation.

Site		1		2		3		4		5		6	
Vegetation (C) /diaspore rain (dr)		C	dr	C	dr	C	dr	C	dr	C	dr	C	dr
Height (m)	Tree layer (T)	–		–		–		–		–		7.0	
	Shrub layer (S)	–		–		0.4		–		–		2.0	
	Herb layer (H)	0.3		0.3		0.4		0.3		0.4		0.9	
Cover (%)	Tree layer (T)	–		–		–		–		–		15	
	Shrub layer (S)	–		–		3		–		–		10	
	Herb layer (H)	25		20		65		55		80		50	
	Bryophyte layer (B)	95		100		95		40		5		1	
I T	*Betula pubescens* agg.		x		x		x		x			2	x
H	*Calluna vulgaris*	2		1		3	x	3	x	5	x	3	
H	*Andromeda polifolia*	1	x	1	x	1		1		+			
H	*Rhynchospora alba*		x	2	x	2	x						
H	*Molinia caerulea*			1		1		1	x		x	2	x
B	*Sphagnum magellanicum*	5		2		4	x	2					
B	*Sphagnum capillifolium*	1	x	1	x	2	x	2					
B	*Polytrichum strictum*	1		+		1		1	x				
II S	*Pinus mugo* agg. f. *prostrata*					1							
S	*Picea abies*											1	
S	*Frangula alnus*	2										2	
S	*Rubus fruticosus* agg.	+										+	
H	*Vaccinium oxycoccus*	1		1				1					

Table 1 continued

Site	1		2		3		4		5		6	
Vegetation (C) /diaspore rain (dr)	C	dr	C	dr	C	dr	C	dr	C	dr	C	dr
H Eriophorum vaginatum	2		1		1		1					
H Drosera rotundifolia	1											
H Scheuchzeria palustris	1		1									
B Sphagnum angustifolium					1							
B Sphagnum papillosum			2									
B Sphagnum cuspidatum			2		1							
B Sphagnum subsecundum					+							
B Pleurozium schreberi							1		1			
B Leucobryum glaucum/ juniperoideum									1			
B Lophocolea heterophylla											+	
B Cladonia spp.					+							

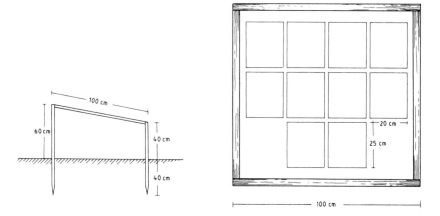

Figure 2. Diaspore trap and sampling design.

these sites, except *Pinus mugo*, was covered. At the end of trapping, the foil was cut into 10 pieces of 20 cm x 25 cm, which were evaluated for each stand under the microscope.

The diaspore bank was studied by taking soil samples with a Damman-corer (Janssens, 1987) in May 1987. The corer had an outer diameter of 15 cm (inner diameter 14.6 cm). Four replicates were taken from each stand. Samples were taken down to a depth of 40 cm in the Wieninger Filz and 30 cm in the Kollerfilze.

Living plants and fragments were removed immediately (roots and rhizomes of dwarf shrubs, roots and old leaf sheaths of *Eriophorum vaginatum*). Parts of bryophytes that appeared photosynthetically active were separated (heads and stems of Sphagna to a depth of 2 to 4 cm).

Each replicate sample was placed in a plastic bag and transported to the laboratory. The soil structure in the cores remained practically unchanged. The core was cut into discs of 5 or 10 cm, from which an edge of 1 to 2 cm was cut off to avoid contamination with other soil layers during soil sampling and transport, leaving each disc with an area of about 100 cm^2. Each disc was spread out on a sterile peat substrate and cultivated in an unheated glasshouse from May 1987 to August 1988, so that the samples were stratified in winter. Samples were irrigated with demineralised water. To exclude contamination during cultivation, pots with sterile peat substrate were put between the cultivated samples. During the cultivation time only some *Betula* sp., one *Marchantia polymorpha* and several *Funaria hygrometrica* plants germinated in these pots. In one case the last species developed in a sample too.

The growth of the seedlings of spermatophytes and pteridophytes was very slow, so they were only counted in October 1987 and at the end of the experiment in August 1988.

An estimation of the number of shoots of bryophytes was made in October

Table 2. Quantitative data of the diaspore rain in the Kendlmühlfilz. Sites 1 to 6, see Table 1; sites 7 to 10 are peat areas mined by milling with a bare peat surface. The quantitative data represent the number of trapped diaspores m^{-2}.

A: species with diaspore rain at all sites,
B: species with diaspore rain only in the natural stands and peat cut areas,
C: species with diaspore rain only on peat sites mined by milling.

	Species	Type of diaspore	Sites									
			1	2	3	4	5	6	7	8	9	10
A	*Betula pubescens*	Fruit	324	276	540	2806	3746	6974	758	438	312	226
	Rhynchospora alba	Fruit	14	130	76	–	–	–	–	2	–	–
	Molinia caerulea	Fruit	–	–	–	18	6	18	–	2	4	–
	Sphagnum capillifolium	Branch	2	4	2	–	–	–	–	2	–	–
		Leaf	–	–	–	–	–	–	–	–	2	2
B	*Calluna vulgaris*	Seed	–	–	2	4	16	–	–	–	–	–
		Fruit with seeds	–	–	–	–	14	–	–	–	–	–
	Andromeda polifolia	Seed	2	2	–	–	–	–	–	–	–	–
	Sphagnum magellanicum	Leaf	–	–	10	–	–	–	–	–	–	–
	Polytrichum strictum	Shoot	–	–	–	2	–	–	–	–	–	–
C	*Juncus effusus*	Seed	–	–	–	–	–	–	–	–	6	328
		Fruit with seeds	–	–	–	–	–	–	–	–	–	2
	Trichophorum alpinum	Fruit	–	–	–	–	–	–	2	2	4	4
	Typha latifolia	Fruit	–	–	–	–	–	–	12	2	–	–
	Sphagnum papillosum	Leaf	–	–	–	–	–	–	–	2	–	–

1987. During the first few weeks and months after sampling the young shoots were examined to see if they had developed from protonemata (detached spores were not found in any case; see also Clymo & Duckett, 1986) or from vegetative parts or propagules (stems, leaves; tubers were not found, although they are produced by many of the investigated species). Subsequently, only the presence of new species was recorded until the first sporophytes were produced in May 1988 (some liverworts, *Campylopus pyriformis*, *Dicranella cerviculata*).

RESULTS

Diaspore rain

The results showed that in stands with a vegetation cover (Tables 1 and 2, 1–6) in almost all cases the diaspore rain consisted of those species which grew close to the trap. Only the winged nuts of the birch occurred in all traps, even if the nearest birches were more than several hundred metres away. The next most abundant species after birch were *Rhynchospora alba* on the wet sites and *Calluna vulgaris* and *Molinia caerulea* on the dry sites. In the year studied, the diaspores of *Eriophorum vaginatum* were not dispersed because they adhered to the mother plant in the wet early summer.

On the peat sites mined by milling, only diaspores of *Betula pubescens* agg. and *Juncus effusus* were abundant. Other species were *Rhynchospora alba*, *Trichophorum alpinum* and *Molinia caerulea*.

Vegetative parts of bryophytes, which are potentially able to regenerate (Oehlmann, 1898; Poschlod & Pfadenhauer, 1989; Poschlod & Schrag, 1990), were trapped on almost all sites. They included branches and leaves of *Sphagnum capillifolium*, *S. magellanicum* and *S. papillosum*.

Diaspore bank along a transect in a natural stand (Wieninger Filz)

The studied transect (Figure 3) represented a gradient from a dry *Calluna* heath through a wet *Calluna* heath to a wet scrub with dwarf pine on the raised bog surface (Table 3). A diaspore bank only occurred down to a depth of 30 cm.

Site 1: dry Calluna *heath*

The vegetation was dominated by *Calluna vulgaris* (cover > 90%). The moss layer (cover < 1%) consisted of *Pleurozium schreberi* and *Cladonia* spp. (Table 3). The surface was bare peat. The peat over the whole investigated horizon was an *Eriophorum–Sphagna cymbifolia* peat (degree of humification, H6–H7 (von Post scale). The mean water table during the vegetation period in 1986 was at 71 cm below surface (maximum 56 cm, minimum 79 cm).

In the diaspore bank, *Calluna vulgaris* was dominant with >40,000 viable seeds in 1 m^2 (Table 4). Viable seeds could be found down to a depth of 15 cm. A small diaspore bank was formed by *Rhynchospora alba* (700 seeds m^{-2}) in the depth

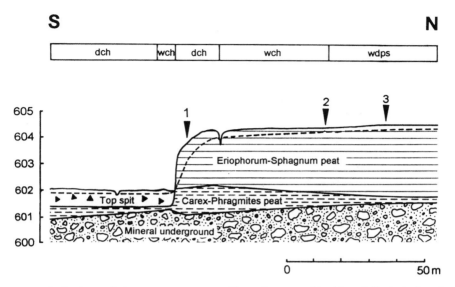

Figure 3. Surface of the transect, peat profile and water table (dotted line) during the vegetation period of 1986 in the Wieninger Filz; dch, dry *Calluna* heath; wch, wet *Calluna* heath; wdps, wet dwarf pine scrub (*Pinus mugo*).

from 5 to 15 cm. Only a few diaspores of other spermatophytes were found in the uppermost layer (*Eriophorum vaginatum, Juncus effusus*). The diaspore bank of bryophytes consisted only of typical species of the bare peat (Table 5). The most abundant species was *Campylopus pyriformis*.

Site 2: wet Calluna *heath*

The herb layer of the vegetation was formed by *Calluna vulgaris, Eriophorum vaginatum, Rhynchospora alba*, rarely *Andromeda polifolia* and *Vaccinium oxycoccos* (Table 3). In the bryophyte layer, *Sphagnum capillifolium* was dominant. Other species were *Sphagnum magellanicum, S. cuspidatum, Dicranum undulatum, Pleurozium schreberi* and some liverworts like *Cephalozia pleniceps* and *Mylia anomala*. The peat comprised the living moss layer (0–3 cm) then an *Eriophorum–Sphagna cymbifolia* peat, from 10 to 40 cm with macro-remains of *Rhynchospora alba, Scheuchzeria palustris* and *Sphagna cuspidata* (degree of humification, von Post H3–H5). The mean water table was 15 cm below surface (maximum 8 cm, minimum 22 cm).

As in the first site, the diaspore bank of spermatophytes was formed by *Calluna vulgaris* and *Rhynchospora alba* and a few seeds of *Drosera rotundifolia* (Table 4). But here diaspores occurred only to a depth of 10 cm. In the diaspore bank of bryophytes (Table 5) peat mosses (*Sphagnum capillifolium, S. cuspidatum*) were found. Brown stems and branches could regenerate down to a depth of 15 cm. In

Table 3. Vegetation and diaspore bank in the soil along a transect in the Wieninger Filz. Sites: 1 = dry *Calluna* heath, 2 = wet *Calluna* heath, 3 = wet dwarf pine scrub. Time of soil sampling: 10 May 1987. C, estimation of vegetation cover after the method of Braun-Blanquet. Dates of relevés: 10 May 1987, 11 August 1987 & 5 October 1987. db, diaspore bank; g, generative; v, vegetative; g/v? an exact association to the generative or vegetative diaspore bank was not possible). I, species only in the actual vegetation; II, species in the actual vegetation and diaspore bank; III, species only found in the diaspore bank.

Site			1		2		3	
Size of the vegetation relevée (m^2)			4		4		16	
Height (m)	Tree layer (T)		–		–		2.0	
	Shrub layer (S)		–		0.4		0.4	
	Herb layer (H)		0.3		0.3		0.3	
Cover (%)	Tree layer (T)		–		–		30	
	Shrub layer (S)		–		3		1	
	Herb layer (H)		90		55		65	
	Bryophyte layer (B)		1		60		60	

Vegetation/diaspore bank			C	db	C	db	C	db
I	T	*Pinus mugo* agg. *f. prostrata*					3	
	S	*Pinus mugo* agg. *f. prostrata*			1		+	
	H	*Betula pubescens agg.*			+			
	H	*Vaccinium myrtillus*					+	
	H	*Vaccinium uliginosum*					+	
	H	*Vaccinium vitis-idaea*	1				1	
	H	*Andromeda polifolia*			+		+	
	H	*Vaccinium oxycoccos*			+		+	
	B	*Sphagnum tenellum*			+			
	B	*Dicranum polysetum*					+	
	B	*Dicranum undulatum*			1			
	B	*Pleurozium schreberi*	+		1		+	
	B	*Cladonia* spp.	+		+		+	
II	H	*Calluna vulgaris*	5	g	2	g	4	g
	H	*Eriophorum vaginatum*		g	2		2	
	H	*Rhynchospora alba*		g	2	g		
	H	*Drosera rotundifolia*			+	g	+	g
	B	*Sphagnum magellanicum*			1	v	2	g/v
	B	*Sphagnum capillifolium*			3	v	3	g/v
	B	*Sphagnum angustifolium*				g	2	v
	B	*Sphagnum cuspidatum*			2	v		v
	B	*Aulacomnium palustre*				g/v?	1	v
	B	*Cephalozia pleniceps*			+	g/v?		g/v?
	B	*Mylia anomala*			+			g/v?

contd

Table 3 *continued*

Site		1		2		3	
Vegetation/diaspore bank		C	db	C	db	C	db
III	H *Juncus effusus*		g				
	H Pteridophyta		g				
	B *Sphagnum papillosum*						g/v?
	B *Campylopus pyriformis*		g/v?				g/v?
	B *Pohlia* sp.		g/v?				g/v?
	B *Polytrichum longisetum*		g/v?		g/v?		g/v?
	B *Calypogeia neesiana*						g/v?
	B *Cephalozia connivens*						g/v?
	B *Cephalozia loitlesbergeri/ macrostachya*				g/v?		
	B *Kurzia pauciflora*		g/v?		g/v?		g/v?

the uppermost layer a few plants of *Sphagnum angustifolium* regenerated by a protonema development. The diaspore bank of three liverworts (*Cephalozia loitlesbergeri/macrostachya, Cephalozia pleniceps, Kurzia pauciflora*) was found in the uppermost layer. Only *C. pleniceps* was present in the actual vegetation.

Site 3: *wet dwarf pine scrub (with* Pinus mugo)

This was the most natural habitat along the transect, formed by the dwarf pine shrubs typical for the raised bogs of the foothills of the Alps (Table 3). In the herb layer *Andromeda polifolia, Calluna vulgaris* and different *Vaccinium* species were dominant, but *Eriophorum vaginatum* and *Drosera rotundifolia* also occurred. The bryophyte layer had a cover of 60%; *Sphagnum magellanicum, S. capillifolium* and *S. angustifolium* were the most abundant species. The peat profile was similar to that of site 2. The mean water table was not recorded.

Only two species of spermatophytes occurred in the diaspore bank (Table 4). *Calluna vulgaris* was found down to a depth of 20 cm, *Drosera rotundifolia* to 10 cm. The diaspore bank of bryophytes had its highest diversity at this site (Table 5). All peat mosses occurring in the actual vegetation could regenerate vegetatively down to a depth of 10 cm, although the vegetative shoot parts were brown and partially decomposed. *Sphagnum cuspidatum* and *S. papillosum*, which did not occur in the actual vegetation, were recovered from the deeper layers regenerating probably by spores (previous protonema development). One of the five liverworts, *Mylia anomala*, regenerated down to a depth of 15 cm.

Diaspore bank of the 'top spit' in old peat pits (Kollerfilze)

The vegetation on the surface of all the old peat pits in the Kollerfilze was dry *Calluna* heath with *Molinia caerulea* and with little or no cover of *Sphagnum* species in the bryophyte layer (Table 6). *Campylopus pyriformis, Polytrichum longisetum* and other bryophytes species occupied the bare peat.

The 'top spit' consisted of an *Eriophorum–Sphagnum cymbifolia* peat (degree of decomposition, von Post H6–H7), sometimes with subrecent vegetative parts of plants in it, caused by setting it aside.

Table 4. Quantitative data of the generative diaspore bank of the spermatophytes and pteridophytes along a transect in the Wieninger Filz. Sites 1, 2, 3 (see Table 3). Depth (cm) of soil layer. Quantitative data represent number of germinated diaspores or spores m^{-2}.

Site	Depth (cm)	1	2	3
Calluna vulgaris	0–5	9175	11950	8250
	5–10	31600	19100	28050
	10–15	2450	–	2950
	15–20	–	–	50
	20–30	–	–	–
Eriophorum vaginatum	0–5	75	–	–
	5–10	–	–	–
	10–15	–	–	–
	15–20	–	–	–
	20–30	–	–	–
Rhynchospora alba	0–5	–	18450	–
	5–10	525	4550	–
	10–15	175	–	–
	15–20	–	–	–
	20–30	–	–	–
Drosera rotundifolia	0–5	–	200	200
	5–10	–	–	2000
	10–15	–	–	–
	15–20	–	–	–
	20–30	–	–	–
Juncus effusus	0–5	75	–	–
	5–10	–	–	–
	10–15	–	–	–
	15–20	–	–	–
	20–30	–	–	–
Pteridophyta	0–5	75	–	–
	5–10	75	–	–
	10–15	–	–	–
	15–20	–	–	–
	20–30	–	–	–

Table 5. Quantitative data of the diaspore bank of the bryophytes along a transect in the Wieninger Filz. Sites 1, 2, 3 (see Table 3). Depth (cm) of soil layer. The quantitative data represent the number of shoots in 0.01 m² divided into five classes: 1 = 1 shoot, 2 = 2–5 shoots, 3 = 6–25 shoots, 4 = 26–100 shoots, 5 = more than 100 shoots. If the identification of the type of regeneration was possible, it is marked in brackets (p, regeneration resulted from a protonema; v, regeneration resulted from vegetative parts such as shoots, leaves or tubers).

	Depth (cm)	Site 1	Site 2	Site 3
Calypogeia neesiana	0–5	–	–	2
	5–10	–	–	1
	10–15	–	–	–
	15–20	–	–	–
	20–30	–	–	–
Cephalozia connivens	0–5	–	–	–
	5–10	–	–	5
	10–15	–	–	3
	15–20	–	–	–
	20–30	–	–	–
Cephalozia loitlesbergeri/ macrostachya	0–5	–	5	–
	5–10	–	–	–
	10–15	–	–	–
	15–20	–	–	–
	20–30	–	–	–
Cephalozia pleniceps	0–5	–	5	5
	5–10	–	–	4
	10–15	–	–	–
	15–20	–	–	–
	20–30	–	–	–

	Depth (cm)	Site 1	Site 2	Site 3
Kurzia pauciflora	0–5	–	4	5
	5–10	–	–	4
	10–15	5 (p)	–	–
	15–20	–	–	–
	20–30	–	–	–
Mylia anomala	0–5	–	–	3
	5–10	–	–	2
	10–15	–	–	2
	15–20	–	–	–
	20–30	–	–	–
Sphagnum angustifolium	0–5	–	1 (p)	3 (v)
	5–10	–	–	2 (v)
	10–15	–	–	–
	15–20	–	–	–
	20–30	–	–	–
Sphagnum capillifolium	0–5	–	4 (v)	5 (v)
	5–10	–	1 (v)	3 (v)
	10–15	–	2 (v)	–
	15–20	–	–	2 (p)
	20–30	–	–	–

contd

Table 5 *continued*

	Site		
Depth (cm)	1	2	3
Sphagnum			
cuspidatum			
0–5	–	5 (v)	–
5–10	–	3 (v)	–
10–15	–	2 (v)	1 (p)
15–20	–	–	4 (p)
20–30	–	–	2 (p)
Sphagnum			
magellanicum			
0–5	–	–	3 (v)
5–10	–	–	1 (v)
10–15	–	–	–
15–20	–	–	1 (p)
20–30	–	–	–
Sphagnum			
papillosum			
0–5	–	–	–
5–10	–	–	–
10–15	–	–	–
15–20	–	–	1 (p)
20–30	–	–	–
Aulacomnium			
palustre			
0–5	–	2	3 (v)
5–10	–	–	1 (v)
10–15	–	–	–
15–20	–	–	–
20–30	–	–	–

	Site		
Depth (cm)	1	2	3
Campylopus			
pyriformis			
0–5	5 (p)	–	–
5–10	5 (p)	–	3 (p)
10–15	3 (p)	–	4
15–20	–	–	–
20–30	–	–	–
Pleurozium			
schreberi			
0–5	2 (v)	–	–
5–10	1 (v)	–	–
10–15	–	–	–
15–20	–	–	–
20–30	–	–	–
Pohlia sp.			
0–5	–	–	–
5–10	2	–	3
10–15	–	–	5
15–20	–	–	–
20–30	–	–	–
Polytrichum			
longisetum			
0–5	3 (p)	–	–
5–10	3 (p)	1	2
10–15	–	–	3
15–20	–	–	3
20–30	–	–	–

Table 6. Vegetation and diaspore bank in the top spit in the peat pits in the Kollerfilze. Legend: see Table 3.

Site (number of peat pit)		4		1		5	
Age of the top spit (years)		21		6–14		12	
Size of the vegetation relevée (m^2)		4		4		4	
Height (m) Herb layer (H)		0.3		0.3		0.3	
Cover (%) Herb layer (H)		65		5		65	
Bryophyte layer (B)		8		15		1	
Vegetation (v) / diaspore bank (db)		v	db	v	db	v	db
I H	*Betula pubescens* agg.					+	
H	*Vaccinium vitis-idaea*					1	
H	*Eriophorum vaginatum*			1			
B	*Polytrichum strictum*			1			
II H	*Calluna vulgaris*	4	g	2	g	4	g
H	*Carex canescens*			+	g		
H	*Rhynchospora alba*			g	+		g
H	*Molinia caerulea*	2	g	2	g	1	g
H	*Drosera rotundifolia*		g	+	g		
B	*Sphagnum magellanicum*	+		1	g/v?		
B	*Sphagnum capillifolium*	1	v	2	g/v?		g/v?
B	*Sphagnum cuspidatum*		g/v?	1	g/v?		g/v?
B	*Campylopus pyriformis*	1	g/v?	1	g/v?		g/v?
B	*Leucobryum glaucum/ juniperoideum*	+	g/v?		g/v?		g/v?
B	*Polytrichum longisetum*	1	g/v?		g/v?		g/v?
B	*Cladonia* spp.	1	g/v?			+	g/v?
III H	Pteridophyta				g		g
B	*Dicranella cerviculata*		g/v?		g/v?		g/v?
B	*Hypnum cupressiforme*		g/v?				
B	*Pohlia* sp.						g/v?
B	*Calypogeia trichomanis*		g/v?				
B	*Cephalozia connivens*		g/v?		g/v?		g/v?
B	*Cephalozia macrostachya*		g/v?				
B	*Cephalozia pleniceps*		g/v?		g/v?		
B	*Cephaloziella elasticha*						g/v?
B	*Kurzia pauciflora*		g/v?		g/v?		

In the diaspore bank of spermatophyte species of the vegetation (Table 7), *Calluna vulgaris* and *Molinia caerulea* were dominant. *Rhynchospora alba, Drosera rotundifolia* and *Carex canescens* occurred very rarely, mostly in deeper layers. Among the bryophytes, *Campylopus pyriformis* was the most abundant (Table 8). Six liverworts were found, *Cephalozia connivens, C. pleniceps* and *Kurzia pauciflora* on almost all sites in all layers. Four *Sphagnum* species, *S. angustifolium, S. capillifolium, S. cuspidatum* and *S. magellanicum*, mostly regenerating by forming protonemata, were present and represented in all layers. Other mosses were *Dicranella cerviculata, Leucobryum glaucum/juniperoideum* and *Polytrichum longisetum*.

Table 7. Quantitative data of the generative diaspore bank of the spermatophytes and pteridophytes of the top spit in the peat pits of the Kollerfilze. Legend: see Table 4.

Site (number of peat pit)		4	1	5
Age of the top spit (years)		21	6–14	12
Species	Depth (cm)			
Calluna vulgaris	0– 5	3400	675	5050
	5–10	3050	500	1200
	10–20	425	1675	1375
	20–30	–	1500	700
Rhynchospora alba	0–5	–	–	–
	5–10	–	–	–
	10–20	25	–	25
	20–30	–	–	–
Drosera rotundifolia	0–5	–	50	–
	5–10	25	–	–
	10–20	–	25	–
	20–30	–	50	–
Carex canescens	0–5	–	–	–
	5–10	–	–	–
	10–20	–	25	–
	20–30	–	25	–
Molinia caerulea	0– 5	250	1750	50
	5–10	50	1000	25
	10–20	–	1850	75
	20–30	25	250	50
Pteridophyta	0–5	–	–	–
	5–10	–	50	25
	10–20	–	100	–
	20–30	–	–	–

Table 8. Quantitative data of the diaspore bank of the bryophytes of the 'top spit' in the peat pits of the Kollerfilze. Legend: see Table 5.

Site (number of peat pit)		4	1	5
Age of the top spit (years)		21	6–14	12
Species	Depth (cm)			
Calypogeia trichomanis	0–5	2	–	–
	5–10	–	–	–
	10–20	–	–	–
	20–30	–	–	–
Cephalozia connivens	0–5	5 (p)	3	5
	5–10	4 (p)	–	3
	10–20	–	5 (p)	3 (p)
	20–30	–	5 (p)	4
Cephalozia macrostachya	0–5	4 (p)	–	–
	5–10	–	–	–
	10–20	–	–	–
	20–30	–	–	–
Cephalozia pleniceps	0–5	3	–	–
	5–10	–	–	–
	10–20	–	–	–
	20–30	–	5	–
Cephaloziella elasticha	0–5	–	–	3
	5–10	–	–	–
	10–20	–	–	–
	20–30	–	–	–
Kurzia pauciflora	0–5	4	–	–
	5–10	–	–	–
	10–20	–	5	–
	20–30	–	5	–
Sphagnum angustifolium	0–5	–	–	–
	5–10	–	–	–
	10–20	–	–	–
	20–30	–	1 (p)	–
Sphagnum capillifolium	0–5	2 (v)	–	2 (p)
	5–10	–	–	–
	10–20	–	3 (p)	–
	20–30	–	–	–

contd

Table 8 *continued*

Site (number of peat pit) Species	Depth (cm)	4	1	5
Sphagnum cuspidatum	0–5	–	–	2 (p)
	5–10	–	–	–
	10–20	2 (p)	–	2 (p)
	20–30	2 (p)	–	–
Sphagnum magellanicum	0–5	–	–	–
	5–10	–	–	–
	10–20	–	1 (p)	–
	20–30	–	–	–
Campylopus pyriformis	0–5	5 (p)	5 (p)	5 (p)
	5–10	5 (p)	5 (p)	5 (p)
	10–20	5 (p)	5 (p)	5 (p)
	20–30	5 (p)	5 (p)	5 (p)
Dicranella cerviculata	0–5	3	3	–
	5–10	–	3	3
	10–20	–	4	3
	20–30	2	–	3
Hypnum cupressiforme	0–5	2	–	–
	5–10	1	–	–
	10–20	–	–	–
	20–30	–	–	–
Leucobryum glaucum/ *juniperoideum*	0–5	3 (p)	3	3
	5–10	–	2 (p)	–
	10–20	–	3 (p)	–
	20–30	–	–	–
Pohlia sp.	0–5	–	–	3
	5–10	–	–	–
	10–20	–	–	–
	20–30	–	–	–
Polytrichum longisetum	0–5	–	–	2
	5–10	–	–	–
	10–20	2 (p)	2 (p)	–
	20–30	–	–	–
Cladonia spp.	0–5	–	–	x
	5–10	x	–	–
	10–20	–	–	–
	20–30	x	–	–

DISCUSSION

Diaspore rain

The results of the investigation of dispersal through the air show that not all, but some, species of the raised bog community are adapted to long-distance dispersal by the wind. The diaspore rain on the peat-mined sites and the vegetation development after the end of the peat mining on the same sites agreed with the results of Maas & Poschlod (1991). *Juncus effusus* and *Typha latifolia* now dominate the peat-mined areas together with other species like *Eriophorum vaginatum, Carex rostrata* or *Drosera rotundifolia*, species which are also adapted to long-distance dispersal by air or by water (*Carex rostrata, Drosera rotundifolia*; Poschlod, 1990). They were not recorded during the investigated period, maybe because they could not be trapped by the method used. This study only covered one vegetation period. Subsequent studies should therefore include some more years and should use methods to catch both water- and bird-dispersed diaspores. Poschlod (1990) had shown that most of the species of raised and transitional bogs are adapted to long-distance dispersal by water (*e.g. Carex* spp., *Drosera* spp., *Potentilla palustris, Scheuchzeria palustris*); only vegetative parts of *Sphagnum* species seem to be dispersed by the wind. These results agree with those of Salonen (1987), who states that the vast majority (99%) of those species which could be found in the diaspore rain in two areas abandoned after peat harvesting in Finland possessed some kind of transportation device.

Diaspore bank and persistence

The results of this investigation of the diaspore bank are in contrast to those of Moore & Wein (1977), who remarked that in *Sphagnum*-dominated bogs there is no diaspore bank of spermatophytes. In the present study, the diaspores of *Calluna vulgaris* and *Rhynchospora alba* seem to be persistent for several decades (classification of persistence according to Poschlod, 1993). *Calluna vulgaris* had the highest density of diaspores in the soil, which agrees with observations in other habitats where *Calluna vulgaris* is growing (Granström, 1988). Hill & Stevens (1981) and Granström (1988) found diaspores of *Calluna* in afforestations on former heath sites which were more than 45 and 70 years old, respectively. Diaspores of *Calluna vulgaris* and *Rhynchospora alba* may persist for more than 100 years (based on an age–depth relationship; McGraw, 1987). *Drosera rotundifolia* was the only other raised bog species found. The persistence of its diaspores seems to be from several years to a few decades (Pfadenhauer & Maas, 1987). *Molinia caerulea, Carex canescens* and *Juncus effusus* are species of disturbed raised bogs. Their diaspores were only found in the 'top spit'. The persistence of diaspores of *Molinia* is probably a few years or several years to a few decades (Pfadenhauer & Maas, 1987; Bakker, 1989); that of *Carex canescens* and *Juncus effusus* is several decades (Kasahara, Nishi & Ueyama, 1967; McGraw, 1987).

Diaspores of other spermatophyte species were not found on any investigated sites. In most cases these species have a transient diaspore bank (persistence <1 year or 1–2 years, Poschlod, 1993), *e.g.. Eriophorum vaginatum* whose diaspores have no dormancy at all (Poschlod, 1990; although in the tundra of Alaska the diaspore bank of *Eriophorum vaginatum* was determined as persistent (McGraw, 1980)). The dormancy is probably site dependent (Simpson, 1990).

Other species of Ericaceae, like *Andromeda polifolia, Vaccinium* spp. (including *V. oxycoccos, V. uliginosum*), were also not found in the diaspore bank, although these species possess diaspores with an innate dormancy. Dormancy could also be enforced by darkness (Poschlod, 1990). This combination is a characteristic of persistent diaspores (Grime, 1989). It is possible that they have such a sparse density that they could not be caught by the sample design used. Another possibility is that the thin and smooth seed coat of the *Vaccinium* species decomposes very quickly.

In the diaspore bank of bryophytes, six liverworts were found in the Wieninger Filz and in the Kollerfilze, although most species could not be detected in the actual vegetation. All species except *Kurzia pauciflora* have tubers (Smith, 1990). *Cephalozia connivens* and *Kurzia pauciflora* have a subterranean shoot axis. *Calypogeia* species have their shoot axis near the surface (Pocock & Duckett, 1985). Duckett & Clymo (1988) showed that a diaspore bank of liverworts is probably based on the regenerating shoot axis. The depth distribution of liverwort species in this study corroborates their hypothesis in most cases. Protonemata were also often found attached to some individuals, so that a diaspore bank of spores probably also exists.

All *Sphagnum* species typical of raised bogs were found in the diaspore bank, sometimes even diaspores of species not present in the current vegetation. Only *Sphagnum tenellum* was not found, although it occurred at one investigated site. In the upper layers (0–15 cm) of the natural stands and in the 'top spit' new shoots arose from vegetative parts, mostly from the stem, which appeared to be brown and dead (Photograph 1). In deeper layers of the natural stands and in the 'top spit' shoots arose from protonemata (Photographs 2, 3). In most cases they are thought to have grown from germinated spores (*e.g.* Figure 2). Clymo & Duckett (1986) found similar results from bogs in mid-Wales and New Hampshire. They supposed that the matrix from which regeneration took place was 25 to perhaps 60 years old. The possibility of a spore input from outside and a downwash in deeper layers can be rejected (Clymo & MacKay, 1987) so that our results, where regeneration could be found in layers down to 30 cm depth, suggest that the diaspore bank of *Sphagnum* species can be persistent for at least several decades.

The diaspore bank of other mosses seems to consist of spores (During & ter Horst, 1983). Only *Aulacomnium palustre* and *Pleurozium schreberi* regenerated out of brown, apparently dead shoots from upper layers (see Longton & Greene, 1979). Probably in most cases the diaspore bank of these species, which form a spore bank, is very persistent.

Photograph 1. Regeneration from pre-existing shoots of *Sphagnum magellanicum* (Wieninger Filz site 3, depth 5–10 cm).

Photograph 2. Development of *Sphagnum* species (*S. capillifolium, S. cuspidatum*), probably from spores on an *Eriophorum vaginatum* fibre (Wieninger Filz site 3, depth 15–20 cm).

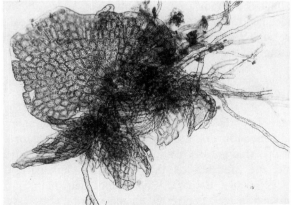

Photograph 3. Detail of a young *Sphagnum* shoot with the protonemal filament and the protonemal plate (see Photograph 2).

Diaspore bank and site factors

Water seems to be an important factor for the persistence of a diaspore bank, at least for the bryophytes. In the natural stand with the deepest water table (Wieninger Filz, site 1) there was no diaspore bank of bryophytes, with the exception of *Kurzia pauciflora*. Spores of some mesic fern species remain viable for a longer time under hydrated than under dry conditions (Dyer & Lindsay, 1992). Results from wet and dry stored 'top spit' from raised bogs of north-west Germany showed no evidence of a diaspore bank of raised bog species in the latter (Roderfeld, 1992), indicating that the top spit should therefore be stored under wet conditions. This can be achieved using excavation methods like the 'Bagger-verfahren' (excavator method, Schmatzler, 1993).

Implication for restoration management of peatland sites mined by milling

The results of studies of vegetation development on bare peat areas (Poschlod, 1990; Maas & Poschlod, 1991; Schuckert *et al.*, 1991) show that at least short term succession towards the former raised bog communities needs intervention. The surface layer or 'top spit' seems to have at least some potential to provide an inoculum for certain important bog species, for example, some *Sphagnum* species seem to have a diaspore bank persistent for several decades. It also seems to have a positive effect on germination and establishment (Roderfeld, 1992). In old peat pits of raised bogs in the foothills of the Alps, excavated by peat cutting by hand or machines, where the 'top spit' was deposited after peat mining, new peat was formed up to a depth of more than 1 m (Poschlod, 1990, 1992). For example, in one peat pit of the Wieninger Filz where peat cutting was finished in 1940, 70 cm of new peat was formed on the 'top spit' after peat mining (Poschlod, 1990). The hydrological conditions in those peat pits were constant water tables during almost the whole year, not more than 15 (20) cm below the surface (Poschlod, 1990). In the investigated region, the foothills of the Alps, the annual amounts of rainfall are between 1100 and 1700 mm (see description of sites, above). The annual distribution is adequate for the growth of *Sphagnum* species typical of raised bogs. Therefore, future studies of the regeneration of peat sites mined by milling should include the spreading of the 'top spit'.

ACKNOWLEDGEMENTS

This study was supported by Bayerisches Staatsministerium für Landes-entwicklung und Umweltfragen. I thank Prof. Dr Pfadenhauer for the opportunity for carrying out this study at his institution, Dipl.-Biol. Hermann Schrag for the photographs and the students of the Technical University of Munich in Weihenstephan, especially Barbara Kaiser, for their help in the field and glasshouse. Ann-Kathrin Jackel corrected the manuscript.

REFERENCES

Bakker, J.P. (1989). Nature management by grazing and cutting. On the ecological significance of grazing and cutting regimes applied to restore former species-rich grassland communities in the Netherlands. *Geobotany*, **14**, 400 pp.

Clymo, R.S. & Duckett, J.G. (1986). Regeneration of *Sphagnum*. *New Phytologist*, **102**, 589–614.

Clymo, R.S. & MacKay, D. (1987). Upwash and downwash of pollen and spores in the unsaturated surface layer of *Sphagnum*-dominated peat. *New Phytologist*, **105**, 175–183.

Duckett, J.G. & Clymo, R.S. (1988). Regeneration of bog liverworts. *New Phytologist*, **110**, 119–127.

During, H.J. & ter Horst, B. (1983). The diaspore bank of bryophytes and ferns in chalk grassland. *Lindbergia*, **9**, 57–64.

Dyer, A.F. & Lindsay, S. (1992). Soil spore banks of temperate ferns. *American Fern Journal*, **82 (3)**, 89–122.

Ehrendorfer, E. (1973). *Liste der Gefäßpflanzen Mitteleuropas*. Fischer, Stuttgart.

Granström, A. (1988). Seed banks at six open and afforested heathland sites in Southern Sweden. *Journal of Applied Ecology*, **25**, 297–306.

Grime, J.P. (1989). Seed banks in ecological perspective. *Ecology of Soil Seed Banks* (eds. Leck, M.A., Parker, V.T. & Simpson, R.L.), p. XV–XXII, Academic Press, San Diego, London.

Hill, M.O. & Stevens, P.A. (1981). The density of viable seed in soils of forest plantations in upland Britain. *Journal of Ecology*, **69**, 693–709.

Janssens, J.A. (1987). Ecology of peatland bryophytes and palaeoenvironmental reconstruction of peatlands using fossil bryophytes. *Limnological Research Center Contribution*, **346**, 67pp.

Kasahara, Y., Nishi, K. & Ueyama, Y. (1967). Studies on the germination of seeds and their growth in rush (*Juncus effusus* L. var. *decipiens* Buchen.) and weeds buried for about fifty years. *Hikobia*, **5**, 91–103.

Longton, R.E. & Greene, S.W. (1979). Experimental studies of growth and reproduction in the moss *Pleurozium schreberi* (Brid.) Mitt. *Journal of Bryology*, **10**, 321–338.

Maas, D. & Poschlod, P. (1991). Restoration of exploited peat areas in raised bogs – technical management and vegetation development. *Terrestrial and Aquatic Ecosystems: Perturbation and Recovery* (ed. O. Ravera), p. 379–386. Ellis Horwood, London.

McGraw, J.B. (1980). Seed bank size and distribution of seeds in cottongrass tussock tundra, Eagle Creek, Alaska. *Canadian Journal of Botany*, **58**, 1607–1611.

McGraw, J.B. (1987). Seed bank properties of an Appalachian *Sphagnum* bog and a model of the depth distribution of viable seeds. *Canadian Journal of Botany*, **65**, 2028–2035.

Moore, J.M. & Wein, R.W. (1977). Viable seed populations by soil depth and potential site recolonisation after disturbance. *Canadian Journal of Botany*, **55**, 2408–2412.

Oehlmann, V. (1898) *Vegetative Fortpflanzung der Sphagnaceen nebst ihrem Verhalten gegen Kalk*. PhD thesis, Freiburg.

Pfadenhauer, J. & Maas, D. (1987). Samenpotential in Niedermoorböden des Alpen-vorlandes bei Grünlandnutzung unterschiedlicher Intensität. *Flora*, **179**, 85–97.

Pfadenhauer, J., Siuda, C. & Krinner, C. (1990). Ökologisches Entwicklungskonzept Kendlmühlfilzen. *Schriftenreihe Bayerisches Landesamt für Umweltschutz*, **91**, 1–61.

Pocock, K. & Duckett, J.G. (1985). On the occurences of branched and swollen rhizoids in British hepatics: their relationships with the substratum and associations with fungi. *New Phytologist*, **99**, 281–304.

Poschlod, P. (1990). Vegetationsentwicklung in abgetorften Hochmooren des bayerischen Alpenvorlandes unter besonderer Berücksichtigung standortskundlicher und populationsbiologischer Faktoren. *Dissertationes Botanicae*, **152**, 331 pp.

Poschlod P. (1992). Development of vegetation in peat-mined areas in some bogs in the foothills of the Alps. *Peatland Ecosystems and Man – an Impact Assessment* (eds. O.M. Bragg, P.D. Hulme, H.A.P. Ingram, & R.A.Robertson,), pp. 287–290. International Peat Society/Department of Biological Sciences, University of Dundee, Dundee.

Poschlod, P. (1993). Zur Dauerhaftigkeit von Diasporenbanken in Böden und deren Bedeutung für den Arten- und Biotopschutz am Beispiel von Kalkmagerrasenstandorten. *Verhandlungen der Gesellschaft für Ökologie*, **22**, 229–240.

Poschlod, P. & Jordan, S. (1992). Wiederbesiedlung eines aufgeforsteten Kalkmagerrasenstandorts nach Rodung. *Zeitschrift für Ökologie und Naturschutz*, **1**, 119–139.

Poschlod, P. & Pfadenhauer, J. (1989). Regeneration vegetativer Sproßteilchen von Torfmoosen – Eine vergleichende Studie an neun *Sphagnum*-Arten. *Telma*, **19**, 77–88.

Poschlod, P. & Schrag, H. (1990). Regeneration vegetativer Sproßteilchen von Braunmoosen. *Telma*, **20**, 291–300.

Roderfeld, H. (1992). *Die ökologische Wertigkeit von Bunkerde in Nordwestdeutschland.* PhD thesis, University of Göttingen.

Salonen, V. (1987). Relationship between the seed rain and the establishment of vegetation in two areas abandoned after peat harvesting. *Holarctic Ecology*, **10**, 171–174.

Schmatzler, E. (1993). Forderungen des Naturschutzes an den künftigen Abbau von Torf. *Telma*, **23**, 287–296.

Schmeidl, H., Schuch, M. & Wanke, R. (1970). Wasserhaushalt und Klima einer kultivierten und unberührten Hochmoorfläche am Alpenrand. *Schriftenreihe Kuratorium für Kulturbauwesen*, **19**, 171pp.

Schuckert, U. & Poschlod, P. (1991). Renaturierung von Badetorfdeponien im Steinacher Ried (Bad Waldsee). *Verhandlungen der Gesellschaft für Ökologie*, **20**, 275–284.

Schuckert, U. & Poschlod, P. (1993). Ansiedlung standortgerechter Moorvegetation auf Badetorfdeponien in Bad Waldsee (Oberschwaben) – Erkenntnisstand nach 3-jährifer Versuchsdauer. *Berichte Institut für Landschafts- und Pflanzenökologie Universität Hohenheim*, **2**, 243–254.

Schuckert, U., Poschlod, P. & Kobert, R. (1991). Vergleichende Untersuchung der Vegetationsentwicklung auf oberschwäbischen Badetorfdeponien. Ursachen und Konsequenzen für die Planung. *Telma*, **21**, 245–262.

Simpson, G.M. (1990). *Seed Dormancy in Grasses.* Cambridge University Press, Cambridge.

Smith, A.J.E. (1978). *The Moss Flora of Britain and Ireland.* Cambridge University Press, Cambridge.

Smith, A.J.E. (1990). *The Liverworts of Britain and Ireland.* Cambridge University Press, Cambridge.

Werner, P.A. (1975). A seed trap for determining patterns of seed deposition in terrestrial plants. *Canadian Journal of Botany*, **53**, 801–813.

32 Blanket Mires in the Upland Landscape

J. H. TALLIS

School of Biological Sciences, University of Manchester, Williamson Building, Oxford Road, Manchester, M13 9PL, UK

SUMMARY

1.   British blanket mires are important both in an international context (as forming a major part of a scarce global resource) and in a national one (as an integral component of the upland landscape).

2.   Many blanket mires exhibit in their development a long period of peat accumulation followed by a more recent phase of degradation.

3.   Degradation involves various types of damage to the mire surface that may lead to exposure of bare peat; failure of the bare peat to revegetate usually results in erosion in the harsh upland environment.

4.   Extensive blanket peat erosion can have serious economic and recreational consequences; most measures to combat peat erosion have concentrated on establishment of a protective plant cover rather than on restoration of the original vegetation.

5.   The commonest type of blanket mire erosion is by gullying. Studies at a limited number of sites indicate three different time-periods for the initiation of gullying, which may represent successive developmental stages: before 1500 BP, 1200–900 BP, and 600–250 BP.

6.   Gullying may have been triggered by the clearance of hillslope forests in later prehistoric times; however, the natural break-up of an intrinsically unstable peat mass cannot be ruled out as an alternative method for the initiation of gullying.

INTRODUCTION

Blanket mire ecology is currently a rather neglected field of study in Britain, though why this should be so is hard to understand, as blanket mires are among the most important of British vegetation types in an international context, comprising more than 2 million hectares of a total global blanket mire resource of perhaps 10–12 million hectares (Figure 1). British blanket mires are an integral and important part of the upland landscape, where their presence contributes substantially to patterns of land-use, water catchment and tourism. Many of these blanket mires still possess an undamaged plant cover over large areas, whereas British raised mires are extensively damaged and essentially curiosities in the lowland

Restoration of Temperate Wetlands. Edited by B.D. Wheeler, S.C. Shaw, W.J. Fojt and R.A. Robertson
© 1995 John Wiley & Sons Ltd.

496

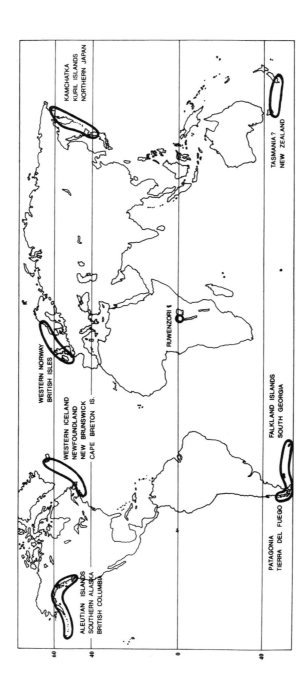

Figure 1. Blanket mires: a scarce global resource. Blanket mires occur only within the regions enclosed by heavy lines. Based on maps in Lindsay *et al.* (1988) and Chambers (1993).

landscape. Both raised and blanket mires have in their peat deposits an archival record that can be used as a proxy source of information about past climatic changes and land-use systems. It is the raised mire record that has been largely used to date. However, rather few raised mires in this country have undamaged peat deposits covering the last 1000–1500 years, when human activity has been most intense, whereas such deposits are commonplace in blanket mires. Moreover, the potential of blanket mires to record the climatic changes already widely recognised in raised mire deposits (as, for example, recurrence surfaces) is just beginning to be realised (Chambers, 1993).

THE RESILIENCE OF THE BLANKET MIRE SYSTEM

Blanket mires have been an evolving part of the upland landscape in Britain for at least 7000 years, though the exact time-span varies from one geographical region to another (Figure 2). During that period blanket mires have accumulated peat at rates substantially similar to those of raised mires (Aaby, 1976) – between 1 and 12 cm per century generally (Figure 3) – to achieve peat depths locally in excess of 5 m. Throughout their history blanket mires have been subjected to the influence of a continually varying climate and human presence, and thus have experienced periodic change and disturbance. Indeed, many blanket mires originated through perturbation, following destruction of the higher-altitude forest and scrub (Jacobi, Tallis & Mellars, 1976; Tallis, 1991; Moore, 1993); nevertheless they subsequently exhibited a considerable inertia or resistance to change ('resilience'; Walker, 1982) as peat built up. The peat archives show clearly that blanket mires in this 'accumulation mode' were able to withstand repeated perturbations to the system that temporarily checked peat growth, but were unable to bring about lasting damage – as witnessed in the peat profiles by recurrence surfaces (Figure 4) and tree stump layers (Birks, 1975; Tallis & Switsur, 1983; Gear & Huntley, 1991), recording periods of drying-out of the mire surface, and the periodic peaks of carbonised plant material, recording major fires across the mire surface (Figure 5).

Many British blanket mires, however, are currently in a damaged or degraded states, with local or more widespread cessation of peat growth. Damage to the mire system can take a variety of forms, representing three different types of process operating on the peat mass (Figure 6):

(a) superficial damage, affecting the general mire surface, and resulting from deliberate or accidental burning, grazing by sheep and deer, trampling (particularly along well-used paths), air pollution and constructional work such as the installation of pipelines;

(b) incision damage, involving local removal of the peat mass by peat cutting, or by ditching and gullying;

(c) marginal damage, involving local or more catastrophic disturbance at the edges of the peat blanket, as a result of sheep grazing or mass movement (peat slides and bog bursts).

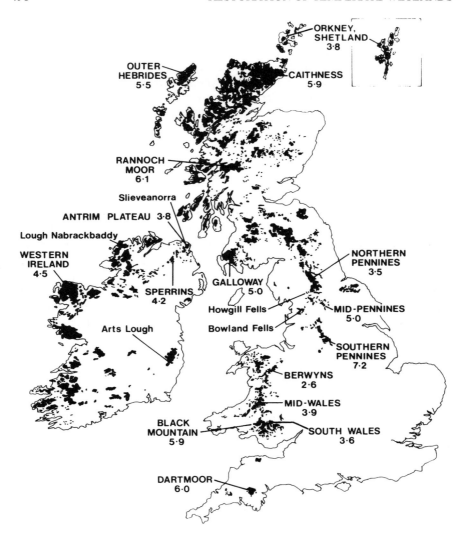

Figure 2. Distribution of blanket peat in the British Isles, and time of onset of widespread peat accumulation in different geographical regions (in thousands of years BP); also shown are locations of certain sites mentioned in the text. Based on maps in Taylor (1983) and Lindsay *et al.* (1988), and on data in Tallis (1994b).

A compilation of data about damage to blanket mires, with particular reference to the Peak District National Park in the Southern Pennines, is given by Phillips, Yalden & Tallis (1981). They identify sheep grazing, regular 'muirburn' (*i.e.* controlled rotational burning), periodic wildfires, air pollution and trampling along long-distance footpaths as major causes of the current degraded state of the Peak

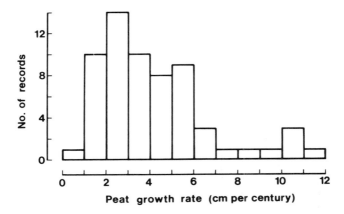

Figure 3. Summary of records of blanket peat growth rates (cm per century), calculated from depths of peat accumulated between successive radiocarbon-dated horizons. Data from Tallis & Switsur (1973), Turner *et al.* (1973), Chambers (1978, 1982, 1983), Pennington *et al.* (1972), Pilcher (1973), Keatinge & Dickson (1979), Pearson (1979), Smith *et al.* (1981), Simmons, Rand & Crabtree (1983), Rowell & Turner (1985), Caseldine & Maguire (1986), Robinson (1987), Robinson & Dickson (1988), Smith & Cloutman (1988), Smith & Taylor (1989) and Tipping, Edmonds & Sheridan (1993).

District moorlands. Commercial peat extraction from upland blanket mires is not generally the important factor that it is in lowland raised mires, though domestic peat cutting is widespread in parts of Ireland and Scotland (Cruickshank *et al.*, 1993).

Damage to blanket mires often results in local or more extensive destruction of the plant cover, so that bare peat is exposed. In some regions such bare peat areas may remain uncolonised by plants for long periods of time. Thus in the Southern Pennines, bare peat areas are known that originated variously from wildfire damage in 1947, 1959, 1976 and 1980 (Phillips *et al.*, 1981; Anderson, 1986); and at one site much of the devastation resulting from a cloudburst in July 1834 is still visible (Montgomery & Shimwell, 1985). A number of factors have been identified that hamper recolonisation of bare peat in the uplands: lack of suitable seed sources, a physically unstable and chemically infertile substrate, and grazing and trampling by sheep (Tallis & Yalden, 1983; North York Moors National Park, 1985). In the harsh climatic conditions of the British uplands, erosion is often the inevitable consequence of the failure of bare peat to revegetate. Once erosion sets in, through the action of rain, snow, frost, wind and drought, peat loss rather than peat growth may proceed quite rapidly (Table 1).

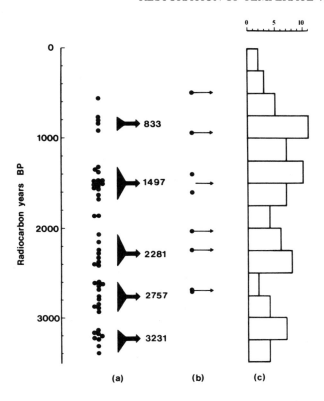

Figure 4. (a) Radiocarbon dates (•1) of recurrence surfaces in six British raised mires, and calculated mean values of apparent date-clusters (data of Dickson (1975), Barber (1981) and Dresser (1985)). (b) Radiocarbon dates of recurrence surfaces in two Southern Pennine blanket mires (data of Tallis & Switsur (1973) and Tallis & Livett (1994)). (c) Number of records of radiocarbon dates for recurrence surfaces in Scandinavian raised mires, grouped in 250-yr time-intervals (data of Aaby (1976) and Tallis (1983)).

Table 1. Rates of peat erosion, as determined by erosion pins; values are mean rates of surface lowering (mm per year) over small areas ± S.D. For sources of data (mostly from sites in the Southern Pennines), see Tallis (1994b).

Superficial erosion (gently-sloping bare peat expanses)		28.7 ± 11.6 (n = 10)
Incision erosion:	gully sides	11.9 ± 5.3 (n = 5)
	gully floors	5.5 ± 2.8 (n = 3)

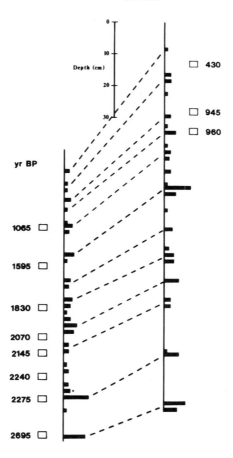

Figure 5. Relative frequency of carbonised plant fragments (black histogram bars) in 1-cm³ samples down two peat columns 3 m apart, from Alport Moor, Southern Pennines; the interrupted lines link corresponding carbonisation peaks in the two profiles. The open rectangles show positions of radiocarbon-dated samples (yr BP).

THE SIGNIFICANCE OF BLANKET MIRE EROSION

Because blanket mires are an important component of many upland landscapes, the onset of erosion may have consequences outside the immediate ecosystem. Thus the removal of the plant cover itself represents lost grazing for animal stock, and lost grazing and shelter for game birds, and can accordingly be quantified in economic terms (Phillips *et al.*, 1981); the peat and soil material removed by erosion can be redeposited in reservoirs lower down the catchment, leading to problems of sediment-infilling (Labadz, Burt & Potter, 1991) and discoloration of drinking water (Butcher, 1992); and the amenity value of upland landscapes may

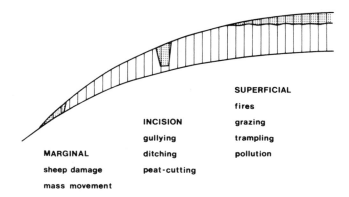

Figure 6. Different types of damage to the blanket mire surface. In this diagrammatic profile through a blanket peat deposit, areas affected are stippled.

also be reduced by erosion – thus severely eroded areas are often visually unattractive, and trampled peat along long-distance footpaths difficult to traverse. Remedial action aimed at alleviating these adverse consequences of erosion has to date concentrated on stabilising and revegetating the bare peat areas, rather than on the restoration of the 'natural' mire vegetation (Tallis & Yalden, 1983; North York Moors National Park, 1985). Revegetation procedures have to overcome the intransigent properties of a harsh upland climate (Phillips *et al.*, 1981; Fullen, 1983), the catotelm peat that is frequently exposed following erosion, and a peat mass whose hydrology has often been irreversibly changed by drainage resulting from gullying.

GULLY EROSION OF BLANKET PEAT

Gullying is the commonest type of damage in most British blanket mires. The gullies are typically linked into a drainage network continuous with the stream systems of the whole landscape, and conformable with the surface contours of the peat mass itself. On sloping ground the gullies run nearly parallel to each other and are sparsely branched, whereas on flat ground there is an anastomosing system of richly-branched gullies (Figure 7): Bower (1960) called these Type 2 and Type 1 gullies, respectively.

Various suggestions have been made regarding the origin of these gully systems (Bower, 1962): that they formed

(a) on a drying mire surface following a natural cessation of peat growth, either as a result of climatic change or as an inevitable consequence of continued decay within the peat mass (Clymo, 1984);

(b) by catastrophic termination of peat accumulation in an increasingly unstable system (Conway, 1954; Pearsall, 1956);

(c) on a damaged mire surface following perturbation to the system – by burning, grazing, ditching, or pollution damage.

Gullying of a peat mass results in enhanced drainage of the surface layers adjoining the gullies, up to a distance of about 5 m from a gully edge (Stewart & Lance, 1983). The longer a gully system is in existence, the greater its effect on the overall water table of the peat mass is likely to be. The hydrology of a deeply and closely gullied peat mass is probably irreversibly changed. Hence a knowledge of the age of blanket mire gully systems is important for assessing the viability of restoration schemes; in addition, it may help in identifying the possible causes of the gullying. Data pertinent to the time of origin of blanket mire gullying are available for a number of sites in the British Isles (Figure 2): Slieveanorra (McGreal & Larmour, 1979), Arts Lough and Lough Nabrackbaddy (Bradshaw & McGee, 1988) in Ireland; Loch Laidon (Rannoch Moor) and the Round Loch of Glenhead, Galloway (Stevenson, Jones & Batterbee, 1990) in Scotland; the Berwyn Mountains (Bostock, 1980) in Wales; and the Howgill and Bowland Fells (Harvey et al., 1981; Harvey & Renwick, 1987; Mackay, 1993), and the Southern Pennines (Tallis, 1964, 1965, 1985, 1987 and 1994a; Tallis & Livett, 1994; Livett & Tallis, 1989) in Northern England. The Southern Pennine studies are the most comprehensive, involving suites of adjoining eroded and uneroded sites at five different locations.

Results from the various studies are summarised in Figure 8. Three clusters of dates for the time of onset of gullying can be recognised:

(1) a set of early dates covering the time-period from c. 4500 to 1500 yr BP;

(2) dates for three areas between c. 1200 and 900 yr BP;

(3) a set of dates from the Southern Pennines and the two Scottish sites covering the time-period from c. 600 to 250 yr BP (AD 1350–1700).

These date-clusters may represent not only regional differences in the time of onset or erosion, but also different phases of erosion within a single region. Thus in the Southern Pennines, dates for Type 2 (linear) gullies fall entirely within the third phase of erosion, while those for Type 1 (reticulate) gullies span the second and third phases (Figure 7). It is probable that the early dates (phase 1), recorded at a number of geographically widely-separated sites, relate to disturbances at the peat margin and to the headward extension of streams into the peat blanket along major drainage lines determined by the pre-peat contours of the landscape. One reason for active cutting-back of upland streams might be forest clearance from the hillslopes, which in many regions of Britain was initiated in prehistoric times (Birks, 1988), and represented a serious perturbation to the upland landscape. Type 1 gullying probably developed when these rejuvenated streams began to draw off water from the pool systems on flatter ground. Type 2 gullying, on the other hand, is more closely related in time, in the Southern Pennines at least, to increasing anthropogenic modification of the mire surface during the last 600 years.

Some check on the likely age of peat gullies can be made from calculations of the time required for gullies of a given size to be incised, at current rates of erosion. Two such studies have been carried out, both in the Southern Pennines

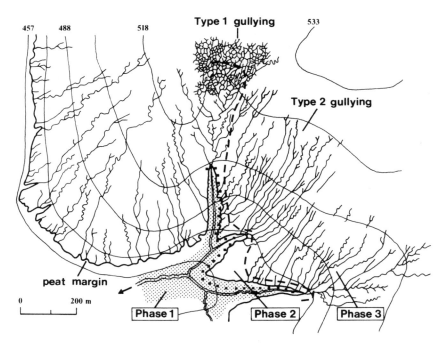

Figure 7. Gully types on Featherbed Moss, Southern Pennines, in relation to surface topography (contour lines in metres), and probable stages in their development (shown for right-hand side of map only. During Phase 1 (prior to *c.* 1200 yr BP), major gullies began to form at the margins of the peat blanket; during Phase 2 (*c.* 1200–900 yr BP), extensive Type 1 gully systems developed; and during Phase 3 (*c.* 600–0 yr BP), Type 2 gully systems were incised.

(Tallis, 1973; Labadz *et al.*, 1991). Both give probable ages of 200–250 years, but for rather small gullies of cross-sectional area 1.0–1.5 m^2. As the larger gullies there have a cross-sectional area of 4–5 m^2, their age is likely to be in excess of 500 years.

If that is so, then gully systems, and the associated lowering of water tables, have been a feature of blanket mires for many centuries. Drying-out of the blanket mire surface has apparently occurred repeatedly in the past also (as evidenced by tree stump layers and recurrence surfaces in the peat), but these drier episodes were mostly of shorter duration. The best available estimate is probably that of Gear & Huntley (1991), who found a pine stump layer in a northern Scottish blanket mire that spanned about a 350-year period. At Alport Moor in the Southern Pennines, Tallis & Livett (1994) found evidence of four dry episodes in the peat stratigraphy between 945 and 2275 yr BP, lasting variously from 35 to 235 years. In many British lowland raised mire peats the most recent drying episode, preceding a return to wetter conditions, is of mediaeval age and radiocarbon-dated to between 550 and 900 yr BP (Figure 4). That return to wetter conditions is not

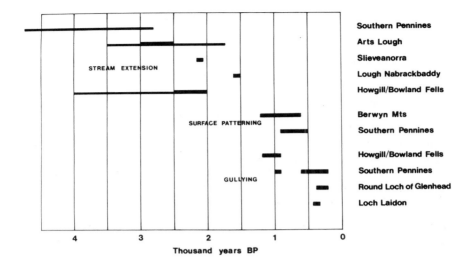

Figure 8. Approximate times of onset of peat erosion at nine sites in the British Isles; where the possible range is large, the most likely time-period is emphasised.

recorded at the more severely eroded blanket mire sites in the Southern Pennines, where a dry mire surface has now been present for a longer period than at any time previously in the last 2700 years. As a result, the hydrology of the peat mass is probably fundamentally altered.

A possible explanation for the development of erosion there might invoke Roman forest clearance as the trigger, and post-mediaeval sheep farming as subsequently accentuating and prolonging indefinitely the effects of the mediaeval dry phase. Whether such an explanation can be extended to other blanket mire regions of Britain is uncertain. The alternative view, that erosion is a natural consequence of peat accumulation, begotten by increasing instability of the peat mass, is still inherently plausible and cannot yet be discounted. Some assessment of the relative roles of the two processes in terminating peat growth is now urgently required if our blanket mire heritage is to be effectively conserved.

REFERENCES

Aaby, B. (1976). Cyclic variations in climate over the past 5,500 yr reflected in raised bogs. *Nature, London,* **263**, 281–284.

Anderson, P. (1986). *Accidental Moorland Fires in the Peak District.* Peak Park Joint Planning Board, Bakewell, Derbyshire.

Barber, K.E. (1981). *Peat Stratigraphy and Climatic Change.* Balkema, Rotterdam.

Birks, H.H. (1975). Studies in the vegetational history of Scotland IV. Pine stumps in Scottish blanket peats. *Philosophical Transactions of the Royal Society of London, Series*

B, **270**, 181–226.

Birks, H.J.B. (1988). Long-term ecological change in the British uplands. *Ecological Change in the Uplands* (eds M.B. Usher & D.B.A. Thompson), pp. 37–56. Blackwell, Oxford.

Bostock, J. (1980). *The history of the vegetation of the Berwyn Mountains, North Wales, with emphasis on the development of the blanket bog.* PhD thesis, University of Manchester.

Bower, M.M. (1960). Peat erosion in the Pennines. *Advancement of Science*, **64**, 323–331.

Bower, M.M. (1962). The cause of erosion in blanket peat bogs. *Scottish Geographical Magazine*, **78**, 33–43.

Bradshaw, R. & McGee, E. (1988). The extent and time course of mountain blanket peat erosion in Ireland. *New Phytologist*, **108**, 219–224.

Butcher, D.P. (1992). The Southern Pennines: peat erosion and reservoir sedimentation. *First International ESSC Congress. Post-Congress Tour Guide* (ed. J. Boardman), pp. 11–17. School of Geography, University of Oxford.

Caseldine, C.J. & Maguire, D.J. (1986). Late glacial/early Flandrian vegetation change on northern Dartmoor, south-west England. *Journal of Biogeography*, **13**, 255–264.

Chambers, C. (1978). A radiocarbon-dated pollen diagram from Valley Bog, on the Moor House National Nature Reserve. *New Phytologist*, **80**, 273–280.

Chambers, F.M. (1982). Two radiocarbon-dated pollen diagrams from high-altitude blanket peats in South Wales. *Journal of Ecology*, **70**, 445–459.

Chambers, F.M. (1983). Three radiocarbon-dated pollen diagrams from upland peats north-west of Merthyr Tydfil, South Wales. *Journal of Ecology*, **71**, 475–487.

Chambers, F. (1993). Late Quaternary climatic change and human impact: commentary and conclusions. *Climate Change and Human Impact on the Landscape* (ed. F. Chambers), pp. 247–259. Chapman & Hall, London.

Clymo, R.S. (1984). The limits to peat bog growth. *Philosophical Transactions of the Royal Society of London, Series B*, **303**, 605–654.

Conway, V.M. (1954). The stratigraphy and pollen analysis of southern Pennine blanket peats. *Journal of Ecology*, **42**, 117–147.

Cruickshank, M.M., Tomlinson, R.W., Dunwoody, C., Bond, D. & Devine, P.M. (1993). A peatland database for Northern Ireland: methodology and potential resource. *Proceedings of the Royal Irish Academy*, **93B**, 13–24.

Dickinson, W. (1975). Recurrence surfaces in Rusland Moss, Cumbria (formerly North Lancashire). *Journal of Ecology*, **63**, 913–935.

Dresser, Q. (1985). University College Cardiff Radiocarbon Dates I. *Radiocarbon*, **27**, 338–385.

Fullen, M.A. (1983). Some changes in air temperature and wind velocity after burning of heather (*Calluna vulgaris*) moor and their relation to moorland surface processes. *The Naturalist*, **108**, 17–24.

Gear, A.J. & Huntley, B. (1991). Rapid changes in the range limits of Scots pine 4,000 years ago. *Science, New York*, **251**, 544–547.

Harvey, A.M. & Renwick, W.H. (1987). Holocene alluvial fan and terrace formation in the Bowland Fells, Northwest England. *Earth Surface Processes and Landforms*, **12**, 249–257.

Harvey, A.M., Oldfield, F., Baron, A.F. & Pearson, G.W. (1981). Dating of post-glacial landforms in the Central Howgills. *Earth Surface Processes and Landforms*, **6**, 401–412.

Jacobi, R.M., Tallis, J.H. & Mellars, P.A. (1976). The Southern Pennine Mesolithic and the archaeological record. *Journal of Archaeological Science*, **3**, 307–320.

Keatinge, T.H. & Dickson, J.H. (1979). Mid-Flandrian changes in vegetation on Mainland Orkney. *New Phytologist*, **82**, 585–612.

Labadz, J.C., Burt, T.P. & Potter, A.W.R. (1991). Sediment yield and delivery in the blanket peat moorlands of the Southern Pennines. *Earth Surface Processes and Landforms*, **16**, 255–271.

Lindsay, R.A., Charman, D.J., Everingham, F., O'Reilly, R.M., Palmer, M.A., Rowell, T.A. & Stroud, D.A. (1988). *The Flow Country. The Peatlands of Caithness and Sutherland*. Nature Conservancy Council, Peterborough.

Livett, E.A. & Tallis, J.H. (1989). *A History of the Kinder Moorlands over the last 1,000 Years*. Internal Report for the National Trust, Edale, Derbyshire.

Mackay, A.W. (1993). *The recent vegetational history of the Forest of Bowland, Lancashire*. PhD thesis, University of Manchester.

McGreal, W.S. & Larmour, R.A. (1979). Blanket peat erosion: theoretical considerations and observations from selected conservation sites in Slieveanorra Forest National Nature Reserve, County Antrim. *Irish Geographer*, **12**, 57–67.

Montgomery, T. & Shimwell, D. (1985). *Changes in the Environment and Vegetation of the Kinder-Bleaklow SSSI, 1750–1840: Historical Perspectives and Future Conservation Policies*. Internal Report for the Peak Park Joint Planning Board, Bakewell, Derbyshire.

Moore, P.D. (1993). The origin of blanket mire, revisited. *Climate Change and Human Impact on the Landscape* (ed. F. Chambers), pp. 217–224. Chapman & Hall, London.

North York Moors National Park (1985). *Moorland Management*. North York Moors National Park, Helmsley, York.

Pearsall, W.H. (1956). Two blanket-bogs in Sutherland. *Journal of Ecology*, **44**, 493–516.

Pearson, M.C. (1979). Patterns of pools in peatlands (with particular reference to a valley head mire in Northumberland). *Palaeohydrology of the Temperate Zone* (eds Y. Vasari, M. Saarnisto & M. Seppälä), pp. 65–72. University of Oulu, Finland.

Pennington, W., Haworth, E.Y., Bonny, A.P. & Lishman, J.P. (1972). Lake sediments in northern Scotland. *Philosophical Transactions of the Royal Society of London, Series B*, **264**, 191–274.

Phillips, J., Yalden, D. & Tallis, J. (1981). *Moorland Erosion Project, Phase 1 Report*. Peak Park Joint Planning Board, Bakewell, Derbyshire.

Pilcher, J.R. (1973). Pollen analysis and radiocarbon dating of a peat on Slieve Gallion, County Tyrone, Northern Ireland. *New Phytologist*, **72**, 681–689.

Robinson, D. (1987). Investigations into the Aukhorn peat mounds, Keiss, Caithness: pollen, plant macrofossil and charcoal analyses. *New Phytologist*, **106**, 185–200.

Robinson, D.E. & Dickson, J.H. (1988). Vegetational history and land-use: a radiocarbon-dated pollen diagram from Mochrie Moor, Arran, Scotland. *New Phytologist*, **109**, 223–251.

Rowell, T.K. & Turner, J. (1985). Litho-, humic- and pollen stratigraphy at Quick Moss, Northumberland. *Journal of Ecology*, **73**, 11–25.

Simmons, I.G., Rand, J.I. & Crabtree, K. (1983). A further pollen analytical study of the Blacklane peat section on Dartmoor, England. *New Phytologist*, **94**, 655–667.

Smith, A.G. & Cloutman, E.W. (1988). Reconstruction of Holocene vegetation history in three dimensions at Waun Fignen Felen, an upland site in South Wales. *Philosophical Transactions of the Royal Society of London, Series B*, **322**, 159–219.

Smith, A.G., Brown, G.C., Goddard, I.C., Goddard, A., Pearson, G.W. & Dresser, P.Q. (1981). Archaeology and environmental history of a barrow at Pubble, Loughermore Townland, County Londonderry. *Proceedings of the Royal Irish Academy*, **81C**, 29–66.

Smith, R.T. & Taylor, A.J. (1989). Biopedological processes in the inception of peat formation. *International Peat Journal*, **3**, 1–24.

Stevenson, A.C., Jones, V.J. & Battarbee, R.W. (1990). The cause of peat erosion: a palaeolimnological approach. *New Phytologist*, **114**, 727–735.

Stewart, A.J.R. & Lance, A.N. (1983). Moor-draining: a review of impacts on land use. *Journal of Environmental Management*, **17**, 81–99.

Tallis, J.H. (1964), Studies on Southern Pennine peats. II. The pattern of erosion. *Journal of Ecology*, **52**, 333–344.

Tallis, J.H. (1965), Studies on Southern Pennine peats. IV. Evidence of recent erosion. *Journal of Ecology*, **53**, 509–520.

Tallis, J.H. (1973), Studies on Southern Pennine peats. V. Direct observations on peat erosion and peat hydrology at Featherbed Moss, Derbyshire. *Journal of Ecology*, **61**, 1–22.

Tallis, J.H. (1983). Changes in wetland communities. *Ecosystems of the World 4A. Mires: Swamp, Bog, Fen and Moor. General Studies.* (ed. A.J.P. Gore), pp. 311–347. Elsevier, Amsterdam.

Tallis, J.H. (1985). Mass movement and erosion of a southern Pennine blanket peat. *Journal of Ecology*, **73**, 283–315.

Tallis, J.H. (1987). Fire and flood at Holme Moss: erosion processes in an upland blanket mire. *Journal of Ecology*, **75**, 1099–1129.

Tallis, J.H. (1991). Forest and moorland in the South Pennine uplands in the mid-Flandrian period. III. The spread of moorland – local, regional and national. *Journal of Ecology*, **79**, 401–415.

Tallis, J.H. (1994a). Pool-and-hummock patterning in a Southern Pennine blanket mire. II. The formation and erosion of the pool system. *Journal of Ecology*, **82**, 789–803.

Tallis, J.H. (1994b). Blanket peat erosion in Britain: a review. Unpublished manuscript.

Tallis, J.H. & Livett, E.A. (1994). Pool-and-hummock patterning in a Southern Pennine blanket mire. I. Stratigraphic profiles for the last 2,800 years. *Journal of Ecology*, **82**, 775–788.

Tallis, J.H. & Switsur, V.R. (1973). Studies on Southern Pennine peats. VI. A radiocarbon-dated pollen diagram from Featherbed Moss, Derbyshire. *Journal of Ecology*, **61**, 743–751.

Tallis, J.H. & Switsur, V.R. (1983). Forest and moorland in the South Pennine uplands in the mid-Flandrian period. I. Macrofossil evidence of the former forest cover. *Journal of Ecology*, **71**, 585–600.

Tallis, J.H. & Yalden, D.W. (1983). *Peak District Moorland Restoration Project, Phase 2 Report*. Peak Park Joint Planning Board, Bakewell, Derbyshire.

Taylor, J.A. (1983). The peatlands of Great Britain and Ireland. *Ecosystems of the World 4B. Mires: Swamp, Bog, Fen and Moor. Regional Studies.* (ed. A.J.P. Gore), pp. 1–46. Elsevier, Amsterdam.

Tipping, A., Edmonds, M. & Sheridan, A. (1993). Palaeoenvironmental investigations directly associated with a neolithic axe 'quarry' on Beinn Lawers, near Killin, Perthshire, Scotland. *New Phytologist*, **123**, 585–597.

Turner, J., Hewetson, V.P., Hibbert, F.A., Lowry, K.A. & Chambers, C. (1973). The history of the vegetation and flora of Widdybank Fell and the Cow Green reservoir basin, Upper Teesdale. *Philosophical Transactions of the Royal Society of London, Series B*, **265**, 327–408.

Walker, D. (1982). The development of resilience in burned vegetation. *The Plant Community as a Working Mechanism* (ed. E.I. Newman), pp. 27–43. Blackwell, Oxford

33 The Growth and Value of *Eriophorum angustifolium* Honck. in Relation to the Revegetation of Eroding Blanket Peat

J. R. A. RICHARDS, B. D. WHEELER & A. J. WILLIS
Department of Animal and Plant Sciences, P.O. Box 601, University of Sheffield, Sheffield, S10 2UQ, UK.

SUMMARY

1. Because the growth form, ecology and distribution of *Eriophorum angustifolium* suggest that it is a suitable species to recolonise and stabilise eroding bare blanket peat, its value in this respect was assessed in field and glasshouse studies.

2. Shoots grown in compost in pots and rooted shoots taken directly from native stands were planted on the eroded plateau (at 630 m) of Kinder Scout, Derbyshire, both within and outside a wired enclosure. A range of treatments was applied, including the addition of lime and fertilisers, and growth was monitored for three years.

3. The best growth was obtained from well-rooted shoots, pre-grown in pots, treated on Kinder with both lime and fertiliser. Grazing and trampling effects were of minor importance here.

4. The most adverse factor influencing the growth of *E. angustifolium* was the extreme acidity of the Kinder peat (pH 2.9–3.0), the best single treatment being the addition of lime. Mineral nutrients were less important, addition of potassium being the most beneficial.

5. Glasshouse experiments, involving solution culture, peat, different concentrations of calcium and different pH values, showed that the promotion of growth by lime was almost entirely attributable to its effect on pH (good growth was made at pH 3.8), the concentration of calcium having very little effect.

6. The extreme acidity of Kinder peat may result in severe proton competition; this may lead to poorer growth on Kinder, relative to two less acid sites studied, in spite of Kinder's apparent greater fertility in terms of mineral nutrients.

7. *E. angustifolium* may well be the most valuable native species for revegetating eroding blanket peat, this being too acidic for many other species. Successful revegetation on Kinder has been achieved by application of 1 t ha^{-1} lime together with 0.5 t ha^{-1} fertiliser.

Restoration of Temperate Wetlands. Edited by B.D. Wheeler, S.C. Shaw, W.J. Fojt and R.A. Robertson
© 1995 John Wiley & Sons Ltd.

INTRODUCTION

Common Cotton-grass, *Eriophorum angustifolium* Honck., a widespread plant of bogs in the British Isles and elsewhere in cool temperate parts of the Northern Hemisphere, has an interlacing rhizome system which shows good potential for stabilising eroding peat surfaces. The rapid expansion of patches of this species, its considerable ecological amplitude, relative unpalatability to sheep and its effectiveness as a pioneer coloniser all suggest that it may have considerable value in revegetating bare areas.

Although much information is available on the biology and ecology of *E. angustifolium* from earlier studies (*e.g.* Pearsall, 1938; Tansley, 1939; Phillips, 1954a; Phillips, Yalden & Tallis, 1981) many features of the growth of the plant in the field remain to be established. To elucidate this situation in relation to the value of *E. angustifolium* in revegetation of eroding, high level, blanket peat, an integrated programme of research involving field and glasshouse studies was carried out from 1987 to 1990. The work was very largely based on the Kinder Estate of the National Trust on Kinder Scout, Derbyshire in the South Pennines.

Position:
  53°23' N, 1°53' W

Study site:
  Grid ref. SK 078873

Altitude:
  c. 630 m

Rainfall:
  1400–1600 mm a^{-1}

Temperature:

January	mean max:	*c.*	1.8 °C
	mean min:	*c.*	−2.8 °C
July	mean max:	*c.*	14.9 °C
	mean min:	*c.*	8.2 °C

Substratum:
  Blanket peat (depth 0–3 (–4) m) upon Millstone Grit

Main plants:
  Eriophorum angustifolium,
  E. vaginatum, Deschampsia
  flexuosa, Empetrum nigrum,
  Rubus chamaemorus,
  Vaccinium myrtillus

Bare peat:
  c. 200 ha (22% of Kinder Estate)

Figure 1. Location and features of the Kinder plateau.

KINDER SCOUT

The much eroded plateau of Kinder Scout, with a substantial cover of strongly acidic peat, was regarded as a suitably harsh environment (Figure 1) to test the value of *E. angustifolium* in revegetation. Deep gullies are frequent, the peat varying in thickness, mostly up to 3 m and occasionally thicker. The underlying Millstone (Kinderscout) Grit, a Carboniferous sandstone, is exposed in some places. Rainfall is high, temperatures low (Garnett, 1956, 1969) and the growing season rather short. Much of the area is bare of vegetation; in 1982, when the National Trust acquired the Kinder Estate, it was established that about 200 ha were completely devegetated. The patchy vegetation is very poor in species (Figure 1), but there was a substantial cover of *Sphagnum* in earlier times.

A wired enclosure of about 0.25 ha was constructed in April 1987 to permit experimental work essentially free of grazing and trampling. This enclosure, which included a number of patches of 'residual' vegetation, mainly of *E. angustifolium, E. vaginatum, Vaccinium myrtillus* and *Deschampsia flexuosa* (Richards, 1990), was on Kinder Low, at the south-west of the plateau, and at an altitude of about 630 m; the highest point is 2088 ft (636 m).

FIELD TRIALS ON KINDER SCOUT

Trial 1

The first field trial aimed to elucidate the relative importance of acidity, fertility, fencing and the nature of the transplant in the growth of *E. angustifolium* on Kinder. The effect of heather brashings in stabilising the peat surface was also investigated.

Plots of 1.5×1.5 m were delimited; there were 13 shoots per plot and four replicates for each treatment. The major treatments, on 11 June 1987, involved the additions of combinations of (7-7-7) Growmore granular fertiliser (NPK), at 100 g m^{-2}, Alginure soil improver (based on seaweed), at 150 g m^{-2}, and ground limestone flour, at 60 g m^{-2} (Table 1). Some treatments were within the enclosure and others outside of it; heather brashings were added (in November) to several plots; some plots received no additions of fertiliser or lime and others were unplanted. Three types of transplants (13 per plot, 52 per treatment) were used: shoots pre-cultivated in pots either in moss peat or ericaceous compost, and shoots (with about 2.5 cm rhizome) used directly from natural populations. All shoots were obtained from vigorous monospecific patches of *E. angustifolium* near the Snake Pass, Derbyshire: some were planted in pots on 22 April 1987 and others transferred directly to Kinder on 11 June 1987. The potted plants were grown in favourable conditions in an open cold frame at Tapton Experimental Garden, Sheffield, for 79 days before the pots, containing the original shoots, and with any daughter shoots attached, were transferred to Kinder on 9 July 1987.

Monitoring the transplanted *E. angustifolium* included an 'end-of-season' (early

Table 1. Effect of major treatments on the growth of *Eriophorum angustifolium* after one season (September 1987) on Kinder.

Fencing	Planting	Growmore granular fertiliser (100 g m^{-2})	Ground limestone flour (60 g m^{-2})	Alginure soil improver (150 g m^{-2})	Mean no. of shoots/ original shoot
Unfenced	Pots + compost	+	+	–	5.7
Fenced	Pots + compost	+	+	–	5.3
Fenced	Pots + compost	–	–	–	3.7
Fenced	Pots + peat	–	–	–	3.0
Fenced	Direct	+	+	–	2.5
Fenced	Direct	–	+	–	1.8
Fenced	Direct	–	–	+	1.8
Fenced	Direct	+	–	–	1.5
Fenced	Direct	–	–	–	1.5
Unfenced	Direct	–	–	–	1.5

September) assessment and was continued for the next two years. Number of shoots per plant (the original shoot and any derivatives) and number and length of leaves per shoot were monitored. The total (*i.e.* summed) length of all living (green) leaves was determined for each plant, mean total leaf length per plant calculated for each treatment and pairs of treatments compared by **t** tests. Treatments were also compared by **t** tests for the number of shoots per plant (in directly-introduced transplants) or by analysis of variance and least significant difference **t** tests (potted transplants). Number of shoots is a coarser measure than total length of living leaves (a good index of growth) and, although similar trends were found for both, significance levels were slightly lower for number of shoots.

Despite the differences in the types of transplants and lack of strict comparability, the simple comparisons of growth in Table 1 give a good indication of the relative importance of the various treatments. The differences in growth shown were maintained and enhanced in the succeeding two years. No spontaneous establishment of higher plants in any plots occurred, although a few tiny seedlings of *E. angustifolium* appeared but were all killed by frost heaving in the winter. Plots treated with fertiliser, lime or Alginure developed a crust of algae, lichens and bryophytes, perhaps reflecting the effect of these treatments in raising pH of the surface peat from about 2.9–3.0 to at least 3.5, a long-lasting effect still evident at the end of the first growing season and beyond.

The effect of enclosure was determined by reference to the treatments with pots containing ericaceous compost in plots with added fertiliser and lime. Plants in the fenced and unfenced versions of this treatment did not differ significantly in either number of shoots or total length of living leaves. Also no significant benefit of exclusion of grazing and trampling was found with shoots introduced directly. The lack of effects of grazing may partly reflect the unpalatability of *E. angustifolium* compared with sown grasses and heather used in other revegetation studies, but no doubt mainly attests to the reduction of grazing pressure achieved on Kinder by the National Trust, with successful rounding up of sheep (indeed, sheep were rarely seen at all on the plateau in the present work). Previous investigations of revegetation on the uplands have concluded that enclosure is important or essential for the successful establishment of plants (Tallis & Yalden, 1983; Turtle, 1984; Bridges, 1986), but species other than *E. angustifolium* have usually been involved and grazing more prevalent.

The much greater growth of the plants previously potted compared with those introduced directly is a striking feature. Between the time of planting and the end of the first season all of the treatments with pot-grown plants showed net growth (increases in total length of living leaves) whereas in shoots introduced directly only those treated with fertiliser and lime gave growth defined in this way. Ericaceous compost was a better medium than moss peat for growth in pots; at the end of the first season, although the difference in number of shoots was not significant, difference in total leaf length (mean 43% greater with ericaceous compost) was significant (P< 0.001). A boost was given to plants pre-cultivated in ericaceous compost when introduced to plots with added fertiliser and lime. The mean number of shoots per plant was significantly greater (P<0.001) than in plots without additions. With directly-introduced plants, fertiliser together with lime was significantly more effective than either on its own, and lime and also Alginure were of significant benefit compared with the control.

Of note was the lack of benefit from fertiliser alone. This may be linked with the short-term acidification shown when fertiliser is added to peat under either field or laboratory conditions (hydrogen ions may be initially displaced by nutrient ions on peat exchange sites but be later dispersed in the peat water).

Monitoring in the second and third years showed that there was a significantly poorer over-winter performance of shoots in the potted plant treatment outside the enclosure than in its fenced equivalent. The difference probably reflected the effect of trampling, but it was overcome by greater production of new shoots in spring and summer, there being no significant differences between the two treatments at the end of the 1988 and 1989 growing seasons.

It was clear by the end of the experiment (31 August 1989) that the performance of directly-introduced shoots had been similarly poor in both fenced and unfenced controls, as well as in plots treated with fertiliser or brashings, there being fewer shoots than at the start. Modest beneficial effects were found in the Alginure and the lime treatments (increases in mean number of shoots per original shoot to 2.3 and 3, respectively) and more substantial ones (5.9 shoots/original) for the fertiliser plus lime treatment, which had provided greater benefit than the sum of the effects of either addition separately. The good performance of shoots pre-cultivated in ericaceous compost was notable even in untreated plots (11.6 shoots/original). Most outstanding, however, were the results given by the potted plants in ericaceous compost which were transplanted to plots treated with fertiliser plus lime. By the end of the trial, the fenced and unfenced versions of this treatment had 19 and 22 shoots per original shoot, respectively.

Trial 2

A second field trial was started in the middle of May 1988 to investigate more fully the effects of combinations of fertiliser and lime in view of the obvious effectiveness in promoting growth found in the first trial of Growmore granular fertiliser at 100 g m^{-2} together with lime at 60 g m^{-2}. Twelve combinations of fertiliser and lime were used, ranging from 40 to 200 g m^{-2} of each (see Figure 2). Plots within the enclosure were 1 × 1 m, two per treatment, and there were 16 directly-introduced plants per plot. Number of shoots was determined on 6 October 1988. For combinations of fertiliser and lime in which both additions were at least 140 g m^{-2}, shoot production was significantly greater (several combinations at P<0.001) than in the untreated control.

The isoline diagram joining points with the same number of shoots (Figure 2) suggests that, with additions of either fertiliser or lime up to 140 g m^{-2}, shoot production was boosted by either increased fertiliser at constant lime or *vice versa*. However, at about 140 g m^{-2} of lime there appears to be a threshold, above which there is a considerable increase in the production of shoots, which is not dependent on appreciable additions of fertiliser. In 1989, when there were drought conditions,

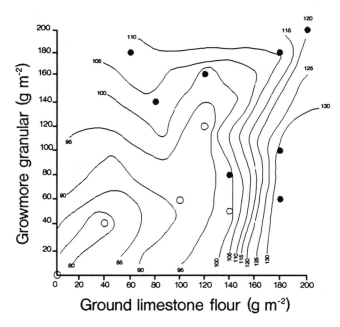

Figure 2. Effect of fertiliser and lime combinations on growth of *Eriophorum angustifolium*: isoline map of total shoot production in two plots for each treatment (May to October 1988); initially 32 shoots per treatment (16 per plot); (●), significantly different from control (o).

comparable results were obtained, plots receiving 180 g m^{-2} lime but either only 60 or as much as 180 g m^{-2} fertiliser having similar mean numbers of shoots per plot. In August 1989, the treatment with 200 g m^{-2} of both fertiliser and lime had the highest number of shoots, nearly four times greater than the control.

Trial 3

This trial was designed to throw light on the effect of major nutrients (N, P, K) on growth of *E. angustifolium*. It was run in the 1989 growing season, when severe drought limited growth on Kinder. The effect of combinations of nitrogen (60 g m^{-2} ammonium sulphate), phosphorus (63 g m^{-2} phosphorus pentoxide) and potassium (26 g m^{-2} potassium sulphate) together with 180 g m^{-2} lime was tested. The indications were that potassium was the most beneficial of the three nutrients, especially at the establishment phase, and nitrogen the least (Richards, 1990), not surprising as the Kinder Scout area is subject to high rates of wet and dry deposition of nitrogen (UKRGAR, 1990).

Conclusions from field trials

The second field trial in particular demonstrated clearly that high rates of lime (around 180 g m^{-2}) gave the greatest increases in growth, with or without additional sources of nutrient. It was also evident from the first field trial that the 'establishment' of shoots in pots with compost, leading to appreciable root development, was also highly beneficial. These findings suggest that lime might enhance rooting and so allow plants to thrive without additional nutrients. With less lime, more fertiliser was needed to compensate, but the initial acidifying effect of the latter was deleterious. Furthermore, the development of roots prior to planting removed the absolute dependence on added lime or lime and fertiliser.

   The benefits of lime observed in the field might be explained in several ways:
(1)   the direct effect of raised pH (*i.e.* fewer hydrogen ions in solution);
(2)   the indirect effects of raised pH, with possible increase in available concentrations of nutrients and decrease of available concentrations of toxic metals;
(3)   the direct effect of calcium on the growth of *E. angustifolium*, considered important by previous workers including Phillips (1954b) and Goodman (1968);
(4)   the indirect effects of calcium in the retention of other nutrients, such as phosphates, in peat.

GLASSHOUSE-BASED EXPERIMENTS

To try to elucidate the nature and relative importance of the beneficial effects of lime on Kinder, a number of experiments were conducted under glasshouse conditions. For experiments involving solution culture, shoots of *E. angustifolium*, supported by polystyrene floats, were grown in bowls containing 8 litres, in a heated glasshouse at Tapton Experimental Garden, Sheffield, with lighting augmented as appropriate.

Concentration of calcium and pH

The growth of E. angustifolium was monitored in solution culture (10% Rorison's solution) in which calcium and pH were varied independently. Three concentrations of calcium (1, 8 and 50 mg l^{-1}, supplied as calcium chloride) and three values of pH (2.8, 3.0 and 3.8), adjusted by means of sulphuric acid, were used, with 16 shoots per treatment, but not all combinations were included.

The results (Table 2) give clear evidence that pH rather than the concentrations of calcium has the major effect on growth. Strongly significant differences in respect of pH, but only minor effects of the concentrations of calcium, were found in both shoot growth (expressed as total length of living leaf per plant) and root growth. The effect of pH on rooting was especially pronounced. With 1 mg l^{-1} Ca, the mean length of living (white) root per plant was almost three times greater at pH 3.8 than at pH 3.0 (and also greater than with 50 mg l^{-1} Ca). Rooting at pH 2.8 was very poor indeed.

The experiment shows that, in the pH range of relevance to Kinder, the benefits from lime were far more likely to derive from raised pH than from increased concentrations of calcium. The effects on rooting appear especially important. Rooting was poor at pH values typical of eroding bogs such as Kinder (2.8 and 3.0), but was promoted considerably at pH 3.8, the pH representative of bogs in the South Pennines which retain vegetation cover, have a water table close to the surface for much of the year, and are reducing.

Effect of pH in phostrogen solution culture

A similar experiment to that above compared growth in solution cultures with 0.25 g l^{-1} phostrogen (N, P, K and other elements) at pH values of 2.9, 3.1 and 3.7 (Figure 3). Growth at the two lower pH values was fairly similar and limited, there being much greater growth of both the shoot system and the root system at pH 3.7. As in the previous experiment, the effect on root production was considerably

Table 2. The effect of calcium concentration and pH on the growth of *Eriophorum angustifolium*. Plants grown in 10% Rorison's solution for 52 days under glasshouse conditions. Treatments followed by the same letter do not differ significantly.

Ca (mg l^{-1})	Mean total length of living leaf per plant (mm)			Mean total length of living root per plant (mm)		
	pH 2.8	pH 3.0	pH 3.8	pH 2.8	pH 3.0	pH 3.8
1	–	938bc	1185a	–	716cd	1957a
8	716d	1004bc	–	449d	823c	–
50	–	961bc	1106ab	–	813cd	1521b

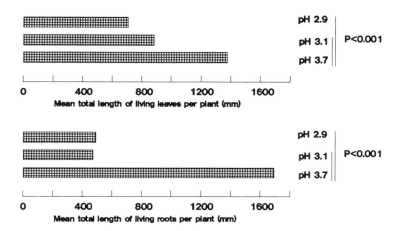

Figure 3. Effect of pH on growth of *Eriophorum angustifolium* in solution culture: phostrogen (0.25 g l⁻¹) at three pH values for 76 days under glasshouse conditions.

greater than on leaf production, the mean length of root per plant at pH 3.7 approaching four times that of plants at pH 2.9 and 3.1, a very highly significant difference.

Effects of raised pH on growth in Kinder peat

The benefits of raised pH compared with increased concentration of calcium were tested by the use of sodium carbonate, a procedure employed by Boatman (1962) in studying *Schoenus nigricans*.

Shoots of *E. angustifolium* were grown in 160 ml of Kinder peat in plastic cups, 10 cups receiving 2 ml of 0.3M sodium carbonate and 10 receiving distilled water only. The untreated peat was pH 2.9; the sodium carbonate treatment was pH 3.6. After growth for 7 weeks, the mean total length of living leaves per plant in the treated peat was 38% greater than the control (Figure 4), significantly different at $P<0.01$.

NUTRIENTS IN PEAT WATERS AND PROTON COMPETITION

The above experiments show that the benefits to growth of *E. angustifolium* of increased concentrations of calcium in solution were limited whereas raised pH, in both solution and peat water, was distinctly beneficial, especially in enhancing root production. These findings strongly indicate that growth is restricted by the direct effect of the very low pH of eroded blanket bogs. While complex effects may operate on Kinder, a simple approach is to consider possible competition between nutrient cations and hydrogen ions. Of interest in this connection is the growth of *E. angustifolium* on Parys Mountain, Anglesey, on a substrate which

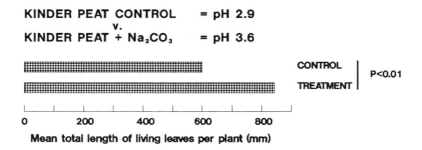

Figure 4. Effect of pH on growth of *Eriophorum angustifolium* in Kinder peat: experiment with sodium carbonate run for 48 days under glasshouse conditions.

may be as low as pH 2.0, with however – at this mine site – high concentrations of minerals, including calcium, in solution. Also, an experiment (Richards, 1990) using various strengths of phostrogen and two pH values (2.9 and 3.7) indicated that stronger solutions are more beneficial at lower and weaker ones at higher pH.

Culture solutions are clearly much richer in nutrients than the waters of blanket bogs such as Kinder. It may therefore be appropriate to consider the greater effects of proton competition in sites with acid peat. A comparison was made in May 1988 of the levels of nutrients in the peat waters of a bare hummock on Kinder, an intact blanket bog at Ronksley Moor (SK 138958) and acid grassland at Blackley Hey (SK 148885), all sites within the National Trust High Peak Estate.

Table 3 shows that, with the dialysis cell technique (Wheeler & Giller, 1984), the peat waters of Kinder, although leached of potassium, are richer in nitrogen and magnesium than those of the other two sites, the concentration of calcium also being joint highest. However, this apparent fertility may be seen in truer perspective if pH is taken into account, Kinder being by far the most acidic.

When the ratio of the number of hydrogen ions to the number of the four other cations assayed is considered (Table 3), Kinder appears rather more infertile than Ronksley, Blackley Hey being very much richer. The likely potassium deficiency on Kinder is highlighted by 29 hydrogen ions per potassium ion as compared with 12 at Ronksley and only one at Blackley Hey.

CONCLUSIONS AND PROPOSALS FOR MANAGEMENT

The field and glasshouse experiments give abundant evidence that the pH of the peat on Kinder is sub-optimal for growth of *E. angustifolium*. Oxidation in eroding bogs contributes to low pH, and acid rain has exacerbated the situation. Skiba *et al.* (1989) present strong evidence that acid rain has reduced the pH of some bog peats in Scotland by as much as half a pH unit; such acidification has almost certainly reduced the vigour of *E. angustifolium*. Control of pollution by

Table 3. Concentration of nutrients, pH and ionic ratios in peat waters at Kinder (bare hummock), Ronksley (intact bog) and Blackley Hey (grass moor). Concentrations are given in mg l^{-1} in peat water.

	Kinder	Ronksley	Blackley Hey
NH_4-N	2.1	0.6	0.3
K	1.1	1.3	2.5
Ca	4.7	3.4	4.7
Mg	0.9	0.5	0.3
pH (water)	3.1	3.4	4.2
H^+	0.8	0.4	0.06
$H^+ : NH_4^+$	7	12	4
$H^+ : K^+$	29	12	1
$H^+ : Ca^{2+}$	7	5	0.4
$H^+ : Mg^{2+}$	22	20	4

sulphurous compounds may lead to a gradual rise in pH of the substrate (Skiba *et al.*, 1989) but active measures are needed to promote revegetation.

The Kinder trials show positively the value of *E. angustifolium* in revegetation of bare blanket peat. Indeed it may well be the most useful naturally occurring species. A single patch of *E. angustifolium* can provide hundreds of large, ready-rooted transplants which may be established rapidly in treated plots, without artificial stabilisers. In a first season the transplants can generate a vegetation cover largely resistant to frost-heaving and trampling and relatively unattractive to sheep (the latter an important consideration in sites where there is severe grazing pressure). Such patches of vegetation have persisted and spread on Kinder since the introduction of transplants in 1987. Furthermore, the apparently destructive separation of patches of *E. angustifolium* to provide transplants can increase overall cover as separated shoots are freed from intraspecific competition which leads to degeneration in centres of naturally occurring patches.

The first field trial showed the great advantage of establishment of roots by growth in pots with compost before planting. This treatment may be impractical on a large scale, although it may be noted that 13 such transplants created continuous cover on Kinder over more than 2 m^2 in three growing seasons. Subsequent fieldwork with directly-introduced shoots showed that these grew well in areas treated with lime and fertiliser at optimal rates. As the best month for planting is usually May, it is advisable to collect shoots earlier and establish them under glasshouse conditions. Dieback is generally complete by October and shoots transferred to a heated glasshouse at or after this time will begin rapid growth almost immediately. There is therefore good opportunity to produce well-rooted transplants in a first growing season that is effectively extended by some six months. Even if only basic conditions exist for growth in a glasshouse or cold frame there is much advantage in promoting early season growth.

When transplants are introduced to field sites, planting depth is likely to vary with the size of shoots and depth of the medium in which they have been grown. Greater planting depth may reduce susceptibility to drought, but this may be important only in the driest years. Although *E. angustifolium* grows better in wetter microsites, it can tolerate, and indeed spread, in the drier conditions of the tops of peat hummocks. Tolerance of drought has been shown in glasshouse experiments and in the field during the abnormally dry years of the late 1980's. The only prerequisite for good growth in such conditions is the establishment of a substantial root system, which is favoured by 'luxury growth' prior to planting or by raising pH of the substratum in the field.

The experiments on Kinder well illustrate the promotion of growth of *E. angustifolium* by raising the pH of the peat by lime; benefits were particularly apparent with more than 140 g m^{-2} of lime. The strong response of *E. angustifolium* to liming of ombrotrophic peat is perhaps not surprising as in many more continental parts of Europe it is more typically associated with fens than with bogs. In the UK it is also widespread in fens and a soil pH range of 2.2–7.6 (median = 5.2, n = 550) has been recorded (B.D. Wheeler & S.C. Shaw, unpublished). It is recommended that, on eroding blanket bogs, lime and fertiliser should be used together, but that the addition of fertiliser (if similar to Growmore) is between one-third and one-half that of lime to counter any initial acidifying effect of the fertiliser. Because of this effect, added fertiliser without lime is not recommended for very acid sites.

On Kinder, nitrogen seems to be relatively abundant, but growth may be limited by availability of potassium and phosphorus. Use of fertilisers richer in these two latter elements, with lime, is therefore desirable here.

Large-scale attempts at revegetation could be based on a series of plots treated by hand with lime and fertiliser. Alternatively, transplants could be introduced at regular intervals to peat treated with lime and fertiliser by helicopter. This procedure has been used successfully by the National Trust over a wide area of Kinder, which received about 1 t ha^{-1} lime and 0.5 t ha^{-1} fertiliser. Glasshouse experimentation showed that, even after 7 months, peat treated in this way was a significantly better medium for *E. angustifolium* than untreated peat.

ACKNOWLEDGEMENTS

A CASE studentship to J.R.A. Richards from the Natural Environment Research Council, partnered by the National Trust, is gratefully acknowledged. Thanks are also due to many of the personnel of the National Trust for assistance in the N.T. Kinder and High Peak Estates and the Manpower Services Community Programme for constructing the enclosure on Kinder.

REFERENCES

Boatman, D.J. (1962). The growth of *Schoenus nigricans* on blanket bog peats. I. The response to pH and the level of potassium and magnesium. *Journal of Ecology*, **50**, 823–832.

Bridges, M. (1986). Stabilisation and revegetation of fire damaged deep peat on Glaisdale Moor. *Moorland Management*. North York Moors National Park, Helmsley, York, pp. 84–96.

Garnett, A. (1956). Climate. *Sheffield and its Region* (ed. D.L. Linton), pp. 44–69. British Association for the Advancement of Science, Sheffield.

Garnett, A. (1969). Climate. *Flora of Derbyshire* (ed. A.R. Clapham), pp. 29–48. County Borough of Derby Museum and Art Gallery.

Goodman, G.T. (1968). The role of mineral nutrients in *Eriophorum* communities. I. The effects of added ground limestone upon the availability and uptake of inorganic elements in an *E. angustifolium* community. *Journal of Ecology*, **56**, 545–563.

Pearsall, W.H. (1938). The soil complex in relation to plant communities. III. Moorlands and bogs. *Journal of Ecology*, **26**, 298–315.

Phillips, J., Yalden, D. & Tallis, J.H. (eds) (1981). *Peak District Moorland Erosion Study: Phase 1 Report*. Peak Park Joint Planning Board, Bakewell, Derbyshire.

Phillips, M.E. (1954a). Biological Flora of the British Isles: *E. angustifolium* Roth. *Journal of Ecology*, **42**, 612–622.

Phillips, M.E. (1954b). Studies in the quantitative morphology and ecology of *E. angustifolium* Roth. III. The leafy shoot. *New Phytologist*, **53**, 312–343.

Richards, J.R.A. (1990). *The potential use of* Eriophorum angustifolium *Honck. in the re-vegetation of blanket peat*. PhD thesis, University of Sheffield.

Skiba, U., Cresser, M.S., Derwent, R.G. & Futty, D.W. (1989). Peat acidification in Scotland. *Nature*, **337**, 68–69.

Tallis, J.H. & Yalden, D.W. (1983). *Peak District Moorland Restoration Project: Phase 2 Report: Re-vegetation trials*. Peak Park Joint Planning Board, Bakewell, Derbyshire.

Tansley, A.G. (1939). *The British Islands and their Vegetation*. Cambridge University Press, London.

Turtle, C.E. (1984). *Peat erosion and reclamation in the southern Pennines*. PhD thesis, University of Manchester.

UKRGAR (1990). *Acid Deposition in the United Kingdom 1986–1988*. Third Report of the United Kingdom Review Group on Acid Rain. Department of the Environment, London.

Wheeler, B.D. & Giller, K.E. (1984). The use of dialysis cells for investigating pore water composition in wetland substrata, with particular reference to dissolved iron and sulphide. *Communications in Soil Science and Plant Analysis*, **15**, 707–716.

34 Restoration of Wet Heathland after Opencast Mining

D. W. MERRILEES, G. E. D. TILEY & D. C. GWYNNE

Environmental Sciences Department, Scottish Agricultural College, Auchincruive, Ayr, KA6 5HW, UK

SUMMARY

1.   In line with current land management policy, designated opencast sites on low quality marginal land will be reinstated with a vegetation cover compatible with the ecology of the area.
2.   Reinstatement methods being assessed include regeneration of native grasses and heather (*Calluna vulgaris*) from direct replacement of fresh peat, application of surface litter and seeding with natural grasses and *Calluna* capsules.
3.   Treatments were established with and without cultivations, lime and fertilisers to assess the most appropriate establishment methods.
4.   Rapid revegetation after opencast mining was best achieved by direct transfer of the indigenous turf and associated fresh peat. Revegetation using litter was a practical alternative but rate of establishment was much slower.
5.   The most successful method of *Calluna* establishment was from turf transfer. Broadcasting *Calluna* capsules was relatively ineffective.
6.   Application of base fertiliser significantly improved the rate of establishment and number of species on most treatments.
7.   Liming had very little effect overall, but initially reduced the establishment of *Calluna*.
8.   In the short term, 1–3 years, it has not been possible to recreate exactly the previously existing vegetation, but the establishment methods tried have produced a diverse ground cover of native species capable of being managed for a range of end uses.

INTRODUCTION

Opencast mining has a vital role to play in the low-cost recovery of shallow coal reserves which cannot be extracted by deep-mine methods. Restoration of opencast sites in the UK has been developed to a high standard with possibilities of restoring land to a wide range of end uses. In the past, restoration has primarily been to agriculture (Proctor, 1989). More recently the trend has been to blend ecological needs with agricultural viability. However, at the present time of

Restoration of Temperate Wetlands. Edited by B.D. Wheeler, S.C. Shaw, W.J. Fojt and R.A. Robertson
© 1995 John Wiley & Sons Ltd.

agricultural surplus within the UK, the future trend will more likely be to restore for nature conservation.

In line with the current land management policy proposed within the Scottish Agri-Environment programme, designated opencast sites on low quality marginal land will thus be reinstated with a vegetation cover similar to the vegetation of the surrounding area. In southern Scotland, the vegetation of rough grazings on poorly drained acid peaty soils comprises moorland communities, containing *Molinia caerulea* (purple moor grass), *Juncus* spp. (rushes) and *Calluna vulgaris* (heather). *Calluna* occurs in many of the communities in varying amounts and restoration of *Calluna*-rich vegetation was a primary aim of the reinstatement process in this study. The objective was to assess the most cost-effective methods of establishing *Calluna vulgaris* and native vegetation cover on opencast sites and to provide a management programme for maintaining this vegetation during the 5-year aftercare period.

Earlier studies on heathland regeneration (Grant, 1968; Bridges, 1985) considered methods of *Calluna* reinstatement following overgrazing or burning rather than complete vegetation reinstatement on a totally denuded soil environment. The restoration of vegetation on disturbed sites in general has been reviewed by Bradshaw & Chadwick (1980). The methods and techniques employed depend on the soil-forming material, climatic conditions and the purpose for which the revegetated surface will be used, for example, amenity, grazing or forestry. Techniques for the restoration of heathlands were reviewed by Putwain, Gillham & Holliday (1982) and by British Gas (1988). Seed viability and germination in *Calluna* were discussed by Gimingham (1960, 1972).

The practical recommendations given by British Gas (1988) for bare or eroded sites indicate the importance of:

- stabilisation of the substratum, with possible pre-treatment such as rotavation;
- introduction of suitable propagules of *Calluna*, which must originate from local sources as bulk quantities of seed are not available commercially;
- possible use of fertiliser and lime inputs on nutrient-poor sites;
- protection of the site from grazing for a minimum of 5 years.

The use of litter from the upper 40–50 mm of the soil profile beneath an existing stand of *Calluna* proved a useful technique for the introduction of native *Calluna* and other species. The litter layer has the advantage of containing vegetative propagules of heathland species in addition to the seed bank. It was essential that the upper layer should not be diluted with greater depths of soil (Putwain & Gillham, 1990). The transfer of turves from adjacent moorland sites also resulted in a complete restoration of the natural cover. Where *Calluna* shoots or seed-bearing capsules were harvested from November onwards, the use of a thinly sown companion grass often favoured *Calluna* establishment. However, it was important that non-competitive species such as *Agrostis capillaris* or *Deschampsia flexuosa* sown at low seed rates were used to avoid shading out the *Calluna*.

On nutrient-poor substrata, mineral fertiliser (6–20–10 NPK) was found to encourage the establishment of *Calluna*. Lime and fertilisers were essential if a grass companion crop was sown. The fertiliser rates should be balanced so as to avoid over-stimulation of the grass. Management after establishment may involve further fertiliser inputs, mainly of nitrogen (N) and phosphorus (P) to promote *Calluna* growth, accompanied by exclusion of animals and other forms of disturbance.

Among the factors required for the germination of *Calluna* seeds, Putwain *et al.* (1982) regarded low pH and continuous moisture as essential. Gimingham (1960) also stressed the importance of pH and light. *Calluna* seeds retain viability for a number of years, especially if dried. Natural germination occurs in both the autumn and spring. The importance of integrating the restoration process into the engineering programme has also been emphasised (British Gas, 1988).

STUDY AREA

The study was carried out on the Headlesscross Opencast Site near Forth, Lanarkshire (National Grid Reference: NS 905580), on the drumlin topography of the Carboniferous shales and sandstones at an elevation of approximately 240 m asl. Soil cover varied from blanket peat, 50–100 cm of amorphous peat, to stagnohumic gley soils of the Quothqhan Series, (Bown & Shipley, 1982) with < 50 cm of peat topsoil on slowly permeable clay subsoil. The peat was very poorly drained, strongly acid (pH: 3.9) in the upper horizon, and nutrient deficient (NPK status very low and Mg status moderate).

The indigenous vegetation cover is a wet heath/acidic grassland mosaic, the predominant species being *Calluna vulgaris, Eriophorum vaginatum, Juncus acutiflorus* and *Agrostis* spp. (Nature Conservancy Council, 1990). Prior to opencast mining the land had been managed for intensive and extensive grazing, after drainage improvement by shallow ditches and introduction of a *Lolium perenne/Trifolium repens* sward on the drier areas. The climate is fairly warm, with an average annual rainfall of 1050 mm, a potential summer soil moisture deficit of 0–25 mm and an accumulated temperature (day degrees C) of 1100 (Birse & Dry, 1970). The Land Capability Classification for Agriculture is 5.2 (Dry, Gauld & Bell, 1986).

Where possible, land is progressively restored as coal extraction is completed to minimise the length of soil storage time. This can vary from one to five years and entails soil being stored in bunds up to 5 m high, inevitably resulting in degradation in the physical, chemical and biological properties of the peat.

TREATMENTS AND METHODS

Once the overburden and subsoil had been replaced to the agreed contour (3% slope), peat that had been stored for 5 years was spread on the experimental area to a depth of 0.5 m. The trial layout (Figure 1) consisted of five main unreplicated treatments in large plots of 400 m^2 and 8 sub-treatments with plot sizes of 50 m^2.

A buffer area, 30 m wide, was left untreated around the site.

The main treatments established in August 1991 were:

(A)   *Fresh peat*: The surface vegetation plus the upper peat layer was stripped to a depth of 300 mm by excavator bucket from the next section to be opencast and spread directly on to the reinstatement plot.

(B)   *Litter*: Coarse vegetation was removed from the next section to be opencast and the litter layer (L and F horizons) rotavated to a depth of 40 mm, collected and spread onto the reinstatement plot at the rate of 3 kg m^{-2}. A germination test on a sub-sample of the litter gave satisfactory germination and establishment rates.

(C)   Calluna *capsules and nurse grass*: A nurse grass of the same species mix as used in Treatment D was sown at a rate of 20 kg ha^{-1} and later overseeded in November 1991 with *Calluna* capsules at a rate of 1 kg ha^{-1}. *Calluna* seed rate was based on a germination rate of 10% achieved under mist conditions in the glasshouse. The capsules were collected from native *Calluna* on the site.

(D)   *Native grasses*: The following grass seeds mixture was sown in August 1991 at the rate of 50 kg ha^{-1}:

Agrostis capillaris	25%	*Festuca longifolia*	15%
Cynosurus cristatus	10%	*Festuca rubra*	40%
Deschampsia flexuosa	5%	*Anthoxanthum odoratum*	5%

The primary aim was to establish rapidly a vegetation cover similar to the indigenous acidic grassland, using species which were available commercially and which previous assessments had shown were viable on acid peat.

(E)   *Control*: Stored peat spread and left untreated to assess the seed bank survival from the storage heaps.

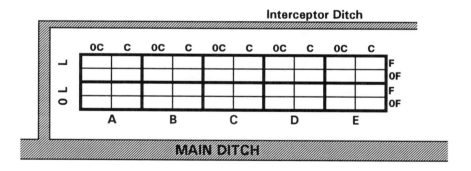

Main treatments
A   Fresh peat
B   Litter
C   *Calluna* capsules & native grass
D   Native grass mixture
E   Control (stored peat)

Sub-treatments
Cultivation (C) *vs* No cultivation (OC)
Lime (L) *vs* No lime (OL)
Fertiliser (F) *vs* No fertiliser

Figure 1. Layout of main and sub-treatments established in August 1991.

The following sub-treatments were superimposed on each of the main treatments.

(a)   *Cultivation*: The cultivation treatment was applied to half of the main plot to a depth of 50 mm with Aitkenhead harrows to improve seed:soil contact.

(b)   *Lime*: The lime treatment, 10 t ha^{-1} of magnesian limestone to raise the pH to 4.8, was applied to half of each cultivation sub-treatment.

(c)   *Fertiliser*: A 5–22–22 NPK base fertiliser was applied at 400 kg ha^{-1} to half of each cultivation x lime sub-plot. As ground cover establishment was slow in Year 2, the fertilised plots were further split, half receiving a maintenance fertiliser (5–22–22 NPK) in years 2 and 3 at 250 kg ha^{-1}.

(d)   *Rolling*: All treatments were lightly rolled after establishment to conserve surface moisture.

MONITORING

A botanical assessment of the total vegetation cover and percentage species' establishment was carried out twice a year for each sub-treatment, using visual scores and randomly placed quadrats. Soil pH and nutrient status were determined each spring to monitor any treatment differences and a photographic record was kept of the progress of establishment.

RESULTS

Rate of vegetation establishment and diversity of species were used as indicators of the reinstatement success and its conservation value. British Coal was particularly interested in the rate of *Calluna* regeneration. Results for each treatment are described below and rate of total vegetation establishment (1991–93) on the main treatments is shown in Figure 2.

(A)   *Fresh peat*: The transplanted vegetation gave an initial ground cover of 100% but subsequently died back during the immediate post-establishment period. In Year 2 there was a rapid recovery resulting in a 95% vegetation cover in Year 3. *Calluna* cover increased from 0 to 6% over this period.

(B)   *Litter*: 16% ground cover was achieved in the initial establishment period but this was reduced to 5% by winter kill. Total vegetation cover increased to 34% in year 2 and 61% in year 3. *Calluna* was slow to establish from the litter seed bank, giving a ground cover of only 1% after 2 years.

(C)   Calluna *capsules*: *Calluna* establishment from overseeding into the nurse grass was unsuccessful, producing <1% ground cover after 2 years. A more successful establishment may be possible by direct drilling of capsules into the nurse grass rather than by surface broadcasting.

(D)   *Native grasses*: Application of base fertiliser was a significant factor in grass establishment. After 3 months the fertilised plots had 62% cover compared with 22% cover where no fertiliser was applied. Total vegetation cover on the

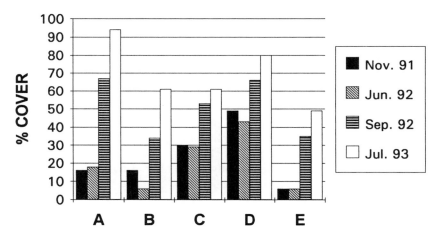

Figure 2. Changes in mean percentage of vegetation establishment (1991–93) on main treatments: A: fresh peat; B: litter; C: *Calluna* capsules and nurse grass; D: native grasses; E. control.

main plot increased from 48% in year 1 to 80% in year 3. *C cristatus* and *A. odoratum* were the dominant species in year 1, but were subsequently replaced by *Agrostis/Festuca* species in year 3.

(E)   *Control*: Vegetation cover, mainly *A. stolonifera,* on the untreated, stored peat was 6%, after 9 months, increasing to 35% during the following 3 summer months. In Year 3 cover was 50%, dominated by *D. flexuosa* and *A. stolonifera*.

FERTILISER EFFECT

Application of a base fertiliser increased ground cover by approximately 50% in all treatments except A, fresh peat (Figure 3). Fertiliser also increased yield. This effect was particularly visible in treatment E where it enhanced germination from the seed bank. Application of maintenance fertiliser had a similar effect in maintaining growth rates and establishment of the sown grass treatments, C and D. Initial assessments indicated that fertiliser had increased the number of species present but had no effect on *Calluna* establishment.

LIMING EFFECT

Lime application had a minimal effect overall (Figure 4). Vegetation cover in the sown grass treatments (C and D) increased and germination from the stored peat, (E), was enhanced .

The limed plots had a higher percentage cover of *F. rubra* and a lower percentage cover of *Sphagnum* spp. and *Calluna* than the unlimed plots.

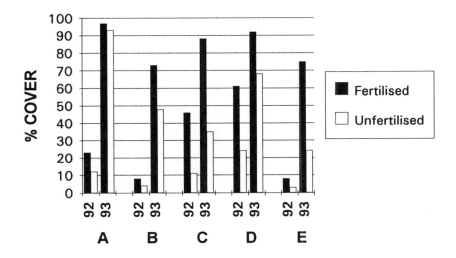

Figure 3. Effect of base fertiliser on mean vegetation cover (June 1992 and July 1993) for main treatments. A: fresh peat; B: litter; C: *Calluna* capsules and nurse grass; D: native grasses; E. control.

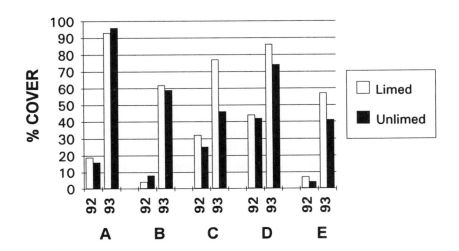

Figure 4. Effect of pH increase from 3.8 to 4.8 on mean vegetation cover (June 1992 and July 1993) on main treatments. A: fresh peat; B: litter; C: *Calluna* capsules and nurse grass; D: native grasses; E. control.

Table 1. Species' establishment (% cover) after two years on main treatments (July 1993). A: fresh peat; B: litter; C: *Calluna* capsules and nurse grass; D: native grasses; E. control. * indicates < 1% cover.

| | TREATMENT | | | | |
	A	B	C	D	E
Total	94	61	61	80	49
Deschampsia flexuosa	50	23	2	1	4
Festuca rubra	2	25	18	34	4
Agrostis spp.	40	4	55	60	24
Holcus lanatus	20	6	2	1	15
Anthoxanthum odoratum	–	–	22	12	1
Juncus effusus	1	1	1	6	10
Calluna vulgaris	6	1	*	–	*
Eriophorum vaginatum	3	*	*	*	*
Potentilla erecta	1	*	*	*	*
Sphagnum spp.	12	1	–	–	–
Other mosses	2	15	1	1	6

SPECIES' ESTABLISHMENT

Conservation value of the reinstated heathland is dependent on the recreation of the original complement of heathland species. Two years after reinstatement, species establishment on the main treatments was assessed (Table 1). Treatment A resulted in the highest number of species, 23, compared with the lowest, 10 species, in treatment C.

After 2 years, grasses were beginning to dominate all plots at the expense of other vegetation. Tall grassy vegetation on all treatments was cut over in September 1993 to prevent smothering of the less competitive plants. *Sphagnum* spp. and other mosses were transferred successfully in the fresh-stripped peat and litter. *Calluna* establishment was slow initially but appeared likely to be successful in the fresh peat and litter treatments based on the frequency of young plants which emerged. *Calluna* establishment from capsules was not successful. *Juncus* spp., which often quickly colonise and dominate reseeded grass swards on poorly drained opencast soils, established on the open swards of treatments D and E.

DISCUSSION

Rapid revegetation of heathland after opencast mining was achieved by direct transfer of turf plus fresh peat from the stripping phase to the reinstatement phase of operations. Following initial die-back of surface vegetation, regeneration from the turf was rapid with complete ground cover being achieved in 2 years. A diverse range of species developed in the sward, which was very similar in species composition to the previously undisturbed sward. This method also provides the best option for *Calluna* regeneration where the original stripped vegetation contains a high content of this species. Revegetation by litter application could readily be achieved on a large scale at low cost with available equipment, *i.e.* rotavators and manure spreaders. Desiccation risk, even during a cool wet period, was high resulting in a poor establishment and a potential erosion risk. Further study is required to assess the optimum rate of litter application. *Calluna* establishment from seeding capsules into the nurse grass was ineffective. Direct drilling may provide a better seed environment and improved establishment.

Application of a base fertiliser at seeding and a maintenance fertiliser during the initial 2 years' establishment period was shown to be essential for grass establishment in the nutrient-deficient peat. Fertiliser also improved seedling establishment from the stored peat. If the sward is to be managed for conservation rather than production, no further fertiliser application is likely to be required after Year 2. In year 3 the vegetation cover on fresh stripped peat showed no increase following fertiliser applications indicating that added nutrients are required for establishment only. Elevation of the pH from 3.9 to 4.8 improved grass establishment from seed and enhanced establishment from the stored peat. However, there was no response in establishment from liming the fresh stripped peat or litter, whilst *Calluna* establishment appeared to have been depressed.

Vegetation establishment will continue to be monitored for a further 2 years in line with the statutory aftercare programme. In commercial practice, sheep would be introduced to the restored site in year 2 as part of an extensive grazing management. On a plot scale this could only be simulated by selective cutting during the growing season. Treading during grazing, would, however have a more manipulative effect on the ground vegetation and possibly result in physical damage to young *Calluna* plants. Vegetation management will therefore be required to provide a balance between controlling the more competitive grass species and minimising any poaching damage to establishing *Calluna* plants.

Opencast mining operations have a major impact on the local rural environment and land use. Reinstatement of the disturbed land and its vegetation is now a legal requirement. It is not possible to replace exactly the previously existing vegetation. However, a number of techniques are available for developing a substantially similar vegetation and to cater for a range of end uses whether for conservation, landscape or agriculture. Indeed, it might be possible to create a mosaic of revegetated surface by using a mix of techniques on the same site.

This study tested establishment methods on the difficult medium of blanket peat and demonstrated that a satisfactory diversity of grasses and wet heathland plants, including *Calluna*, can be developed, at least in the short term. Future management will clearly determine the subsequent development of this vegetation.

ACKNOWLEDGEMENTS

We are grateful to British Coal Opencast (Scotland) for funding the above study and to Alistair Duncan and other support staff for technical assistance in establishing and monitoring the site. The Scottish Agricultural College is partly funded by the Scottish Office Agriculture & Fisheries Department.

REFERENCES

Birse, E.L. & Dry, F.T. (1970). *Assessment of Climatic Conditions in Scotland, Number 1*, Macaulay Land Use Research Institute, Aberdeen.

Bown, C.J. & Shipley, B.M. (1982). *Soil and Land Capability for Agriculture*. Macaulay Land Use Research Institute, Aberdeen.

Bradshaw, A.D. & Chadwick, M.J. (1980). *The Restoration of Land*. Blackwell Scientific Publications, Oxford.

Bridges, M.K. (1985). Stabilisation and re-vegetation of fire damaged deep peat on Glaisdale moor. *Moorland Management.* pp. 84–96. North York Moors National Park, Helmsley, York.

British Gas (1988). *Heathland Restoration: A Handbook of Techniques*. British Gas plc, London.

Dry, F.T., Gauld, J.H. & Bell, J.S. (1986). *Land Capability for Agriculture – Sheet 65*. Macaulay Land Use Research Institute, Aberdeen.

Gimingham, C.H. (1960). Biological Flora of the British Isles. *Calluna vulgaris* (L) Hull. *Journal of Ecology*, **48**, 455–483.

Gimingham, C.H. (1972). *Ecology of Heathlands*. Chapman and Hall, London.

Grant, S.A. (1968). Heather regeneration following burning: a survey. *Journal of the British Grassland Society*, **23** (1): 26–33.

Nature Conservancy Council (1990). *Handbook for Phase I Habitat Survey*. Peterborough.

Proctor, R. (1989). *Proceedings of Symposium – Surface mining: future concepts, 3–4*. Marylebine Press Limited, Manchester.

Putwain, P.D. & Gillham, D.A. (1990). The significance of the dormant viable seedbank in restoration of heathlands. *Biological Conservation*, **52**, 1–16.

Putwain, P.D., Gillham, D.A. & Holliday, R.J. (1982). Restoration of heather moorland and lowland heathland, with special reference to pipelines. *Environmental Conservation*, **9**, 225–235.

35 Impacts of Conifer Plantations on Blanket Bogs and Prospects of Restoration

A. R. ANDERSON, D. G. PYATT & I. M. S. WHITE

Forestry Authority, Northern Research Station, Roslin, Midlothian, EH25 9SY, UK

SUMMARY

1.   The impacts of forestry plantations on blanket bogs need to be understood before the question of restoration can be addressed.

2.   The flora of blanket bogs is affected by fencing off the land for afforestation. The reduction in grazing and in some cases the cessation of burning cause changes in the composition of the vegetation.

3.   At an experimental site in Caithness, both forestry ploughing and ditching lowered the water table of a blanket bog. The influence of ditch spacing disappeared within 19 years owing to a reduction in the effective ditch depth. On deepening the ditches to their original depth their influence increased.

4.   Ploughing also changed the vegetation within 3 years, from a community dominated by *Trichophorum cespitosum* and *Cladonia portentosa* to one dominated by *Calluna vulgaris* and *Erica tetralix*. Where P and K fertilisers were applied to the plough ridges, *Eriophorum vaginatum* became dominant.

5.   Artificial rewetting would be needed to restore the original vegetation at this site. However, cracking of well-humified peat beneath the closed tree canopy, where sufficiently advanced to form an effective drainage system, would make artificial rewetting impossible in most situations.

INTRODUCTION – AFFORESTATION OF BLANKET PEAT

There are some 190,000 ha of forest on peat over 45 cm deep in Great Britain, the vast majority of this being on blanket bogs in the uplands (Pyatt, 1993). The wetness, low pH and low nutritional status of bog peat restricts the choice of tree species which can be grown. Peatland forestry trials during the 1920s and 1930s showed that seven species of conifer grew reliably, if slowly, on unflushed peat (Zehetmayr, 1954). *Pinus contorta* grew the most vigorously on unflushed peat and was planted extensively, while *Picea sitchensis* has been grown on the more

Restoration of Temperate Wetlands. Edited by B.D. Wheeler, S.C. Shaw, W.J. Fojt and R.A. Robertson
© Crown copyright 1995. Produced with funding from the Department of Health. Published by consent of the Secretary of State for Health and with the permission of the Controller of Her Majesty's Stationery Office. The views expressed are those of the author and do not necessarily reflect the views or policy of the Forestry Commission or any other government department. Published by John Wiley & Sons Ltd.

fertile flushed peats. It is now common practice to plant mixtures of these species, the pine nursing the spruce by drying the peat and making more nitrogen available but later being suppressed by the faster-growing spruce, which forms a more valuable timber crop. Timber yields of 10–12 m^3 ha^{-1} a^{-1} are likely on unflushed peats and yields of 14 m^3 ha^{-1} a^{-1} are achievable on flushed peats, both provided that early windthrow does not occur (Pyatt, 1990). Twin-throw spaced-furrow ploughing is needed for successful establishment of the trees and if the furrows are limited to 30 cm deep, tree roots can cross them, giving the trees a wider root system and improving their chances of remaining wind-firm (Pyatt, 1990).

THE IMPACTS OF AFFORESTATION ON BLANKET BOGS

The impacts of conifer plantations on blanket bogs are considered by looking at four distinct stages of the forest rotation and identifying the operations and processes which affect the hydrology, nutrition and other site conditions (Table 1).

The establishment stage

A change in land use, most often from rough grazing or grouse-moor, to forestry brings about a reduction in, or sometimes a cessation of, grazing by sheep and deer. The practice of regular light burning of rough grazings and patch burning of grouse-moor, both used as means of increasing their nutritional value, are also

Table 1. A summary of the changes to a blanket mire brought about by four stages in a forest rotation: + represents a raising of the water table or a nutrient enrichment; − represents a lowering of the water table; ++ and -- indicate large effects.

Stage in Rotation	Changes due to afforestation		
	Lowering of water table	Nutrient enrichment	Other effects
Establishment			Reduced grazing and
− fencing			cessation of burning
− ploughing	−	+	Increased habitat diversity
− ditching	−		
− fertilising		++	
Before canopy closure	−	+	Increased shelter
			Increased shade
After canopy closure	− −	+	Greatly increased shelter
			Dense shade
Harvesting			
− leaving residue	++	++	Decreased shelter
			Decreased shade
− removing residue	++	+	Removal of shelter
			Removal of shade

discontinued when afforestation begins. Chapman & Rose (1987) reported a change of vegetation on the shallower peat areas of Coom Rigg Moss, a bog enclave within Kielder Forest, from *Sphagnum*-dominated types to communities dominated by *Calluna vulgaris* and *Deschampsia flexuosa*[1]. They suggested that the vegetation changes may have resulted from the cessation of grazing and regular burning 28 years previously when the surrounding land was planted with conifers. Smith & Charman (1988) classified the vegetation of 34 bog enclaves in Kielder Forest and found that the cover of ombrogenous mire, wet heath and 'dry' moorland species was related to their edge:area ratio and the age of the surrounding forest. The smaller the edge:area ratio and the younger the surrounding trees, the greater the dominance of ombrogenous over dry moorland species. In a further study, Charman & Smith (1992) found that ombrogenous species were also associated with the deeper peat and that distance to the site edge was less important than peat depth to the number of bog species. This evidence supported the hypothesis that vegetation change was attributable to the cessation of burning and grazing rather than to a forest edge effect. However it is difficult to draw conclusions from this work, because of the high colinearity between peat depth and distance from the forest edge.

Spaced-furrow ploughing, carried out prior to planting trees on deep peat, produces a well-drained, bare ridge on which to establish tree seedlings (Taylor, 1970). A raised ridge has a more extreme soil temperature regime than a flat surface (Burrows, 1963; Mahrer & Avissar, 1985) and the increased accumulated temperature above a threshold around 5°C favours root growth (Tabbush, 1986; Coutts & Phillipson, 1987). Nitrogen mineralisation accelerates with the change in temperature regime (Strathers & Spittlehouse, 1990). The ridges are about 2 m apart and the furrows spaced at four intervals (or at 2 m apart in the case of older plantations ploughed with a single-throw plough). The surfaces of the ridges and furrows start off as bare peat. Their microclimate, soil temperature and moisture conditions are different from those of the original bog; they constitute new habitats. Drainage ditches 70–90 cm deep, at variable spacing, and their associated spoil heaps, also provide new habitats. Their primary function is to remove water from the plough furrows, which can be achieved by wide spacing (*e.g.* 100-m intervals), but on some peat types drainage ditches are also installed to control the water table and encourage deeper rooting. This requires a more closely spaced system (*e.g.* 20-m intervals). The effect of ditching on the water table was measured in a drainage experiment (see below).

Current forest fertilisation practice in Britain is to apply phosphate and potassium when planting conifers on blanket peat, repeating the dressing when the trees are 6–8 years old (Taylor, 1991). A typical application would consist of 450 kg ha^{-1} unground or granulated rock phosphate, supplying 60 kg P ha^{-1} as P_2O_5, and 200 kg ha^{-1} of muriate of potash, providing 100 kg K ha^{-1} as K_2O. For Sitka spruce (*Picea sitchensis*), a third application may be needed at 12–16 years. A

---

[1] Species names used are those given in Stace (1991) or, in the case of mosses, Smith (1978).

dose of nitrogen fertiliser, typically 150 kg N ha^{-1} as urea, every three years is recommended when growing Sitka spruce on unflushed peat but this can be avoided by planting a mixture of Sitka spruce and a 'nurse' species, such as lodgepole pine (*Pinus contorta*).

Before canopy closure

It takes 10–20 years for the branches of conifers to form a closed canopy on blanket bog sites. In the first three years after planting, the trees are too small to have any effects additional to those of the operations already discussed. For the remainder of the period up to canopy closure there is a gradual increase in shade, shelter, rainfall interception and pollutant deposition as foliage and branches develop.

After canopy closure

Closure of the canopy causes dense shading of the ground and after some two or three years the surface vegetation changes from a bog to a forest floor community. Some shade-intolerant species are lost from the ground flora and a litter layer of dead needles forms. Nutrient recycling within the ecosystem replaces the uptake of available soil nutrients as the dominant nutritional process (Miller, 1981).

Canopy closure also results in an increase in interception loss and total evaporation so that the water table falls well below the level of the furrow bottoms during dry summers and water uptake by the trees during these periods replaces drainage as the main cause of drying of the peat (Binns, 1959). Blanket bog peat is usually highly humified (Pyatt, Craven & Williams, 1979) and is therefore subject to shrinkage and cracking when it dries (Binns, 1968; Pyatt & John, 1989), these effects being irreversible (Hobbs, 1986; Schnitzer, 1986; Lindsay *et al.*, 1988). The ground surface subsides due to the shrinkage of the peat (Pyatt *et al.*, 1992), but this process eventually reaches a point where the peat's resistance to tearing is less than its resistance to subsidence, so it cracks (Pyatt & John, 1989). At first the cracks appear in the bottoms of the plough furrows and ditches, where tear resistance is reduced owing to the removal of the more fibrous acrotelm. As further drying takes place, cracking develops between the furrows, forming a reticulate network (Binns, 1968; Howell, 1984), which can act as a drainage system. When the ditches which drain these cracks become blocked, the water table rises during wet weather and water stands in the cracks, but, because peat shrinkage is irreversible, they do not close up. We do not know whether any areas of blanket bog with fibrous catotelm peat actually exist, but if so, we would expect them to be less subject to cracking than the vast majority in which the catotelm peat is pseudofibrous or amorphous.

Harvesting

Harvesting the timber causes the most abrupt change in ground conditions during a forest rotation. Interception loss is greatly reduced and transpiration virtually stops. Usually this causes a sudden rise of the water table (Pyatt *et al.*, 1985). Incident light increases dramatically and the climate near the ground becomes wetter and windier and has a more extreme temperature regime. These changes will normally be tempered because the harvesting debris consisting of branches and tops is left on the ground and continues to intercept both water (Titus & Malcolm, 1987; Anderson, Pyatt & Stannard, 1990) and light as it weathers down to a surface mat over approximately five years. The changes would be more abrupt if the branches and tops were removed from the bog (*e.g.* by chipping for the board or landscaping markets). Nutrient release from the dead foliage would also be much reduced if branches were removed.

Little is known about the reversibility of the impacts of afforestation mentioned above. Because drainage has been used universally for afforesting blanket bog any attempts to restore such areas of bog require an understanding of how the hydrology has been affected. There are few published studies of the hydrological effects of afforestation of blanket bog so we have conducted a study of this subject using two experiments.

EFFECTS OF AFFORESTATION ON BLANKET BOG HYDROLOGY

Introduction

The first experiment was based on an old drainage experiment set up in 1968 to compare the effects of different drainage techniques on tree growth. We started work on the present study in 1987 with these objectives:
(1) to compare water table depths after 20 years' tree growth with those measured in the first four years and with undisturbed bog;
(2) to repeat this after deepening all the intercepting ditches to their original depth.

A second experiment on the same site was set up in 1989; its objectives were to measure:
(1) the effects on effluent water quantity and quality of three planting treatments and a control;
(2) the physical, chemical and microbiological changes in the peat as it progressively dries.

The first objective is not directly relevant to the subject of this paper and will be published separately. The chemical and microbiological results are not yet available, but the early effects of ploughing on water levels and the associated peat shrinkage are described, together with results showing the effect of ploughing and fertilisation on the ground vegetation.

Experimental site

The forest drainage experiment, Rumster 3, and the hydrology experiment, Rumster 17, were both situated on an area of ombrogenous 'Eastern' watershed blanket bog (Lindsay *et al.*, 1988) at Bad a' Cheo in Caithness, Highland Region (National Grid Reference ND167500). The bog surface was 90–95 m above sea level and the peat was 3–5 m deep. A fibrous layer, 10 cm thick, overlay pseudofibrous peat with a von Post humification value of H7–9. The vegetation was dominated by *Trichophorum cespitosum* and *Cladonia portentosa*; *Sphagnum capillifolium*, *Eriophorum angustifolium*, *E. vaginatum*, *Erica tetralix*, *Sphagnum papillosum*, *Narthecium ossifragum* and *Calluna vulgaris* were abundant. The mean annual precipitation at the site was *c.* 1000 mm and evaporation *c.* 500 mm.

Methods

The drainage experiment was laid down in 1968 in four randomised blocks of six, 45 x 100 m treatment plots (Table 2 and Figure 1). The first three treatments consisted of shallow double-mouldboard (D30) ploughing (*i.e.* ridges thrown up on both sides of the 30-cm-deep furrows), intercepted at right angles by 90-cm-deep ditches at intervals of 9, 14 or 18 m respectively. The next two treatments consisted of deep ploughing: D60 (double mouldboard ploughing with 60-cm-deep furrows) and S90 (single mouldboard ploughing, in which a ridge is thrown up on one side only of the 90-cm-deep furrows), both of these having no intercepting ditches, except at the plot ends. The final treatment was an undisturbed control. All except the control were planted with *Pinus contorta*. Three 90 cm deep boreholes, situated mid-way between the intercepting ditches in the case of the D30 treatments, were used to measure the borehole water level (BWL), *i.e.* the distance from the water table to the ground surface, in each of the 24 plots, monthly from 1969 to 1973 and weekly from 1987 to 1988. The ditches, which became shallower over their 20-year life by accumulating peat debris and pine needles and by shrinkage of the top 90 cm of the peat, were deepened to 90 cm depth over the winter of 1988–89 and a further series of weekly BWL measurements was made from 1989 to 1990. The slope of the ground surface before drainage in each plot was estimated from a topographic survey of the site in 1966. This was used as a covariate in the analyses of variance of BWL.

The hydrological experiment began in 1989, when the four control plots of the

Table 2. Details of the six treatments of the drainage experiment. The control treatment was not ploughed or ditched and was left unplanted.

Name	Plough furrows		Intercepting ditches	
	Depth (m)	Spacing (m)	Depth (m)	Spacing (m)
D30/9	0.3	4.5	0.9	9
D30/14	0.3	4.5	0.9	14
D30/18	0.3	4.5	0.9	18
D60	0.6	4.5	0.9	–
S90	0.9	2.4	0.9	–
Control	–	–	–	–

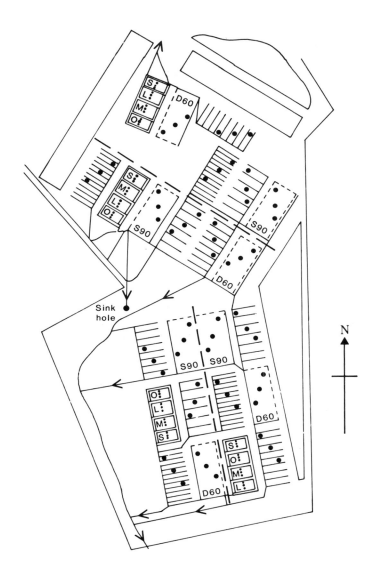

Figure 1. Sketch map of the Rumster 3 drainage experiment and Rumster 17 hydrology experiment. The ditch layout and positions of the boreholes are shown. Thick broken lines separate blocks and thin broken lines represent plot edges not defined by ditches. The D30/9, D30/14 and D30/18 treatment plots of Rumster 3 (see Table 2) are not labelled but can be distinguished by their ditch spacings.

drainage experiment were sacrificed to provide the four replicates and four small treatment plots laid down in each (Table 3 and Figure 1). These were 42 m x 20 m with 90-cm-deep perimeter ditches and were separated by 6-m-wide strips on which the drain spoil was heaped. The first three treatments consisted of D30 ploughing and then planting with *Pinus contorta, Picea sitchensis,* or a 50:50 mixture of the two. Each of these treatments received a different fertiliser regime; the *Picea sitchensis* was given P and K, the mixture was given P only and the *Pinus contorta* received no fertiliser at planting, but had to be given P in May 1991 because the trees were showing symptoms of P deficiency. The fourth treatment was an unploughed, unplanted control.

The main purpose of this experiment was to monitor the quantitative and qualitative water balance of these three types of plantations; the results, which are not yet available, will be published separately. Three boreholes in each plot were used to measure the water level weekly from 1989 to 1991. In each plot a set of six brass marker plates was installed at depth increments of 25 cm down to 150 cm below the surface. Each marker plate was fixed to a steel rod, the end of which protruded above the surface. The vertical height of each plate was measured at roughly 6-month intervals by surveying the height of the rod end relative to a vertical datum (the top end of a steel rod pushed down to the base of the peat and hammered into the underlying till). Vegetation was surveyed, using 40 quadrats (20 cm x 20 cm) on a randomly chosen diagonal transect of each plot, in summer 1992. Only 20 quadrats were used in the control plots, where the greater variability caused by ploughing was absent. The plough ridges in the M and S treatments were sprayed with glyphosate in September 1990 to kill *Epilobium angustifolium*, which can damage young trees by rubbing during the winter.

Results

Drainage experiment

Winter period mean borehole water levels, BWL_w (the mean of all the measurements made during December, January, February and March), have been used as a measure of treatment effects. A surplus of rainfall over evaporation is

Table 3. Treatment details for the hydrological experiment. All plots had a perimeter drain 90 cm deep. Phosphorus was applied at 58 kg ha^{-1} and potassium at 108 kg ha^{-1}.
*: In the third growing season, treatment L was given phosphorus because the trees showed deficiency symptoms.

Treatment name	Ploughed	Species Planted	Fertiliser applied at planting
L	Yes	Lodgepole pine (LP)	– *
S	Yes	Sitka spruce (SS)	PK
M	Yes	LP+SS 50:50 Mixture	P
O	No	–	–

normal during the winter months so the height of the water table depends largely on the effectiveness of the drainage network and progress of cracking. Evaporation is more important in summer and, during dry spells, is the main factor controlling the water table height. While the extent and duration of lowering of the water table during the summer were regarded as the driving forces of long-term hydrological change, its level during the winter was thought better to reflect the progress of this change. This would be especially so in the context of restoration because, after removal of the trees, and the consequent reduction in evaporation, we would expect the water table to be controlled, even during the summer, by the system of drains and cracks. Analysis of variance was used to compare BWL_w between treatments. Wherever results are described as significant, the 95 % probability level, or greater, is implied.

The drainage treatments caused a significant lowering of the water table in the first four years compared with the control (Table 4, Period 1). There was also a trend of increasing BWL_w with intensity of drainage, the S90 treatment, by far the most intensively drained, having a significantly lower water table than all other treatments, and the D30/9 having a significantly lower water table than the D30/18, showing the influence of intercepting ditch spacing.

By the time the trees were 19 years old (Table 4, Period 2) and had had a closed canopy for several years, the significant difference between the drainage treatments and the control remained but the relationship between intensity of drainage and BWL_w was no longer significant; and neither was the difference between D30 treatments with different intercepting ditch spacings.

After deepening the ditches to their original 90 cm depth (Table 4, Period 3) the BWL_w in the three D30 treatments, although not significantly different, again fell into the same order as their ditch frequency. The change in BWL_w consequent on deepening the ditches (Table 4, Change 2 to 3) was significantly greater in these

Table 4. Winter mean depth to water table (cm) for the six treatments described in Table 2. The least significant difference ($P < 0.05$) between treatments for each comparison is given below. The means for Periods 2 and 3 and the change between Periods 1 and 3 have been adjusted for the significant ($P < 0.05$) covariate, slope.

Treatment Name	Winter mean depth to water table (cm)				
	Period 1 (1969–73)	Period 2 (1987–88)	Period 3 (1989–90)	Change 2 to 3	Change 1 to 3
D30/9	23	26	43	17	20
D30/14	20	23	38	15	19
D30/18	18	24	37	13	19
S90	30	30	33	3	2
D60	20	33	38	5	19
Control	2	2	--	--	--
LSD	4	12	13	6	11

three ditched treatments than in those without ditches.

The overall change in BWL_w between the first few years and the period after ditch deepening (Table 4, Change 1 to 3) was significantly greater in all other treatments than in the most intensively drained (S90) and the undrained control., The S90 treatment had possibly had such a large and immediate effect that the drying effect of the trees was less important.

The original slope of the ground surface influenced BWL_w significantly in the second and third measurement periods, but not in the first. Every 1% slope of the ground surface was associated with a 24-cm increase (95% confidence interval = $\pm$ 14 cm) in the plot mean BWL_w. The values in Table 4 have been adjusted for this covariate where it was significant.

Hydrological experiment

In the hydrological experiment, shallow ploughing significantly lowered the water table compared with the control (Table 5). In the control the drainage effect of the perimeter ditch seemed to have caused a slight lowering of the water table, indicated by comparison with the BWL_w in the control treatment (O) of the drainage experiment (Table 4, Period 2). However, this cannot be tested statistically because the same boreholes were not used in both cases.

The lowering of the water table caused subsidence of the ground surface by 6 cm and 2 cm, measured near the centre of the ploughed and control plots respectively, in the first 2 years. The rate of subsidence slowed down thereafter. The changes in level of the marker plates at depths of up to 1.5 m below the surface indicated that the subsidence of the surface was due to consolidation of the peat at all depths, rather than shrinkage of the surface layer alone.

The vegetation survey showed that the control plots were dominated by *Trichophorum cespitosum* and *Cladonia portentosa* (Table 6). Ploughing, but with no fertiliser applied until the third growing season, when an application of P was given, caused a change on the undisturbed ground between plough ridges, to a community dominated by *Erica tetralix* and *Calluna vulgaris*, while ploughing and fertilising with P and K at the time of planting caused *Eriophorum vaginatum* to become dominant on these undisturbed areas. In all three ploughed treatments,

Table 5. Winter mean borehole water level (cm) in the hydrological experiment for the periods November 1989 to March 1990 and November to December 1990. The least significant difference is for the $P < 0.05$ probability level.

Treatment	Borehole water level (cm)	
	1989–90	1990–91
Ploughed	16	12
Control	8	7
LSD	4	3

Table 6. Vegetation survey results for the hydrological experiment. Figures represent percentage of quadrats with the given species more dominant than any other. The columns headed O, L, M and S are for vegetation on the undisturbed strips of ground between plough ridges in each treatment (see Table 3).

	Treatment				Ridges (L only)	Furrows
	O	L	M	S		
Number of quadrats	80	40	40	40	20	30
Species						
Calluna vulgaris	6	30	28	15	14	5
Erica tetralix		27	7	6	16	5
Eriophorum angustifolium	5	2	13	12	57	16
Eriophorum vaginatum	10	6	13	27	2	1
Trichophorum cespitosum	29	19	10	25		1
Bryum caespicitium						15
Campylopus introflexus						5
Campylopus pyriformis						35
Cladonia portentosa	29	10	4	5	1	1
Dicranella heteromalla					7	13
Hypnum cupressiforme			1			
Hypnum jutlandicum	2	4	12	7		
Pleurozia purpurea			3			
Sphagnum capillifolium	11	1	5			
Sphagnum cuspidatum	3		1			
Sphagnum papillosum	2			3		
Sphagnum subnitens	3	1	3			
Others					3	3

Campylopus pyriformis had become the most dominant species in the plough furrows. *Epilobium angustifolium* had become common on the plough ridges in the fertilised M and S treatments by the summer of 1990 and it had been necessary to spray these with glyphosate to prevent the trees from being damaged by rubbing. This problem did not arise in the unfertilised L treatment, illustrating that this species can quickly colonise plough ridges on poor peat after phosphate fertiliser has been applied. Because the ridges in the M and S treatments received this herbicide, only the survey results for the ridges in the L treatment are included in Table 6. *Eriophorum angustifolium* had become by far the most dominant species on the ridges, followed by *Erica tetralix* and *Calluna vulgaris*.

Discussion: hydrological effects of afforestation

The use of depth to water table for comparisons of the drying effect of plantations is justified by its importance for recolonisation by bog plants after removing the trees. The absolute change in height of the water table (*i.e.* the change in its height above the mineral substratum), may be much larger than the change in depth to water table, in a situation where the peat has consolidated and the surface has subsided due to drying. However, it is the distance between the water table and the surface which affects the conditions for plant growth.

There are very few published studies of the effects of drainage and afforestation on blanket bog peat or vegetation; most drainage studies have concentrated on the effects on tree growth. Fraser (1933) made observations on pseudofibrous peat adjacent to ditches and concluded that, while ditching can reduce its water content, it does not necessarily improve the aeration. This, we suggest, was due to the peat shrinking as it lost water but remained saturated so that air did not intrude. Binns (1968) compared the water content profile of peat under 30-year-old *Pinus contorta* with that in failed plots of the same experiment, and in adjacent unplanted areas. The experiment had been drained by hand-digging 15-cm-deep furrows at 2-m intervals. The plots where the tree crop had failed demonstrated almost no drying effect due to drainage alone, while those where the crop had succeeded demonstrated marked drying of the peat due to the combination of draining and tree growth. He concluded that drying of this afforested peat was due not to the shallow drainage but to the evapotranspiration of the trees. Farrell (1985) measured the depth to the water table in a forest fertiliser and liming experiment on blanket bog and found a positive correlation between depth to water table and growth of the 20-year-old *Picea sitchensis*. No information on the effect of ditching and ploughing on the water table was reported, because these had been uniformly applied over the whole experiment.

Farrell also reported subsidence of the ground surface, averaging 18 cm over the 14-year period starting when the trees were 5 years old and related to tree growth. This relationship between tree growth and ground surface subsidence indicates that we can expect further subsidence in the Rumster hydrology experiment, where the early subsidence, due to drainage, of 6 cm, had almost stopped after the first 2 years. This prediction is supported by the observed subsidence, by 30–55 cm, of the ground surface beneath the 20-year-old trees of the Rumster drainage experiment (Pyatt *et al.*, 1992).

PROSPECTS FOR RESTORING AFFORESTED BLANKET BOG

One option for restoring blanket bogs after afforestation is to leave the site to revert naturally after removal of the first-rotation trees. There is plenty of evidence, stored in the peat, of forests which invaded ombrogenous mires during the Sub-Boreal period and were eventually succeeded by the further accumulation of ombrogenous peat (*e.g.* Lewis, 1911; Tansley, 1939). However, those forests were not sustained by artificial drainage or fertilisation, as are the plantations of today. We cannot be confident, in the face of a change in global climate, that the high rainfall and relative humidity which currently favour peat formation in areas of blanket bog will be sustained in the next century. Thus we cannot restore an afforested blanket bog simply by leaving it to nature, at least not within a reasonably short period of time.

Positive management is needed in any attempt to restore the original blanket bog vegetation quickly. Blocking or filling in ditches and furrows, which might have taken many years to fill in naturally, would reduce the time it would take for the water table to return to within a few centimetres of the surface. Leaving the trees to succumb to a renewed high water table, an option successfully practised on raised bogs colonised by pines in Switzerland (A Grünig, personal communication) would only be an option if the investment in the afforestation costs were being sacrificed for the sake of restoration. We have no evidence that this option would be successful on blanket bog, and its main advantage, that of saving the harvesting costs, would only apply if the harvesting costs exceeded the value of the timber. One further advantage would be in avoiding the risk of damaging the site during harvesting operations. Removing the trees would restore light and exposure conditions to the bog surface far more quickly than leaving them to die on their feet and would remove the nutrients stored in the timber. Good *et al.* (1990), reporting on a survey of vegetation in conifer plantations in Kielder Forest, found that most plantations less than 20 years old on deep peat retained sufficient remnants of their original vegetation to warrant restoration and at higher elevations crops up to 40 years old retained a representative ground flora. Vegetation management, such as herbicide spraying to control heather, would be unnecessary if the water table were successfully restored, but might be considered justified if it increased the rate of recolonisation by *Sphagnum* mosses. However, livestock might be necessary to restore the original character of the vegetation where it had been artificially created and sustained by grazing prior to afforestation (Good *et al.*, 1990).

Raising of the water table by damming ditches is normal practice in mire restoration and appears to be successful, although little hydrological or botanical monitoring has yet been reported. Much work in restoring bogs drained for forestry has been done on the Border Mires, a series of bogs within Kielder Forest, Northumberland, the wetter parts of which were not planted. Only recently has monitoring of the vegetation and water levels been started so results are not yet available. The Border Mires are of a type transitional between raised and blanket bogs and, to our knowledge, no attempts have yet been made to restore true blanket bog after afforestation. Vasander, Leivo & Tanninen (1992), describing an attempt to restore drained ombrotrophic bog in central Finland, reported limited success in raising the water table by damming ditches. They found that more dams were needed than had been installed initially and that dams designed to retain the water flowing in one direction leaked because the damming reversed the direction of flow. Problems may arise when trying to raise the water table in cracked peat. There are no reports in the literature of attempts to do this so we can only speculate on its feasibility. If the cracking is confined to the furrow and ditch bottoms then it should be possible to install dams which go down deeper than the cracks. However, if the cracking has spread through the whole mass of peat between the furrows, the network of cracks would presumably by-pass dams in the furrows and ditches, rendering them ineffective. The water level in the cracks will largely be controlled by their depth or by their height above an outlet such as a ditch crossing an unplanted ride. On very flat ground, large areas could be restored hydrologically by blocking a small number of these controlling outlets, but, on the gentle slopes more characteristic of blanket bogs, the areas affected by damming these outlets would be a small proportion of the whole.

ACKNOWLEDGEMENTS

We thank Alan Grant and James Munro for taking borehole readings, Arkle Fraser, Ian Forshaw, Gordon Watson and Colin Lesley for their co-operation and support, Neil Redgate for doing the vegetation survey and Julian Philipson and Gordon Patterson for their constructive comments on an earlier draft.

REFERENCES

Anderson, A.R., Pyatt, D.G. & Stannard, J.P. (1990). The effects of clearfelling a Sitka spruce stand on the water balance of a peaty gley soil at Kershope Forest, Cumbria. *Forestry*, **60(1)**, 51–71.

Binns, W.O. (1959). *The physical and chemical properties of deep peat in relation to afforestation*. PhD thesis, University of Aberdeen, UK.

Binns, W.O. (1968). Some effects of tree growth on peat. In: *Proceedings of the Third International Peat Congress, Quebec, Canada*, National Research Council, Ottawa, Canada, 358–365.

Burrows, W.C. (1963). Characterisation of soil temperature distribution from various tillage-induced microreliefs. *Soil Science Society of America Proceedings*, **27**, 350–353.

Chapman, S.B. & Rose, R.J. (1987). Vegetation change at Coom Rigg Moss NNR. *The NERC Institute of Terrestrial Ecology Report for 1986–87* NERC, Swindon, UK. 100–101.

Charman, D.J. & Smith, R.S. (1992). Forestry and blanket mires of Kielder Forest, northern England: long term effects on vegetation. *Peatland Ecosystems and Man: An Impact Assessment* (eds O.M. Bragg, P.D. Hulme, H.A.P. Ingram, & R.A. Robertson), pp. 226–230. International Peat Society/Department of Biological Sciences, University of Dundee. Dundee.

Coutts, M.P. & Phillipson, J.J. (1987). Structure and physiology of Sitka spruce roots. *Proceedings of the Royal Society of Edinburgh*, **93B**, 131–144.

Farrell, E.P. (1985). Long-term study of Sitka spruce on blanket peat: 2. Water-table depth, peat depth and nutrient mineralisation studies. *Irish Forestry*, **42(2)** 92–105.

Fraser, G.K. (1933). Studies of certain Scottish moorlands in relation to tree growth. *Forestry Commission Bulletin No. 15*. HMSO, London.

Good, J.E.G., Williams, T.G., Wallace, H.L., Buse, A. & Norris, D.A. (1990). *Nature Conservation in Upland Conifer Forests*. Unpublished report to the Nature Conservancy Council and the Forestry Commission.

Hobbs, N.B. (1986). Mire morphology and the properties and behaviour of some British and foreign peats. *Quarterly Journal of Engineering Geology*, **19**, 7–80.

Howell, J.H. (1984). *Morphological and microbiological changes in peat following afforestation.* MSc thesis, Dept. of Soil Science, University of Aberdeen, UK.

Lewis, F.J. (1911). The plant remains in the Scottish peat mosses. *Transactions of the Royal Society of Edinburgh*, **47**, 793–799.

Lindsay, R.A., Charman, D.J., Everingham, F., O'Reilly, R.M., Palmer, M.A., Rowell, T.A., & Stroud, D.A. (1988*). The Flow Country. The Peatlands of Caithness and Sutherland.* Nature Conservancy Council, Peterborough. 174pp.

Mahrer, Y. & Avissar, R. (1985). A numerical study of the effects of soil surface shape upon the soil temperature and moisture regimes. *Soil Science*, **139(6)**, 483–490.

Miller, H.G. (1981). Forest fertilization: some guiding concepts. *Forestry*, **54(2)**, 157–167.

Pyatt, D.G. (1990). Long term prospects for forests on peatland. *Scottish Forestry*, **44(1)**, 19–25.

Pyatt, D.G. (1993). Multi-purpose forests on peatland. *Biodiversity and Conservation* **2(5)**, 548–555.

Pyatt, D.G. & John, A.L. (1989). Modelling volume changes in peat under conifer plantations. *Journal of Soil Science* **40**, 695–706.

Pyatt, D.G., Craven, M.M. & Williams, B.L. (1979). Peatland classification for forestry in Great Britain. *Classification of Peat and Peatlands* pp. 351–366. International Peat Society, Helsinki,.

Pyatt, D.G., Anderson, A.R., Stannard, J.P. & White, I.M.S. (1985). A drainage experiment on a peaty gley soil at Kershope Forest, Cumbria. *Soil Use and Management* **1(3)**, 89–94.

Pyatt, D.G., John, A.L., Anderson, A.R. & White, I.M.S. (1992). The drying of blanket peatland by 20-year-old conifer plantations at Rumster Forest, Caithness. *Peatland Ecosystems and Man: An Impact Assessment* (eds O.M. Bragg, P.D. Hulme, H.A.P. Ingram, & R.A. Robertson), pp. 153–158. International Peat Society/Department of Biological Sciences, University of Dundee. Dundee.

Schnitzer, M. (1986). Water retention by humic substances *Peat and Water. Aspects of Water Retention and Dewatering in Peat.*(ed. C.H. Fuchsman), pp. 159–176. Elsevier Applied Science Publishers, London.

Smith, A.J.E. (1978). *The Moss Flora of Britain and Ireland.* Cambridge University Press, Cambridge.

Smith, R.S. & Charman, D.J. (1988). The vegetation of upland mires within conifer plantations in Northumberland, northern England. *Journal of Applied Ecology*, **25**, 579–594.

Stace, C.A. (1991). *New Flora of the British Isles.* Cambridge University Press, Cambridge.

Strathers, R.J. & Spittlehouse, D.L. (1990). Forest soil temperature manual. *Canada-British Columbia Forest Resource Development Agreement Report 130.* Forestry Canada, Victoria, B.C.

Tabbush, P.M. (1986). Rough handling, soil temperature and root development in outplanted Sitka spruce and Douglas-fir. *Canadian Journal of Forest Research*, **16**, 1385–1388.

Tansley, A.G. (1939). *The British Islands and their Vegetation.* Cambridge University Press, Cambridge.

Taylor, C.M.A. (1991). Forest fertilisation in Britain. *Forestry Commission Bulletin*, **93**. HMSO, London.

Taylor, G.G.M. (1970). Ploughing practice in the Forestry Commission. *Forestry Commission Forest Record* **73**, 44pp. HMSO, London.

Titus, B.D. & Malcolm, D.C. (1987). The effect of fertilisation on litter decomposition in clearfelled spruce stands. *Plant and Soil*, **100**, 297–322.

Vasander, H., Leivo, A. & Tanninen, T. (1992). Rehabilitation of a drained peatland area in the Seitseminen National Park in Southern Finland. *Peatland Ecosystems and Man: An Impact Assessment* (eds O.M. Bragg, P.D. Hulme, H.A.P. Ingram, & R.A. Robertson), pp. 381–387. International Peat Society/Department of Biological Sciences, University of Dundee. Dundee.

Zehetmayr, J.W.L. (1954). Experiments in tree planting on peat. *Forestry Commission Bulletin No. 22.* HMSO, London.

36 The Basis of Mire Restoration in Finland

H. HEIKKILÄ
National Board of Waters and the Environment, Research Centre of Nature Reserve 'Friendship', Tönölä, FIN-88900, Kuhmo, Finland

T. LINDHOLM
National Board of Waters and the Environment, Nature Conservation Research Unit, P.O. Box 250, FIN-00101, Helsinki, Finland

SUMMARY

1.   In Finland 60% of the 10.4 million ha of mire has been drained for forestry, with the aim of improving tree growth in peatlands.
2.   Drainage favours hummock and lawn-level mire plants together with forest species; flark-level species disappear rapidly.
3.   In Finnish National Parks and mire reserves there are numerous drained mires, covering an area of 5851 ha. In areas planned for conservation, there is an additional 50000 ha of drained mires.
4.   The hydrological conditions of protected drained mires are restored by filling-in the ditches. It is also necessary to remove trees which have grown after drainage in order to decrease evapotranspiration and to restore the landscape mosaic. The filling of the ditches is mainly done by excavators.

MIRES IN FINLAND

The southern half of Finland contains a zone of raised bogs (Figure 1), while the northern half is occupied by aapa mires (Ruuhijärvi, 1983, 1988). Most of Finland is slightly continental, western coastal areas being slightly maritime (Ahti, Hämet-Ahti & Jalas, 1968; Tuhkanen, 1984). Finland lies on the Baltic bedrock shield. The rocks and soil are mainly acid and poor in nutrients. On average about 30% of the land area in Finland is covered by mires, *i.e.* about 10.4 million ha.

Only large mire-basins form true complex types. Small mires usually do not have the structures of the mire complex, such as hummock–hollow or pool–string systems. Also lagg, margin slope and true central plateau are usually lacking in small raised bogs. Many small mires may, however, form large representative networks between mineral hills. These mire systems, as well as true complex types

Restoration of Temperate Wetlands. Edited by B.D. Wheeler, S.C. Shaw, W.J. Fojt and R.A. Robertson
© 1995 John Wiley & Sons Ltd.

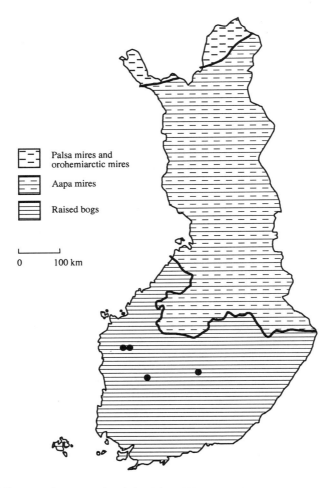

Figure 1. Mire complex zones in Finland (Ruuhijärvi, 1988). The locations of sampling areas are indicated with dots.

with their drainage basins, are important units in conservation and restoration strategies.

UTILISATION

Cultivation of permanent fields in the nineteenth century was the start of mire exploitation in Finland. It is estimated that 1 million ha of mires has been converted into arable fields in Finland (Heikkilä, 1989). The local nutrient load from agriculture and other pollution sources has had little effect on virgin mires. The mire areas used for peat production or reserved for it occupy about 0.1 million ha (Eurola *et al.*, 1991). Large water reservoirs cover about 50,000 ha of mires. By far the most intensive form of mire exploitation is drainage for forestry, which covers about 6 million ha or 60% of Finnish mires (Aarne, Uusitalo & Herrala-Ylinen, 1990). The drained area is about four times greater than the total mire area of the United Kingdom (mire areas according to Göttlich, 1990).

DRAINAGE FOR FORESTRY: METHODS AND RESULTS

The most intensive decades of draining for forestry were the 1960s and 1970s, when about 80% of all drainage was carried out. In the 1990s the draining of virgin peatlands has almost ceased, and nowadays the main goal is the maintenance of ditches for continued drainage.

The purpose of mire drainage is to induce better tree growth, usually *Pinus sylvestris*, by deepening the aerobic peat layer. This is achieved with ditches usually 30–50 m apart and 1 m deep (Päivänen, 1990). Surface peat outside the ditches is left untouched. Draining plans included large areas, and even the narrowest strips of mire were drained. Different areas were often joined by ditches in the mineral soil. In large areas it is therefore very difficult to find examples of undrained mires. Even ombrotrophic bogs were often drained (Heikkilä, 1984; Eurola *et al.*, 1991). The tree growth on poorly-drained areas was increased by fertilisation, mainly PK and NPK (Päivänen, 1990). Marginal areas of raised bogs have been systematically drained or used for agriculture, so that very few wholly undisturbed raised bogs remain, even if the central parts are untouched. Aapa mires can also be affected by drainage in the catchment areas, so that they are even more vulnerable than raised bogs.

The annual tree growth in all the Finnish peatland forests was 10 million m^3 according to the third inventory of Finnish forests (1951–53). In the seventh inventory (1977–84) the estimation was 15 million m^3, the increase being 5 million m^3 (Paavilainen & Tiihonen, 1988). The aim of the forest drainage is to have an increase of 25 million m^3 annually from peatland forests by the end of the twenty-first century (Heikurainen, 1982), even if this may be an overestimation. The increase will be mostly due to the increase in growth in areas now drained, because drainage has almost ceased. Most of the increase has occurred in mires which were originally forested. Tree growth in open mires has usually been poor.

EFFECTS ON VEGETATION

The vegetation of mires that have been drained for forestry gradually changes towards the vegetation of forests of similar nutritional status, although it does not become identical (Heikurainen, 1959; Sarasto, 1961). Only a few Finnish mires have reached this state (*c.* 4% of the drained mire area) (Keltikangas *et al.*, 1986). All others are in transitional stages.

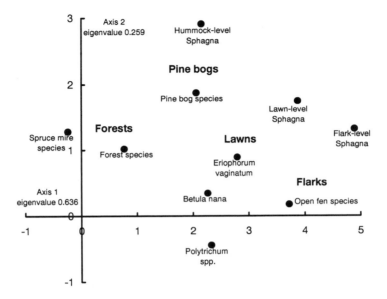

Figure 2. Detrended Correspondence Analysis ordination of mire species groups from virgin and drained mires in southern Finland

The species of pine bogs usually survive drainage, even some *Sphagnum* species. Poor-fen species disappear from drained surfaces but they often find refuge in ditches or poorly drained patches as drainage is not equally effective everywhere. Many mire species, for example *Carex heleonastes*[1], *Saxifraga hirculus* and *Drepanocladus vernicosus* (Mitt.) Warnst., vanish rapidly and are endangered owing to the extensive drainage (Heikkilä, 1992).

Fertilisation increases the growth of some species, such as *Eriophorum vaginatum* and *Betula nana*. Weeds are usually uncommon in drained mires. *Polytrichum* species dominate in some unsuccessfully-drained areas.

The change of vegetation is illustrated by analysis of 188 sample plots (4–5 1 x 1 m² relevés) from virgin and drained mires in southern Finland (Figure 1). The species were ordinated by Detrended Correspondence Analysis (DCA) ordination (Figure 2). After drainage, flark-level species are replaced by lawn-level species or dwarf shrubs in all places. Depending on the effectiveness of drainage and nutrient status, the hummock level may turn into a forest species community or stay practically unchanged. In Figure 3, DCA-ordination of the sample plots shows the possible successional direction of transitional drainage areas. Fertile mires change towards forest-like biotopes and nutrient-poor mires turn into dwarf-shrub-dominated types.

---

[1] Nomenclature of vascular plants: Hämet-Ahti *et al.* (1986).

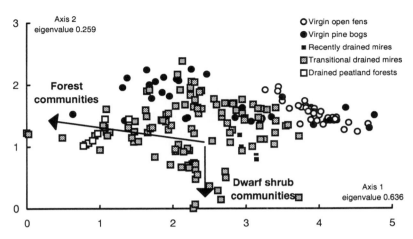

Figure 3. Detrended Correspondence Analysis ordination of Finnish mire vegetation. Possible successional directions are indicated with arrows.

PROTECTION

In the course of the 1960s the rapid destruction of mires was noticed and the first protection plans in state-owned territory were made. The National Park Committee suggested a large and thorough scheme, which included invaluable mire areas among other biotopes (Tallgren *et al.*, 1976). This programme was not implemented fully and mire areas in particular were excluded. The first part of the nationwide Mire Conservation Programme included both private and state-owned areas (Haapanen *et al.*, 1977). In the second part, mires were included, especially those with endangered species and site types (Haapanen *et al.* 1980). The whole programme was ratified in 1981. It includes 600 mires, with an area totalling 500,000 ha.

The mire conservation programme has now been largely completed with regard to the state-owned areas. Because they were protected so late, many of these mires had already been drained in the 1960s and 1970s. The acquisition and protection of privately-owned mires is still incomplete. Ministry of Environment data indicate that more than 50,000 ha of these mires has been drained since the ratification of the programme (P. Salminen, personal communication). Prime virgin mires that were previously excluded have now been included within a complementary conservation programme for about 500 mires, covering 120, 000 ha.

At present, 0.7 million ha of mires is protected, 75% of which are situated in northernmost Finland. The proportion of drained mires in protected areas varies considerably in different parts of Finland (Table 1).

Table 1. The area of protected mires in different regions of Finland, and the proportion of these that are drained.

Park Region	Mire area	Virgin		Drained	
	(ha)	(ha)	(%)	(ha)	(%)
S Coast	7406	6564	89	842	11
W Finland	29997	27169	91	2828	9
E Finland	18522	16444	94	1079	6
Ostrobothnia	96375	95569	99	806	1
Kainuu	24670	24430	99	240	1
N Finland	184434	184378	100	56	0
N Lapland	336424	336424	100	0	0
Total	697827	691977	99	5851	1

RESTORATION IN PROTECTED MIRES

The protected drainage areas will be restored following the plans of the Forest and Park Service (Metsähallitus, 1993) and the Ministry of Environment. Until now the restoration has taken place in only parts of the few mires. Plans have been now made to restore whole mire complexes and their surroundings.

In the restoration of mires drained for forestry, rewetting of the surface is most important: the flora and the fauna will respond in due time. Because most mire plants are usually still present in the mire or in nearby places, they can readily re-invade, and the natural vegetation cover redevelops relatively easily. In fertilised mires the removal of species such as *Betula nana* may be necessary. Re-introduction of lost species is planned in some special cases, for example planting of *Saxifraga hirculus* in some of its former localities in the south. Data are not available about the seed bank in mires drained for forestry.

Until now wooden dams have been built across the ditches in order to retain water in the mire (Vasander *et al.*, 1992), but in many places this does not seem to be a powerful tool. In future, restoration will be done mainly by in-filling the ditches with the peat originally taken from the same ditches using excavators. The filling of ditches which separate mires from the surrounding mineral soil is the only way to get the water from mineral soils to reach the mire again. This is one of the main problems in drained minerotrophic mires.

Cutting of the tree stand is usually needed to reduce water losses by evapotranspiration. Cutting also restores the original landscape mosaic of mires and forests including large marginal zones which are important for biodiversity. Restoration of the landscape pattern is also considered important in national parks where recreation is important.

RESTORATION IN UNPROTECTED AREAS

In unprotected areas, restoration takes places only occasionally. Unprofitable drainage areas are not maintained and it is likely that the ditches will eventually become occluded and the hydrology will be restored naturally. In some cases restoration of mires is needed to restore valuable adjacent watercourses.

REFERENCES

Aarne, M., Uusitalo, M. & Herrala-Ylinen, H. (1990). Metsätilastollinen vuosikirja 1989. (Yearbook of forest statistics 1989.) *Folia Forestalia*, **760**.
Ahti, T., Hämet-Ahti, L. & Jalas, J. (1968). Vegetation zones and their sections in northwestern Europe. *Annales Botanici Fennici*, **5**,169–211.
Eurola, S., Aapala, K., Kokko, A. & Nironen, M. (1991). Mire type statistics in the bog and southern aapa mire areas of Finland (60° N). *Annales Botanici Fennici*, **28**,15–36.
Göttlich, Kh. (1990). *Moor- und Torfkunde*, E. Schweizerbart'sche Verlagsbuchhandlung (Nägele u. Obermiller), Stuttgart.
Haapanen, A., Havu, S., Häyrinen, U., Lehtimäki, E., Raitasuo, K., Ruuhijärvi, R. & Salminen, P. (1977). Soidensuojelun perusohjelma. [The basic programme for mire conservation.] *Komiteanmietintö*, **1977:48**, Helsinki.
Haapanen, A., Havu, S., Häyrinen, U., Lehtimäki, E., Raitasuo, K., Ruuhijärvi, R. & Salminen, P. (1980). Soidensuojelun perusohjelma II. [The basic programme for mire conservation II.] *Komiteanmietintö*, **1980:15**, Helsinki.
Hämet-Ahti, L., Suominen, J., Ulvinen, T., Uotila, P. & Vuokko, S. (1986). *Suomen retkeilykasvio. (Summary: The field flora of Finland.)*, 3rd revised edition. Suomen Luonnonsuojelun Tuki, Helsinki.
Heikkilä, Raimo (1984). Karujen rämeiden ja nevojen ojituksista, erityisesti Etelä-Pohjanmaalla. (Summary: Unprofitable forestry drainage of sparsely tree covered and treeless poor mires, especially in Southern Ostrobothnia, Western Finland.) *Suo*, **35**, 41–46.
Heikkilä, Raimo (1992). Changes in the distribution of some plant species of the eutrophic fens of southern Finland. *Peatland Ecosystems and Man: An Impact Assesment* (eds O.M. Bragg, P.D. Hulme, H.A.P. Ingram & R.A. Robertson), pp. 244–249. International Peat Society / Department of Biological Sciences, University of Dundee, Dundee.
Heikkilä, Reijo (1989). Soiden maataloudellinen merkitys nyt ja tulevaisuudessa. (Summary: Peatlands in Finnish agriculture now and in the future.) *Suo*, **40**, 111–113.
Heikurainen, L. (1959) Tutkimus metsäojitusalueiden tilasta ja puustosta. (Referat: Über waldbaulich entwässerte Flächen und ihre Waldbestände in Finnland.) *Acta Forestalia Fennica*, **61**, 1–279.
Heikurainen, L. (1982). Peatland forestry. *Peatlands and their utilization in Finland* (ed. Laine, J.). Finnish Peatland Society and Finnish National Committee of the International Peat Society, Helsinki.
Keltikangas, M, Laine, J., Puttonen, P. & Seppälä, K. (1986). Vuosina 1930–1978 metsäojitetut suot: ojitusalueiden inventoinnin tuloksia. (Summary: Peatlands drained for forestry during 1930–1978: results from field surveys of drained areas.) *Acta Forestalia Fennica* **193**, 1–94.
Metsähallitus (1993). Luonnonsuojelualueiden hoidon periaatteet. Valtion omistamien luonnonsuojelualueiden tavoitteet, tehtävät ja hoidon yleislinjat. [Principles of

management of nature conservation areas. The objectives, tasks and main lines of management in the state-owned nature conservation areas.] *Metsähallituksen luonnonsuojelujulkaisuja B* **1**.

Paavilainen, E. & Tiihonen, P. (1988). Suomen suometsät vuosina 1951–1984. (Summary: Peatland forests in Finland in 1951–1984.) *Folia Forestalia*, **714**, 1–29.

Päivänen, J. (1990). *Suometsät ja niiden hoito.* [*Peatland Forests and their Management.*] Kirjayhtymä, Helsinki.

Ruuhijärvi, R. (1983). The Finnish mire types and their distribution. *Ecosystems of the World. 4B. Mires: Swamp, Bog, Fen and Moor. Regional Studies* (ed. A.J.P. Gore), pp. 47–67. Elsevier, Amsterdam.

Ruuhijärvi, R. (1988). Suokasvillisuus. [Mire vegetation]. *Atlas of Finland*, **141** (ed. P. Alalammi). Maanmittaushallitus, Suomen Maantieteellinen Seura, Helsinki.

Sarasto, J. (1961). Über die Klassifizierung der für Walderziehung entwässerten Moore. *Acta Forestalia Fennica*, **74**, 1–47.

Tallgren, C.O., Väisänen, P.O., Kangas, I., Seiskari, P., Kivilaakso, T., Hellman, L., Ojala, O., Tuomainen, E., Korpela, T., Havu, S., Kellomäki, E., Häyrinen, U. & Lovén, L. (1976). Kansallispuistokomitean mietintö. [National Park programme]. *Komitean-mietintö*, **1976:88**, Helsinki.

Tuhkanen, S. (1984). A circumboreal system of climatic-phytogeographical regions. *Acta Botanica Fennica*, **127**, 1–50.

Vasander, H., Leivo, A. & Tanninen, T. (1992). Rehabilitation of a drained peatland area in the Seitseminen national park in Southern Finland. *Peatland Ecosystems and Man: An Impact Assesment* (eds O.M. Bragg, P.D. Hulme, H.A.P. Ingram & R.A. Robertson), pp. 381–387. International Peat Society/Department of Biological Sciences, University of Dundee, Dundee.

Index

Note: Page references in **bold** refer to main chapter or section topics, those in *italics* to tables and figures.

acidification, 65, 79, 80, 83, 108, **262**, **263**, *264*, **273**
acrotelm, 8, 262, 293, **296**, **305**, *308*, *309*, **317**, 406, 407, 417, 448, 536
aluminium, 53, **96**, 291
Anthoxanthum odoratum, *151*, 160
Araneae, **225**
archaeology. *See also* palaeoecology.
  restoration and, **19**
atmotrophiation. See acidification
Australia; Northern Tablelands, **183**

base richness, **53**
biodiversity, 49, 187, 253, 254
birds, 7, 20, 21, 122, 260
  habitats, **208**, *210*
  management for, 262
  of raised bogs, **360**, *365*
  rare species, *210*
  restoration for, **207**, **359**, **451**
bog, 80, *94*, **287**; *See also* vegetation; wetland
  blanket, 10, 16, 36, *103*, **287**, **495**, **533**
    degradation, **495**, *502*, **509**
    development, 495
    distribution, 289, 495, *496*, *498*
    restoration, 503, **509**, **533**, **544**
  concept of, **13**
  raised, 16, 35, 36, *103*, 213, **287**, 497, *500*
    definition, 380
    development, **24**, 25, **262**, **379**
    distribution, 35, 289
    ecology, **380**
    regeneration, **379**
    restoration, 8, 29, 42, **305**, **315**, **331**, **347**, **349**, **359**, **379**, **405**, **423**, **435**, **451**, **471**, **549**

  vegetation, 6, **349**, **405**, **471**, *480*, *485*
  regeneration: definition, **383**
  restoration, **33**, 551
  vegetation, *36*, 38, *44*, 263, 306, **359**, **379**, **435**, 453
  key species, **392**
bryophytes, 38, *44*, 52, **108**, 174, *179*, 180, 185, **251**, **273**, 274, 281, 282, *284*, **379**, **471**. *See also Sphagnum.*
carr, 29, *44*, *256*, 258, 261, 263, 274
charophytes, 185

calcium, 53, 75, *84*, **96**, **279**, *281*, *282*, *283*, 290, *292*, 293, *295*, 297, 408, **409**, *410*, **413**, 415, *416*, 418, 439, 455, **509**, 515, *519*
Calluna vulgaris, 351, *352*, **523**
Canada, **423**
  Pokesudie Bog, New Brunswick, **451**
  Ste-Marguerite peatland, Quebec, 426
carbon, *156*, 160, 439
  C:N ratio, 127, 144, 157, *160*, 297, 444
  C:P ratio, *160*
Carex aquatilis, *155*
Carex dioica, **176**, *178*
Carex lasiocarpa sere, *256*, 262, 266, 267, *268*
CARICION DAVALLIANAE, 35, 53, 56, 68, 74, 78, 256
catotelm, 262, 263, 293, 296, **305**, 321, 323, 536
chemistry. *See* peat and water chemistry
chloride, *292*, *295*
Cladium mariscus, 27, 40, 51, 54, 67, 224, 241
climate, **51**, 261
  microclimate, 300, 374, **435**, 535

Coleoptera, **225**, **244**, *247*
conservation, **33**, 122, 218, 267, 347, 436, **549**
  birds, 359
  evaluation, **247**
  objectives, **5**, **173**, **208**, 241, **251**, 274
  rarity, 7, **34**, **37**
  value, **34**, 50, 51, 225, 255, 527, 530
Crepis paludosa, *155*

Dactylorhiza majalis, *155*
diaspore
  bank, 10, 106, 131, 140, 144, 163, 554
    studies on, **183**, **189**, **471**
    persistence, 184, *185*, **489**
    types of, **197**, *198*
  dispersal, 285, **471**
  regeneration from, 412, **423**, *432*
Diptera, **243**
drainage. *See* hydrology.
dune slack wetland, 80

Erica tetralix, *352*, 353
ERICO-SPHAGNION, *36*
Eriophorum angustifolium, 79, *298, 352*, 353, 387, **509**
Eriophorum vaginatum, *352*, 353, **437**, *438, 440, 491*
Estonia, *365*
eutrophication, 57, 75, **91**, 263, 265, **273**

fen, **91**, *94*, **121**, **451**. *See also* wetland; vegetation
  concept of, **12**
  definition, 74
  development, **77**, *78*, 79, 80, *101, 106*, **113**
  distribution, 35, **50**
  diversity, 36
  floating. *See* vegetation, floating raft
  meadow, 84, **143**, 167
  poor fen, 13, 35, **53**, 54, 83, *103*, **109**, 251, 385, 552
  restoration, 29, **33**, 42, **49**, **73**, *86*, **91**, **113**, **121**, **129**, **143**, **167**, **189**, 220, **223**, **241**, 251, **273**, **549**
  rich fen, 13, 35, 37, **53**, 54, 73, 78, 83, *103*, **104**, **108**, **167**, 251, **273**
  soil types, **121**. *See also* peat

spring, 75, 83, 171
system, **74**, **77**
valleyhead, 37, **40**, *41*, 52, **67**
vegetation, 7, 29, 36, *44*, **73**, *78*, 80, *84*, 126, *133,* 171, *177, 179,* **189**, **223**
fertiliser,
  control of application, 266
  experimental addition, 104, 105, *298*, **405**, **423**, **509**, **523**
  agriculture, 121, **143**, *146, 147, 169,* 170
  forestry, **533**, 535, 552
fertility, **56**, 63, 121
Finland, *365*, **549**
fire, 261, 384, 388
  regeneration following, 384
forestry
  effects of, 80, *534,* **549**
  restoration following, **533**, **549**

Germany, 80, *365*, 382, 384, 394
  Bavaria, **189**; Bissendorfer Moor, **362**; Fettsee, *82*, *84*; Kendlmuhlfilz, **472**; Kollerfilz, **473**; Kulbinger Filz, 385; Lieper Posse, *82*, *84*; Lower Saxony, **347**; Silleruper Moor, *386*; Südliches Wietingsmoor, **362**; Tinner Dose, **363**; Upper Rhinluch, **121**; Wieninger Filz, **473**

habitat
  bird, **359**, **451**, **466**
  quality, 38, 40
  rarity, **34**
  structure, 373
Hemiptera, **225**
Holcus lanatus, *151*, 159
hydrology, 79, **305**, 534
  aquifer yield, *310*
  drainage, 130, 266, **308**
    effects of, 41, 75, 77, 78, 80, 107, **113**, **121**, 163, 332, **533**, **549**
    types of, **129**
  evapotranspiration, 79, 308, 316, 318, **319**, 344, 447, 544, 554
  groundwater, 59, 74, 83, **93**, *94,* 95, 114, 261, 267, *268,* 275
    flow, *75, 81, 86, 276*
  management, **85**, **218**, **265**

model, 85, **123, 315, 331, 336**, 394
  groundwater mound, **305**, *311, 312,*
    337
  SIMGRO, **339**, *340*
  SWAMP, **336**, *338*
monitoring, 351, **353, 407, 540**
regional, 307
restoration management, 10, 42, 79, 80,
    82, 107, 118, **127**, *128,* **129, 144,**
    187, 214, **217**, 220, **273, 305, 315,**
    325, **331**, *333,* **347**, 362, 375, 392,
    460, *461,* **545**, 554
  archaeology and, **28**
  buffer zones, **332, 335**
  bunds, 312, 334
  creation of open water, 128, **334**
  ditch blocking, 309, **333, 349**, 463,
    554
  ditch clearance, **242**, *243, 244*
  drainage, **275**
  research needs, **343**
  supplementary water supply, 94,
    107, 108, 109, 325, *326*
run-off, 310, 316, **321**
seepage, 145, **308, 315, 331**, *335, 338,*
    344, 393
water balance, *309,* **316**, *317,* **318**, *333,*
    336, 347, 407, 540
water budget, 123, 215, **307**
water flow, *81, 94,* 101, 108, 299, 315,
    326, 335
water regime, 13, *15*, 29, 58, 59, *94,*
    114, 115, *116,* **183**, 220, **267**, 282,
    412

invertebrates
  fossil remains, 22
  management for, **219, 223**, 241, 262
  rare species, **223**
  species richness, **226**, *227*
Ireland, 406, 503
iron, 53, 58, **96**, 99, 291, 296, 298, *410,*
    439

Juncus acutiflorus, 150, *151*

light, *63*, 162, **427**, 447, 525, 536
lime; experimental addition, **413, 425,**
    509, 523

Lycaena dispar, **2**

magnesium, 53, **279**, *281, 282, 283,* 290,
    292, 293, *295*, 439, 455, 518, *519*
mammals, 122.
  impacts of, **25**, *27*, 39; *See also*
    vegetation management, grazing
manganese, 53, 296, 439
microbial activity, 96, 297
mineralisation, 58, 59, 75, **95, 102**, 118,
    147, 263, 265, 269, 437
mining, coal - restoration following, **523**
models, **382**
  agricultural, 169
  fen development, 77, *78*
  hydrological. *See* hydrology
  ICHORS, 267
Molinia caerulea, 175, **176**, *178*, 180

Netherlands, 7, 77, **85, 91, 251, 379**, 394
  Bergschenhoek, **20**; Bourtanger Moor,
    24; Engbertsdijksvenen, **35**, 335, 337,
    338; Groote Peel, 339, *340*, 390, 394;
    Meerstalblok, 33; Molenpolder, *96, 97*;
    Peel, 386, **387**, *389*; Stobbenribben, *96,*
    97; Stroomdallandschap, Drentsche A,
    143; Vechtplassen, **273**; Westbroek, *96,*
    97
nitrogen, 52, 56, 59, 95, *96, 97, 148, 156,*
    160, 283, *284, 292,* 298, 299, 408, 409,
    439, 518, 520, 525, 535. *See also*
    fertiliser; mineralisation; nutrient
  ammonium, *284,* 290, 298, *410,* 419,
    455, **515**, *519*
  atmospheric deposition, 10, 81, *92, 93,*
    103, 146, *147*, 299, 515
  availability, **106**
  cycle, *161*
  inputs, 147, *148*
  limitation, 102, *103,* **143, 158**
  mineralisation, 147, **160**, *161*, 163, 298,
    535
  nitrate, *284,* 290, 296, *410,* 455
  nitrification, **160**
Norway, 373
  Sølendet Nature Reserve, **167**
nutrient. *See also* fertiliser; N; P; K,
    eutrophication
  accumulation, 143

availability, 75, 92, **143**, *159*, 274, 299
  reduction through management, 95,
    102, 106, *107*, **143**
cycling, 101, 144, 296, 536
dynamics, **143**
addition, 457, 465. *See also* fertiliser
enrichment, *534*, 409
limitation, **102**, *103*, **143**, **158**
sources, **91**, 97

Odonata, **243**, *248*
Opiliones, **225**
organic matter, 101, 147, *160*, 291

palaeoecology, **19**, 79, 171, 255, **259**, 261,
  263, **379**, **495**
  carbon dating, 387, *500*, *501*
  lead dating, 387
  macrofossils, 20, 22, 25, **386**, *389*
  pollen record, 20, 27, **386**
  recurrence surfaces, 383, 392, 497, *500*
Papilio machaon, 3, **232**
peat *See also* soil; fen; bog
  accumulation, 65, **113**, **262**, 269, 385,
    390, *391*, **392**, **394**, 497, *498*, *499*
  bare; recolonisation, 499, **509**, 524
  chemistry, *53*, *55*, **290**, **435**
    C:N ratio, 78
    fertility. *See* fertility
  decomposition, *114*, 115, 319, 322,
    323, 390, 392
  depth, **123**, 320, 322, 333, 456
  erosion, 457, **495**, *500*, *504*, *505*, 524
  humification, 296
  physical properties, **113**, *114*, 117, 127,
    307, **317**, **321**, **331**, **435**, 537
    bulk density, 322
    hydraulic conductivity, 296, 307,
      308, 320, 321, 322, *323*, 327,
      333, 336
    moisture content, 114, *127*, 374
    porosity, 115
  stratigraphy, 80, **385**, *388*, *479*
  types of, *391*
    effect on revegetation, *442*, *443*
peat extraction, 213
  as management tool, 28, 42, 67, 80,
    144, **260**, **273**, 334

commercial, 3, 64, 323, 350, 362, 405,
  423
'traditional', 3, 24, **61**, 65, **67**, 241,
  274, 350, 362
effects of, **64**, 316, 332, *437*
recolonisation, 79, **65**, *66*, *67*, **251**, *256*,
  257, *264*, **379**, 392, **405**, **406**, **423**,
  435, **451**, **471**
Peucedanum palustre, 3, 232
pH, 52, 83, 96, 97, 99, 100, 101, 107, 127,
  160, 220, **279**, *280*, *282*, *283*, *292*, 293,
  295, 296, 298, 409, *410*, **413**, 415, *416*,
  425, 439, 455, **509**, **516**, *519*, **523**, 525.
  See also acidification; calcium; lime
phosphorus, 52, 56, 75, 94, 95, *96*, *97*, **98**,
  99, *100*, 127, *156*, *160*, 281, 283, *284*,
  297, *298*, 299, *410*, **413**, 415, *416*, 419,
  439, 455, **515**, 520, 525.
  See also fertiliser; nutrient
  availability, **97**, **106**, 274
  limitation, **102**, *103*, **143**, **158**
  mineralisation, 147
Phragmites australis, 29, 66, 224, *244*,
  247, 258, 259, 262, 269.
  See also reedbeds
  Phragmites-sere, *256*, *268*
physical properties. *See* peat
phytogeography, **51**
Plantago lanceolata, *152*
Poland, 83, 105, **114**
pollution, 266
  atmospheric, 55, 75, 274, 283, 299,
    348, 409, 518. *See also* nitrogen
Polytrichum alpestre, **436**, *438*, *440*
Polytrichum strictum, **426**, *432*
potassium, 56, 75, 127, *156*, 291, *292*,
  297, *410*, 439, 455, **515**, **518**, *519*, 520,
  535. *See also* fertiliser; nutrient
  limitation, 102, *103*, **143**, **158**
prairie pothole wetlands, **129**

Ranunculus repens, *152*
redox potential, 52, 57, 59, **99**, 296
reedbeds, 7, 24, 29, 35, **220**, **223**
restoration
  concept of, 34
  constraints on, 4, **10**, **215**, 265, **266**
  definition, **4**, **208**, 252, 453
  feasibility, **6**, **214**, *215*

objectives, **5**, *49*, **118**, 144, 155, 213, 224, *265*, 275, 322, **359**, **391**, 406, **453**, **467**
planning, **207**, *212*, 254, 266, 332, 341, **451**, *455*, 525
principles, *468*
scales of, **266**
strategies, **8**, 9, **91**, **105**, *106*
Rhinanthus angustifolius, *152*
RHYNCHOSPORION ALBAE, 36, 53, 74

salt marsh, **451**, 457
Scheuchzeria palustris, 24, **27**
Schoeno-Juncetum subnodulosi, 35, *37*, 40, 56, 67
Schoenus ferrugineus-community, 190, 193, **195**
Scirpus lacustris sere, *256*, 258, *268*
season, **184**, 197
seed bank. *See* diaspore bank
sodium, 290, *292*, 293, *295*, 439, 455
soil *See also* peat, fen, bog
    chemistry, *160*
    moisture content, 95, *160*
    physical properties, 9, *160*
Sphagnum angustifolium, **424**, **425**, *427*, *429*, *430*
Sphagnum auriculatum, *414*
Sphagnum capillifolium, *491*
Sphagnum cuspidatum, 353, **409**, *411*, *414*, *417*, *491*
Sphagnum fallax, **439**, *441*, *442*, *445*, 446
Sphagnum fuscum, **425**, *429*, *430*, **439**, *441*, *442*, 446
Sphagnum magellanicum, *352*, 353, **409**, *411*, **424**, **425**, **426**, *427*, *429*, *430*, *432*, **439**, *441*, *442*, *491*
Sphagnum nemoreum, **425**, *429*, *430*, **431**
Sphagnum papillosum, *352*, 353, **424**, *428*
Sphagnum recurvum, **409**, *411*, *414*, *417*
Sphagnum rubellum, **424**, *427*
Sphagnum species, 65, *78*, 79, 102, 103, 262, 263, *264*, 274, *284*, 296, 299, 306, *318*, 319, 321, 332, 344, **349**, 379, **435**, 453, 462, 465, **471**
    experimental studies, **405**, **423**, **435**
    regeneration, **412**, **424**, **471**
Sphagnum tenellum, *352*, 353

sulphate, *100*, 290, *292*, *295*, 296, 408, 409, *410*, 419, 455
sulphide, 296; sulphur, 298
Sweden, 103, **360**, *365*
Switzerland, **436**

temporary wetlands, **183**
topography, 16, **123**, *125*, *126*, 215, 259, 334, **451**, *456*, *462*, *463*, *464*, 535
    microtopography, **359**, 462, 463

UK
    England, 373, 503
        Broadland (East Anglia), 3, 35, 39, 42, *50*, 66; Dartmoor, *292, 294, 295*; East Anglia, 37, 61, 67; Fenland (East Anglia), 2, 38; Glasson Moss, **349**; Holme Fen, 39; Jenny Hurn, 292; Kinder Scout, Derbyshire, **509**; Leighton Moss, 7; Malham Tarn Moss, *292, 294, 295, 298*; Nene Washes, **215**; Ouse Washes, **215**; Peak District, **498**, *501*, *504*, **509**; Redgrave & Lopham Fens, 40; Skoyles Marsh, Hickling, **223**; Somerset Levels, **22**, *23*, **25**, *26*, *27*, 39, **215**; Thorne Moors, 35, *292*, **315**, *324*, 385, **407**, *408*; Wedholme Flow, **349**; Wicken Fen, 38, 40, 177, **241**; Woodwalton Fen, 2, 38
    Scotland, 373, 503
        Bad a' Cheo, **537**; Benn Eighe, *292*; Carn a'Ghlinne, *292*; Headless Cross, **525**; Insh Marshes, 35
    Wales, 39, 503
        Cors Caron, 33, **35**, 36, 42; Cors Fochno, 36; Cors Geirch, 42; Llyn Cerig Bach, 29
    USA: prairie pothole region, **129**; Windover, Florida, **21**

vegetation, 215. *See also* bog; fen
    competition, 58, 59, 157
    composition; controls on, **49**, **52**, *54*, *55, *129*, 157, **167**
    dispersal, 140, **143**, 155, 156, 157, 164
    diversity, 184, 363
    floating raft, **65**, **101**, **251**, **273**, 393, 394, **405**, **407**, 408

management, 57, 60, *61, 62, 172*, **184**, 241, 263. *See also* fertiliser
  agricultural, 126, 144, 145, **168**, 274
  cessation of, 41, 179, 261, 274
  fire, 534
  for birds, **218**
  for invertebrates, **223**
  grazing, 144, 219, 261, 384, 512, 531, 534, 545
  haymaking. *See* mowing
  mowing, 62, 75, 84, 95, 102, 143, 144, **167**, *177, 179*, 192, **224, 232**, 256, **261, 269**, 274
  peat extraction. *See* peat extraction
  revegetation methods, **523**
  scrub/tree removal, 29, 172, 177, 225, 263, 309, 312, 375, 541, 545, 554
  top-spit application, **460**, 465, **471**
  traditional, 3, 24, **61, 169, 171**
  transplantation, 11, 85, 188, 376, **509**, 519, **523**, 554
nutrient content, *156*, 159
  N:P ratios, **104**
plant mineral nutrition, **297**
productivity, 56, 74, 75, 81, *106*, 144, *149, 150*, 158, *159*, 163, **173**, *174*, **175**, *176*, 297, 299, 394
rare species, 38, *44*, 51, 57, 59, 66, 74, 79, 83, 84, 85, 126, **143**, 154, 156, 171, 173, 218, 256, *257*
recolonisation, **129**, *133, 137*, **183**, 219
refugia, 138, 407
scrub encroachment, 64, 179, **260**
species richness, 51, *55*, 59, *62*, 78, 135, *136*, 137, *138*, 143, 144, 157, 274
  fertility and, 57, *157*
structure, **363**, *368*
succession, **60**, 66, 79, 80, **101, 143**, 167, 172, 179, 249, **251**, *256*, **274, 379**, 381, 390, **435**, *438, 440*, **454**, 472

zonation, **129, 134, 456**
Viola palustris, 155

water. *See also* hydrology
  abstraction, 40, 41, 59, 80, 85, 266
  chemistry, **52**, *53*, **97**, *98*, 267, **273, 287, 408**, *410*, 418, **455, 517**, *519*
    alkalinity, 52
    bicarbonate, **279**, *281, 283*
    chloride, *281*, 290; chlorine, 455
    conductivity, 52, **279**, *280, 282, 283*, **408**
    groundwater, *98, 268*, **279**, *281, 282, 283*
    rainwater, *98*, **290**, *291, 292*
    river water, **93**, *98*
    salinity, *256*
    seawater, *292*
    surface water, 83, **279**, *281, 282, 283, 284*, **290**, *292, 294, 295*
  level, 41, 114, 217, **309**, 311, *312*, 318, 319, *320*, **332**, *343*, 390, 460, *479*, *534, 536, 541, 542*
    effect on vegetation, 57, **183, 349, 412, 423, 435**, *442*, 492, 520
    fluctuation, 41, **183**, 309, 318, 321, 332, 334, 335, 336, *338*, **349**, *354*, 393, 407, *408*, 417, *426*
    archaeological remains and, 29
  river, **93**
  surface, 83, **93**
wet grassland; restoration for birds, **214**
wet heath, 263, 406, **523**
wetland. *See also fen. See also bog*
  concept of, **11**
  development, 19, 22, 60, **113**
  human impacts on, **1**, 19, **24**, 77, 168, **253, 379**. *See also* peat extraction; vegetation management
  losses of, **1**, 9, **38**, 130, 144, 550
  types of, **11**, *14, 15*, **34**, 36, **113, 114**, *116*, 549